The
HARPER HANDBOOK
of College Composition

The
HARPER HANDBOOK
of College Composition

By **GEORGE S. WYKOFF**, Professor of English, Purdue University, and **HARRY SHAW**, Formerly Director, Workshops in Composition, New York University

SECOND EDITION

New York
HARPER & BROTHERS, PUBLISHERS

THE HARPER HANDBOOK OF COLLEGE COMPOSITION, Second Edition

Portions of this book are adapted from
Writing and Rewriting, by Harry Shaw.
Copyright, 1937, 1945, 1949, 1951, 1955,
by Harper & Brothers.

Library of Congress catalog card number: 57-6260

Contents

Foreword   ix

Part 1. GETTING UNDER WAY

1· **You and the Process of Communication** 3
2· **Your First Themes** 14

Part II. THE HARPER HANDBOOK

1· **The Whole Theme**

Manuscript Form 27
Theme Topics 31
The Title 37
Analysis of Subject 40
Substance 47
Outlines and Outlining 50
Proportion 62
Beginning the Theme 63
Ending the Theme 71
Unity 76
Coherence 78
Clearness 80
Consistency 94
Effectiveness 99
Revision 103
The Basic Forms of Writing 114
The Précis and the Paraphrase 126
Using the Library 139
Taking Notes 160
The Research Paper 163

2· **The Paragraph**

Definition and Characteristics 193
Mechanics 195

Contents

The Topic Sentence or Statement 196
Substance 201
Unity (Oneness) 219
Order 224
Proportion and Length 228
Transition 233
Appropriateness 237
Revision 243

3 · The Sentence

Sentence Fragment 249
Comma Splice 257
Fused or Blended Sentences 263
Sentence Unity (Oneness) 265
Incompleteness of Meaning 268
Mixed and Illogical Constructions 273
Faulty Coordination 280
Faulty Subordination 286
Logical Dependent Clauses 288
Word Order 291
Dangling Modifiers 294
Split Constructions 301
Transition 304
Conciseness 309
Parallelism 312
Consistency 320
Choppy Sentences 323
Position and Arrangement 325
Variety 331
Appropriateness 334

4 · The Word

Using the Dictionary 341
Spelling 360
Obsolete and Archaic Words 384
Localisms 386
Colloquialisms 387
Idiomatic English 390
Illiteracies 395

Contents

Improprieties 398
Slang and Neologisms 403
Precise Diction 409
Technical Words 413
Mixed Figures 414
Emphatic Diction 417
Appropriateness 420
Triteness 424
Fine Writing 427
Conciseness 429
Useless Repetition 433
Euphony 436
Glossary of Faulty Diction 440

5· Grammar

Words 462
  Naming Words: Nouns and Pronouns 463
  Asserting Words: Verbs and Verbals 471
  Modifying Words: Adjectives and Adverbs 476
  Joining Words: Prepositions and Conjunctions 479
Phrases 482
Clauses 485
Sentences 489
Case 496
  Nominative or Objective Case 500
  Possessive (Genitive) Case 502
Agreement of Subject and Predicate 508
Pronoun and Antecedent 518
Linking and Auxiliary Verbs 530
Principal Parts of Verbs 539
Tense and Tone 549
Voice (Active and Passive) 561
Mood (Mode) 567
Adjectives and Adverbs 572
Conjunctions 579
Grammatical Terms Defined 586

6· Punctuation and Mechanics

The Period 612

Contents

Exclamation Points and Question Marks 614

The Comma 617

  Commas to Introduce 619

  Commas to Separate 620

  Commas to Enclose 627

The Semicolon 646

The Colon 653

The Dash 657

Parentheses, Brackets, and Less Frequently Used Marks 661

The Hyphen 664

The Apostrophe 669

Quotation Marks 674

Italics 680

Capitals 683

Abbreviations 690

Numbers 693

Glossary of Applied Punctuation 701

Appendix A. Writing Letters 709

Appendix B. Sentence Analysis and Diagraming 741

Index 751

Foreword

A COURSE in Freshman English—depending upon a freshman's pre-college training—means many things to many people, as it should. For some teachers its important aim is training students to read critically and carefully. For others the course provides opportunity to teach literature, a sort of survey leading to advanced or specialized literary work. With still others first-year English constitutes an approach to aesthetics, a method of fostering "good taste." And some instructors use the discipline of the course to emphasize speaking or listening or principles of clear thinking.

We are content to agree with any of these approaches. Each is important, legitimate, defensible. Yet many years of classroom experience have convinced us that no course can be a successful coverall, that primary emphasis must be placed somewhere, that one unassailable charge against the efficacy of the first-year English course is that in attempting much it sometimes accomplishes too little.

We believe that the needs of most beginning college students—perhaps all—are best served by genuinely solid work, under supervision, in thinking, writing, and rewriting. *The Harper Handbook of College Composition* has only these major aims: *to help students to think and write correctly, clearly, effectively, and appropriately, and to assist teachers in achieving these aims for their students.* Such aims, we hold, are important and significant. Learning to think clearly and learning to write correctly, clearly, effectively, appropriately, are worth-while intellectual processes valuable not only in composition classes but in all other outreachings of the mind.

In every line of this textbook—whenever the information has been available—we have relied upon the recordings of various reputable dictionaries, dictionaries which through their prefatory articles and through their consulting editors have the backing and approval of the foremost linguistic authorities in the United States. To these reputable dictionaries English teachers constantly refer their students. We have tried—perhaps many times in vain—to avoid the minor embarrassments that occur or might occur when what the teacher or handbook says disagrees with what the student's reputable dictionary says.

In both the preceding edition and the present edition we have tried to follow the advice given by Alexander Pope:

> Be not the first by whom the new are tried,
> Nor yet the last to lay the old aside.
> —*Essay on Criticism*, II, 135, 136

Our attempts to follow this advice lead us to make the same comment that W. Cabell Greet made about following a middle course for pronunciation in *The American College Dictionary:* "This middle course may grieve young radicals and old conservatives, but it is hoped that it will please the judicious" (page xxii).

Our attitude toward language and usage is that stated in the conventional definition of good English—written and spoken English used correctly, clearly, effectively, appropriately in carrying on the business, professional, and social affairs of our country (pp. 14, 339). In applying this definition to various parts of this handbook, we have been influenced by the prefaces of the various reputable dictionaries to which we refer students: for example, applying more widely the attitude toward pronunciation expressed in *Webster's New Collegiate Dictionary* (page ix) that correctness is a flexible term, that a word or expression is correct and standard when it is in actual use by a sufficient number of cultivated people or when it "prevails among the educated and cultured people to whom the language is vernacular."

We also agree with the comments made by one of our consultants, Professor George E. Grauel of John Carroll University—bearing in mind that appropriateness is also an important characterizing word:

1. Good usage *is not* merely numerical preponderance among all users of the language any more than correctness of surgical technique is a matter of decision by a Gallup poll.

2. Good usage *is* a matter of preponderant usage among the informed users of the language.

3. The *occasional* use of a form or construction by an "elite" speaker

Foreword

or writer does not in itself establish the practice as equally good or desirable with the forms or constructions *heavily favored* by good writers and speakers. Even careful users of the language are guilty of errors or indulge in occasional eccentricities; for teaching purposes, the conventionally preponderant practices of good writers and speakers are best.

The Harper Handbook of College Composition is filled with specific recommendations and definite suggestions. If some consider them to be rules and regulations, such may be the needs of students seeking positive answers. Agreeing that much about language and grammar is descriptive, we believe that the application of much of this information is prescriptive, that there must be much that is prescriptive in giving directions to students about writing. Our belief, further, is that improvement in thinking and writing involves replacing bad habits with good, that learning composition—or any intellectual or social activity—is necessarily negative in part.

Experience suggests that there is no ideal plan of organization or order of assignments in Freshman English. Any teacher will naturally follow the order of assignments which he has found most satisfactory and will vary this order from year to year according to the needs of his or her students. Since many students are weak in more than one division of writing, we recommend prompt assignment of the two prefatory chapters in this book dealing with communication and early themes. The six major divisions of the text ("The Whole Theme," "The Paragraph," "The Sentence," "The Word," "Grammar," and "Punctuation and Mechanics") may be taken up in any order. The authors have each started at various times with every one of the six divisions save punctuation.

As a textbook for teaching, *The Harper Handbook of College Composition* is designed for three purposes: as a text for profitable use in the classroom; as a text for independent use and consultation on the student's desk; and as a text useful to the teacher in marking themes and to the student in making corrections. This last purpose explains partly the predominating use of the imperative mode (for variety, at the risk of being considered inconsistent, we have occasionally been impersonal or used the passive voice). It also explains some of the detail in certain sections, the comma, for example, Section **88**; our own experience has been that a student learns more from a specific reference than he does from searching for an answer in several pages of print. We have done everything we (and our colleagues and consultants) could do to make the book as easy to use, as sensibly comprehensive, as flexible, and as attractive as possible. If our efforts are successful, we owe much to those who have shared their professional experiences, to former teachers, and to students from whom we have learned perhaps more than we have taught. Many of these students have permitted us to use, anonymously, both their good and their bad writing; some have been unconscious victims. Most of the illustrations and exercises in this handbook are based upon or have been adapted from a careful perusal of some 3000 freshman themes.

Particularly do we extend our hearty thanks to the gifted and experienced teachers whose suggestions and advice have immeasurably improved this book. Names of 25 of these were recorded in the "Foreword" of the first edition (pages x and xi). For this new edition we have received suggestions from other eminently successful teachers who have used this book in their classrooms. We can give only this record—inadequate as it is—of our deep indebtedness to the following: Orville Baker, Northern Illinois State College at DeKalb; Dudley Bailey, University of Nebraska; Rosa Bludworth, San Angelo College; Weller B. Embler, Cooper Union; George E. Grauel, John Carroll University; Richard L. Greene, Wesleyan University; James B. Haman, Georgia Institute of Technology; Willoughby Johnson, University of Missouri; Herbert C. Kalk (and staff), Woodrow Wilson Branch of The Chicago City Junior College; Beatrice Law, West Virginia University; Albertine Loomis (and staff), Highland Park Junior College; Claude H. Neuffer, The University of South Carolina; Paul A. Orr, Georgetown University; E. Arthur Robinson, University of Rhode Island; Kenneth W. Scott, Long Island University; Macklin Thomas, The Chicago City Junior College; and Marjorie Thurston, St. Paul Campus, University of Minnesota.

We are also most appreciative of the comments and suggestions of some sixty staff members of the Department of English at Purdue University.

Finally, we can never adequately express our appreciation to two most efficient helpers, Jocelyn T. Shaw and Brenta H. Wykoff.

GEORGE S. WYKOFF
HARRY SHAW

xii

PART I

GETTING UNDER WAY

CHAPTER 1

You and the Process of Communication

THE AFFAIRS of the world—its business and its pleasure—are carried on through communication: the exchange and interchange of thoughts and ideas between two people or more. It is even possible for one person to commune or communicate with himself.

The means, or the media, of communication are various. Messages can be conveyed through pictures, including painting, graphic representation, photographs, sketches, cartoons; through sculpture; through architecture; through music; through dancing. The most common medium is language, the use of words: the written or printed page and the spoken word. Communication can be limited to two persons, or it can be extended to include hundreds or thousands or millions. When large numbers of people are involved, we use "mass media" of communication: books, magazines, newspapers; radio and television; motion pictures, in which obviously, as in TV, words and pictures combine.

Applied to language, communication consists of two major divisions, each containing two closely related parts: (1) writing and reading, (2) speaking and listening.

Achieving communication can be likened to the successful use of the telephone and radio because a sender and a recipient are always involved. The writer writes for, or sends to, a reader; the reader reads or receives what the writer has sent. The speaker speaks for a listener; the listener receives what the speaker has transmitted. Between the sender and the receiver is, of course, the subject, the material being transmitted. When the recipient understands what the sender has wanted to convey, communication is completed. The more

3

clearly and effectively the reader or listener understands the subject presented, the more successful the communication is.

The process is illustrated by the following diagram:

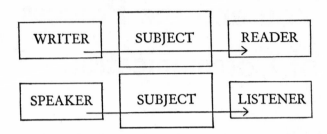

Through all parts of effective communication runs the thread of straight thinking—that is, of forward movement of thought, of a clear, orderly plan and arrangement of ideas. In addition, there must be attention to methods of correct reasoning, so that conclusions are not based on faulty or insufficient evidence and so that good evidence is not misused to support seemingly correct but actually unsound conclusions. Writers and speakers are responsible for logical thinking in their parts of the communication process; readers and listeners must avoid being misled by illogical thinking in what they read or hear. (See also Section 12c.)

No recent statistics are available concerning the proportion of time an average adult spends in some form of communication. Tremendous increases in the number of copies of books, magazines, and newspapers, and continuing expansion of motion pictures, radio, and especially television have made obsolete the estimates of a quarter of a century or even a decade ago.

If you were to keep account for a week of your communication activities, what do you think *your* results would be? How much time do you spend reading? writing? speaking? listening, even though your listening may include seeing? The percentages might show that the time spent in writing activities is somewhat small, the time spent in reading somewhat more, and that spent in speaking and listening most of all.

Such statistics would not and do not prove that any area of communication is unimportant. Each *is* important. Each has its uses;

each is necessary; each demands certain skills on the part of the user if he is to make the process of communication successful.

When you write, or read, or speak, or listen, you are thereby engaged in one of the four parts of communication. So closely are these four parts related that the training you give yourself and the skills you develop in any one part will contribute to your mastery of all the others. Although this handbook is designed primarily to assist you in writing, your own mastery of written language can be more easily and quickly attained if you give adequate attention to your speaking, reading, and listening.

WRITING

Your written papers should express ideas. You may wish to record these ideas for your own use, as in note taking or diary entries. More commonly, however, you write to convey your ideas to a reader or readers—your instructor, classmates, or some other designated person or persons.

For effective communication of ideas, there must be a *controlling purpose* and *ample substance,* but even with these a paper may fail unless it passes an accurate, final test of its worth: Does it correctly, clearly, effectively, and appropriately convey ideas from writer to reader? Correctness, clearness, effectiveness, and appropriateness are essential to a good theme or a well-written paper. If one is lacking completely, or is lacking to an unusual degree, the theme or paper is weak. Remember, also, that readers get no help from a writer's voice, gestures, or facial expression. Words must therefore be easily recognizable, i.e., conform to accepted spelling; must carry the maximum meaning so as to keep the reader's attention; must be so arranged as to present the writer's ideas accurately; and must be punctuated so as to provide the clearness normally achieved by the intonation of a speaker's voice.

A well-written paper, therefore, must be *correct* in its (1) grammar, (2) punctuation, (3) mechanics, and (4) spelling. It must be correct, clear, effective, and appropriate in its (5) diction, (6) sentence construction, and (7) paragraph structure. A paper which receives a passing grade is reasonably correct, and any careful user of a composition handbook and a good dictionary can learn to achieve correctness, which is or should be assumed in formal and informal writing designed for readers both inside and outside college or university boundaries. An *excellent* paper has as its chief merits *clearness, effectiveness,* and *appropriateness,* and writing a paper which possesses these qualities is a real achievement.

The writer, not the reader, is the one who must make communication successful. "Easy writing makes hard reading, but hard writing makes easy reading." A much-loved and highly successful teacher of writing used to add: "You may think you have done enough if you write so that you can be understood. Well, you haven't. You must write so that *you can't be misunderstood.*"

SPEAKING

Correctness, clearness, effectiveness, and appropriateness apply to both written and spoken communication—those aspects of communication are the "sending" part of the circuit. For speaking, the same emphasis is needed on a controlling purpose and ample substance, and on grammar, diction, sentence construction, and paragraph structure—a structure usually made clear in speaking by means of key words like "in the next place," "for example," "as a result," and "finally." The speaker does not worry, fortunately, about punctuation marks or misspellings; unlike the writer, however, he must be concerned about pronunciation, for it is as unforgivable for him to mispronounce words as it is for the writer to misspell.

The speaker has one other heavy responsibility. The writer can expect—perhaps unreasonably—his reader to reread materials which he does not immediately understand or from which his attention has momentarily wandered. In speaking, the communication is given only once, and unless it is received by the listener as the speaker desired it to be, communication fails. Except in conversation, the speaker has no opportunity to repeat. He must, therefore, be *immediately* clear and effective.

Successful speaking, like successful writing, comes only through constant practice, but for the technical details of speaking—such as use of voice, posture, gestures, audience approach, type of speech—formal instruction is necessary through the aid of both teacher and textbook.

Can speaking help you in writing? Certainly. Since you speak many more times a day and on many more occasions than you write, your habits of correct, clear, effective, and appropriate speaking assist materially in correct, clear, effective, and appropriate writing. On the negative side, watch your speaking—conversation, especially—for serious errors in grammar and word use. Such errors easily become habits and are frequently carried over into your writing.

READING

As a reader you are at the other end of the communication process, "receiving" through the printed or written word what some other writer has sought to communicate. Your part in the process cannot be passive, unless you read merely to be entertained or to skim through for an idea here and there. If you are reading for information and instruction, you will be an *active* reader and will have at least one of three major purposes in your reading: (I) to understand the content of the reading material; (II) to evaluate it, agreeing or disagreeing, or possibly agreeing only in part; (III) to use the reading material for improving your own writing and speaking.

So important has the idea of effective reading become that books are being written on the subject, and colleges and universities are adding courses and counsellors to help students improve. These books and courses are not designed for the handicapped reader—this aid is called *remedial reading.* They are designed to help the comparatively slow or average or even superior reader to increase his reading speed and his comprehension of what he reads—this aid is called *developmental reading.* If such help is available, use it; lacking such help, you can improve your reading effectiveness through specific directions.

I. *In reading for information about ideas and content, use the following suggestions:*

1. Read and understand the title. Look also for any subtitle, prefatory note by the author, material about the author, any introductory summary, any footnotes giving additional information.

2. Determine the kind of reader (degree of education, occupation, age level, sex) for whom the author is writing. Determine also how well the author has adapted his material to this reader and what the occasion or the circumstances were for his writing.

3. Look for a sentence or a paragraph in which the author states his central purpose. Whether it is expressed or implied, formulate it in your own words. Look also for a sentence or paragraph in which the author summarizes his content—the *theme* sentence of the *theme* paragraph.

4. Look for mechanical aids that the author has used to help you: subheads; numbering of sections (I, II, III, etc.); blank spaces between sections; italicized words or sentences; paragraph divisions.

5. Read the entire article, chapter, or section rapidly, and then reread it paragraph by paragraph. Near the beginning, as suggested in (3) above, look for a sentence or a paragraph in which the author summarizes his content, or in which he gives the *theme* or central thought and the point of view to be used in developing it. Underline the topic sentence or topic phrase or topic word of each paragraph. Notice how these topics are developed within each paragraph (see pp. 196–200). Use pen or pencil to indicate which paragraphs belong together. Look for transitional devices (see pp. 233–237) which indicate how successive paragraphs are linked or change the direction of the discussion. Note the length of the paragraphs and try to account for those which are extremely short or extremely long.

6. As you read, underline the words whose meaning you do not know and whose meaning you cannot guess from the context. Look them up in a good dictionary, choose the definition which fits the context, and write it in the margin.

7. Make a formal outline (see pp. 50–60) of the material, using for your main heads and subheads the underlining and grouping which you have done according to Suggestion 5.

II. *In evaluating what you have read—deciding to what extent you accept it, believe it, let it influence your thinking or guide your actions—answer the following questions:*

The Process of Communication

1. Is the author an authority? an expert witness? Is he close enough to the situation he is writing about to know it thoroughly? Has he had sufficient experience?
2. Is the author biased? Or is he sufficiently detached from the situation to give an objective view?

If you are reading nonfiction of the expository or argumentative type, ask yourself, in addition:

3. Has the author presented enough data to support his generalizations?
4. Has the author reasoned logically, avoiding common fallacies? (See Section 12c.)

If you are reading fiction, ask yourself:

1. Has the author succeeded in creating an illusion of reality?
2. Has the author helped me to understand myself and my fellow human beings better than before?

III. *In reading to help yourself write and speak correctly, clearly, effectively, and appropriately, use the following suggestions:*

1. Occasionally underline a word or a group of words and identify it grammatically by definition and use. Assist your review of grammar by choosing various grammatical terms and looking for examples of these in your reading.
2. Look at the punctuation marks in three or four paragraphs. Do they follow the conventional principles of punctuation? If any marks are used in a striking or unconventional manner, give a reason for their use, the purpose they serve.
3. Look on each page for three or four examples of words spelled according to rules and for words which are exceptions to the rules.
4. Underline a certain number of words which you know and which are effectively used. Underline a certain number of words which you do not have in your active vocabulary but which you will hereupon add with the aid of your dictionary.
5. Study a certain number of the sentences. Examine them for their use of phrases and clauses, of subordination and coordination. Determine which sentences are simple, complex, compound, compound-complex (see pp. 490, 491). Which are loose or periodic (see pp. 492, 493)? Which use inverted word order? What is the proportion of long and short sentences? Examine the ways in which sentences begin and end. Use all this material for a brief analysis of the

9

author's style and compare it to that of your own written work. 6. Restudy the author's paragraphs according to suggestion 5, p. 8. Apply to your own paragraphs whatever methods of effective paragraphing the author has used. 7. Study the author's use of title, of a *theme* statement, of a controlling purpose, of a point of view, and of a plan of organization. If these are clear and effective, adapt them to your own writing, where appropriate.

LISTENING

Listening, perhaps the most commonly used form of communication, is difficult to utilize effectively. Most people are not effective listeners. They have only a haphazard and inaccurate idea of what they have heard, partly because of lapses in attention and partly because memory is faulty. Listeners normally have but one opportunity to hear what is spoken. Therefore, aside from conversation and other informal talks purely for entertainment, some note taking is advisable when you listen to classroom lectures, formal speeches, radio addresses, forum and panel discussions, and the like. Good notes are not mere verbatim reports of what is said; in fact, a knowledge of shorthand is not necessary to, and does not insure, good note taking, for you will have to think and understand as well as record.

To obtain the most from your listening, your notes should follow specific suggestions or contain answers to specific questions.

Listening to classroom lectures.

Lecture notes have various uses, such as a possible source for themes, material for basic research, or review material for examinations. In reading, you have all the time you need to reflect and to condense and organize your ideas, but in listening to and taking notes on lectures, you have to think and write rapidly. Thus, taking lecture notes is more difficult than making notes on reading.

The majority of students take lecture notes in bound or loose-leaf notebooks; some prefer using cards or card-size slips of paper (3 x 5, 4 x 6, or larger). Whatever the mechanical method, keep together all the notes taken in a single course. Record the date and the subject of each lecture. Utilize the following aids:

The Process of Communication

1. "Stop, look, and listen" before you write. Do not record the introductory words dealing with a subject unless they are really important; wait until the point can be summarized.

2. Do not try to take down everything the lecturer says. The best lecture notes are always condensed; they contain in summary and outline form the gist of what was said.

3. Abbreviate in order to save time. Make up a list of abbreviations, such as $\overline{c}$ for "with"; $\therefore$ for "therefore"; $=$ for "equal"; & for "and"; tr. for "translation," etc.

4. Keep your mind on the lecture and concentrate on what is being said so that your "attention lapses" will be infrequent and of short duration.

5. Read over your notes on a lecture as soon as possible after they are taken. If they are blurred, jumbled, or difficult to read, copy them over neatly; if your abbreviations may later lose meaning for you, write them out at once.

Listening to speeches.

1. What was the occasion for the speech? What were the circumstances under which it was given?

2. Was the address given before a miscellaneous group or a specialized one (college assembly, classroom lecture group, specific society, etc.)? Was it appropriate or inappropriate for this specified audience?

3. What was the subject of the speech? Did the speaker give early a phrase or sentence stating his central theme?

4. What was the purpose of the speech: to entertain, inform, convince, persuade, or incite to action? Did the speaker use chiefly logical and intellectual materials or did he make an emotional appeal?

5. What materials did the speaker use in support of his central theme? How did he organize them? How did he indicate his plan of organization? (Watch for such clues as "there are three reasons," "in the second place," "as an example," "by way of contrast," etc., and for other linking or transitional devices.)

6. How did the speech begin (challenging statement, personal experience, anecdote, quotation, historical incident, etc.)?

7. What devices were used to hold attention throughout the speech (specific examples, personal experiences, definitions, allu-

sions, questions, humor, familiar or unusual materials, repetition, stories or anecdotes or incidents, etc.) ?

8. How did the speech end (concise summary, repetition of central theme, quotation, appeal for belief or action, etc.) ?

9. What striking or unusual words were used? Did the general tone seem impartial or were words used to "slant" the subject in a given direction? List some of these striking, unusual, or "slanting" words.

Listening to radio, television, and movie programs.

Two widely popular forms of "receiving" are radio and television listening. Programs in these mediums of communication are varied, most of them being primarily for entertainment. Some combine information and entertainment, but you will probably not take notes on such a program unless it be a formal radio or TV address. However, if your listening is to be active and critical, you must answer three basic questions: (1) What *kind* of program is it (news broadcast, news commentary, radio drama, dramatized biography, address, forum, quiz program, etc.) ? (2) What is *the general purpose* (information, recreation, inspiration, argument, etc.) ? (3) At what *general or specific class* of listeners is it aimed? If some of this information can be obtained *before* the time of listening, the listening process is facilitated and strengthened.

Most useful to you in learning to write, speak, read, and listen effectively will probably be news broadcasts and commentator programs. Such programs provide lessons in the selection of materials to arouse and hold interest. Moreover, in listening to news commentators, you will need to differentiate conjecture and opinion from facts and to evaluate the speaker's impartiality or bias.

Note also these devices: the use of short sentences, the placing of transitional devices at the beginning of sentences, the use of simple and vigorous words, repetition to make ideas effective, and, in general, the use of a conversational tone.

In listening to radio or TV drama, try to discover—either before or early in the broadcast—what kind of drama is being presented: light, serious, farcical, satirical, biographical, etc. Determine the central theme of the play and state it in a sentence or two. Note the contributions made by the announcer or commentator and by the

12

The Process of Communication

different characters. In addition to their appearance, how do what they say and the way they say it help to characterize them, make them definite, vivid, convincing? What sound effects are used and what specific purposes do they serve? Note also how music influences the mood or tone of the play, indicates passage of time or change of scene, and sometimes even replaces words.

Movie programs, like TV programs, are also varied, but their major contribution is dramatic presentation. Note the similarities and differences between radio drama and movies or television. In these latter two, note how sound and sight, hearing and seeing, complement each other: as an experiment close your eyes for part of the program and hold your ears shut for a part. How much did you miss? Again, answer for yourself questions about the type of drama, subject matter, central theme, development of character. Also, since you are seeing as well as hearing, determine how well the speeches are adapted to or appropriate for each speaker. For the best critical and active listening to movie and television programs, some advance preparation is essential, a preparation becoming increasingly easy through reviews and comments in newspapers and magazines. (For a discussion of written criticism in general, see p. 120.)

As outlined above, informal listening and careful formal listening with note taking can contribute to the clearness and effectiveness of your writing, for they will give you experience in organizing and evaluating ideas.

CHAPTER 2

Your First Themes

REGULARLY through your freshman year and occasionally in later college assignments you will be required to write papers of varying length. The chief purpose of this writing is to establish and confirm habits of correctness, clearness, effectiveness, and appropriateness in written work, so that in future years your writing will measure up to the standards expected of one with your degree of education.

FRESHMAN ENGLISH

Your college writing will begin in the first week or two of your freshman year with so-called formal training being given in freshman English. The aim of this course is to give you practice in the correct, clear, effective, appropriate expression of your own ideas, emotions, reactions, thoughts. It is not a course designed for the training of professional writers. Hundreds of thousands of students preceding you have benefited from such a course, have improved in their writing. Why not you? The course makes no demands beyond the ability of the ordinary student. The instructor will grade your written work by giving you constructive criticism and by marking all your major errors and many of your minor ones. Only as you profit by this criticism and as you eliminate these errors will your writing conform to acceptable standards of "good English"—written and spoken English used correctly, clearly, effectively, appropriately in carrying on the business, professional, and social affairs of our country.

ATTAINING STANDARDS OF GOOD ENGLISH

"Good English" is necessarily a broad term, and what is "good English" at one time and place may not be "good English" at an-

14

other time and place. A discussion in some detail of language and the occasions for its variations in use is given on pages 337–346 and pages 420–423.

Here it is sufficient to say that good English is correct, clear, effective, appropriate English in speaking and writing. Applied to writing, what in brief do these characterizing words mean?

Correct writing is writing that is free of errors in grammar, spelling, punctuation, diction, mechanics—serious or ludicrous or even minor errors that distract your reader from your subject.

Clear writing is writing that permits no possibility of confusion, that is, understandable with little or no difficulty by the reader for whom it is written.

Effective writing is writing that makes a favorable impression on the reader, writing that he remembers because it catches his attention and holds it, writing that he remembers with pleasure and profit.

Appropriate writing is writing that is adapted to the reader—his age, education, interests, understanding; writing also that is suitable for the occasion and the purpose of its creation.

To attain these standards of good English, you need *constant* practice in writing. You will get limited practice by writing papers in your freshman English course. You cannot, however, make much progress merely by letting your first draft be your final draft or by giving either your first or last draft a hasty rereading before calling it finished. Nor can you establish satisfactory habits by writing carefully only one or two papers a week for freshman English. Careful planning, composing, rereading, and checking—these steps you should apply to *everything* you write, even to the letters you send to relatives and friends. Remember that any improvement in writing comes only through your own efforts. The best teacher and the best textbooks can only assist; they can never do the job for you.

SEVEN PRACTICAL SUGGESTIONS FOR WRITING THEMES

How can you improve in theme-writing from the very beginning? The following suggestions apply to both your early and succeeding papers.

15

1. Follow the work-sheet method of preparing a paper or a theme —a method designed to help you write easily, effectively, even quickly and painlessly. (See pp. 25, 26.)

2. *Analyze* the theme subject carefully. What are its possibilities? List as many divisions of the subject as you can. Determine your *central purpose.* There is no such thing as good *purposeless* writing. (See pp. 40–46.)

3. Gather *ample substance* for the fulfillment of your central aim. Draw upon your *own experience* and the *experience of others* as revealed in newspapers, magazines, books, and conversation. Make use of your own *observation, curiosity, imagination,* and *reflection.* (See pp. 47–49.)

4. *Arrange* the material you have collected. Reject all that is irrelevant to your purpose and accept and classify that which remains. Many good themes have been written without the aid of a formal outline, but no good theme has ever been written which did not have a *definite* plan of some sort. (See pp. 50–60.)

5. Write your first draft—slowly and thoughtfully if that is the best way for you; or rapidly, if you want to get your thoughts on paper and then spend time on their improvement. Revise your first draft; better still, entirely rewrite it. Remember that there is no such thing as good writing; there is only good *rewriting.* Keep asking yourself these questions: Have I tested my paper for its *organization* and the *relevance* of all material to my subject? Will my reader see exactly what I have in mind? Will he be interested in my presentation? Have I made my writing clear, effective, and appropriate?

6. After completing step 5, read and reread your theme for errors in mechanics, grammar, punctuation, spelling, and diction. If you find that you are making several kinds of errors, reread each paper several times for similar errors of a specific kind; that is, reread once for misspellings, once for errors in punctuation, once for errors in grammar, and so on. If your paper has been written outside class, make a final, clean draft to turn in.

7. Proofread your final draft, pencil or pen in hand, pointing to every word and punctuation mark. Reading aloud, when possible, will help, for it slows down your proofreading speed, and your voice will help you to find errors that your eyes will overlook.

Your First Themes

How long should you spend in the preparation of a paper or theme? No one can say. Subjects vary in difficulty. Students differ in their abilities: some write easily and rapidly; others write slowly and laboriously. However, *every student* should spend *at least two hours* on each 400- or 500-word assignment. If you make serious errors in your writing, work at them first. If you have few such errors, work at them and concentrate also on improving your sentences and word choice. Usually there is only one answer to the question, "How can I make my themes better?" It is the uninspired but eminently true "Take more time."

AIDS IN ATTAINING STANDARDS OF GOOD ENGLISH

To help you attain standards of good English, your instructor will give during your freshman English course—in addition to new material—some review or memory-refreshing assignments in grammar, punctuation, spelling, diction, and sentence construction. Unfortunately, these assignments cannot be given simultaneously, nor can they always be given in the order in which you may need them. Your early writing, for example, may show errors in spelling, or diction, or punctuation, or grammar, while your assignments are dealing with the whole theme, choice of subject, planning, or paragraphing. You may feel aggrieved that your themes are being graded down for errors that you have not yet studied in your review assignments or classwork. When this happens, your task, and it is *your* task, no one else's, is as follows:

1. Utilize to the fullest extent any comment that your instructor makes on your themes. Note carefully the errors he marks and reference numbers indicating sections of this handbook. Through his aid you will find where your weaknesses lie, and you will be in a strategic position to make the necessary revisions and to avoid making the same errors in later themes.

2. As a part of this strategy, keep a record of your most common errors in writing (see chart on back of page facing inside back cover) and consult it each time you have any writing to do.

3. Study and master the specific directions concerning the elimination of the error or errors that you are making. A worthy ideal is to

try never to make the same mistake twice, or even the same kind of mistake.

4. An additional valuable aid is to make a "correction sheet" for every paper that is returned to you. A sample form, filled out, is given on this and the next page. In the left margin put the symbol and handbook section number. In the left column copy the material from the theme exactly as it is; in the right column copy the same material but make sufficient change for the correction of the error. Do not, however, change the wording or phrasing so much that there is no apparent relation between the error and the correction. Be sure to include enough in both columns so that both the error and the correction are immediately understandable, even weeks afterward, without further reference to the theme. Consult these correction sheets when you are assigned additional writing. As the number of your correction sheets increases, you will have a personal guide to both the kinds of errors that you habitually make and the methods by which these errors can be corrected.

CORRECTIONS FOR THEME No. x

	Incorrect	*Correct*
sp 52e	admited	admitted
p 94a	a students first task	a student's first task
sp 52b	to many activities	too many activities
CS 32	Many a freshman becomes a reporter for the student newspaper, this activity aids him in his writing.	Many a freshman becomes a reporter for the student newspaper; this activity aids him in his writing.
SF 31	Another activity that everyone needs involves physical exertion. If he wants to keep in good physical condition.	Another activity that everyone needs involves physical exertion, if he wants to keep in good physical condition.
gr 76b	The major activity of many students are in the field of athletics.	The major activity of many students is in the field of athletics.
gr 75d	An individual activity appeals to my roommate and I.	An individual activity appeals to my roommate and me.

18

FS 33	Such in brief are our extracurricular activities every student should choose one of them and take an active part.	Such in brief are our extracurricular activities; every student should choose one of them and take an active part.

SAMPLE FORM FOR "CORRECTION SHEET" FOR THEMES

Your instructor may, of course, have different suggestions concerning corrections. Some instructors ask that writing be done on alternate lines so that corrections can be made in red or green ink above the errors. Other instructors ask that corrections be made on the backs of the theme pages. The plan suggested above applies when correction sheets are returned to students but themes are retained in the instructor's office for reference and for consultation with students.

SERIOUS ERRORS TO BE AVOIDED

As a short cut to more rapid improvement in writing, concentrate on avoiding all of the serious errors discussed below. If any of these appear in your writing, consult immediately the pages listed. You should answer satisfactorily each of the following questions about each of your early themes and continue applying the practice to all your written work.

1. IMPROPER CHOICE AND LIMITING OF SUBJECT.

Have I chosen a subject and narrowed it so that, in the number of words at my disposal, I have given my reader a clear and complete, not a vague, general, and rambling account of what he expects to learn from my writing? (See pp. 31–35.)

2. FAULTY PLANNING.

Have I followed an orderly plan in the writing of my paper? Always make a brief written or mental outline, dividing your subject into two, three, four, or more related parts and writing a paragraph on each part. (See pp. 50–60.)

3. IMPROPER PARAGRAPHING.

Is each of my paragraphs an adequate treatment of one phase or division of the subject? Does a paragraph include material that belongs elsewhere in the paper? Does a paragraph omit material necessary to clear development of the paragraph's topic, or is the material included illogically in some other paragraph? Is any paragraph too long or detailed? Too short and concise? (See pp. 193–246.)

4. SENTENCE FRAGMENTS.

Have I written any unjustifiable sentence fragments? Remember that a sentence—to be clear, for most practical purposes, to your reader—should contain a subject and predicate, should make sense by itself, or should convey a sense of complete meaning to the reader. When punctuated like a sentence, dependent clauses and various kinds of phrases—verb phrases, participial phrases, infinitive phrases, absolute phrases, appositive phrases, and prepositional phrases—serve in general only the undesirable purpose of confusing your reader. Such sentence fragments can usually be corrected (a) by attaching each to an independent statement or (b) by making each complete, with its own subject and predicate. (See pp. 249–254.)

5. FUSED SENTENCES.

Have I written two sentences together, with no mark of punctuation between, and thereby confused my reader by not indicating to him where one complete thought ends and another complete thought begins? (See pp. 263, 264.)

6. "COMMA SPLICES."

Have I avoided making any unjustifiable "comma splices"? A "comma splice" results from using a comma to separate two complete sentences, or, in grammatical terms, using a comma between two independent clauses not joined by one of the simple conjunctions, *and, but, or, nor, neither, yet.* If your rereading shows you an unjustifiable "comma splice," it is a very simple matter to correct: (a) replace the comma with a period or a semicolon; (b) use one of the simple conjunctions just mentioned immediately after the

20

comma; or (c) change one of the independent clauses to a dependent clause or a phrase, and let the comma remain. (See pp. 257–260.)

7. MISUSE OF SEMICOLON.

Have I misused the semicolon by using it to set off a dependent clause or a phrase? Ordinarily, the semicolon serves the same purpose as the period: to indicate the end of one complete thought and the beginning of another; it is this "break" in thought that your reader expects when he sees a semicolon. One guide is this: no period, no semicolon. Setting off dependent clauses or phrases with semicolons leads to the same confusion in your reader's mind as is caused by the *sentence fragment*. (See pp. 646–650.)

8. SERIOUS ERRORS IN GRAMMAR.

Have I avoided making any serious errors in grammar that would distract my reader's attention from what I am saying to the way I am saying it?

a. *Have I made my subjects and predicates agree in number?* This is a subtle principle more easily violated than observed, partly because of the position of the subject, or the way nouns form their plurals, or the way two or more members of a compound subject are connected. (See pp. 508–513.)

Incorrect: More freshmen is needed for the football squad.
Correct: More freshmen are needed for the football squad.

Incorrect: In this house lives my sister, her husband, and their two children.
Correct: In this house live my sister, her husband, and their two children.

Incorrect: Neither my sister nor her husband have a college education.
Correct: Neither my sister nor her husband has a college education.

b. *Have I used adjectives and adverbs correctly, and not used an adjective when I should have used an adverb, or vice versa?* (See pp. 572–576.)

Incorrect: Things are going *good* with me now.
Correct: Things are going *well* with me now.

21

Incorrect: I have never smelled anything so *fragrantly*.
Correct: I have never smelled anything so *fragrant*.

c. *Have I used the correct form of the verb?* Serious errors in verb use, in addition to misusing singular-plural forms, are mistaking the past tense for the past participle, or vice versa, and confusing similar verbs like *lay—lie, sit—set, raise—rise.* (See pp. 539–545.)

Incorrect: The cattle were laying on the grass.
Correct: The cattle were lying on the grass.

Incorrect: John seen the car coming and done his best to avoid the accident.
Correct: John saw the car coming and did his best to avoid the accident.

Incorrect: Father has ran for public office numerous times.
Correct: Father has run for public office numerous times.

d. *Have I used the correct case forms of pronouns when these are the objects of verbs or prepositions?* (See pp. 496–502.)

Incorrect: Did you telephone John or *I* last evening?
Correct: Did you telephone John or *me* last evening?

Incorrect: Your amusing letter to Harry and *I* was greatly enjoyed.
Correct: Your amusing letter to Harry and *me* was greatly enjoyed.

Incorrect: The purpose of *we* students now is to learn to write correctly.
Correct: The purpose of *us* students now is to learn to write correctly.

9. MISSPELLING

Have I checked the spelling of all words about which I am in doubt? Have I carefully proofread once for any misspellings due to carelessness?

REMINDER: Only after a theme has been carefully planned, written, rewritten, checked for all kinds of errors, and proofread is it likely to approach correctness in all its details of grammar, punctuation, mechanics, spelling, diction (including idiom), and sentence and paragraph structure. Always study *systematically* and *conscientiously* the handbook sections dealing with your particular weaknesses so as to forestall making errors.

PART II

The
Harper
Handbook

The Whole Theme

"ENGLISH" may be difficult for some students and easy for others, but everyone can learn to write and speak decently and competently if he is earnest in his efforts and is willing to devote the necessary time and energy to mastering his *own* language. After all, for most of us—except the non-English born—English is our own, our native tongue, and we should take pride in using it correctly, clearly, effectively.

Through study of the principles of writing—the whole theme, paragraphs, sentences, words—we can approach desired competency and decency: "Good English—the written and spoken English used effectively in carrying on the business, professional, and social affairs of our country."

To learn to write correctly, clearly, and effectively, you may require a semester of theme writing, or a year, or two years, or more —depending upon your background training and upon the time and energy you may, or may not, have given to the problem in the past. *Everyone* can improve his ability to write if he will conscientiously try.

You can eliminate certain types of errors in your writing and you can become aware of other types of errors to be on guard against by doing carefully the exercises at the ends of the various sections which follow. Such exercises are no substitute for writing. There is infinite truth in the familiar statement: *The only way to learn to write is to write.*

Other sections of this book deal with the paragraph, the sentence, and the word. This section deals with the whole theme or composition and with specific approaches to writing such longer units.

To write decently, competently, even *painlessly,* many students have found effective the following process, done step by step:

Prepare a number of work sheets, 5½ by 8½ inches in size (half-size standard stationery), a desirable size since each work sheet will contain all necessary step-by-step information.

25

The Whole Theme

Work Sheet 1. On this sheet, put preliminary miscellaneous information: The number of the theme. The number of words required. Reader or readers aimed at. General title. Specific title, or titles, if given; otherwise, several specific titles suggested by the general title. General tone of paper (see Section 4f). *Theme* sentence, the sentence that summarizes the content of the theme you plan to write.

Work Sheet 2. Here put your preliminary analysis for possible content (see Section 4d). List 13 to 24 items which might be included and which might serve as the topic or subject for a paragraph each.

Work Sheet 3. From the 13 to 24 items on Work Sheet 2, make a tentative outline (see Section 6). Your outline can be changed later, if necessary, as you develop it in writing.

Work Sheet 4. On this work sheet write topic sentences—one for each paragraph—for the paragraphs that you plan for your theme. The number will depend upon the major divisions of your outline. Preferably, make each topic sentence a simple sentence (see Section 23).

Work Sheet 5, and *6, 7, 8, 9,* etc., depending upon the number of paragraphs, using one work sheet for each paragraph. On each work sheet copy a topic sentence from Work Sheet 4. Expand this topic sentence into an adequate paragraph (see Section 24).

When you have expanded the last topic sentence into its paragraph, you have written your theme. Do your rereading, revising, and correcting on these work sheets. When you are satisfied with your revisions and corrections, copy your material on regular theme paper. Make a final rereading of your theme before you turn it in. Your instructor may ask you to make a final draft of your outline and to turn it in with your theme. He may also wish to see all your work sheets.

But before you turn your theme over to a reader, there are questions that you should ask yourself about any composition that you write:

→1. Does my theme have a *central purpose?*
→2. Have I carefully *analyzed* the subject?
→3. Does my theme have *ample substance?*

→4. Is the substance *arranged* logically and effectively?

→5. Is my theme *unified?*

→6. Is my theme *clear?* Will it mean to my reader exactly what it means to me?

→7. Does my theme have *interest?* Is my substance presented interestingly and emphatically so that it will make a *definite appeal* to the reader?

→8. Is my theme *correct* in all mechanical and grammatical details?

If you can truthfully and correctly answer "yes" to these eight questions, your task is completed. If you cannot answer "yes" to these eight questions, you need the guidance and constructive criticism that both your instructor and your textbook will give. None of these requirements is beyond the ability of the ordinary student. That is, none is too difficult for the ordinary student who will work intelligently, industriously, and faithfully. The following sections are designed to help you give "yes" answers to the foregoing questions.

MANUSCRIPT FORM

1. Consider carefully the importance of neatness and legibility in the themes which you submit. Many a good composition has received a poorer grade or made a poorer impression than its actual content deserved because it was so improperly prepared and so untidily written that the reader lost patience in trying to decipher it. Conversely, many a thin theme or composition has received a comparatively high grade because of its extreme neatness and legibility. As a conscientious writer, give your ideas the outward form which will best insure their ready communication. Here, then, are some suggestions for the preparation of your final draft.

1a. Conform to specific standards in preparing manuscript.

If in your English composition or other classes there are particularized directions for the preparation of manuscript, follow those directions unvaryingly. Otherwise, use the following as a guide:

1. *Paper.* Use only standard-sized stationery, 8½ by 11 inches in size. Ruled paper is convenient for longhand, but most standard paper is unruled. Use paper of good quality, clean white bond,

which will take ink without blurring. Write on only one side of each sheet.

2. *Title.* Write the title on the first line, or about two inches from the top of the page. Center the title. Capitalize the first word and all other important words in the title (see Section **97a**). Do not use a period after the title, but use a question mark or exclamation point as necessary for interrogative or exclamatory titles.

3. *Beginning.* Begin the theme about one inch below the title. If the paper is ruled, write on every line; if unruled, leave about one-half inch between lines.

4. *Margins.* Leave a margin of about one inch on the left side of each page. Standard theme paper has a margin of one inch ruled off; leave a similar blank space on paper not having this vertical line. Leave a margin of about a half-inch at the right. Make the margins even and fairly uniform down the page.

5. *Indentations.* Indent the first line of every paragraph about one inch. Use indentations of equal length for all paragraphs in the same paper. Make no exception if you have occasion to use *numbered* paragraphs. On the second page and following pages, indent the first line *only* if it is the beginning of a paragraph.

Pay attention to the ending of the paragraphs. Leave part of a line blank *only* at the end of a paragraph. You thus indicate to the reader that a new paragraph will begin on the next line; he should not find that line beginning flush with the left-hand margin.

Indicate a paragraph division not shown by indentation by placing the sign ¶ before the word beginning the paragraph. Cancel a paragraph division by writing "No ¶" in the margin. But, in general, avoid the use of the marks ¶ and "No ¶." Preferably, you should recopy the entire page, correcting the indentation.

6. *Insertions.* Use a caret (∧) when inserting an omitted expression (see Section **92g**).

7. *Cancellations.* Draw a straight line through material that you wish to cancel. Do not use parentheses or brackets to cancel words. These marks have their own particular uses (see Section **92**) and should never be used to indicate deletion.

8. *Order.* Number and arrange the pages of your composition in correct order. Use Arabic numerals in the upper right-hand corner

of each page. Arrange the pages in proper order: 1, 2, 3, etc. No reader likes to open a manuscript and find page 2 or page 3 before him.

9. *Endorsement.* With the pages in proper order, page 1 on top, fold the theme lengthwise through the middle. On the right-hand side of the back of the last page write your name, your course, your instructor's name, the date, and the number of the paper. Write these items in the order desired by your department or your instructor.

NOTE: For other "basic mechanics" in the preparation of manuscript, see "The Hyphen" (Section **93**), "Capitals" (Section **97**), "Abbreviations" (Section **98**), "Italics" (Section **96**), and "Numbers" (Section **99**).

1b. Make your handwriting legible.

Illegible writing taxes the patience of a reader and causes him to give so much attention to the words themselves that his thought is turned away from the important ideas which should engage his interest. Make your handwriting easily readable by

1. *Not crowding your writing.* Do not run words together; do not run consecutive lines too closely together; do not crowd the writing at the bottom of the page.

2. *Not leaving gaps in your writing.* The consecutive letters in a word should be joined. Do not leave a line partly blank, for no good reason, at the bottom of a page.

3. *Forming your letters carefully and correctly.* Dot every small-letter *i* and *j*. (Use dots, not circles.) Cross every *t*. Make small letters *m* and *n* and *u* distinct, and small letters *a* and *o*. Do not carelessly write small letters as capitals, or capitals as small letters (see Section **97g**).

4. *Writing with a good pen using clear ink* (preferably black or blue-black), and *writing legibly.* Avoid the reader's possible comment on your theme: "This *looks* like a very interesting theme, but I can't *read* it!"

1c. If possible, type your themes and other written work.

Typescript is more legible than handwriting; also, errors are more

29

easily detected in typescript than in handwriting. Observe the following conventions in typing:

1. Indent paragraph beginnings either 5 or 10 spaces.

2. Leave margins at both the left and right: an inch or an inch and a half at the left, about an inch at the right.

3. Leave a blank space of at least an inch at the bottom of each page.

4. Double-space all lines (never single-space, except in business letters).

5. After terminating marks of punctuation (period, question mark, exclamation point), use the space bar twice or thrice; after internal punctuation marks, use it once.

The endorsement on a typewritten manuscript is usually placed in the upper left-hand corner of the first page. If the paper is folded, it should also be endorsed like a handwritten theme (see "Endorsement," **1a**). If the manuscript is being submitted for printing, this endorsement contains, on three lines, the writer's name, his street address, and his city and state. For such submission, a manuscript is folded once through the middle, horizontally, or, if it is not bulky, like a business letter for a long-sized envelope.

1d. Avoid numerous and unsightly erasures and corrections.

1. *Recopying.* Everyone is likely to make errors even in preparing a final draft. If such errors are numerous, it is far better to recopy an entire page than to leave it filled with blots, blurs, and canceled and inserted words. If only one or two corrections must be made on a page, follow the directions given above **(1a)** under "Indentations," "Insertions," and "Cancellations."

2. *Proofreading.* Every manuscript should be reread slowly and carefully for errors of all kinds, and especially for careless errors. ("Oh, I knew better than that" is, afterward, slim excuse for the writer.) Though typescript makes detection of errors easier, typed papers often contain more errors than papers written in longhand because of the insidious way in which letters seem to change places and because of careless proofreading. For a guide to proofreading, see Section **15**.

3. *Final Draft.* Always reread the final draft of a manuscript before passing it on to a reader.

THEME TOPICS

2. Every writer has had the discouraging experience of writing something with great care, something which pleased him and seemed to be correct and clear, only to find that others did not enjoy reading it, that it did not get across. Although everything has interest for somebody, it is equally true that some objects are inherently more interesting than others and can be presented more effectively.

Students manage to turn in both conventional and outstandingly interesting themes when definite topics are assigned by their instructors, but they are often puzzled when required to write compositions on topics of their own choosing. There are five simple tests which will enable you to choose subjects that you can handle effectively (Section 2a, b, c, d, e).

2a. Choose a topic of interest to yourself.

It is difficult to write effectively unless you are actually interested in the material. Vagueness, aimlessness, dullness, and sketchiness are sure evidence of uninterested writing; force and vigor are usually present when you are wrapped up in your subject and let yourself go. You can write more vigorously and interestingly about people and activities that you have been intimately associated with, either pleasantly or unpleasantly, than you can about people and activities that you have known about only through reading or the experience of others.

For example, you may not have been interested in labor unions, but if members of your family or intimate friends have been favorably or adversely affected by labor unions, you are likely to discover that unions are a genuinely interesting topic.

Do not neglect, either, the possibilities of subjects suggested by your reading or by your conversations with others.

You necessarily will write several themes on topics in which you are not really interested—an experience not uncommon for any speaker or writer. Usually even when theme topics are assigned by your instructor, there is opportunity for you to choose that aspect of the subject that comes closest to your interests.

2b. Choose a topic of interest to your readers.

Except on rare occasions, like keeping a diary or taking notes, all writing is done primarily for a reader or a group of readers, with the purpose of giving either information or entertainment, or both. Far more important than yourself as writer are your readers. These may be your classmates, your friends, your relatives, readers of campus publications, or your instructor. Your paper may be specifically required as a class exercise, but you can indicate for what type of reader you intend it. Your instructor then becomes a kind of editor, a "reader over your shoulder," who visualizes himself as one of your designated readers and who judges whether your writing is appropriate.

A writer is a salesman: he has to "sell" his ideas to his readers. He will quite profitably spend considerable time in analyzing the likes and dislikes of his readers, their backgrounds, their general range of information on the chosen subject. He will plan ways to overcome their "sales resistance" by interesting them in his material, or presenting in new or different ways material in which they are already interested.

In general, the following subjects and phases of these subjects have a genuine appeal for most people:

1. *Timely topics:* new ideas or late facts, or the development of some old idea by emphasis upon its contact with recent developments.

2. *People:* unique, prominent, familiar, or unforgettable (even personal reminiscences and reactions).

3. *Places:* historical, unusual, scenic, even uncommon features of common places, and especially familiar features of familiar places.

4. *Travel:* not so much the places themselves but the actual experiences and people encountered in getting from place to place.

5. *Important matters:* those which involve the life and property of others and which have a relation to the reader's own welfare.

6. *Conflict:* contests between people, between man and nature, and internal conflicts (within the individual).

7. *Amusements, hobbies, recreation.*

8. *Occupations.*

9. *Religion.*

10. *Nature:* in all of its animate and inanimate appearances—

animals, plants, flowers, trees, metals, atoms, antibiotics, geology, astronomy, cosmic forces, etc.

NOTE: You may be aided in choosing topics by keeping in mind the general purposes of the four kinds of writing: to tell a story (narrative); to give a picture in words (description); to explain (exposition); or to convince (argumentation).

2c. Choose a topic about which you know something.

Just as one cannot expect to handle a tool or machine efficiently and expertly without some previous experience, some first-hand acquaintance, so one cannot expect to write effectively without some experience and first-hand acquaintance with the topic of the composition. Most current magazine articles and nonfiction books, and fiction too, are based on many months or years of direct observation, study, and personal familiarity with the materials treated. Have you enjoyed the novels of Thomas Hardy, Joseph Conrad, or Herman Melville? Read a biographical sketch of each and note the use they made of their experiences when they wrote. Melville, for example, shipped as a sailor before the mast in 1839. Two years later he sailed around Cape Horn in the whaler *Acushnet* and the following year lived briefly with cannibals in the South Seas. These experiences— and his keen observation of men and the sea—he utilized in *Typee, Redburn,* his great novel *Moby Dick,* and other writings.

Every writer goes to his own experience—to those things he knows or has thought or seen or heard. You, likewise, can do so profitably and effectively.

2d. Choose a topic which you can treat adequately.

You should have in mind, in choosing a topic, approximately the length of the paper that you plan to write. A short paper requires a limited subject; a longer paper naturally permits a broader subject, a more extended treatment, a wider point of view, the inclusion of more details.

The word *theme* implies a single, well-defined *phase* of a subject. It is impossible to write an effective 500-word theme on a subject which requires 5,000 words. If you choose a broad subject and fail to limit it, you are likely to write sketchily and superficially. *College Fraternities, Professional Football, Chicago,* and *Aviation* are

33

examples of such topics. A small composition on a large subject is necessarily a fragmentary, disconnected, ineffective treatment.

General topics or broad subjects must therefore be narrowed. *The Duties of a Fraternity Pledge, How Professional Football Players Are Recruited,* and *When in Chicago, See the Planetarium* are examples of such limitation. *Aviation* is a hopelessly broad subject; limited to *Aviation in America,* it is still too large, even for a book; *The Career of Wilbur Wright* might be developed in a very long paper; *Wilbur Wright's First Flight* would be more suitable for ordinary-length theme treatment.

2e. Choose a topic which is concrete and specific.

Even though you have a topic which can be adequately treated in the number of words allotted, many topics are uninteresting because they are general, vague, or abstract. If any of these words describe your selection, restudy it to make it concrete and specific.

Consider these successive narrowings of a broad general subject, in the light of a student's interest, observation, and experience. The asterisk (*) indicates the broader subject which is narrowed in the next group of topics.

Very general:	College Activities.
General:	Fraternities and Sororities.
	Physical Activities.
	Intellectual Activities.
	Social Activities.
	Studies in College.
	*Student Organizations.
Less general:	Our Intramural Sports.
	College Dramatics.
	Weekends on the Campus.
	Departmental Clubs (Science, Chemistry, French, Debating, etc.).
	Interest Clubs (Camera, Model Railroads, Painting, Ceramics, etc.).
	*Musical Organizations.
Fairly specific:	Our Student Chorus.
	Our All-Campus Musical Show.
	Student Dance Bands.
	Impromptu Music.

Broadcasting Music to the Dormitories.
*Our Glee Club.

Limited: How I Joined the Glee Club.
Why I Joined the Glee Club.
How to Become a Member of the Glee Club.
What Our Glee Club Does.
How Our Glee Club Helps Our College.
Join Our Glee Club and See Our State!
Let's Sing!

2f. Be prepared to write on assigned topics.

Many of the composition subjects in your college classes will be assigned. They may need some adaptation or limitation; they may need none.

Writing on such assigned subjects is excellent experience and also practical training for post-college work, since much routine writing (and speaking) is done on assignment. Answers to letters, research reports in business and industry, newspaper reporting, feature articles, and many of the nonfiction articles in general and trade magazines (as well as formal lectures and informal talks) are examples of assigned materials.

EXERCISES

NOTE: In addition to the theme subjects below, some 150 theme topics are suggested in the Exercise at the end of Section 16, page 122.

A. For each of the 10 classes of subjects on page 32, make a list of 5 to 10 limited topics, each suitable for a 350-word to 500-word theme.

B. Using the following as general subjects, for each write three to · five limited topics which you think will interest specific readers whom you designate: Animals, Athletics, Atoms, Bravery, Business, Campus Activities, Childhood, Contests, Education, Food, Friends, Health, Heroes, Illness, Medicine, Memories, Music, Nature, Night, One Week, Personal Experience, Recreation, Relatives, Soil Conservation, Sorrow, Success, Superstition, Tall Stories, Vacations, Weather.

C. Using the following as general subjects, for each write three to five limited topics which you think will interest specific readers whom you designate: Airplanes, Ancestors, Automobiles, Birthdays, Cities, Cooking, Country, Crises, Dormitories, Dramatics, Embarrassments, Etiquette or Good Manners, Failure, Favorites, Fishing and Hunting, Future, History, Jobs, Jokes, Military Service, Money, Patriotism, Photography, Radio and TV, Reading, Sportsmanship, Taking Stock, Teachers, Thoughtfulness, Water.

D. Using the following official or unofficial American holidays as general subjects, for each write three to five limited topics which you think will interest specific readers whom you designate: New Year's Eve, New Year's Day, Lincoln's Birthday, Washington's Birthday, St. Patrick's Day, Good Friday, Easter, April Fool's Day, May Day, Memorial Day, Fourth of July, August Vacation Days, Labor Day, Columbus Day, Homecoming, Halloween, Armistice Day (Armed Services Day), Thanksgiving, Christmas Eve, Christmas Day.

E. Prepare a list of 10 limited theme topics designed to be developed by telling a story (narrative). Prepare a list of ten designed to be developed by giving a picture in words (description); ten to be developed by explaining (exposition); ten to be developed by convincing (argument).

F. Make a list of five incidents in your life which you think might be interesting to your readers, your instructor and the members of your class.

G. List five subjects about which you think you know details not known to your classmates.

H. Apply the five tests (2a, b, c, d, e) for topics to the following suggestions for themes and suggest what readers you have in mind:

1. An interview with a well-known campus personality.
2. An account of a visit to a law court during a criminal trial.
3. The history, including a description, of one of the buildings of the college.
4. A description and character sketch of one of the best-known employees of the college.
5. A description of the college cafeteria during the luncheon hour.
6. Description of college "types": the athlete, the aesthete, the iconoclast, the bluffer.
7. A description of, and commentary upon, a popular radio or TV program.
8. A criticism of a motion picture currently being shown.
9. An account of the conversation among a group of friends after a college dance.
10. A commentary upon the "easiest" and the "most difficult" courses and professors in the college.
11. Favorite magazines and newspapers.
12. Personalities of high school and college teachers.
13. Likes and dislikes (radio announcers, tabloid newspapers, practical jokes, eight-o'clock classes, trailers, etc.)

14. An account of how you budget your time for a day, a week, a month of college life.
15. What you want to be, and to be doing, ten years from now.
16. Politics on the campus.
17. The greatest personal disaster you can imagine.
18. A list of five books, with reasons for their choice, which you would take with you if you were to be marooned on a desert island for the remainder of your life.
19. Desirable qualities you want your friends (future wife, future husband) to have.
20. The ideal preparation for college.

THE TITLE

3. A well-chosen title serves two purposes. It helps you stick to your subject throughout a theme, reminding you that all material included should be relevant, should have bearing upon the subject. A well-chosen title is also a most effective means of gaining the attention of the reader. Who has not been led to read a certain book, magazine article, or story because of its attractive title? Motion picture producers frequently have paid thousands of dollars merely for the use of an effective title. Give your theme a good title and you have already taken an important step in making the whole composition effective.

3a. Avoid confusion of title and subject.

The term *subject* is broader and more inclusive than the word *title*. If the instructor asks for a composition on "Reading Habits," he has assigned a *subject,* not a *title,* and you should sharpen this subject to a more specific and more interesting title. Conversely, if the actual title is assigned, you must discover precisely what subject it covers. Do not assume that the title of a specific paper should be the same as a general subject which has been assigned. The best titles indicate not a general subject but the actual *theme* of the composition.

3b. Make the title suggest or indicate the material contained in the theme.

It is impossible, of course, for a title to mention everything which the theme contains, but it should give at least a hint of the contents. Do not announce a title and then develop ideas which have no relation whatever to it. Above all, do not use a title, no matter how catchy, which is deliberately misleading.

3c. Use effective phrasing in the title.

1. *Avoid long titles.* As a title, *Browsing Among Magazines* is certainly more effective than *How to While Away an Afternoon Among the Magazines in the Periodical Room of the Belvedere Library.* Lovers of William Wordsworth's poetry refer to a well-loved poem as *Tintern Abbey* rather than by the title the poet gave it: *Lines Composed a Few Miles Above Tintern Abbey, on Revisiting the Banks of the Wye During a Tour, July 13, 1798.*

2. *Rephrase vague and commonplace titles.* Titles like *College Football Is Overemphasized, A Camping Trip, Contemporary Etiquette,* and *The Importance of Using Short Words* can be rephrased for greater concreteness and uniqueness: *Dollar Marks on the Gridiron, Alone in a Civilized Wilderness, Best Foot Forward,* and *Little Words, but Mighty.*

At the other extreme, however, titles which puzzle, mislead, or are too strained and bizarre are questionable. To be effective, a title should be short, informative, fresh, and definite. In these 10 titles, the first five are informative; the second five are fresh, challenging. All are short and definite.

1. *On Various Kinds of Thinking.*
2. *The Method of Scientific Investigation.*
3. *How Americans Choose Their Heroes.*
4. *TV: A Prospectus.*
5. *Portrait Photography.*
6. *The Great Sports Myth.* (A criticism of the American system of sports)
7. *That Burrowing Bean.* (An article about peanuts)
8. *Is It Anyone We Know?* (An article criticizing advertisements designed to appeal to women)
9. *Snapshot of America.* (A brief survey of American culture)
10. *Look Out, Here I Come!* (A study of the reasons for our increasing number of automobile fatalities. Another article on the subject was titled —*And Sudden Death!*)

3d. Place and punctuate the title correctly on the page.

Center the title on the page, on the first line of ruled paper or 2 inches from the top of unruled paper. Leave a space between the title and the first line of the theme. (See Section **1a**.)

Capitalize important words (see Section **97a**), but do not italicize the title or enclose it in quotation marks unless it is itself a quotation or unless you quote it in the theme.

Do not place a period after the title; a question mark or exclamation point may be used if needed.

3e. Avoid vague, indirect reference to the title in the first sentence of the theme.

The title is independent of the composition. The first sentence, therefore, should be complete in its meaning, self-explanatory, without need for reference to the title. Avoid the vague reference of words like *this, that, such* in your opening lines.

Ineffective,
less clear:
1. This is one of the best books I own, and I find it invaluable.
2. It was in the winter of 1955 when it happened. I was driving . . .
3. From early childhood I have been interested in this subject.
4. I was not exactly a tourist when I visited these countries.
5. Many times I have asked myself this same question.

Improved:
1. My dictionary is one of the best books I own, . . .
2. My most serious accident occurred in the winter of 1955.
3. From early childhood I have been interested in music.
4. I was not exactly a tourist when I visited England, Scotland, and Ireland.
5. Many times I have asked myself whether a college education is worth the price.

EXERCISES

A. Buy, or consult in your library, current copies of three or four magazines like *The Saturday Evening Post, Esquire, The American Scholar, The Atlantic Monthly, Harper's Magazine.* Look at the titles of the articles; then skim through the content of these articles and decide whether the titles are commonplace, intriguing, novel (or too novel), appropriate. Copy those titles that you think skillfully chosen, and put in parentheses the general subject of the articles.

B. Follow the procedure listed in Exercise A but apply it to the short stories in the same magazines.

C. Comment on the titles of the selections in your book of readings. Do for eight or ten of these selections what is asked under Exercise A, above.

D. Make the following titles more interesting and effective:

1. A Day in New York City.
2. Spring Sports.
3. A Canoeing Trip.
4. Flying.
5. Why I Came to College.
6. Cold Weather.
7. My Religion.
8. Spending Money.
9. Radio (or TV) Programs I Dislike.
10. Table Manners.
11. A Theme About Myself.
12. Thoughtfulness.
13. Autumn Activities on the Farm.
14. Aboard Ship.
15. My Budget.
16. Campus Clothes.
17. A Rainy Day.
18. Study Habits.
19. Blind Dates.
20. College Vacations.

ANALYSIS OF SUBJECT

4. The first step in writing a theme, after you have chosen or have been assigned a subject and have limited it, is a careful analysis of the subject. You should attempt to understand what the subject involves by asking yourself and by answering satisfactorily certain questions. Your answers to these questions can well be your overall *controlling purpose* to guide you in planning and writing. There should be an objective for your paper other than the completion of a required assignment, for there can be no such thing as good purposeless writing.

Consider carefully answers for these important questions:

→1. How long is my paper to be?

→2. For what reader or readers am I to write? (The teacher is a "reader over your shoulder," an adviser, a kind of editor.)

→3. What is my specific purpose in writing this paper, the purpose that controls and centralizes my writing? Can I express the content of my planned paper in a single summarizing sentence, a thesis sentence, a theme-topic sentence?

→4. What do I already know about the subject? Where can I find additional material, and what kind of material do I want or need?

→5. What type of writing will best suit my subject: narrative, descriptive, expository, argumentative?

4a. Begin your analysis on the basis of the number of words you are to write.

Themes vary in length. Some may be as brief as 250 or 300 words, others may be 500 words or 1,000 words, and long research papers may run up to 5,000 or 8,000 words. Similarly, in the presentation of a speech, you may be asked to speak for 2 minutes, or 5 minutes, or 10 or 15 or 20.

Your choice of subject, your narrowing of a fairly broad subject, your choice of details, and your plan of organization to be followed —all these are directly affected by the number of words that you are to write.

4b. Make your analysis according to your prospective reader.

Nearly every piece of writing is a project for communicating to someone a series of thoughts and emotions. That "someone" may be a specially chosen individual, like the recipient of a business or friendly letter, or he may be one of a group. Narrow "the reader" or "the group" for whom you are writing. The group should not be too large, too broad. Such labels as "the average reader," "any one interested," "city people," "college students," "high school graduates" include people of such varied interests and backgrounds that a composition aimed at them can at best be general. Make sure, too, that your choice of reader is appropriate. It is inappropriate to choose a reader that you talk to a dozen times a day, such as your roommate, or, if you live at home, a member of your family.

Writing aimed at a specific, appropriate person or group is likely to be clear, concise, and effective. Often, your English teacher is one who tries to judge how appropriately and effectively you have written for the reader or readers you have designated. For example, a theme on the subject, *My Background in English,* may be written for your present English teacher to indicate the strong and weak points of your training. It may be written for your high school principal, suggesting changes in the course for those students who go to college. It may be written to your former high school English teachers and may give a critical evaluation of their courses in the light of your present course.

4c. Determine the *central purpose* of the theme.

Before you begin to write, state in a single sentence—which may or may not be included in the theme later—your central purpose, your controlling idea. To play upon words, what is the *theme* of your theme? Write a *thesis* statement, a *topic sentence* for the paper, a sentence that summarizes your entire material. Until you have done this, you have not fully or clearly defined your purpose. (For examples of thesis or summarizing statements, see pp. 53 and 60.)

On the general subject, *A Camping Trip,* you might clarify your purpose and procedure by jotting down for your own guidance:

Limited subject:	*Advice to a Beginning Recreational Director.*
Possible title:	*Let's Take the Boys Camping.*
Reader:	A recreational director or assistant director who is starting his first summer of service.
Length:	1,000 words.
Thesis sentence (general):	Boys between 12 and 15 enjoy most those group activities—especially out-of-doors—which call for vigorous physical exertion.
Or	
Thesis sentence (specific):	The kinds of recreational activities that appeal to boys between 12 and 15 years of age are (1) athletic and competitive (softball, baseball, tennis, swimming, horseshoes); (2) athletic and social (rowing, canoeing, hiking, woodcraft); (3) handicrafts; (4) mental (reading appropriate books, group discussions).

4d. In determining your central purpose, list 15 or 20 details that you might possibly use.

Make an inventory of what you know of the subject. If you know little, make specific plans to find out more, through various means (see Section 5).

Put your inventory into words. Make a list of, say, 15 to 20 or 25 items that *might* be included, that *might* serve as the topic for a paragraph each. The items at first listing may come in no special order, and you may wish to prepare from them a revised list.

For example, in a theme on *When in Chicago, Visit the Planetarium,* your list might include:

1. What a planetarium is.
2. History of the Planetarium.
3. Location.
4. Cost.
5. Description of building (exterior).
6. Description of building (interior).
7. Special exhibits.
8. Special lectures.
9. Maintenance of Planetarium.
10. Personnel.
11. Comparison of Chicago's Planetarium and New York's.
12. Value of planetariums.
13. Mechanics of the projecting machine.
14. Famous astronomers who have lectured there.
15. Best days to go ("free" days or "fee" days).
16. Necessity of making two or three visits.
17. My outstanding experiences there.
18. My personal recommendations to the visitor.

Or, on a simpler subject, like *Meet My High School, The High School I Attended,* or *Important Facts Concerning—High School,* your list might include, as they come to mind:

1. Size.
2. Building.
3. Location.
4. History and name.
5. Number of students.
6. Kinds of students.
7. Number of teachers.
8. Kinds of teachers.
9. Courses of study.
10. College prep courses.
11. Commercial courses.
12. Vocational courses.
13. Athletic program.
14. Basketball championships.
15. Publications.
16. Social activities.
17. Class trips.
18. Dramatic presentations.
19. Musical activities.
20. English courses.

Naturally you would not include all such details in your theme nor in this first-draft order. But such a listing gives you an "overview" and can suggest direction and what details to include or exclude. Your central purpose, after a study of the Planetarium list, might be limited to giving directions for reaching the Planetarium and to calling attention to special exhibits and lectures. From the list about your high school, your central purpose might be a discussion or an evaluation of extracurricular activities, or a discussion of how well your high school work (studies and activities) prepared you for college.

4e. Choose a consistent method of development.

Even when you have sharply limited your subject to fit the number of allotted words, when you have chosen a specific reader or readers, and when you have made a list of possible items to include, you must do still more in your analysis. You must choose some method of development and treatment which will most clearly and effectively accomplish your purpose.

You may wish primarily to use narrative (anecdote, history, biography, etc.); to describe (details of persons or places); to explain (give directions, define, classify, tell how a mechanism works or a process develops, etc.); or to argue (give reasons for and against, give advantages and disadvantages, show the need for or value of, etc.). Or one type of development may be aided by another: by the use of specific narrative incidents in an expository paper, or by a number of descriptive details, or by comparisons and contrasts. (See Section 16.)

4f. Maintain a consistent tone, style, or prevailing character.

Find a word or two, an adjective or noun, which will describe your purpose and planned treatment. Keep this characterizing word constantly in mind as you write. When you have finished writing, check your written material for consistency in the light of this specific descriptive word. Among such words, the following are examples: *serious, dignified, solemn, formal, elevated, critical, humorous, flippant, facetious, light, light-hearted, cheerful, genial, gentle, conversational, familiar, breezy, racy, witty, breathless, whimsical, tranquil, peaceful, sad, mournful, eerie, persuasive, contentious, pungent, ironical, satirical, savage, vitriolic.*

Notice, as examples, the differences in tone in the following. Woodrow Wilson used a *serious* and *dignified* tone in defining liberty:

What is liberty?

I have long had an image in my mind of what constitutes liberty. Suppose that I were building a great piece of powerful machinery, and suppose that I should so awkwardly and unskillfully assemble the parts of it that every time one part tried to move it would be interfered with by the others, and the whole thing would buckle up and be checked. Liberty for the several parts would consist in the best possible assembling and adjustment of them all, would it not? If you want the great piston of the engine to run with absolute freedom, give it absolutely perfect alignment and adjustment with the other parts of the engine, so that it is free, not because it is let alone or isolated, but because it has been associated most skillfully and carefully with the other parts of the great structure.

What is liberty? You say of the locomotive that it runs free. What do you mean? You mean that its parts are so assembled and adjusted that friction is reduced to a minimum, and that it has perfect adjustment. We say of a boat skimming the water with light foot, "How free she runs," when we mean, how perfectly she is adjusted to the force of the wind, how perfectly she obeys the great breath out of the heavens that fills her sails. Throw her head up into the wind and see how she will halt and stagger, how every sheet will shiver and her whole frame be shaken, how instantly she is "in irons," in the expressive phrase of the sea. She is free only when you have let her fall off again and have recovered once more her nice adjustment to the forces she must obey and cannot defy.

Human freedom consists in perfect adjustments of human interests and human activities and human energies.[1]

In contrast, consider the *satirical, half-humorous, half-serious* tone that James Thurber uses in discussing "The Case Against Women":

Another spectacle that depresses the male and makes him fear women, and therefore hate them, is that of a woman looking another woman up and down, to see what she is wearing. The cold, flat look that comes into a woman's eyes when she does this, the swift coarsening of her countenance, and the immediate evaporation from it of all humane quality make the male shudder. He is likely to go to his stateroom or his den or his private office and lock himself in for hours. I know one man who surprised that look in his wife's eyes and never afterward would let her come near him. If she started toward him, he would dodge behind a table or a sofa, as if he were engaging in some unholy game of

[1] From *The New Freedom*. Copyright by Doubleday and Company.

tag. That look, I believe, is one reason men disappear, and turn up in Tahiti or the Arctic or the United States Navy. . . .

I have a lot of other notes jotted down about why I hate women, but I seem to have lost them all, except one. That one is to the effect that I hate women because, while they never lose old snapshots or anything of that sort, they invariably lose one glove. I believe that I have never gone anywhere with any woman in my whole life who did not lose one glove. I have searched for single gloves under tables in crowded restaurants and under the feet of people in darkened movie theatres. I have spent some part of every day or night hunting for a woman's glove. If there were no other reason in the world for hating women, that one would be enough. In fact, you can leave all the others out.[2]

EXERCISES

A. Comment on the following as the readers for whom papers in the past have been written, according to students in freshman English classes. Which seem appropriate or inappropriate, which too general, and which properly specific: (1) Anyone who has an older sister. (2) Anyone who has a young brother. (3) Anyone with patience. (4) People who have not lived on a farm. (5) Any unmarried person. (6) Basketball lovers. (7) Anyone interested in traveling to Mexico. (8) A boy or girl, 14 to 17 years old. (9) A pen pal in England. (10) Anyone not from New York City.

B. Make a list of five theme subjects suitable for treatment in 250 to 500 words; five for treatment in 1,000 to 1,500 words; and five for treatment in 4,000 to 6,000 words.

C. Choose one subject from each of the three length groups in Exercise B and write a sentence or two for each, stating your central purpose (see Section 4c and Section 6g).

D. For one subject chosen in Exercise C, list 15 or 20 details that you might consider using in developing the theme.

E. For each of the subjects chosen in Exercise C, indicate your probable method of development (see Section 4e).

F. Choose five of the *tones* listed in Section 4f, and for each list three theme subjects which might be developed illustrating the particular tone chosen.

G. Restrict the following broad subjects to some phase which can be treated within the limits of an assigned theme-length paper:

[2] From *Let Your Mind Alone!* published by Harper & Brothers, 1937. Copyright, 1936, by James Thurber.

1. Communism in America—Past and Present.
2. The Cosmetics Industry.
3. How People Lived in the Depression '30's.
4. My College Career.
5. Games of Chance.
6. Campus Politics.
7. Campus Activities.
8. Academic Activities.
9. Misunderstandings Between Americans and Europeans.
10. TV Advertising
11. The Motion Picture Industry.
12. Atomic Energy.
13. Atomic Weapons.
14. Week-end Recreations.
15. National and State Parks.

H. Using one of the limited subjects you have prepared for Exercise G, discuss various methods of development to suit different purposes and different kinds of readers.

I. Make a list of 10 subjects which are likely to be uninteresting to your fellow students. Mention methods of analysis and treatment which might make these subjects interesting.

SUBSTANCE

5. The substance or content of a theme may come entirely from your own experience, observation, or imagination, or in part from what you have read and heard about the experience of others. The successful theme depends upon your genuine effort to collect material *before* you actually begin to write.

5a. Gather substance from your own thought and experience.

Many students believe that their own ideas and experiences are not significant or interesting. Actually, personal experience has a freshness and interest which can be effectively conveyed to the reader. As we are interested in what others say to us, others are interested in what we say to them. Significant and interesting materials are available from our own *observation, curiosity, imagination,* and *reflection.*

Indeed, every writer necessarily puts something of himself into everything he writes. The more of himself he puts into his writing

—his own ideas, reactions, and observations—the more likely he is to write with full, interesting, concrete detail. There is no better source of substance than one's self.

5b. Gather substance from the thought and experience of others.

Although a writer necessarily gathers substance from himself, he should not neglect the material he may derive from others.

The easiest and perhaps most pleasant way of getting material for themes from other people is *discussion*. This may take the form of an *interview* in which the ideas of the interviewed person may constitute almost the whole of the theme. Or it may be merely a *conversation* with a member of your family, an acquaintance, or an instructor, in which there is an interchange of ideas, a give-and-take which results in clarified and expanded thought. Classroom discussions are often an excellent source of material for compositions.

Another important way of getting substance from people is *reading*. Magazines, newspapers, and books are almost inexhaustible sources of material which may be utilized. Half-formed ideas of your own may be intensified and expanded by reading. Entirely new phases of thought may be suggested, which, when put through the hopper of your mind, may legitimately be used as your own. A fruitful source of material—a combination of conversation and reading—is discussing with your classmates and instructor the ideas, and their significance, in book-of-readings assignments.

For special information a *letter of inquiry* to a company or to a recognized authority may provide valuable substance, a method especially useful for a longer research paper. Likewise, you may obtain material for themes from *radio* and *television programs, motion pictures,* and *plays.* Although these are usually listened to or seen, not read, they do constitute the experiences and thoughts of other people and as such are fruitful sources of substance.

In drawing upon the experiences and impressions of others, be careful to make them your own by assimilating the ideas and expressing them in your own words, unless you quote directly. When you make use of an idea new to you, either in your own or in quoted words, acknowledge your indebtedness courteously and fully. Sometimes a phrase is sufficient: "As Thomas Carlyle points out in *The French Revolution, . . .*" or "These novelists, Joseph Warren

Beach says in *American Fiction, 1920–1940,* were profoundly affected by the social conditions. . . ." Sometimes—in a research paper, for example—fuller acknowledgment is necessary; for the proper method and forms of documentation in research papers, see Section 20f. The charge of plagiarism must be avoided; taking the ideas and words of another and passing them off as your own is plagiarism.

EXERCISES

A. For each of the following groups make a list of five limited subjects which can be developed using your own thought, experience, and observation:

1. Past and Present Physical Activities.
2. Past and Present Social Activities.
3. My Environment (home, community, college).
4. Recreation and Avocation.
5. Education.
6. Vocational Experiences (full-time; part-time).
7. Financial Responsibilities.
8. Religion.
9. Politics.
10. Philosophy of Life.

B. Mention some personal experience or an incident which you have witnessed that could be used in developing a theme based on one of the following topics:

1. Intercollegiate Football Should (Should Not) Be Abolished.
2. Activities and Studies Do Not Mix.
3. Buying Second-Hand Books.
4. Earning and Saving Money.
5. The Value of a Time Budget.
6. Kindness to Animals.
7. A "Never Again" Experience.
8. The Earth from Above.
9. Drive-Ins.
10. Safe Automobile Driving.

C. What is the most successful theme you have written? How much of its material was based upon personal thought and experience? How much was derived from other people?

OUTLINES AND OUTLINING

6. After you have analyzed your subject, gathered ample substance, and, perhaps, selected a title, you must consider the problem
of *arranging* the material which you have chosen. *Order* is of great
importance in the whole theme. A confused and confusing arrangement confuses the reader, and a clear arrangement is essential in
making your material clear.

The most frequently used method to insure clear ordering of the
parts of a theme is an *outline*. An outline is a sort of blueprint, a
skeleton, a framework for the builder-writer of the theme; in one
sense it is a recipe which contains the names of ingredients and the
order in which they should be used. Outlines need not be elaborate
or overly detailed; they are only a guide to the writer, to be consulted as he writes, to be varied, if need be, when other important
ideas are suggested in the actual writing. In fact, as you write, you
may find certain changes in plan effective and necessary. Sometimes,
too, outlines are of greater value in revision than in the writing of
the first draft.

Why have outlines? Many instructors require them for themes
which are to be submitted because they know that a theme must
be clearly ordered and proportioned to be effective, and because an
outline aids the advisory reader as well as the writer in grasping
immediately the organization. Certainly, no one can write an orderly
composition without using *some kind* of outline, formal or informal,
actual or implied. A writer must know where he is going, whether
his outline be actually written or only in his mind.

A mental outline, one existing only in the mind, is of course of
no help for a teacher who would like to make constructive suggestions about the ordering and subdivision of ideas. Even a brief
outline might well be written—and written *before* you write the
theme. Only apparently logical is any student's statement that he
cannot make an outline until he finishes his theme and knows what
he has said. Would you like to live in, buy, and be proud of a house
which the contractor built first and then made the plans for after
he knew what the house contained?

There are three types of outlines: the *topic outline,* the *sentence
outline,* and the *paragraph outline.* Each type is distinctive and
serves its own special purpose.

6a. Use a topic outline to make clear to yourself the arrangement of your ideas.

The topic outline consists of words, phrases, or dependent clauses —not sentences. It has meaning primarily to the writer and then only for immediate use; perhaps 6 weeks later even the writer would not know what some of the topics mean. Such an outline may be very simple, like the following:

MY BIG DAY

I. The evening before
II. The day itself
III. The morning after

WHY "GO ON" WITH LATIN?[1]

I. The popular reason why people go on with any subject (136 words)
II. The practical reason why people go on with any subject (75 words)
III. The attractive reason why people go on with any subject (148 words)
IV. The effective reason why people go on with any subject (134 words)
V. Application of "the effective reason" to Latin (199 words)
    A. An enlightened perspective (97 words)
    B. An accompanying sense of intellectual mastery (102 words)

NOTE: The figures in parentheses indicate how proportion and proper length (see Section **6f**) can be achieved. In addition, in the article written from this outline, an introductory paragraph had 44 words and a concluding paragraph had 59 words.

The topic outline may be more elaborate, more detailed:

CAMPUS VERSUS CLASSROOM[2]

I. The problem of the classroom (scholarship)
    A. Vacation
        1. Its length
        2. Its lack of relation to post-college life

[1] For a 995-word article from this outline, see Warren E. Black, "Why 'Go On' with Latin?" in *School and Society*, 69 (May 7, 1949), 334, 335.
[2] For a 2,800-word article from this outline, see Burges Johnson, *Campus Versus Classroom*, 1946. The outline is based on the selection, "Campus Versus Classroom," in *Readings for Opinion*, pp. 79–82, edited by Earl Davis and William C. Hummel (New York: Prentice-Hall, Inc., 1952). A paragraph outline of this selection appears in Section **6c**.

    3. Its supposed justification
    4. Why it persists
  B. The college "year" (32 weeks) and the time that is lost
    1. Enrolling and examinations (over 5 weeks)
    2. "Hell Week"
    3. Athletic program
    4. A "prom"
    5. "Senior Week" or "Junior Week"
    6. The cut system
    7. Saturday holidays
II. The problem of the campus (its activities)
  A. Its war with scholarship
  B. What its activities are
  C. Woodrow Wilson on the life and work of a college
  D. The confusion of the two (campus and classroom) in the minds of administrators
III. Possible solutions to the problems
  A. The original old-world setup
    1. Not wanted
    2. Probably not workable
  B. A complete merger of campus and classroom

6b. **Use a sentence outline to make clear to yourself and to a reader the arrangement of ideas.**

The *sentence outline* consists of sentences—grammatically complete sentences, containing subjects and predicates. Such an outline is clear, now and later, to the writer; it is equally clear to any reader who would make constructive suggestions about it. For this latter reason many teachers insist upon sentence outlines. The outline may be simple:

MY BIG DAY

  I. I spent the previous evening putting my soap-box racer into perfect condition.
  II. I won all my preliminary heats, the semifinals, and came in first in the finals.
  III. I was greeted with a parade in my home town and given all kinds of civic honors.

The outline may also be more elaborate, more detailed:

UNIVERSITY DAYS[3]

Thesis sentence: I never could pass botany, but I passed all the other courses that I took at the university: economics, physical education, and military drill.

I. I never could pass botany.
  A. I was unable to see through a microscope.
  B. I repeated the course.
    1. The professor vowed that he would make me see.
    2. I did see, but it was only the reflection of my own eye.
II. I did not like economics but I managed to pass it.
  A. I had my own troubles with the course.
  B. They were nothing to the troubles of a football tackle, Bolenciecwcz.
III. I had more anguish in gymnasium work than I had in botany and economics.
  A. I could not see to do the exercises or play the games.
  B. I could not pass the swimming requirement.
  C. I disliked the physical examination.
IV. I did not have the trouble with journalism that a certain agricultural student had.
V. I had trouble passing the military drill requirement.
  A. We drilled with outmoded rifles and studied Civil War tactics.
  B. I spent four years on military drill.
  C. I had one moment of military glory in the presence of General Littlefield.
  D. I had an interesting interview with General Littlefield the next day.

6c. Use a paragraph outline primarily as a first step in outlining the work of others.

The paragraph outline consists of groups of sentences—perhaps, but not necessarily, the topic sentences (see Section 23), indicating the contents of whole paragraphs.

Such an outline is valuable to the writer when the theme is to consist of only two, three, four, or five paragraphs. His outline consists of his topic sentences or summarizing sentences, usually designated by Arabic numbers.

The paragraph outline is especially useful as the first step in out-

---

[3] For this well-known and widely reprinted essay, see James Thurber, *My Life and Hard Times* (1933).

lining someone else's work, such as a magazine article or an essay. Topic sentences are chosen, perhaps revised a little, or summary sentences are written to represent the thought of successive paragraphs in a selection being studied. From these sentences a topic outline or sentence outline can be built which reveals major and minor divisions.

Here, as an example, is a paragraph outline of Burges Johnson's "Campus versus Classroom," from which paragraph outline the topic outline on page 51 was prepared:

1. The serious-minded boy who goes away to college dreams that he is about to dedicate four years of his life to higher education.
2. Tradition says that 20 of the annual 52 weeks shall be given over to "vacation," perhaps on the theory that a student needs to regain the physical strength he has lost in long hours of hard study.
3. Today this long break in the college year is continued partly from habit and partly because it has become a vested right of the teacher, whose underpayment in salary is counterbalanced by overpayment in leisure.
4. I should like now to examine the 32 weeks in terms of classroom and study hours, in the prewar era.
5. One-sixth of the time of the classroom has been taken from it for the business of organization and tests.
6. Then come other fixed demands made by the campus and enforced by tradition.
7. A "prom" with attendant house parties is more than an evening dance after the day's work is over.
8. In many colleges "Senior Week" or "Junior Week" is a fixture, with festivities supplanting study for 5 or 6 consecutive days.
9. In order to regularize student attendance, or from some other reason now known to God alone, each individual student is allowed a fixed number of unexplained and pre-excused "cuts" to provide for emergencies. . . . All of these drains upon class time have reduced the 32 weeks to 22.
10. I add to this list the Saturday holidays which are a matter of routine at a majority of our universities and colleges.
11. It seems that activities which began spontaneously as outlets for youthful energy in a day when the campus and the surrounding community offered too little variety have now jelled into conventional forms.

12. These activities have not only been thieves of time, but they have been at war with scholarship, many of them secretly and some of them openly and brazenly.

13. The list is long, and if some champion denies the war, the answer is: then why is the activity not a part of the curriculum and an adjunct of the classroom?

14. All of them (the list) are potential enemies of the classroom, and all are actual enemies in one college or another.

15. "*Life* at college," wrote Woodrow Wilson, "is one thing, the *work* of the college another, entirely separate and distinct."

16. A fundamental absurdity of our undergraduate administration is this: it will not admit frankly that classroom instruction is no longer its sole excuse or even its chief excuse for being.

17. The fact is that in ruling over two separate jurisdictions an administrator confuses them in his own mind or thoughtlessly allows them to clash with each other.

18. Many worth-while experiments in college organization have been tried, but no American college has dared to try going all the way back to the original old-world setup; this would mean devoting itself solely to the business of scholarship.

19. Probably such an experiment in American undergraduate college administration has not been tried because no one wants it; it would not work, the chief reason being the immaturity of American college boys and girls.

20. President Hopkins once remarked that the most effective college would be a combination of orphanage and penal institution.

21. The representatives of the former republic of Czecho-Slovakia, after visiting many American colleges, assembled at Vassar College to compare notes and draw up a message of advice to Czechoslovak students who might follow them.

22. The Czech women observed that the life of the campus did much to develop self-reliance and initiative in American women students.

23. My only reason for suggesting that an undergraduate college might try the experiment of complete indifference to campus life is to bring out in sharper relief the obvious alternative—that some college might try bringing about a complete merger of campus and classroom.

6d. Make your outlines correct in form.

The real purpose of an outline is to detect and reveal the structure—the plan, the arrangement—of a piece of writing. The mechanical correctness of an outline is important only as it serves this purpose. There is really neither correctness nor incorrectness of outline form; writers in the past have followed certain conventions, and it is these conventions which are described in this and the next section.

The outline, whether topic, sentence, or paragraph, is based, first of all, on division of material into major parts. Your analysis of your subject shows what the major divisions of your topic are and in what order you can best discuss them. You then make the divisions the foundation of your outline and examine these main points to determine what subtopics you need to include to make your discussion complete.

The examples of outlines given under Section **6a, b,** and **c** show the conventional use of symbols, indentation, and punctuation.

Arabic numbers are used in the *paragraph outline*. Roman numerals could be used, but for some 30 to 50 paragraphs the numbering might be complicated (see Section **99d**). A period follows the symbol; a period or a question mark comes at the end of the sentence. The beginning of each sentence may be indented, or it may begin flush at the left margin, with run-over lines indented.

In making the *topic outline,* follow these directions:

1. Indicate the major divisions by using Roman numerals, I, II, III, IV, etc. Begin flush at the left margin.

2. Indicate the first series of subdivisions under each main division by using capital letters, A, B, C, D, etc. These should be indented equally.

3. Indicate the next series of subdivisions (if needed) by Arabic numbers, 1, 2, 3, 4, etc., also equally indented; and if still further subdivisions are needed, use small letters, a, b, c, d, etc., also equally indented. But do not divide too minutely; avoid cluttering an outline with excessive detail; keep the number of main headings and major subdivisions to a minimum, consistent with clearness, order, and meaning.

4. Use a period after each symbol. Periods at the ends of topics are optional, but be consistent in their use or omission.

In making the *sentence outline,* follow the directions given just above for the topic outline. The only difference is the use of some terminating mark of punctuation—period, question mark, exclamation point—at the end of all divisions and subdivisions.

6e. Make your outlines consistent in their divisions and their wording.

A few words and phrases jotted down at random are not an outline. A usable outline requires thought. You must give it a consistent structure if the theme you write from it is to be well arranged and clear. Therefore, you must critically examine your first draft of the outline and carefully revise it. Remove repetitions and overlappings; add specific details, where necessary; remove illogical relationships; reorganize parts for the most effective organization.

To attain these aims in outlining, follow these suggestions.

1. Be sure that the first main heading—or any main heading—does not merely repeat the title. A main heading is a division of the title or subject.

Wrong: ADVICE TO A HIGH SCHOOL STUDENT

  I. Advice to a high school student
  II. Types of courses to take in high school

HOW TO BE A GOOD FRIEND

 I. Friend—a definition
 II. Types of friends
  A. Fair-weather friends
  B. True friends
 III. How to be a good friend
  A. Be loyal
  B. Be sincere
  C. Be helpful
 IV. Rewards in being a good friend

2. Use parallel phrasing (see Section **45**). Be consistent by using words or the same kind of phrases or the same kind of clauses or the same kind of sentences for all main divisions and subdivisions. Do not use a word for one topic, a dependent clause for another, and do not mix the two kinds of outlines—the topic outline and the sentence outline.

WHO I AM

Wrong:	Improved:	Improved:
I. About my name	I. My name	I. What my name is
II. About my home	II. My home town	II. Where I come from
III. Occupation	III. My occupation	III. What I am doing

3. Do not put in a subhead any matter that should be in a larger division, and do not put in a main heading any matter that should be in a subdivision.

MEET MY ROOMMATE

Wrong:	Wrong:
I. Physical appearance	I. Physical appearance
A. His name	II. Height, weight, age, complexion
B. His outstanding character trait	
C. His worst fault	

4. Remember that outlining is division, that subdivision means division into at least two parts. If a single minor topic must be mentioned, express it in, or as part of, its major heading, or add another coordinate minor topic.

Wrong:

WHY ACCIDENTS HAPPEN

    I. Major reason for accidents
      A. Drivers at fault
   II. Minor reason for accidents
      A. Roads and highways at fault
  III. Proposed solution
      A. Better driver training

However, do not artificially seek for a subdivision B or a subdivision 2 to correspond to an A or a 1. Carry such a single subdivision in your mind or add it as part of the larger division. Some teachers accept and advise a single subdivision when it is to serve as one example or one illustration, since an outline can be a plan of additions as well as of divisions.

Advisable:
  I. Major reason for accidents: drivers at fault
 II. Minor reason for accidents: roads and highways at fault
III. Proposed solution: better driver training

Acceptable:

KINDS OF RESTAURANTS

 I. Those specializing in American food
II. Those specializing in foreign foods

   A. Italian
      1. Antonelli's in Pittsburgh for spaghetti
   B. Chinese
      1. Fu Yung in St. Louis for chop suey
   C. Swedish
      1. Swenson's in Detroit for smorgasbord

5. Avoid meaningless headings such as *Introduction, Body, Conclusion.* If you know what these parts are to contain, put your ideas into words and use them as the headings. Even such headings as *Reasons, Causes, Results, Effects* should be avoided unless they are accompanied by explanatory material or subheads.

6. If your theme is to contain a short introductory or concluding paragraph, such paragraphs need not be indicated by outline topics. For example, the article written from the outline, "Why 'Go On' with Latin?" on page 51, has a brief introductory paragraph of 44 words and a brief concluding paragraph of 59 words.

6f. Use an outline to give your theme proportion.

A good outline will enable you to achieve proper order, and it will assist you in achieving proportion and appropriate length—an adequate number of words for each major division and subdivision for purposes of clearness and effectiveness.

Careful thought, planning, and estimating in both outline and theme are necessary if you are to write a paper that is neither too long nor too short. If you do not plan your themes and if you do not follow some guide to proportion, you may write a narrative of five pages, of which four deal with relatively unimportant details and only one with the really important part of the story. Or in an expository theme, you may write 400 words of introductory material and then suddenly realize that you have only 100 left; into these few you may attempt to compress the important ideas which needed most of the 400-word space.

As a practical suggestion for proportion, place in parenthesis marks after each part of your outline the number of words you plan to write on that division or subdivision. The sum of the subdivision words should equal the major division; the sum of the major divisions should equal the total number of words required. This allocation is, of course, only tentative; you may find expansion or contraction necessary as you proceed. (For an example of such allocation, see the outline of "Why 'Go On' with Latin?" on p. 51.)

6g. Use a *thesis sentence* in the preparation or development of your outline.

Some teachers advise and many writers like to use a *thesis sentence*—one sentence providing the gist of the whole paper or a kind of topic sentence (see Section 23) not for one paragraph but for all. The thesis sentence may summarize a writer's thinking before he begins making his outline; it may serve to tie together his various thoughts after the outline has been written. Your teacher may ask you to prepare such a thesis sentence for each theme and to place it between the title and the outline. (See the thesis sentence for "University Days" on p. 53.)

A thesis sentence for "Campus versus Classroom," page 51, might read:

"Campus versus Classroom" contrasts the scholarship activities of the classroom and the extracurricular activities of the campus; it shows how little actual time there is for academic training, how extracurricular activities conflict with activities of the classroom, and how there may eventually be a solution in their merger.

EXERCISES

A. Rewrite the following outlines, eliminating all errors:

(1)   ARE COLLEGE BOYS STUDENTS?

I. Definition of word, *student.*
    a. Reference to several dictionaries.
II. Many boys come to college to engage in athletics.
    A. Some come to enjoy the social life.
    B. Others to keep from working.
III. A minority come to get a real education.
    1. Preparation for various professions.
        a. Medicine, dentistry.
        1. Law, teaching.
IV. Summary and Conclusion.

Exercises

(2) THREE 4-H ACTIVITIES

I Junior leadership
  a) age
  b) experience
  C) girls' and boys' projects
II Clothing
  a) Age

B) experience
C) Time
D) Cost
III Freezing
  a) where purchased
  B) Cost

(3) AN INTRODUCTION TO THE FIELD OF
TEACHING HOME ECONOMICS

I. Introduction to the Field of Teaching Home Economics.
A. Cooking

B. How to sew
C. Drawing and ceramics

(4) MEET MY ROOMMATES

I. Roommates
  a. Their names and where their home towns are
  b. Their hobbies
  c. What we have in common

d. Physical and Mental characteristics
e. What I like about them
f. What I dislike about them

(5) SOME POPULAR SUPERSTITIONS

I. Introduction
II. Body

III. Conclusion

(6) THREE AIRPLANE RIDES

I. First was slow and gentle
II. Long

III. Wild

(7) CHRISTMAS AT HOME

I. Christmas at Home
  A. A delightful occasion

II. Opening my presents
III. Christmas Day

(8) AN AMERICAN PASTIME

I. One of the American Pastimes
  A. Movies
    1. Western

2. Romance
3. Murder

(9) MY FIRST GUN

A. Out Hunting
B. Showing my Cousin

C. Getting shot
D. Lesson Learned

(10)   THE HIGH SCHOOL I ATTENDED

I. Bldgs
   a. size
   b. location
II. Students
   No. of
   Kind of Students
III. Teachers

   1. Kind of teachers
   2. No. of teachers
IV. Course of Study
   1. College prep
   2. General course
   3. Vocational study

B. Make correct topic outlines for the three themes indicated by the topics you chose in Exercise C on page 46.

C. Make a correct sentence outline for five themes that you could write on the topics chosen in Exercise B on page 46.

D. Make a paragraph outline of one of the essays in your book of readings.

E. Change the paragraph outline (Exercise D) into a sentence outline.

F. Change the sentence outline (Exercise E) into a topic outline.

G. After you have prepared the topic outline (Exercise F), write after each of your main divisions and subdivisions the number of words used by the author. Study this word-numbered outline with the essay or article from the point of view of proper or inadequate proportion.

PROPORTION

Much of the discussion of outlines (Section 6) deals with proportion in planning themes. Proportion is important also as it concerns the amount of space, or detail of treatment, for the various parts of the whole composition.

7. Develop divisions of a theme in proportion to their importance.

Proportion requires that the development given each division of a theme—each paragraph or each group of paragraphs—be in accord with the relative importance of the division. Note the word *relative;* importance is not absolute. In determining which parts of a theme should be developed at length and which less fully, you must be guided by the *purpose* of the theme and the *readers* for whom it is written. Ordinarily, do not give disproportionate space to less closely related or incidental sections of your theme; ordinarily, also, give greater space to sections which may be difficult to understand otherwise, or which are to be emphasized.

For example, if your purpose in writing on *TV Advertising* is to show that such advertising is brazenly overdone, your theme will be badly proportioned if you devote more than half the space to a discussion of the origin and growth of general advertising or of TV broadcasting and only a small part of the composition to the central theme.

Similarly, if you are writing a composition on *Campus Customs* for your classmates, you can appropriately give less space to many important details well known to them than if you are writing on the same subject for a group of foreign students. Even for your classmates, if you argue for the abandonment of certain customs and the retaining of others, the ones you wish to change will get more space than the ones with which you have no quarrel.

The principle of proportion is simply that of giving any part of a theme the space and attention which are commensurate with its importance in relation to the reader and the subject itself.

EXERCISES

A. Study the amount of space given each division of one of your recent themes. Can you justify the proportion from the standpoint of both subject and reader?

B. Look up in a good dictionary these words: *perspective, distortion, proportion, allocation, apportionment.* Discuss the meaning of each as it applies to your writing.

BEGINNING THE THEME

8. After you have gathered material and correctly outlined and proportioned this substance, you are faced with the problem of *beginning* the composition.

Do not make the mistake of thinking that the body of a theme is the only important element and that beginnings and endings are merely tacked on as appendages. Introductory and concluding sentences or paragraphs are of genuine importance to the whole theme because they are first and last impressions. Beginnings and endings should be direct, clear, and effective, not abrupt or wordy. If such material is not carefully composed, the whole theme is likely to lack proportion.

8a. Avoid a beginning referring indirectly and vaguely to the title.

Remember the advice given under Section **3e:** the opening sentences of a theme should be self-explanatory. The reader should never have to refer to the title for the meaning of "This subject . . . ," "On this trip . . . ," "Such an accident . . . ," "These evils. . . ." Here are four improved understandable opening sentences that do not make reference to titles:

Collecting matchbooks as a hobby is fascinating.
On our trip to Mexico we met interesting people and saw memorable scenes.
A head-on collision of two automobiles traveling at high speed is the worst kind of motor accident.
The evils of TV advertising are numerous.

8b. Avoid unnecessary formal introductions.

Write an introduction only when your theme requires one. Usually, only long papers require a formal beginning giving an extended definition of terms, a history of the subject, or a long statement of its significance. Be careful not to make a formal series of general statements or to give needless explanations and details.

8c. Avoid wordy beginnings.

Many writers ramble for some time before they warm to their subject and really come to grips with it. They seem to be building a platform from which to "take off." By the time the reader reaches the "take-off point," if he ever does, he has lost interest in the subject.

Look at the second or third paragraph of your theme. If your theme really begins there, you can throw away everything before it.

Occasionally, a student labors through much introductory material and finally turns up something worth talking about near the end. He unfortunately stops at that point, exhausted by his efforts.

8d. Avoid beginnings that are too abrupt.

Too much introductory detail is ineffective. On the other hand, you must not bewilder your reader by beginning so abruptly that he is unable to understand what follows. If preliminary details are needed, you must give them.

Direct, clear, and effective beginnings serve one major purpose:

orientation. At the end of your first paragraph, ask yourself: "Does my reader have his bearings in the discussion? Does he know where he is and in what direction he is moving?" If your answer is "No" to these questions, throw away what you have written and try again.

For your beginnings the happy medium between *too much* and *too little* is assurance that your reader will continue reading with interest and pleasure.

8e. Begin themes directly and clearly.

If you will think through what you have to say, you can make the important opening position really count by attacking the heart of the subject and avoiding false starts and loose generalities.

Four direct and clear beginnings are illustrated in the following, on *The Evils of TV Advertising:*

1. *Repetition of the title in the opening sentence.*

The evils of TV advertising project like pinnacles above the lesser evils of other forms of advertising.

2. *Rephrasing or paraphrasing the title in the opening sentence.*

Of all forms of advertising, that broadcast by TV is the most brazen and least effective.

3. *A setting or framework within which the subject will develop.*

Everyone is familiar with TV broadcasting, but not everyone realizes that many TV programs are used not only to give information and entertainment but also to enrich those who prepare, present, and pay for them.

4. *A summary or outline paragraph enumerating the main divisions to be discussed.*

TV advertising at the present time is guilty of four deadly sins: the sin of exaggeration, the sin of false taste, the sin of usurpation, and the sin of greed.

These four beginnings are further illustrated in these opening sentences of magazine articles:

1. The method of scientific investigation is nothing but the expression of the necessary mode of working of the human mind. . . .
—Thomas Henry Huxley, "The Method of Scientific Investigation"

2. I shall explain at once what I mean by the "three voices." . . .

—T. S. Eliot, "The Three Voices of Poetry"

3. A few months ago the editors of *Fortune* went into a huddle and, after elaborate and careful calculations, produced the statement that as many as nine million people have moved to the suburbs of American cities since 1947, and that as a result there are now thirty million suburbanites in the United States—a record number, and by a large margin. . . .

—Frederick Lewis Allen, "The Big Change in Suburbia"

4. There are a number of channels of propaganda that are important to the average American. They are, in no special order, personal contacts, newspapers, magazines, radio programs, books, and visual media, such as motion pictures, the theater, and television. There is nothing final in this list.

—William Hummel and Keith Huntress,
"The Media of Propaganda"

Such direct beginnings—a kind of topic sentence for the whole composition—immediately inform the reader of the subject to be discussed. Each such beginning gives the central thought or *theme* of the theme.

8f. Begin themes effectively.

A good beginning gains the reader's attention and so interests him that he wishes to continue reading. Direct and clear beginnings—like those suggested in Section 8e—are usually emphatic. Other specific ways—*alone* or *in combination*—are effective and are illustrated by the opening sentence or sentences of many magazine articles and chapters in books. Some of the most frequently used of these beginnings are the following; compare them with the titles given after the authors' names:

1. *An illustrative incident or anecdote.*

In the year 1830 a French customs official unearthed, in the valley of the Somme, strange implements of flint now recognized by the learned as the weapons with which men of the Old Stone Age made war. These stones are called *coups de poing,* or "blows of the fist," for one end was rounded to be grasped in the hand, while the other end was pointed for persuasion. With these modest tools of death, it seems, the Neanderthal men from what is now Germany, and Cro-magnon men from what is now France, fought fifty thousand years ago for the mastery of the continent, and, after a day of lusty battle, left perhaps a score of dead on the field. Twenty years ago [1917] modern Germans and modern Frenchmen fought again, in that same valley, for that same prize, with magnificent tools of death that killed ten thousand men in a day. One art alone has made indisputable progress in history, and that is the art of war.

—WILL DURANT, "Why Men Fight"

My wife's grandmother, the wife of a distinguished lawyer, once declined to dine with the Cartiers of jewelry fame because they were, as she put it, "in trade." Life for grandmother was relatively simple where social distinctions were concerned, but while there are still a few people who think and act much as she did, the passage of time has eliminated a great deal of that particular snobbishness from American society.

—RUSSELL LYNES, "Highbrow, Lowbrow, Middlebrow"

2. A combination of narrative and descriptive details.

Late last autumn, when the first snow flurries dusted across the northern half of the United States, an estimated three million pairs of knees began to twitch. This mass flexing was the first symptom of a seasonal phenomenon that has progressed in twenty years from the status of a foreign foolishness to that of a national mania. Although still in early stages of development, this phenomenon has reversed migratory instincts, cut scars in the faces of ancient mountains, created an economic revolution in rural areas, upped the income of the medical profession, and released several million inmates of modern society into flights of ecstatic freedom.

—ERIC SWENSON, "Let Fly Downhill"

3. A significant or startling or paradoxical statement.

Such a statement should not be used for attention and interest alone; it should have some connection with what is to follow.

In the past twenty-five years more than seven hundred thousand people have been killed by automobiles in the United States. This is almost twice as many as have been killed in all the wars in which this country has ever been engaged. Some fifteen to twenty million others have been injured, more than a million of them permanently disabled. As a cause of death the automobile ranks just behind diabetes and tuberculosis.

—BERGEN EVANS, "Look Out, Here I Come"

Podunk, as a place name, is older in American history than New York, Philadelphia, and Baltimore, and only six years junior to Boston, yet the lexicographers still pass it over with titters, and try to give the impression that the place itself is a mere hypothetical entry.

—H. L. Mencken, "The Podunk Mystery"

4. *A use of "I" or other first-person reference.*

Between ten and seventeen I did the major bulk of my reading. I have never read as many books (I don't mean manuscripts) per year since, nor do I expect to in the future.

—Clifton Fadiman, "My Life Is an Open Book"

The day I was graduated from college I believed—modestly, and yet with a nice warm glow of conviction—that I was an educated young woman. I had salted away an impressive supply of miscellaneous information. My mind, after constant limbering up with fancy mental gymnastics, was as supple as a ballerina. I was all set to deal with Life.

—Marion Walker Alcaro, "Colleges Don't Make Sense"

5. *A "you" opening, frequently as a polite command, an invitation, or a direct personal appeal.*

How do you measure your weight or waist line, the length of your garden, a bit of butter, a few drops of water? Do you use pounds and ounces, feet and inches? Or grams and kilograms, meters and centimeters? The measurements you use depend upon where you live, what you do for a living—and perhaps even how law-abiding you happen to be.

—Darrell Huff, "Should We All Go Metric?"

I should like you to consider with me a characteristic and fundamental phase of the structure upon which our society is built—its morale.

—Charles E. Wyzanski, Jr., "The Anatomy of Courage"

Note: Use the *you* beginning carefully and appropriately, not as an impertinent or buttonholing device to involve your reader by mechanical means. Make sure that the *you* is a genuine and appropriate address to your reader, that the *you* and the problem stated really concern him. Otherwise, to obtain essential interest at the beginning, use better, more effective devices.

Ineffective and inappropriate for most readers:
    Have you ever built a bird house?

Have you ever climbed a mountain peak in the Himalayan Mountains?

Did you know that the air we breathe is often called ozone?

Appropriate:

Your local, state, and national taxes are high and may go higher? What are you going to do about them? (Group of tax-paying citizens)

Are you observing the necessary precautions for safety in your school laboratory? (Laboratory students)

Your eyes are your most precious possession. Learn about them and their proper care. (College students)

6. *A direct question.*

Have any people ever played such a trick on themselves as we have with the automobile?

—BERGEN EVANS, "Autointoxication"

A bright-eyed woman, whose sparkle was rather more of eagerness than of intelligence, approached me at a party one afternoon and said, "Why do you hate women, Mr. Thurber?"

—JAMES THURBER, "The Case Against Women"

7. *An "if" opening or statement-of-condition.*

If you were suddenly chosen from a group and asked to make an informal luncheon talk, or address a business meeting, or even speak to millions of people over radio and TV, how would your voice sound to your listeners?

—STEPHEN S. PRICE, "Put Your Best Voice Forward"

If the universities had not recently brought the social sciences into the curriculum, they would have saved themselves a lot of trouble. Their freedom would have been attacked very little in the twentieth century.

—ZECHARIAH CHAFEE, JR., "The Freedom to Think"

8. *An observed experience.*

Everyone has heard people quarreling. Sometimes it sounds funny and sometimes it sounds merely unpleasant; but however it sounds, I believe we can learn someting very important from listening to the kind of things they say.

—C. S. LEWIS, "Right and Wrong as a Clue to the Meaning of the Universe"

9. *Directly or indirectly quoted material of some kind or the report of a conversation.*

"Habit a second nature! Habit is ten times nature," the Duke of Wellington is said to have exclaimed; and the degree to which this is true no one can probably appreciate as well as one who is a veteran soldier himself.

—WILLIAM JAMES, "Habit"

Once, in the course of his magnificent wartime broadcasts, Winston Churchill introduced certain lines from *Say Not the Struggle Naught Availeth,* by the English poet, Arthur Hugh Clough. The reader may remember them. They ended: "But westward, look, the land is bright."

—CLIFTON FADIMAN, "The Art of Quotation"

10. *References to people—contemporary or historical, prominent or unknown.*

When I was in St. Augustine, Florida, in the winter of 1932, Helen Keller appeared at the Cathedral Lyceum, and I went to see and hear her there, drawn by curiosity, such as one feels for any world-famous person.

—VAN WYCK BROOKS, "Helen Keller"

The celebrated French criminologist, Alphonse Bertillon, is supposed to have said that it is impossible for a bird to fly through a cloud without leaving traces.

—ROBERT BENDINER, "The Man Who Reads Corpses"

In a dim hut in the Wild Arctic Circle region of Sweden, an area of impenetrable forests and howling storms, a doctor knelt by a stricken patient to wrestle with death.

—RALPH WALLACE, "Doctor at the End of the World"

11. *Timely news events or seasonal occurrences.*

On the morning of December 7, 1951, in the General Sessions Court in New York City, fourteen tall young men stood before Judge Saul S. Streit. The scene was the climax of the notorious basketball scandals in which players had been convicted of receiving bribes from professional gamblers for throwing basketball games in Madison Square Garden.

—HAROLD W. STOKE, "College Athletics: Education or Show Business"

Each spring, with the coming of the crows, the campus of every college that can boast an engineering school undergoes its annual invasion. Recruiting agents from large industrial firms descend on the students with attractive offers of employment; some blue-ribbon institutions receive proposals from a single company to hire the entire senior class.

—George S. Odiorne, "The Trouble with Engineers"

12. *Posing a problem.*

The late Albert Jay Nock used to remark that the most acute observers of the cultural pattern in America have been not social scientists, educators, clergymen, jurists, philosophers, but humorists. A strong case may be made out for this opinion.

—Bernard Iddings Bell, "Perennial Adolescence"

From my boyish days I had always felt a great perplexity on one point in *Macbeth*. It was this:—The knocking at the gate which succeeds to the murder of Duncan produced to my feelings an effect for which I never could account.

—Thomas De Quincey, "On the Knocking at the Gate in 'Macbeth' "

13. *Creation of suspense.*

My career as a mining engineer has this much in common with many success stories—it was founded on an accident. Otherwise, there is no comparison, because mine is not a success story.

—Emily Hahn, "B.Sc."

In Moulmein, in Lower Burma, I was hated by large numbers of people—the only time in my life that I have been important enough for this to happen to me.

—George Orwell, "Shooting an Elephant"

ENDING THE THEME

9. Like the beginning, the ending is an important position. Because it has the last words that the reader sees, it should be emphatic and effective; it should make a final impression upon the reader.

9a. Avoid unnecessary formal or rambling conclusions.

The most important thing to remember in ending themes is this: When you have said all you intended to say, stop. A short composition usually requires no formal conclusion; a summarizing or rounding-off sentence will suffice. A rambling and wordy ending will destroy the effect of what has been said. Except in argumentative writing, there can be little excuse for concluding statements like "thus we see" and "in conclusion, let me state."

Try, therefore, to find a concise effective ending (see Section **9c**), but if you can't, stop anyway instead of trailing off or padding. Apply the story of the guest leaving at the end of a long evening and lingering at the door mumbling: "There was something else I wanted to say," to which the hostess replied, "Perhaps it was 'Good-by.'"

9b. Avoid abrupt and incomplete endings.

Like an effective beginning, there is for an effective ending a happy medium between formal or rambling conclusions and endings that are too abrupt, too sudden or incomplete. Your theme should leave an impression of completeness, of having rounded out a discussion and reached a goal. Avoid closing with a statement that concerns only some detail. Bring your reader back to some phase of the main thought of your theme or leave him with a thought that is a real contribution to the subject.

9c. End themes effectively.

Various specific methods—*alone* or *in combination*—can be used to make the endings of themes effective. Like beginnings, these endings are illustrated in the closing sentence or sentences of magazine articles and chapters in books. Some of these endings are the following. Again, compare them with the titles of the articles:

1. *Reference to or restatement of title or central idea.*

. . . Only the free can be educated, but only the truly educated will find the spiritual spark of genius and morality necessary to remain free.
—Sidney J. French, "Only the Educated Shall Remain Free"

. . . Works of art, in my opinion, are the only objects in the material universe to possess internal order, and that is why, though I don't believe that only art matters, I do believe in Art for Art's Sake.
—E. M. Forster, "Art for Art's Sake"

2. *A summarizing or clinching of the theme of the article.*

The right approach to mathematics, then, is to unbridle the imagination. But this can only be done after the mistaken ideas and feelings about it have been cleared away.
—Mario G. Salvadori, "Math's a Pleasure"

. . . He is that rare statesman—perhaps the only great one of his time —who has kept his feet in the mud of today but his eyes on the stars of tomorrow.

—Hanson W. Baldwin, "Churchill Was Right"

3. *A statement of significance, or some new or practical application.*

One thing is certain: men are no longer taking grass for granted, and we have only begun to discover what may be done with the commonest and potentially the most valuable of all our plants.

—Milo Perkins, "Grass Made to Your Order"

. . . And no matter what some anthropologists, sociologists, and geneticists may tell us, we shall go on believing that man, unlike other forms of life, is not a captive of his past—of his heredity and habits— but is possessed of infinite plasticity, and his potentialities for good and for evil are never wholly exhausted.

—Erich Hoffer, "The Role of the Undesirables"

4. *A generalized statement or logical conclusion growing out of the material presented.*

One is forced to the conclusion that the American woman—according to the advertisements—has a wonderful life until she's twenty-five. After that she'd better be dead.

—Agnes Rogers Allen, "Is It Anyone We Know?"

You can't escape reading fifteen minutes a day, and that means you will read half a book a week, two books a month, twenty a year, and 1,000 or more in a reading lifetime. It's an easy way to become well read.

—Louis Shores, "How to Find Time to Read"

5. *Linking the subject with some matter of current interest.*

No one knows. Nor can any one safely predict. We are at about the same stage in atomic energy today as those in the field of electricity attempting to predict its future uses only ten years after Franklin experimented with his kite.

—Gordon Dean, "Atomic Energy for Peace"

. . . The progress achieved so far is the accomplishment of the many generous public-spirited men and women whose patient aid and unswerving conviction that cancer must and will be solved are making, with the working scientist, the vital steps towards its solution.

—C. P. Rhoads, "Chemicals for Cancer"

6. *Suggesting a course of action or giving advice.*

Educators now find that what was once the recreation of students in school has been transformed into a responsibility of the educational system to supply the public with entertainment. It is essential that educators carry through a fundamental revision of concepts of athletic management appropriate to this transformation.

—HAROLD W. STOKE
"College Athletics: Education or Show Business"

We can make America safe for tree farms only by making every citizen take personal responsibility for keeping fires out of the woods.

—WILLIAM B. GREELEY, "Man-Made Fires"

7. *Offering a warning.*

But silence and inaction mean tacit acquiescence, defeat by default. And unless we act soon to reform our mass media, they will almost certainly succeed in wholly deforming us.

—ALEXANDER KLEIN, "The Challenge of Mass Media:
Movies, Radio, Television"

Most important of all, the contest for technical pre-eminence must not lead us into the trap of encouraging that type of technician who has been called the "skilled barbarian"—the specialist tightly fitted into his own slot and serenely indifferent to the "unscientific" turmoil in which the rest of us live. Such a luxury we can ill afford.

—GEORGE S. ODIORNE, "The Trouble with Engineers"

8. *A direct or indirect quotation.*

Finally, in defense of a habit that it is too late for me to change and that is part of my equipment as a writer, may I call upon Isaac Disraeli? "Those who never quote," he says in his *Curiosities of Literature,* "in return are seldom quoted."

—CLIFTON FADIMAN, "The Art of Quotation"

And if any of your friends come to you with the message that the problems of public life have become intolerable and require some immediate and total solution, I think you might do well to bear in mind the reply which a distinguished European statesman, Bismarck, once gave to certain of his more impatient and perfectionist contemporaries, who wanted him to solve all his country's problems right away, and entirely.

"Let us leave just a few tasks," Bismarck suggested, "for our children to perform; they might be so bored in this world, if they had nothing to do."

—George F. Kennan, "The Illusion of Security"

9. *A direct question.*

What is security for but to give human beings their chance to achieve their full stature of humanity?

—Irwin Edman, "The Elite Among Us"

All of this will, of course, affect every one of us—directly whenever we buy a postage stamp and indirectly through the effect of the rate changes on newspapers, magazines, and books. But it will probably still leave unanswered the basic question: just what part of the postal operations is business and what part is public service?

—Stacy V. Jones, "Who'll Pay the Postage?"

10. *An "if" ending.*

. . . There is hope that law, rather than private force, may come to govern the relations of nations within the present century. If this hope is not realized, we face utter disaster; if it is realized, the world will be far better than at any previous period in the history of man.

—Bertrand Russell, "The Future of Man"

We ought when we put down a book to feel a deeper sense of completion of self, not of escape from it. We ought to understand that self better and feel in closer accord with it and more content with it. If we do, then the book is literature, and literature has made its contribution to life.

—Pearl Buck, "Literature and Life"

11. *An "I" or other first-person reference.*

The public as a whole—that is, the public barring the Intellectual Snobs—shows its sensible preference for having its artists in sufficient possession of their faculties to put us all, and immediately, in possession of their meaning. The artist who does not know his own intentions is a pretender. If he does know them and cannot express them, he is merely incompetent.

I hope I have made myself plain.

—Ivor Brown, "The Case for Greater Clarity in Writing"

75

EXERCISES

A. Choose six articles from your book of readings and study their beginnings: (1) What methods do they use to begin directly and clearly (Section 8e)? (2) What methods, or combination of methods, do they use to gain effectiveness (Section 8f)? (3) Have you discovered other methods in addition to those listed in Sections 8e and 8f?

B. Study the beginnings of all articles in one issue of a magazine such as *The Atlantic Monthly, Harper's Magazine, The Saturday Evening Post, Fortune, The Reader's Digest.* Apply to these beginnings the directions given in Exercise A.

C. Of the articles that you choose in Exercise A, examine the endings: (1) What methods of effective ending are used (Section 9c)? (2) Are there other methods in addition to those listed in Section 9c?

D. What methods of effective ending are used in the articles that you consulted for Exercise B? Are there other methods in addition to those listed in Section 9c?

E. Analyze the beginning and ending of two of your recent themes. If necessary, rewrite the beginnings and endings to make them clearer, more direct, and more effective.

UNITY

10. A *theme* (a short paper, a composition in words) contains and treats a *theme* (subject of a discussion, meditation, composition). Keep in mind constantly "the *theme* within the *theme*" so that you will be sure of treating a *single* phase of one subject. A composition should clearly and fully develop this one phase, but it should not contain unrelated material or padding. It should stick to the oneness of its central idea, its controlling purpose. If it does, it is said to have unity.

10a. Discuss in your theme only one phase of a subject.

A writer is not likely to violate unity so grossly as to discuss completely unrelated subjects, such as, for example, a game of baseball in a composition whose theme is the horrors of war. The danger is that he may thoughtlessly slip from one phase of his subject into another phase which is remotely related but which has no bearing upon the central theme. There is nothing more confusing or irritating to a reader than the insertion of irrelevant detail whose connection with the main theme is not obvious.

The principle of unity in a written composition is violated by the following:

1. An irrelevant introduction or conclusion that is useless or merely tacked on to meet a word quota (see Sections **8b, 9a**).

2. Material which has nothing to do with the subject but is included merely for its own sake.

When a student has a scarcity of ideas and a great need for words, he is likely to resort to padding; that is, he may fill a paragraph or two with words that deal with a phase of the subject other than the particular one being treated. As an illustration, many student-written book reviews give too much space to facts about the author and too little space to the book. A student, writing on the subject, *The Ingenuity of Robinson Crusoe on the Desert Island,* began his theme: "Before giving a discussion of Robinson Crusoe's ingenuity on the deserted island, I think it well to give the main facts of Daniel Defoe's life." Over half the paper was devoted to Defoe's biography.

3. Material which bears on the general subject but which has little bearing on the particular topic discussed. For example, the title of a theme is *My High School*. The particular phase of the subject is the *instruction* in the school. The purpose of the theme is to prove that the school which you attended furnished you with instruction which enables you to do your college work successfully. If in this composition you enter upon a discussion of the school building itself, attempting to point out that it is badly in need of repair, you will have shifted the purpose, the central idea, of the theme.

10b. Give your theme unity of purpose and tone.

In addition to keeping clearly in mind your specific purpose—treating adequately a single phase of one subject—you should seek to achieve also a twofold *general* purpose: (1) If you wish to inform, amuse, interest, arouse to action, be consistent in this aim of your writing. (2) Decide on the basic form of writing that you will use (see Section **16**). If you plan to write narration, do not overburden your writing with description. If you plan to explain, do not become involved in detailed arguments over applications. If you plan to argue, do not introduce anecdotes which have little or no bearing on the evidence.

Also, make your theme consistent in its tone or mood. Do not unnecessarily mix tragedy and comedy, pathos and satire, humor and stateliness, reverence and irreverence, dignity and absurdity, or any two similar extremes. For examples: a serious paper on Abraham Lincoln's last day should not introduce the humorous anecdotes of which Lincoln was fond; a witty paper on the pleasures of eating should not conclude with serious moralizing about the dangers of overindulgence; a fair-minded discussion of international relations on the campus should not include comical or satirical stories about any particular race or nation.

EXERCISES

A. Try to find places in a recent theme where you have dealt with more than one phase of a subject or where you have not confined yourself to both a central and a general purpose.

B. Show how a theme may lack unity even if all its component sentences and paragraphs are themselves unified.

C. Discuss violations of unity in the following plan for a theme:

MY ROOMMATE'S FATHER

I. My roommate's father is an excellent dentist.
II. He studied hard while he was in college and dental school and took many scholastic honors.
III. His mother died during his last year at dental school.
IV. My roommate is not a good student; he is more interested in dancing and campus dramatics.
V. After he was graduated, my roommate's father studied abroad for several years.
VI. He now has a large and lucrative practice in Mobile.
VII. His health is poor, and he has engaged an assistant.
VIII. My roommate has many excellent characteristics.

COHERENCE

11. Coherence means "holding together." It is an essential quality of the good theme because, without coherence, there can be no clear communication of thought from writer to reader. A composition is coherent when its parts have been so carefully woven together that the reader is never confused about the relationships of ideas.

11a. Check your theme and your outline for orderly arrangement.

There is no easier way to confuse your reader than to develop your theme in a series of unrelated steps or in a puzzling order. Test each part of your outline; test each paragraph; and test each sentence within each paragraph. Does each element lead logically and clearly to the element that follows? Are there any gaps? Have you omitted necessary transitions which will indicate orderly development? Make sure not only that you *have* order in the theme but that you *reveal* this order to the reader.

11b. Do not leave any gaps in thought.

In writing a composition remember that your reader cannot read your mind. The relationships of ideas that are clear to you will not be clear to him unless you make them so.

For example, a student may be writing on *Rules for Safe Driving,* in which he jumps from a paragraph dealing with the running of red lights and stop signs to a paragraph discussing ice and snow. The relation of the two paragraphs should be made obvious to the reader in some such manner as this: "In addition to necessary driving precautions, certain measures are necessary also because of road conditions."

11c. Attain coherence by the use of transitional devices.

If the parts of a composition have orderly arrangement and if no gaps in thought occur, coherence is usually attained. Occasionally, however, the progress of thought must be actually *marked* so that the reader will immediately know when one point has been finished and another is taken up.

Transitional devices—literally, bridging or crossing-over devices— which accomplish this purpose are the following:

1. Transitional words and phrases, such as *moreover, however, consequently, in addition, in the second place,* etc. (for longer lists of transitional words and phrases, see pp. 305, 582, 583.)
2. Transitional sentences. Such sentences come usually at the be-

ginning or the end of paragraphs, that is, between integral parts of the theme. An example (in addition to that at the end of Section 11b): "The greatness of a college depends not only upon its buildings and equipment; it depends also upon its faculty and students."

3. Transitional paragraphs, each usually consisting of one or two sentences which look back to the preceding paragraph and point forward to the paragraph which is to come.

The thoughtful writer remembers that he is attempting to *transfer* ideas to readers, and in this effort he will ask, "Will my readers understand this? What will insure their seeing exactly what I have in mind? Shall I summarize here? Shall I warn my readers that I am taking up a slightly different idea here?"

In a coherent theme each paragraph must seem to grow out of the preceding one, and each group of paragraphs dealing with one division of the theme must be clearly connected with other paragraph groups, just as within each paragraph each sentence is logically and coherently related to the sentences that precede and follow. Finally, the reader must be able to see clearly that the whole theme has made orderly progress from beginning to end, without gaps in thought, without obscurity, without fruitless backward movement.

(For supplementary discussion of transition within and between paragraphs, see Section 28.)

EXERCISE

In your book of readings or in the nonfiction articles of a current magazine, look for examples of the three kinds of transitional devices described in Section 11c. Prepare for class a brief discussion of your findings.

CLEARNESS

12. Every writer, both student and professional, can profitably apply the advice of Anthony Hope, British author of the novel, *The Prisoner of Zenda:* "Unless one is a genius, it is best to aim at being intelligible."

Correctness, clearness, and effectiveness are essentials of all good writing. In some respects, clearness is the most important of the three. An idea may be incorrectly and ineffectively expressed, and yet, if it is understood by others, communication, the purpose of all writing, has been achieved.

On the other hand, a theme may be substantially correct in the details of writing and not be clear to the reader. It is theoretically impossible for writing to be effective without being clear; yet many a reader has read and reread material which was obviously correct and seemingly emphatic without being able to understand its central meaning.

Thus, because clearness is essential, nearly every section of this book deals with it. Two specific suggestions and one general suggestion for attaining clearness deserve particular attention.

12a. Restate in simple, direct language the meaning of any passage not clear.

A sentence or series of sentences may be clear to you but not to your reader. Put yourself in his place and read through his eyes. Perhaps your teacher as "reader over your shoulder" may imply, "This is almost or quite opaque," but he will probably say, "Now just tell me in your own words what you had in mind here." Such a secret thought and such a voiced comment concern the sentence or paragraph which is grammatically acceptable and seems to have a kind of meaning playing over its surface but which is still far from communicating anything definite. Use simple, direct language to make your meaning clear.

12b. Define all terms which are not completely clear.

A writer aiming at clearness will never take too much for granted on the part of the reader. It is the writer's responsibility to make sure that the reader understands.

Certain terms familiar to you may be foreign to your reader. Since thinking begins with terms (ideas, concepts, names), the reader cannot understand your thought unless he understands the terms used. Strange or unusual words may puzzle a reader; even in context he may be unable to guess their meaning. An attentive reader should, of course, be willing to look up words if he expects to grow in wisdom and word power, but the writer should not assume that all readers will take this trouble. Appropriateness of words—for the occasion and to the reader—is a fair test; the writer should use words that he can reasonably expect the reader to understand.

If it is necessary to use technical words—that is, terms peculiar to and generally understood only by members of a certain sect, class, or occupation—define them clearly. Such terms as the following are not everyday words: *cassock, quinazoline, gravamen, counterpoint, idiopathy,* and *syncope.* If you use them, define. Again, you should consider the reader or class of readers for whom you are writing; for example, if you are writing a paper for a group of musicians, you need not explain words like *counterpoint.*

12c. Test your statements for evidence of clear thinking.

Clear, orderly thinking must underlie effective writing and speaking. Its presence in the writing and speaking of others should similarly be evident as you read and listen.

In narrative (storytelling), description (word painting), and some forms of exposition (explanation), your material follows a clear, orderly plan—each part leading logically to the part that follows (see Section **6**).

In other forms of exposition (such as fact-finding and in accounts of experiments, in both of which a chain of reasoning is necessary to lead to a definite conclusion) and in argumentative writing or speaking (designed to convince or persuade of the truth or falsity of a proposal or statement), the process of clear thinking becomes more complicated than mere planning and arrangement.

Errors in thinking often occur in fact-finding and experiment-describing exposition and in argumentative writing and speaking, especially when writer or speaker is concerned with establishing his "case" and yields to the temptation to ignore, twist, or even falsify the evidence. For clear and straight thinking, therefore, guard against the errors briefly discussed below when you write or speak.[1] Train yourself to know what they are by looking for them in the writings and speeches of others.

[1] Those who do much writing and speaking of the kinds mentioned (exposition and argument) will find in the following books an excellent extended treatment of methods for attaining clear thinking: Monroe C. Beardsley, *Thinking Straight,* 2nd ed. (Englewood Cliffs, N.J.: Prentice-Hall, Inc., 1956); Richard D. Altick, ch. 3, "Patterns of Clear Thinking," in *Preface to Critical Reading,* 3rd ed. (New York: Henry Holt and Company, 1956); and Manuel Bilsky, *Logic and Effective Argument* (New York: Henry Holt and Company, 1956).

Two common methods of clear thinking, used and violated every day, are *induction* and *deduction.*

Induction seeks to establish a general truth, a comprehensive principle, an all-embracing conclusion. The inductive process begins by using observation of a number of specific facts; it classifies these facts, looks for similarities among them, and from a sufficient number of these facts or particulars draws a conclusion or "leads into" a principle. Once the principle is stated, other particulars or examples are sought to support or verify it. The movement is always *from the particular to the general.*

Deduction, on the other hand, seeks to establish a specific conclusion by showing that it conforms to or "leads down from" a general truth or principle. The movement, implied or expressed, is always *from the general to the particular.*

Let us look at some examples of these processes. Very early in the history of the human race men became convinced from their observation of many particular instances that no man lives forever, that sooner or later all men die. Through *inductive* thinking, then, mankind arrived at a general conclusion about itself, a conclusion that the Greek philosophers phrased: "All men are mortal." A generalization so well established that it no longer needs to be re-examined and tested to be widely believed is sometimes called a major premise, and is used as the starting point in a piece of *deductive* thinking. Thus in the light of the general truth that all men are mortal, we examine the particular truth that Samuel Samson is a man, and we come to the conclusion that therefore Samuel Samson is mortal—that he will die sooner or later. This deductive process is as follows:

Major premise: All men are mortal.
Minor premise: Samuel Samson is a man.
Conclusion: Therefore, Samuel Samson is mortal.

Trouble in clear thinking frequently arises when one of the premises is not stated, but implied, and assumed to be true when it may not be. True reasoning: Samuel Samson is mortal because he is a man. False reasoning: Joe Browne is a poor student because he is an athlete. (Query: Has the statement, "All athletes are poor students," been proved true?)

Through *inductive* reasoning the "laws" (here meaning "principles" or "descriptive, generalized statements") of any science, such as medicine, biology, chemistry, or physics, have been arrived at; and through *deductive* reasoning they are being applied every day in particular situations—the development of a vaccine, the building of a bridge, the manufacture of a complicated business machine.

Similarly, with the "laws" or "rules" (i.e., principles) of language—pronunciation, grammar, word-use, punctuation. Most students do not develop their own punctuation rules by *induction,* although they could if they wanted to spend the time and effort required. If you were to read several hundred pages of prose and make note of how commas are used, you would doubtless reach the conclusion that a comma is usually placed after an introductory adverbial clause—a *when* or *if* or *although* or *because* clause standing at the beginning of a sentence. This process is also *descriptive.* You could then apply this principle *deductively* to your own writing, a process which is also *prescriptive.* Ordinarily, however, you will be content to accept the generalization from your instructor or from a handbook, doing your inductive thinking in fields where the principles have not been so thoroughly investigated and established.

Among specific types of errors which violate principles of clear thinking are the following:

1. *Not distinguishing fact from opinion* is an error that appears in much thinking. A fact is based on actuality and can be positively proved or verified. If it is a statistical fact—such as the population of a city, the number of students in a college or university, or the cost-of-living index for January in a specified year—it is the result of systematic enumeration and mathematical calculation. If it is a historical or biographical fact—the invasion of England by the Normans in 1066; the stock market crash on October 29, 1929, preceded by a lesser panic on October 24; the unenthusiastic reception of Abraham Lincoln's speech at Gettysburg in 1863—such a fact is attested by a record of some sort: a newspaper story, an entry in a private journal or letter, a government document, or, if we go back far enough in time, a tapestry, a rock carving, or a fossil. A generalization, such as that all men are mortal, is con-

sidered a fact only when the evidence in support of it is so overwhelming that its acceptance is virtually unanimous.

Opinion, on the other hand, is a personal inference or preference drawn from facts. That is, it is a belief, the value of which is determined by the validity of the facts which support it and the judgment of the person holding or expressing it. In the following sentence the italicized phrase is opinion; the remainder is fact: Robert Louis Stevenson, *the world's greatest informal essayist,* was born on November 13, 1850. A favorite trick of propagandists is so to mingle opinions with facts as to obscure the difference between them.

2. *Hasty generalization* is one of the great sins against clear thinking. Frequently in induction we observe only a few instances and then are inclined to jump to a dogmatic conclusion, but in most situations it is impossible to draw a sound conclusion from a limited number of instances. Proverbs and other very general statements are often of this kind, some true and some false, such as "Oh, well, you know how women are!" or "Isn't that just like a man?" Or statements like "He would forget; after all, he's an absent-minded professor!" A true proverb, warning also against all hasty generalization, is this: "Let's remember that *one* swallow or *one* robin does not make a summer."

A variation of the *hasty generalization* error is the error of *post hoc ergo propter hoc* (Latin for "after this, therefore on account of this"), the mistake in clear thinking which holds that a happening which precedes another must naturally be its cause, or when one happening follows another, the latter is the direct result of the first. Many popular superstitions began or continue in this way—"No wonder I had bad luck today; yesterday I walked under a ladder (or saw a black cat cross my path, or drew the number 13, or broke a mirror, etc.)." "I have to work my way through college; naturally, I cannot make high grades in my courses." "Bill Smythe has all the spending money he needs; naturally, he does not make high grades in his courses."

3. *Insufficient or biased or suppressed evidence* should be guarded against in any attempt to think clearly. Evidence consists of facts which furnish ground for belief, which tend to prove an assumption or proposition. You have already seen that the use of insuffi-

cient evidence results in the making of hasty generalizations. The use of biased evidence results in equally unwarranted assumptions; suppression of evidence—evidence in favor of another view or casting some doubt on our own presentation—is completely dishonest.

Even figures or statistics can lie if evidence is insufficient, biased, or suppressed.[2] Much of the so-called truth about advertising, or national income, or the value of sports, or similar materials designed to impress the public comes from biased sources, from paid propagandists and directly interested apologists. The testimony of a full-time secretary of a national fraternity is insufficient in itself to support a contention that fraternities are not undemocratic; the evidence of a girl to whom no sorority ever paid any attention may be biased and insufficient to prove that sororities are socially undesirable.

4. The *it-does-not-follow error* (*non sequitur*) is an error common in deductive thinking just as hasty generalization is in inductive thinking. The *non sequitur* is an inference or conclusion that does not follow from the materials upon which it is apparently based. For example, you may know that all the women on the campus are enrolled in the department of chemistry, and you may know also that Student X is taking chemistry, but that does not justify the conclusion that Student X is a woman. Similarly, you may know that gentlemen prefer blondes, but it does not follow that if a girl is a blonde she will be preferred by all the gentlemen of her acquaintance. Many great men have been wretched penmen, but no one is justified in inferring from his own bad penmanship that he is destined to greatness. In other words, unless the material from which you are drawing a conclusion is included in the expressed or implied *all*-group of the generalized statement, the conclusion is not valid.

5. *Begging the question* consists of taking a conclusion for granted before it is proved. Three common forms are *name-calling, slanting,* and *shifting the meaning of a word. Name-calling* appeals to prejudice and emotion, not to intellect. Our minds are so quick to accept epithets that we fail to look behind the propaganda. Fre-

[2] Darrell Huff's "How to Lie with Statistics," *Harper's Magazine,* August, 1950, gives an entertaining and revealing account of nine tricks by which statistical presentations can be made misleading.

quently name-calling appears as sarcasm and invective. Examples are "this wolf in sheep's clothing," "a lousy football player," "this rabble rouser," "second-rate college," "a Caspar Milquetoast." *Slanting* uses colored, unfairly suggestive words to create an emotional attitude for or against a proposal or movement. Its approach is subtle and cumulative. Examples are "these *undemocratic* fraternities and those *snobbish* sororities," "this *undesirable* proposal," "such a *sly* act," "an *unworkable* and *makeshift* substitute," "*dangerous* tendency." *Shifting the meaning of a word* consists in using the same ambiguous word several times with a shift in meaning that, it is hoped, will escape the reader or listener. College *unions* are one thing, labor *unions* are another. So, too, are *sport* and *sports*. *Literature* as *belles lettres* is not *literature* as the written record of the entire life and thought of a people. Should everyone vote the *Republican* ticket because this is a great *republic,* or should he vote the *Democratic* ticket because this is a great *democracy?*

6. *Evading the issue* occurs most frequently in heated personal arguments but is common everywhere. It consists of ignoring the point under discussion and making a statement that has no bearing on the argument. When you tell a classmate that his study habits need improvement and he retorts that you do not handle your allowance properly, he has ignored the question. He may be quite right, but he has not won the argument. He has merely employed what logicians call *ad hominem* argument (argument against the person). Dealing with personalities rather than principles, it seeks to discredit proposals by emphasizing alleged undesirable characteristics of men or groups who favor or are associated with those proposals. *Ad hominem* argument is especially common in political campaigns where issues are not met squarely. A candidate or his supporters may attack the past record, character, and even family of his opponent without once confronting the issues themselves. Appeals to passion and prejudice may gain the votes of the shallow or the ignorant, but they should not convince listeners or readers who have trained themselves against the pitfalls of illogical thinking.

7. *Faulty analogy* occurs when we infer that because two objects or ideas are similar in one or more respects they must necessarily be similar in some further way. Analogy itself can be both accurate

and effective; otherwise, we could never make use of two rhetorical devices based upon it: simile and metaphor. When we use figurative-language analogy, we are not trying to prove something; we are trying to make something clear. When William Shakespeare wrote

> That time of year thou mayst in me behold
> When yellow leaves, or none, or few, do hang
> Upon those boughs which shake against the cold,
> Bare ruin'd choirs where late the sweet birds sang. . . .

he was not attempting to prove a point; he was seeking to give a vivid and moving picture of old age, and he succeeded memorably. If, in an argument about social security, someone were to say, "Look here. We don't do anything to help or protect or comfort trees when they lose their leaves and the autumn winds shake them. Why, then, should we provide assistance to old men and women?" —if anyone were to argue thus, he would be so clearly committing false analogy that he would make himself ridiculous. Sometimes even literal analogies are faulty because the stated points of similarity are not essential; they are either superficial or less important than the differences. Although a certain type of student government—say, the honor system—has worked well in a small college, it does not necessarily follow that it will work equally well in a state or city university of some 20,000 or 30,000 students. Analogy, therefore, is more effective in other forms of discourse than in closely reasoned or argumentative writing. In all writing and speaking it is effective only to the extent that it is illustrative, because in most analogies the differences outweigh the similarities.

Errors in clear thinking—technically, fallacies in logic—not only are common but frequently overlap. We should all try to find and analyze evidence; we should not permit emotional bias and prejudice to take the role of sound reason in our thinking, speaking, and writing; and we should not let unsound reason corroborate our prejudices. In short, we should attempt to acquire honest habits of thought and to express this honesty in speaking and writing.

12d. Revise or rewrite your material to show evidence of clear thinking.

Although you may have checked your statements according to

the directions given in Section **12c,** your material may need further improvement. Your instructor may refer you to one of the following, to guide you in revising or rewriting parts of your paper:

1. The statement needs qualification; it is too sweeping or dogmatic. (This comment refers to assertions which are *not* necessarily false or hasty but simply cover too much ground too positively and need to be guarded with a limiting phrase such as "It is likely that," "As far as my observations go," "Some if not all," etc.)
2. The evidence supplied is pertinent but falls far short of proof.
3. There is such a thing, believe it or not, as being too specific. More general or comprehensive reasons are needed to support this kind of conclusion.
4. Your argument is good so far as it goes, but it is quite unconvincing because you have failed to dispose of some obvious and overriding arguments that can be made on the other side.
5. The facts cited are not such as you can normally verify. You should supply informally in the current of your text some authority, occupational experience, or other reason why you should be believed. (This suggestion is different from documentation—see Section **20f, g;** it applies to the short, informal essay where footnotes would be out of order.)
6. You owe it to your reader not to waste time in naïve exploration of religious or philosophical questions that have been canvassed for thousands of years by experts without being brought to an issue. No logical conclusion on this point is possible because the assumptions with which you begin are untestable.
7. Your treatment here is obviously marked by particular bias and prior emotional commitment. This does not necessarily make your conclusions false but it does make them all suspect.
8. Your approach here is essentially moralistic and directive rather than analytical. There is no law against preaching, but distinguish preaching from investigation, analysis, and reasoning.[3]

EXERCISES

Without paying too much attention to the exact, logical names for the errors in reasoning, reply in your own words to the directions in the following:

A. Point out any errors in clear thinking in the following sentences:

[3] For these suggestions the authors acknowledge their indebtedness to Professor Macklin Thomas of the Chicago City Junior College.

12

1. I have a big day this afternoon, three hours of chemistry lab.
2. We proceeded backward to where we thought we had lost the money.
3. To get through this year I shall have to pitch pennies.
4. The next time I woke up, I was sound asleep.
5. The 35 churches in our city include Catholics, Lutherans, Protestants, and those who belong to the Church of Rome.
6. On my 21st birthday I awoke and found a man in my bed.
7. My teacher is an internationally known scholar on Browning; 20 years ago he published an article explaining one of Browning's shorter poems.
8. During the day my greatest pleasure is engaging in nocturnal frolics.
9. We're having a good dinner tonight; I heard Mother say she was too busy to go down town, she had other fish to fry.
10. I don't know why Jones should be condemned for that fault. At least two other people have exactly the same fault.
11. There are no bluebirds in Indiana. I am positive, because I've never seen any.
12. My alarm clock rang exactly at 6 o'clock A.M. this morning.
13. The score of this shoddily played game was 0 to 0, a scoreless tie.
14. Many an automobile stops along the roadside and picks blueberries.
15. Too many people would like the pork barrel to fall right on their heads.
16. The sky became dark and night fell in the middle of the day, when it became light again.
17. Vespers and sunrise services were held Thursday night, Friday morning, Friday night, and Sunday morning.
18. Many a morning when Mother is upset, she burns the toast, and she burns the toast because she is upset.
19. Some pessimists believe that if women were entirely eliminated, the population of this planet would increase.
20. When I said that I had never traveled to any extent, my facetious roommate said that Any Extent was a mighty nice place to visit.

B. Directions given in A.

1. I studied all night yesterday.
2. Only red hair and plenty of freckles made Queen Elizabeth I the great queen that she was.
3. Evening services were held Thursday night, Friday afternoon, and early Sunday morning.
4. When John learned that poetic license was needed, he decided to quit trying to write poetry.

5. I know she must be wicked because she comes from Paris, France.
6. There goes another bad driver; naturally, it's a woman.
7. I understand that in Greece some very old coins have been discovered having the date on them of 312 B.C.
8. My one brother's name is Robert William; he is my twin and also my only brother or sister.
9. On August 2, 1940, I was born to my parents; I was only a baby then.
10. In a hundred years, I predict that the events of the present will be a thing of the past.
11. Until the late 19th century there was no need for telephones because people did not do much telephoning before then.
12. The reason for this lack of time is because of the fact that I am still getting adjusted.
13. I plan to hibernate this summer in a camp in northern Michigan.
14. The reason he didn't laugh is because he has no sense of humor.
15. I don't like some kinds of bologna. They taste like dead camel's meat.
16. This is a good book. I know, because I wrote it. And why am I an authority? Because I have written the book.
17. I have performed a miracle; I have carried water in a sieve for 15 miles and never spilled a drop.
18. I should not like anything to happen to my husband before we are married.
19. When the real estate agent asked me if I would like to see a model home, I said, "Sure! What time does she get off work?"
20. In high school I attained my goal, which was to graduate from college.

C. Directions given in A.

1. I was born at a very early age in Louisville, Kentucky.
2. When a man's trapped, he's trapped; and vice versa.
3. John is the youngest of three boys in the family, the other two brothers being older.
4. The fact that our stadium was filled to capacity for the Notre Dame game in 1949 is clear evidence that we need a much bigger stadium.
5. George, Mary, and Henry were really very normal people in every way except that they were friends of mine.
6. I have had some very interesting teachers, and then I've had some good teachers too.
7. Being the youngest in our family, I was naturally born last.

8. Most of the plays that we gave in high school were great successes, considering the fact that some were taken from the writings of famous authors.

9. Half of my teachers in high school were men; the other half, strange to say, were women.

10. I have selected all my college activities thoughtfully at random.

11. The farmer takes his many wives to the state fair every year.

12. About a week before he died, a stroke claimed my grandfather's life.

13. I dropped up to the third floor for a conference with my instructor.

14. My seven brothers were all born one year after each other.

15. My father earns his living as manager of a drug store, and he also works some.

16. The attendance at our football games has doubled by a third in the past several years.

17. The doctor was surprised to find three babies in that set of twins.

18. Our annual 4-H Round-Up is held biennially.

19. Every year and sometimes twice a year, we have an annual street carnival.

20. In some of the disastrous shipwrecks of the past, even the women and children had to man the lifeboats.

D. How would you reply to the following questions or suppositions?

1. Suppose you hear a U.S. Government official quoted as saying, "The greatest enemy in America is the United States Government," what would you think?

2. What is your opinion when you learn that the official was speaking against Federal support of price controls for agricultural commodities, and his sentence, *in toto,* read: "The greatest enemy of free economic institutions in America is the United States Government"?

3. You receive through the mail literature including a "Free Information Certificate" entitling you to receive free information on the White Cross Plan of hospitalization. Give reasons why you think you would or would not receive this information if you wrote without making reference to the "Free Information Certificate."

4. Mother once said to Father: "Honey, lend me 10 dollars. But just give me 5 now. Then you'll owe me 5, and I'll owe you 5, and we'll be even."

5. We students believe that we go to college to improve our faculties. Our faculties are our teachers. Therefore, we go to college to improve our teachers.

6. If you think I am dead, please awaken me thoroughly; I do not wish to be buried alive. —Note by the hotel bedside of an 80-year-old.

7. If you do not receive this order, please write me and I shall send it to you again. —Letter to a mail-order house from a newly arrived immigrant.

8. Three copies of this test are missing. Those who have them should make an A. Therefore, anyone who makes an A presumably is one of the three who has seen a copy of this test.

9. Mary loves Bill; Bill loves Sue; Sue loves Mike; Mike loves Sally; and Sally loves Henry. Therefore, Henry loves Mary.

10. Woman is an antonym for man, and man is an antonym for beast; therefore, woman is an antonym for beast.

11. When Professor Sheehan was asked how many students there were on our campus, he immediately replied, "About one out of ten."

12. Poison ivy won't hurt anybody. My brother and I have played in it often, and never had any trouble.

13. Smoking isn't the least harmful; otherwise, there wouldn't be so many doctors that smoke.

14. I haven't acted like an old fool because an old fool must be at least 30, and I'm only 19.

15. It is either raining or not raining. It is *not* raining. Therefore, it must be raining.

E. Directions given in D.

1. I don't know why I should reduce; my doctor is just as fat as I am.

2. Strange as it seems, a pound of feathers weighs more than a pound of lead.

3. I will never, never tell a lie, except once in a while, on very special occasions.

4. "Brothers and sisters have I none, but this man's father is my father's son."

5. A truck driver on a U.S. highway was fined $11.85 for neglecting to *put out* flares while his truck was parked. *Query:* Was he fined because he failed to place lighted flares around his truck, or was he fined because he failed to extinguish already lighted flares after he parked his truck off the highway?

6. If you swear that to the best of your knowledge and belief, something did or did not happen, what do you think a judge or jury would decide in regard to the alleged occurrence?

7. A equals B and B equals C and C equals D and D equals E. Therefore A equals E.

8. You say you have never been very good in English, and you aren't interested in it. What you mean is that you don't care for the lan-

guage of your native country, you don't care for your native country, and you would like to be counted with Philip Nolan in "The Man Without a Country": "Damn the United States; I hope I never hear those words again."

9. Point out the logical inconsistencies in these lines from Stephen Foster's popular folk-song, "Oh, Susannah":

> It rained all night the day I left,
> The weather it was dry,
> The sun so hot I froze to death,
> Susannah, don't you cry.

10. As a democratic organization, we must respect each other's opinions and abide by the will of the majority; but if any one DARES to disagree with my recommendations he is just a plain, low-down, no-good, lousy, stinking skunk.

11. Those who enter college for the first time with a full schedule are called freshmen; you are entering college with a full schedule; therefore, you are a freshman.

12. Those who enter college for the first time with a full schedule are classed freshmen; you are entering college for the first time; therefore you are a freshman.

13. When they drive, some people look back and immediately turn into telephone poles.

14. When you mention my brain and my mind, may I remind you that you are hitting below the belt?

15. Our farm is on a hill and our neighbor's farm is on level ground. When we and he build a perpendicular fence of palings and place them 4 inches apart, we have to use many more palings than he does. Why do we?

CONSISTENCY

13. To write clearly and effectively a writer must be *consistent* in his approach to his material and in its development.

Consistency concerns *mood, style,* and *point of view,* this last a phrase with several meanings: (1) a point or position from which a view is obtained, actually something which is seen; (2) through whose eyes something is seen or through whose mind something is considered—one person's, another person's, or the eyes or minds of many persons.

13a. Be consistent in the personal point of view.

In discussing a subject, you may use one of four personal points of view, i.e., through whose eyes are you looking or through whose mind are you considering? Your choice will depend upon appropriateness to the reader or readers and appropriateness to the subject.

1. *The first person* (*I, my, mine, me, we, our, ours, us*), i.e., the person writing or speaking. First person, singular or plural, is usually used in telling first-hand experiences, thoughts, decisions.

2. *The second person* (*you, your, yours*), the person or persons written or spoken to. Remember that the *you* should not be vague but should refer directly to your reader or readers (listener or listeners), in giving information, asking direct questions, making requests, giving invitations.

3. *The third person* (*he, his, him, she, her, hers, they, their, theirs, them*). Third person is used when you are writing (or speaking) about some one—male or female—or about some group.

4. *The impersonal,* from which point of view all personal pronouns (1, 2, and 3, above) are omitted in favor of indefinite pronouns (*one, a person, everybody, anyone,* etc.)—see Section **71e**—or the passive voice. (See Section **81**.) The impersonal point of view is frequently used in descriptive, expository, and argumentative writing.

For the use of various points of view in writing narrative, see Section **16a**.

Do not carelessly shift the point of view in any discussion from *I* to *we* or *you* or *one,* or from anyone of these to another. When a shift is necessary or effective, as it sometimes is, give your reader warning of what you are doing.

13b. Be consistent in a subjective or objective approach.

When you are *subjective,* you let your own feelings, emotions, prejudices control your attitude. You are personal: everything is seen through your eyes or through your mind as a thinking *subject.*

When you are *objective,* you refuse, or try to refuse, to let your own feelings, emotions, prejudices, control your attitude. You are impersonal: everything is seen or considered outwardly, as it is related to the *object* of thought. An "objective" test, for example, is a test on which the grader's own feelings or beliefs count for nothing; no matter who grades the test, the result is absolutely the same.

One kind of writing may demand a subjective approach and attitude. When it does, guard against letting any objective words or phrases creep in. Another kind of writing may demand an objective approach and attitude. When it does, guard against letting any subjective words or phrases creep in.

13c. Be consistent in the use of a physical point of view.

A physical point of view can concern a point in *space* or a point in *time*. For certain kinds of writing you must choose a point in *space* (inside or outside a building, an elevation, a point of the compass, etc.) or *time* (hour, season, weather, year), from which the subject is to be considered. The selection of a definite point of view is particularly important in descriptive and narrative writing. After you have chosen your position and time, do not needlessly shift them; and, when a shift is necessary, make such shift clear to your reader by using adequate transitional phrases.

If you are describing a building, for example, do not shift carelessly and without warning from the back to the front of it, or from the inside to the outside, or from one floor to another. The reader will be confused if he thinks that you are looking at the outside of the house and suddenly you begin to describe one of the bedrooms or the furnace in the basement.

A confusion in *time* is just as mystifying to the reader. Do not carelessly jump from one year to another or go suddenly from night to the afternoon of the next day. If the time is midwinter, do not without warning interject details about June beetles or growing cotton.

13d. Be consistent in the use of a mental point of view.

For certain kinds of writing, especially expository and argumentative, you must choose a mental point of view, a position or "point in the mind" as it were. You have heard about a doctor's point of view, or a teacher's, a clergyman's, a lawyer's, an undergraduate's. When you attribute views to people, make them consistent and appropriate.

Furthermore, after you have chosen a mental point of view from which to consider a subject, keep this point of view constantly before you. If you are discussing intercollegiate athletic competition, you may properly present arguments for and against it, but you must make perfectly clear when you shift from one side to the other. Similarly, if you are arguing that intramural sports are preferable to intercollegiate athletics, do not present arguments in favor of the latter unless you use them to further your central point. And do not subtly shift to a different phase of the subject, such as women's part in intramural sports, without indicating the shift. Never cause confusion in the mind of your reader about the mental point of view.

13e. Make your writing consistent in *mood*.

Occasionally you will wish to establish a certain *mood* for your reader, to create a certain *impression* in his mind. To succeed, choose words and phrases that will *express that mood for you.*

Here are a few of the many moods from which you can choose: *peacefulness, cheerfulness, lightheartedness, optimism, sarcasm, bitterness, anger, carelessness, sadness, hopelessness, pessimism, weirdness, eeriness, gloom.* You can add many more. (See also Section 4f.)

Notice how the italicized words in the following build the mood or atmosphere or impression of gloom and fear:

During the whole of a *dull, dark,* and *soundless* day in the *autumn* of the year, when the clouds hung *oppressively low* in the heavens, I had been passing *alone,* on horseback, through a *singularly dreary* tract of country, and at length found myself, as the *shades of the evening* drew on, within view of the *melancholy* House of Usher. I know not how it was—but, with the first glimpse of the building, a sense of *insufferable gloom* pervaded my spirit. I say *insufferable;* for the feeling was *unrelieved* by any of that half-pleasurable, because poetic, sentiment with which the mind usually receives even the *sternest* natural images of the *desolate* or *terrible.* I looked upon the scene before me—upon the mere house, and the simple landscape features of the domain—upon the *bleak* walls—upon the *vacant* eye-like windows—upon a few *rank* sedges—and upon a few white trunks of *decayed* trees—with an utter *depression* of soul which I can compare to no earthly sensation more properly than to the after-dream of the reveller upon opium—the *bitter lapse* into everyday life—the *hideous dropping off of the veil.* There was an *iciness,* a *sinking,* a *sickening of the heart*—an *unredeemed dreariness* of thought which no *goading* of the imagination could *torture* into aught of the sublime. What was it—I paused to think—what was it that so *unnerved* me in the contemplation of the House of Usher?

> —EDGAR ALLAN POE, "The Fall of the House of Usher"

13f. Make your writing consistent in style.

Let us think of *mood* as the atmosphere that a writer creates to surround his reader, the impression that the writer wants the reader to receive. Let us think of *style*—which occasionally may include mood—as mainly the manner in which a writer expresses himself. In that expression, variety of phrase, clause, and sentence patterns is not inconsistent, but desirable; however, consistency in style is mainly, although not exclusively, a matter of word choice. What kind of style are you aiming at? Formal? Dignified? Conversational? Simple? Archaic? Quaint? Whimsical? Flippant? Humorous? Breezy? Breathless? Concise? Whatever it is, be consistent in the choice and arrangement of words so that you will achieve the desired aim.

Notice how consistent is the concise, pithy style in this paragraph from Francis Bacon's essay, "Of Studies":

> Some books are to be tasted, others to be swallowed, and some few to be chewed and digested; that is, some books are to be read only in parts; others to be read, but not curiously; and some few to be read wholly, and with diligence and attention. Some books also may be read by deputy, and extracts made of them by others; but that would be only in the less important arguments, and the meaner sort of books; else distilled books are like common distilled waters, flashy things. Reading maketh a full man; conference a ready man; and writing an exact man. And therefore, if a man write little, he had need have a great memory; if he confer little, he had need have a present wit; and if he read little, he had need have much cunning, to seem to know that he doth not.

EXERCISES

A. Determine the *personal* point of view in several essays and short stories that you have read recently.

B. Determine the *physical* point of view (in *space*) of some piece of description which you have read. Does this point of view shift? If so, explain.

C. Determine the *physical* point of view (in *time*) of some narrative that you have read. Does this point of view shift?

D. Determine the mood or impression created in one or more of several essays that you have studied recently. List some of the effective words used.

E. Determine the mood or impression created in one or more pieces of description which you have read. List some of the effective words used.

F. Write a paragraph in which you create the mood or impression of one of the suggestions in Section 13e.

G. Write a paragraph using words which illustrate one of the kinds of style suggested in Section 13f.

EFFECTIVENESS

14. Effectiveness in writing is dependent upon correctness and clearness, but their presence does not insure effectiveness. In order to communicate ideas effectively, you must *interest* your readers. Many students, with the aid of textbooks and instructors, learn to write correctly and clearly. Just as necessary is the expression of ideas in such a manner as to gain and hold the attention of those who read.

The title of an opera by Verdi, *Aïda,* contains the letters of a memory device which can apply to writing: A—Attention; I—Interest; D—Desire; A—Action. That is, a theme should first command the attention of the reader, then attract his interest so that he will desire to read it, perhaps agree or disagree with what is said, and then do what the theme suggests.

14a. Achieve effectiveness by conveying an actual sense of fact.

Many papers are not genuinely effective because of abstractness, indefiniteness. Good writing is definite, concrete; it contains specific details which arouse interest. In other words, it either contains facts or conveys a sense of fact. It should go further and tell what the facts are for.

A composition on taxation will hardly be effective so long as you abstractly discuss the theory of taxation. When you show that every-one of us pays taxes in large or small amounts, even on small every-day items, including food; and when you show also the concrete ways in which tax money is spent for local, state, and national services, your paper comes alive and conveys an actual sense of fact; it has suggested what the facts are for.

Not every writer can be witty or urbane, but everyone can make occasional use of dialogue, or humor, or satire, or human interest, or of a series of questions or exclamations, and everyone can get concrete, definite *movement* of some kind into his writing.

Specific answers to the questions Who? What? Where? When? Why? How? are effective. They furnish realistic touches, clear imagery, which the reader has a right to expect. To help you convey effectively an actual sense of fact:

→1. Enumerate specific details.
→2. Narrate specific and dramatic incidents.
→3. Use specific people as examples, whenever possible.
→4. Use comparison and contrast.
→5. Show definite relationships of causes and effects.

14b. Achieve effectiveness by variety of sentences and paragraphs.

Variety is the spice of writing; it makes writing effective. Try using a variety of sentences: (1) those which vary in grammatical form—simple, compound, complex, compound-complex (see pp. 490, 491); (2) those which vary in meaning and purpose—declarative, interrogative, imperative, exclamatory (see pp. 491, 492); those which vary in the use of suspense—loose and periodic (see pp. 492, 493); those which vary in length—long, short (see Section **49c**). Vary the beginnings of your sentences: start some with the subject, others with one of the numerous kinds of phrases, and others with dependent clauses.

So, too, with your paragraphs: observing the principles of good paragraphing, vary the length of your paragraphs. Just as a reader will tire of pages with no paragraph breaks at all, he will lose interest in a group of paragraphs which are monotonously alike in length or in the kinds of sentences they contain.

14c. Achieve effectiveness by the use of parallel structure.

Parallel structure means that two or more ideas, two or more parts of a sentence, are expressed in the same grammatical form: prepositional phrases, participial phrases, predicate phrases, dependent clauses, independent clauses, and the like. A simple example of parallelism is the oft-quoted line: "To err is human; to forgive divine," in which the subjects (two infinitives) and the adjectives are balanced:

To err	is	human
To forgive	(is)	divine

(For more detailed discussion of parallelism within the sentence, see Section **45**.)

Sometimes separate sentences and even paragraphs are made parallel. Examine carefully the following: check each sentence and the structure of each sentence in the first paragraph with each sentence and the structure of each sentence in the second paragraph.

Verse is patterned language. That is, verse is composition in which words are arranged according to a pattern, a form which is metrical, rhythmical. Verse may be mere doggerel, such as
> "Here lies the body of Samuel Blank;
> He dropped a match in a gasoline tank."

These lines are verse because they consist of words arranged according to a pattern.

Poetry is patterned language, plus. That is, poetry is composition arranged in a pattern. But poetry is more than verse. It signifies high thought, imagination, or emotion.
> "Heard melodies are sweet, but those unheard
> Are sweeter; therefore, ye soft pipes, play on."

These lines are poetry because they are patterned language which contains genuine thought and imagination. All poetry is verse, but not all verse can be called poetry.

14d. Achieve effectiveness by the skillful repetition of words.

Faulty and useless repetition of words and ideas can prevent effectiveness (see Section **68**). Skillful use of repetition can help to achieve it. Reread the illustration of parallelism in Section **14c** and note the effectiveness achieved by the repetition of words like *verse, patterned language, poetry*.

Note the effectiveness of the repetition of the two words, *I know,* in the following, creating the feeling of intimate personal experience:

I know how a prize watermelon looks when it is sunning its fat rotundity among pumpkin vines and "simblins"; I know how to tell when it is ripe without "plugging" it; I know how inviting it looks when it is cooling itself in a tub of water under the bed, waiting; I know how it looks when it lies on the table in the sheltered great floor space between house and kitchen, and the children gathered for the sacrifice and their mouths watering; I know the crackling sound it makes when the carving knife enters its end, and I can see the split fly along in front of the blade as the knife cleaves its way to the other end; I can see its halves fall apart and display the rich red meat and the black seeds, and the heart standing up, a luxury fit for the elect; I know how a boy looks behind a yard-long slice of that melon, and I know how he feels; for I have been there. I know the taste of the watermelon which has been honestly come by, and I know the taste of the watermelon which has been acquired by art. Both taste good, but the experienced know which tastes best.[1]

14e. Achieve effectiveness through effective diction.

Aim at explaining, describing, or narrating from a *fresh* point of view; use vivid, concrete words which suggest feeling, which appeal to the reader's sense of shape, color, sound, touch, taste, and smell. Replace with more colorful, more expressive words the comparatively colorless verbs like *to be* (various forms), *to make, to have, to do, to cause, to seem.* Apply the suggestions for effective diction—use emphatic, appropriate, concise, euphonious diction; avoid trite diction, useless repetition, fine writing—discussed in Sections 63 through 69.

14f. Achieve effectiveness by using the active voice instead of the passive voice.

Make your themes have life, move, or create an impression of movement, with the subjects of your sentences acting and not being passive or acted upon (see Section 81.) To say "The motor was started" or "The way was lost" is not so effective as "I started the motor" or "We lost our way." Use verbs in the active voice whenever you want to express or imply action, mental or physical, unless the purpose of the sentence is to represent the subject as being acted upon. Even in sentences emphasizing inanimate things, choose carefully the appropriate voice: "The fluid runs through the tube at a constant rate" is preferable to "The fluid is run through . . ." When you have chosen the grammatical voice you want, be con-

[1] Mark Twain, *Autobiography,* (New York: Harper & Brothers, 1924), I, 111.

sistent: shifting from active to passive confounds sense and tends to confuse your reader (see Section **46b**).

EXERCISES

A. Choose an article from your book of readings or from a current magazine. Prepare for class discussion an analysis of the devices used for effectiveness in three or four of the paragraphs.

B. Analyze several articles in one issue of *Time* in order to determine the reasons for its effective style.

REVISION

15. "There is no such thing as good writing; there is only good *rewriting.*" Some students may not accept this statement; they maintain that if they really "get going," they turn out first drafts which are superior to anything they have laboriously revised, or they recall having heard of successful writers who never rewrote. The statement, nevertheless, is basically sound.

An Irish author, Frank O'Connor, says of himself: "I write a story with a feeling of slight regret for poor Shakespeare's lack of talent and wake up with a hangover that makes poteen look like cold water. Then, having cursed life and forsworn literature, I start rewriting. If I can work up the Shakespeare mood often enough, I may get it right in six revisions. If I don't, I may have to rewrite it fifty times. This isn't exaggeration."[1]

Like professional writers, students differ in their abilities: some write easily and rapidly; others write slowly and painstakingly, revising as they go. No one, not even an accomplished professional writer, can plan, write, and proofread a paper all at one time. Perhaps the best plan to follow is this: First, gather material for your theme and then plan and arrange it. Next, write the theme with all the vigor and interest you can. If you are a slow, methodical writer, you may wish to compose carefully each phrase, clause, and sentence, checking for spelling, grammar, punctuation, and word-use as you go. Or if you want to get something down on paper, as many writers do, proceed as rapidly as you can without paying spe-

---

[1] Quoted in the head-note to Frank O'Connor, "The Wreath," *Atlantic Monthly,* CXCVI (November, 1955), 65.

cial attention to grammatical, rhetorical, or mechanical details until your first draft is finished. Simply follow the plan that best assures your writing a good theme. After that, and preferably some time later, revise the theme carefully, before you make the final copy.

15a. Revise your theme for unity, coherence, emphasis.

Read your theme once to make sure that it is unified, coherent, and effective as a whole. Delete any extraneous material; recheck to assure that everything in the theme is relevant to the subject; rephrase all vague or rambling thought; substitute specific details for broad generalities.

15b. Revise your theme to secure better sentences.

Read again the preliminary draft to improve the sentences in phrasing and structure. Make certain that all the sentences are unified and complete (Sections **31, 35**); that all ideas are properly coordinated or subordinated (Sections **37, 38**); that there are no "sentence fragments," "comma splices," or "fused sentences"; that the sentences are clearly and effectively phrased; and that the sentences are varied in structure (Section **49**).

15c. Proofread your theme for accuracy and correctness.

In the haste of composing a first draft, you may frequently make careless slips not due to ignorance or you may neglect to check matters about which you are not sure. After you have written your first draft, reread it, correct it, and even entirely rewrite it, eliminating all possible errors.

→1. Go through the theme once for the sole purpose of making sure that all the words are *spelled correctly* (see Section **52**).
→2. Read the theme through again to insure *grammatical correctness*.
→3. Read the theme through again to insure *correct punctuation*.
→4. Read the theme again to insure *effective diction*.

15d. Revise after an interval of time.

Allow as much time as possible to elapse between writing a paper and revising it. If there is sufficient time between the two steps— the actual composition and the suggested rereadings—you will see errors that were not apparent to you when you just completed writing. You can approach your theme more objectively; errors not seen before will be prominent. You have probably noted that most of us can detect errors in another's work more easily than in our own. If you will allow your work to jell, you can see it almost as objectively as if it were the work of someone else.

Another helpful suggestion is to proofread aloud if it is possible. Instructors admit that when they read student themes to the class, they find errors that they overlooked in previous silent readings. Your voice slows down your eyes; you will see errors you have already missed; you will catch harsh or awkward-sounding word combinations; and you will detect involved sentences which need simplification and clarification.

15e. Proofread your final draft.

If you have carried out your revision thoroughly, there should be no flaws in the final draft except those that result from slips of the pen or from errors in typing. Because such slips do occur, you will need to proofread the final draft with care. Do this with pen or pencil in hand, pointing to every word and punctuation mark as you check its correctness. Read aloud this final draft also.

Helpful hints for the first and final drafts of written papers are also given on pages 14–22, "Your First Themes."

15f. Revise your graded and returned theme according to a specific plan.

As in many other activities, one does not improve merely by having his attention called to his errors. He must correct those errors under supervision. So, too, with theme writing.

When your theme is graded and returned to you, observe carefully the errors that are marked and profit by the comments that your instructor has written.

If there are errors in organization or in various types of sentence structure, you may be asked to rewrite and resubmit the theme. If there are errors in spelling, grammar, punctuation, or diction, you may be asked to make corrections on the theme itself, on the back of the theme, or on a separate sheet, labeled "Corrections for Theme No. —." Your instructor will indicate by some method, such as underlining the symbols, which errors are to be corrected, and he may further indicate by some mechanical device such as brackets [. . . .]

the/	Every man has in him possibility	*insert word*
,/,/	Every man they say has in him the possibility	*insert commas*
;/	Every man has in him the possibility but	*insert semicolon*
⊙/	Every man has in him the possibility	*insert period*
:/	They say Every man has in him the possibility	*insert colon*
?/	Has every man the possibility	*insert question mark*
’/	Every mans possibilities lie within him	*insert apostrophe*
“/”/	Every man has in him the possibility	*insert quotation marks*
(/)/	Every man they say has in him the possibility	*insert parentheses*
=/	Some men sidestep the possibility	*insert hyphen*
1/m //	Every man that is, most has in him the	*insert em dashes*
1/	Every man has in him the possibility	*insert superior number*
₰/	Every man has in him thee possibility	*take out*
⁀/	Every man has in him the possi bility	*close up*
₰/	Every man has in him the possibillity	*take out and close up*
tr/	Every man in him has the possibility	*transpose*
stet/	Every man has in him the possibility	*stet, let it stand*
#/	Every man has in him thepossibility	*insert space*
⁀/#/	Ever yman has in him the possibility	*close up and insert space*
eq#/	Every man has in him the possibility	*even spacing*
□/	Every man has in him the possibility	*indent one em*
¶/	purpose. Every man has in him the	*start new paragraph*
[/	[Every man has in him the possibility	*move to left*
]/	]Every man has in him the possibility	*move to right*
(q/?)	Every man has in him the possibilities	*query to author*
cap/	every man has in him the possibility	*set in capitals*
sc/	Every man has in him the possibility	*set in small capitals*
lc/	Every Man has in him the possibility	*set in lower case*
rom/	Every *man* has in him the possibility	*set in roman*
ital/	Every man has in him the possibility	*set in italic*
bf/	Every man has in him the possibility	*set in boldface*
(sp)	Two out of 3 have in them the possibility	*spell out*
9	Every man has in him the possibility	*invert*
wf/	Every man has in him the possibility	*wrong font*
⊥/	Every man has in him the possibility	*push down space*
x/	Every man has in him the possibility	*broken letter*
=/	Every man has in him the possibility	*straighten line*
‖/	Every man has in him the possibility	*align*

Proofreader's Symbols, Listed and Illustrated. (From Dorothy Thompson, *Author's Manual,* rev. ed. Copyright, 1956, by Harper & Brothers.)

At recess Tom continued his flirtation with Amy with jubilant self satisfaction. And he kept drifting about to find Becky and lacerate her with the performance. At last he spied her but there was a sudden falling off of his mercury. She was sitting cosily on a little bench behind the schoolhouse looking at a picture-book with Alfred Tample—and so absorbed were they, and their heads so close over the book together, that they did not seem to be conscious of anything in the world besides. Jealousy ran red-hot through Tom's veins. He began to hate himself for throwing away the chance Becky had offered for a reconciliation. He called himself a fool, and all hard names he could think of. He wanted to cry with vexation. Amy chatted happily along, as they walked, for her heart was singing, but Tom's tongue had lost its function. He did not hear what Amy was saying, and whenever she paused expectantly he could only stammer an awkward assent, which was as often misplaced as otherwise. He kept drifting to the rear of the school house, again and again, to sear his eyeballs with the hateful spectacle there. He could not help it. And it maddened him to see, as he thought he saw, that Becky Thatcher never once suspected that he was even in the land of the living. But she did see, nevertheless, and she knew she was winning her fight too, and was glad to see him suffer as she had suffered.

Amy's happy prattle became intolerable. Tom hinted at things he had to attend to; things that must be done, and time was fleeting. But in vain the girl chirped on. Tom thought, "Oh, hang her, ain't I ever going to get rid of her." At last he must be attending to those things—and she said artlessly that she would be "around" when school let out. And he hastened away, hating her for it.

"Any other boy!" Tom thought, grating his teeth. "Any boy in the whole town but that St Louis smarty that thinks he dresses so fine and is aristocracy! Oh, all right, I licked you the first day you ever saw this town, mister, and I'll lick you again! You just wait till I catch you out! I'll just take and—" And he went through the motions of thrashing an imaginary boy—pommeling the air, and kicking and gouging.

—MARK TWAIN, *Tom Sawyer*

Proofreader's Symbols, Applied. (From Dorothy Thompson, *Author's Manual*, rev. ed. Copyright, 1956, by Harper & Brothers.)

107

or double parallel lines || . . || how much material is to be included on the correction sheet. These correction sheets can be valuable guides in future writing. Save them and study them, especially just before you make the final revision of succeeding themes. (For further discussion of correction sheets—their importance, use, and form—see pp. 18, 19.)

Helpful also is the keeping of a Theme Record, with the kind and number of errors from each theme. For your own guidance you can use the Theme Record facing the inside of the back cover. Your instructor may ask you to make a copy of the Theme Record on a separate sheet, so that he can check it for and with you from time to time.

15g. Follow conventional practice in proofreading printed materials.

In anticipation, perhaps, of your future needs as a campus newspaper or magazine writer, or as a post-college author of articles or books, you are in this section offered advice on preparing material for printing and on proofreading printed materials.

1. Check to see that your manuscript is double-spaced, clearly typed, with double spacing used also for quoted materials and footnotes. Use one side only of white paper, 8½ x 11 inches in size, and *never* use onionskin or other very thin paper. Leave margins of an inch at top, right, and bottom, of an inch and a half at the left. Put your name and address in the upper left corner of the first page. Type the title in capitals about two inches from the top, and put under it your name as you want it printed. Number pages consecutively, top right or top center. Always keep a carbon copy.

2. Be sure your typewritten material is exactly as you want it. Your printer will follow your copy as you have it, misusing grammar, punctuation, spelling, and diction in accordance with your manuscript. For italicized words, underscore once; for small capitals, underscore twice; for large capitals, type them as CAPITALS, or underscore three times; for boldfaced or blackface type, use one wavy line.

3. When you receive galley proofs (single-column sheets about 22 inches long), read them word by word, or even letter by letter, pointing to each with a pencil. If you make changes not occurring

in your manuscript, be prepared to receive an additional bill for these changes.

4. Mark all errors and indicate them also in the margin opposite. Learn to mark printers' proof according to conventional proof-reader's marks. See the illustrated list on page 106 and see how the symbols are applied on page 107. If these will not serve, write out your changes.

5. After you return the galley proofs, you may receive page proofs. Reread these carefully to be sure that all corrections indicated on the galley proofs have been made; that there are no new errors; and that all errors previously missed are now marked. Any additional changes not in the galley proofs will also be made at your expense.

Remember, finally, in all proofreading that you as the author bear the final responsibility in seeing that all errors are marked and corrected.

EXERCISES

A. Make an honest analysis of the time spent on three of your themes. Estimate the amount of time spent on *preparation* for writing, the *actual* time spent in writing, and the time spent in *revising*.

B. Write a short paper discussing the meaning and application of the following statement: "Technical errors hinder communication in writing as much as stammering does in conversation."

C. Below are six short themes, three of them accompanied by their outlines. All were written in class, in a 50-minute period. Proofread each theme carefully, marking all the errors that you see and giving each theme a grade. Assume that the writers have had 10 weeks of college English instruction. Write for each theme a paragraph of comment that should aid the writers in future themes.

WHY ACCIDENTS HAPPEN

I Reasons for Accidents
  A. Careless
  B. Drinking
II Types of Accidents
  A. Women drivers
  B. Men drivers

III What to do about then
  A. Age
  B. People thenself

What are some of the main reason why we have so many accident now days. Is it that the people don't care about thenself, or don't they care about the next guy. Why do they just jump in, start the car and take off without even looking where there going. These kind of drivers are the ones that kill most of the people in auto accidents. They are the ones that drive without care for other people they may know how to drive a car, but do they know how to drive it carefully. A safe driver will drive his car with care, and drive it under the speed laws. Then there is the driver that drinks while driving his car. This kind of driver should not be alound to drive a car. About 90% of all are accidents in the United States are cause by drunken drivers.

There are many types of peopl that drive a car, and about the worst of these are women drivers. Women drivers are always getting in accidents. They may not be the ones that cause these big accidents, but they are the ones that causes the little ones. They hardly ever know where there going or what there doing while driving. And when they do get in an accident there so scare that they just don't know what to do, so they just faint. There are also the hot roders, who drive there car as fast as they can. (*Unfinished.*)

THREE SERIOUS ERRORS IN ENGLISH

There were three reasons why I didn't get through English 101 the first time. One of them being the sentence fragment. Time and time again I made this error. I did just about everything I could to prevent this error, but it seem to be a hopeless case. I could recognize the mistake when it was pointed out to me, but in proff reading I couldn't find them.

The sentence fragment gave me quite alot of trouble and kept my grades low; but another error, which put my grades down even lower, was spelling. In most cases it was'nt not knowing how to spell a paticular word, it was carelessness more then anything else. I would misspell "there" and "their" all of the time. I knew the differences between the two; I was just careless in writing them.

The last and biggest of my problems was the run-on-sentence. This I think was my biggest and worst mistake; if none of the other errors were on my themes you could be sure that the run-on-sentence was there to take care of the grade.

AN ENCOUNTER WITH THE POLICE

The embarrassing encounter I had with the police was the night our basketball team had played a home game with one of the stronger teams in the state. The game had been close all the way and we had findly won with the help of an overtime period. The school was having a dance after the game in the gym, so while the peopl cleared the gym I decided to go to the druge store, that was my mistake. I had been too the druge store and was entering the parking lot behind the school when the trouble started. I was pulling into a vacant spot to park when I saw the rest of the team in another car waitting for me. So I pulled my car into the parking place and do the fact that I have an all modle car I always park it in reverse. Well they were in a hurry and I was too, so when I parket the car I didn't let the motor stop turning over before I let out on the clutch and the car went backward quite fast for a short distance. This would have been all right if that cop hadn't parked his ploice car so close behind me. When my car rolled backward it hit the police car and boy was he mad. He was so mad that before he got though with me he had four other cops their to help arrest me. But it didn't end so bad as it might have sounded because of the fact that I had just played for the highschool and that the ploice were frindly with the basketball team I got off fairly well. It all goes to show that when you hit a police car your in for trouble.

WHO I AM

I. Whats my name?
   1. Nickname
   2. Meaning of name
II. Where am I from?
   1. Jackson, New York
   2. Albany, Pennsylvania
III. What Am I Doing?
   1. Present
   2. Future

My name is Margaret Ellen Jones, but all my friends call me Peg. The name Margaret comes from a Greek word meaning pearl. Since the pearl is a precious jewel and symbolizes quietness and peacefulness, you might get the impression that I am the quiet and meek type. Much as I hate to disillusion you I have to tell the truth. As my father says when he tries to quiet me, "You're the noisiest girl in the house." Of course that wouldn't be saying much if there were only one girl in the house; but my father has four daughters and none of them are quiet. I don't really think I'm any noisier than the average girl but my father thinks differently on the subject. So as the name Margaret doesn't seem to fit me, I glad my friends call me Peggy.

I was born in Jackson, New York, in 1939 and continued to live there for nine years. It was such a quiet peaceful little town that I rather wish we had stayed, but Dad had his office changed and we moved to Albany. Since I was quite young the change of scenery and friends affected me very little; but mother says she caught me day-dreaming about Jackson several times.

I finished grade school and high school in Albany and graduated from the latter on June 6, 1956.

Albany has five large high schools therefore you can imagine what the basketball season meant to the teen-agers. Our high school career was made up of basketball games, just enough studying to get by, and more basketball games. That's the way it went for three years and then we realized college was just a year away and then we began studying.

I took a college preparatory course in high school in case I had the chance to go to college. I'm glad I did because here I am enrolled in State University. History is my favorite subject and I think I would like to teach it when I'm through college. I'm working and studying now to accomplish my aim. This is my answer to "What am I doing?"

FIGURES OF SPEECH

Figures of speech is a word or group of words which translated or interpreted literally might not make sense; but if they are interpreted liberally, the word or words could convey a definate meaning that would otherwise be necessary to write a paragraph to describe. Figures of speech are used very often, not only in written articles, but also in informal conversation. It would be odd to listen to someone who didn't use figures of speech. A very vivid description of an article or an action of someone would probably necessitate the use of at lest one figure of speech.

The three most commonly used figures of speech which we find in written articles are: metaphor, simile, and personification. Metaphor is the substituting of a word or group of words in the description of an object to give a desired effect, but the description might not make sense if interpreted literally. The moon is a large green cheese is a metaphor which can't be translated literally but gives a desired effect.

Exercises **15**

Simile is the comparing of two objects which aren't the same but resemble each other. For instance, he is fleet as a deer, or he walks like an elephant, are examples of simile. The sentences each use some other object to compare with the object or person being described. Personification is the giving to an inanimate object qualities which the object can't posess. The personification the mountain looked down at the valley is a good illustration of the giving to an inanimate object qualities that it can't posess. The mountain can not see, but the personification gives a more vivid description and created a sense of feeling about the mountain which couldn't be otherwise created. Figures of speech are necessary to create a specific feeling in the reader and to give a vivid description of the object being described. Thus, figures of speech are very important in writing an article.

MEET CHICAGO

I. Introduction to Chicago
II. Description of City
   A. Its layout
   B. Its parks
III. Sketch of City.
IV. Detriments
V. Conclusion

I'd like you to meet my home town, Chicago. To really introduce you to the city would take days and days, therefore it's nearly impossible to do anything now but give you a brief sketch of my favorite home.

Of course, you know the city has a "North Side", a "West Side", the "Loop", and last but not the least a "South Side" with Lake Michigan acting as a boundary line on the east of the city. Although Chicago has it's fill of parks we (the Southsiders) agree that our parks are the best. And who can dispute with us, for there is nothing as beautiful as the Loop at night seen from the vantage point of a lonely deserted beach.

Naturally the darkness of night hids some of the "Windy City's" dirt, but since the weather is so unpredictable the rain or snow will soon wash or cover this detriment. When people ask me how I can stand that filthy place, I can never find an answer. Maybe I'm crazy like the rest of the Chicagoans, or maybe I love the way the city reacts. I love the small town atmosphere of carolers at Christmas time; the bustling frantic shopping for last minute items in a bustling frantic department store as the whole town seems to be ready to burst with some of that lost Christmas spirit; the suppressed murmurings of chil-

113

dren gazing in awe at some modern or ancient device in the Museum of Science and Industry; the sailors and their girls walking quietly in the park filled with blooming cherry trees; Buckingham fountain conceitedly showing it's splendid colors to a multitude of it's freinds; the people, young and old, lining up to drop their hard earned money into a box so that a child may someday walk without crutchs. All this I love and so much more that I'm afraid if I tell it you really might begin to think I'm quite conceited and that I'm hiding some of the facts, the true facts, about Chicago.

Yes, we have slums, horrible dirty places where ten humans exsist where two people could comfortably call home, but we are doing something about it and today you can see block after block of undefined rubble being cleared away and clear modern housing units going up in it's place.

Chicago has gansters and law breakers for which it is notorius, but I won't go into that as I can honestly say that I've never been afraid to walk home at night alone. If there are violators of law, I've never seen them. Now I'm not saying I haven't heard about them but . . . oh, lets drop this subject.

I can't write a conclusion for there isn't any. Chicago isn't concluded and never will be. We have just gotten started and if Texas doesn't watch out we may call her our suburb in another year or two.

THE BASIC FORMS OF WRITING

16. All writing can be classified according to one of four forms or types: narration, description, exposition, and argument. *Narration* (or *narrative*) tells a story; *description* gives a picture in words; *exposition* explains; *argument* seeks to convince. No one form exists alone, pure and unmixed; for example, descriptive details may be used in narrative or in exposition; narration helps to clarify in exposition or argument; and argument may be used in exposition. Predominating tone and purpose and characteristics (Section **4c, f**) determine the classification of any piece of writing.

Cutting across boundaries and classifiable according to content are such varieties of writing as the précis (see pp. 127–129), the paraphrase (see pp. 129–132), the research paper (see pp. 163–192), and letters (see pp. 709–738).

Deceptively simple when so labeled, these basic forms of writing and their subdivisions vary in difficulty. The following discussion is brief; you can receive further help from examples in your book of readings, from class discussions and lectures, and from books, magazines, and articles on specific basic forms. For a guide to finding these in your library, see Section **18.**

16a. Use narration to tell a story, true or imagined.

Narration, in telling a story, answers the questions: "What happened? How? When? Why? Where? With or by whom?" It varies in length from extremely long to extremely short materials: novels, novelettes, dramas, biographies and autobiographies, histories, news stories, short stories, incidents, and anecdotes. Longer types of narrative are beyond the scope of freshman writing, as are some of the shorter ones; one-act plays, news writing, and short stories require specialized study.

The plan or order in simple narrative is chronological; that is, you relate the various events as they occurred in time. The narrative is told from a certain *point of view,* the phrase here meaning: through whose eyes and thoughts do we get the story? Do we get it from a major character, from a minor character, or from an omniscient or all-knowing angle? The author is *omniscient;* that is, he knows all that his characters think, feel, and do, and he tells events and thoughts that could not possibly be known by *all* the other participants or characters. The story can be told in the first person (*I*), in the third person singular (*he* or *she*), or with multiple persons (*he, she,* and *they*). In writing narrative, the author must be consistent in point of view.

Shorter or shortened forms of narrative and narrative-exposition that you may choose or be assigned are the anecdote, incident, autobiography, interview, and profile.

1. The *anecdote* is a narrative bit told or written to illustrate some specific point. Its chief characteristic is that it presents individuals in an action which illustrates some definite idea, illuminates some aspect of personality or character. Dialogue, setting, and characters are subordinate to the main point. The anecdote rarely stands alone but is a powerful method of making understandable a possibly difficult idea.

2. An *incident* is a short narrative told for its own sake. It deals

115

with a single, simple situation. Its primary emphasis is upon the character of the narrator or some person involved in the action, or upon the action itself. The incident involves characters, setting, action, and dialogue, but it is simple in structure, brief, and without undue emphasis upon dramatic conflict. Good examples are in the department, "Life in These United States," in each month's *The Reader's Digest*. The following is an example:

When I handed my son a carton of cigarettes, he informed me he had stopped smoking, but insisted on taking the cigarettes anyway. I noticed he put the box on his bureau in plain view; I feared that such temptation would not help the cause.

About two weeks later he returned the full carton to me. "Thanks, Mom," he said. "Now you can give this away—I don't need it any more."

The lid was almost detached from being opened and closed so often. Inside I found a crumpled piece of paper on which was written, "Go ahead and take one—WEAKLING!"[1] [102 words; other examples run to 300 words]

3. In *autobiography,* you give a rounded and understandable picture of yourself, just as in biography you give such a picture of another person. In analyzing your subject (*you*) and gathering material, give consideration to the following: a brief account of your heredity and environment—ancestry, birthplace, places of residence; a series of descriptions of people, places, and events, including education, which have genuinely influenced you; your social beliefs; your religious beliefs; your political beliefs; your moral beliefs; your interests, likes and dislikes, hobbies; your ambitions; your qualities of character; your ideas of happiness. An autobiographical theme composed in whole or in part of a smoothly articulated discussion of these and similar important matters should be genuinely significant and revealing to both writer and reader.

4. The *interview* is a narrative account of some person's opinions, beliefs, and attitudes told through dialogue and direct quotation. The person need not be a VIP—"very important person"; almost anyone who has an interesting occupation or hobby is a good subject. Before the interview, find out as much as you can about the

---

[1] By Alys L. Brennan, in *The Reader's Digest,* February, 1956, pp. 87, 88. Used by permission.

person. Plan in advance the questions you are going to ask and the topics which you would like to have discussed. According to circumstances, modify these as necessary during the interview. Be inconspicuous in the use of a notebook or in taking notes; try to rely upon your memory in the subject's presence. Avoid an exclusive use of a "question and answer" style in writing up the report of the interview. Try to give something of the background of the person. Build your interview around some high point or central thesis of the conversation. Finally, be careful to insure the mechanical accuracy of your interview, such as the use of punctuation marks and the paragraphing of conversation.

5. The *profile* combines biographical material with character interpretation. The profile differs from biographical writing in that it contains more anecdotes, human-interest stories, and humorous or ironic comment. As its name indicates, it is not a full-length portrait; it merely seizes upon highlights and bears somewhat the relation to a full-length biography that a short story does to a novel. Anyone, regardless of who he is, is a potential subject for a profile.

Include in your profile much more than merely "who's who" detail, which ordinarily constitutes a minor part of the whole. Be thorough in getting information, not only from the subject himself but from his friends and acquaintances, the members of his family, his roommate, his enemies, his teachers or students. Do not make your profile didactic: you are not writing a sermon, a moral lecture, or a piece of propaganda. Build the major portion of the profile around some dominant characteristic of the subject. Use incidents, anecdotes, description of appearance and actions, direct quotations, and account for his attitudes toward various topics.

Follow some clear plan of organization. A good and typical profile may be written as follows: First, describe your subject's physical appearance and follow up with a few "flashes" of him or her in action—teaching a class, serving a customer, treating a patient, etc. After that, give a rapid story of the subject's life, stressing those details of heredity and environment which have an important bearing. Then come back to him as of the present, showing why he is important, interesting, amusing, or is bitter, frustrated, or happy, or what not. Here you will develop his guiding "philosophy of life," his primary motives, his aims and hopes, the worth of his actual achievements. Such an outline is merely a suggestion; rearrangement of the items is permissible.

16b. Use description to give a picture or an impression.

Description is that kind of writing which tells how something looks, tastes, smells, sounds, feels, or acts. It deals with objects, people, places, scenes, animals, moods, or impressions. It may supplement narrative, exposition, or even argumentative writing. The primary purposes of description are to portray a sense impression and to indicate a mood.

1. Maintain a consistent point of view to make description clear and effective. As in narrative, choose through whose eyes and mind the subject is presented, and be consistent. Furthermore, are the materials described outside the person: physical things that you help the reader to *see*, or *hear*, or *smell*, or *taste*, or *touch*—concrete *physical* things? Or are the materials within the mind, a *mental* outlook, by which you create for the reader a specific mood or tone (Section 4f)?

2. Use the "space order," ordinarily, in writing description. Space order means choosing some point in space or geography, from which point your description moves: from north to south or east to west, from left to right or right to left; from near to remote or remote to near; or, in personal description, from head to foot. Sometimes you can develop description by beginning with prominent characteristics and moving to the less prominent.

3. For effective description, use words that appeal to one of the senses or that portray a mood: shape, size, color (*rectangular, bulbous, bluish*); sound words (*tinkling, harsh, melodious*); smell words (*pungent, acrid, rose-scented*); taste (*sweet, sour, tangy, bitter*); touch words (*hard, hot, soft, cold, caressing, velvety*); mood words (*sad, brooding, mournful, melancholy*). A piece of descriptive writing should have a single effect, provide a unified dominant impression.

4. A common form of descriptive writing is the *sketch*, a study of character or setting or mood. It contains little action or plot but places emphasis on descriptive details. Unlike the anecdote, it is not concerned with making a point or illustrating a thesis; unlike the

incident, it puts emphasis upon characterization to the virtual exclusion of action.

16c. Use exposition to explain or clarify or interpret.

Exposition includes the greatest part of what we write and read: textbooks; long and short magazine articles; newspaper editorials; and criticisms of books, motion pictures, radio and television programs, and musical compositions. All of these except the first you may be called upon to write.

1. Follow a logical plan or order in writing exposition. Choose one of the following:

a. *Known to Unknown.* Begin with what your reader knows and proceed to the unknown material about which you are to give information.

b. *Simple to Complex.* Begin with easily understood matters; proceed logically to the more difficult.

c. *Classification.* Divide your subject into its various parts according to a consistent, logical plan and discuss each part in order.

d. *Time.* Develop your subject according to the way its phases develop in time, as, for example, giving instructions on how to paint furniture.

e. *Space.* Follow the order that the parts of your subject occupy in space, such as a discussion of regional characteristics or of particular attitudes or habits in various countries.

f. *Deductive.* Begin with a general statement or truth and show how it applies to specific or particular instances or examples.

g. *Inductive.* Discuss particular instances or examples from which you draw a general conclusion or make a generalized statement.

h. *Analogy and Contrast.* Explain your subject, or some part of it, by using analogy, which shows a similarity to some familiar object, or by using contrast, which emphasizes differences.

2. Choose the form of exposition which will most appropriately and effectively develop your subject.

a. *Expanded Definition.* Other than giving a simpler synonym to define a term, most definition assigns a term to a general class (*genus*) and then shows how it differs from other members of this class (*differentia*). In all such definitions, use simple words; exclude everything from the definition that does not belong in it; include

119

everything that does belong; and avoid using the term being defined or any derivative of it. Expanded definition proceeds by giving further details or examples; by using comparison or contrast; by showing cause or effect; or by dividing the term into its component parts. Some of the varied methods of paragraph development discussed in Section 24b can be applied to writing definitions.

b. *Narrative Exposition.* So called because it explains by telling a story and usually follows a time order, narrative exposition is commonly used in the explanation of a process. Subjects using the words "how," "the method," "the principle," and the like, are developed by narrative exposition—for example, *How Petroleum Is Refined* and *Methods of Obtaining Penicillin from Mold.*

c. *Giving Directions.* An important subdivision of narrative exposition is giving directions. Subjects may be impersonal, *How to Ride a Bicycle,* or personal, *How I Learned to Ride a Bicycle.* In either, directions should be so clear that your reader will have no trouble in following them.

d. *Descriptive Exposition.* So called because it explains by describing and ordinarily using space order, descriptive exposition is commonly used in the explanation of mechanical objects like a spark plug, the telephone receiver, a fishing reel. Frequently, descriptive exposition and narrative exposition are used together; excellent examples appear in any issue of a semitechnical or popular scientific magazine.

e. *Criticism.* Whether of a book, magazine article, movie, radio or television program, or musical composition, a criticism is an estimation of worth or value. Ordinarily, as critic, you will answer four questions: What was the author's purpose? What methods did he use in accomplishing his purpose—scope, characters, setting, kind of plot, dialogue, point of view, style, etc.? Was the purpose successfully accomplished? Was it worth accomplishing?

The following suggestions for writing a critical review may be helpful: Always give some indication of the contents. Select a controlling idea and mold your review around it. Make some use of quotations from the work. Be specific; avoid vague terms. Do not hesitate to inject yourself and your ideas into the review. Avoid contradictions and afterthoughts which destroy the unity of purpose and tone of your review.

f. *Informal and Formal Essays.* The informal or personal essay is usually a friendly and conversational explanation of the writer's attitudes or opinions or moods toward some specific subject, using some dominant tone such as whimsy, satire, irony, humor. The formal essay or article is a dignified and usually impersonal treatment of some serious subject; it may be descriptive or argumentative, but it is usually expository. Examples of both informal and formal essays can be found in contemporary magazines: the former is fairly infrequent in this decade; the latter is a preponderant or integral part of the contents of almost all modern magazines. Formal essays are usually specialized types of exposition. However, by following the directions already given for the writing of themes (choosing and limiting and analyzing subjects, Sections **2, 4;** getting material, Section **5,** and organizing, Section **6**), and by adapting the directions for writing the research paper (see Section **20**), you should approach successful writing of the formal essay or article. Bear in mind only that the formal essay is now usually written in an appropriately popular style and, although based on fact, is not accompanied by the paraphernalia of documentation (footnotes and bibliography).

16d. Use argument to persuade or convince.

Formal argument is a complicated subject, using four specialized steps: establishing the proposition, analyzing the proposition, formulating the argument, and preparing the brief, a special form of outline.

Less formal argument—usually used in themes, magazine articles, and occasional newspaper editorials—is built around subjects containing the words "advantages," "disadvantages," "value," or "why": *The Advantages of Belonging to a Social Fraternity, The Value of Intramural Athletics, Why Mission College Should Abolish Final Examinations.*

The order or plan to follow in informal argument is classification: a listing of the reasons for or against, sometimes in the order of climax, i.e., progressing to the most important, sometimes in a more or less arbitrary order. Under each reason discuss the facts or materials, known as evidence, which support and establish that particular phase of the argument. Guard against any weaknesses or errors that would destroy the effectiveness of the chain of reasoning or logical thinking (see pp. 82–89).

Make all argumentative substance lead to an inevitable conclusion. But sometimes you may give both sides and leave the reader to make his own decision about the conclusion: *The Advantages and Disadvantages of Final Examinations.*

EXERCISES

In writing on any of the following subjects, remember that you should have in mind, and indicate, a specific reader or limited group of readers (see Section 4b, p. 41).

A. Examine three selections in your book of readings; determine how many of the four basic forms of writing (narration, description, exposition, argument) are contained in each selection.

B. From the vantage point of a window overlooking a busy street, observe details which are primarily expository, descriptive, argumentative, and narrative. For each type of writing, compile a list of ten subjects based on your observation.

C. Write a 400-word narrative, preferably but not necessarily from personal experience, which will exemplify an old proverb. Do not explain the expository idea of the proverb; simply state at the end the proverb which the narrative exemplifies.

1. A stitch in time saves nine.
2. Better late than never.
3. He who hesitates is lost.
4. Little strokes fell great oaks.
5. Procrastination is the thief of time.
6. There's no fool like an old fool.
7. Fools rush in where angels fear to tread.
8. Pride goeth before a fall.
9. A rolling stone gathers no moss.
10. It's a long lane that has no turning.
11. He who laughs last laughs best.
12. Haste makes waste.
13. Make hay while the sun shines.
14. Two heads are better than one.
15. All's well that ends well.
16. A bird in the hand is worth two in the bush.
17. Half a loaf is better than no bread.

18. One good turn deserves another.
19. A friend in need is a friend indeed.
20. You can't have your cake and eat it too.

D. Write an anecdote to "prove" or "disprove" any one of the following statements.

1. Women are more emotional than men.
2. Men are better automobile drivers than women.
3. Young people are no ruder than their elders.
4. Chivalry among youth is nonexistent.
5. Few people have the courage of their convictions.
6. Informal education is more valuable than formal education.
7. Most important people have inferiority complexes.
8. The honor system on our campus is successful.
9. Athletes receive special consideration from their instructors.
10. Our campus does not know the meaning of "campus politics."

E. List five incidents in which you have recently been involved and which you think would be of general interest.

F. Read the department, "Life in These United States," in several issues of *The Reader's Digest*. From your own experience write several similar incidents (limit, 300 words).

G. Write a brief autobiographical theme (about 500 words), introducing yourself to your instructor.

H. If you do not write a fairly complete autobiography, you may be assigned (or wish to write) sections or divisions of your autobiography: Ancestry; Early Childhood; Environment; Early Education; College; Summer Activities; People, Places, and Events That Have Had Influence; Friends; Religion; Politics; Travel; Ambitions; Interests and Hobbies; Personal Characteristics; Ideals.

I. Choose someone on or near the campus who has a responsible position or who is known for some achievement or activity. Plan, carry out, and write an interview with this person. Suggestions: A Dean; A Head of a Department; An Interesting Teacher; The College Business Manager; A Student Pastor; The Manager or Owner of a Cafeteria; A Bookstore Owner or Manager; The Librarian; The President of Some Class or Organization; The Manager of a Student Activity; A Campus Band Leader; A Campus Policeman; A Janitor; A Night Watchman; A Bus or Taxicab Driver, etc.

J. Write a *profile* of one of the people mentioned in Exercise I or in Exercise N.

K. Copy from a guidebook a formal description of some place which you have visited. Then write a brief description in which you try to convey to the reader some idea of the *impression* which the place made upon you. Make liberal use of your five senses.

L. Make each of the following specific; then write a brief, literal description of any two: A Soda Fountain; A Chemistry Laboratory; A Student Room; A Dentist's Office; A Bus Station; The College Cafeteria; A Professor's Office; A Chain Grocery Store; A Skyscraper; A Filling Station; Back Stage at a Theater; A Projection Booth; A Student's Notebook; An Airport; A Stadium; A Golf Course; A City Park; A Bridge; A Modernized Farm; A Mountain.

M. Assume that a friend of yours in a distant city has agreed to meet at the station someone he or she has never seen. Write for that friend an adequate description of a relative, your roommate, a classmate, or a close friend.

N. Make individual and write a character sketch of one of the following: A College Dean; A Typical Clubwoman; A Member of My Family; My Best Friend; The Cashier at a Motion Picture Theater; A Camp Counselor; A Fraternity Brother; A Coed; An Actress as She Appears in the Part of a Specific Character; Our Family Physician; A Good Teacher; My High School Principal; A Campus Leader; An Unforgettable Character; Man (or Woman) of the Year.

O. Write an informal or expanded definition (300 to 500 words long) of one or more of the following: Dictatorship; A Roommate; An English Composition Class; A Theme; Hydroponics; A State Fair; Sorority Tea; Fraternity Rush; A Good Sport; The Ideal Wife (or Husband); Television; Student Government; 4-H Club; Campus Politics; Code of Honor; Rewriting; S O S; Cut-throat Competition; Scholars and Students; any limited term in sport (Lateral Pass; Offside; Strike; Net Ball; Three-Bagger; Technical Foul; Knockout; Hole in One; etc.).

P. Write a narrative exposition explaining one of the following processes:

1. How an Automatic Washing Machine Works (or any similar mechanism).
2. The Manufacture of Paper (or any similar process that you know about or have observed in a factory).
3. Producing an Amateur Play.
4. Dressing for a Formal Dance.
5. The Principle of Jet Propulsion.
6. Mimeographing.
7. Cooking with a Pressure Cooker.

8. Fluorescent Lighting.
9. The Method of Electing Class Officers.
10. Air Conditioning in the Home.

Q. Write a "giving directions" theme on one of the following:

1. How to Make a Tossed Salad (or some other appetizing food).
2. How to Lead a Boy Scout (Girl Scout) Troop.
3. How to Change an Automobile Tire.
4. How to Study Successfully.
5. How to Make an Eight-O'clock Class.
6. How to Prepare for an Examination.
7. Rules for Driving in City Traffic.
8. A Guide to (or Through) a Building, Factory, Park, Campus, Historical Site, etc. (make definite).
9. Directions for Getting to (name some place).
10. How to Make a Strike in Bowling (or any other limited action in a sport).
11. How I Learned to Swim (or some other physical activity).
12. How I Budget My Time.
13. How I Earn My Spending Money.
14. How I Taught My Dog Tricks.
15. How I Developed My Hobby of —.

R. Write a theme for a named person on a subject beginning: "So You Want to Learn to . . . ."
S. Write a descriptive exposition on one of the following: Automatic Washer, Deep-Freeze Unit, Electric Fan, Camera, Opaque Projector, Movie Film, Ball Point Pen, Desk Calendar, Microscope, Lawn Mower, Can Opener, Storm Windows, Drawing Board, Model Airplane, Electric Shaver, etc.
T. Choose from each of the following groups one that you liked (or like) best and one that you liked (or like) least. Write a criticism of each: book (fiction), book (nonfiction), magazine, newspaper, movie, radio program, television program, musical composition, dramatic production, short story.
U. Write a theme for a named person on one of the following subjects. Begin each theme title with the words "This is a . . . ."
Town You Should Visit; Program You Should Hear; Meal You Would Enjoy; Girl (Boy) Whom You Should Know; Professor Whom You Should Have; Activity You Should Enter; Book You Should Read; Profession You Should Enter; Hobby You Should Have; Movie You Should Not Miss.

V. Make a list of twelve theme subjects to be developed as argument. Distribute your subjects equally among the following:

1. The Advantages of —.
2. The Disadvantages of —.
3. The Value of —.
4. Why I Am in Favor of —.
5. Why I Am Opposed to —.
6. Why — Should — (Example: Why Mission College Should Adopt the Honor System).

THE PRÉCIS AND THE PARAPHRASE

17. "You went to the movies last night, didn't you? What was the picture about?" "What did you do in the city this afternoon?" "Write a brief statement concerning the essential ideas in Thackeray's essay on Addison." All such questions, asked in conversation and on examinations, require summarizing answers—an indispensable form of communication in modern college life. Many times each day we are called upon to give, in written or oral form, condensed versions of events, ideas, or impressions.

In fact, the method of summary is generally prevalent. Such a popular magazine as *The Reader's Digest* is largely composed of summaries of more detailed articles in other periodicals, and the editorial technique involved—that of preserving so far as possible the exact wording of the full-length article but dropping out substantial portions of it—has been employed by dozens of imitative "digest" magazines. Certain periodicals publish digests of entire books. Radio news commentators furnish what are essentially summaries of the latest news developments, and they say: "For further details, see your daily newspaper." Magazines such as *Time* and *Newsweek* contain short articles which are, in one sense, condensations of events. Business and industrial executives frequently have occasion to ask their employees to submit brief reports concerning developments in their departments or trends in business or research, or to write brief introductory summaries of longer reports. The illustrations need not be continued; all of us could mention other examples of the use of summaries.

A summary, as a condensed version of a longer passage or a more extended account, has several forms: the *abstract,* the *digest,* the *synopsis,* the *résumé,* the *epitome,* the *précis.* Of these forms of summary, the most widely used is the précis.

THE PRÉCIS

A précis (form both singular and plural, pronounced *pray-see'*) is a brief summary of the essential thought of a longer composition. It attempts to provide a miniature of the original selection, reproducing the same proportions on smaller scale, the same ideas, and the same mood and tone, so far as possible. The maker of a précis cannot interpret or comment; his sole function is to give a reduced photograph of the original author's exact and essential meaning. Nor can he omit important details.

Instructors frequently require précis in both oral and written form because they realize how effective the summarized method is in developing students' capacities for *careful reading, constructive thinking,* and *exact writing.* The composition of a good précis is difficult, requiring time and effort. In making a précis, follow these suggestions:

17a.   Select carefully the material to be condensed.

Some selections can be reduced satisfactorily but others are so tightly knit that condensation is virtually impossible. You can make précis of novels, short stories, plays, and speeches, but not of short material whose style is especially compact and epigrammatic.

17b.   Read the selection carefully.

The purpose of a précis is to present, as briefly and clearly as possible, the important ideas of the selection being condensed. In order to grasp the central ideas, you must read carefully, analytically, and reflectively. Look up the meanings of all words and phrases about which you are in doubt. Look for important or key expressions that must be used in your précis if it is to preserve the essential meaning and flavor of the original selection. Before starting to write, you must, to use Francis Bacon's phrase, "chew and digest" the selection, not merely "taste" it or "swallow" it whole in a single gulp. You must see how the material has been organized, what devices the writer has used, what kinds of illustrations support the main thought. You may want to question critically some of the writer's statements, but if your purpose is to write a précis, you must report faithfully and without comment what he has said.

17c. Use your own words.

Quoting sentences—perhaps topic sentences—from each paragraph results in a sentence outline, not a précis. You must use your own words for the most part, although a little quotation is permissible. Ordinarily, the phrasing of the original will not be suitable for your purposes. Once you have mastered the thought of the selection, your problem is one of original composition. You are guided and aided by the order and wording of the material, but the précis itself represents your own analysis and statement of the main thought.

17d. Set limits to the number of words you use.

The length of a condensation cannot arbitrarily be determined, but it is safe to say that for purposes of summary most prose can be reduced by two-thirds to three-fourths. A précis, therefore, should usually be about one-third to one-fourth as long as the original. Nothing of real importance can be omitted, but you must remember that the central aim of a précis is condensation.

17e. Follow the plan of the original.

Follow the logical order of the original so that the condensation will be accurate. Thoughts and facts should not be rearranged; if they are, the essence of the original may be distorted. Give attention to proportion. Try to preserve as much as possible of the mood and tone of the original.

17f. Write the précis in good English.

The condensation should not be a jumble of disconnected words and faulty sentences. It should be a model of exact and emphatic diction and clear, effective sentence construction, because it must be intelligible to a reader who has not seen the original. Transition from sentence to sentence must be smooth and unobtrusive, emphasizing the unity of the summarization. Although the précis is not often likely to be so well written as the original, it should read smoothly and possess compositional merit of its own.

The following example of a précis was written by a student. Criticize it in the light of the suggestions given above.

ORIGINAL

For a hundred years and more the monarchy in France had been absolute and popular. It was beginning now to lose both power and prestige. A sinister symptom of what was to follow appeared when the higher ranks of society began to lose their respect for the sovereign. It started when Louis XV selected as his principal mistress a member of the middle class, it continued when he chose her successor from the streets. When the feud between Madame Du Barry and the Duke de Choiseul ended in the dismissal of the Minister, the road to Chanteloup, his country house, was crowded with carriages, while familiar faces were absent from the court at Versailles. For the first time in French history the followers of fashion flocked to do honor to a fallen favorite. People wondered at the time, but hardly understood the profound significance of the event. The king was no longer the leader of society. Kings and presidents, prime ministers and dictators, provide at all times a target for the criticism of philosophers, satirists, and reformers. Such criticism they can usually afford to neglect, but when the time-servers, the sycophants, and the courtiers begin to disregard them, then should the strongest of them tremble on their thrones. (208 words.)

—DUFF COOPER, *Talleyrand*

PRÉCIS

For more than a hundred years the monarchy in France had been absolute and popular. But Louis XV lost the respect of the upper ranks of society by choosing his mistresses from lower classes. When the feud of the Duke de Choiseul with Madame Du Barry resulted in the Minister's dismissal, the court turned its attention to him, away from the king. The king, no longer the leader of society, could well tremble for his throne. (76 words.)

THE PARAPHRASE

The paraphrase is not a form of summary but another type of "report on reading" frequently required in college work. Whereas a précis is a digest of the essential meaning of an original passage, a paraphrase is a full-length statement of that meaning. It is a free rendering of the sense of a passage, fully and proportionately, but in different words; or, as *Webster's New International Dictionary* says: "A restatement of a text, passage, or work, giving the meaning in another form, usually for clearer and fuller exposition." A paraphrase does not include translation from one language to another, the technical name for which is *metaphrase*.

The paraphrase is most frequently used to make clear any wording which is vague, obscure, or difficult, a process usually consisting of both simplification and modernization. Each of you has read a particularly difficult poem or an especially abstruse discussion which you could not make sense of until you put it in your own words. After you did so, its meaning was clear, and you felt that you had actually translated the passage into your own thought processes. Much of the discussion in English and social science classrooms begins with a paraphrasing of the ideas expressed in assignments from textbooks. In other words, every student has almost daily need for reshaping source material to suit his own discussional purposes.

Three common uses of paraphrase, therefore, are the following: (1) paraphrasing technical, semitechnical, or otherwise difficult materials into understandable nontechnical English; (2) paraphrasing poems into clear prose; (3) paraphrasing poetry or prose of a bygone era into understandable, present-day prose.

If the material to be paraphrased is poetry, remember: (1) A line of poetry is a *poetic* unit, not a *sense* unit; it need not be and very likely is not a sentence. As a first step, copy the poem as if it were prose; then reread it with special attention to the punctuation marks and the purposes they serve. (2) Poetry, for poetic reasons, often uses inverted, suspended, or transposed word order. Rearrange these words in normal, straightforward English word order: subject and modifiers, predicate and modifiers, object and modifiers.

In making a paraphrase, follow these additional suggestions:

17g. Study the original passage.

"Study" here means that you should read the original passage as often as necessary in order to understand its full and exact meaning. It is impossible properly to paraphrase a passage until you have mastered its essential content, until you are familiar with its purposes, organization, and method of getting at the central idea. As in making a précis, you must read and think as consistently as you can.

Some phrases and sentences you will probably have to reread several times, carefully and reflectively, before their meaning becomes clear to you. If the passage contains obscure words and allusions, consult a dictionary or other reference book to determine their meanings.

17h. Use your own words.

Try to find understandable equivalents for words and phrases which are obscure, but do not strain for synonyms. You should feel free to use words from the original material if their meaning is unmistakably clear, but do not hesitate to use your own words and phrases where simplification, clarity, or modernization requires them.

17i. Leave out nothing of importance.

A paraphrase is a restatement and, as such, should contain the thought of the original in its entirety. Omitting significant detail is a violation of the original and results in distortion.

17j. Add nothing which is not in the original.

A paraphrase is not designed to be a *full* interpretation, in which the paraphraser adds his own comments. Interpretation and explanation should be confined to making clear what the original author had in mind. Whether you like or dislike what the writer has said, whether you agree or disagree with him, whether you think his logic is sound or faulty—these considerations do not enter into the making of the paraphrase. As a writer, your making of a paraphrase does not mean that you cease to think; it means that your thinking produces a full-length statement of another's meaning.

17k. Retain the tone of the original.

As closely as clarity will permit, follow the tone, the spirit, the mood, the atmosphere of the material being paraphrased. Do not change the purpose, mood, treatment, or tone of the original; be careful not to distort, to parody, to give a wrong meaning. Obviously, a paraphraser can hardly hope to achieve the same mood and tone quality as the author of, say, a great poem, but he should try to preserve as much of these existing qualities as possible.

17l. Use good English.

Any paraphrase of a good poem or prose passage is worth far

131

less than the original, but the better the paraphrase, the less the difference between it and the original. In addition to careful reading and constructive thinking, the making of a good paraphrase, just as of an effective précis, requires exact writing. Correct, clear diction and sentence structure are indispensable to the successful paraphrase.

The following is a paraphrase made by a student. Criticize it in terms of the suggestions given above.

ON FIRST LOOKING INTO CHAPMAN'S HOMER

> Much have I travell'd in the realms of gold,
> And many goodly states and kingdoms seen;
> Round many western islands have I been
> Which bards in fealty to Apollo hold.
> Oft of one wide expanse had I been told
> That deep-brow'd Homer ruled as his demesne:
> Yet did I never breathe its pure serene
> Till I heard Chapman speak out loud and bold:
> Then felt I like some watcher of the skies
> When a new planet swims into his ken;
> Or like stout Cortez, when with eagle eyes
> He stared at the Pacific—and all his men
> Look'd at each other with a wild surmise—
> Silent, upon a peak in Darien.

—John Keats

PARAPHRASE

I have read widely in the great classics of literature and have noted many examples of great poetry. I had often been told of the work of Homer and the poetry which he had created, but I never really understood or appreciated its great beauty and power until I read Chapman's translation. Then I felt as awed as some astronomer who unexpectedly discovers a new planet, or as surprised and speechless as Cortez (Balboa) and his followers when they saw the Pacific Ocean for the first time, from Panama.

EXERCISES

A. Look up in your dictionary these words: *précis, abstract, summary, epitome, outline, compendium, synopsis, abridgment, digest, résumé.*

B. Write several précis of materials from your book of readings. Include one narrative and one expository selection.

C. Select several articles in a current issue of *The Reader's Digest*. In your library obtain the magazines referred to. Write a comment on the shortened versions compared with the original versions.

D. Choose an article in a current magazine and condense it as *The Reader's Digest* would.

E. Write a précis of the following selection from James Harvey Robinson's "On Various Kinds of Thinking":

A third kind of thinking is stimulated when anyone questions our belief and opinions. We sometimes find ourselves changing our minds without any resistance or heavy emotion, but if we are told that we are wrong we resent the imputation and harden our hearts. We are incredibly heedless in the formation of our beliefs, but find ourselves filled with an illicit passion for them when anyone proposes to rob us of their companionship. It is obviously not the ideas themselves that are dear to us, but our self-esteem, which is threatened. We are by nature stubbornly pledged to defend our own from attack, whether it be our person, our family, our property, or our opinion. A United States Senator once remarked to a friend of mine that God Almighty could not make him change his mind on our Latin-America policy. We may surrender, but rarely confess ourselves vanquished. In the intellectual world at least peace is without victory.

Few of us take the pains to study the origin of our cherished convictions; indeed, we have a natural repugnance to so doing. We like to continue to believe what we have been accustomed to accept as true, and the resentment aroused when doubt is cast upon any of our assumptions leads us to seek every manner of excuse for clinging to them. The result is that most of our so-called reasoning consists in finding arguments for going on believing as we already do.[1]

F. Write a précis of this final paragraph of Jack London's "To Build a Fire":

Then the man drowsed off into what seemed to him the most comfortable and satisfying sleep he had ever known. The dog sat facing him and waiting. The brief day drew to a close in a long, slow twilight. There were no signs of a fire to be made, and, besides, never in the dog's experience had it known a man to sit like that in the snow and make no fire. As the twilight drew on, its eager yearning for the fire mastered

[1] From *The Mind in the Making*, by James Harvey Robinson. Copyright, 1921, by Harper & Brothers.

it, and with a great lifting and shifting of forefeet, it whined softly, then flattened its ears down in anticipation of being chidden by the man. But the man remained silent. Later, the dog whined loudly. And still later it crept close to the man and caught the scent of death. This made the animal bristle and back away. A little longer it delayed, howling under the stars that leaped and danced and shone brightly in the cold sky. Then it turned and trotted up the trail in the direction of the camp it knew, where were the other food-providers and fire-providers.

G. Write précis of these two paragraphs, the opening and closing of Joseph Addison's *Spectator* Paper No. 26, "On the Tombs in Westminster Abbey":

When I am in a serious humour, I very often walk by myself in Westminster Abbey, where the gloominess of the place, and the use to which it is applied, with the solemnity of the building, and the condition of the people who lie in it, are apt to fill the mind with a kind of melancholy, or rather thoughtfulness, that is not disagreeable. I yesterday passed a whole afternoon in the churchyard, the cloisters, and the church, amusing myself with the tombstones and inscriptions that I met with in those several regions of the dead. Most of them recorded nothing else of the buried person, but that he was born upon one day and died upon another: the whole history of his life being comprehended in those two circumstances that are common to all mankind. I could not but look upon these registers of existence, whether of brass or marble, as a kind of satire upon the departed persons, who had left no other memorial of them, but that they were born and that they died. They put me in mind of several persons mentioned in the battles of heroic poems who have sounding names given them, for no other reason but that they may be killed, and are celebrated for nothing but being knocked on the head. The life of these men is finely described in Holy Writ by *the path of an arrow,* which is immediately closed up and lost. . . .

I know that entertainments of this nature are apt to raise dark and dismal thoughts in timorous minds, and gloomy imaginations; but for my own part, though I am always serious, I do not know what it is to be melancholy, and can therefore take a view of nature in her deep and solemn scenes with the same pleasure as in her most gay and delightful ones. By this means I can improve myself with those objects, which others consider with terror. When I look upon the tombs of the great, every emotion of envy dies in me; when I read the epitaphs of the beautiful, every inordinate desire goes out; when I meet with the grief of parents upon a tombstone, my heart melts with compassion; when I see the tomb of the parents themselves, I consider the vanity of grieving for those whom we must quickly follow. When I see kings lying by those who deposed them, when I consider rival wits placed side by side, or the holy men that divided the world with their contests and disputes, I reflect with sorrow and astonishment on the little competitions, factions, and debates of mankind. When I read the several dates of the tombs, of some that died yesterday, and some six hundred years ago, I consider that great day when we shall all of us be contemporaries, and make our appearance together.

H. Look up in your dictionary the meaning of *paraphrase, metaphrase, translation, parody, version, interpretation.*

I. Write a paraphrase of the following poems, according to the directions given in Section **17g–1.** Your instructor may also ask you to write a précis of your paraphrase.

From SONNETS
XXIX

When, in disgrace with Fortune and men's eyes,
I all alone beweep my outcast state,
And trouble deaf heaven with my bootless cries,
And look upon myself and curse my fate,
Wishing me like to one more rich in hope,
Featured like him, like him with friends possessed,
Desiring this man's art, and that man's scope,
With what I most enjoy contented least;
Yet in these thoughts myself almost despising,
Haply I think on thee; and then my state,
Like to the lark at break of day arising
From sullen earth, sings hymns at heaven's gate;
    For thy sweet love remembered such wealth brings
    That then I scorn to change my state with kings.

—WILLIAM SHAKESPEARE

ON HIS BLINDNESS

When I consider how my light is spent
Ere half my days, in this dark world and wide,
And that one talent which is death to hide
Lodged with me useless, though my soul more bent
To serve therewith my Maker, and present
My true account, lest he returning chide;
"Doth God exact day-labor, light denied?"
I fondly ask. But Patience, to prevent

That murmur, soon replies, "God doth not need
Either man's work or his own gifts. Who best
Bear his mild yoke, they serve him best. His state
Is kingly: thousands at his bidding speed,
And post o'er land and ocean without rest;
They also serve who only stand and wait."

—JOHN MILTON

THE WORLD IS TOO MUCH WITH US

The world is too much with us: late and soon,
Getting and spending, we lay waste our powers.
Little we see in nature that is ours;
We have given our hearts away, a sordid boon!
This sea that bares her bosom to the moon,
The winds that will be howling at all hours,
And are up-gathered now like sleeping flowers;
For this, for everything, we are out of tune;
It moves us not.—Great God! I'd rather be
A pagan suckled in a creed outworn;
So might I, standing on this pleasant lea,
Have glimpses that would make me less forlorn;
Have sight of Proteus rising from the sea;
Or hear old Triton blow his wreathèd horn.

—WILLIAM WORDSWORTH

WHEN I HAVE FEARS THAT I MAY CEASE TO BE

When I have fears that I may cease to be
Before my pen has gleaned my teeming brain,
Before high-pilèd books, in charact'ry,
Hold like rich garners the full-ripened grain;
When I behold, upon the night's starred face,
Huge cloudy symbols of a high romance,
And think that I may never live to trace
Their shadows, with the magic hand of chance;
And when I feel, fair creature of an hour,
That I shall never look upon thee more,
Never have relish in the faery power
Of unreflecting love—then on the shore
  Of the wide world I stand alone, and think,
  Till love and fame to nothingness do sink.

—JOHN KEATS

HOW DO I LOVE THEE?

How do I love thee? Let me count the ways.
I love thee to the depth and breadth and height
My soul can reach, when feeling out of sight
For the ends of Being and ideal Grace.
I love thee to the level of every day's
Most quiet need, by sun and candlelight.
I love thee freely, as men strive for Right;
I love thee purely, as they turn from Praise.
I love thee with the passion put to use
In my old griefs, and with my childhood's faith.
I love thee with a love I seemed to lose
With my lost saints—I love thee with the breath,
Smiles, tears, of all my life!—and, if God choose,
I shall but love thee better after death.

—ELIZABETH BARRETT BROWNING

SONNET I *from* DIVINA COMMEDIA

Oft have I seen at some cathedral door
A laborer, pausing in the dust and heat,
Lay down his burden, and with reverent feet
Enter, and cross himself, and on the floor
Kneel to repeat his paternoster o'er;
Far off the noises of the world retreat;
The loud vociferations of the street
Become an undistinguishable roar.
So, as I enter here from day to day,
And leave my burden at this minster gate,
Kneeling in prayer, and not ashamed to pray,
The tumult of the time disconsolate
To inarticulate murmurs dies away,
While the eternal ages watch and wait.

—HENRY WADSWORTH LONGFELLOW

DOVER BEACH

The sea is calm to-night,
The tide is full, the moon lies fair
Upon the Straits;—on the French coast, the light
Gleams, and is gone; the cliffs of England stand,
Glimmering and vast, out in the tranquil bay.
Come to the window, sweet is the night air!

137

Only, from the long line of spray
Where the sea meets the moon-blanch'd sand,
Listen! you hear the grating roar
Of pebbles which the waves suck back, and fling,
At their return, up the high strand,
Begin, and cease, and then again begin,
With tremulous cadence slow, and bring
The eternal note of sadness in.

Sophocles long ago
Heard it on the Aegean, and it brought
Into his mind the turbid ebb and flow
Of human misery; we
Find also in the sound a thought,
Hearing it by this distant northern sea.

The sea of faith
Was once, too, at the full, and round earth's shore
Lay like the folds of a bright girdle furl'd;
But now I only hear
Its melancholy, long, withdrawing roar,
Retreating to the breath
Of the night-wind down the vast edges drear
And naked shingles of the world.

Ah, love, let us be true
To one another! for the world, which seems
To lie before us like a land of dreams,
So various, so beautiful, so new,
Hath really neither joy, nor love, nor light,
Nor certitude, nor peace, nor help for pain;
And we are here as on a darkling plain
Swept with confused alarms of struggle and flight,
Where ignorant armies clash by night.

—MATTHEW ARNOLD

SAY NOT THE STRUGGLE NAUGHT AVAILETH

Say not the struggle naught availeth,
The labor and the wounds are vain,
The enemy faints not, nor faileth,
And as things have been they remain.

If hopes were dupes, fears may be liars;
    It may be, in yon smoke concealed,
Your comrades chase e'en now the fliers,
    And, but for you, possess the field.

For while the tired waves, vainly breaking,
    Seem here no painful inch to gain,
Far back, through creeks and inlets making,
    Comes silent, flooding in, the main.

And not by eastern windows only,
    When daylight comes, comes in the light,
In front, the sun climbs slow, how slowly,
    But westward, look, the land is bright.
        —ARTHUR HUGH CLOUGH

USING THE LIBRARY

18. A library is virtually a laboratory where deposits of the written word and the graphic portrayal of thought preserved in manuscripts, print, and picture are available to the reader, the investigator, and the creative worker. A knowledge of what these resources are and an understanding of how they are organized are prerequisites for your effective use and enjoyment of this library-laboratory.

As a preliminary step, use one of your free hours for a trip to the library. Get its physical setup clearly in mind; the number of rooms and their use—the main reading room, study alcoves, and reserved-book room; the labels on the different offices of the library personnel indicating the activities that make a library effective; the different sections for reference books, new acquisitions, fiction, bound magazines, current magazines and newspapers, and the like. Stroll beside the reference shelves and note the kind and location of the books there.

Libraries differ in actual content and physical arrangement, but the basic principles which determine the organization of library resources have been sufficiently standardized to enable the student familiar with them to proceed with an investigation in any library.

The regulations established for its users by a particular library may appear in various forms. Before losing time by a trial-and-error method of learning to use your library, and especially before beginning research on any subject or for any paper or article, you should find out whether your library has a guide, handbook, or pamphlet which explains or interprets its organization.

Whether familiar or not with library organization, you are urged to examine one or more of the following guides. The first one, probably kept at the library reference desk, is comprehensive and invaluable. Each of the other three is smaller, but adequate and inexpensive.

Winchell, Constance M. *Guide to Reference Books,* 7th ed., 1951. *Supplement, 1950–1952,* 1954.

Barton, Mary M. (comp.). *Reference Books: A Brief Guide for Students and Other Users of the Library,* 3rd ed. (Baltimore, Maryland: Enoch Pratt Library, 1954).

Cook, Margaret G. *The New Library Key.* (New York: The H. W. Wilson Company, 1956).

Russell, Harold G., and others. *The Use of Books and Libraries,* 8th ed. (Minneapolis: University of Minnesota Press, 1955).

Look up in these guidebooks some or many of the titles listed below, for the rich information that is given, such as full bibliographic details and helpful critical discussions of materials on various subjects.

There are three important kinds of material which a student has at his disposal in every library: reference works, periodicals, and the general collection of books.

18a. Become familiar with the reference works in your library.

Unless you know in advance what books and magazine articles are best suited to your research needs, you should start with a study of condensed, authoritative articles in reference books. Any book may be used for reference purposes, but reference books "are usually comprehensive in scope, condensed in treatment, and arranged on some special plan to facilitate the ready and accurate finding of information."[1] Such works are usually segregated as a special collec-

---

[1] Isadore G. Mudge, "Reference Work and Reference Books," in Constance M. Winchell, *Guide to Reference Books,* 7th ed. (Chicago: American Library Association, 1951), p. xvi. Mudge's brief introduction, pp. xv-xvii, gives valuable suggestions for consulting and studying reference books.

tion on shelves open to the student in the main reading room or in a nearby reference room.

The following lists contain the titles of works which are likely to be most valuable to the undergraduate student. Several titles may deal with the same general or specific subjects, and your library is virtually certain to have one or more of these books. Remember, however, that the preparation of a reference book is expensive in time and money. It cannot be revised and reprinted very often. Always a good starting point, its materials may become "dated," and you should supplement any dated materials by consulting annual publications and current indexes. (See Section **18b.**)

1. BOOKS OF GENERAL INFORMATION.

A. General Encyclopedias.

> *Collier's Encyclopedia.* 20 vols. (Kept up to date with an annual volume, *Collier's Year Book Covering National and International Events.*)
> *Columbia Encyclopedia,* and supplement.
> *Encyclopaedia Britannica.* 24 vols. (Kept up to date with an annual volume, *Britannica Book of the Year, a Record of the March of Events.*)
> *Encyclopedia Americana.* 30 vols. (Kept up to date with an annual volume, *The Americana Annual, an Encyclopedia of Current Events.*)
> *New International Encyclopaedia.* 25 vols. (Kept up to date with an annual volume, *New International Year Book, a Compendium of the World's Progress.*)

B. General Dictionaries.

> *Funk and Wagnalls New Standard Dictionary of the English Language.*
> Murray, Sir James A. H., and others (eds.). *A New English Dictionary on Historical Principles,* reissued as *The Oxford English Dictionary.* 13 vols. (Commonly referred to as the NED, N.E.D., OED, or O.E.D.)
> *Webster's New International Dictionary of the English Language.*

C. Special Dictionaries and Wordbooks.

> Berrey, Lester V., and Van den Bark, Melvin. *American Thesaurus of Slang: A Complete Reference Book of Colloquial Speech.*

Crabb's English Synonyms.

Craigie, Sir William A., and Hulbert, James R. (eds.). *A Dictionary of American English on Historical Principles.* 4 vols.

Fowler, Henry W. *A Dictionary of Modern English Usage.*

Mathews, Mitford M. (ed.). *A Dictionary of Americanisms on Historical Principles.* 2 vols.

Partridge, Eric. *A Dictionary of Slang and Unconventional English.* 4th ed.

Roget's *International Thesaurus of English Words and Phrases.* (Revised constantly and title may vary slightly.)

Webster's Dictionary of Synonyms.

D. Yearbooks, in addition to the annual yearbooks of the various encyclopedias (See 1-A, above).

American Year Book: An Annual Record of Events and Progress.

Annual Register: A Review of Public Events at Home and Abroad (British).

Information Please Almanac (Miscellaneous information).

International Yearbook and Statesmen's Who's Who.

Statesman's Year-book: Statistical and Historical Annual of the States of the World. (Over 90 annual volumes have been published.)

Statistical Abstract of the United States.

United Nations Yearbook.

World Almanac and Book of Facts (Miscellaneous information).

Some of these books have been published annually for many years; some are comparatively recent. Like most of the books listed in this entire section (**18a**), their general nature is evident from their title or from their subtitle. Outstanding events, changes, statistics, and progress in the fields of industry, government, literature, and education should be sought in these yearbooks for the period. The *Statesman's Year-Book,* for example, gives data regarding the government, area, population, education, religion, and industries of every nation and state in the world, including the United States.

2. BOOKS OF SPECIAL SUBJECT INFORMATION.

A. Some Basic Reference Works in Various Fields.

Adams, James Truslow (ed.). *Dictionary of American History.* 5 vols.

Apel, Willi. *Harvard Dictionary of Music.*

Bury, J. B., and others (eds.). *Cambridge Ancient History.* 12 vols.

Catholic Encyclopedia. 15 vols.

Chambers, R. *The Book of Days.* 2 vols. (Old, but still interesting as "a miscellany of popular antiquities in connection with the calendar, including anecdotes, biography and history, curiosities of literature, and oddities of human life and character.")

Damon, Charles R. (comp.). *American Dictionary of Dates, 458–1920.* 3 vols.

Douglas, George W. *The American Book of Days.*

Fielding, Mantle. *Dictionary of American Painters, Sculptors, and Engravers.*

Grove's Dictionary of Music and Musicians. 9 vols.

Gwatkin, H. M., Whitney, J. P., and others (eds.). *Cambridge Medieval History.* 8 vols.

Handlin, Oscar, and others. *Harvard Guide to American History.*

Harper's Encyclopedia of Art: Architecture, Sculpture, Painting, Decorative Arts. 2 vols.

Harper's Encyclopaedia of United States History from 458 A.D. to 1912. 10 vols.

Hastings, James (ed.). *Dictionary of the Bible.* 5 vols.

Hastings, James (ed.). *Encyclopedia of Religion and Ethics.* 13 vols.

Jewish Encyclopedia. 12 vols.

Jones, Franklin (ed.). *Engineering Encyclopedia.* 2 vols. (Treats 4,500 important engineering subjects.)

Keller, Helen Rex. *Dictionary of Dates.* 2 vols.

Monroe, Paul (ed.). *Cyclopedia of Education.* 5 vols.

Morris, Richard B. *Encyclopedia of American History.*

New Schaff-Herzog Encyclopedia of Religious Knowledge. 12 vols.

O'Rourke, Charles E. *General Engineering Handbook.*

Oxford History of Music, 2nd ed. 7 vols.

Schlesinger, Arthur M., and Fox, D. R. (eds.). *A History of American Life.* 12 vols.

Scholes, Percy A. *Oxford Companion to Music.*

Seligman, Edwin R. A., and Johnson, Alvin (eds.). *Encyclopaedia of the Social Sciences* (Commonly known as E.S.S.). 15 vols. (Its information is supplemented by that in the *American Year Book.*)

Thompson, Oscar (ed.). *International Cyclopedia of Music and Musicians.*

Universal Jewish Encyclopedia. 10 vols. (More up-to-date than the *Jewish Encyclopedia.*)

Van Nostrand's Scientific Encyclopedia.

Ward, A. W., and others (eds.). *Cambridge Modern History.* 13 vols.

Subject encyclopedias are usually broader in scope than their titles indicate. They are especially useful for supplying a brief history of a special subject, together with a selected bibliography (a list of books, booklets, and articles about a certain subject or subjects, or about a person or persons). In general, therefore, students should prefer the special encyclopedias for subjects within their scope. *Encyclopaedia of the Social Sciences* (E.S.S.), for example, is usually superior to the general encyclopedias for treatment of political, social, and economic subjects and for all topics relating to human welfare and relationships. The "best" encyclopedia to use for a given topic often depends upon the phase of a subject being investigated. For example, *advertising* is touched upon in the general encyclopedias, but *advertising* as a business is more satisfactorily treated in E.S.S.

In addition to the titles listed, you will find in your library scores of other handbooks, dictionaries, or encyclopedias. A random sampling reveals handbooks on the following: air conditioning, art, automotive engineering, aviation, banking and finance, business administration, chemistry and physics, civil engineering, educational research, electrical engineering, geography, heating and ventilating, history of science, industrial relations, marine diesels, mechanical engineering, modern European literature, plastics, portraits, radio electronics, radio engineering, rare metals, refrigeration engineering, sociology, songs, structural engineering, welding, wool, world history, world literature.

There are also innumerable special bibliographies, i.e., lists of books and magazine articles. A random sampling shows bibliographies on these subjects: American natural history, American game mammals and birds, ceramics, costume, dancing, detective short story, fairy tales, foreign affairs, handicrafts, labor articles, meteorites, North American folklore and folksong, paper making, printing, stainless steel, swimming.

B. Biography.

Biography Index, 1946—. (A cumulative[2] index to biographical material in books and magazines.)

Current Biography: Who's News and Why, 1940—. (Eleven monthly issues which are cumulated in one alphabet annually "of personalities prominent on the international scene, in the arts, sciences, industry, politics, education, and entertainment.")

Dargan, Marion. *Guide to American Biography, 1607–1933.* (Suggests original and secondary sources.)

Johnson, Allen, and Malone, Dumas (eds.). *Dictionary of American Biography.* 21 vols. (Commonly known as D.A.B. or DAB. It includes outstanding Americans who are no longer living.)

Kunitz, Stanley J., and Haycraft, Howard (eds.). *American Authors, 1600–1900.* (Includes 1,300 biographies and 400 portraits.)

Kunitz, Stanley J., and Haycraft, Howard (eds.). *British Authors Before 1800.* (Includes 650 biographies and 220 portraits.)

Kunitz, Stanley J., and Haycraft, Howard (eds.). *British Authors of the Nineteenth Century.* (Includes 1,000 biographies and 350 portraits.)

Kunitz, Stanley J., and Haycraft, Howard (eds.). *Twentieth Century Authors.* (Includes 1,850 biographies and 1,700 portraits.)

Preston, Wheeler. *American Biographies.* (Excludes living people.)

Stephen, Leslie, and Lee, Sidney (eds.). *Dictionary of National Biography.* 63 vols. originally: reissued in 22 vols. Several supplements. (Commonly known as D.N.B. or DNB. It includes outstanding Englishmen who are no longer living.)

Who's Who (principally British). (Includes only living people.)

Who's Who in America (Includes only living people. For those who have recently died, see earlier volumes or volumes entitled *Who Was Who in America.*)

Webster's Biographical Dictionary.

There are also brief biographies of contemporary people in various fields and in foreign countries, such as *American Men of Science; Directory of American Scholars; Leaders in Education; Who's Who in American Art; Who's Who in Engineering; Who's*

---

[2] *Cumulative* or *cumulation:* increasing by successive additions. As used in connection with indexes, it means that lists of authors, titles, and subjects are arranged alphabetically and published in several issues of a magazine; then periodically—for example, quarterly, semiannually, annually, or over a 2- or 3-year period—all the lists are combined in one alphabet, and the earlier separate issues are discarded.

Who in the Theatre; and "Who's Who" in the Middle West, Canada, France, Latin America, the United Nations.

Your library will have special bibliographies for biographical and critical materials about older authors. A random sampling shows such special bibliographies of the following: George Ade, Geoffrey Chaucer, Cervantes, James Fenimore Cooper, Stephen Crane, Charles Dickens, Robert Frost, Oliver Wendell Holmes, Thomas Hardy, John Keats, Abraham Lincoln, Edgar Allan Poe, James Whitcomb Riley, Walter Scott, William Shakespeare, Booth Tarkington, Mark Twain, Walt Whitman.

C. Literature—General Reference Books, Guides, Special Indexes, and Quotation Books.

> *A.L.A. Index . . . to General Literature.* (With *Supplement,* a guide down to 1910; a subject index, still useful for older books.)
>
> Baker, Ernest A. *Guide to Historical Fiction.* (Lists about 5,000 novels dealing with the past, but its publication date, 1914, renders it useless for the last 40 years or more.)
>
> Baker, Ernest A., and Packman, James. *Guide to the Best Fiction, English and American, Including Translations from Foreign Languages.*
>
> Bartlett, John. *Familiar Quotations.* (First published in 1855, the book has been constantly revised by succeeding editors.)
>
> Bateson, F. W. (ed.). *Cambridge Bibliography of English Literature.* 4 vols.
>
> *Book Review Digest,* 1905—. (An index to reviews of some 4,000 general books appearing in some 75 American and British periodicals. It is published 11 times a year, but it is cumulative semiannually and annually.)
>
> Burke, William J., and Howe, W. D. (eds.). *American Authors and Books,* 1640–1940.
>
> Cary, M., and others (eds.). *Oxford Classical Dictionary.*
>
> Cook, Dorothy E., and Monro, Isabel S. *Short Story Index: An Index to 60,000 Short Stories in 4,320 Collections.* (Entries are listed by author, title, and subject.)
>
> Cruden's *Complete Concordance to the Old and New Testaments.* (Notes and Biblical proper names under one alphabetical arrangement. This is an old book which has been constantly revised by later editors.)
>
> *Cumulative Book Index: A World List of Books in the English Language,* 1929—. (Author, title, and subject entries are in one

alphabet. It is published monthly, except August, and cumulated frequently during the year, annually, and in four- or five-year cumulations. Information given includes publisher, price, and date of publication. For books in print before the *Cumulative Book Index* started, see *United States Catalog,* 1st, 2nd, 3rd, and 4th editions.)

Essay and General Literature Index, 1900—. (An index to essays and articles in volumes of collections of essays and miscellaneous works; supplements the *A.L.A. Index,* above; published semi-annually.)

Firkins, Ina Ten Eyck. *Index to Plays,* 1800–1926, with *Supplement* to 1934. (The two volumes index 11,156 plays by 3,538 authors.)

Granger, Edith. *Index to Poetry.* (The fourth edition, 1953, indexes 577 volumes of poetry anthologies.)

Hart, James D. *Oxford Companion to American Literature.*

Hartnoll, Phyllis (ed.). *The Oxford Companion to the Theatre.*

Harvey, Paul. *Oxford Companion to Classical Literature.*

Harvey, Paul. *Oxford Companion to English Literature.*

Hoffman, Hester R. *Bessie Graham's Bookman's Manual, a Guide to Literature,* 7th ed.

Magill, Frank N. (ed.). *Masterplots.* First Series, 2 vols. Second Series, 2 vols. (Also published under the title, *Masterpieces of World Literature in Digest Form.*)

Mencken, H. L. (ed.). *A New Dictionary of Quotations on Historical Principles from Ancient and Modern Sources.*

Miller, Madeleine S., and Miller, J. Lane. *Harper's Bible Dictionary.*

Nield, Jonathan. *A Guide to the Best Historical Novels and Tales,* 5th ed. (Useful down to 1929.)

Oxford Dictionary of Quotations.

Smith, Horatio (ed.). *Columbia Dictionary of Modern European Literature.* (Contains 1,167 articles by 239 specialists, dealing with later nineteenth and twentieth century authors; 31 literatures are represented.)

Sonnenschein, William S. *Best Books: A Reader's Guide to the Choice of the Best Available Books in Every Department of Science, Art, and Literature.* 6 parts. (Lists about 100,000 books. First appeared in 1887; final edition in 1910–1935.)

Spiller, Robert E., and others (eds.). *Literary History of the United States.* 3 vols.

Steinberg, S. H. (ed.). *Cassell's Encyclopaedia of Literature.* 2 vols.

Stevenson, Burton E. *Home Book of Quotations, Classical and Modern.*

Technical Book Review Index, 1935—. (A guide to reviews of scientific and technical books in scientific, technical, and trade journals. It is published monthly except July and August, and is cumulative annually.)

Trent, William P., and others (eds.). *Cambridge History of American Literature.* 4 vols.

Ward, A. W., and Waller, A. R. (eds.). *Cambridge History of English Literature.* 15 vols.

18b. Become familiar with indexes to periodicals.

If you are doing research on a subject of contemporary or revived interest or of recent occurrence, you will need to consult magazine files and, perhaps, bound volumes of newspapers. Libraries usually display current issues of the best general magazines and some of special interest—some libraries even have special periodical rooms for such magazines—but older issues are bound in book form and can be obtained most easily after you have consulted the index books which are a guide to the contents of the magazines.

In each of these indexes, look for the directions to the reader, ordinarily given in the preface, so that you can interpret the entries and find your material without loss of time. The front of each index volume will usually tell you which magazines are indexed and will give full instructions for use. For example, here are two entries from *Readers' Guide to Periodical Literature:*

Author entry:

> **LINDBERGH, Charles Augustus, 1902-**
> Our best chance to survive. por Sat Eve Post
> 227:25 Jl 17 '54
> Thoughts of a combat pilot. pors Sat Eve
> Post 227:20-1+ O 2 '54

This entry means that during the time covered by this issue Charles A. Lindbergh (born 1902) published two articles. One, "Our Best Chance to Survive," with his portrait, was published in *The Saturday Evening Post* for July 17, 1954, in Volume Number 227, page 25. The second, entitled "Thoughts of a Combat Pilot," with portraits also, was published in *The Saturday Evening Post* for October 2, 1954, in Volume Number 227, beginning on page 20, and continuing on page 21 and other later pages. (For unbound magazines, the date of issue is your guide; when the magazines are bound into book form, the volume number is your guide, with the date of issue being important only when each issue is paged separately.)

Subject entry:

> **COLLEGE students**
> Americans as students. P. Emmanuel. Atlan
> 194:59-62 Ag '54; Discussion. 194:77-9 O; 19
> N '54

This entry means that an article dealing with college students, entitled "Americans as Students," by P. Emmanuel, appeared in the *Atlantic Monthly* for August, 1954, pages 59 to 62; the volume number, when the magazine is bound, is Volume 194. There was discussion of the article in the October, 1954, issue, pages 77 to 79, and in the November, 1954, issue, page 19; both issues are still part of Volume 194.

The most helpful of the periodical indexes are those given below. To keep readers entirely up to date, with little loss of time on the part of the reader, most of them are cumulative; that is, articles are indexed by subject, author, and, sometimes, title, in several issues; then, all these entries including any new entries are combined in one alphabet. This cumulation may cover 3 months, 6 months, a year, and, eventually, several years—all in all, a method that saves tremendous time for the investigator.

1. *Agricultural Index,* 1916—
   This is a cumulative subject index to a selected but extensive list of agricultural magazines, books, and bulletins.
2. *Annual Magazine Subject-Index,* 1907–1949.
   This is a subject index to a selected list—dealing mainly with history, travel, and art—of American and British periodicals and professional or cultural society publications.
3. *Art Index,* 1929—
   This is a cumulative author and subject index to magazines and bulletins dealing with the fine arts, such as architecture, painting, ceramics, sculpture.
4. *Bibliographic Index, A Cumulative Bibliography of Bibliographies,* 1937—
   This is a subject index to separately published bibliographies and to

bibliographies included each year in several hundred books and approximately 1,500 periodicals.

5. *Bulletin of the Public Affairs Information Service*, 1915—

This is a cumulative subject index to current books, pamphlets, periodicals, government documents, and other library material in the fields of economics and public affairs.

6. *Catholic Periodical Index*, 1930—

This is a cumulative author and subject index to a selected list of Catholic periodicals.

7. *Dramatic Index*, 1909–1949.

This is, or was, an annual index to articles and illustrations concerning the stage and players in American and British periodicals.

8. *Education Index*, 1929—

This is a cumulative author and subject index to magazines, books, bulletins, and reports in the entire field of education.

9. *Engineering Index*, 1884—

With changes over the years, this index has been since 1928 a selective subject-author index to periodicals in all engineering fields. It is published annually, but technical libraries receive weekly cards containing the information eventually published in the annual volumes.

10. *Facts on File*, 1940—

This is a weekly world news digest with cumulative index, including world, national, and foreign affairs, Latin America, finance and economics, arts and science, education and religion, sports, obituaries, and other miscellany.

11. *Index to Legal Periodicals*, 1908—

This is a cumulative subject and author index to articles in law journals.

12. *Industrial Arts Index*, 1913—

This is a cumulative subject index to a selected but extensive list of business, finance, applied science, and technology periodicals, books, and pamphlets.

13. *International Index to Periodicals*, 1907—

This is a cumulative author and subject index to articles in domestic and foreign periodicals dealing with literature, history, social science, religion, drama, and pure science. It is really a supplement to *Readers' Guide*, below.

14. *Music Index*, 1949—

This is a cumulative index to current music periodical literature.

15. *The New York Times Index*, 1913—

This is a cumulative guide to events of national importance by reference to date, page, and column of The New York *Times*. Material is entered by subjects, persons, and organizations. The only index to an American newspaper, it is an indirect guide to events in other newspapers.

16. *Nineteenth Century Readers' Guide to Periodical Literature,* 1890–1899, with supplementary indexing, 1900–1922. 2 vols.

17. *Poole's Index to Periodical Literature.*
    This is an index of articles, by subject only, in American and British periodicals from 1802 to 1906. 7 vols.

18. *Quarterly Cumulative Index Medicus,* 1927—
    This is an author and subject index to medical magazines and books. For materials before 1927, see *Index Medicus,* 1879–1899, 1903–1926, a classified index of medical literature.

19. *Readers' Guide to Periodical Literature,* 1900—
    Most useful to the general reader, this is a cumulative index to over 100 popular and semipopular magazines. Entries are according to author, subject, and fiction title.

20. *Subject Index to Periodicals,* 1915—
    This is a cumulative index, arranged by subject, to articles in British magazines.

21. *Writings on American History,* 1906–1940, 1948—
    This is an annual index, arranged by author, title, and subject, to materials in books and periodicals dealing with United States history.

18c. Become familiar with the general collection of books in your library.

The most important part of a library is the main collection of books. In order to obtain them for your own use, you need to consult the card catalog. This catalog is the index of the whole library. It consists of 3 x 5-inch cards which are filed alphabetically in long trays or drawers in a series of filing cabinets; on the front of each drawer is a label—A–ABN—giving the alphabetical limits of the cards there.

Book information is filed in the card catalog in three ways: (1) by author, (2) by title, and (3) by subject. Each book in the library is therefore represented in the card catalog by several cards, which are printed and supplied by the Library of Congress and which are thus uniform in all libraries. These cards are usually identical, except that certain lines may be typed across the top, giving the title, joint author, or subject headings, i.e., entries for the subject with which the book deals and which are obtained from the Library of Congress card.

On this page are examples of one of the simpler cards in the card catalog. The typed numbers at the left are the call number of the book, in this case the Dewey Decimal Classification (see pp. 154–156). The typed words show that one card is indexed by title, one by subject (for this book, there is also another subject entry); one card is filed according to author. The first line gives the author's last name, his given name, and his date of birth. On the second, third, and fourth lines are the title, the author's name again, the collaborating author, the edition, the place of publication, the publisher,

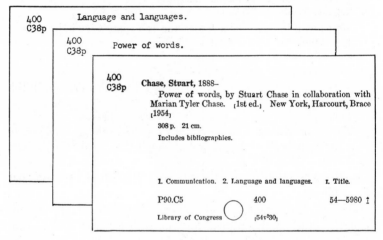

Sample Cards, Library Card Catalog.

and the year of copyright (no brackets around date would indicate that the date is printed on the title page). Line five gives the number of pages and the size (height) of the book in centimeters. Line six indicates that the book has bibliographies. Line seven tells that, in addition to the author card, there should be in the card catalog three additional cards, one under the subject "Communication," one under the subject "Language and languages," and one under title. In line eight, the "P90.C5" is the call number of this book in libraries using the Library of Congress system; the middle number, "400," is the initial number for libraries using the Dewey Decimal

Classification. The other figures have a specialized meaning intelligible only to librarians; for example, "54—5980" is the number of this card, when copies of it are ordered from the Library of Congress, which prepares and prints it. The round hole is for the insertion of a rod in the filing drawer so that if the drawer is accidentally dropped, the hundreds of cards in the drawer are not hopelessly mixed up.

A library card with more complicated information on it (can you explain it?) is illustrated on this page. In addition to the other information typed in, this particular card now very likely has typed in after the author's birth year the date "1956," since Mencken died

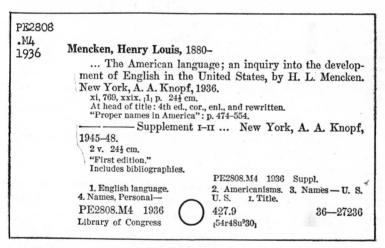

Specimen Library Card, Card Catalog.

in that year. When you think that the information on any library card is important to you and you do not understand how to interpret it, ask a member of your library staff.

When you want a book, and if you know the author or the title of the book you want, you can most easily get the needed information from the author or title card. If you know neither author nor title, turn to the cards that list books dealing with the subject upon which you are working and make your choices from the collection there. If the author is not given, as may be true of many bulletins or pamphlets, or if there is no author, as is true of bound volumes of magazines, look for the title or the organization responsible for the publication.

In addition to revealing the resources of the library, the card catalog gives the call number by means of which each book is located on the shelves. This number appears in the upper left-hand corner (see illustrations) and corresponds exactly to the number placed on the cover and the number placed inside the front cover of the book. Some libraries are so arranged that all or part of the books are placed on open shelves easily accessible to students. In other libraries the main collection is shelved in enclosed stacks. To obtain a book in this case, you must fill out a "call slip" furnished by the library and present it at the Circulation or Loan Desk. On this call slip you write the call number of the book, the author, the title, and your own name and address; the library attendant then obtains the book for you from the stacks.

The student who has access to the book collection will soon discover that the books are arranged according to a definite system, the concrete expression of which is the first part of the call number. The two classification systems most commonly used in this country are the Dewey Decimal Classification and the Library of Congress Classification. Books classified by either system are arranged according to the subjects they treat.

In the Dewey Decimal Classification, the entire field of knowledge is arranged in nine groups plus one group for reference books. Each primary class as well as each subclass is represented by a three-digit number; further subdivisions are indicated by the use of numbers after a decimal point. The 10 main classes and some of the nine subclasses under the main classes are illustrated in the following:

000 General works
  010 Bibliography
  020 Library science
  030 General encyclopedias
  040 General collected essays
  050 General periodicals
  060 General societies, museums
  070 Journalism, newspapers

630 Agriculture
640 Home economics
650 Communication, business
660 Chemical technology
670 Manufactures
680 Trades
690 Building
700 Arts and recreation
  710 Landscape gardening

080 Polygraphy, general collections
090 Rare books
100 Philosophy
200 Religion
300 Social sciences
310 Statistics
320 Political science
330 Economics
340 Law
350 Administration
360 Associations and institutions
370 Education
380 Commerce, communication
390 Manners and customs
400 Linguistics
500 Pure science
510 Mathematics
520 Astronomy
530 Physics
540 Chemistry
550 Geology
560 Paleontology
570 Biology, anthropology
580 Botany
590 Zoology
600 Applied science
610 Medicine
620 Engineering
720 Architecture
730 Sculpture
740 Drawing, decoration, design
750 Painting
760 Engraving
770 Photography
780 Music
790 Amusements
800 Literature
810 American
820 English
830 German
840 French
850 Italian
860 Spanish, Portuguese
870 Latin
880 Greek
890 Other literatures
900 History
910 Geography, description, and travel
920 Biography
930 Ancient history
940 Europe
950 Asia
960 Africa
970 North America
980 South America
990 Oceania and the polar regions

Examples of further subclassification:

Applied Science is numbered 600; Engineering, 620; Radio, 621. A book, *Microphone Technique for the Speaker,* by Verl Bratton, has as classification number 621.384193/B73m. The B73m is placed under the longer number; B is the first letter of the author's last name; m the first letter of the first word of the title.

American Literature is numbered 810–819; an edition of Henry Wadsworth Longfellow's *Evangeline* is numbered 811/L86e. English Literature bears the numbers 820–829; English Drama is 822;

Elizabethan Drama is 822.3; an edition of Shakespeare's *Julius Caesar* is numbered 822.3/S5jA, in which the last letter, A, stands for *A*rden Edition.

The Library of Congress Classification uses letters of the alphabet followed by additional letters or by Arabic numerals. The main classes are these:

A	General works	N	Fine arts
B	Philosophy, religion	P	Language and literature
C	History, auxiliary sciences	Q	Science
D	History and topography (except America)	R	Medicine
		S	Agriculture, plant and animal industry
E and F	American history		
G	Geography, anthropology	T	Technology
H	Social sciences	U	Military science
J	Political science	V	Naval science
K	Law	Z	Bibliography and library science
L	Education		
M	Music		

The letters, I, O, W, X, and Y, have not yet been used and will allow for expansion by five additional classes. Each general class has subclasses: PB—PH classifies modern European Languages; PN, PR, PS, and PZ classify, respectively, General Literary History, English Literature, American Literature, and Fiction and Juvenile Literature.

Under PS, for example, PS 303–324 is American poetry; PS 700 on, individual authors; PS 2250–2298, Henry Wadsworth Longfellow; PS 2263, Longfellow's *Evangeline*.

In filing cards in the card catalog, libraries in general observe the following rules:

All libraries file by entry, i.e., according to what appears first on the card, whether author, subject, or title. The articles *the, a, an* appearing as the first word of a title are ignored. Most libraries file letter-by-letter to the end of the word. This means that the title card, *The American Way,* is filed in front of the subject card, AMERICANISMS, just as all cards beginning "New York" are filed in front of cards with "Newark" as the entry word. Libraries which file in strictly alphabetical order, of course, place *-isms* before *way* and

-*ark* before *York*. Incidentally, encyclopedias, as well as library catalogs, differ in this fundamental respect.

Books *about* an author—when his name is a subject entry, it is typed in black capitals or in red—are filed before or after all books *by* that author.

Cards for authors having the same last name as the entry word are filed according to the given name; always make a note of the first name, or at least the initials, of an author and of the *exact* title of the book you want.

Abbreviations and numerals are filed just as they would be if the word they represent were spelled out.

When the entry word is the same, all authors by that name precede all subjects, and all subjects precede all titles. For example, Washington, George (books by), WASHINGTON, GEORGE (books about), *Washington merry-go-round* (title) are entered in that order.

EXERCISES

A. After you have become familiar with your college or university library, choose two or three or four of the following sentences, or write similar ones. Use each as the first sentence, the topic sentence, in a paragraph. Expand each sentence into a fair-sized paragraph, a half-page or three-fourths of a page long.

1. I have made my first visit to our library.
2. I have made a thorough tour of our library.
3. Several things impressed me about our library.
4. The library has many uses.
5. The ————— room in the library is an interesting place.
6. The library has a newspaper room.
7. The library has a periodical room.
8. The library has a study room.
9. The library has a main reading room.
10. The library has a reserved-book room.
11. The card catalogue is very helpful.
12. This is how you borrow books from the library.
13. Fiction books are kept in a special place.
14. The New York *Times* is both bound and kept on microfilm.
15. Our library has encyclopedias and other reference books.
16. This is how you find material in bound magazines.

17. It is fun to browse through the bound magazines in the library.
18. You can even have dates in the library!
19. My high school (home town) has a satisfactory (unsatisfactory) library.
20. I have (hope to have) a private library.

B. Answer the following. Give, if not already indicated, the source of your information.

1. Make a floor plan of the main reading room of your college or university library, showing the location of the more general kinds of reference books such as encyclopedias, dictionaries, biographical books, magazine indexes.

2. Where in your library are kept bound magazines, current magazines, bound newspapers, current newspapers, novels, reserved books, the card catalog?

3. Go to your library and fill out call slips or cards for six nonfiction books you would like to read. Get one of the books and bring it and the other five call slips to class.

4. Make a list of five widely different (alphabetical) subject headings that are used in the *Industrial Arts Index, Education Index, Legal Index, Public Affairs Information Service,* and *Art Index.*

5. Choose a word in the *New English Dictionary (Oxford English Dictionary)* with at least 20 lines of type, and prepare a brief account of its history.

6. Consult a dictionary of Americanisms and discuss a half-dozen words that have specialized meanings in America of the past or present.

7. Where would you find information about a prominent living American, Englishman, musician, engineer, scientist, educator?

8. Who wrote the following and in what poems?
   a. "A little learning is a dangerous thing."
   b. "What is so rare as a day in June?"
   c. "In the spring a young man's fancy lightly turns to thoughts of love."
   d. "God's in His heaven—All's right with the world!"
   e. "Where ignorance is bliss, 'tis folly to be wise."
   f. "Bliss was it in that dawn to be alive,
      But to be young was very heaven!"

9. How many books were published last year on the subject of cookery, canals, landscape gardening, reading, oil, clothing?

10. Find the name, birth place, birth date, and death date of a prominent nineteenth-century architect, a painter, a musician, a teacher.

11. Identify the following Bible characters: Habbakuk, Saul, Obed, Jesse, Naomi, Jezebel, Bartholomew, Jude, Obadiah, Nicodemus.

12. Prepare a list of historical novels dealing with the Crusades, seventeenth-century England, the American Civil War, the American Middle West, old Louisiana.

13. In your library what is the (a) most recent book by Ernest Hemingway, (b) most recent book about Ernest Hemingway, (c) the most recent magazine article or story by Ernest Hemingway, (d) the most recent magazine article about Ernest Hemingway?

14. What company (or companies) publishes the works of Thomas Wolfe, Stephen Spender, William C. DeVane, John R. Tunis, Aldous Huxley?

15. How many books does your library have about Charles Dickens, Theodore Roosevelt, John J. Pershing?

16. Compare the treatment (i.e., number of pages) in four encyclopedias of ceramics, pumps, Oxford University, silk.

17. Who are the authors of the following: *The Barretts of Wimpole Street, Barrack Room Ballads, Leaves of Grass, Vanity Fair, The Journal of the Plague Year?*

18. Who were the people who wrote under the pseudonyms of O. Henry, Mark Twain, Saki, George Eliot, Acton Bell, Lewis Carroll?

19. Who were the following? What did they do? When did they live? When did they die? (a) Thomas à Becket; (b) Thomas à Kempis; (c) Thomas Aquinas; (d) Thomas Browne; (e) Thomas Hughes; (f) Thomas Hardy; (g) Thomas Henry Huxley.

20. What system of classification is used in your college library? Get the call number of a book on each of the following: ceramics, education, poetry, travel, biography. What is the title of each book? When and where was it published? Who is the publisher?

C. Answer the following questions after you have filled in the blanks or have had them filled in for you by your teacher:

1. Give the name, birth date, and death date of one of the persons whose biographies are listed on page _____ of Volume _____ of the *Dictionary of American Biography.*

2. For the last word which is treated fully at the bottom of the first column (not carried over to the second column) on page _____ of Volume _____ of *A Dictionary of American English,* give (1) its origin and (2) the sentence containing its earliest recorded use.

3. Give the volume and page number of the volume of the *Encyclopedia Americana* which discusses _____.

4. From the card catalog obtain the name of a book on _____ which was published in the 1940's.

5. According to the *Readers' Guide to Periodical Literature* for _____ _____, did John Steinbeck in that year publish any stories in *The Saturday Evening Post,* the *Atlantic Monthly,* or *Collier's?* If so, list the titles of the stories.

6. Does the library have any copies of *Time* magazine for the year _____? of *The New Yorker* for the year _____? of *Newsweek* for the year _____?

7. Were any articles on _____ published during November, _____? If so, list one and the name of the magazine in which it appeared.

8. According to *The Engineering Index,* were any articles published in foreign magazines in _____ on _____. If so, list one, and the name, date of publication, and country in which it appeared.

9. Give page and volume number of the article in the *Encyclopedia of Religion and Ethics* on _____.

10. Give the name of the author, the title, and the publisher of the latest book about _____ listed in the card catalog.

TAKING NOTES

As a college student you will spend much time taking notes in your room, in the library, and in the classroom. Both now and later you will be faced with the problem of taking notes on books and articles for research or other subjects about which you may write, or for use in reviewing for examinations. You will need, too, to take usable notes on lectures and other speeches (see pp. 10–13). Much of your success or failure depends upon your ability to take notes which are really helpful.

19. Take careful notes from your reading.

Note taking is, or should be, a process of systematic thinking. Too frequently it is the hurried setting down of jumbled, carelessly selected ideas on scraps of paper or miscellaneous jottings here and there in a notebook. If you really wish to get maximum benefit from your reading, with the most intelligent labor-saving, you should organize both the materials and the methods of note taking.

In order to preserve notes until a long paper is written, or until an examination is over, or for possible use at any future time, you can employ a uniform method of taking notes.

Materials. 1. Many instructors and students believe that the most efficient note taking can be done on *cards* or *slips of paper* (3 x 5 or 4 x 6 inches, or larger), *one note to a card*. All notes taken should be placed on similar cards, a heading put on each, and the cards filled for later reference. The advantage of this system is that all notes on the same subject, even when taken at widely separated intervals, can be kept together.

2. Some students prefer to take notes on full-size or half-size sheets of paper, or *loose-leaf notebook* paper. (Bound notebooks are usually unsatisfactory.) If you use such materials, remember to keep notes on a particular book or article together and organize your notes on the various phases of the subject as you proceed.

Methods. More important than the materials used for recording notes are the methods employed. In order to save time and trouble later and to prevent assembling a hodgepodge of quotations and undigested raw material, follow this technique, however tedious and cumbersome it may seem:

1. Before you begin to take notes on a book, study its Preface and Table of Contents. From these you will find out the scope and purpose of the book. If you are going to read only one chapter from a book, or a magazine article, skim through it first, and then begin to read carefully and take notes. If the book has an index, you may save time by examining it for your particular subject or for related materials.

2. Record accurately and fully the details about the source of information: author, book, titles, article or chapter titles, magazine titles, dates, volume and page numbers, and the like.

3. Record accurately and fully the information itself. If you write a précis (p. 127) or a paraphrase (p. 129), check it on the spot with the original. If you are quoting directly, to use the material later for either direct quotation or summarizing, make a word-by-word check at once. Be careful to copy *exactly* all direct quotations, preserving original spelling and punctuation; mark clearly any such variations in your *first* notes, and do not forget to use quotation marks.

Your notes must be clear and full, or you will have to make trip after trip to the library to supply missing information. Get all the information you need and *get it the first time.* Notes must be *clear,* so that you can read and understand them later; *full,* so that you can supply adequate information about sources in both footnotes and bibliography; *exact,* so that you can quote or paraphrase accurately; *organized,* so that you can make ready use of what you have assembled.

4. Condense your notes. They should be as full as needed but not

As Volunteer   (Lincoln)

Black Hawk War
Two reasons for volunteering:
1. Job as clerk would soon be gone.
2. "And he was running for the legislature; a war record, in any kind of war, would count in politics."
He enlisted; friends said they would elect him company captain.
P. 154
Carl Sandburg, *Abraham Lincoln, the Prairie Years,* Vol. I, N.Y.: Harcourt, Brace & Co., c. 1926.

As Captain   (Lincoln)

Lincoln as captain drilled his men. One day he had two platoons advancing toward a gate.
Couldn't think of order to get them in column of two's. Commanded:
"This company is dismissed for two minutes when it will fall in again on the other side of the gate."
P. 155
Carl Sandburg, *Abraham Lincoln, the Prairie Years,* Vol. I, N.Y.: Harcourt, Brace & Co., c. 1926.

so lengthy that main ideas are obscured in a mass of detail. Make frequent use of topic sentences (see Section 23) and summaries.

5. Rearrange and regroup your notes as your work proceeds. Keep your notes on a single subject together, not mixed with others even on the same general subject. This segregation is especially important whenever numerous books or articles are consulted.

If you are writing a research paper (see Section 20), you will of course be analyzing your subject, and you will be making—through your analysis and through the arrangement and grouping of your notes—a preliminary outline of your paper. In this way you will be able to keep on the main track of the investigation and not be totally surprised at the end of your note taking by the manner in which your investigation has run away with you. You will also be more thoroughly prepared for the next major step in the preparation of your paper.

6. Be careful to distinguish fact and opinion in your reading and in the notes themselves. In weighing opinions, consider the facts upon which the opinions are based, the expert knowledge and possible bias of the author, and the date of publication of the material.

The specimen cards on page 162 illustrate use of the methods suggested. Note that the upper right corner gives the author or general subject, the upper left the specific subject; then follow a direct quotation, summary, or paraphrase, and full bibliographical details. If a number of note cards come from the same source, you can work out an abbreviated system whereby your bibliographical references will be explained by your preliminary or final bibliography cards.

Not all cards will be notes of material directly quoted. Some will be *précis* digesting or summarizing in your own words the ideas of the source (see pp. 127–129). Some will be *paraphrases* giving in your words a full-length statement of the meaning of the source material (see pp. 129–132). All cards should be so complete that you will not need to return to the source to discover how much of the material is direct quotation, how much paraphrase, or what the bibliographical facts are.

THE RESEARCH PAPER

20. The *research paper*—also called an *investigative theme* or a *term report* or a *term paper*—is a long theme, usually from 1,500 to 6,000 words, assigned in most college courses which require outside reading. Such a paper is designed to be more than a mere report; its purpose is to make a careful investigation of some subject and to present and interpret the source material in the light of the researcher's findings.

It should not be merely a reading report based on several books or articles read more or less haphazardly. It should not be a jumbled series of quotations and paraphrases. In fact, you should learn how to put the ideas of others into your own words, give proper credit, but avoid overuse of short or extended direct quotations.

A good research paper is a study, carefully controlled, which sets out with a definite purpose and accomplishes that purpose. The best research papers are usually extensions of phases of work actually mentioned in connection with courses for which they are prepared; such courses are also fruitful sources for subjects.

The preparation and writing of a successful research paper depend upon four major steps: (1) choosing and analyzing the subject; (2) making a thorough investigation of the subject; (3) preparing an outline; and (4) writing and revising. As a preliminary to these four steps, review "The Whole Composition," Sections 1 through 17, pages 25 to 139.

20a. Choose and analyze your subject carefully.

The choice of a good subject will save you much time later. Keep these points in mind:

1. If possible, choose a subject in which you are already interested or one in which you think that you can become interested. Furthermore, do not select so abstruse or technical a subject that your readers cannot be interested.

2. Do not select too large or too small a subject. Some subjects can be treated adequately in one thousand words; an attempt to develop such subjects in 5,000-word papers results in padding, repetition, dullness. On the other hand, do not choose a subject which cannot be handled in the assigned space.

3. Choose a topic upon which enough has been written for you to obtain adequate information. Always keep in mind the resources of the library in which you will do your investigating; for example, avoid a subject which will depend heavily upon back copies of mag-

azines which your particular library does not have. Remember that your paper should be based upon material from *several* sources: reference books, periodicals, books, perhaps newspapers, and personal interviews.

4. Select a central purpose, a controlling idea, and state it in a thesis topic or theme sentence. Any assembling of material presupposes the support of some proposition, some general statement or idea, and all the facts you gather should lead toward your conclusions, the really important part of any research paper. You may have to change your attitude toward and treatment of your subject when you have assembled and digested your materials, for you should never start out with a rigid, preconceived idea that you want to establish in spite of all contrary facts and evidence. A research paper, like any theme, must develop one phase of a subject, fairly and convincingly, in order to achieve one central purpose.

5. Select, but modify if necessary, the basic type of writing for your research paper. Your report may be *descriptive exposition;* it may describe and explain the processes involved in making rayon. It may be *narrative:* a report of exactly what took place at the time of the sinking of the *Andrea Doria.* It may be *argumentative:* the setting forth of facts in favor of or opposed to some plan, movement, proposal, such as reasons for or against making 18 the legal voting age in a certain district or state. Or it may be *analytical;* a comparison of socialism and communism treating the likenesses and differences of the two systems. But whatever type of writing you choose, your research paper must have a clear, unmistakable *purpose.*

Choice of topic depends upon your own interests and the interests of your prospective reader or readers. Literally hundreds of topics are suggested by these broad fields:

applied science	language
biography	literature
economics	manufacturing
education	politics
fine arts (music, painting, sculpture, ceramics, architecture, etc.)	psychology
	pure science
	religion
history	warfare

Other hundreds of subjects are possible from somewhat more limited but still general topics, as for example:

An outstanding or memorable episode, or day, or month, or year in a well-known person's life (like "Lincoln the Soldier," see pp. 178–187, below).

An account of the relatives of a famous person.

An achievement by a well-known person.

The friendship of two well-known people, or some phase of that friendship.

The reception, influence, effect of some book, some invention, some process, or the reputation of such 10, 25, 50, 100 years later.

Famous scientific discoveries or inventions (see "Black Magic," pp. 187–192, below).

Famous historical events, trials, sporting events, etc.

Famous or well-known battles or phases of battles (land, sea, air).

Famous or memorable shipwrecks, storms, fires, floods, cyclones, tornadoes.

A famous structure (harbor, canal, bridge, building, ship, tower, cathedral, pyramid, dam, tunnel, train, automobile, airplane, etc.).

As suitable limitations of some of the foregoing, consider as examples:

Dwight Eisenhower's First Day as President.

Lincoln's Son.

Noah Webster's First Dictionary.

Thomas A. Edison's Minor Inventions.

Abraham Lincoln and His Secretary of State, William H. Seward.

Early Results of the Discovery of Anesthesia.

Mark Twain's *Huckleberry Finn*—Its First Ten Years.

April 19, 1775 (or July 4, 1776, or April 6, 1917, or November 11, 1918, or December 7, 1941).

The First Kentucky Derby.

The Siege of Corregidor.

The Final Day of the Battle of Gettysburg.

The Sinking of the *King George V*.

The Straits of Mackinac Bridge.

A Tunnel Under the English Channel.

The Development of the Flying Boxcar.

20b. Make a thorough investigation of the subject.

The conscientious researcher ferrets out all the information he can about a given subject. A student, pressed for time, is not likely to ascertain *all* the facts, but at least he should make as thorough search as possible for pertinent detail. You must utilize the information to be found in reference books, periodicals, the general collection of books in your library, and newspapers. It is an illusion that using an encyclopedia and writing a term paper are one and the same thing. A term paper has no real value unless it does more than merely dip into a subject.

In order to make a thorough investigation of the subject:

1. Learn how to use efficiently the resources of your library: reference works, periodical indexes, the card catalog and general collection of books (see Section **18a, b, c**). From these resources—notably the first three—prepare a preliminary bibliography on

Sandburg, Carl
Abraham Lincoln, the Prairie Years
2 vols.
New York: Harcourt, Brace & Co. c. 1926

Preliminary Bibliography Card.

3 x 5-inch cards, that is, a list of books and magazine or newspaper articles that are *likely* to contribute material—with one title to a card. You will save time if you give complete information on this preliminary bibliography card, since it will serve as your information for your final bibliography. See this page for sample.

2. Take careful notes from your reading (see Section **19**). Give full details about sources after each note. If there is no possibility

of confusion, you can use an abbreviated reference to the full information on your bibliography card.

20c. Prepare an adequate outline for your paper.

Not until you have read and taken notes on available material will you be in a position to outline your research paper completely and accurately. It is helpful, however, if you have in mind, early, some general plan you might follow, a plan you can adapt, change, and rearrange as you assemble your material and become familiar with it. When you have worked long enough to reach definite conclusions and to see the framework of the whole structure, you can then rearrange your notes in final form, under the appropriate headings, and from them prepare a topic or sentence outline. (See Section **6a** and **b**.) The actual writing of the paper should begin *only* after you have prepared and revised carefully such an outline.

In making an outline for your paper, bear in mind that the object of your investigation is to find out the facts, arrange and interpret them, and present conclusions based upon them. The writer of a research paper is not necessarily a propagandist—rather is he a discoverer of fact—but he must assimilate and absorb what seems to him the truth so that he can present it to a reader who will see what definite purpose he had in mind.

20d. Write your research paper correctly, clearly, and forcefully.

After you have investigated the field thoroughly and have organized your notes and prepared an outline, you are ready to write the paper. If you have taken careful notes and arranged them properly, your work is much more than half done. But be careful to give the results of your study correct, clear, and forceful expression. To this end, you should write the body of your paper as clearly and forcefully as you can; you must take great care with footnotes and bibliography; and you must revise your paper to insure correctness and accuracy.

There is no reason why a term report should be dull and lifeless. If you have chosen an attractive subject and investigated it thoroughly, you should have little difficulty in making your paper "come alive." No penalty is attached to an occasional bit of humor in a research paper; the vitality which can be achieved by vigorous diction and neatly turned phrases will add effectiveness to the thoroughness and accuracy which the paper must have. Careful investigation, vigorous writing, and pleasant, easy reading need not be exclusive of one another.

20e. Revise your research paper carefully.

After you have written the report with all the vigor and interest which you can muster, and after you have correctly indicated the footnotes and bibliography (see Section 20f and **g**), you should allow the paper to "jell"; that is, if time permits, put the report aside and forget about it for some time, several days if possible. After this "cooling" process, you will be able to come back to it with more impartiality than was possible just after you finished it. The errors which everyone makes will be more apparent to you, and you can at this time give the theme its final polishing. Give your research paper the rereadings suggested on pages 103–109, and to them add another for the sole purpose of making certain that the footnotes are accurately and uniformly listed and that the bibliography is correctly and consistently arranged.

In addition to being correct, clear, effective, and appropriate, every investigative theme worthy of the name must be carefully documented. The suggestions which follow should enable you to provide your paper with adequate and accurately listed footnotes and bibliography, *provided your notes on your reading were carefully taken.*

20f. Use footnotes to document your research paper adequately and properly.

The purpose of a footnote is to mention the authority for some fact stated or some material quoted, or to develop some point more or less incidentally referred to in the body of the paper.

Generally known facts do not require substantiation in footnotes, nor do well-known quotations, usually. With other materials the charges of plagiarism must be avoided, and unless the idea and the phrasing are completely your own, you should refer the reader to some source for your statement. In order to be entirely honest, you will acknowledge every source of indebtedness, even when no direct quotation is used.

Occasionally the writer wishes to develop, interpret, or refute some idea but does not wish an extended comment to interfere with the unity of his paper. He uses a footnote, but too many footnotes for such purposes can become distracting to the reader.

How many footnotes should appear in a research paper? Only as many as are necessary, in the light of the discussion above. One investigation may call for twice as many as another. Some pages of your paper may require a half dozen or more footnotes, others may need none or only one or two. A good guiding principle is the following: Use footnotes to acknowledge credit where it is due and to supply discussion-explanations only when necessary for understanding.

1. Adopt a standard form of footnote and be consistent in its use.

Methods of footnoting are numerous, but whatever system you employ should be consistent throughout your paper and immediately clear to any intelligent reader. The Modern Language Association of America *Style Sheet* favors the following forms—content, arrangement of details, punctuation—for books and periodicals.

For books: (1) *author's or authors' name,* i.e., given name(s) followed by last name, followed by a comma; (2) *title of chapter or part of book cited,* enclosed in quotation marks, followed by a comma inside the final quotation marks (used when the article is part of a collection, anthology, etc.); (3) *title of the book,* in italics (i.e., underlined), followed by a comma; (4) *editor's or translator's name* (if any) in normal order, preceded by "ed." or "trans." and followed by a comma; however, if the work of the editor or translator is considered of first importance, his name comes first, followed by "ed." or "trans." in parentheses—(ed.) or (trans.)— followed by a comma, followed by the work; (5) *edition used,* whenever the edition is not the first, in Arabic numerals (e.g., 3rd ed.), followed by a comma; (6) *the series,* if book is part of a series, followed by a comma, followed by the number of this book in the series; (7) *the number of volumes* if more than one (e.g., 4 vols.) but this information is not needed if the reference is to a specific passage instead of to the book as a whole; (8) *place(s) and date(s) of publication,* within parentheses, followed by a comma; if it is desirable, the publisher's name may be given—following the place of publication, preceded by a colon, and followed by a comma; (9) *volume number,* if one of two or more, in capital Roman numerals, preceded and followed by a comma; (10) *page number(s)* in Arabic numerals (unless the book or part of it referred to has small Roman numerals), preceded by a comma, followed by a period.

NOTE: Naturally, for many books used in preparing student-written research papers, certain of the foregoing items will not appear, especially (4), (6), and possibly (2).

For articles or stories in periodicals (first references): (1) *author's name,* given name(s) followed by last name, followed by a comma; (2) *title in full,* enclosed in quotation marks (not underlined), followed by a comma inside the final quotation marks; (3) *name of the periodical* (or its standard abbreviation, if any) in italics (i.e., underlined), followed by a comma; (4) *volume number* not using the abbreviation "Vol." but using capital Roman numerals, followed by a comma unless material in parentheses follows; however, for newspapers and for many weekly or monthly magazines which page each issue separately, the volume number may be omitted in favor of the complete date, enclosed in commas, followed by the use of "p." or "pp." and the page numbers in Arabic numerals; (5) *issue number* or *name,* if periodical is quarterly, like "Winter" or "Spring"; (6) *year,* preceded by month if needed (i.e., when each issue is paged separately), enclosed in parentheses, followed by a comma; (7) *page number(s)* in Arabic numerals, not preceded by "p." or "pp." but followed by a period.

NOTE: The use of (5) above may be rare. Also, some teachers believe that if periodicals use Arabic numerals for their volume numbers, these should be used instead of Roman numerals, or when the Roman numerals become unwieldy, such as CCXXVII for 227.

The foregoing directions for footnotes are illustrated in the following examples:

BOOKS

A. Book by one author:

[1] John R. Tunis, *This Writing Game* (New York: A. S. Barnes & Company, 1941), p. 26.

[2] Henry Louis Mencken, *The American Language,* 4th ed. (New York: Alfred A. Knopf, Inc., 1936), p. 168.

B. Book by two or more authors:

[1] John Tasker Howard and Arthur Mendel, *Our American Composers* (New York: Thomas Y. Crowell Company, 1941), p. 82.

C. Book of two or more volumes:
¹ Douglas S. Freeman, *George Washington* (New York: Charles Scribner's Sons, 1948), II, 142.

D. Book prepared by an editor:
¹ *Representative English Comedies*, ed. Charles Mills Gayley (New York: The Macmillan Company, 1916), I, xxiii.
² Richard Aldington (ed.), *Great French Romances* (New York: Duell, Sloan, and Pearce, 1946), p. 17.

E. A Translation:
¹ Homer, *The Odyssey*, trans. George Herbert Palmer (Boston: Houghton Mifflin Company, 1891), p. 46.

ARTICLES (ESSAYS, STORIES)

A. From a magazine:
¹ Walter D. Edmonds, "Arrival of the Lily Dean," *The Saturday Evening Post*, CCX (May 7, 1938), 5.
or
¹ Walter D. Edmonds, "Arrival of the Lily Dean," *The Saturday Evening Post*, May 7, 1938, p. 5.
² Roger Angell, "A Walk in Washington," *Holiday*, XIX (May, 1956), 37.
or
² Roger Angell, "A Walk in Washington," *Holiday*, May, 1956, p. 37.
³ "What to Do about the Draft?" *Life*, XL (May 14, 1956), 69.
or
³ "What to Do about the Draft?" in *Life*, May 14, 1956, p. 69.
(Note the alternate expression after the question mark, just above.)

B. From a collection:
¹ Katherine Mansfield, "Bliss," *A Study of the Short Story*, ed. Henry S. Canby and Alfred Dashiell (New York: Henry Holt and Company, 1935), p. 303.
² Burges Johnson, "Campus versus Classroom," *Readings for Opinion*, ed. Earl Davis and William C. Hummel (New York: Prentice-Hall, Inc., 1952), pp. 79–82.

C. From a newspaper:
¹ "Summer's Children," The New York *Times*, June 19, 1954, p. 14.
² "The U.S. and Its Critics," The New York *Times*, April 15, 1956, Section 4, p. 8.

NOTE: The first reference above is to the daily edition, the second to the Sunday edition.

2. Use the following standard footnote abbreviations.

In footnotes in research papers, abbreviations are permissible and desirable. If the need for abbreviations occurs, employ these forms:

1. anon. anonymous
2. ante before
3. art. (plural, arts.) article (articles)
4. bk. (plural, bks.) book (books)
5. c. copyright, copyrighted
6. cf. compare. Never use "cf." in the meaning of "see."
7. ch. (plural, chs.) chapter (chapters)
8. comp. compiler, compiled
9. ed. (plural, eds.) editor (editors) edition (editions)
10. e.g. for example
11. f. (plural, ff.) following line (following lines), following page (following pages)
12. fig. (plural, figs.) figure (figures)
13. *ibid.* "the same." If a footnote refers to the same source as the one referred to in the footnote *immediately* preceding, the abbreviation *ibid.* (from the Latin *ibidem* meaning "in the same place") may be used. If the volume, page, title, and author are the same, use *ibid.* alone. If the volume and page differ, use, for example, *Ibid.,* III, 206. *Ibid.* usually comes at the beginning of a footnote and is capitalized for that reason only.
14. i.e. that is
15. l. (plural, ll.) line (lines)
16. *loc. cit.* "the place cited." If the reference is to the *exact* passage covered by an earlier reference not immediately preceding, use *loc. cit.* (from the Latin *loco citato* meaning "in the place cited"). Never follow *loc. cit.* with a page number.
17. MS (plural, MSS) manuscript (manuscripts)
18. n. (plural, nn.) note (notes)
19. N.B. *nota bene*—"take notice, mark well"
20. *op. cit.* "the work cited." After the first full reference to a given work, provided no other work by the same author is mentioned in the paper, succeeding references may be indicated by the author's surname, followed by *op. cit.* (from Latin *opere citato* meaning "in the work cited") and the volume and page.

Many teachers and editors believe that *op. cit.* is the most abused of all abbreviations in research writing; they advocate, instead, the author's name alone with a short title for footnote references after the first. The following examples illustrate:

First entry:
[1] Sir Arthur Quiller-Couch, *On the Art of Writing* (New York: G. P. Putnam's Sons, 1930), p. 84.

Subsequent entry for the same book:
Allowed:
[5] Quiller-Couch, *op. cit.*, p. 92.
Preferred:
[5] Quiller-Couch, *Art of Writing*, p. 92.

First entry:
[1] Clifton Fadiman, "Herman Melville," *The Atlantic Monthly*, CLXXII (October, 1943), 88.

Subsequent entry for the same article:
Allowed:
[4] Fadiman, *op. cit.*, p. 90.
Preferred:
[4] Fadiman, "Melville," p. 90.

21. p. (plural, pp.) page (pages)
22. par. (plural, pars.) paragraph (paragraphs)
23. *passim.* To be employed when no specific page reference can be given; it means "everywhere," "throughout," "here and there."
24. pseud. pseudonym
25. pt. (plural, pts.) part (parts)
26. q.v. which see
27. sec. (plural, secs.) section (sections)
28. *sic.* thus, so. Used between brackets in someone's quoted material, to show that the material is followed exactly even if there is an error in spelling, grammar, punctuation, word use.
29. v. (plural, vv.) verse (verses)
30. vol. (plural, vols.) volume (volumes)

The abbreviations *ibid., op. cit.,* and *loc. cit.,* and the words *passim* and *sic* are always italicized (underlined).

3. Place the footnote numeral and the footnote properly.

A footnote is referred to by an Arabic numeral placed above and to the right of the word to be commented upon. If the reference is to a statement or a quotation, place the numeral at the end of the passage, and always after the punctuation.

Before the actual footnote at the bottom of the page repeat the number used in the text. Do not use asterisks or other symbols in place of Arabic numerals.

Footnotes should be numbered consecutively throughout the paper. Although a few writers number them anew for each page, most instructors and editors prefer the consecutive numbering plan, since it facilitates everyone's work—including the writer's—if the paper needs to be retyped after revision or to be prepared for printing.

Footnotes may be put at the bottom of pages, between lines in the manuscript proper, or all together at the end of the paper. Most instructors greatly prefer the first of these methods; the second method distracts from the continuity of reading; and the third makes easy reference difficult and may have the footnotes conflicting with the bibliography for position. If the footnotes are placed at the bottom of the page, they should not be crowded. Always leave a clearly defined space between the text and the footnotes; you can even draw part of a line or a full line between. If you typewrite, be guided by your instructor's advice concerning single or double-spacing in the footnotes.

20g.   Use a bibliography to document your research paper properly and adequately.

A *bibliography* is a list of books or magazine or newspaper articles relating to a given subject and—in the research paper—placed at the end of the manuscript. It is usually a list—in one alphabet, or classified—containing the names of all the works actually quoted from or used generally in the paper and its preparation. Thus a bibliography may contain more references than the sum of all the footnote references. Every formally prepared research paper should contain a bibliography.

Arrange bibliographical items correctly and consistently, in regard to content, order of details in each item, and punctuation. Usage in the arrangement of bibliographies varies, but, subject to adaptation by your instructor, keep the following suggestions in mind as your guide. Since *The MLA Style Sheet,* designed for the preparation of research articles only, has no suggestions for the preparation of a bibliography, the following suggestions are based on *A Manual for Writers of Term Papers, Theses, and Dissertations,* Revised Edition, by Kate L. Turabian (Chicago: University of Chicago Press, 1955).

Arrange the items alphabetically by the last names of the authors. Each author's last name is followed by a comma, and then by his given name(s) or initial(s) as they appear in the source. If the author's name is not given or is not known, list the item alphabetically according to the first word (except *the, a,* or *an*) in the title. List titles by the same author chronologically according to dates of publication. When more than one work by the same author is cited, use a blank line about one-half inch long or eight typewritten spaces in place of the author's name after its first appearance. To make the author's name stand out (it may even be put in capital letters throughout), place it flush with the left margin, and indent all run-over lines.

Punctuation: A comma follows the author's last name and precedes his given name or initials. A period, not a comma, follows the complete name. If the person is the editor or compiler or translator, abbreviations for these in parentheses—(ed.), (comp.), (trans.) —follow the name and have a period both within and without the parentheses. The title of a book is followed by a period; the place of publication, the publisher, and the date of publication are *not* placed in parentheses, as they are in footnotes. The titles of articles and of the periodicals in which articles appear are treated as they are in footnotes (see p. 170), except that the inclusive pages (beginning and ending page) of the article should be shown. The use of italics in the bibliography for titles of books and of periodicals is optional and depends upon the desires of the writer or of those who are directing his work.

If the items in a bibliography are numerous, you may classify them in groups—books, magazine articles, public documents, reports, and newspaper accounts. Such classification is illustrated below, although the items there are not so numerous as to require separate listings. An optional method is to have *all* bibliographical items in one alphabetical arrangement.

A sentence or phrase following each item in the list is sometimes helpful and desirable. Such statements should indicate the scope or content of the book or article; they comprise what is known as a *descriptive bibliography* and they begin on the line following the entry.

Place the bibliography at the end of the research paper, and begin it on a separate page, not on the last page of the text. If the paper is typewritten, spacing is single or double, according to desire or instructions; if it is single, use double spacing between the items.

The following is an example of a short bibliography:

Bibliography

A. Books

Allen, Hervey. *Israfel, the Life and Times of Edgar Allan Poe.* New York: Farrar & Rinehart, Inc., 1934.

Boyd, Ernest Augustus. *Literary Blasphemies.* New York: Harper & Brothers, 1927, pp. 163–185.

Campbell, Killis. *The Mind of Poe and Other Studies.* Cambridge, Mass.: Harvard University Press, 1933.

"Edgar Allan Poe," *Encyclopaedia Britannica* (1955 ed.), XVIII, 104, 105.

Ostrom, John Ward (ed.). *The Letters of Edgar Allan Poe.* 2 vols. Cambridge, Mass.: Harvard University Press, 1948.

Robertson, John W. *Edgar A. Poe: a Psychopathic Study.* New York: G. P. Putnam's Sons, 1922.

————. *Bibliography of the Writings of Edgar A. Poe.* 2 vols. San Francisco: Russian Hill Private Press, 1934.

Woodberry, George Edward. *Life of Edgar Allan Poe, Personal and Literary, with His Chief Correspondence with Men of Letters.* 2 vols. Boston: Houghton Mifflin Company, 1909.

B. Magazine Articles

Cooke, A. L. "Edgar Allan Poe—Critic," *Cornhill Magazine,* LXXII (November, 1934), 588–597.

Eaves, T. C. D. "Poe's Last Visit to Philadelphia," *American Literature,* XXVI (March, 1954), 44–51.

Huxley, Aldous Leonard. "Vulgarity in Literature," *Saturday Review of Literature,* VII (September 27, 1930), 158, 159.

Macpherson, Harriet Dorothea. "Dumas and Poe Again," *Saturday Review of Literature,* VI (February 22, 1930), 760.

Wilson, James Southall. "Devil Was in It," *American Mercury,* XXIV (October, 1931), 215–220.

Given below are two student-written research papers. They have many merits, among which are their organization, content, and interest appeal. They show that any student who will expend time, patience, and energy can produce research papers not only good in themselves but of interest to a wide variety of readers. One paper deals with one of the most prominent figures in American history; the other deals with one of the most important of modern scientific developments. "Lincoln the Soldier" (approximately 1,900 words) and "Black Magic" (approximately 1,400 words) were, respectively, Themes No. 12 and No. 9 in second-semester composition at the University of Illinois.[1]

As you study these examples, bear in mind several facts: (1) Although here reproduced in typewriter type, these papers in type-written manuscript form would have a page size of 8½ x 11 inches (standard size), with the lines double-spaced, and with the foot-notes consistently either double-spaced or single-spaced. (2) Note how direct quotations are used within the body of the paper, not only in phrases and sentences but also in paragraphs. In manuscript form, quoted paragraphs would be single-spaced or, if double-spaced, would be indented an inch more on the left and an inch more on the right. (3) Note the use of ellipsis periods within the quoted paragraphs, to indicate omissions (see Section **86g**). (4) Note in the footnotes that when only two consecutive pages are re-ferred to, the documentation reads: "pp. 464, 465"; when more than two consecutive pages are referred to, the documentation should read: "pp. 212–214." (5) In manuscript form, the papers would have the bibliography begin on a separate page at the end.

LINCOLN THE SOLDIER
Mortimer Hitt

Although Abraham Lincoln spent fifty-one days in the armed service of the United States, in the Black Hawk War, few writers have more than mentioned the fact, probably because of the general lack of authentic accounts and the meager wording of official reports and records of this phase of his career.

Lincoln was yet to be recognized by the world when hostilities broke out. To be sure, he al-

---

[1] "Lincoln the Soldier" and "Black Magic" were published in *The Green Caldron, A Magazine of Freshman Writing,* the University of Illinois, Urbana, Illinois, the former in Vol. 16 (October, 1946), pp. 27–32, the latter in Vol. 19 (May, 1950), pp. 9–12. Copyrighted by Charles W. Roberts, and reproduced by permission.

ready had made a name for himself in New Salem and Sangamon County. He was noted for his skill in athletics, particularly in wrestling, a sport in which he had held his own against all comers,[1] and he already was making plans for his political career.[2]

Carl Sandburg suggests that Lincoln enlisted for two reasons: first, he would soon lose his clerking job; and second, "he was running for the legislature; a war record, in any kind of war, would count in politics."[3] Whatever may have been his motives, the fact remains that Lincoln, on the twenty-first of April, 1832, enlisted in the militia, which was at that time called into the service of the national government.[4]

Lincoln was chosen captain by the men of his company, in accord with the custom of those days. An interesting account of his election is given by Leonard Swett:

> Together with the talk of organizing a company in New Salem, began the talk of making Lincoln captain of it. His characteristics as an athlete had made something of a hero of him. . . . But when the day of organization arrived, a man who had been captain of a real company arrived in his uniform, and assumed the organization of the company. The mode of it was as follows: A

[1] Leonard Swett, "Mr. Lincoln's Story of His Own Life," in <u>Reminiscences of Abraham Lincoln by Distinguished Men of His Time</u>, ed. Allen Thorndike Rice (New York: North American Publishing Company, 1886), pp. 463, 464.

[2] Carl Sandburg, <u>Abraham Lincoln, The Prairie Years</u> (New York: Harcourt, Brace & Company, 1926), I, 154.

[3] <u>Ibid</u>.

[4] Abraham Lincoln, <u>Muster Roll of Captain Abraham Lincoln's Company</u> (MS in State Historical Library, Springfield, Illinois).

line of two was formed by the company, with
the parties who intended to be candidates
for officers standing in front. The candidate for captain then made a speech to the
men, telling them what a gallant man he was,
in what wars he had fought, bled and died,
and how he was ready again, for the glory of
his country to lead them. Then another candidate; and when the speech-making was
ended, they commanded those who would vote
for this man, or that, to form a line behind
their favorite. . . .

   When the real captain with his regimentals
came and assumed control, Lincoln's heart
failed him. He formed in the line with the
boys, and after the speech was made they began to form behind the old captain, but the
boys seized Lincoln, and pushed him out of
line, and began to form behind him . . . and
when they counted back he had two more than
the other captain, and he became real captain. [5]

His captaincy was the first electoral job he
ever held, and in his own words, it was "a success which gave me more pleasure than any I have
had since."[6]
That Lincoln was obviously untrained and inexperienced in the ways of the military is evi-
denced by an account of his drilling his company
during the first few days of his service. The
men were marching across a field, formed in what
today most probably would be termed a "company
front," when they came to a gate at the edge of
the field. Lincoln, unable to recall the proper
command for getting the company into a column,

[5] Swett, "Mr. Lincoln's Story," pp. 464, 465.
[6] <u>Abraham Lincoln From His Own Words and Con-</u>
<u>temporary Accounts</u>, ed. Roy Edgar Appleman
(Washington: Government Printing Office, 1942),
p. 2.

shouted, "This company is dismissed for two minutes, when it will fall in again on the other side of the gate!"[7]

Lincoln's ignorance of drill regulations was not the only thing that caused him trouble. He was arrested and his sword was taken away from him for a day because he broke a general order that forbade the discharge of firearms within a radius of fifty yards from the camp.[8] It may have been that he was not familiar with the orders or that he was careless in judging his distance. Whatever the reason, he showed clearly that he was not taking his responsibilities very seriously.

Lincoln's company was not amenable to discipline. To his first order he received the reply, "Go to the devil, sir."[9] The attitudes of the men are described very well by Theodore Pease:

> Allow the man whom they had recently honored by electing captain—a man whom they knew thoroughly as no better than themselves —allow such a one to take advantage of his position to direct an action undesirable to them? Incomprehensible! To the recently elected captain this point of view seemed entirely reasonable.[10]

Yet another example of the obvious lack of discipline is witnessed by the following incident. One of the men broke into the officers' quarters one night and stole a quantity of liquor which

[7] Sandburg, _Abraham Lincoln_, p. 155.

[8] William H. Herndon and Jesse W. Weik, _Herndon's Lincoln_ (Springfield: The Herndon's Lincoln Publishing Co., 1921), I, 95.

[9] Norman Hapgood, _Abraham Lincoln, The Man of the People_ (New York: The Macmillan Company, 1900), p. 32.

[10] Theodore C. Pease, _The Centennial History of Illinois_ (Chicago: A. C. McClurg and Co., 1919), II, 161.

he shared with his comrades. When the army began
to march the following morning, the men of Lincoln's company dropped out right and left until
only a few remained in the ranks. It was late in
the evening before the entire company was together again. As a result of the investigation
that followed, Lincoln, though innocent of com-
plicity in or knowledge of the affair, was arrested and forced to undergo the humiliation of
wearing a wooden sword for two days.[11]

This theft may be partly excused on the
grounds that the men were not given adequate rations. Lincoln's company, between April 25 and
May 17, received the following:

Corn	118 bu., 18 pecks	Powder	1 keg
Meal	10 qts.	Lead	50 lbs.
Flour	1 bbl., 252 lbs.	Flints	265
Bread	66 lbs.	Candles	20
Salt	42 lbs.	Tape	144 yds.
Pork	1 bbl., 160 lbs.	Buckets	50
Whiskey	10½ gals.	Coffee Boilers	7
Sacks	48	Tin Pans	7
Blankets	3	Tin Cups	16[12]
Soap	[Amount unreadable]		

Some authors have mentioned that the men would
make expeditions to nearby farms, and return
loaded down with sundry items of food. This
seems entirely probable, for there were, including Lincoln and his lieutenants, seventy men in
the company. One can readily see that the rations listed above would hardly suffice for that
number of active men for a period of twenty-
three days, let alone the additional ten days of
their enlistment during which time no rations
were drawn.

The closest contact Lincoln had with the In-

---

[11] Herndon, Herndon's Lincoln, pp. 95, 96.
[12] William Thommas, Quarter Master's Book (MS
in State Historical Library, Springfield, Illinois), p. 14.

dians during the war was with an old Indian who
had a safe conduct from General Cass and who was
captured by some of the men. They were about to
kill the aged savage, but Lincoln intervened and
saved his life.[13] There are several accounts of
this episode by various reputable authors, but
as none of them is documented, it may be apocry-
phal.

On the twenty-seventh of May, Lincoln's company was demobilized at Ottawa, Illinois, because of the increasing dissatisfaction of the
men.[14] Lincoln and several of the other men from
his company re-enlisted for a period of twenty
days in Captain Elijah Iles' company of Independent Rangers,[15] a company composed of gen-
erals, colonels, captains, and other distinguished men of the disbanded army. It was an
unique organization—the men had no camp duties
and could draw rations as often as they desired;
their arms and equipment were of the best. In
the final analysis, Lincoln was much better off
as a private in this company than he had been as
captain of his old organization.[16] Captain Iles'
company saw no action whatever during the twenty
days of Lincoln's enlistment. In fact, though
many historians have written about the war, and
more still have written biographies of Lincoln,
there is no account of his individual actions
during this enlistment.

Lincoln's second period of enlistment ended on
the sixteenth of June, and although he re-
enlisted the same day, he was not actually mus-

[13] Ida M. Tarbell, The Early Life of Abraham
Lincoln (New York: S. S. McClure, Ltd., 1896),
p. 141.
[14] Isaac H. Elliott, Adjutant General's Report
(Springfield: Journal Co., 1902), IX, 100.
[15] General Robert Anderson, Muster Rolls, etc.,
etc., Black Hawk War, 1832 (MS in State Historical Library, Springfield, Illinois), p. 7.
[16] Tarbell, Early Life, p. 144.

tered into service again until the twentieth.[17]
The officer who mustered Lincoln into service
the second and third times was Major Robert
Anderson, later to be commander of Fort Sumter
during the early part of the Civil War. From his
own account:

> I also mustered Abraham Lincoln twice into
> the service and once out. He was a member of
> two of the Independent companies which were
> not brigaded. The first time I mustered him
> into the service was at the mouth of the Fox
> River, May 29, 1832, in Captain Elijah Iles'
> company. . . . I mustered him out of the
> service at the "Rapids of the Illinois,"
> June 16, 1832, and in four days afterwards,
> at the same place, I mustered him into serv-
> ice again in Captain Jacob M. Early's com-
> pany. . . . Of course I had no recollection
> of Mr. Lincoln, but when President he re-
> minded me of the fact.[18]

Surely if Lincoln had had any of the qualities
of a good soldier he would have been remembered
by some of the officers, such as General Anderson, and most likely would have been promoted.
Many of the accounts build up Lincoln's accom-
plishments during his military career into proportions far beyond what seem to have been the
actual facts as illustrated by surviving primary
sources. The very fact that he remained a private during his second and third enlistments
speaks for his military abilities.

BIBLIOGRAPHY

Anderson, General Robert. Letter dated May 10,
1870, to E. B. Washburn. (MS in State Historical Library, Centennial Building, Springfield,
Illinois.)

[17] Anderson, Muster Rolls, p. 23.
[18] General Robert Anderson, Letter dated May
10, 1870, to E. B. Washburn (MS in State Historical Library, Springfield, Illinois), p. 4.

———. <u>Muster Rolls, etc., etc., Black Hawk War,</u>
<u>1832</u>. (MS in State Historical Library, Cen-
tennial Building, Springfield, Illinois.)
Appleman, Roy Edgar (ed.). <u>Abraham Lincoln</u>
<u>From His Own Words and Contemporary Accounts</u>.
Washington: Government Printing Office, 1942.
Arnold, Isaac N. <u>Address: November 19, 1868</u>.
Chicago: Fergus Printing Co., 1877.
———. <u>The Life of Abraham Lincoln</u>. Chicago: A. C.
McClurg and Co., 1901.
Barber, Joseph. <u>War Letters of a Disbanded Vol-</u>
<u>unteer</u>. New York: Frederic A. Brady, 1864.
Barrett, Joseph H. <u>Life of Abraham Lincoln</u>. New
York: Moore, Wilstach and Baldwin, 1865.
Brooks, Noah. <u>Abraham Lincoln: His Youth and</u>
<u>Early Manhood</u>. New York: G. P. Putnam's Sons,
1901.
———. <u>Abraham Lincoln and the Downfall of Ameri-</u>
<u>can Slavery</u>. New York: G. P. Putnam's Sons,
1908.
Browne, Francis F. <u>The Every-Day Life of Abraham</u>
<u>Lincoln</u>. Chicago: Browne and Howell Co., 1913.
<u>Collections of the State Historical Society of</u>
<u>Wisconsin</u>. Vol. XIV. Madison: Democrat Print-
ing Co., 1898.
Dunne, Edward F. <u>Illinois, The Heart of the</u>
<u>Nation</u>. Chicago and New York: Lewis Publishing
Co., 1933.
Elliott, Isaac H. <u>Adjutant General's Report</u>.
Vol. IX. Springfield: Journal Co., 1902.
Ford, Governor Thomas. <u>A History of Illinois</u>.
Vol. I. Chicago: R. R. Donnelley and Sons Co.,
1945.
Hapgood, Norman. <u>Abraham Lincoln, The Man of the</u>
<u>People</u>. New York: The Macmillan Co., 1900.
Herndon, William H., and Weik, Jesse W. <u>Hern-</u>
<u>don's Lincoln</u>. Vol. I. Springfield: The Hern-
don's Lincoln Publishing Co., 1921.
Iles, Major Elijah. <u>Sketches of Early Life and</u>
<u>Times</u>. Springfield: Springfield Printing Co.,
1883.
Lincoln, Abraham. <u>Muster Roll of Captain Abraham</u>
<u>Lincoln's Company</u>. (MS in State Historical

Library, Centennial Building, Springfield, Illinois.)

Malone, Thomas J. "Soldiering with Captain Abraham Lincoln," American Legion Weekly, February 6, 1925, pp. 5, 6, 18, 19.

Moses, John. Illinois, Historical and Statistical. Chicago: Fergus Printing Co., 1895, pp. 357-378.

Nicolay, John G., and Hay, John. Abraham Lincoln, A History. Vol. I. New York: The Century Co., 1914.

Pease, Theodore C. The Centennial History of Illinois. Vol. II. Chicago: A. C. McClurg and Co., 1919.

Report and Collections of the State Historical Society of Wisconsin for the Years 1877, 1878, and 1879. Madison: David Atwood, 1879.

Report and Collections of the State Historical Society of Wisconsin for the Years 1883, 1884, and 1885. Madison: Democrat Printing Co., 1888.

Sandburg, Carl. Abraham Lincoln, the Prairie Years. Vol. I. New York: Harcourt, Brace & Co., 1926.

Second Annual Report and Collections of the State Historical Society of Wisconsin for the Year 1855. Madison: Calkins and Proudfit, 1856.

Smith, George W. History of Illinois and Her People. Vol. II. Chicago and New York: American Historical Society, Inc., 1927.

Smith, Henry. "Indian Campaign of 1832," Military and Naval Magazine of the United States, August, 1833, pp. 321-333.

Swett, Leonard. "Mr. Lincoln's Story of His Own Life," in Allen Thorndike Rice (ed.), Reminiscences of Abraham Lincoln by Distinguished Men of His Time. New York: North American Publishing Company, 1886, pp. 455-468.

Tarbell, Ida M. The Early Life of Abraham Lincoln. New York: S. S. McClure, Ltd., 1896.

———. The Life of Abraham Lincoln. New York: Lincoln History Society, 1900.

Thommas, William. Quarter Master's Book. (MS in
   State Historical Library, Centennial Building,
   Springfield, Illinois.)

BLACK MAGIC

Marvin E. Mayer

Many years ago there lived in Bologna, Italy,
a cobbler named Vincenzo Cascariolo, who pursued
the interesting art of alchemy. During an expedition to Mt. Pesoro, his attention was attracted by the sparkle of a heavy rock which
glistened with an unearthly brilliance.[1] Greatly
excited, he lugged it home and heated it in his
furnace, hoping it would enable him to produce
gold. But much to his sorrow, it did not.
   In the spring of 1944, three hundred and
forty-two years later, a scientist, not an al-
chemist, brought another rock back from the
mountains. Beneath ordinary light it was a drab,
gray stone which no one would look at twice. But
in darkness, under ultra-violet light, it burst
into a mass of exuberant red, flecked with spots
of vivid green.[2] In the last few years, dozens
of men like him have been bringing home rocks,
natural and synthetic, grinding them up, causing
them to emit weird hues, and doing astonishing
things that the old cobbler never dreamed of
doing. Where Cascariolo failed, they have succeeded, producing wealth that would have made
the old man dizzy.
   They call this peculiar behavior "fluorescence," a word that will do as well as any
other. The name was first used because fluorspar
is one of the long list of substances which
emit light of various specific colors upon
stimulation by certain wave lengths from a part
of the spectrum which man does not ordinarily

[1] "Fluorescence," Encyclopaedia Britannica, IX
(1946 ed.), 422.
[2] Judith Richardson, "Color Magic with Black
Light," Popular Mechanics, June, 1945, p. 107.

use. The cobbler's curious find sparkled as it did because the ultra-violet part of the sun's rays evoked its fluorescence. If he had possessed the equipment of our modern laboratories, he would have been even more astonished by its brilliance.

Armed with invisible ultra-violet light and varieties of materials which fluoresce, physicists and illumination engineers are playing a fascinating game these days. From the array of bottles, they pour little mounds of powder on a bench, powders which are all white under daylight or ordinary lamp light. When the "black light" is turned on in the dark laboratory, each mound glows with its own characteristic fluorescence color, and the experimenter is confronted with a dazzling rainbow spectacle of pastel blues, greens and yellows. The familiar color of an object which happens to possess fluorescence has no relation to its hue when stimulated by ultra-violet. We call a fresh egg white or brown because it looks that way under ordinary light. Under ultra-violet of the right wave length, it has a reddish glow. "Black light" can analyze a pretty girl's face with very uncomplimentary keenness: the powder around the roots of a girl's hair is purple; the dye in her hair is gray; the wash applied around her eyes to make them sparkle is yellow; her rouge is yellow, and if she smokes, there is a yellowish color around her mouth due to nicotine stain.[3]

However, the difference does not stop there. The light which comes from an object under daylight is only a reflection, but a fluorescent object activated by ultra-violet becomes an extraordinarily efficient converter or middleman of light on its own account. Because of this property, the "black magic" of 1602 is a modern tool which within a single decade has become in-

[3] Jim Marshall, "That New Black Magic," Collier's, September 30, 1944, p. 66.

dispensable in industry, commerce, and scientific analyses. "Fluorescence," which yesterday was an obscure and poorly used word used only by physicists, is now on everyone's tongue, and there is hardly a street in America where its effect is not visible.

When the big fairs of New York and San Francisco opened their gates in 1939 with their bright prophecies of a brave new world, one of the first things that impressed the visitors was a glass wand which gave out a new kind of light.[4] At the Flushing spectacle, more than ten miles of these tubes produced a soft, diffused, yet powerful illumination, unlike anything that had been seen before. Glowing in many colors, they flooded the streets and exhibits with hues unrivaled in purity and brilliance and played a major part in creating the atmosphere of a futuristic wonderland.

What people saw was the public unveiling of fluorescent light, the first radical departure in illumination since Edison's invention of the filament electric bulb. Dazzled by the glittering parade of novelties, spectators dismissed the luminous tube as only another new toy for the decoration of fairs and carnivals. In this opinion, they were not alone. Even many lighting experts who recognized the revolutionary nature of the new light believed that it would be used only for advertising and display, like a neon sign. All doubters were caught off balance, for, since that time, fluorescent lighting has swept the country in a boom of amazing proportions.

The new lamp uses a completely new method for converting electricity into light. It has no filament like the ordinary light bulb. Mercury vapor in the tube gives off ultra-violet light when the current is passed through it, and the

---

[4] Harland Manchester, New World of Machines (Toronto: Random House of Canada, Limited, 1945), pp. 66, 67.

ultra-violet light, striking a chalklike chemical coating with which the tube is lined, is
converted into light suitable for illumination.[5]
It is pleasanter, cooler, easier on the eyes,
and vastly more efficient than any other light
ever invented for general use.

In offices, stores, and restaurants, the
quality of the new light is quickly noticeable,
for every corner of the room appears to be
flooded with soft, evenly distributed light.
Overhead in clusters, or perhaps fixed vertically on the walls, are the gleaming tubular
fluorescent bars, sometimes bare, sometimes partially shielded with grids made of glass or a
translucent porcelain-like plastic. In either
case, you can look at the tubes without hurting
your eyes. You will notice that, like Peter Pan,
you have lost your shadow. This is because the
sharp "point lighting" of the ordinary bulb has
been eliminated. The tube has ten times the
surface area of a regular light bulb of the same
wattage, so the light is spread out as evenly as
melted butter on a piece of toast.

But this use is only one phase of the fluorescent boom. The active principle of the lamp has
been adapted to a score of important uses. It
has given pathologists a valuable new weapon in
the study of disease; it saves the crops of the
potato farmers, detects mold and adulteration
in foodstuffs, and it has a multitude of combat
uses where "seeing in the dark" may save lives.[6]
Reactivated fluorescent dye powders have saved
many aviators forced down at sea as the addition
of this powder to the water tints a large area,
making it visible to rescue planes. Maps may be
encased in a fluorescent plastic which makes
them visible when exposed to a "black light."[7]

[5] Ibid., p. 69.
[6] "Safer Future Promised," Science News Letter,
XV (May 13, 1944), 317.
[7] Ibid.

Another modern achievement is the answer to the problem of marking laundry. People mark their clothing with a fluorescent dye and the man who makes up the packages and sorts the garments works under invisible light.

Many years ago, Dr. Robert W. Wood, noted for his brilliant contributions to the knowledge of fluorescence as well as for his scientific pranks, brought forth the spectacular stage effect by which a line of chorus girls could be suddenly transformed into dancing skeletons or a row of bodiless shoes, gloves and hats.[8] This is done by painting the costumes with fluorescent material which cannot be seen under ordinary theatre lights. When the lights are turned out and the stage flooded with invisible ultra-violet light, only fluorescent markings are visible; advertising billboards have used the same technique to make a sign carry a double message at night, when lit alternately with ordinary bulbs and "black light." Night clubs also use it. At the turn of a switch, walls which are ordinarily blank blossom forth with romantic, tropical vistas. These uses and numerous others make this mystery of yesterday the hope of the future.

From the cobbler's discovery of the "Bologna stone," as it was then called, to the experimentations of today, fluorescence has helped revolutionize the modern age.

BIBLIOGRAPHY

"Fluorescence," Encyclopedia Americana (1946 ed.), XI, 401.

"Fluorescence," Encyclopaedia Britannica (1946 ed.), IX, 422–426.

Luckiesh, M. The Lighting Art. New York: McGraw-Hill Book Co., Inc., 1917.

Manchester, Harland. New World of Machines.

[8] Manchester, New World of Machines, p. 79.

Toronto: Random House of Canada, Limited, 1945.

Marshall, Jim. "That New Black Magic," <u>Collier's</u>, September 30, 1944, pp. 66–75.

"More Light Urged," <u>Business Week</u>, May 11, 1946, pp. 39–41.

Richardson, Judith. "Color Magic with Black Light," <u>Popular Mechanics</u>, June, 1945, pp. 106–112.

"Safer Future Promised," <u>Science News Letter</u>, May 13, 1944, p. 317.

The Paragraph

WRITING is a process of building. Just as letters of the alphabet are combined into words, and words are linked to form phrases, clauses, and sentences, so sentences are combined to form paragraphs. Good themes or compositions are built with good paragraphs, which are fundamental to all good writing and which are predicated upon clear thinking.

Good paragraphs are not difficult to compose. Anyone can create them who has ideas, will think clearly about them, will develop them, will relate them to one another, and will write and rewrite thoughtfully. We may speak in sentences, but we should and must think and write in larger units.

To achieve good paragraphs, therefore, you should understand the meaning, the purposes, and the characteristics of paragraphs and paragraphing.

DEFINITION AND CHARACTERISTICS

21a. Understand clearly the meaning and purpose of paragraphing.

A paragraph is a group of sentences, sometimes one sentence, developing either one single topic or a specific part of a larger topic.

The purpose of the paragraph is to aid in communicating ideas by setting off the single topic which is developed or by providing clear distinctions between the separate parts of a longer composition. A complete theme or short paper may consist of one paragraph only (see Section **29d**). Or a theme or paper may have two or three or as many paragraphs as the writer decides are necessary to give his subject adequate treatment.

193

21b. Make your paragraphs correct, clear, effective, and appropriate.

A well-constructed paragraph should be *correct, clear, effective,* and *appropriate*—characteristics dependent upon careful thinking.

Good paragraphing is essential for clearness. Properly separated groups of sentences enable the writer to plot his course and see the progress he is making. To the reader, too, they make the structure and development of ideas easily apparent by serving as signposts or road markers to guide him along the paths of thought which the writer is developing. The reader, following the signs laid out to help him, can obtain, quickly and clearly, a grasp of the parts and of the whole which they constitute.

Good paragraphing is also essential for effectiveness, partly because readers easily tire unless a page of writing is broken into smaller units. The sign of the paragraph, *indentation,* is a helpful lure to the reader; he feels that he has completed a unified section of writing and can go on to another unit. Books, magazine articles, and even short stories are often divided into chapters or sections, or their parts otherwise typographically are set off from one another not so much to keep closely related ideas or parts of the action together as to furnish the reader a breathing space.

For convenience and ready reference, seven desirable paragraph characteristics are listed below; each one will be fully discussed in later sections. For the most part, these characteristics refer to the "normal" paragraph, that is, the paragraph as we commonly think of it. They do not apply to paragraphs appropriate for special purposes (see Section 29).

1. A good paragraph is *mechanically* correct. It is properly indented. In dialogue, it correctly represents every change of speaker. (*Correctness*)

2. A good paragraph contains a *topic statement,* expressed or implied. (*Clearness*)

3. A good paragraph depends upon proper *analysis* of its topic; it contains a *body of thought,* not a mere fragment. The well-developed paragraph is never sketchy or incomplete. (*Clearness*)

4. A good paragraph must be *unified.* Oneness of purpose and content is essential; unrelated details must be eliminated. Each

paragraph contains the words that belong with it, not with the preceding or following paragraph. (*Clearness and effectiveness*)

5. A good paragraph has its ideas arranged in proper *order*. The sentences in it are so worded and arranged that each sentence flows naturally out of the one that precedes it and leads naturally into the one that follows. (*Clearness and effectiveness*)

6. A good paragraph is well *proportioned* and has appropriate *length*. If the thought of the paragraph is important, the paragraph will be fairly long. If the paragraph discusses an idea, or a group of related ideas, of comparatively less importance, the paragraph will be shorter. Usually a series of short, choppy paragraphs, or a group of very long ones, should be avoided. (*Effectiveness and appropriateness*)

7. A good paragraph contains *transitional aids:* words, phrases, clauses, and sentences serving as links or bridges. The thoughts within paragraphs should make orderly, clear progress, and there should be clear, smooth passage from one paragraph to another. (*Clearness and effectiveness*)

MECHANICS

22. Mechanical correctness in paragraphs is simple to attain because the conventions are few and easily learned. Absence of errors is a mechanical and negative aspect of writing, but it is an element without which any writing loses much of its effectiveness.

22a. Indent the first line of every paragraph.

Indentation, although mechanical, is important. Indent the first line of every paragraph three-quarters of an inch or more; or, if you typewrite, about five or ten spaces.

The break of distinct paragraph indentation is a real aid to both writer and reader in recognizing the divisions of thought within the whole theme. Paragraph indentation also aids in reading; the break serves as a signal that a clear distinction between separate parts of the whole composition is about to be made.

Use indentations of equal length for all the paragraphs in the same theme. Make no exception for *numbered* paragraphs.

Avoid in general the use of the marks "¶" and "no ¶," meaning, respectively, "a new paragraph intended" and "not a new paragraph." Preferably, you should recopy the entire page, correcting the indentation.

Do not indent the first line of the second page or succeeding pages unless the indentation marks the beginning of a new paragraph.

22b.   Do not leave part of a line blank within a paragraph.

Unless a new paragraph begins on the next line, do not leave part of a line blank within a paragraph. Blanks in lines which are not last lines of paragraphs mislead your reader, who expects such a break to finish the discussion of one phase of a subject. Furthermore, such blanks in lines not only cause a jagged appearance but also make less efficient the mechanical process of reading—the eye, in sweeping over the line, has to make several extra movements in order to adjust itself and to transfer meaning to the brain. Margins at the left of the page should, of course, always be uniform for the same reasons and should not meander toward the right.

(For the conventional and appropriate use of very short paragraphs—conversation, short introductory and concluding paragraphs, transitional paragraphs, business letters, directions, summaries, conclusions, and recommendations—see Section 29.)

THE TOPIC SENTENCE OR STATEMENT

23. A topic sentence or statement gives the gist of the paragraph; it contains the heart of the idea which is to be, is being, or has been, developed. It contributes to the unity, the clearness, and the effectiveness of the paragraph by pointing out the topic, the central thought with which the group of sentences is concerned.

23a.   Use a topic sentence or topic statement to aid in gaining paragraph unity.

The topic sentence, although so called, may not be a "sentence" at all. It is the statement containing the subject or topic, which may be expressed in various forms: (1) as one of the clauses in a compound sentence; (2) as the main clause of a complex sentence;

(3) as a phrase within the sentence; or (4) even as a single word. A short, simple sentence, however, is usually the most effective kind of topic sentence.

The reason for such flexibility is that a writer may use part of the sentence containing the topic to serve as transition or to indicate the manner in which the topic is to be developed or the direction in which the discussion is to continue. Whatever its grammatical form, the topic sentence, or statement, always is or contains the subject of the paragraph.

Not every well-constructed paragraph contains an expressed topic sentence, but every good paragraph is so well knit that it at least *implies* one. The reader, reflecting, can sum up the central thought of the paragraph in his own "topic sentence." Perhaps a study, however, of a number of paragraphs would show that the clearest and most effective paragraphs are those in which the topic is expressed, and the least effective those in which it is implied. Consideration for the reader is certainly an argument in favor of an expressed topic.

A topic sentence or statement or word, therefore, is a guide to both writer and reader. For the writer, it is the guide by which he keeps on the subject and avoids introducing irrelevant material. It may be—perhaps should be—a simple sentence, at least in its first draft. Simple sentences are easier to phrase than other kinds, and a writer can write all the topic sentences or statements for a theme, or even a long paper, before he begins the more difficult task of developing them.

A well-planned topic outline, in which you have already decided the divisions to be expanded into paragraphs, will readily provide the key words for topic statements; a sentence outline will present topic sentences ready-made. The paragraph outline, usually made of others' writing, shows us how other authors have composed their topic sentences. (See Section 6a, b, c.)

As an easy check on the presence or absence of a paragraph topic and its effective phrasing, reread carefully each paragraph that you write. Put in the margin the one or two words that are the subject of the paragraph. Or apply the methods of some textbooks which print in blackface type the paragraph topic at the beginning of the paragraph. If you follow any of these suggestions, be sure to eliminate all mechanical uses of the paragraph topic from your final draft.

23b. Vary the kind of sentences containing the topic.

Although simple sentences are clear and effective as topic sentences, you can include topics in the phrases or clauses of compound, complex, and compound-complex sentences. For variety use declarative and interrogative sentences, and when they are appropriate, use exclamatory or even imperative sentences. You can use any of these kinds of sentences also to make a topic sentence which generalizes, or summarizes, or particularizes.

23c. Vary the position of topic sentences within the paragraph.

Ordinarily, since the purpose of writing is clearness of communication, the first sentence of the paragraph—especially in expository and argumentative writing—should be or contain the topic. The reader should be told immediately what he is to read about. Since a series of paragraphs beginning with topic sentences may become monotonous, a writer can experiment with placing each paragraph topic in the second, third, or fourth sentences, and letting the earlier sentences lead up to it. Occasionally, the last sentence may be or contain the topic. Occasionally, too, the thought of the topic sentence may be repeated in other sentences in the paragraph.

Study the following three examples. Note the unifying, clarifying effect of the topic sentences; note also their position and form. To emphasize their position, they are here italicized.

1. The topic sentence is the first sentence, a declarative sentence; it tells what is to follow.

Two main courses of study are offered at Milldale High School. One is the academic course and the other is the commercial course. The high school freshman is required to choose the course he plans to follow during the next four years. The academic course consists of the subjects which are required for college entrance, such as written composition, English and American literature, mathematics, history, and some science. This course does not include typing, shorthand, or bookkeeping, although a student may elect one or more of these. The commercial course is designed for girls and boys preparing to become stenographers and secretaries. It does not include English literature or any of the sciences or higher mathematics courses. It is concerned mainly with the commercial courses, like shorthand, typing, bookkeeping, business English, and office etiquette. (Student theme)

2. The topic statement is the dependent clause in the second sentence, an answer to a question; note, too, that it is repeated in the fourth sentence.

In the face of this, one may ask: Why does the great and universal fame of classical authors continue? The answer is that *the fame of classical authors is entirely independent of the majority.* Do you suppose that if the fame of Shakespeare depended on the man in the street it would survive a fortnight? *The fame of classical authors is originally made, and it is maintained, by a passionate few.* Even when a first-class author has enjoyed immense success during his lifetime, the majority have never appreciated him so sincerely as they have appreciated second-rate men. He has always been reënforced by the ardor of the passionate few. And in the case of an author who has emerged into glory after his death, the happy sequel has been due solely to the obstinate perseverance of the few. They could not leave him alone; they would not. They kept on savoring him, and talking about him, and buying him, and they generally behaved with such eager zeal, and they were so authoritative and sure of themselves, that at last the majority grew accustomed to the sound of his name and placidly agreed to the proposition that he was a genius; the majority really did not care very much either way. (From Arnold Bennett's "Why a Classic Is a Classic.")[1]

3. The topic sentence is the fourth sentence; the sentences before and after it illustrate and expand the idea expressed.

Suppose, however, that we had called that same animal a "mongrel." The matter is more complicated. We have used a word which objectively means the same as "dog of mixed breed," but which also arouses in our hearers an emotional attitude of disapproval toward that particular dog. *A word, therefore, cannot only indicate an object, but can also suggest an emotional attitude toward it.* Such suggestion of an emotional attitude does go beyond exact and scientific discussion because our approvals and disapprovals are individual—they belong to ourselves and not to the objects we approve or disapprove of. An animal which to the mind of its master is a faithful and noble dog of mixed ancestry may be a "mon-

[1] From *Literary Taste: How to Form It,* by Arnold Bennett, Hodder, Hodder, & Stoughton, 1930.

grel" to his neighbor whose chickens are chased by it. (From Robert Thouless' "Emotional Meanings.")[2]

These illustrations indicate a few positions for the topic sentence and a few of the ways in which it is expressed. The important thing to remember is this: One criterion of the good paragraph is that it must be so unified that its gist, or pith, is stated in a topic sentence or can be when a topic is not expressed. Only thus can you be certain that you have kept to the subject; only thus can the reader follow clearly the development of your idea. Keep in mind, too, that a topic sentence contains only the main point or points of a paragraph, not every idea mentioned.

EXERCISES

A. Three assignments in one: Underline the topic sentences or topic statements of a number of paragraphs in one of your textbooks; in an article in a current magazine; in an article in your book of readings. Discuss the position in the paragraph of these topic sentences and the kinds of sentences they are.

B. From your reading, select a seemingly well-constructed paragraph which has no topic sentence or topic statement. Give the implied topic.

C. By means of the author's topic sentences, make an outline of some essay in your book of readings.

D. Write five or more topic sentences to be used in developing each of the following theme subjects:

1. Why I Am Attending _____ College.
2. The Honor System on Our Campus.
3. The Best Way to Sell Second-Hand Cars.
4. The Most Remarkable Character in Our Town.
5. How to Improve in Writing.
6. Let's Ignore the Saturday Football Games.
7. Reading as a Substitute for Travel.
8. Why Golf Makes Walking Interesting.
9. See Your Dentist Twice a Year, but Your Doctor Only Once.
10. Are You Here to Study or to Have a Great Time?

E. Using the following simple sentences as topic sentences, expand one or more into paragraphs of 150 to 300 words.

[2] From *How to Think Straight,* by Robert H. Thouless. Copyright, 1939, by Simon and Schuster, Inc.

1. A good farmer can always make a comfortable living.
2. Conservation of water depends upon conservation of our forests.
3. Basketball in our state is overemphasized.
4. It is women who make a home out of a house.
5. Careless driving is responsible for serious accidents.
6. Basketball is a better spectator-sport than bowling (or some similar game).
7. Bowling (or some similar game) is a better sport for individuals than basketball (or some similar game).
8. Our college's greatest need is _____.
9. May I recommend a good television (or radio) program?
10. John Doe (or another name) is having trouble in English.
11. The nickname of my state is _____.
12. Being the oldest (youngest, only) child in a family has its advantages (disadvantages).
13. A satisfactory roommate has few faults and many virtues.
14. The recent snowstorm created a new world.
15. What would universal military training mean to the youth of America?
16. High school English is different from college English.
17. The illness was diagnosed as _____.
18. A traveler has many unusual experiences.
19. Life on a farm (in a city) has its exciting moments.
20. A budget is an efficient way to conserve time (or money).

SUBSTANCE

24. After you have determined the thought to be developed in the paragraph and put it in a topic sentence, expressed or implied, you encounter the problem of developing the thought. Topic sentences are only the beginning, the foundation, the summary sentence of the thought to be presented. Neither hazy generalizations nor mere repetition of the central thought builds good paragraphs.

Clear and effective paragraphs are completely developed and contain an abundance of pertinent detail. Ineffective paragraphs are weak not because the central ideas are necessarily weak but because their substance is thin, dull, and meaningless. In other words, fully developed paragraphs require genuine mental activity. An effective, clear theme is the sum total of a series of paragraphs rounded with ample substance.

24a. Gather substance from your own thought and experience and from the thought and experience of others.

After you have phrased the topic sentence, you must draw upon your own experience and the experience of others as revealed in newspapers, magazines, books, and conversation. Make use of your own observation, curiosity, imagination, and reflection. Since one paragraph may be a complete short theme or one of a series of paragraphs making up a theme, the suggestions concerning substance for the whole theme (Section 5) apply equally to the paragraph.

To this substance apply also the analysis suggested for theme topics in Section 4. Your paragraph topic is simply a more limited subject: What are its component parts? What, from your various materials, will you jot down concerning it?

For example, for a long theme, "Important Facts Concerning My High School," designed to inform his freshman English instructor of his precollege background, a student chose for one paragraph subject, "Courses of Study Offered." As a starting place and in no special order, his jottings consisted of the following:

1. Two main courses
2. Academic course
3. Commercial course
4. General course for a few weaker students
5. Time of choosing courses
6. Content of academic course (composition, literature, history, science, mathematics, etc.)
7. Content of commercial course (typing, shorthand, bookkeeping, business English, etc.)
8. Purpose of academic course
9. Purpose of commercial course

The following outline for the paragraph resulted from these jottings:

I. General information about courses
   A. Kinds
   B. Purpose
   C. Time of choosing

II. The academic course
   A. Subjects included
   B. Subjects not included
III. The commercial course
   A. Subjects included
   B. Subjects not included

For the paragraph as finally written from this outline, see p. 198.

24b. Follow a consistent method, or methods, in developing the idea contained in the topic sentence.

There are various methods by which a topic can be expanded into an effective paragraph. Your topic sentence, if well chosen and phrased, will often indicate the most desirable method; sometimes it will suggest several methods from which you should choose the one that will most clearly, effectively, and appropriately accomplish your purpose. The choice of any one method does not exclude use of other methods of paragraph development. Bear in mind also that a short illustration—a sentence or two at the most—may always be inserted into the course of development by any method without destroying the unity of the paragraph or the directness of the thought.

The most frequently used methods of developing a paragraph topic are the following: particulars and details, illustration or example, comparison or contrast, division, causes or effects, reasons and inferences, and definition.

1. Development by *particulars and details* means explaining the various aspects of the idea contained in the topic sentence by a series of specific details or concrete particulars, arranged in a logical order. Since any topic is broader or more general than its supporting material, every paragraph is in a sense developed by particulars and details. Apart from other methods, however, this method uses ideas related to or suggested by preceding ideas, and all taken together amplify, make vivid, make definite the idea of the topic. Notice how particulars and details support the topic, italicized, in the following paragraphs:

Miscellaneous *details:*

In an elevator, ascending with strangers to familiar heights, the breath congeals, the body stiffens, the spirit marks time. These brief vertical journeys that we make in a common lift, from street level to office level, past the missing thirteenth floor—they afford moments of suspended animation, unique and probably beneficial. Passengers in an elevator, whether wedged tight or scattered with room to spare, achieve in their perpendicular passage a trancelike state: each person adhering to the unwritten code, a man descending at five in the afternoon with his nose buried in a strange woman's back hair, reducing his breath to an absolute minimum necessary to sustain life, willing to suffocate rather than allow a suggestion of his physical presence to impinge; a man coming home at one A.M., ascending with only one other occupant of the car, carefully avoiding any slight recognition of joint occupancy. What is there about elevator travel that induces this painstaking catalepsy? A sudden solemnity, perhaps, which seizes people when they feel gravity being tampered with—they hope successfully. Sometimes it seems to us as though everyone in the car were in silent prayer.[1]

Narrative *details:*

The bare, indisputable facts in the life of Mary Todd Lincoln are few and simple. She was born of a good Kentucky family, in 1818, ten years after her husband. In 1839 she came to live with her sister, Mrs. Edwards, in Springfield. After a stormy courtship Lincoln married her in 1842. Her life then led her through Illinois law and politics to the White House, and the war, and the culminations of triumphant peace. All the triumph and hope were blasted by the assassination of her husband, and her remaining years, in spite of a brief sojourn in Europe, were darkened by sorrow and misfortune till a temperament, always impulsive and intense, was unbalanced to a point of oddity approaching and at times reaching actual derangement. She died in 1882.[2]

Descriptive *details:*

About noon we came out upon *a long, shallow sheet of water* which the guide called Bloody-Moose Pond, from the tradition that a moose had been slaughtered there many years before. Looking out over the silent and lonely scene, his eye was the first to detect an object, apparently feeding upon lily-pads, which our willing fancies readily shaped into a deer. As we were eagerly waiting some movement to confirm this impression, it lifted up its head, and, lo! a great blue heron. Seeing us approach, it spread its long wings and flew solemnly across to a dead tree on the

[1] From E. B. White, *The Second Tree from the Corner,* Harper & Brothers. Copyright by E. B. White.

[2] From *Wives,* by Gamaliel Bradford. Copyright, 1925, by Harper & Brothers.

other side of the lake, enhancing rather than relieving the loneliness and desolation that brooded over the scene. As we proceeded, it flew from tree to tree in advance of us, apparently loth to be disturbed in its ancient and solitary domain. In the margin of the pond we found the pitcher-plant growing, and here and there in the sand the closed gentian lifted up its blue head.[3]

Expository *details:*

We all appear to ourselves to be thinking all the time during our waking hours, and most of us are aware that we go on thinking while we are asleep, even more foolishly than when awake. When uninterrupted by some practical issue *we are engaged in what is now known as a reverie.* This is our spontaneous and favorite kind of thinking. We allow our ideas to take their own course and this course is determined by our hopes and fears, our spontaneous desires, their fulfillment or frustration; by our likes and dislikes, our loves and hates and resentments. There is nothing else anything like so interesting to ourselves as ourselves. All thought that is not more or less laboriously controlled and directed will inevitably circle about the beloved Ego. It is amusing and pathetic to observe this tendency in ourselves and in others. We learn politely and generously to overlook this truth, but if we dare to think of it, it blazes forth like the noontide sun.[4]

2. Development by *illustration* or *example* uses a series of sentences which furnish an example or a specific instance representative of the more general statement in the topic sentence. Because an example familiar to the reader carries its own explanation, there is no surer way of anticipating the reader's question about your topic sentence, "What does it mean?" Several short instances, or a longer single example, serve to answer this question, to drive home to the reader the idea expressed.

The following paragraph from Robert Louis Stevenson's essay, "El Dorado," is developed by several *specific instances:*

One who goes touring on foot with a single volume in his knapsack reads with circumspection, pausing often to reflect, and often laying the book down to contemplate the landscape or the prints in the inn parlour; for he *fears to come to the end of his entertainment,* and be left com-

---

[3] From "The Adirondacks," by John Burroughs, in *Wake-Robin.*
[4] From *The Mind in the Making,* by James Harvey Robinson. Copyright, 1921, by Harper & Brothers.

panionless on the last stages of his journey. A young fellow recently finished the works of Thomas Carlyle, winding up, if we remember aright, with the ten notebooks upon Frederick the Great. "What!" cried the young fellow, in consternation, "is there no more Carlyle? Am I left to the daily papers!" A more celebrated instance is that of Alexander, who wept bitterly because he had no more worlds to subdue. And when Gibbon had finished the *Decline and Fall,* he had only a few moments of joy; and it was with a "sober melancholy" that he parted from his labours.

In the following, one *example* is the major means of developing the topic:

There are many people, especially older people, who are inclined to underestimate their talents and who lead lives unworthy of their full abilities. But there are many more (the younger generation is well represented here) who believe they have no limitations; they consider themselves capable of doing everything and anything all at one time. It is a member of this latter group who endangers not only himself, but also those with whom he associates. I once had a grade-school teacher notorious for her personal self-confidence (and public failure) in her ability to handle alone a job really needing three people. She was school principal, teacher of the fifth and sixth grades, and librarian. As a result of her triple task, my classmates and I were never quite certain who discovered the Fountain of Youth, or what eleven times four equaled. To be sure, we were all perfect at the techniques involved in pasting labels in books, but many other parts of our sixth-grade education were sadly neglected because teacher was usually flitting about attending to her various other duties. To make matters worse, nervous strain frequently wrought havoc in her easily-upset emotional state. I remember one particularly trying day when nothing seemed to go right for her. Lazy janitors, school board troubles, and several missing encyclopaedias combined to wear her patience thin. A spilled bottle of ink was the final straw. She burst into tears, picked up a three-volume set of *Our Latin American Neighbors,* hurled them blindly at the class, and locked herself into the closet. "Bolivia" hit me; "Mexico" gave another boy a black eye. The class was thereafter in a state of humiliation. On that day I learned a lesson I'll never forget: *Never undertake more than you can handle, and handle well.*[5]

[5] "Know Thyself," one-paragraph theme by Nancy Hieronymus, DePauw University student. From *Indiana English Leaflet,* February, 1955.

3. A topic may be made clear and effective by the use of *comparison* or *contrast*. Comparison shows the likeness between the topic and some idea or object familiar to the reader; contrast shows differences. Not infrequently both comparison and contrast are used within the same paragraph.

By *comparison:*

The emotion of a mob is like a flooding river. The river is at first quiet and still, but as the rain continues to fall day by day, and the waters rise higher, it begins to build up tremendous pressure. The river is no longer quiet. There is a murmur that grows in volume, grows louder and louder until finally the river breaks loose and surges over its banks, gathering momentum as it goes, rolling over everything in its path, wrecking homes, killing people. When the rampage is over, the river is once more quiet and still, showing no signs of its late turmoil, unmindful of the damage it has caused. So it is with the mob. It is one of the most destructive instruments on earth when aroused. It loses all power of reason and can only follow its leaders, roaring, destroying everything in its path, until the individuality of its members reasserts itself. Then the mob begins to break up, to disperse itself. Each member, going his own way, hardly remembers what the common bond was that had held them together. Even the memory of what has happened finally disappears.[6]

By *contrast:*

It is a misfortune of the English language in modern times *that the word "disinterested" is commonly confused with the word "uninterested."* The modern lexicographers who work on the principle that whatever is the usage of people is acceptable are beginning to accept the confusion, and perhaps they are very wise in their principle, but in this instance the usage of people—or at least of some people—has deprived us of our only word for a very important virtue. Up until recently the meanings of the two words were kept distinct, and it was a mark of ignorance to confuse them. "Disinterested" meant that one had nothing to gain from the matter at hand, that one was objective in one's judgment, that one had no selfish motive but was impartial and unbiased. "Uninterested" meant that one was bored by the matter at hand, that it did not engage one's attention. The distinction is still in force among almost all careful writers and speakers; they blame, say, a labor arbitrator who

---

[6] "Mob," one-paragraph theme by Phyllis Hahn, DePauw University student. From *Indiana English Leaflet,* February, 1955.

is *uninterested* in the case he is hearing, but they praise him for being *disinterested* in the way he decides it.[7]

4. Developing a topic by *division* means that the writer calls attention to two or more parts of the topic and discusses each one briefly within the same paragraph. The following paragraphs are developed by this method:

The eagle in all cases uses one nest, with more or less repair, for several years. Many of our common birds do the same. *The birds may be divided, with respect to this and kindred points, into five general classes.* First, those that repair or appropriate the last year's nest, as the wren, swallow, bluebird, great-crested flycatcher, owls, eagles, fish hawk, and a few others. Secondly, those that build anew each season, though frequently rearing more than one brood in the same nest. Of these the phoebe-bird is a well-known example. Thirdly, those that build a new nest for each brood, which includes by far the greatest number of species. Fourthly, a limited number that make no nest of their own, but appropriate the abandoned nests of other birds. Finally, those who use no nest at all, but deposit their eggs in the sand, which is the case with a large number of aquatic fowls.[8]

To the fatalism of the Orient and the other-worldliness of the Christian Middle Ages must be added a second idea opposed to the concept of progress—that is, *utopianism. This idea takes two forms.* In the minds of some thinkers it is related to the past; there has been a golden age, in the "good old days of the fathers" or in some remote period of the early evolution of mankind. In seeking to escape the evils of the present, we must return to the perfection of long ago when people lived in peace, happiness, innocence, and plenty. But, in other minds, utopianism is related to the future: by doing this or that we can establish a static order of bliss—a fixed scheme of things so nearly perfect that they will never have to be changed. A variant on these aspects of dreaming may be called the utopianism of whitewash: the present order is so nearly perfect that it is almost profane to inquire into its evils or to propose modifications, for the possibility of doing harm is always greater than the chances of doing good. Historians, with all their searching, have not been able to find the golden age in the past, and skeptics doubt the perfection of the

[7] From Lionel Trilling, prefatory note to Matthew Arnold's "The Function of Criticism at the Present Time," *Major British Writers.* Copyright, 1954, by Harcourt, Brace and Company.

[8] From "Birds'-Nests," by John Burroughs, in *Wake-Robin.*

present. Still the illusion of utopianism shadows all human thought about public and private affairs, challenging the idea of progress.[9]

5. Development by *cause* (*causes*) or *effect* (*effects*) is ordinarily used for topic statements regarded as facts and hence is common in much expository writing. The material is tangible, concrete. The topic sentence gives the generalized statement or conclusion drawn from the data; these data make up the supporting material of the paragraph, the causes or reasons. Or the supporting material tells what the various results or effects are of the general statement in the topic.

By *cause:*

The birth of a volcanic island is an event marked by prolonged and violent travail: the forces of the earth striving to create, and all the forces of the sea opposing. The sea floor, where an island begins, is probably nowhere more than fifty miles thick—a thin covering over the vast bulk of the earth. In it are deep cracks and fissures, the results of unequal cooling and shrinkage in past ages. Along such lines of weakness the molten lava from the earth's interior presses up and finally bursts forth into the sea. But a submarine volcano is different from a terrestrial eruption, where the lava, molten rocks, gases, and other ejecta are hurled into the air through an open crater. Here on the bottom of the ocean the volcano has resisting it all the weight of the ocean water above it. Despite the immense pressure of, it may be, two or three miles of sea water, the new volcanic cone builds upward toward the surface, in flow after flow of lava. Once within reach of the waves, its soft ash and tuff are violently attacked, and for a long period the potential island may remain a shoal, unable to emerge. But, eventually, in new eruptions, the cone is pushed up into the air and a rampart against the attacks of the waves is built of hardened lava.[10]

By *effect:*

To most participating nations, *a modern war brings complex economic results.* Science and industry are occasionally advanced by researches derived from the stimulus and energy of war. Life and property are destroyed; vast sums are consumed in armament; impossible debts accumulate. Repudiation in some form becomes inevitable; currencies are de-

[9] From *A Century of Progress,* by Charles A. Beard. Copyright, 1932, by Harper & Brothers.

[10] From Rachel L. Carson, *The Sea Around Us.* Copyright, 1950, 1951, by Oxford University Press, Inc.

preciated or annulled, inflation relieves debtor governments and individuals, savings and investments are wiped out, and men patiently begin to save and lend again. Overexpansion in war is followed by a major depression in peace. International trade is disrupted by intensified nationalism, exalted tariffs, and the desire to develop at home all industries requisite in war. The vanquished are enslaved—physically, as in antiquity, financially and by due process of law today. The victorious masses gain little except in self-conceit; the ruling minority among the victors may gain much in conquered lands, markets, spheres of influence, supplies, and taxable population.[11]

6. Development by *reason* or *inferences* is a method usually used for topic statements regarded as opinions and hence is common in exposition of ideas and argumentative writing. The material is intangible, abstract—for the most part. Supporting material gives the reasons used in establishing the opinion or the data from which the statement of the topic sentence was inferred.

The only plausible alternative to the conclusion that earth and sun will continue the even tenor of their ways for an inconceivably long period of time *is that the sun will some day imitate the supernovae* occasionally detected among the stars *and terminate the existence of the entire solar system by a gigantic explosion.* Precisely one such supernova has been observed within the galaxy of the Milky Way and several such in all the other galaxies of stars during the past few decades. The astronomers could therefore calculate for us the chances on a statistical basis that any individual star—the sun, for example—would suffer such a fate within any given period of time. The result would be a figure so infinitesimal as to set at rest the mind of even the most jittery of questioners. Pending the discovery of the kind of premonitory symptoms displayed by stars about to blow themselves to atoms, the best that can be done is to rest content in history. Since the earliest records of living creatures were left as fossils, if not indeed since the earliest sedimentary rocks were formed, the sun has faithfully maintained its energy output within a fairly narrow range and has given no evidence of any fluctuations that might suggest any significant change in its behavior.[12]

Has electricity lightened the housewife's work? No, it has only altered the type of work. Although modern appliances have supposedly re-

[11] From Will Durant, "Why Men Fight," *The Saturday Evening Post,* July 10, 1937.

[12] From Kirtley F. Mather, "The Future of Man," *The Scientific Monthly,* March, 1940.

moved the pioneer drudgery from tending a home, the wife of today not only must be a cook, baby sitter, mother, cleaning woman, gardener, laundress, mechanic, diplomat, tutor, seamstress, interior decorator, and caterer; she must also be an electrician. Narcissa Whitman did not have to worry about pennies in the fuse box or an electric dryer which got rust spots on her wash. However, she is a heroine in our history while the contemporary housekeeper is classified as a sluggard. Men wonder why women are taking over their jobs in the business world. If they had a centigram of sense and would do a minute bit of repair work at home, their over-worked wives would not seek a career for a release from the sweat-shop domiciles. Edison's tinkering was theoretically fine and dandy, but he failed to consider that woman might destroy herself by fixing her iron with a hairpin. Men, this is an open letter to you suggesting that "the little woman" may not have the "lead-pipe" cinch you think she has—electricity or no electricity.[13]

7. Development of a topic by *definition* involves the use of substance which answers the implied question of the reader, "What do you mean by this?" To be clear and effective, the paragraph developed by this method also uses some of the foregoing methods: details and particulars, illustration and example, comparison or contrast, cause or effect. A straightforward definition is the following:

Science is a method of knowledge that arose and first proved its usefulness within the realms of mechanics, physics, and chemistry. In essence it is remarkably simple. The first step is to discover the pertinent facts. Next, you make a guess as to the law which accounts for these facts. And finally, you test the correctness of this guess by experiment. If your experiments do not verify the first guess, you admit that you were wrong, and make another guess. And so on, until you have found a piece of demonstrable knowledge, or demonstrated that the truth with regard to that particular matter is so far unknown.[14]

A more personalized or humanized definition is the following:

The jazz man is a modern maestro, and mood music is his business. From dusk to dawn he wraps his soul around a mournful tune, weaving a soft, magical pattern in blue as his skillful fingers ripple fiddle-faddle

[13] "Has Electricity Lightened the Housewife's Work?"—a one-paragraph theme by Diane Bosse, Purdue University student. From *Indiana English Leaflet*, February, 1955.
[14] From Hugh Stevenson Tigner, "The Pretensions of Science," *The Christian Century*, September 14, 1938.

on the heartstrings of barflies and patrons of dingy nightspots. He stands, a tall, black Joshua, pouring his lonely, liquid melodies into each bleak corner, floating them across the bar where, night after night, a million miseries and heartaches are ground into the polished mahogany or whisked away with a swish of the bar rag. The jazz man is a bit of flotsam in a frantic world. A sad-eyed trumpeteer with a ragged tune and a honey-colored horn, he fashions a new tonight for faceless puppets in smoke-filled basements and pieces together the remnants of yesterday's happiness. Transient in mind and body, he carries his heart in a trumpet case, and his home is a bandstand in a noisy, obscure room in a nameless city. Where he goes there is sweat and smoke and stomping feet—and laughter.[15]

24c. Combine various methods of developing the topic sentence when they are necessary and appropriate.

You can write clear and effective paragraphs by developing them according to *one* of the methods described above, whichever is most appropriate for the purpose. On the other hand, it is frequently not only impossible to eliminate the overlapping of some of the methods, but doing so would be illogical and undesirable. As some of the illustrations show, the use of several methods is effective; in fact, a few of the methods virtually require the use of others. An analysis of many well-written paragraphs, therefore, will show that the method of development cannot be rigidly exclusive, that the important point is not to demonstrate any particular method but to achieve adequate development of the topic.

In the following paragraph from Aldous Huxley's "Comfort" are elements of particulars or details, illustration, comparison, contrast, and even repetition:

Another essential component of modern comfort—the adequate heating of houses—was made impossible, at least for the great ones of the earth, *by the political structure of ancient societies.* Plebeians were more fortunate in this respect than nobles. Living in small houses, they were able to keep warm. But the nobleman, the prince, the king, and the cardinal inhabited palaces of a grandeur corresponding with their social position. In order to prove that they were greater than other men, they had to live in surroundings considerably more than life-size. They re-

[15] "Jazz Man," one-paragraph theme by Nancy L. Mullenix, University of Illinois student. From *The Green Caldron,* October, 1955.

ceived their guests in vast halls like roller-skating rinks; they marched in solemn processions along galleries as long and as draughty as Alpine tunnels, up and down triumphal staircases that looked like the cataracts of the Nile frozen into marble. Being what he was, a great man in those days had to spend a great deal of his time in performing solemn symbolical charades and pompous ballets—performances which required a lot of room to accommodate the numerous actors and spectators. This explains the enormous dimensions of royal and princely palaces, even of the houses of ordinary landed gentlemen. They owed it to their position to live, as though they were giants, in rooms a hundred feet long and thirty high. How splendid, how magnificent! But oh, how bleak! In our days the self-made great are not expected to keep up their positions in the splendid style of those who were great by divine right. Sacrificing grandiosity to comfort, they live in rooms small enough to be heated.[16]

Not infrequently a single topic is developed in a series of paragraphs. To establish a certain statement, a number of illustrations may be given, each in a separate paragraph. Similarly, a series of paragraphs may support the truth of a major division or topic; they may give the causes; they may give the effects. Such a paragraph series usually results from the desire of the writer to make his materials convenient to the reader, as opposed to one long, complicated paragraph, and to attain both clearness and effectiveness.

After practice and experience you will find choice and use of the various methods of paragraph development to be almost automatic. All methods of paragraph development have essentially the same purpose, and their names are of little importance. The primary aim in writing paragraphs is that the writer develop his paragraphs adequately and that the reader see exactly and fully the developed ideas contained in expressed or implied topic sentences. The test of the substance of a paragraph is that of clear and effective communication.

24d. Avoid developing paragraphs with hazy generalizations.

Adequate substance consists of definite, concrete ideas, impressions, reflections, and observations. Generalizations are frequently trite, vague, and ineffective. Note the lack of worth-while substance in this student-written paragraph:

[16] From *Proper Studies,* by Aldous Huxley, Doubleday, Doran, & Company, Inc., 1928.

Cheating never pays. After all, "honesty is the best policy"; also when one gets something for nothing he does not appreciate it. I think that every student should be on his own, even if his "own" is not good enough for him to pass his course. One should be honest, no matter what the cost. The student who thinks cheating is a sin only when it is detected is fooling nobody but himself. Sooner or later, his sins will find him out, and he will have nobody but himself to blame.

After revision the paragraph attained greater effectiveness through the use of specific illustration:

Cheating does not pay. A friend of mine, whose identity I shall conceal by merely calling him J., thought that it did. He frequently said to me in high school: "Why should I study when it is so easy to get the desired results without work? The only sin in cheating is being caught." And so J. was dishonest all through his four years at school. But when he took the college board examinations, he could not cheat because of the nature of the questions and the efficiency of the proctors. He failed, and was bitterly disappointed, since he wanted very badly to enter ——— University. As he read his letter of failure, he was convinced that cheating does not pay, that it is not a substitute for honest hard work.

24e. Avoid meaningless, ineffective repetition of the topic sentence.

Repeating the topic sentence in different words is a device auxiliary to other methods of paragraph development. Such repetition should be meaningful; to be effective, it should add clearness and should expand and develop the idea by the use of specific details. Note the effective use of repetition in the Aldous Huxley paragraph on page 212, and in the following student-written example:

The residents of our town can look toward the future and say that they are proud to live here. Why can they be proud? Why are they proud now? They are proud because there are no large industries in Scotch Plains! They are proud because there are no cheap housing developments in Scotch Plains! They are proud because there are no dirty railroads in Scotch Plains! They are proud because there are no degrading slums in Scotch Plains! The town is more than a town of houses. It is a town of homes!

Repetition alone, no matter how varied the words, is rarely used as the sole or major method of developing a paragraph. Repetition which adds nothing new is merely thought going round in circles. Note the inadequacy of this repetitious paragraph:

Some people pay too much attention to their diet. They spend hours every day wondering if they should eat this or that. They are too concerned about their digestive processes. One would think their greatest concern was low-calorie food, and their talk shows that it is. Diet is not nearly so important as these people think it is; it's the amount they eat. Paying so much attention to diet does not warrant so much concern. They just pay too much attention to it.

EXERCISES

A. Write 14 sentences which you would like to develop into paragraphs. Compose these topic sentences so that you could develop two paragraphs according to each of the following methods: (a) particulars and details, (b) illustration or example, (c) comparison or contrast, (d) division, (e) causes or effects, (f) reasons and inferences, (g) definition.

B. Choose seven of the topic sentences (Exercise A) and write seven paragraphs, one illustrating each of the methods listed.

C. From your reading, select two paragraphs which illustrate each of the methods of development discussed in Section 24b.

D. Develop each of the following topic sentences into a paragraph, each paragraph to illustrate a method of development listed in Exercise A:

1. Saturday night is a busy time in our town.
2. Driving on icy roads is dangerous.
3. My favorite spectator sport (activity sport) is _____.
4. Smoking cigarettes is a harmful habit.
5. Is courtesy to women a custom of the past?
6. Living in a dormitory (fraternity, sorority) is preferable to living in a private home (fraternity, sorority).
7. I have had an embarrassing encounter with the police.
8. Girls seem to be better students in English than boys.
9. What is a good student?
10. My grandfather (or someone else) is a "character."
11. There are several aids to correct spelling.
12. I admire (dislike) my roommate for his (her) _____.
13. There are numerous ways to earn money at college.
14. A large college has more advantages (disadvantages) than a small college.

24 Exercises

15. The greatest need of our college is _____.
16. We need longer (shorter) vacations.
17. An engineer and a mechanic are not exactly the same.
18. Many mistakes are made because of ignorance (or carelessness).
19. There is a difference between "a practical joke" and "a mean trick."
20. Experience is a good but an expensive teacher.

E. Directions given in D.

1. Most lectures are forgotten in a day or so.
2. Grandfather's generation lived a happier life than ours does.
3. A telephone contributes to the conveniences (inconveniences) of living.
4. The future of America depends upon the proper conservation of its (oil, soil, water, manpower, inventive ingenuity, etc.)
5. The era of the small independent farmer is (is not) passing.
6. There is (is not) a vast difference between sports and athletics (or between amateur and professional athletics).
7. Television and radio are distinctly 20th-century forms of entertainment.
8. An effective use of connectives reveals more clearly than anything else a writer's mastery of his material.
9. I believe that _____ is the most interesting magazine published in America today.
10. A man's best friend is his _____.
11. College is a poor (good) place in which to get an education.
12. I offer three solutions to the problem of the increase in traffic fatalities.
13. My last summer vacation was one that I shall long remember.
14. Here are directions for _____.
15. Atomic energy will change our daily life in many ways.
16. The view from the top of _____ is one of sheer beauty (fascinating interest).
17. What is an Honor System in campus life?
18. A good theme is characterized by _____.
19. Getting involved in campus activities (politics) brings complex results.
20. Nature is a wonderful artist.

F. Study the following paragraphs. Choose the topic sentence or topic statement of each, or phrase the topic if it is merely implied. Identify the dominant method of paragraph development. What other methods are used in addition to the main method? Is a combination of methods used, with no one method outstanding?

1. This is a delicious evening, when the whole body is one sense, and imbibes delight through every pore. I go and come with a strange liberty in Nature, a part of herself. As I walk along the stony shore of the pond in my shirt sleeves, though it is cool as well as cloudy and windy, and I see nothing special to attract me, all the elements are unusually congenial to me. The bull-frogs trump to usher in the night, and the note of the whippoorwill is borne on the rippling wind from over the water. Sympathy with the fluttering alder and poplar leaves almost takes away my breath; yet, like the lake, my serenity is rippled, but not ruffled. These small waves raised by the evening wind are as remote from storm as the smooth reflecting surface. Though it is now dark, the wind still blows and roars in the wood, the waves still dash, and some creatures lull the rest with their notes. The repose is never complete. The wildest animals do not repose, but seek their prey now; the fox, and skunk, and rabbit, now roam the fields and woods without fear. They are Nature's watchmen—links which connect the days of animated life.[17]

2. College athletics *is* public entertainment. Last year football audiences numbered 40 million, and now basketball is outstripping football in attendance. It is estimated that the public pays $100 million a year to the colleges for admission tickets, and television has added enormously to the number of spectators and to the revenue. Public interest as measured in publicity, newspaper coverage, and attention is far beyond that given to any educational activity. In no major school does the attention given to the appointment of a president compare with that given to the appointment of a coach, and the general public can name many more coaches than presidents.[18]

3. The migratory passage of birds, like the movements of the stars, can be a great consolation to men whose minds continually search for an established order and progression in the universe. The knowledge that, whatever we may make of ourselves in the moment of our existence, the stars will continue in their appointed courses, the seasons will move in their confirmed order, the birds will pursue their destined bi-

[17] From Henry David Thoreau, "Solitude," in *Walden.*
[18] From Harold W. Stoke, "College Athletics: Education or Show Business?" *The Atlantic Monthly,* March, 1954.

annual migrations, carries with it a sense of ultimate security which the works of man alone fail to convey. It seems to give us the intimation of a will that directs us. It belies our orphaned state in the universe. Order, harmony, regularity, these elements implicit in the recurrent flight of birds, are beyond the touch of the good and evil that men do in the numbered hours of their survival. Knowledge of the integrated pattern of the universe in which the birds share, of the final cosmic autocracy whose imposed limits no organism may transcend, secures us from the nightmare of anarchy.[19]

4. Life for most of these attractive, brown-skinned Micronesian peoples is simple and primitive. They have no literature. Few of them have any but the most elementary education. For centuries before the white man came they maintained a fairly happy existence, developing a culture admirably adapted to the conditions under which they lived. Theirs was a subsistence economy undisturbed by worries of buying and selling. Mother Nature is for the most part kindly in the South Seas. Coconuts, bananas, breadfruit, pandanus, taro, and fish are easily to be had; clothing presents no trouble—the less the better; and shelter is easily furnished by the leaves of pandanus or palm. Sustained work was quite unnecessary. A strongly developed communal family or clan system removed the fear of individual want or capacity, and promised care in time of sickness or old age.[20]

5. The real attraction of skiing is probably the fact that it is a magnificent form of escape. For those great numbers of Americans who are too deeply mired in the complexities of present-day society to attempt permanent simplification of their lives, skiing offers a brief, uninhibited respite. The sensation of complete freedom, both physical and mental, that overcomes a skier while flying down a mountainside can be almost miraculous. For a short space of time his life is his private property, dependent on no time schedules, restricted not one whit by his own intellectual limitations or by those of others. His whole being is absorbed in what he is doing and in where he is doing it, and both considerations are physical. In the concentration essential to the moment, the past of desk calendars, time clocks, phone calls, social forms, train schedules, personal relationships, self-examinations, and world idiocies is blotted out; and the only perceivable future is involved with the pine tree that marks the turn ahead. The sensation of grace and speed, independent

---

[19] From Louis F. Halle, Jr., *Birds Against Men*, The Viking Press, Inc., 1938.

[20] From Francis B. Sayre, "The Pacific Islands We Hold," *The Atlantic Monthly*, January, 1950.

of devices, that a skier feels while competing with nature and with himself may be elusive, and it may end abruptly with a crash into the underbrush, but once felt it gains a grip which again and again brings him out of his cave and up to the timberline in winter.[21]

6. Daily themes in my day had to be short, not over a page of handwriting. They had to be deposited in a box at the professor's door not later than ten-five in the morning. A classmate of mine, when an epigram was called for, once wrote, "An epigram is a lazy man's theme written at ten-three A.M." And because of this brevity, and the necessity of writing one every day whether the mood was on you or not, it was not always easy—to be quite modest—to make these themes literature, which, we were told by our instructors, is the transmission through the written word, from writer to reader, of a mood, an emotion, a picture, an idea. I hate to think how few, in fact, of all the thousands that were poured into that yawning box were literature, how seldom the poor instructors could dip their pens into their pots of red ink and write the magic "A" on the back. Their sarcastic comments were surely excusable. I have even forgiven the young man with hair like yellow corn-tassels, who scrawled on verses of mine, required to be written in imitation of some poet, "This may be O'Shaughnessy, it isn't poetry." Did he think thus to kill two song birds with one stone? Well, the effort of those of us who were sincere and comprehending in our pursuit of the elusive power to write was to make our themes literature as often as possible, and to do this the first essential was the choice of a subject. Not everything one sees or does or thinks can take shape on a page of paper and reproduce itself for the reader. Selection was the first requirement.[22]

UNITY (ONENESS)

25. A paragraph, consisting of a series of related sentences, should develop consistently the larger idea which binds these sentences together as a unit. If a paragraph contains substance, no matter how excellent, which is irrelevant to the central thought, it is not unified. There are two standard tests for unity, whether the writing be a theme, a paragraph, or a sentence: (1) *omit* all material which is not an essential, logical part; (2) *include* all material which is an essential, logical part.

[21] From Eric Swenson, "Let Fly Downhill," *Harper's Magazine,* January, 1948.
[22] From Walter Pritchard Eaton, "The Daily Theme Eye," *The Atlantic Monthly,* March, 1907.

25a-b

25a. Omit material not related to the main thought of the paragraph.

Material which is not related to the main thought of the paragraph, i.e., to the topic which is the subject of the paragraph, should be omitted or placed in another paragraph where it does belong. In planning and writing, you will find that your mind does not always work logically, and, frequently, unrelated ideas will occur to you. Test each idea by asking this question: Does this material refer to the thought contained in the expressed or implied topic sentence? If it does not, exclude the material from your paragraph; its inclusion will both confuse and irritate your reader in his attempt to see what the relationship is. Let each paragraph develop and convey one idea, its own idea—and no other.

The following paragraphs do not possess unity:

Grandmother loved the wild flowers which grew near her home. Nearly every day she would go into the fields and meadows and return with an armful of daisies or violets or Queen Anne's lace, which she would carefully arrange in bowls of water. *These bowls were of all kinds: pewter, silver, and copper. They had been in our family for generations. Grandmother's mother had bought them at Woodward and Lathrop's many years ago.* She would put the flowers in every room in the house and walk from room to room admiring their texture and color.

Lake-of-the-Woods is an excellent place for the sportsman to spend the summer. If you like to fish, there are all kinds of fresh-water fish to be found, the most common of which is the pike. A few miles away, up in the mountains, the streams are filled with brook trout. *For people who like to winter-fish, there is ice-fishing nearly every day.* People who are fishing there for the first time can obtain guides, leaving the town early in the morning before the weather gets hot and returning in the cool of the evening.

25b. Include all material necessary for adequate development of the topic sentence.

Lacking adequate thought and careful consideration, too many student-written paragraphs are brief and underdeveloped. Two or three sentences, at the most, are used, supposedly to give full development to the topic. Obviously, such paragraphs lack unity: they are too short, too underdeveloped; they omit a number of important ideas and details necessary to the development and unity of the paragraph.

The following paragraph is representative of this kind. Aside from a question of order, the writer presumably wanted to prove the statement in the last sentence:

When you do your own freezing at home and grow your own fruits and vegetables, the cost is very little as compared to the frozen food in the stores. It's no wonder why the 4-H clubs in Ohio are the largest in the United States.

The paragraph might have been revised and expanded somewhat as follows:

When you grow your own fruits and vegetables and do your own freezing at home, the cost is very little compared to the cost of frozen food in the stores. More and more Ohio families have learned the truth of this statement, and not only on farms but in many small towns and on vacant lots in cities, people are setting out vegetable gardens and fruit trees. The younger generation is in large part responsible; they are learning through 4-H clubs how to grow fruits and vegetables and how to freeze them. And this is only one of many 4-H activities. It's no wonder that the 4-H clubs in Ohio are the largest in the United States.

In the following paragraph, one of the two ideas forming part of the topic statement—the man's education—has not been adequately discussed:

John Johnson was qualified for the position of City Sanitary Engineer by both education and experience. He had been assistant to the City Sanitary Engineer of Indianapolis for five years; during one of those years, when his superior was ill, he had been in sole charge. He then became a consultant for the Indiana State Conservation Commission, which was making a survey of stream pollution. Two years of private practice in Louisville followed. When our city decided that it had grown large enough to need a sanitary engineer, our City Council looked over the field of applicants carefully, and felt fortunate in obtaining the services of John Johnson.

In revision, this writer has two choices. He can omit mention of "education" as part of the topic, or he can include adequate developing materials. A third possibility is, of course, a separate paragraph on education.

In contrast to the underdeveloped paragraph is the overdeveloped one. Frequently you may be tempted to expand a single paragraph to greater length than you should by including too much material—even though pertinent—suggested by the method or methods of development that you are using. In choosing substance to achieve this purpose, check carefully to see that you have included *all* essential information, that you have left no unanswered questions to puzzle your reader, but that you have included *only* that material that will make complete the discussion of your topic sentence. When there is additional pertinent material, consider the possibility of including it in a separate paragraph.

25c. Attain unity by consistently following specific methods of paragraph development.

Various specific methods of paragraph development have been discussed in Section 24. Skillful use of one method or of a combination of two or more methods can guide you in including, expanding, or excluding material so as to produce a well-rounded, unified paragraph.

EXERCISES

A. Show why the following paragraphs do not possess unity.

1. The year Robert, my oldest brother, first entered college, the war was just beginning to show its effects but not to any great extent. When he first started, he commuted for a while and had a locker at Craven Hall, where he threw his coat and books along with perhaps three or four hundred other boys. He sometimes ate lunch there and once in a while at the Union, where the freshmen who lived on the campus ate. At that time there were no graduate students living on the campus.

2. During the greater part of the last century, Cuba was ruled by a captain-general, later called governor-general. The population of Cuba was divided into four classes: (1) the Spaniards, who occupied the offices and positions of power; (2) the Creoles, who were the planters, business men, and lawyers of the island; (3) the free mulattoes and Negroes, making up one-sixth of the population; and (4) the slaves, estimated at one-third the total population. The third class was excluded by law from holding any civil office; the fourth class were mere chattels. Although the native Cubans had little civil, political, or religious free-

dom, they were heavily taxed to maintain Spanish military forces on the island and a large number of Spanish officials.

3. Malta lies almost in the middle of the Mediterranean—55 miles from Sicily and about 150 miles from Africa. Its area is less than one hundred square miles. The island was originally all rock, no soil whatever. Legend has it that all the soil was shipped in from Sicily years ago. The island is under the control of the British. The highest point on the island is the small town of Rabat, 700 feet above sea level. Malta's strategic location made possible raids on Italian and German shipping to Africa, when Rommel was in Egypt and Tunisia. This was during World War II. The population is mainly Italian. The poet, Samuel Taylor Coleridge—he wrote "The Rime of the Ancient Mariner"—was for a time the Secretary to the Governor of Malta.

B. Write constructive advice for the student-authors of the following paragraphs. Show them why their paragraphs lack unity and give suggestions for unifying and developing each.

1. I was graduated from Rock City High School in May, 1954. Then in July, 1956, I married a girl from my home town that I had been going with for over two years. I enlisted in the Army in the fall of 1954.

2. The town of Springfield was settled by Kentuckians. In 1789, James Demont built his log cabin beside Buck Creek. In 1801 Springfield was planned and in 1818 Clark County was created and in 1827 Springfield was incorporated. In 1902, A. B. Graham, a school superintendent in Springfield, Clark County, Ohio, organized the first 4-H Club. Clark County was the home of the famous Indian Chief Tecumseh. He was born in 1768, not far from Springfield. Later he migrated to Indiana, where his brother, the Prophet, was defeated in the Battle of Tippecanoe by General William Henry Harrison. The present population of Springfield is between 85,000 and 90,000.

3. I live in Aurora, Indiana, with my brother, sister, and my parents. We have a small garden out in back, and we live in a two-story brick house. My grandfather lives on a farm eighteen miles away. Aurora has a population of seven thousand people and it is located near the states, Ohio and Kentucky. Father's name is Martin, and he attended high school in Uniontown, Pennsylvania. Grandfather's farm contains over three hundred acres. Most of it is fertile, but some of it is hilly.

4. Every spring our high school Junior class sponsors the prom. Last year we took an all-night trip up and down the Ohio River in the *Delta Queen*. My best friend was captain of the football team, and he lives next

door. My partner at the dance was his sister. Our basketball team has never won the state championship, but one of our players is now here on our college team. In high school, mathematics was my favorite subject; I never liked English.

ORDER

26. One major problem in writing a paragraph is securing full, interesting, unified material. A second major problem is *arranging* the material. Even excellent substance will lose much of its effectiveness if it is incorrectly and illogically arranged.

26a. Arrange sentences in a paragraph in clear sequence.

Hasty and inaccurate thinking causes a lack of paragraph unity and may also result in the sentences of a paragraph being arranged not in order but in disorder. Because our minds do not always work logically, we tend to insert ideas as they occur to us, to place ideas ahead of the place where they belong, or to forget them and add them later in the paragraph. Anyone who has attempted to tell a long story or who has heard one told ("Oh, I should have said" or "I forgot to say") knows how difficult it is to arrange ideas in their proper order.

An illustrative analogy is the comparison of a well ordered paragraph to a good dinner. At such a dinner, we expect our food in this order: soup; meat, potatoes, and vegetables; salad; dessert and coffee. The order is logical and clear. So, too, with the sentences in a paragraph: each should have a definite position in the arrangement; each should lead clearly to the one that follows. Keep related parts together; finish one phase of the thought before you begin another.

26b. Make the arrangement of sentences show clear progress or a clear forward movement.

The arrangement of sentences within a paragraph depends upon the substance itself; there is no standard rule. However, there is one essential of order: it requires progress, a forward movement of some sort. The thought must go from some place to some other place.

This progress may be of several kinds, and sentences may be arranged in the following ways:

224

1. *Chronological* (time) *order,* which serves for much narrative writing, expository processes, and descriptions—all of which progress as the writer changes his temporal point of view. That is, one sentence follows another in the order that the events discussed followed one another in the order of their occurrence in time.

2. *Space order,* as in description, in which details are arranged according to the position and progress they have in space: from near to remote, or remote to near; from outside to inside or from inside to outside; from left to right, or from right to left.

3. *Order of logic,* in which the writer makes a general statement and then supplies details to support it, or he presents a series of details or particular statements, all of which lead up to a generalized statement at the end of the paragraph (inductive method), or the writer makes a general statement or conclusion and then applies it in the succeeding sentences to a particular instance or example (deductive method).

The following paragraph is arranged according to the order of *logic,* the inductive method; that is, the first sentence is a generalized statement, and the remaining sentences establish its truth (see also methods 5 and 6 under Section 24b):

From time immemorial work has been glorified. Song and story yield their homage to the solid merits of work, however romantically they may extol the delights of indolence, while essay and biography axiomatically acclaim work as the sure means to personal success and social esteem. The more prosaic and academic discussions of contemporary life, in their exaltation of work as the great social panacea, do but reëcho the words of Carlyle, who describes it as "the grand cure of all the maladies and miseries that ever beset mankind." The Rotarian mind makes work co-equal, if not identical, with service. Nowhere has this doctrine been better summed up than in the words of that past master of pious platitudes, Calvin Coolidge: "To provide for the economic well-being of our inhabitants, only three attributes, which are not beyond the reach of the average person, are necessary—honesty, industry, and thrift." (Oh, if it were only so simple!)

—Henry Pratt Fairchild in *Harper's Magazine*

26c. Arrange sentences in a paragraph in effective order.

Order in the paragraph involves not only clearness but effectiveness. There are three easily attainable methods of effectiveness in the arrangement of sentences within the paragraph.

1. *Beginning and ending as effective positions.* Ordinarily, sentences developing the most important phase of the idea of the paragraph should be placed at the beginning or the end. The most trenchant statement of the paragraph should certainly not be embedded somewhere in the middle. First and last impressions of paragraphs, as of sentences and of people, are genuinely important.

2. *Order of climax.* When the most important of a series of ideas in a paragraph or the most important thought is placed at the end, the arrangement is called the order of climax. Each successive idea is followed by a more important one, the most important and dramatic coming last. The reader reads on, lured by the prospect of the concluding, climactic statement.

Study the two examples following for their use of climax. The first passes from negative to affirmative ideas, from reason to emotion to religion. In the second example—a 121-word, one-sentence paragraph—a series of important statements builds up to a decisive conclusion.

The problem of social salvation, as I see it, is not a problem of science but one of emotion, value, and loyalty. It is not a problem of being open-minded, or objective, or dispassionate, or of mental discipline, or of learning to suspend the judgment. It is a problem of loving and hating the proper things, a problem of calling only beautiful things beautiful, a problem of cherishing values of universal validity rather than those of limited worth. It is a problem of turning passion in a life-furthering direction, of replacing lower loyalties by higher ones. It is a matter of indoctrination and propaganda in behalf of high moral ends. In other words, it is a religious problem.[1]

—HUGH STEVENSON TIGNER, "The Pretensions of Science"

So, after four years of seeing everything there is to see in big-time college football—victories, defeats, publicity, hospitals, championships, and bowls—of being known as a "football player" rather than a human being, of seeing myself and my teammates misrepresented and misquoted by sportswriters who seldom attempted to know the players personally, of playing in a 97,000-seat stadium in which my nonpaying student friends were forced to sit in the end zone, of having my natural desire for physical exercise corrupted and commercialized, of giving up pleasant afternoons in favor of kicking and rolling in the dust and muck

---

[1] From *The Christian Century*, September 14, 1938.

of the practice field—I have decided that big-time football is a poor bargain for the boys who play the game.²

—ALLEN JACKSON, "Too Much Football"

If you consistently fail to keep something in reserve, if you always fully inform your reader in advance of what your statement implies, appropriate as that method is for certain kinds of writing, you will lose the effectiveness that climactic arrangement affords.

3. *Miscellaneous order.* When several ideas, related and coordinate, are presented in one paragraph, and when neither of the two preceding methods applies, the writer can choose the order of arrangement which he believes his designated reader will find interesting and attractive. For example, there are "three ways to study," or "three places to eat," or "three reasons for joining some organization." Whether developed in one paragraph or in three paragraphs, these ideas—if of equal importance—can be presented in an order which is purely arbitrary.

EXERCISES

A. Write three topic sentences for which the development will emphasize clearness according to the respective methods mentioned in Section 26b. Write the paragraphs.

B. Write three topic sentences for which the development will emphasize effectiveness according to the respective methods mentioned in Section 26c. Write the paragraphs.

C. Below are four paragraphs in which the sentences have been jumbled. Write these paragraphs with the sentences in an order which makes sense.

1. One of the men stood up abruptly. 2. Once the set crackled loudly and a high-pitched whine filled the cramped cabin, but then that too died away. 3. In the dim yellow light his face showed annoyance and contempt for his companion's fear. 4. Below decks two men huddled silently over a small radio set, feverishly turning dials in an attempt to send a message. 5. Somewhere a bell buoy rang at measured intervals, incessantly keeping time with the waves while the small cabin cruiser tossed restlessly about in the cottony grey mist.

1. He has the apparatus for producing and receiving sound; however, his skill in using a language is acquired. 2. We do know, however, that

² From *The Atlantic Monthly,* October, 1951.

language is not a natural and inherent activity of human beings although man is biologically equipped for the use of languages. 3. There are other possible ways that language could have begun, but none of the theories seem completely satisfactory. 4. Language may have developed from man's attempts to reproduce the sounds of other animals, or it may have been an elaboration of the involuntary noises that were uttered to indicate pain, joy, or other emotions. 5. The origin of language is not known.

1. It has grown to a billion-dollar business from the day of grandmother's rose water and rice powder. 2. The paint-powder-and-perfume industry is no small business. 3. Oddly enough, shaving materials are excluded from this last figure. 4. Cosmetics is really an all-embracing field now—both in the age groups affected and the industrial aspects involved. 5. Beauty is indeed a big business. 6. And it is said that a woman uses three times her weight in cosmetics during her lifetime. 7. For instance, babies need oils and talcum powder; the pigtail set requires hair trainer and rough skin cream; our teen-agers consume quantities of lipstick and shampoo; most mature women use skin creams and facials; even the men require 40 million dollars worth of skin-conditioning creams and colognes.

1. Compounding terms to make new words is the most popular method of enlarging a vocabulary. 2. Two words can also be combined to produce new words such as typewriter, blackbird, and schoolhouse. 3. This method of compounding is more useful as a means of word development because the components of the word are known and the new concept is more easily grasped. 4. As a third example, television is a new development but the components of the word have been in existence for centuries. 5. The resulting word means under the water, but its meaning is restricted to this type of underwater vessel. 6. From the word "intend," which is a French loan word, we are able to make a dozen or more commonly used terms: intended, intentional, intentionally, unintentional, unintended, are only a few possibilities. 7. A second example: When the underwater ship was developed, it was named by taking the word "marine," which pertains to the sea, and attaching the prefix "sub," which means under. 8. The English language has a vast number of prefixes and suffixes that can alter the meanings of a basic word.

PROPORTION AND LENGTH

27. Paragraphs should have adequate substance, unity, and correct order of sentences. They need also right proportion. One paragraph should not, through its writer's carelessless or thoughtlessness, be made unduly long, another unduly short. Proportion means that the ideas in a paragraph are developed according to their importance and that all paragraphs are planned and written carefully and thoughtfully in relation to one another and to the whole theme.

27a. Make sure that paragraphs are correctly proportioned.

In writing a theme of 500 words, a student may compose a long introductory paragraph, follow it with a transitional paragraph, and have left only 100 words or so for the final paragraph which contains the actual *theme,* the central idea of the paper, the purpose for which it was written. Such a composition, obviously, is badly proportioned.

If a paragraph contains discussion of a proportionately important idea, its length should be greater than that of a paragraph which develops a comparatively minor topic. Occasionally, the inclusion of many or important details may need greater space, but remember that readers are likely to attribute importance to ideas on a basis of the length of the paragraphs in which they are discussed.

In general, do not expand ideas that are relatively subordinate or treat sketchily ideas that are of fundamental importance. Between these two extremes of overexpansion and underdevelopment there is a golden mean: the writing of paragraphs which adequately deal with their topics and which, added together, give a unified, well-proportioned discussion of the subject.

27b. Achieve proportion through careful overall planning.

Correct proportion demands careful planning. The writer who dwells at length upon some phase of the theme because he is interested in that phase or knows it thoroughly may not be taking into account its importance in relation to the reader. To achieve correct paragraph proportion, the thoughtful writer must consider the relation of the paragraph to the whole subject, and also his reader's reaction. Study the following suggestions:

→1. Consider the subject as a whole before writing an individual paragraph.
→2. Think of the reader; determine the central purpose which each paragraph is to have in communicating ideas to him.
→3. Shorten paragraphs if they are out of proportion in relation to the subject and the reader, even though they contain favorite

ideas and their revision will sacrifice proudly written, precious words.

→4. Lengthen paragraphs if they contain ideas that need amplification, illustration, or repetition, so that their significance may really be felt by the reader.

Length, like proportion, is determined by the relative importance of the thought unit the paragraph embraces. No specific rule for paragraph length can be laid down, save the principle just mentioned, and the principle of appropriateness (see Section 29). Two general recommendations may serve as guides.

27c. Avoid a series of short, choppy paragraphs.

A series of short, choppy paragraphs is usually a sign that a writer has not thought carefully about analyzing his topic sentence and has not developed fully and clearly the central idea of each paragraph, or that he has failed to see the relationship of ideas and has divided into several paragraphs what should have been united into one of greater length.

Note the choppy, disconcerting effect of the following short paragraphs:

I admit 10 acres are big for a garden, but I had grandiose ideas about getting money to help me on my college career.

As my various vegetables came on, I was happy. Every morning at an early hour I arose and set out for Louisville.

Louisville has a large farmers' market, and I wanted to be among the first traders there.

I arrived there before most people were awake and had my produce neatly arranged before the housewives set out to market.

Because my vegetables were fresh and attractively displayed, I usually had little difficulty in selling them.

Sometimes on rainy days people were slower in arriving and buying. By noon of each day, however, on the average, I had completed my sales and returned to my gardens.

Then I worked in the fields until sunset, and spent the rest of the evening preparing for the next day's market.

Thanks to the long hard days and nights I put in, I am able to finance my first 2 years in college.

To correct such short paragraphs, a writer should follow one of two suggestions: (1) review and apply the methods of analysis and expansion discussed in Section **24**, or (2) examine his paragraphs which precede or follow; perhaps with minor revisions these can be combined into a paragraph of adequate length.

Short paragraphs are not always to be avoided. They may be correctly used for emphasis and they have other appropriate uses. For example, in description or narration, short paragraphs often aid in achieving a vigorous, emphatic style. Frequently they are necessary in dialogue to indicate change of speakers. But very short paragraphs should not be written except for a definite stylistic effect, as is sometimes done in newspapers and advertisements.

27d. Avoid a group of long, heavy paragraphs.

A series of very long paragraphs is likely to strain your reader's attention. It is better to furnish him with an occasional paragraph break which will afford an opportunity to catch his breath and summarize the thought. Moreover, very long paragraphs may contain material which does not properly belong; they thus violate the principle of unity. Usually it is difficult to write a unified paragraph of over 250 or 300 words.

When paragraphs are unduly long, it is often possible to break each one into two or more shorter paragraphs without violation of unity, provided that appropriate transitional words or phrases are used.

27e. Choose long or short paragraphs in accordance with your central purpose.

There is no special reason to avoid either long or short paragraphs. Use them according to the proportionate value of the thought units they express. It is only a *series* of either that may prove ineffective. Writers today tend to shorter paragraphs than formerly were used, but in scholarly or technical papers paragraphs still run to considerable length. In popular magazines and newspapers, the average length is about 100 words or even less. The use of long or short paragraphs, or a compromise between the two, is often a matter of convention and appropriateness. (See Section **29**.)

You might well give consideration, therefore, to this advice from the Modern Language Association *Style Sheet:* "For the sake of both appearance and emphasis, avoid writing many very short or very long paragraphs, especially in sequence. Remember that brief paragraphs on your typed page will usually look even briefer in print." Also, brief paragraphs in longhand look even shorter when typewritten.

EXERCISES

A. Study one of the essays in your book of readings. Comment upon the paragraph proportion.

B. Comment upon the apportioning of space (time) in some lecture or debate you have recently heard. Did some phases (paragraphs) seem unduly long or unduly sketchy?

C. Choose three topics for 500-word themes and estimate the proportionate importance of the several developing paragraphs.

D. Indicate the number of words proportionately correct for each paragraph of a 500-word theme based on a theme subject, "Learning to _____." Follow or adapt this plan:

LEARNING TO SWIM
1. Correct mental attitude for the beginner.
2. Correct body position.
3. How to handle the arms.
4. How to handle the feet.
5. How to breathe.
6. Errors to be avoided.
7. Summary.

E. Compare the average length of the paragraphs in an article in *The Atlantic Monthly* with the length of those in an article in *The Saturday Evening Post.*

F. Ascertain the average length of the paragraphs in a newspaper story and in a full-page advertisement printed in a popular magazine. What effects are achieved by the brief paragraphs?

G. Count the number of words in several consecutive paragraphs of some essay in your book of readings.

H. Compare the number of words in the opening three or four paragraphs of several essays in your book of readings.

I. Rewrite so as to place in larger units these choppy paragraphs:

Every year, except during years when civilian production is curtailed, thousands of people buy new TV sets for the first time. Other thousands replace their old sets with new ones.

Why?

All these people want entertainment. Buying a TV set is buying a seat for the big show.

Who gives the show?

The advertisers give the show. They want the attention of the public, and they are willing to pay heavily to get it.

But some advertisers seem to forget that the entertainment value of the programs they provide is, for the public, of paramount importance. The advertising message is accepted only if it is not too insistent and blatant.

If advertisers wish to be repaid for the show, if they wish to win good will, they must avoid antagonizing the public with too obvious intrusion of the advertising message into the entertainment of the program.

J. What advice, in writing, would you give concerning paragraphing to students who write themes like this:

THIS IS MY SISTER

Her name is Charlotte Ann and she is a junior at Millvale State Teachers College. She has light brown hair and brown eyes, and is an attractive young lady.

She has a quick smile and a word of greeting for everyone. Everyone who knows her thinks very highly of her. She has many friends.

She is going to college on a scholarship. She has a part-time job during the school year and a full-time job during the summer. The scholarship does not pay for everything.

She has been a success in college, both at making good grades and at making good friends. She has to keep her grades up to a certain level to keep her scholarship. She is also vice-president of the Women's Residence Hall Student Council.

She wants to learn to drive an automobile. Almost every time I see her during the summer, she wants me to give her a driving lesson. I usually do give her one, but since I am seldom home it doesn't help her too much.

To sum everything up, I am proud of my sister and I hope she thinks the same of me.

TRANSITION

28. *Trans* literally means *over, across, beyond, on* or *to the other side of.* *Transition,* in general, means passage or change from one position, part, place, state, stage, or type to another.

Applied to writing, transition means showing evidence of the links or bridges between related units. This evidence may be a word, phrase, clause, sentence, or group of sentences. The tangible evidence of relation may link parts of sentences or two sentences; it may link paragraphs. Transition within or between sentences is discussed in Section **43**; the present section deals with paragraph transitions.

When we say that a theme should be coherent, we mean in part that the paragraphs should be properly tied together. If the order of the sentences within the paragraph is clear and fully logical, then the secret of coherence lies in the use of connectives, transitional expressions, between the paragraphs.

28a. Make the relationship between paragraphs clear by using transitional words and phrases.

Shifts in thought are always puzzling to a reader unless he is prepared in advance for them. Transitions are similar in function to signs on highways, such as "Curve, 100 yards" and "Slow Down: Double Lane Ends." By definition, a paragraph is a series of sentences dealing with one phase or idea of a larger topic. When the discussion of this phase has been finished, the careful, considerate writer will inform his reader of that fact and prepare him for the next phase of the discussion. Sometimes he finds it necessary to sum up what has been said. More often, he points out the "road" to be followed in the next paragraph: in the same direction, a pause to give examples, a reversing to show contrast, a paralleling to make a comparison. Such direction-pointing to the reader is a major aid to clearness and effectiveness.

Important as transitions are, they should be relatively brief and inconspicuous. Virtually a mechanical feature of style designed to make the machinery run smoothly and easily, they should not be labored or artificial, nor should they protrude so awkwardly that they distract the reader's attention from *ideas*. Since transition *reveals* relationships, transitional devices are inherent in the material, should grow out of the nature of the material, and need only be put into adequate words to show the nature of the already existing relationships.

The competent writer has a knowledge of connectives and their proper use. (See the comparative list of conjunctions and their meanings on pp. 582, 583.) The following is a list of some of the more frequently used transitional words and phrases. The classification is not rigid but merely suggestive to show some of the kinds of relationships that transitional words and phrases serve:

In the same, or similar, or parallel direction: *and, again, moreover, furthermore, likewise, besides, similarly, again, another reason, in like manner, as I said.*

Comparison or example: *as an illustration, for instance, for example, let us compare, by way of comparison.*

Contrast: *but, yet, nor, neither, however, nevertheless, otherwise, whereas, on the other hand, on the contrary, in contrast.*

Result or summary: *for, because, since, as, hence, accordingly, thus, therefore, consequently, in short, as a result, to summarize.*

Others: *in the first place, second, finally, meanwhile, while, then, in conclusion.*

Employed at the beginning of a paragraph, although not necessarily as the opening words, such connectives serve to link what is to follow with the thought in the preceding paragraph. An entire sentence may also be used transitionally.

. . . The valence of certain elements varies in different compounds.

But first let us discuss the valence of two common elements, oxygen and hydrogen, which . . .

We have seen how words, phrases, and sentences can be used as transitional aids; let us now consider the transitional paragraph. For clear and effective writing, . . .

28b. Make the relationship between paragraphs clear by repetition.

Often coherence may be shown by using the same key words at the close of one paragraph and the beginning of the next. Pronouns, as words referring to something that has preceded, can occasionally be used, but an effective paragraph usually begins with a strong word or words, the topic of the paragraph and its relation to the topic of the theme. Repeating such key words is also effective transition. In the following examples, the repeated material is italicized.

. . . This concludes the author's explanation of *taxation.*

But *taxation* is not the only problem which *he* discusses.

There are three reasons why I believe in the Honor System. In the first place, . . .

My second reason for believing in *the Honor System* is . . .

Finally, I support the *Honor System* because . . .

From these examples, you will note that a combination of methods of paragraph transition (**28a** and **28b**) is not only possible but effective.

28c. Make the relationship between paragraphs clear by using transitional paragraphs.

Sometimes the shift in thought between two paragraphs, or two groups of paragraphs, is so marked that a word or phrase, or repetition, is not sufficient fully to indicate the transition. In such a situation a short transitional paragraph of one or two sentences may be used to give a summary of what has been said and to suggest what is to follow. The second example under **28a** above could have served as such a transitional paragraph. The writer, considering effectiveness and appropriateness, must decide whether to paragraph such sentences separately or include them at the ending or beginning of other paragraphs. In the following example, the italicized material is a transitional paragraph:

Four characteristics mark the good theme: correctness, clearness, effectiveness, and appropriateness. If a theme lacks any one of these elements, it is not a good theme; if it lacks more than one, or lacks any one to an unusual degree, it is a very poor theme.

These elements, then, are essential. It now remains for us to define each of these terms and apply them to such matters as diction, punctuation, and sentence structure.

A good theme must be correct in its diction. Correct diction implies . . .

28d. Make transitions clear by leaving no gaps in thought.

Frequently, in certain kinds of writing, paragraph connection is faulty because the writer fails to give all pertinent details of relation. For example, in a descriptive theme one paragraph may end with a description of the exterior of a house and the next begin with a discussion of the view from an upstairs room. A transitional phrase is needed. Or one paragraph may discuss the value of good roads, and the next begin: "Good roads, however, are a menace to life and property." The reader naturally asks why? A gap has been left in the thought and must be filled in with, perhaps, a statement that good roads, because they are a temptation to speed and reckless driving, are also a menace.

Good writing is always characterized by skill in the revelation of thought relationships. Transitional aids are indispensable to the writer who wishes fully, smoothly, and effectively to *communicate* his thoughts, and the exact shadings of his thought, to his reader.

EXERCISES

A. From your book of readings, select an expository or argumentative essay. Make a list of the devices used for transition between the paragraphs. Classify these devices according to some such plan as that suggested in Section 28a. Write, for reading to the class, your discoveries, under the title, *Effective Paragraph Transition*.

B. Restudy the essay you chose for Exercise A. Note and discuss the position of the transitional devices: at the beginning, between, or at the end of paragraphs.

C. Repeat Exercises A and B, but use for your study an article in a current magazine.

D. Underline all the transitional words and phrases which occur between paragraphs in one of your recent themes. In the light of Section 28a-d, can you make these transitions more effective?

E. Expand into a short transitional paragraph some linking word or phrase which you have used in a recent theme.

APPROPRIATENESS

29. Depending upon your purpose, you choose certain kinds of paragraphs which most appropriately and effectively accomplish that purpose. In addition to the "normal" paragraph or series of paragraphs which develop the various phases or divisions of a subject and are unified by being built around a specific topic (Sections 23–28), other paragraphs—having brevity or length, or consisting of loosely related or even single statements—perform special and specific functions. The following suggestions concern the appropriateness of such paragraphs.

29a. Use short paragraphs in writing dialogue or quoting conversations.

In *writing dialogue* or *quoting conversations,* use a separate paragraph for each speaker's words. Most of these paragraphs will be short, some very short. Such is conventional practice, although you may find several separate speeches included in one paragraph—to the possible confusion of the reader.

The following example illustrates the very short speeches of dialogue:

Larry spooned a generous portion onto his plate, speared a piece of beef, and lifted it to his mouth.

"How is it?" asked Polly.

"Pretty good," said Larry.

"Only pretty good?"

"I mean it's wonderful."

"How wonderful?"

"If you served it to a maharajah, he'd probably send you around a trunkful of rubies in the morning."[1]

In the following example, three particulars may be observed: correct paragraphing of conversation, correct paragraphing of explanatory material, and correct form for introductory and explanatory words within paragraphs which contain dialogue.

"Are we *here?"* she called to the driver, and something inside her seemed trying to burst.

"You bet," he answered. "See that building? That's the church. And d' yer see that one? That's the school."

Such funny little houses they were. Not at all like a church and a school.

"And here's the post office," said the driver, drawing up before a building that was really a grocery store.

Mother hadn't said anything for a long time, but she had reached over for Joan's hand, and was squeezing it very hard. "I see Father," she cried out all at once, in a choky sort of voice.

"Yeah, that's him," said the driver.[2]

29b. Use short paragraphs for introductory, concluding, and transitional paragraphs.

For long or fairly long papers, or long sections, a brief *intro-*

[1] From *This Week,* April 10, 1949.

[2] From *Story,* May, 1937.

ductory paragraph is sometimes desirable, especially of the outline-beginning kind. The following is an introductory paragraph listing the topics to be expanded in the following paragraphs:

> The causes of war are psychological, biological, economic, and political —that is, they lie in the impulses of men, the competition of groups, the material needs of societies, and fluctuations of national power.[3]

Similarly, for long or fairly long papers, a brief *concluding* paragraph is sometimes desirable. For the material introduced by a preceding paragraph and discussed in detail in the article, the following serves as a brief summary and conclusion:

> These, then, are the causes of war. How natural it seems now, in the perspective of science and history; how ancient its sources and how inscrutable its destiny![4]

For a discussion of *transitional* paragraphs, see Sections **28b** and **28c.**

29c. Use short paragraphs in business letters.

Paragraphs in *business letters* vary from one or two to six lines. Longer paragraphs are seldom used; they make it difficult to get the message at a single glance, a major purpose of most business letter paragraphs. (For examples, see pp. 717–720. On 8½ x 11 business stationery, the paragraphs of the sample letters would take even fewer lines.)

29d. Use a single, complete-in-itself paragraph to develop a simple subject or a single topic.

In treating briefly *a single topic* or *a simple subject,* use only one paragraph. Such a paragraph is of course independent and complete; it is really a short theme or theme in miniature. Many newspaper editorial writers, columnists, advertising writers, magazine editors, and textbook editors, among others, make frequent use of independent paragraphs. Examples are common in the editorial columns of newspapers; news items in newspapers; editorial or commentary paragraphs in magazines, especially the news weeklies; brief introductory notes or biographical sketches in books of read-

[3] From Will Durant, "Why Men Fight," *The Saturday Evening Post.*
[4] *Ibid.*

ings; and narrative or expository material in semitechnical or popular science magazines.

At the beginning of the term especially, freshman English students are often required to write independent paragraphs. Later they are required to write on larger topics, and their paragraphs become units of longer compositions. Here is an example of the independent paragraph developing a single topic, "crab grass":

> With lawnmowing just about over for the year, it was a pleasure the other morning to find a letter in the *Tribune* in defense of crab grass. The letter was from Mr. Gilbert G. Brinckerhoff, a retired schoolteacher living in Radburn, New Jersey, and it was the first piece of original thinking we had come across in weeks. Mr. Brinckerhoff, probably alone among homeowners in the United States, has taken the pressure off crab grass and off himself: he has come up with the discovery that you can just leave the stuff alone and survive; you don't have to fight it. Brinckerhoff has developed a lawn that is one hundred per cent crab grass; not a spear of anything else mars its lovely green surface. It makes, he says, a very presentable lawn. What this discovery will do to the Scott Lawn Company, what steps against Brinckerhoff will be taken by an aroused citizenry of Radburn—these are subjects for conjecture. But at least there is one man in America whose energies are not flowing into silly channels and who can stand erect and look something in the face. We admire Brinckerhoff and wish him a long, indolent retirement, much of which can be spent in a rocker on the porch overlooking the weedy plain.[5]

For other examples, see the quoted paragraphs in Section 24.

29e. Use a paragraph of not too closely related sentences for a summary, conclusions, recommendations, or directions.

Many longer papers require for their rounding out and for effective endings a paragraph giving a *summary, conclusions,* or *recommendations.* Such a paragraph consists of sentences which are not too closely related; that is, as the paragraph develops, the last sentence is somewhat removed from the thought of the first sentence. The same kind of paragraph is used in writing which gives certain kinds of *directions.* The unifying topic of such paragraphs, usually implied, is one of the foregoing italicized words.

[5] From E. B. White, *The Second Tree from the Corner,* Harper & Brothers. Copyright by E. B. White.

The following is a summarizing paragraph, a conclusion to a 2,600-word article on cosmetics, entitled "A Dab of Paint":

The field of cosmetics is of necessity a vast field. It would hardly do to have only one type of cream. If the various cosmetics are to accomplish their general purpose of caring for the skin, they must be designed and used for specific purposes. The bare essentials for a treatment with creams include three types: a cleansing cream chosen for the type of skin it is to be used on, a lubricating cream that provides a tonic effect, and a vanishing cream that acts as a powder base. All three types are essential for a cream treatment. As personal needs dictate, various other special creams may be used. Beauty is too personal to prescribe specific preparations without some knowledge of personal needs.[6]

As a good example of the summary of an entire book, study the following:

Robert Gunning, the author of *The Technique of Clear Writing*, accomplishes what he sets out to preach. This whole book is one of the best examples of clear writing written about the subject. The opening chapters tell what has been learned about the habits and preferences of readers. The closing chapters review causes and cures for foggy writing in business, journalism, law, and the technical fields. The main body of the book consists of Ten Principles of Clear Writing: (1) Keep sentences short; (2) Prefer the simple to the complex; (3) Prefer the familiar words; (4) Avoid unnecessary words; (5) Put action in your verbs; (6) Write like you talk; (7) Use terms your reader can picture; (8) Tie in with your reader's experience; (9) Make full use of variety; (10) Write to express, not impress.[7]

The following is an example of a paragraph *giving directions*. The general subject was "preparing reports"; there were paragraphs of advice about selecting a topic, building a bibliography, keeping an idea page, outlining the paper in detail, and then this:

Write the paper; dash it off from the outline and polish it later. It is difficult to keep many things in mind as you write. Devote your initial writing efforts to getting your ideas stated; this initial draft can be gone over later in order to correct English mistakes and to put in headings, references, and footnotes. Dashing this first version off helps a writer

---

[6] From *The Scientist*, May, 1952.
[7] From "Reading about Writing," *Effective Letters Bulletin*, New York Life Insurance Company.

keep his attention on his theme rather than getting lost in details, and the sentence ideas tend to flow into each other much better. Usually all needed corrections can be inserted in this first draft, but if necessary, parts can be cut out and pasted in order.[8]

29f. Use paragraphs of isolated statements to emphasize summaries, conclusions, recommendations, directions, or important statements.

For effectiveness in writing *summaries, conclusions, recommendations,* certain kinds of *directions,* or *important statements,* use paragraphs of isolated statements; that is, paragraphs consisting of single sentences or parts of sentences. Such paragraphs are frequently numbered. Their position in a theme or an article may vary: summaries may come at the beginning or end, conclusions and recommendations at the end, directions and important statements anywhere in the paper where they are most effective. Here is an example:

As a result of this investigation, our conclusions are as follows:

1. Weather conditions that morning were not suitable for flying.

2. The engine of this plane had mechanical defects that should have been corrected before the take-off.

3. The pilot, and owner, of the plane was comparatively inexperienced in flying under unfavorable weather conditions.

4. The Brooktown Municipal Airport authorities, since their advice and commands were ignored, should be absolved of responsibility for the accident.

Not infrequently such paragraphs of isolated statements come within the body of an article. For example:

Part of the [water-famine] solution is to stop the reckless waste. The engineers of the Department of Water Supply estimated that it would be possible for the eight million New Yorkers to conserve 196.8 million gallons of water per day. They urge that citizens

1. Repair, or have the landlord repair, any leaking faucet or other wasting fixture.

2. Don't wash dishes under an open faucet.

3. Don't heat or cool the baby's bottle under a running faucet.

[8] From Francis P. Robinson, *Effective Study,* Harper & Brothers. Copyright, 1941, 1946.

4. Keep a bottle of water in the refrigerator to get a cool drink quickly.

5. Don't overrinse in using washing machines.[9]

EXERCISES

A. From a magazine or your anthology, choose a short story and examine the paragraphing of dialogue. Note how much, if any, explanatory material is included in the paragraphs giving quoted speeches.

B. Write a short paper in order to illustrate paragraphing and the use of quotation marks (see Section **95**) on the subject, *A Dialogue Between — and —.*

C. In one article in a magazine or in your book of readings, mark all the short paragraphs (two to six lines). Determine what purpose they serve: introductory, concluding, transitional, etc.

D. Look through such magazines as *The New Yorker, The Nation, The New Republic,* or *The Reader's Digest* for one-paragraph articles or discussions. Estimate their length. Find the topic sentence or statement and discuss the method or methods of paragraph development used.

E. Comment on the length and purpose of the paragraphs in several business letters written to you or to relatives and friends.

REVISION

30. Give time and thought to careful revision of every paragraph.

Although the preceding sections have discussed the paragraph as something separate from a theme or a longer paper, the distinction is at best artificial. A paragraph may be a theme, or a theme may consist of one paragraph, or two paragraphs, or many paragraphs. In fact, a common definition of a theme, a paper, an article is that it is a series of related paragraphs.

The clearness and effectiveness of a theme depends upon the clearness and effectiveness of its paragraphs. Using the work-sheet method suggested on pages 25, 26, anyone can put on paper the words and sentences that constitute a paragraph. The real work then begins—*revision*. Every paragraph should be carefully considered in the light of the preceding sections: characteristics, mechanics, topic statements, analysis, substance, unity, order, proportion and

[9] Arthur H. Carhart, "Turn Off That Faucet!" in *The Atlantic Monthly,* February, 1950, p. 39.

length, transitions, and appropriateness. In addition, every sentence, even every word, should be checked with the handbook advice given about Sentences, Diction, Grammar, and Punctuation.

Revision is important. Perhaps your own writing of paragraphs can be improved through careful study of the following material. It consists of two versions of the same theme, which was revised *paragraph by paragraph* by the student himself in the light of constructive criticisms given by the instructor in personal conference with the student.[1] The two versions show how much improvement is possible in a total theme when careful attention is given to paragraph detail, organization, and transitions.

As you study these revisions, you might keep in mind the following summary of the instructor's constructive comments made concerning the unrevised paper:

"1. On any controversial subject, it is good psychology to take into account, or at least show an awareness of, what an opponent would claim for the subject.

"2. Use of detail is inconsistent. Although the three main arguments are concretely illustrated, opportunities to be more convincing are lost because of vague generalities instead of facts, as in paragraphs one and three.

"3. The original and most compelling of the arguments should be chosen and pointed up with the most effective composition devices possible.

"4. Each paragraph should be examined and revised in the light of the foregoing and with the thought in mind that while a paragraph has a beginning, a middle, and an end much as a theme has, each paragraph here is also a part of a larger whole."

I Didn't Pledge a Fraternity

Original

I have learned from various sources about fraternities and I don't think that I should join one.

Revised

I have talked to many fraternity men and independents about fraternities. I listened to what they had to say and decided that I shouldn't join

[1] For permission to use this material, the authors gratefully acknowledge their indebtedness to the student-author, Ronald Van Putte, his instructor, Professor William Stafford of Purdue University, and the *Indiana English Leaflet,* where this material first appeared in print.

a fraternity. It is true that fraternity life has some benefits, such as living in a close knit group, getting a feeling of responsibility, and learning the social graces. Since the disadvantages offset the advantages, however, I don't think that I should join one.

Original

Fraternity life takes up too much time. Everyone, especially the freshmen, has special jobs to do. These jobs may range from serving dinner to cutting the lawn. All of these jobs take time away from studying. The bad part about Hell-week and initiation is that it takes up the time a student should be using to build a firm foundation of studies. Although it is not supposed to, initiation takes preference over studies during Hell-week. The members of a fraternity are required to go to the various social events whether or not they desire to.

Revised

One of the disadvantages of living in a fraternity is that the extra-curricular activities take up too much time. Everyone, especially the freshmen, has special jobs to do. These jobs may vary from serving dinner to cutting the lawn. All of these jobs take time away from studying. Another time-consumer is the various social functions that a member must attend, many of them whether he wants to or not. Hell-week and initiation also take valuable time—and from that crucial part of the semester when the new student should be acquiring good study habits. Little free time, then, is available to the fraternity member when he is pledging.

Original

Another one of the sore spots of fraternity life is the money problem. The cost of a fraternity is usually above that of a university-sponsored dormitory. The cost usually doesn't include the price of parties, picnics, dances, trade functions, or displays for the fraternity lawn. Fraternity life is fine for the person who has a lot of money to throw away, but a student with a limited amount of money has a tough time. He will usually break his budget and the back of his bank account.

Revised

Another one of the sore spots of fraternity life is the money problem. According to the Inter-fraternity Council, the average cost per year at a Purdue fraternity is $675. The cost of living at a university-sponsored dormitory is $630. Although $45 is not much money, it does become a major factor when the cost of parties, picnics, dances, trade functions, and lawn displays is added to it. Fraternity life is fine for the student who has a great deal of money to spend, but a student with a limited amount of money has a difficult time. He will usually break his budget and the back of his bank account if he joins a fraternity.

Original

Living in a clique may lead to prejudiced thinking. The fraternity may not allow foreign students, colored students, or students having a certain religion to pledge the fraternity. The fraternity member will not get a chance to meet these students and may get the wrong ideas about them. These rejected students will tend to cling together and worsen the problem by getting false ideas.

Revised

The most important disadvantage of living in a fraternity, however, is the effect that it may have on a person's mind. Living in a clique may lead to prejudiced thinking. The fraternity may not allow foreign students, colored students, or students having a certain religion to pledge the fraternity. The member will not get a chance to be in close contact with these people and may misinterpret their ideas and beliefs. The rejection of some students may lead to rejection of others of the same race, nationality, or religion and thus instill in the student an intolerant attitude for the rest of his life.

Original

In general, I can't see that a fraternity can do a person much good, but I can see where it is possible to do him harm. The fraternity may provide a person with the social graces, but if his thinking is prejudiced and narrow-minded, what good can they possibly do?

Revised

In general, I can't see that a fraternity can do a person much good, but I can see how it is possible to do him harm. The fraternity may provide a person with the social graces, but if his studies suffer from lack of time, his money is wasted, and his thinking is prejudiced and narrow-minded, what good can it possibly do?

The Sentence

GOOD themes, good articles, good papers are built with good paragraphs, which, in turn, are built from good sentences. Clearly, good themes cannot be made from faulty paragraphs, nor can good paragraphs be built from awkward, incomplete, rambling, or choppy sentences. The paragraph can be only so good as its component parts, its sentences, the units of expression. A successful writer, therefore, must know how to achieve unity, clearness, effectiveness, and appropriateness in his sentences.

To obtain such characteristics in sentence structure requires a solid foundation, a substantial framework. You must first know what a sentence *is;* you must understand grammatical structures and functions, and upon that foundation and framework construct sentences that are correct, clear, effective, and appropriate.

A fairly satisfactory definition of a sentence is that it is a word or group of words conveying a sense of complete meaning to the reader. Although there are exceptions, the word or group of words conveying complete meaning *usually* has a subject and a predicate; the subject may be expressed or it may be understood; either subject or predicate may also be understood from the context. (See pp. 489–493.)

It is important to remember that the foregoing statements refer to *grammatical* completeness. In one sense we do not have a complete thought until we have read or written a whole series of sentences, perhaps an entire paragraph or theme. A pronoun in one sentence may take its meaning from an antecedent in another. Such words as *thus, these, another,* and *again,* and such phrases as *for example* and *on the other hand* frequently show that the thought about to be presented in a new sentence is intimately related to the thought in a preceding sentence or paragraph.

247

When we say, then, that a sentence conveys a sense of complete meaning to the reader, we do not mean that we can dispense with its context. We mean only that we have a group of words so ordered as to be *grammatically* self-sufficient. For example, the statement, "He wrote that music when he was only 19 years old," is grammatically complete. It has a subject, the pronoun *he,* and it has a main predicate verb, *wrote;* moreover, the dependent clause, "when he was only 19 years old," is properly integrated into the sentence by the subordinating conjunction *when.* In this sense the entire statement is complete and must be begun with a capital and be followed by a period. So far as total meaning is concerned, however, we need other sentences to tell us that *he* refers to the musician Mendelssohn and *that music* refers to the incidental music for *A Midsummer Night's Dream.*

Because punctuation and capitalization are governed in part by grammatical rather than logical completeness, understanding the grammar of the sentence is basic for clear and effective writing. Sentence clearness and effectiveness, however, are more than matters of punctuation and capitalization; they depend also upon the forms and patterns of sentences, of which a full discussion is given on pages 489–493. A review of this material may be helpful before you study the following sections, which deal specifically with errors frequently made in writing the sentence and suggest definite ways of avoiding them.

Like problems dealing with themes, paragraphs, and words, the problems of writing sentences may be classed under three main heads: *correctness, clearness,* and *effectiveness.* As it concerns the sentence, *appropriateness,* the fourth characteristic of good writing, is considered here as an important aid to effectiveness. Sections 31–50 deal with these three divisions as follows:

Correctness
  Sentence fragment—Section 31
  Comma splice—Section 32
  Fused or blended sentences—Section 33

Clearness
  Sentence unity (oneness)—Section 34
  Incompleteness of meaning—Section 35

Mixed and illogical constructions—Section **36**
Faulty coordination—Section **37**
Faulty subordination—Section **38**
Logical dependent clauses—Section **39**
Word order—Section **40**
Dangling modifiers—Section **41**
Split constructions—Section **42**
Transition—Section **43**

Effectiveness

Conciseness—Section **44**
Parallelism—Section **45**
Consistency—Section **46**
Choppy sentences—Section **47**
Position and arrangement—Section **48**
Variety—Section **49**
Appropriateness—Section **50**

Such a listing as this may help you to keep in mind the three main problems you are attacking. You should note, however, that these topics are not mutually exclusive. Effective sentences result from both correctness and clearness; sentence unity is probably as much a problem of correctness as of clearness and could have been placed under either heading. Or, for another illustration, both proper coordination and subordination are necessary for clearness and effectiveness. As you study the sections which follow, keep your attention focused on the larger problem: how to make sentence *correctness,* sentence *clearness,* sentence *effectiveness,* and sentence *appropriateness* contribute to the correctness, clearness, effectiveness, and appropriateness of the longer units—paragraphs, themes, papers—that you write.

SENTENCE FRAGMENT

31a. Use justifiable sentence fragments for clear and effective writing.

Grammatically defined, a sentence consists of a subject and predicate and expresses a complete thought. Yet various kinds of statements express a complete thought without an expressed or implied subject or predicate.

1. Not sentence fragments but clear, effective statements are the following non-subject-and-predicate statements:

Interjections: *Hush! Ouch! Indeed! Alas! Ah! Oh! Oh, oh! Pshaw!*
Greetings: *Hello. Good morning. Good evening. Good night. Good-by.*
Expressive, exclamatory, or transitional statements: *What a day! Never again! To summarize. Now another point. One other important matter.*

2. Considered as sentence fragments but justifiable and effective are elliptical sentences. An elliptical sentence is a grammatically incomplete sentence, a part of a sentence without a subject or predicate, or both. These omitted parts are understood from the context, from what precedes or follows. Ellipsis is common in recording dialogue or answers to questions, or even in some of the exclamatory expressions in (1) above: *What a day* (*that was*)! *Never again* (*will I do that*)!

Elliptical answers to questions are words like *yes, no, never, always, of course,* or statements such as the following (combinations of conversation and questions-answers):

"Was that coat on sale?"
"Yes."
"A bargain?"
"Naturally."
"Did you buy it?"
"Of course."
"For how much?"
"Thirty-five dollars."

3. For certain kinds of writing—not sustained formal or informal prose—sentence fragments are peculiarly appropriate, as in descriptive notes on books in a bibliography or reading list:

Charles Major, *When Knighthood Was in Flower*. A romantic novel dealing with Renaissance England. Of interest to the older teen-age group. Especially valuable for its vivid life and swift movement.

31b. Avoid using unjustifiable sentence fragments.

An unjustifiable sentence fragment is a word or group of words (1) which does not make sense to the reader, or (2) which is not clear or effective because it is set apart from other words with which the reader expects it to be naturally attached or associated. The error is also called the "period fault," since it can be considered an error in punctuation, but it is more commonly considered an error in sentence construction. (Review the correct uses of the period, Section **86.**)

Common kinds of unjustifiable sentence fragments are dependent clauses or phrases. (See "Phrases" and "Clauses," pp. 482–488.) Each kind is given special discussion in Sections **31c** and **31d.** Unjustifiable sentence fragments can be effectively eliminated by one of several methods:

→1. Attach each fragment to an independent statement or to a statement making sense—if the fragment naturally and logically belongs with that statement.

→2. Revise so that the fragment becomes included as part of a complete statement (compound subject, compound predicate, compound sentence, complex sentence, etc.).

→3. Make each fragment complete by providing it with a subject and predicate and fulfilling the grammatical definition of a sentence.

31c. Avoid setting off a dependent clause as a sentence.

The dependent clauses which are frequently mistaken for sentences are adverbial clauses and adjective clauses. The adverbial clause may be wrongly set off when it logically should be at the beginning or end of an independent clause. The adjective clause may be wrongly set off when it logically should be at the end of an independent clause.

Wrong: I had no money for a trip to Europe. *When suddenly I was left a small fortune.* (Adverbial clause)
Unless you can't find anything else. We don't advise you to take this job. (Adverbial clause)
The governor decided not to veto the bill. *Even though there were parts of it that he did not like.* (Adverbial clause)
I was a student for four years at Oriole High School. *From which I was graduated in June, 1956.* (Adjective clause)
I have talked with a businessman. *Who thinks that the prospects for the next 12 months are excellent.* (Adjective clause)

251

Correction of the dependent clause sentence fragment usually involves no change in the wording. A change in capitalization (from a capital to a small letter) and in punctuation (from a period to a comma or no mark—see Sections **88f, 88m**) is enough. Or the dependent clause may be made independent by omitting the subordinating conjunction from the adverbial clause, or by changing the relative pronoun to a personal pronoun in the adjective clause.

Correct: I had no money for a trip to Europe. Suddenly I was left a small fortune.

Unless you can't find anything else, we don't advise you to take this job.

The governor decided not to veto the bill. There were parts of it, however, that he did not like.

The governor decided not to veto the bill, even though there were parts of it that he did not like.

I was a student for four years at Oriole High School, from which I was graduated in June, 1956.

I have talked with a businessman who thinks that the prospects for the next 12 months are excellent.

I have talked with a businessman. He thinks that . . .

31d. Avoid setting off a phrase as a sentence.

The phrases that cause trouble as sentence fragments are usually the following: participial, infinitive, absolute, prepositional, prepositional gerund, appositional, subject (noun with modifiers), and verb (as the second member of a compound predicate).

To correct such sentence fragments, (1) attach the phrase to or incorporate it in the sentence with which it logically belongs, or (2) make the phrase a sentence by giving it a subject, predicate, and completeness.

Study the following illustrations carefully. There are at least two parts to each: the first contains a sentence fragment with a label as to its kind; a corrected version follows, achieved by use of one of the methods just suggested.

Incorrect: *Having worked in a garage for four years.* John thinks he is an experienced mechanic. (Participial phrase)

Correct: Having worked in a garage for four years, John thinks he is an experienced mechanic.

Incorrect: I studied for hours every night. *Preparing myself to take and pass the College Entrance Board examinations.* (Participial phrase)

Correct: I studied for hours every night, preparing to take and pass the College Entrance Board examinations.

Incorrect: Harry has now two goals in life. *To graduate from college and to establish himself in business.* (Infinitive phrase)

Correct: Harry has now two goals in life. He wishes to graduate from college and to establish himself in business.
Harry has now two goals in life: to graduate from college and to establish himself in business.

Incorrect: *Winter having come early that year.* The mountain passes were soon blocked by the snow. (Absolute phrase)

Correct: Winter having come early that year, the mountain passes were soon blocked by the snow.
Winter came early that year, and the mountain passes were soon blocked by the snow.

Incorrect: *After a long hard day of classes and studying.* A student is ready to tumble into bed early. (Prepositional phrase)

Correct: After a long hard day of classes and studying, a student is ready to tumble into bed early.

Incorrect: Some people constantly discuss politics. *Without really knowing what they are talking about.* (Prepositional gerund phrase)

Correct: Some people constantly discuss politics without really knowing what they are talking about.

Incorrect: My mother spent her girlhood on a farm near Wildwood. *A small town in southeastern Ohio.* (Appositional phrase)

Correct: My mother spent her girlhood on a farm near Wildwood, a small town in southeastern Ohio.

Incorrect: We were fascinated by the scene at timberline. *Especially the stunted, twisted trees.* (Appositional phrase)

Correct: We were fascinated by the scene at timberline, especially the stunted, twisted trees.

Incorrect: *One of my neighbors, who killed all the weeds in his lawn by spraying them with a weed killer.* (Subject phrase)

Correct: One of my neighbors killed all the weeds in his lawn by spraying them with a weed killer.

One of my neighbors, who killed all the weeds in his lawn by spraying them with a weed killer, now has the most beautiful lawn in town.

Incorrect: *Even the winters, which are very long and severe in that climate.* (Subject phrase)

Correct: Even the winters are very long and severe in that climate. Even the winters, which are very long and severe in that climate, cannot compare with the winters I remember as a boy.

Incorrect: That night the river overflowed its banks. *And flooded the lowlands.* (Verb phrase)

Correct: That night the river overflowed its banks and flooded the lowlands.

What seem like—and are—sentence fragments are frequently used by skilled writers for stylistic purposes. For example: "He walked as though he were dreaming. Dreaming? Hardly. He was more detached than that. He was hypnotized! Far away. Lost in another world."

Students frequently complain that their instructors mark all fragmentary sentences as incorrect, even those deliberately written for stylistic effect. The truth is that most teachers wish their students to use fragments for rhetorical purposes only after they have demonstrated their knowledge of sentence completeness. After you have shown that you know what a sentence is, you may be allowed to experiment.

EXERCISES

A. Read carefully an article in your book of readings or in a recent magazine. Underline any sentence fragments that you find. Do you think they are justifiable? Do you think they, or some of them, would be more effective if they were sentences?

B. Correct the unjustifiable sentence fragments in the following by attaching them logically to materials with which they belong:

1. I said that I was going to St. Louis to visit my uncle. And that my uncle was going to take me to a major-league baseball game.
2. The Reference Room contains many different types of material. Collections of encyclopedias, yearbooks, indexes, and biographical dictionaries.

3. A great time, the Christmas season.
4. I have never found life dull in the town where I was born. The town of Mooresville, Minnesota.
5. After we walked down the stairs from the top of the monument. We walked around the lagoon and through the rows of cherry trees.
6. I liked the theme, "Public Enemy Number One." In which the public enemy turns out to be fog.
7. The hardest part came next—waiting. Just waiting for the judges to reach a decision.
8. I must close now. Looking forward to hearing from you.
9. We spend a great deal of time talking to our mountain neighbors. These being more interesting than you would imagine.
10. I think the best way to learn how to study is to improve your reading. Not only speed it up, but learn to read with more exactness.
11. Electricity, man's valuable but unseen friend!
12. I spent my entire time in the Navy in schools. Almost 2 years as a student and the other 2 years as an instructor.
13. There are three high schools in my home town. Washington High being the one I came from.
14. The circus was a glorious sight! All the colors, animals, and people.
15. College is the last step in education. The step which will, in most cases, determine the future.

C. Correct the unjustifiable sentence fragments in the following by expanding them into sentences:

1. My family consists of my father, my mother, my brother, and my sister. Also my grandfather because he lives with us.
2. Sunday, the only time that I can sleep late.
3. There wasn't much activity around the campus at Thanksgiving. At least none that I could see.
4. I don't know much about a ship. Only that it floats on water and is used for hauling freight and passengers.
5. If you like being out in the wilds, and I really mean wilds. You will like this camp site.
6. Since I had been there only once before. I had a hard time finding my way around.
7. It is a small town, but we can go swimming in the summer. And to basketball games in the winter.
8. A recreational program can be set up in any situation. For example, at a picnic, where such games as horseshoes can be played.
9. Bill played varsity basketball for three years. Holding down the position as first-string center.

10. Mackinac Island, which rises out of the Straits of Mackinac between Lake Huron and Lake Michigan.
11. Today I started a new life. A fresh clean life. Full of new adventures and of new opportunities in a different world. Here in college.
12. After the plants are growing and the beautiful flowers are in full bloom.
13. I had the usual English and reading courses. The ones where you learn to read, write, and spell.
14. Twin Cave, which is a large cave and which has never been completely explored. It reveals many large room-like areas cut from the rock.
15. Certain rules must be learned about the library. What books can be taken out and what books must be used there.

D. Correct the unjustifiable sentence fragments in the following by attaching the fragments or by expansion:

1. My uncle owns two cabins. One log cabin 20 years old and another which has just been built.
2. Thanksgiving was a bleak cold wintry day. The kind of day that you like to sit by the fire.
3. Small sailing craft and power boats swaying in the rough, roaring waters.
4. Eight o'clock is no time for a lecture. Especially on Monday morning after we have just had a busy week end.
5. Have you taken a walk in the woods in the spring? Noticing all the leaves bursting out on the trees.
6. Then I had my first look at the Washington Monument. Standing there stately and tall in the night.
7. Springfield has 225 acres of park area. The largest one being Snyder Park.
8. You would like Friendliness Restaurant on the north shore. A friendly atmosphere with the employees acting as hosts instead of waiters.
9. I am joining the Music Union in St. Louis next week. Because I have a job with a dance band there.
10. Trees which are centuries old all around you.
11. I finally did pass English. Because I think the teacher didn't want me in her class any more.
12. The fog was bad that day. So bad, in fact, that the plane couldn't land at the Chicago airport.
13. People rushing around at Christmas buying presents for their friends.

14. The breaking of a mirror will result in severe punishment. No less than seven years' bad luck.

15. Football, a game that has 11 players on each side.

COMMA SPLICE

32. Like the sentence fragment, the comma splice may be considered either an error in punctuation or an error in sentence construction. With either label, the unjustifiable comma splice is a serious error which causes confusion to the reader, since the writer does not show him where one sentence ends and another begins.

The comma splice—also called the "comma fault" or "illiterate comma"—is not an ordinary misuse of the comma. Instead, it is the error of using a comma to join two sentences; literally, the comma "splices" or links the sentences. More strictly defined, in grammatical terms, the comma splice is the error of using a comma between two independent clauses not joined by one of the pure or simple coordinating conjunctions, *and, but, or, nor, neither, yet.* (See Section **88d.**)

32a. Avoid unjustifiable comma splices.

The unjustifiable comma splice, as defined above, appears in several specific forms:

1. *Two statements which have no grammatical relationship but which are related by content.*

Incorrect: There will be a meeting of the Science Club on Friday evening, several important matters are to be discussed.

2. *Two related statements, the second of which begins with a personal pronoun whose antecedent is in the first.* Remember that personal pronouns, though they often refer to antecedents in other sentences, do not make *grammatical connections* between clauses; only relative pronouns perform that function.

Incorrect: The office is on the 35th floor, it overlooks the Hudson River. The trees on the campus are old and sturdy, they were planted over 100 years ago.
The Dean considered a few minutes and then shook his head, he did not say a word.

3. *Two related statements, the second of which begins with a demonstrative pronoun or adjective* (*this, that, these, those, such*). Like the personal pronouns, demonstrative pronouns and adjectives do not make *grammatical connections* between clauses.

Incorrect: Go south until you come to the corner of State and Madison Streets, this is one of the busiest intersections in the world.

4. *Two statements, the second of which begins with or contains a conjunctive adverb* (see list of conjunctive adverbs in Section **89b** and on pp. 582, 583). Despite the word *conjunctive,* such adverbs (*however, accordingly, then, nevertheless,* etc.) do not make the close *grammatical connections* between independent clauses that are made by the pure conjunctions. Conjunctive adverbs show only a logical relationship; hence, the comma is not a strong enough mark of punctuation to stand between the clauses.

Incorrect: We had taken a wrong turning near Northville, thus we found ourselves traveling miles out of our way.
    The spring vacation ended on Thursday morning, however, I did not return from the South until Sunday evening.
    The University imposes no penalties for absences, you are, however, expected to make up all work that you miss.

The comma splice error can be corrected in several effective ways:
1. Use a period after the first statement and a capital at the beginning of the second. This method is partly objectionable because of resulting short, choppy, jerky sentences (see Section **47**). It is effective if the ideas are not too closely related and if a *series* of short, choppy, jerky sentences is avoided.

Incorrect: There was no reason for my going, I was not invited.
Correct: There was no reason for my going. I was not invited.
    There will be a meeting of the Science Club on Friday. Several important matters are to be discussed.

2. Use a semicolon between the statements (see Section **89a** and **b**). This method is preferable when a conjunctive adverb is used to make clear the kind of relationship between the two statements.

Incorrect: My roommate spent money faster than he anticipated, therefore he had to drop out of school at the end of the first semester.
    I was able to borrow money to complete my first year, other-

wise I should have had to leave at the end of the first semester.

Correct: My roommate spent money faster than he anticipated; therefore he had to drop out of school at the end of the first semester.

I was able to borrow money to complete my first year; otherwise I should have had to leave at the end of the first semester.

The University imposes no penalties for absences; you are, however, expected to make up all work that you miss.

3. Insert a pure conjunction between the statements, or as an appropriate substitute for the conjunctive adverb, and retain the comma (see Section 88d). If the ideas are closely related, this is an effective method, for the pure conjunction makes the close relationship evident.

Incorrect: Classes will begin on September 20, freshmen should be on the campus for orientation the preceding week.

Correct: Classes will begin on September 20, and freshmen should be on the campus for orientation the preceding week.

The spring vacation ended on Thursday morning, but I did not return from the South until Sunday evening.

4. Subordinate one of the statements and retain the comma. This is usually the most effective method if the thought expressed is not radically changed by the subordination. In fact, the comma splice error is often the result of an attempt to show a causal relationship without proper subordination. One of the statements can be reduced to a dependent clause or to a phrase.

Corrected by using dependent clauses:

Although the University imposes no penalties for absences, you are expected to make up all work that you miss.

There was no reason for my going, since I was not invited.

If I had not been able to borrow money to complete my first year, I should have had to leave at the end of the first semester.

Go south until you come to the corner of State and Madison Streets, which intersection is one of the busiest in the world.

Corrected by using phrases:

On Friday evening there will be a meeting of the Science Club, in order to discuss several matters. (Adverbial phrase)

The office is on the 35th floor and overlooks the Hudson River. (Verb phrase)

Having taken a wrong turning near Northville, we found ourselves traveling miles out of our way. (Participial phrase)

Go south until you come to the corner of State and Madison Streets, one of the busiest intersections in the world. (Appositional phrase)

In correcting the comma splice, do not make a "frying pan" error, an error worse than the one you have already made. Merely omitting the comma does not correct the comma splice; it replaces it by the even more serious error of the fused or blended sentence (see Section 33).

32b. Use a <u>justifiable</u> comma splice when it is appropriate and effective.

The foregoing discussion has dealt with the *unjustifiable* comma splice. Although occasional examples may be found in print, many writers and editors are careful to avoid the error, using instead the punctuation suggested above.

Certain kinds of comma splice are appropriate and effective, but be sure first that they are justifiable:

1. *When the independent clauses are very short, with the subjects usually the same.*

I came, I saw, I conquered. (Julius Caesar's famous sentence)

We rested a bit, then we resumed play.

2. *When the independent clauses, neither one very long, express contrast.* Sometimes the first clause makes a negative statement, the second an affirmative one, or, as in one form of question in English, the first statement is affirmative, the second one negative (see Section 88j).

This is Henry, that is George.

Biology comes from two Greek words: *bios* means *life*, *logos* means *study*.

We are not spending the summer in Maine, we are spending it in Wisconsin.

You have a copy of the assignment, haven't you?

EXERCISES

A. Read carefully an article in your book of readings or in a magazine such as *The Atlantic Monthly, Harper's, The Saturday Evening Post,* or *Newsweek.* Encircle all "comma splices." Are they justifiable or unjustifiable? Comment on the kinds of clauses spliced, such as "short independent clauses," "first clause is negative, second is positive," "conjunctive adverb seems to relate clauses closely enough for the comma." Which of the sentences containing comma splices could be made clearer or more effective by changing the comma to a stronger mark of punctuation?

B. Correct all the unjustifiable comma splices in the following sentences. If it is possible, correct each one by all the methods suggested above. Arrange your corrected versions in the order of most effective to least effective.

1. I overslept this morning and did not get to class, however, my theme was finished.
2. With people who like their home towns as I do mine, I would not argue, I would only agree, "There's no place like home."
3. Aurora has five grade schools, two are parochial schools and three are public schools.
4. The students and the teacher did not get along properly, therefore, about all I remember was a riot each day.
5. One defect is incorrect spelling, the other is the occasional use of faulty diction.
6. Speaking, writing, and reading habits are first begun at home, then they are continued in school.
7. The streets are not clean, the buildings lining the streets are old, dirty, and broken down.
8. Radio City is larger than our Music Hall, both are similar in design, however.
9. My home town is located in northwest Indiana, it is about 25 miles southeast of Chicago.
10. Let a friend proofread for you, he's not as liable to look over your mistakes.
11. You drive up and down these steep hills for about three miles, then you come out of this rough area to level ground.
12. Let's share our vacation experiences, here are mine.
13. My parents have both had the opportunity to ride a plane, now they are eager for me to fly.
14. It seemed to me that the day nursery school would be much more

suitable to me than teaching, consequently I changed my course of study.

15. Only three companies had a picture of their firm on the letterhead, one had theirs at the top and the others had theirs at the bottom of the page.

16. Christmas comes on Monday this year, this means that our church will have two morning services.

17. Small towns are also known for their peace and quiet, there are no police sirens and constant honking of horns.

18. I won't have very much money to spend during the holidays, in fact, by my last calculation, I'll be 10 dollars short.

19. Edward did not want to listen to my story, all he wanted was to borrow some money.

20. Chicago's railroad center forms one of the largest junctions of track in the world, its stockyards are the largest in the United States.

C. Directions given in B.

1. Professional players are playing for money, they play football as if it were a job.

2. "It won't work," he said, "I'm too old."

3. Baseball would probably die out if people in America didn't like to criticize, thus when they attend a game, they can really blow off their steam.

4. My main objective in life is to be some one important, I would like to be a business executive in some large firm.

5. A town that should be interesting to you is Harrisburg, it is the capital city of Pennsylvania.

6. The average freshman does not find the subject matter too hard, instead he finds it hard to adjust himself to the new way of college life.

7. In high school I spent very little time studying, as a matter of fact I never so much as took a book home.

8. Our farm is not too large, it consists of 200 acres.

9. I had no intention of ever using chemistry in later life, consequently I did not take the high school course offered.

10. "We do not have a 13th floor," he explained, "it is a superstition of the hotel."

11. To enter graduate work, the student must have a good college record, also he must have a great desire to specialize.

12. Most people write the same as they speak, therefore, if you speak correctly, you will write correctly.

13. The long struggle was well rewarded, I had landed a 2-foot catfish.
14. "One thing was accomplished," I said to Mother, "I passed my written test with a perfect score."
15. I once heard the story about a man who was driving along in his automobile, all at once a black cat ran in front of him.
16. This is big money in anybody's "book," at least I think so.
17. English is difficult for me for two reasons, I will try to explain them in this theme.
18. At Indianapolis turn east on Route 40, that road will take you straight into Columbus.
19. I have broken many superstitions and no harm has come to me, thus I have lost my belief in all superstitions.
20. I have been telling you about the advantages of my home town, now I would like to say something about the disadvantages.

FUSED OR BLENDED SENTENCES

33. *Fused* or *blended* sentences are two grammatically complete sentences which are joined or run together with *no* mark of punctuation between.

33a. Do not write two sentences with no punctuation whatever between them. Use a terminal mark (period, question mark, exclamation point) or a semicolon.

Fused or blended sentences are a serious grammatical error, an error in punctuation, and a violation of the principle of unity. It is an even more flagrant violation of correctness than the comma splice, for the writer of a comma splice shows that he senses the need for punctuation of some sort.

A sentence is a complete and meaningful statement and should always be followed by a full stop, that is, by a terminal mark of punctuation (see Sections **86, 87**).

Incorrect: That night the river overflowed its banks and spread over the lowlands thousands of people were left homeless by the time the waters receded.

Judged by the grammatical form, this "sentence" contains two independent statements. Each may be written as a separate sentence, or, if the writer feels that the statements are sufficiently related in thought, a semicolon. The result is a compound sentence with a semicolon separating the clauses and the terminal mark at the end.

Correct: That night the river overflowed its banks and spread over the lowlands. Thousands of people were left homeless by the time the waters receded.
That night the river overflowed its banks and spread over the lowlands; thousands of people were left homeless by the time the waters receded.

Concerning possible fused sentences, you might ask yourself: Have I written two sentences together, with no mark of punctuation between, and thereby confused my reader by not indicating to him where one complete thought ends and another complete thought begins?

33b. Never correct fused sentences by placing a comma between them.

If you correct the fused-sentences error by using a comma, your error is of course the comma splice (see Section **32**). The four methods, therefore, for the correction of the comma splice should be carefully studied for application to similar correction of fused-sentence errors.

EXERCISES

Copy the following sentences and use capital letters (see Section **97**), periods, question marks, exclamation marks, or semicolons where they are needed:

1. I'll tell you one thing it surely is hard to eat peas in an airplane.
2. I have had two accidents in my lifetime I hope I will not have any more.
3. My analytical geometry is taking entirely too much of my time therefore I'm going to drop it and spend more time on my other subjects.
4. This will introduce my father, Mr. J. E. Connolly he was born in Pittsburgh, Pennsylvania, on May 28, 1915.
5. I didn't go to our high school football game instead I watched a college game over television.
6. I am interested in a number of famous composers among them are Tchaikowsky, Beethoven, Offenbach, and Wagner.

7. The college preparatory course could eliminate this difficulty also this course should include subjects that would help the student in college.

8. Spending money is not a hard thing to do it seems as though it is gone before a person knows it.

9. We didn't have dinner at home instead we had dinner at Grandmother's house.

10. Indiana has many soils and special soil types many of these latter are in the southern part of the state.

11. The American is not only wasteful and careless he takes no thought for the future.

12. Maybe people had bad luck three or four times on a Friday then they began to believe that Friday was an unlucky day.

13. I have been able to raise 170 bushels of corn an acre this is the record in our county.

14. In 1953 Mt. Comfort had its first excitement the high school basketball team went to the semifinals in the state tourney.

15. The evening of the day I played hookey I told my parents what I had done well they just about went through the ceiling.

16. We did not go to camp just for recreation much of our time was spent on woodcraft and in meetings of several kinds.

17. I plan to practice medicine until I have saved some money then I will give up my practice and travel for a while.

18. Four years of high school English is a great help in college however I am still very poor in English.

19. Muncie, Indiana, is an average American city it was once described as Middletown, U.S.A.

20. Private homes do not offer social functions therefore those who live in private homes miss the various social activities offered by the dormitories and sororities.

SENTENCE UNITY (ONENESS)

34. Unity means *oneness, singleness of purpose,* or, as the *New World Dictionary* defines it, "an arrangement of parts or material that will produce a single, harmonious design or effect in an artistic or literary production." Unity applies to the whole composition (Section 10) and to the paragraph (Section 25). It also applies to the sentence.

For clearness, a sentence conveys complete meaning, but sentence unity does not mean that only one object or idea should be mentioned, or that the sentence must be short. A unified sentence may refer to several people, places, objects, or ideas, and may extend to considerable length. For example, this is a unified sentence: "Although the weather had turned warmer during the night, Jim and I decided to pack our provisions and sharpen our skates in the hope that our guide would decide the ice was still safe for skating." The sentence is long and refers to several things and people, but it is unified because it has a singleness, a oneness of purpose and of content. The ideas are closely related and form a unit of thought.

Another sentence could be one-fourth as long as this and refer to only one person, and yet violate the principle of unity: "Joe was a good student, being the possessor of a new hat." The reader of this sentence very properly comments that the two ideas have nothing in common.

Unity in the sentence, essential to clear writing, is violated by (1) introducing too many details and (2) combining unrelated ideas. (Also, see Section 37.)

34a. Avoid rambling sentences which introduce too many details.

Wrong: We accepted the invitation to have the State High School Golf Tournament at Moose Junction, a small town in Minnesota, which has only 5,000 inhabitants, but which contains several supermarkets, a number of churches, two good hotels, a number of motels, being on the junction of one United States highway and two state roads, and, since 1946, a drive-in restaurant as well as a golf course owned by a wealthy man named Putt.

At least approaching unity, because of an attempt to keep the idea of golf as the central or single purpose, a revision might read:

Revised: We have accepted the invitation to have the State High School Golf Tournament at Moose Junction, Minnesota, because of the facilities it offers. It is easily accessible by railroad and by several highways, United States Route 39 and two state roads, 138 and 139, which intersect there. There are two good hotels and several motels; in addition, quite a number of the city's 5,000 inhabitants have agreed to open their homes to the high school students. Restaurants are adequate, including a new large drive-in near the golf course. Naturally, the deciding factor in choosing Moose Junction has been this golf course. One of the best, in every sense, in the Midwest, it is owned and maintained by a golf enthusiast and wealthy man named, appropriately, Mr. Putt. He has guaranteed that the course will be in excellent condition for the high school tournament.

34b. Avoid placing incongruous ideas in the same sentence.

Incongruous ideas are unrelated ideas, and the error can occur not only in the same sentence but in different sentences, in the same paragraph, or even in the same theme. When incongruous ideas occur in the same sentence, unity can sometimes be attained by making one idea subordinate to the other or otherwise trying to show some evidence of relationship. If the ideas are not closely related, they might be placed in separate sentences; if there seems no relationship at all, one of the ideas should be omitted.

Wrong: Mary wore a white dress, and she had a good time at the dance.

Improved: Wearing a white satin dress and a purple orchid, Mary was the most popular girl at the dance, where she naturally had a wonderful time.

EXERCISES

Revise the following sentences to give them unity.

1. The town of Aurora has a population of 7,000, and there are no farmers living in the town.
2. One hundred years ago John E. Sherman was elected mayor of our city; however, the present mayor is Wendell G. Orson.
3. We feel that our fraternity is the best at State College, which was founded in 1899 by two brothers, George and Daniel Slate; they founded the fraternity, not the college, which was established by an act of the State Legislature in 1870, and the moving spirit there was Morton Dowhill, the Speaker of the Senate.
4. As I grew older, my desire to play basketball grew also, and when I entered high school I was too small to play my first 2 years of school, being only five feet tall, so I had to sit on the bench, but later in high school I began to grow, and before I graduated my senior year I was playing center on the first team, for I had grown 13 inches in 2 years.
5. "If I had a million dollars, I would buy me a new car and a new

suit and a new pair of shoes and go all around the world and see it all and when the car got something wrong I would not wait to get it fixed, I would buy me another new car and give the old one to some kids and keep going and if it was water I would buy me an airplane and just keep going." (Schoolboy's theme on "What I Would Do with a Million Dollars," in *This Week,* July 3, 1949.)

INCOMPLETENESS OF MEANING

35. Justifiable sentence fragments convey complete meaning to your reader; unjustifiable sentence fragments do not (see Section 31). On the other hand, there are sentences which are grammatically complete and yet which are incomplete or vague in meaning. A sentence should contain a single thought, or a group of closely related ideas, and it should be clear.

Because of inaccurate thinking, many writers do not express their ideas completely enough to make them fully understandable units of thought. The fault is that the writer knows, or thinks he knows, what he has in mind but does not take the trouble fully to convey his ideas. Likewise, some "sentences" are incomplete because the writer does not know the grammatical essentials of a sentence. Sound thinking and a minimum understanding of the grammar of a sentence will enable you to avoid both unjustifiable sentence fragments and two other serious kinds of incompleteness: (1) the omission of *words* necessary for clear, full expression and (2) the omission of essential *ideas.*

35a. Do not omit a necessary main verb or an auxiliary verb.

Both formal and informal usage sanctions omission of words in writing and speaking. Such sentences as "He made such a speech as only a politician can [make]" and "I play a better game of tennis than my roommate [does]" are complete and correct without the added *make* and *does.* The following sentences, however, involve more serious breaches of clearness and correctness; in each there are two clauses or a compound predicate, but the auxiliary verb (Section 78) or the main verb (Section 79) is improperly understood to be correct:

Doubtful: The lawn *was* mowed and the hedges neatly trimmed.
Improved: The lawn *was* mowed and the hedges *were* neatly trimmed.

Doubtful: I never *have* and probably never *will write* excellent themes.
Improved: I never have *written* and probably never *will write* excellent themes.

Doubtful: My roommate *has* and always *will study* hard to be an honor student.
Improved: My roommate has *studied* and always *will study* hard to be an honor student.

35b. Do not omit a necessary article, pronoun, preposition, or conjunction.

Doubtful: The president and chairman of the committee accepted my petition.
(This sentence means that one man is both president and chairman.)
Improved: The president and the chairman of the committee both accepted my petition.

Wrong: My father's name is Martin and has been a lifelong resident of Highland Park.
Clear: My father's name is Martin, and he has been a lifelong resident of Highland Park.

Doubtful: I have great interest and high regard for your work.
Improved: I have great interest *in* and high regard for your work.

Doubtful: I am asking that statement be made clearer.
Improved: I am asking *that* that statement be made clearer.

35c. Do not omit words necessary in a comparison.

Do not omit the standard of comparison or an essential word to make the comparison clear. (For mixed and illogical comparisons, see Section 36c, d, e.)

Doubtful: He is so sick.
Improved: He is so sick that he cannot attend class today.
He is really sick.

Doubtful: Country life is so friendly and peaceful.
Improved: Country life is so friendly and peaceful that many people will not live anywhere else.

Doubtful: Your speech has been the greatest success.

Improved: Your speech has been the greatest success of any given thus far.

Your speech has been a great success.

Doubtful: Mathematics interested Henry more than Nora.
Improved: Mathematics interested Henry more than it did Nora.

Mathematics interested Henry more than Nora did.

Doubtful: His hands are bigger than any man I know.
Improved: His hands are bigger than those of any man I know.

35d. Include all words essential for the clear expression of ideas.

In addition to the suggestions in Section **35a, b,** and **c,** revise any statement that is not clear because other essential words are omitted.

Not clear: As far as that, we students would not be in favor.
Clear: As far as that proposal is concerned, we students are not in favor of having tuition fees increased.

Not clear: The girl across the hall wears the clothes my sister in Chicago wears.
Clear: The girl across the hall wears clothes such as those my sister in Chicago wears.

Not clear: Like all the rest of the Home Economics students, my first 2 years of study are already planned.
Clear: Like the curriculum of the other Home Economics students, my curriculum for the first 2 years is already planned.

35e. Do not let punctuation marks replace necessary words.

Sometimes a careless writer lets a mark of punctuation, usually a comma, replace a needed subordinating conjunction like *that* or a relative pronoun.

Incomplete: We asked, she should consider being our candidate for Prom Queen.

Henry always believed, he could become an honor student.

The man, I wrote to was the Registrar.

People in Fayville are so friendly, I could live here forever.
Improved (by omitting the commas and inserting any words necessary for clearness):

We asked that she should consider being our candidate for Prom Queen.

Henry always believed that he could become an honor student.

The man I wrote to (or, The man that I wrote to) was the Registrar.

People in Fayville are so friendly that I could live here forever.

35f. Avoid a telegraphic style in formal and informal writing.

Because every word telegraphed, cabled, or radioed costs money, we have developed a telegraphic style for such messages. In this style we omit subjects or main verbs or auxiliary verbs or adjectives or adverbs or conjunctions or prepositions or pronouns; in other words, we try to make ourselves understood with the least possible number of words and at lowest cost.

Such writing can be understood even when important words are omitted. Otherwise, many important telegrams would be misinterpreted. The following message serves its purpose:

Letter received. Leaving tomorrow noon. Reserve room Carter Hotel. Get theater tickets Saturday matinee, night.

Such a style is not effective in either formal or informal writing. Appropriate for telegrams, day letters, night letters, cablegrams, and radiograms, it is inappropriate for ordinary prose communication.

EXERCISES

A. Make complete the sense of the following sentences by inserting or substituting the necessary words or by revising or rewriting.

1. I believe the standards of our college are considerably higher than many colleges.
2. My childhood was the same as most boys and girls who grow up in a small community.
3. Our American workers are paid more than any other country.
4. I can usually park our car much better than Mother.
5. Let's put students through high school on the assumption that each one is going on to or some other form of advanced training after graduation.
6. The major activity on our campus is the Student Union Building.
7. In our town there is always something to do, and is not as small as Plymouth or Lakeville.

8. When we left for our vacation, the windows were firmly closed and the front door locked.
9. My first college semester has not been so bad.
10. Paved roads are more comfortable and last longer.
11. In our college there is a course for almost everyone except modern American poetry.
12. Our football team always has and always will play clean.
13. To quote a phrase I read somewhere, a person can choose his friends but not his relatives, sounds just a bit vicious.
14. When the toys have been put away and the house cleaned, Christmas is over.
15. I never have and I never will celebrate a birthday on February 29.

B. Directions given in A.

1. Seems to me this is the most beautiful building on the campus.
2. In summarizing my thoughts on what you could do to help prepare high school students for college, or whatever else they want to do is, first, have them take aptitude tests to find out what they are most interested in.
3. I am now in the process of taking aptitude tests which if I had taken when I first entered high school, I might now be sure I was studying the thing I am most interested in.
4. Among the leading products produced in our city are as follows: hosiery, paper, motors, records, and refrigerators.
5. In high school constant supervision was not as evident as it was in grade school and therefore made me have a growing sense of independence.
6. There hasn't and there won't be a more wonderful artist than Nature.
7. My name is Ted Johnson and come originally from the South Side of Chicago.
8. I hope everyone has and will enjoy their future vacation as much as I did mine.
9. Not being accustomed to living away from home, to all the homework with so little time for relaxing, and to doing fairly bad in my school work (at the beginning), made it very difficult for me to finish my first year.
10. This dislike of English I feel was due to the teacher that I had was old and was slipping in her ways of teaching.
11. A freshman should feel his school work comes first.

12. As I was very timid in a gathering of such important people, stupidly forgot all about introducing myself.
13. My young brother's hair is always combed neatly and his hands washed clean.
14. I am very enthusiastic and fond of my art teacher's sketching.
15. Jane's mature attitudes and capacities were superior to most individuals of her age.

MIXED AND ILLOGICAL CONSTRUCTIONS

36. You have studied how lack of clearness is caused by the use of unjustifiable sentence fragments (Section **31**), unjustifiable comma splices (Section **32**), and, even worse, fused sentences (Section **33**). You have also seen how the cause of clear writing is hindered by the omission of important, necessary words (see Incompleteness of Meaning, Section **35**). Supplementing those sections is the following discussion dealing with additional hindrances to clear writing. Such hindrances are mixed and illogical constructions.

Construction in sentence formation is the grouping of words with other words or word combinations. A statement that is contrary to reason, does not make good sense, violates some principle of regularity, and thus is not clear, is illogical. Sentence structure should make sense to a reader; if it doesn't, the reason is frequently ignorance of grammar or slovenly thinking, or both.

You may expect your reader to give careful attention to your writing, but you cannot expect him to spend time untangling involved and mixed constructions or to correct your mistakes in thinking. He may make the necessary corrections as he reads, but his attention is unwillingly attracted to the errors and away from the important communication of ideas. Therefore, if you wish to present your thoughts clearly and effectively, heed the following warnings.

36a. Do not start a sentence with one construction and then stop, or shift to another, leaving one or more sentence elements incomplete.

Sometimes a writer begins a sentence, changes his construction and direction, forgets where he is, keeps adding words while moving in a different direction, and then stops before he has given meaning to the words with which he started. Such an unfinished construction results in the following:

Wrong: A high school friend of mine, who because he ran out of funds, had to leave college at the beginning of his sophomore year and go to work in a local factory.

Our college band, not being accustomed to the new conductor and resenting his extremely critical manner.

These constructions result in sentence fragments (see Section 31d). Fragments may be completed by the addition of pertinent material:

Right: A high school friend of mine who, because he ran out of funds, had to leave college at the beginning of his sophomore year and go to work in a local factory, saved enough money in 3 years to return to college and finish his education.

Our college band, not being accustomed to the new conductor and resenting his extremely critical manner, soon lost its morale and its high standing.

In other constructions there is an independent clause or the equivalent of a sentence, but there are also additional words with no logical and grammatical relationship to what precedes or follows.

Not clear: An automobile, unless you take good care of it, you will soon have to have it repaired.
Improved: Your automobile will soon have to be repaired unless you give it proper care.

Not clear: With these 11 men functioning as a team is the reason for our successful season.
Improved: With these 11 men functioning as a team, we had a successful season.
Because these 11 men functioned as a team, we had a successful season.

In the following, the italicized part begins with a word, *anyone,* presumably going to be the subject, modified by an adjective clause; the construction stops there, and an independent clause follows. In the first correction the italicized part is used as the writer apparently planned to use it; in the second correction it is used, logically and grammatically, as the object of a verb.

Wrong: *Anyone who can be really happy,* most people would look upon him with envy.

Clear: *Anyone who can be really happy* is looked upon with envy by most people.

Most people would envy *anyone who can be really happy.*

36b. Avoid mixed, confusing "blends."

Unless we are careful, certain "blends" will creep into our thinking and writing. In such a sentence as "He had no automobile in which to ride in," we have blended *in which to ride* and *to ride in.* Similarly, blending *where* (*at* or *in which*) with *at which* results in a statement such as "Where do you live at?" or "The room where I live in . . ." In speaking, we might say, "Despite of what you say, I think you are wrong." Here we have blended *in spite of* and *despite.* Such constructions are as much a result of careless thinking as of grammatical ignorance. When we write, "Irregardless of that, he decided to stay," we have carelessly blended *regardless* and *irrespective.*

A confusing sentence blend is that in which the writer begins with an indirect question and blends the direct question into the statement (see also Section **95k**).

Confused: If I had to do it over again, sometimes I wonder would I come to this college or go to work.

Improved: If I had to do it over again, sometimes I wonder whether I would come to this college or go to work.

Unfinished construction and a blend of confused ideas:

To me this is truly a book that, after read, you will never be the same again.

36c. Avoid a mixed or double comparison.

A frequent and special example of the mixed and confused blend occurs when a writer tries to include two comparisons in the same statement: (1) the grammatical positive and comparative degree of an adjective or an adverb: (2) a member of a class or group and yet a unique member. Good use sanctions the double comparison in the same sentence, but, for clearness and effectiveness, it demands that the second come after the first has been completed. (For omissions of necessary words in comparisons, see Section **35c.**)

Wrong: He is *as* strong, if not stronger, *than* Fred.

For a short distance a man can run *as* fast, if not faster, *than* a horse.

Improved: He is *as* strong *as,* if not stronger *than,* Fred.

For a short distance a man can run *as* fast *as,* if not faster *than,* a horse. (These are improved but awkward.)

Preferable: He is *as* strong *as* Fred, if not stronger.

For a short distance a man can run *as* fast *as* a horse, if not faster.

Wrong: My father is *one of the tallest, if not the tallest man* in town.

The Battle of Waterloo was *one of the greatest if not the greatest battle* in all history.

Preferable: My father is *one of the tallest men in town, if not the tallest.*

The Battle of Waterloo was *one of the greatest battles in all history, if not the greatest.*

36d.   Avoid including within the class or group the object or term being compared, if it is part of the class or group.

Inaccurate: Straziboski is older than any man on the football team.

Clear: Straziboski is older than any *other* man on the football team.

Inaccurate: Henry has a higher scholastic average than any student in the College of Arts.

Clear: Henry has a higher scholastic average than any *other* student in the College of Arts.

36e.   Do not use the word <u>other</u> when the superlative degree indicates that the object or term compared is included within the group or class.

Inaccurate: Straziboski is the oldest of all the *other* men on the football team.

Clear: Straziboski is the oldest of all the men on the football team.

Inaccurate: Henry has the highest scholastic average of all the *other* students in the College of Arts.

Clear: Henry has the highest scholastic average of all the students in the College of Arts.

36f. Avoid confusing double negatives.

One common violation of clear phrasing is the unjustifiable double negative. Illiterate speech abounds with such expressions as "can't hardly," "can't scarcely," "haven't scarcely." In formal and good informal English, however, they should be avoided.

Although rigid double negatives have been allowable in past centuries, they are now currently out of style and unacceptable. We are not likely to say or write "I didn't get no food" or "I didn't see nobody" or "Nobody isn't going to tell me anything," but we should always be careful in using *not* with such "negative words" as *no, but, nor, only, hardly, scarcely,* and *except.*

Questionable: I have *not had but* 4 hours' sleep last night.
You *can't help but* admire the man's courage.
Some students have *not scarcely* enough money to pay for their bare necessities.

Improved: I have had *but* 4 hours' sleep last night.
You *can't help* admiring the man's courage.
Some students have *scarcely* enough money to pay for their bare necessities.

Allowable and occasionally effective, however, are certain double negatives expressing a weak positive, such as using *not* with a negative prefix or suffix of an adjective or adverb.

A spare tire is a *not unnecessary* piece of equipment.
This position calls for a *not irresponsible* person.
Despite the punishment the boxer walked *not unsteadily* to his corner.

Sentences may of course contain more than one negative when the sense justifies the use:

That I was *not* present in class today is *not* true.
I can *not* tell why I was *not* able to concentrate in that test.
You *couldn't* have known that I was *not* present if you had *not* been present yourself.

EXERCISES

A. Correct the mixed or illogical constructions in the following sentences:

1. At the day's end I was so tired I couldn't hardly stand up.
2. I think fraternities are very educational as well as going to school.
3. Campus activities as far as college goes I have only one, a fraternity, of which I am now a pledge.
4. John has the kind of personality in which I wished that I possessed.
5. I do not see my grandparents but once a year.
6. My hobbies, I have done that are outstanding.
7. For weeks I had counted the days until the beginning of one of the shortest—or seemed the shortest—2-week vacation of my life.
8. I often wondered why people smoked; therefore I thought to myself, but could not find very many good reasons.
9. We put the injured girl in the man across the street's car and took her to the hospital.
10. It is on icy roads that kills half of the people in the United States.
11. In the preceding paragraphs I have tried to convey how my family usually spends Easter, as I have known it in my youth, will always be cherished by me.
12. This is the kind of movie that you can't hardly get to see no more.
13. During the 500-mile race there are pits along the rails and any repairs that are needed during the race.
14. We didn't have but little choice in our high school subjects.
15. His father being a manufacturer of cigars explains his social status.
16. Pittsburgh isn't the cleanest city in the United States, by no means.
17. There are pictures and diagrams which illustrate a number of words that only illustrations will complete their definitions.
18. I haven't hardly had time to get all my assignments done.
19. I know from my own experiences with different subjects at college the subjects I had been exposed to before I could better understand.
20. I didn't pay no attention to what my teachers said.

B. Rewrite the following sentences, correcting the mixed or illogical constructions:

1. Football will teach a man how to work with others as a team, good sportsmanship, a better body, and a good clean mind.
2. Women have proved themselves to be just as competent, or more competent, as men.
3. I wasn't receiving no monetary reward for my labors.
4. The high school I attended was a great one, and, in my opinion, will continue to be one as long as it is occupied.
5. By serving as a Junior Leader in the 4-H Club gave Marie a broader and more practical experience.
6. After a test I usually think that I just don't know nothing.

7. Mother's name is Norma and is a 4-H leader and very active in community work.
8. This city is "home," and though I have traveled over a large portion of the earth's surface, where the pasture remains the greenest.
9. Looking back and thinking if I were a beginning freshman again, what would I do, I would like to do many things differently; but, when we really stop and think that what we are here for is to learn and if we already know it all there would be no real reason for coming to college in the first place.
10. Five minutes later, maybe not that long but anyway it was a State cop.
11. In all his efforts to get up on his feet made his wound bleed more.
12. This is the identical pillar where the prisoner of Chillon was chained to.
13. The dormitory chairman stated that if we wanted Reilly for secretary let us get his name on the printed ballot.
14. With two beds, two dressers, two desks, and two chairs, is it any wonder that we have no space in which to exercise in?
15. Our dog has never learned that it can't eat but one mouthful at a time.
16. The cartoonists exaggerate all a politician's mistakes, which, I know from personal acquaintance, some are deserving of it and some are not.
17. The many large dormitories with their hundreds of cell-like rooms, house students who after 4 years do not even know or recognize their classmates, seems cold and unfriendly.
18. After being up for two whole nights, I was so tired when the initiation came I wasn't hardly able to keep my eyes open.
19. It was a good speech but, disregardless of that, I was not convinced.
20. The fact that you can't take but one girl to the dance, you should not invite two; irregardless, some fellows get in that predicament.

C. Directions given in B.

1. Our Homecoming displays thrilled the alumni as much, if not more than they did the students.
2. After I have owned for 25 years a drug store like my uncle, I hope to be able to retire and live well.
3. A vacation is a good and the fastest way to spend money that I know of.
4. I enjoyed especially a trapeze act which consisted of a man and a woman.

5. Another kind of excitement is after hard work, great care, and training, your livestock wins first prize at a county fair.
6. This service gives us a better understanding and true meaning of Christmas.
7. Father grew up on a farm, and, like my mother, he did the chores of a farm boy.
8. People are always kindest and more generous during the holiday season.
9. The streets of our city need more parking meters on them like other cities.
10. Colorful Colorado is the highest and one of the most scenic states in the United States.
11. There are many other types of work available such as the production chemist.
12. Living in a dormitory will give a student as much education if not more than he will get from the classroom.
13. The library is too vast of a territory to grasp very much of its wealth in so little time.
14. The American Farm Bureau has as many, if not more, members than most labor unions.
15. This is the first abridged dictionary to be prepared by a staff larger than most unabridged dictionaries.
16. The city of Indianapolis is as large, if not larger, than Pittsburgh.
17. My dormitory, I was told, when, after what seemed like running through a maze, I set my eyes on what was to be my abode for the rest of the semester.
18. Coney Island has rides for the young and the old and fun houses that you'll laugh your head off.
19. The Ohio River is fully as deep, if not deeper, than the Wabash River.
20. By a good fraternity I mean one that is a place for the boys to have fun, but also helps the boys get their lessons by having study hours and such things as that.

FAULTY COORDINATION

37. In order to be correct and clear, sentences must be unified and complete. In order to be clear and effective, they must be so constructed that the relative importance of their elements is fully apparent. Are these elements coordinate, of equal rank? Are some of them subordinate? In clear and effective sentences, appropriate coordination and subordination are observed.

The immature writer will phrase his sentences as a child speaks. That is, he will construct a series of independent clauses loosely held together by coordinating conjunctions. A child very naturally might say: "We went to the circus, and we saw all the freaks, and we drank pink lemonade, and we had a grand time." A more mature person will avoid such running-on sentences. If he thinks carefully, he can express his ideas in constructions which will show their varying importance. He will show that equal ideas are equal and he will subordinate minor ideas so that the important statement may be more emphatic.

Avoid excessive coordination, then, because it is childish, monotonous, and ineffective. Avoid inaccurate and illogical coordination because it reveals that you have not really thought through the relationship of the ideas you wish to express and you thereby give the reader hazy, incorrect impressions of the thoughts presented to him.

37a. Avoid stringy, running-on sentences.

Obviously, a stringy, running-on sentence is one that just goes on and on. Do not overwork the possibilities of the compound sentence. Avoid excessive use of a series of short independent clauses and avoid excessive use of coordinating conjunctions between independent clauses. Reduce predication; that is, change an independent into a dependent clause, a dependent clause into a phrase, a phrase into a single word (see Section **44a**).

Immature: George bought a new automobile; it had free wheeling; it had a heater; it had automatic transmission; it had no radio; and it had no seat covers.
George bought a new automobile, and it had free wheeling, and it had a heater, and it had automatic transmission, but it had no radio and it had no seat covers.

Improved: George's new automobile has free wheeling, a heater, and automatic transmission, but it has neither radio nor seat covers.

37b. Avoid "seesaw" sentences.

"Seesaw" sentences are compound sentences with two independent clauses of approximately equal length, whether or not joined by conjunctions. Alone or used occasionally, such a balanced sentence is effective; a succession of such sentences is monotonous and ineffective. Usually one of the clauses can be subordinated.

Ineffective: There was nothing too much to do between Christmas and New Year's, but I managed to attend a few good movies during this time. New Year's Eve wasn't too exciting either, and there were only the same old things to do. The "old gang" was together, more or less, and we had a fairly good time. Most of my old friends who were not attending college seemed immature, but I guess they will improve with time. All in all, it was nice to go home, but I certainly enjoyed seeing the campus again.

37c. Avoid the overuse of <u>so</u> as a conjunction.

Even though *so* is correctly used as a conjunctive adverb with a semicolon preceding, and even though it is frequently used between independent clauses with only a comma before it, the chief objection to *so* in such constructions is simply *overuse*. Whether the word is *so* or any other word, overuse is ineffective. In constructions like those below, *so* can often be replaced by *therefore, thus, accordingly,* and the like, or predication may be reduced.

Ineffective: He had to study, *so* he did not attend the game.
The bridge was out on Highway 40, *so* we had to make a long detour on Route 28.

Improved: He had to study; therefore he did not attend the game.
Having to study, he did not attend the game.
Since the bridge was out on Highway 40, we had to make a long detour on Route 28.

In correcting the overuse of *so*, guard against a worse error, that of using another conjunctive adverb with a comma before it and thus writing an unjustifiable comma splice (see Section 32).

Wrong: The bridge was out on Highway 40, therefore we had to make a long detour on Route 28.

Sometimes *so* is misused when the writer means *so that* or *in order that:*

Ineffective: Shorter assignments are given *so* more students can master them.

> Do people want the government to spend more money *so* they can pay higher taxes?

Improved: Shorter assignments are given *so that* more students can master them.

> Do people want the government to spend more money *in order that* they can pay higher taxes?

37d. Avoid false coordination: do not join a relative clause to its principal clause by <u>and</u>, <u>but</u>, or <u>or</u>.

Remember that *coordinate* means "of equal rank." An independent clause, therefore, cannot be joined to a dependent clause by a coordinating conjunction. *And, but, or,* and other coordinating conjunctions connect only elements that are equal in rank.

The most frequent violation of this principle is the so-called "and which" construction. Do not use *and which, but which, and who, but who,* etc., unless there is a preceding "which clause" or "who clause" coordinate with it.

Wrong: He showed much energy at first, *but which* soon vanished.

> Tompson is a man of intelligence, *and who* is an industrious worker.

> I do not trust Henry, *or whom* I should like to have as a close friend.

> This is a beautiful golf course, *and which* you will enjoy playing on during your college years.

The simplest method of correcting these sentences is to omit the conjunctions, but remember to apply the principle of punctuation regarding restrictive and nonrestrictive clauses (Section **88m**).

Revised: He at first showed much energy, which soon vanished.

> Tompson is a man of intelligence who is also an industrious worker.

> I do not trust Henry, whom I should not like to have as a close friend.

> This is a beautiful golf course on which you will enjoy playing during your college years.

Another method of correcting this error is the use of parallelism (Section **45**), by adding a "who clause" or "which clause" to be appropriately coordinate.

Revised: I do not trust Henry, whom I have come to know well and whom I should not like to have for a close friend.

> This is a beautiful golf course which is open only to students and on which you will enjoy playing during your college years.
>
> Tompson is a man who is intelligent and who is an industrious worker.

Sometimes such revision is wordy and ineffective, as in the last revised example. Made more concise, the sentence might read:

> A man of intelligence, Tompson is an industrious worker.
> or
> Tompson is intelligent and industrious.

37e. Avoid inaccurate coordination.

When independent clauses, or dependent clauses, or phrases are *genuinely* coordinated with other independent clauses, or dependent clauses, or phrases, use the exact coordinating conjunction that relates them. Do not use *and* if *but* is the exact word, *or* for *but,* and the like.

Inaccurate: I wanted to buy the coat, *but* (not *and*) I had no money. We had a flat tire, *or* (not *but*) we should have been here an hour ago.

EXERCISES

A. Rewrite the following sentences in order to eliminate improper co-ordination:

1. He returned to the dairy farm and asked Tess to marry him and she said she loved him but she could never marry him.
2. They walked for miles and miles but finally they were arrested and Tess was taken to jail, and she was tried, and then she was finally executed.
3. Golf tournaments last about 5 days, if you can continue to win, but if you lose you are assured of staying for at least 3 days, and then sometimes you can enter into what are called consolation matches.
4. I can be around a golf course and continue to play golf and there will be many chances for me to go to different towns and states to play in tournaments.
5. To go out when one should study is one of the worst habits a new student has, therefore one that he has to work the hardest to improve.

6. Aurora, Indiana, is located on the banks of the Ohio River, and it is thirty miles west of Cincinnati, Ohio.
7. Father taught school for a while, then went into the insurance business.
8. I've had a bad day: my math recitation wasn't so hot this morning; our lunch wasn't so hot; then my score on the golf course wasn't so hot, either.
9. Then in a few years there was to be a state road come through one of the towns down close to the river; every one thought it would come through our town; instead it went through another town.
10. In 1801 Springfield was planned, and in 1818 Clark County was created, and in 1827 Springfield was incorporated.
11. The most unusual author is a mother of a teen-ager and a housewife.
12. My brother and I have eye trouble, but we both wear glasses.
13. The train home was crowded, and we stood all the way.
14. The students choose their own subjects, or they report on things they are interested in.
15. We had a good time dancing, then came back to the dormitory.

B. Rewrite the following sentences in order to eliminate the overuse of *so*. Use different methods.

1. The fish were not biting so we came home early.
2. There are many art courses offered so I shall have a wide choice.
3. We had a test every week, so we reviewed constantly.
4. The melodies of the mountains are simple, so they are easily remembered.
5. I was the only one with a car, so I was chosen to transport the group.
6. Many of my friends were home from other colleges, so we had several enjoyable reunions.
7. I don't believe in working all the time, so I'm going to have a two weeks' vacation in September.
8. There was a good movie at one of the theaters so we decided to go.
9. This got to be very boring so I changed jobs the next week.
10. We couldn't find a restaurant so we ate in a sandwich shop.
11. I have bought all my books, so I am ready to begin classes.
12. I never did like English as a subject, so I got started on the wrong foot.
13. None of us could do any studying, so we sat around and discussed the coming game.

14. My first camera was inadequate, so I have been adding to my equipment.
15. My new roommate and I have no major differences, so we should get along quite well.

FAULTY SUBORDINATION

38. Like appropriate coordination, appropriate subordination contributes to clear and effective writing by showing the relationship of less important to more important ideas.

Careful, thoughtful writing contains much subordination. The good writer recognizes that not all of his ideas deserve equal rank, and he judiciously places them in constructions which correspond to their importance. Thus he writes sentences which are unified and effective. His thoughts are more clearly communicated to his readers, for they can see what the relationship of the sentence elements actually is.

The careful writer will avoid excessive and faulty coordination (see Section **37**), but in so doing he should also avoid making errors in excessive and faulty subordination. Reducing predication (see Section **44a**) requires thoughtful care; the writer must be certain that he knows exactly the relationships of his ideas so that his reader is also made aware of exactly the same relationships.

38a. Avoid putting a coordinate idea in a subordinate form.

Inaccurate: My older brother was heavy and slow, *while* my sister was lithe and active.

                Born in Canada in 1900, he became an American citizen in 1925.

                I called to my pouting sister, *though* she refused to answer.

To make these sentences and others like them more effective, change the subordinating conjunction to a coordinating conjunction, or otherwise coordinate the ideas:

More effective: My older brother was heavy and slow, *but* my sister was lithe and active.

                He was born in Canada in 1900, *but* he became an American citizen in 1925.

                I called to my pouting sister, *but* she refused to answer.

38b. Avoid putting the main idea of a sentence into a subordinate construction, or a subordinate idea into a main clause.

Upside-down subordination exists when an idea of lesser importance is put in an independent clause, and the really important idea is put in a dependent clause or phrase. The writer has not evaluated the worth of his statements, and the reader attaches undue importance to a subordinate idea. It is sometimes difficult, however, to determine which *is* the subordinate idea, and the writer should give careful consideration to the problem from the point of view of his reader. Often the most dramatic incident and the effect, rather than the cause, are major ideas; preliminaries, such as time and place, and attendant circumstances are minor—subordinate—ideas.

Ineffective: We were getting tired of walking when we decided to hail a taxicab.

              I saw the truck heading straight toward me, when I was unable to move, from fear.

Improved: Since we were getting tired of walking, we decided to hail a taxicab.

              Although I saw the truck heading straight toward me, I was unable to move, from fear.

38c. Avoid excessive subordination.

Sentences which contain a series of overlapping subordinate statements are not effective. In such a series, each clause or phrase depends upon a preceding clause or phrase. Sentence elements should be linked appropriately, but they should not be built like an accordion, or, to vary the simile, like stairs, where each step is attached to the one just above.

Ineffective: These are inexpensive toys which have been made in Japan where there is cheap labor which depends upon American trade.

              I loved to watch the children who fed the squirrels the nuts which were on sale at the corner stand that was near the park entrance.

EXERCISES

Rewrite the following sentences, correcting the faulty subordination.

1. Whitefish Bay is eight miles north of Milwaukee, having a population of about 12,000 people.

2. I was just drifting off to sleep when my roommate rushed in yelling "We've been pledged!"

3. As the lightning struck the house, Mother was talking on the telephone.

4. Another of my fond memories is the old jalopy which I bought for $25.00 from the man who has a gas station near Tilton where I took the bus that took me to high school.

5. I was not driving fast through the intersection when a policeman shouted "Stop!"

6. During my freshman year I am living in a rooming house which is owned by an elderly lady whose father was a college professor for some 50 years at Marion, which is the other teachers' college in the state supported by public funds.

7. Father had little resistance to disease, because when he contracted pneumonia he spent over 4 weeks in the hospital.

8. This unforgettable character was usually desperate, being out of work, and he had no money.

9. I saw him frequently, when he looked at me queerly, and with his eyes blinking.

10. We lost the last game by a close score in the last few seconds, when the coach rose from the bench, shaking his fist at the referee.

LOGICAL DEPENDENT CLAUSES

39. If you recognize the clearness and emphasis which proper subordination contributes to your sentences, you will use a large number of dependent clauses. But proper subordination is difficult and requires careful thinking. Errors in subordination are in part due to incorrectness, which causes a lack of both clearness and effectiveness. Therefore, make sure that you use dependent clauses correctly and clearly.

All dependent clauses have the functions of separate parts of speech—noun, adjective, adverb. To use one of them for another is like misusing the single-word parts of speech. Specifically, common errors include the following: adverbial clause used for noun clause, adverbial clause used as a substitute for a noun, and a complete sentence used for a noun clause or a noun.

39a. Do not use an adverbial clause as a noun clause.

When a noun clause is grammatically needed as the subject of a verb, the object of a verb, or a predicate nominative noun clause, do not use an adverbial clause in its place. *When, where, because* clauses are frequent offenders. The obvious correction: substitute a noun clause for the adverbial clause, or give the adverbial clause correct grammatical construction.

Dubious: *Because he had no money* was the reason Henry dropped out of school.
I see *where the paper says that colder weather is coming.*
The reason the airplane crashed was *because it had run out of gasoline.*

Correct: *That he had no money* was the reason Henry dropped out of school.
Henry dropped out of school *because he had no money.*
I *see that the paper says that colder weather is coming.*
The reason the airplane crashed was *that it had run out of gasoline.*
The airplane crashed *because it had run out of gasoline.*

For a discussion of the illogical "The reason is because . . ." error, see item 118, Section **70,** "Glossary of Faulty Diction."

39b. Do not use an adverbial clause in place of a single noun or noun phrase.

Similar to the errors mentioned in Section **39a** is the use of adverbial clauses for single nouns or noun phrases. Again, *when* and *where* clauses are the chief offenders in this type of incorrect subordination, especially in explanations or definitions.

To correct, substitute a single noun or a noun with modifiers for the adverbial clause, or change the construction to make the adverbial clause grammatically correct.

Dubious: Plagiarism is *where* you take the work of another and pass it off as your own.
Anemia is *when* the blood has certain deficiencies.
When you graduate from college is the time to take life seriously.

Correct: Plagiarism is the taking of another's work and passing it off as your own.
Plagiarism occurs when you take the work of another and pass it off as your own.

Anemia is a disease in which there are certain deficiencies in the blood.

When you graduate from college, you should take life seriously.

39c. Use a noun clause, not a sentence, as the subject or complement of _is_ and _was_.

To correct, make the sentence (independent clause) into a dependent clause by the use of the proper subordinating conjunction, usually *that,* or change the sentence into a correctly used adverbial clause, or reduce the independent clause to a phrase.

Dubious: I had sprained my ankle was the reason I could not go to the dance.

              Mary's only fault is she has a bad temper.

Correct: The reason I could not go to the dance was that I had sprained my ankle.

              I could not go to the dance because I had sprained my ankle.

              Mary's only fault is that she has a bad temper.

              Mary has only one fault: a bad temper.

A quoted sentence, however, may be used as a noun.

Correct: "Her little face is like a walnut shell" is a line from an English poem.

EXERCISES

A. Compose 12 original sentences, four each of which illustrate, respectively, noun clauses, adjective clauses, and adverbial clauses.

B. Rewrite the following sentences, correcting the misuse of dependent clauses:

1. The main reason I should like to go back to California is because my brother lives there.
2. The Reading Clinic is where I went for the information I desired.
3. Whether two people are in love or not is not decided by the law.
4. Another example of his constant teasing is when he pretends to be deaf.
5. One of the reasons I chose chemistry is because of my love of the subject.
6. Here is where I was surprised.

290

7. Just because you think that you know something doesn't mean that you shouldn't study.
8. One type of blind date is when neither the boy nor the girl knows each other.
9. The reason this is my favorite article is because I can understand the author's point of view.
10. At Colorado Springs is where we spent our vacation.
11. A contest is held where the best paper is chosen and is published in the campus newspaper.
12. About 11 o'clock was when we ran into the fog.
13. The reason I say this is because we have many relatives in that country.
14. The time we miss someone the most is when we are separated from them.
15. The reason Joe is my favorite athlete, I suppose, is because I am biased.
16. Right then is when I started believing in that superstition.
17. Because I have red hair and freckles causes me a lot of teasing.
18. College is where many lasting friendships are formed.
19. The best time to teach young people to swim is when they are very young.
20. The reason small children learn to swim faster than adults is because they do not fear the water.

WORD ORDER

40. In highly inflected languages—where nouns, adjectives, adverbs, and verbs have varied and distinguishing, identifying endings, the relationships of words are usually shown by these endings. Our English language is not highly inflected. Consequently, clearness very often depends in part or solely upon the position of words in a sentence.

A writer should correctly place related words together so that the reader sees their connection and is not misled. It is especially important to place every modifier as close as possible to the word that it modifies.

40a. Place clearly such words as <u>only</u>, <u>not</u>, <u>even</u>, <u>hardly</u>, <u>scarcely</u>, etc.

Words like *only, not, even, hardly, scarcely, today, tomorrow*, as well as other words like correlative conjunctions, *both—and, neither—nor, either—or, not only—but also,* should be clearly placed in a sentence so that they convey precisely the meaning the writer intends.

Consider the difference in meaning of the following:

> I was invited to a luncheon today.
> I was today invited to a luncheon.

> My first teacher's name was Rosemary.
> My teacher's first name was Rosemary.

Or consider how *only* changes the meaning when its position is varied in the same sentence:

> *Only* the teacher told me to write a theme of 300 words.
> The *only* teacher told me to write a theme of 300 words.
> The teacher *only* told me to write a theme of 300 words.
> The teacher told *only* me to write a theme of 300 words.
> The teacher told me *only* to write a theme of 300 words.
> The teacher told me to write *only* a theme of 300 words.
> The teacher told me to write a theme *only* of 300 words.
> The teacher told me to write a theme of *only* 300 words.
> The teacher told me to write a theme of 300 words *only.*

Words like *only* are usually associated with the word or phrase immediately preceding or following. Even when there is no confusion, effectiveness is better served when *only* is placed in its proper place:

Less effective: Henry *only* wanted to borrow 10 dollars.
              I *only* have 2 days left to finish my packing.
More effective: Henry wanted to borrow *only* 10 dollars.
              I have *only* 2 days left to finish my packing.

40b. Place clearly phrases and clauses.

The suggestions about placing words clearly (see Section **40a**) apply also to phrases and clauses. In general, place phrases and clauses as nearly as possible to the words they modify, if there is the slightest chance of confusion. Obviously, writers of the following did not mean what their sentences say:

> A few years ago the White House in Washington was closed for alterations to visitors.

I decorated our Christmas tree with our family.
We all put our presents under the tree, which we had wrapped up the night before.

Nor did these newspaper advertisers really mean what their printed words conveyed:

LOST—A green lady's purse on Main Street last Friday.
WANTED—An apartment by a young couple freshly painted and newly plastered.

Sometimes, rephrasing is necessary:

A few years ago the White House in Washington was closed to visitors while alterations were being made.
We all put our presents, which we had wrapped up the night before, under our Christmas tree.

40c. Avoid a "squinting modifier."

"Squinting," in one sense, means "looking in two directions at once." A modifier is said to be *squinting* when it refers to either of two parts of a sentence, what has gone before or what has followed. The inevitable result is ambiguity: just which of two possible meanings did the writer want his reader to accept?

For clearness, move the modifier and include it with the material it qualifies. If the sentence is still awkward, rewrite it. Punctuation may also help (see Section **88k**), but it is not a safe guide.

Ambiguous: Most boys who have the name John *somewhere along the line* get a nickname.
               All the family sat still *momentarily* with a surprised look on their faces.
Clear: Most boys who have the name John get a nickname somewhere along the line.
               All the family momentarily sat still, with a surprised look on their faces.
               All the family sat still, with a surprised look, momentarily, on their faces.

EXERCISES

Revise the following sentences so as to remove any lack of clearness or effectiveness due to faulty word order:

1. All of us have watched my little sister develop into a healthy little girl with a great amount of pride.
2. After wandering around Chicago for three hours, I was found nearly starved to death by my mother.
3. Mary only has been studying music for 2 years.
4. I am trying to say what I mean more clearly.
5. Indianapolis is not one of the largest cities in the world situated on navigable water.
6. Our town was moved to a new location on the Pennsylvania Railroad, which was called West Lincoln.
7. The theatre will only seat about 250 people.
8. My uncle keeps the trophies and ribbons that he has won with his Holstein cattle on the second floor.
9. The boys did not want to eat grape jelly, which they disliked all winter.
10. We cooked our food in the kitchenette which we bought at a local grocery.
11. Don, our hired hand, comes to work after breakfast on the tractor.
12. Every year there are many mothers who have babies between the ages of 16 and 20 years.
13. I have only been in 4-H work for 6 years.
14. I became conscious of an old man with a beard about a block behind.
15. I met my present girl friend when I came home last winter from a dance on a streetcar.
16. This diploma from Penn State University, which belongs to my father, was granted in 1934.
17. My roommate's father is one of the six men in the world that was shot down twice and survived.
18. I slept at the boy's house that drove me home.
19. At the practice house, a few girls have to manage the whole house from balanced meals to house cleaning on a very small budget.
20. I saw him strike the telephone post with my own eyes.

DANGLING MODIFIERS

41. Dangling modifiers are those which do not properly or clearly depend upon the right words. They are of two kinds: dangling verbal phrases and dangling elliptical clauses. Ambiguity and even ludicrousness frequently result from their use.

41a. Avoid dangling verbal phrases.

Dangling verbal phrases consist of participial, prepositional gerund, and infinitive phrases. Such a phrase dangles when (1) it has no substantive (i.e., noun or pronoun) to modify, or (2) the substantive is the wrong one. Usually the phrase begins the sentence or the independent clause. It should therefore logically modify the subject of the sentence or the clause. The most ludicrous examples are those in which a phrase expressing motion modifies a subject which is stationary, or a phrase expressing fixity modifies a moving subject.

Ludicrous: Walking through the main gate of the park, the swimming pool is just ahead. (Dangling participle)
           Turning the corner, the Post Office Building is seen. (Dangling participle)
           Standing at the intersection, the Greyhound bus roared by. (Dangling participle)
Incongruous: Hanging from the very top of the tree, Grandfather saw a robin's nest. (Dangling participle)
           Buried several inches under ground, our dog tried to locate the bone. (Dangling participle)

Not so serious but still to be avoided are less ludicrous and incongruous modifiers.

In preparing for a test, it is advisable to review thoroughly. (Dangling prepositional gerund phrase)

In business letters, the dangling *enclosed you* phrase is common —does it mean that *you* are enclosed?

Dangling: Enclosed with this letter you will find your membership card.
          Enclosed you will find an order blank.
          Enclosed please find a check for $7.85.
Improved: Enclosed with this letter is your membership card.
          You will find an order blank enclosed.
          A check for $7.85 is enclosed.
          I am enclosing a check for $7.85.

The dangling infinitive phrase is less frequent and incongruous, partly because a writer usually uses, or has in mind, an adverbial *in order to* phrase. Many introductory infinitive phrases state or suggest purpose. Clearness and effectiveness are best served when such infinitive phrases depend upon the noun or pronoun indicating the one who has the purpose in mind.

Questionable: To succeed in life, ambition is necessary.
To play golf well, a good set of clubs is needed.
Improved: To succeed in life, a man must have some ambition.
To play golf well, you need a good set of clubs.

Sentences containing dangling verbal phrases may be corrected in several ways: (1) expand the verbal phrase to a dependent clause; (2) supply the noun or pronoun which the phrase should modify; (3) place the phrase so near the proper substantive that there can be no confusion.

Correct and clear: Walking through the main gate of the park, I saw the swimming pool just ahead.
After you walk through the main gate of the park, the swimming pool is just ahead.

Turning the corner, you will see the Post Office Building.
Just as you turn the corner, the Post Office Building appears.

Standing at the intersection, we saw the Greyhound bus roar by.
As we stood at the intersection, the Greyhound bus roared by.

Grandfather saw a robin's nest hanging from the very top of the tree.

Hanging from the very top of the tree, a robin's nest can be seen.

Our dog tried to locate the bone which was buried several inches under ground.

Buried several inches under ground, the bone baffled all attempts of our dog to find it.

In preparing for a test, a student should review thoroughly.
When a student is preparing for a test, it is advisable to review thoroughly.

> If you want to play golf well, you should have a good set of clubs.

Occasionally, even an introductory preposition phrase is dangling:

> After graduation from high school, my father asked about my future plans.
>
> Better: After I graduated from high school, my father asked about my future plans.
>
>   After graduation from high school, I was asked by my father about my future plans.

Participal phrases tacked on to the end of a statement with *thus, thereby,* and *therefore* are also dangling because they have no noun or pronoun to modify. Clearness is served if these dangling modifiers are removed by (1) making the participle a member of a compound predicate, or (2) rephrasing the sentence.

> Questionable: I was ill for several weeks, thus causing me to fall behind in my work.
>
>   We lost the last game of the season, thereby preventing us from going to the Rose Bowl.
>
> Improved: I was ill for several weeks and thus fell behind in my work.
>
>   We lost the last game of the season and were thereby prevented from going to the Rose Bowl.
>
>   My several weeks' illness caused me to fall behind in my work.
>
>   Our loss in the last game of the season prevented us from going to the Rose Bowl.

When a verbal phrase is used to specify a general action it is not considered a dangling modifier:

> Approved: Generally speaking, tuition fees should not be increased.

Such words or phrases as *considering, concerning, according to, owing to,* etc., are used prepositionally, not as verbals. Thus, *"Considering* everything, the proposal was fair" is a correct and clear sentence.

41b. Avoid dangling elliptical clauses.

Ellipsis means an omission. An elliptical clause, usually a dependent clause, is one from which the subject or verb, or both, have been left out. The reader understands what they are, for presumably they are the same as those in the independent clause.

Clear: When [. . .] in New York last month, we visited the United Nations Building.
When [we were] in New York last month, we visited the United Nations Building.

The *dangling* elliptical clause is one in which the understood subject and predicate are *not the same* as those of the main clause. The usual offenders are clauses introduced by *before, after, while, when, though,* and *if.*

As from dangling verbal phrases, ambiguity and ludicrousness result from dangling elliptical clauses:

Before warmed up, you should never race a motor.
While studying last evening, the lights went out.
When 6 years old, my grandmother died.
Though failing the course, my instructor kept giving me encouragement.

Two ways of correcting dangling elliptical clauses are the following: (1) insert in the dependent clause the subject and verb or verb-part needed to make the sentence clear, or (2) change the subject or subject-verb in the independent clause so that it, or they, would be clear logically, if they were also expressed in the dependent clause.

Clear: Before it is warmed up, you should never race a motor.
Before warmed up, a motor should never be raced.

While I was studying last evening, the lights went out.
While studying last evening, I found myself suddenly in darkness; the lights had gone out.

When I was 6 years old, my grandmother died.
When 6 years old, I grieved because my grandmother had died.

Though I was failing the course, my instructor kept giving me encouragement.
Though failing the course, I was given constant encouragement by my instructor.

EXERCISES

A. In each of the following sentences there is a dangling phrase. Correct each one twice, by using two of the three methods suggested in Section 41a, p. 295.

1. Bottled up in a small jar, I had several fine specimens of butterflies.
2. After spending three hours in the chemistry laboratory, Mother was waiting for me when I came out.
3. Saving my money for weeks, the motorcycle was finally purchased.
4. After winning a Homecoming football game, the alumni are very happy.
5. Enclosed you will find a check for $5.
6. Traveling on most state and national highways, the signs are a great deal of help.
7. After spending 18 months in the Army, Chicago certainly looked good on my return.
8. Having run off and gotten married, my parents were disappointed in my oldest sister.
9. Driving from New York, Philadelphia is about 90 miles.
10. After boiling for 20 minutes, I let the mixture cool slowly.
11. Going into the next room, your eye meets the portrait of the present president.
12. Being farmers, hogs and dairy cows are our main interest.
13. Leaving high school with fairly good grades, the principal recommended me for college.
14. After wandering through the woods all afternoon, my stomach told me that it was time to go home and eat.
15. Taking the pills every day, the doctor soon had me well.
16. Falling over the cliff, you will notice a tremendous waterfall.
17. Being electric, I find it easy to be awakened by my alarm clock.
18. After eating my breakfast, Father told me of the day's plans.
19. Having this kind of woman for a wife, she will be a great help to any man's success.
20. Being new here at college, the traditions are somewhat confusing.

B. Directions given in Exercise A.

1. Besides being dangerous, I am not a skillful driver at high speeds.
2. By using common sense in driving, many accidents can be avoided.
3. Seeing the car was out of gas, it was pushed to the next service station.

4. Before choosing a college, a catalog should be sent for.
5. By having a college education, the chances for securing a good job are numerous.
6. Upon arriving on the campus, everything seemed strange.
7. Being unfamiliar with the university, the dean and his secretary helped me very much.
8. Having completed our placement tests, our programs for the first semester were made out.
9. Going to class for the first time, the stairway seemed awfully steep.
10. After being out of school a year and a half, it is kind of hard to get back into the swing of things.
11. Being a student at this university, spare time is a very rare thing.
12. In pledging a fraternity, certain duties are assumed.
13. After reading the directions carefully, the experiment seemed quite easy to do.
14. October 26, 1953, terminated my service, being honorably discharged.
15. In attempting to learn to spell, the textbook was a great help.
16. Weighing only 150 pounds, football was a rugged game.
17. Driving on past the sign, the stadium appeared.
18. After saying "hello" to everyone, a big dinner is next on the program.
19. Our farm is three miles from town, going north.
20. I watched three men working like beavers putting bricks on top of each other.

C. Correct each of the dangling elliptical clauses in the following sentences by using for each the two methods suggested in Section **41b**, p. 297.

1. When thoroughly stewed, even an invalid will enjoy our prunes. [From an advertisement of a fruit company.]
2. While reading through the magazine, there were several articles that had an eye-catching appeal.
3. When building a drive mechanism, common sense is required.
4. If choosing a summer camp, the cost must be considered.
5. When in New York, my eyes were constantly on top of the skyscrapers.
6. Thoroughly tired, Sunday morning is a good time to stay in bed.
7. When living at home, it is often difficult to study.
8. When studying, it is easy for the mind to wander.
9. If taught the proper method in high school, my problems in college would not be so complex.

10. When in grade school, my teachers did not stress English as they should have.
11. While serving the dessert, one of the pies slid off the tray.
12. When entering a restaurant, the bill of fare is presented.
13. His manners, though well-bred, were not inviting.
14. While showing my livestock at the state fair, the judges complimented me on my exhibit.
15. When in the air, the fields and farms look like a checkerboard.

SPLIT CONSTRUCTIONS

42. So far as correctness is concerned, there is nothing wrong or incorrect about the separation or "splitting" of closely related materials. From the point of view of the reader, the objection is one of clearness and, even more, of effectiveness.

English is not a highly inflected language (Section **40**), and since many English words show little if any inflectional change, it is important to keep logically related elements together. Writers sometimes unnecessarily separate closely related elements, and the result is awkwardness and ambiguity, not clearness and effectiveness.

Closely related parts in a sentence are verbs in a verb phrase, coordinate sentence elements, subject and predicate, verb and object, verb and complement, preposition and object, the two parts of an infinitive, and any other word combinations that logically belong together.

42a. Do not needlessly separate the parts of a verb phrase.

When more than one verb word is involved, the normal verb phrase in English consists of the auxiliary verb and the main verb. Apply the tests of smoothness and logic, clearness and effectiveness in separating these verb forms:

Awkward: I never *shall see* his like again.
          I *shall see* never his like again.
          I *shall see* his like never again.
Effective: I *shall never see* his like again.

Whenever it is possible, however, keep the parts of a verb phrase together, particularly when long phrases or clauses do the splitting.

Awkward: This tree *has,* although you would not think so, *been* here for 80 years.

Improved: Although you would not think so, this tree *has been* here for 80 years.

Awkward: He *is,* despite many objections from his parents, *going* to study music and painting.

Improved: He *is going* to study music and painting despite many objections from his parents.

                Despite many objections from his parents, he *is going* to study music and painting.

42b. Place coordinate sentence elements together.

When two coordinate phrases or two coordinate dependent clauses are used in a sentence, one should not come at the beginning and the other at the end. For effectiveness keep them together and indicate their relationship by the appropriate coordinating conjunction.

Ineffective: *Although he was a good tennis player,* he was not able to make the varsity squad, *although he practiced daily.*

Effective: *Although he was a good tennis player* and *although he practiced daily,* he was not able to make the varsity squad.

Ineffective: *With fair weather,* we should have an enjoyable fishing trip, *with good luck.*

Effective: *With fair weather* and *good luck,* we should have an enjoyable fishing trip.

42c. Avoid unnecessary separation of subject and predicate, verb and object, verb and complement, preposition and object, or other closely related sentence elements.

On occasion, greater clearness may be achieved by separation, as suggested in "Word Order" (Section 40), or greater clearness and smoothness, as in this sentence, where verb and object are split in the improved version:

Vague: In his remarks the psychologist discussed everyday matters and people whom you and I know *as simply as a child.*

Improved: In his remarks the psychologist discussed, *as simply as a child,* everyday matters and people whom you and I know.

Such separation of closely related elements should be made for appropriate and specific purposes, never aimlessly.

42d. Avoid a widely split infinitive.

In some English verb constructions, the infinitive is used without its accompanying sign *to;* in many other verb constructions, the sign of the infinitive *to* is necessary. When words or phrases or even clauses come between the *to* and the verb, the construction is called a *split infinitive.*

The construction has behind it the example and practice of many reputable writers, but a study of these examples shows that in effective writing rarely is more than a single word—an adverb—used between *to* and the verb. In "He failed to *entirely* pay for it," *entirely* is properly and effectively placed next to the verb pay, which it modifies. To place it after *failed* or after *pay* or even after *it* would result in a confusing or awkward construction.

Whenever a split infinitive occurs in your writing, let clearness, naturalness, and effectiveness be the tests for its use. Rarely clear, or natural, or effective is the use of a phrase or a clause as a separating element.

Ineffective: Our family physician telegraphed us *to* as soon as possible *come.*

Improved: Our family physician telegraphed us *to come* as soon as possible.

EXERCISES

Point out and correct all faulty split constructions in the following sentences.

1. I would like to merely and in a few simple words make a few statements about my high school training.
2. My roommate, after a year in college, had, in many different ways, improved.
3. If the coach gives his permission, we can play 36 holes of golf this afternoon, if it does not rain.
4. Jane did all she could to subtly and without showing any intention of doing it vex, cut, and embarrass her rival for the title of Beauty Queen.
5. No one in my community has ever in all these years known such a dry summer.
6. Because it was raining, I did not like to go fishing, because the fish would not bite well.

303

7. Such pleasant memories of my first college year I am not likely to now or ever soon forget.

8. All the members of Eta Kappa Nu were, in the opinion of all their teachers, considered brilliant students.

9. During our visit to Mexico, we found that when the sun sets, the air becomes cooler, when the evening breezes blow.

10. I have found that it is sometimes possible to without much forethought and with some haste in the writing compose a good theme.

TRANSITION

43. Individual sentences may be correct, clear, effective, and appropriate, and yet be neither clear nor effective when they are put together in a paragraph. If the order of the sentences within the paragraph is fully logical, then any lack of clearness probably is due to faulty *transition*. Remember that *transition* means passing from one place, state, or position to another, and that *evidence of transition* consists of linking or bridging devices. As applied to writing, there are three degrees of transition: between paragraphs (discussed in Section 28), within the sentence, and between sentences (discussed in this section). When used within the sentence, transitional devices usually come between clauses; when used between sentences, they occupy a position near or at the beginning or the end of the sentences they link.

Our own processes of thought are so familiar to us that we are likely to forget that our readers do not understand quite so readily and fully as we do the exact relations of our ideas. The writer's thoughts not only must progress logically; they must be *marked* so plainly that the reader can readily grasp both them and their interrelations. Only thus can effective communication be achieved.

43a. Make sentence transitions clear by using transitional words and phrases.

Transitional words and phrases are not needed within or between all sentences, and your best guide is consideration for your reader: have you made the relationship between your ideas evident to him?

Review the discussion concerning paragraph transition (Section 28a): the purpose and examples of transitional words and phrases. Most of these purposes and examples apply to transition between clauses and transition between sentences.

1. Between dependent and independent clauses, the subordinating conjunctions are evidence of relationships: *after, although, though, as, because, before, for, if, lest, in order that, so that, since, than, till, until, unless, when, whenever, where, wherever, whereas, whether, while,* etc.

2. Between independent clauses or between sentences, evidence of relationships is expressed by

the simple or pure conjunctions: *and, but, or, nor, neither, yet;*
the correlative conjunctions: *both . . . and, neither . . . nor, either . . . or, not only . . . but also;*
the conjunctive or parenthetic adverbs: *besides, however, nevertheless, therefore, thus, so, consequently, hence, likewise, furthermore, still, also, then, moreover, otherwise, meanwhile,* etc.

For a comparative table of conjunctions, giving their meaning and grammatical uses, see pages 582, 583.

3. Other words and phrases for sentence transition include *in addition, in fact, as a result, indeed, again, afterward, as I said, fortunately, here, in short, now, of course, naturally, on the contrary, soon, temporarily, truly, well, more than, most of all, too,* etc.

In the use of these transitional words and phrases, remember that the beginnings and endings of sentences are emphatic positions, and effective writing demands variety in the position of these inconspicuous but necessary materials.

Special care should be taken when you move from your own writing to quoting or phrasing others' materials. Examples:

. . . As Abraham Lincoln said, in his "Address at Gettysburg," ". . . ." The result is that . . .

Certain lines from Shakespeare's *Julius Caesar* well summarize this philosophy:

In considering ideals over and beyond our vocational activities, let us remember the Bible verse concerning man's need to live by more than bread alone.

. . . This point is well illustrated in the following sentence from Matthew Arnold's essay, "Literature and Science": . . . As a result, we can apply . . .

43b. Make sentence transitions clear by repetition.
The most effective kind of repetition for sentence transitions is

the use of pronouns referring to preceding nouns and pronouns. Synonyms are also effective. Occasionally, too, key or important words can be repeated in several sentences, but this kind of repetition (see Section **68**) for sentence transition is not nearly so effective as it is for paragraph transition.

Study carefully the following sentences from the first two paragraphs of Thomas Henry Huxley's "The Method of Scientific Investigation." Note how the italicized words illustrate the various devices for sentence transition, discussed above.

The method of scientific investigation is nothing but the expression of the necessary mode of working of the human mind. *It* is *simply* the *mode* at which all phenomena are reasoned about, rendered precise and exact. . . .

You will understand *this better, perhaps, if* I give *you* some familiar example. *You* have all heard it repeated, *I* dare say, that *men of science* work by means of *induction and deduction, and* that by the help of *these operations, they,* in a sort of sense, wring from nature certain *other* things which are called natural laws and causes, and that out of *these,* by some cunning skill of *their* own, *they* build up hypotheses and theories. *And* it is imagined by many that the operations of the common mind can be *by no means* compared with *these processes, and* that *they* have to be acquired by a sort of special apprenticeship to the craft. To hear *all these* large words *you* would think that the *mind* of *a man of science* must be constituted differently from *that* of *his* fellow men; *but if you* will not be frightened by terms, *you* will discover that *you* are quite wrong, *and* that *all these* terrible apparatus are being used by *yourselves* every day and every hour of *your* lives.

43c. Avoid inexact transition.

Use transitional words and phrases as necessary, but use them correctly. Inexact transition is the equivalent of inexact diction (see Section **60**).

Inexact: He did not get the telegram before he left *whereas* it was delivered late.

                I wanted to study architecture, *and* my father wanted me to become a lawyer.

                I know I forgot to pay the bill *whereupon* I have the money in my pocket.

                My roommate wished to spend Christmas vacation in

Florida; *on the other hand,* his parents also wanted him to go.

Improved: He did not get the telegram before he left *because* it was delivered late.

I wanted to study architecture, *but* my father wanted me to become a lawyer.

I know I forgot to pay the bill, *for* I *still* have the money in my pocket.

My roommate wished to spend Christmas vacation in Florida; *fortunately,* his parents also wanted him to go.

43d. Avoid labored and artificial transition in sentences.

The suggestion concerning paragraph transition (Section **28**) about making transitions relatively brief and inconspicuous applies to sentence transition. The major purpose is, of course, to show relationship and the direction of the relationship; a secondary but not unimportant aim is to make evident this relationship smoothly, skillfully, unobtrusively, effectively.

In the first example transitions are needed between short choppy sentences:

Baseball is said to be the national game; I do not like it. If it is the national game, thousands must enjoy watching it, or playing it. I know people who do not ever attend a game; I know people who see as many as 50 games a year. I should not make a dogmatic statement about the appeal of the sport; I have never witnessed a game.

In his first revision, the student inserted transitional words and phrases—here italicized—at the beginning of each sentence or independent clause, as follows:

Baseball is said to be the national game; *however,* I do not like it. *Yet* if it is the national game, thousands must enjoy watching it, or playing it. *To be sure,* I know people who do not ever attend a game; *on the other hand,* I know people who see as many as 50 games a year. *Perhaps* I should not make a dogmatic statement about the appeal of the sport; *you see,* I have never witnessed a game.

After reviewing Section **48,** "Position and Arrangement," and Section **49,** "Variety," and letting pronouns and repetition serve as part of the transition devices, the student produced this more acceptable revision. Note the greater clearness and smoothness caused by the italicized words:

Although baseball is said to be America's national game, I do not like *it. Yet* if *it* is the *national game,* hundreds must enjoy playing the *game* and thousands must enjoy watching *it.* I know people who see as many as 50 or 60 *games* a season and who drive many miles to see *them;* on the other hand, I know people who never attend a *game* and who wouldn't walk across the street to see *one. Perhaps* it is all a matter of *sporting* taste, *and perhaps* I should not make a dogmatic statement about the appeal of *baseball. You see,* I have never seen a *game, and* I prefer a *sport* that I can take part in, peacefully, quietly, badly perhaps, and without "fan"-fare. *I prefer* golf.

EXERCISES

A. Use better connectives for the inexact ones in the following sentences:

1. I did not recite well that day, yet I had not studied my lesson.
2. We don't know yet as we can go.
3. Our fraternity secretary did not arrive by airplane because I was at the airport.
4. When we left the concert early, yet our friends stayed.
5. I was so sleepy when I finished studying until I just tumbled into bed.
6. Joe is not a good musician, while his parents do not encourage him to practice.
7. I asked my blind date to go to the movies and she wanted to go to the dance.
8. As an athlete Harry would not take good care of himself, whereas he contracted pneumonia.
9. We had hardly left town than we had a puncture.
10. The train left at noon, and I hurried to the station, where it was late.

B. Mark all the transitional words and phrases used in two paragraphs of an article in your book of readings. Try to read the sentences, omitting the transitional devices. Then discuss these transitional words and phrases by indicating their meaning and the purposes that they serve.

C. Repeat Exercise B, but apply the directions to an article in a current magazine.

CONCISENESS

44. *Conciseness* literally means "expressing much in a few words; brief and to the point." Logically, therefore, conciseness is primarily a problem in diction, or word use, and as such it is discussed in Section **67**. There the discussion concerns words and word combinations in phrases, such as avoidance of superfluous words, unnecessary repetition, reduction of wordy phrases, circumlocutions and euphemisms, and overuse of modifiers. Conciseness is also a problem in writing sentences.

A sentence may be complete and unified and yet be ineffective because it is wordy. A sentence of 100 words may be concise, and one of 20 may be wordy. No sentence can be effective when it contains too many words or ideas—or too few. Francis Bacon was probably the most concise of English writers (see pp. 98, 318) and somewhat difficult to understand for that reason.

In the clear and effective use of "how many words?" the golden mean of word number applies to parts of sentences, to sentences, to paragraphs, to whole themes. Its guiding suggestion: Do not use so many words that the meaning is lost in a forest of verbiage and do not use so few words that the meaning is obscured through brevity. In other words, do not use any more words than are necessary to express your meaning correctly, clearly, effectively, and appropriately. The problem, however, is not so much one of correctness and clearness; it is one of effectiveness. Wordiness—like long-windedness in speech—is never effective.

In addition to the advice concerning conciseness in word use (Section **67**), three suggestions apply specifically to sentences.

44a. Reduce predication.

At various places—in this handbook and by your instructor—you will be advised to *reduce predication*.

Reducing predication means reducing the number of words to make an assertion—cutting out all unnecessary words by making one word serve the purpose of two or three or more. For example, one synonym can replace several words without jeopardizing in any way the intended meaning. For clearness and effectiveness, a writer will

1. Combine two short sentences into one (see also Section 47):

From: I am a freshman in the School of Home Economics. I am specializing in Applied Design.

To: I am a freshman in the School of Home Economics, specializing in Applied Design.

2. Reduce a compound sentence to a complex or simple sentence:

From: Joe E. Brown has for years been an excellent comedian, and there isn't anyone who doesn't like Joe E. Brown.

To: Everyone likes Joe E. Brown, who has for years been an excellent comedian.

3. Reduce a complex sentence to a simple sentence:

From: Everyone likes Joe E. Brown, who has for years been an excellent comedian.

To: Everyone likes Joe E. Brown, for years an excellent comedian.

4. Reduce clauses to phrases (see preceding example also):

From: . . . a haze which resembled the color of smoke.

To: . . . a haze the color of smoke.

5. Reduce clauses and phrases to single words:

From: . . . waiting until I became frantic.

To: . . . waiting frantically.

From: . . . a haze the color of smoke.

To: . . . a smoke-colored haze.

6. Reduce two or more words to one:

From: . . . a member of a fraternity.

To: . . . a fraternity member.

From: . . . an instructor in the Department of Mathematics.

To: . . . a mathematics instructor.

From: . . . are going to attend.

To: . . . will attend.

Study the following series of reductions. In the first statement are 19 words. In the last statement are seven words. Has the last omitted any essential information not included in the first?

1. In the distance we could see the tops of the Rocky Mountains. These mountain tops were covered with snow.
2. In the distance we could see the tops of the Rocky Mountains, which were covered with snow.
3. In the distance we could see the Rocky Mountains, which were covered with snow.
4. In the distance we could see the Rocky Mountains, covered with snow.
5. In the distance we could see the snow-covered Rocky Mountains.
6. In the distance we saw the snow-covered Rocky Mountains.
7. We saw the distant, snow-covered Rocky Mountains.

44b. Avoid piling up unnecessary details.

This fault is called *prolixity*. A prolix sentence may be unified (see Section **34**), but it is ineffective because its details obscure or weaken the point of the main idea.

> Last summer the local junior golf tournament was won by my brother Harry with a set of golf clubs that he had purchased two years before from a friend of mine who had bought a new set and who sold the boy his old clubs at a bargain price.

Freed of unnecessary details, this sentence says:

> Last summer my brother Harry won the local junior golf tournament with a second-hand set of clubs.

44c. Avoid the useless repetition of an idea.

This fault is called *tautology*. Frequently, a writer who is not thinking carefully will repeat an idea, for no purpose, in different words.

> I was very anxious for him to succeed and eager that he do so. This absolutely new and novel innovation will please them; they will like it very much.

EXERCISES

A. Choose any three paragraphs of explanation in this handbook. Do these paragraphs violate the principles of conciseness? If they do, what are your suggestions for condensation? Send your suggestions to one of the authors in a business letter (see pp. 709–732).

B. Look up in a good dictionary the following nouns: *redundancy, tautology, circumlocution, verbosity, verbiage, periphrasis, prolixity, ple-*

onasm, diffuseness, terseness, succinctness, curtness, brevity, sententious-ness.

C. From your reading find one or two examples, each, for six of the terms in Exercise B.

D. Look up in a good dictionary the following adjectives: *concise, terse, laconic, succinct, pithy, summary, compendious, redundant, prolix.*

E. Examine several of your recent themes. Copy any wordy sentences or parts of sentences and under each write your concise revision.

F. Make more concise the wording of the following:

1. I come from Fountain City, Tennessee. It is a small town located on U.S. 29, just 9 miles south of Richmond, Tennessee.
2. Pictures of our city's industries were compiled into colorful booklets. These booklets were printed in many languages and distributed throughout the world.
3. As I recall our childhood friendships of those earlier childhood days, there were 10 of us who went, one Halloween evening, to pay a call upon Harold, our fellow-playmate, who had been sick and ailing for a long period of time.
4. My favorite sport is baseball. That is a wonderful sport for boys and a sport that keeps an athlete on his toes.
5. We now have a park that was opened not long ago. The land, not long ago, on which the park is now located, was once just a piece of wasteland and swamp that has since been drained.
6. It was a clear, sunny day without a rain cloud in the sky.
7. She was a great talker who spoke well and who often had a great deal to say on each and every possible occasion.
8. Anyone who knows anything about the young people of this day and age knows that the more tactfully and diplomatically they are handled, the better their social behavior will be as far as the other sex is concerned.
9. That side of the structure receives the morning sun but during the time that the sun is in the west and afternoon shadows begin to fall, it is dreary and cheerless.
10. I waited for the signal which would indicate that the hunt had begun, but the dogs with their barking and the horses with their stamping drowned out all other sounds and noises.

PARALLELISM

45. *Parallel*—a word from the field of mathematics—in its usual sense means two or more lines extending in the same direction and at the same distance apart at every point. Teachers of writing have adopted the words *parallelism* and *parallel* to mean "close resemblance, similarity"; that is, when two or more ideas in a sentence are related and serve a similar purpose, they can be phrased in the same grammatical form.

When not overused, parallel construction is an excellent device for correctness, clearness, and effectiveness. It shows the reader immediately what ideas are of equal importance; it helps the writer to make sentences grammatically correct; and, appropriately used, it is one means of attaining or contributing to an emphatic, vigorous style.

The simplest form of parallelism is two or more words in a series. Using more complex forms, the writer can make two or more phrases parallel, or two or more dependent clauses, or two or more independent clauses, or two or more sentences, or even two or more paragraphs.

Words:	Henry is *slow* but *thorough*.
	The American colors are *red, white,* and *blue*.
	My favorite boyhood activities were *hunting, fishing,* and *trapping*.
Phrases:	Both *at home* and *at school* Joe has his mind only on basketball.
	Every afternoon my grandfather is at the barber shop *telling yarns about his youth* or *hearing the yarns that his cronies tell*.
Dependent clauses:	I was desperate *when I arrived late on the campus* and *when I found there were no desirable rooms available*.
Independent clauses:	Julius Caesar's most famous statement was this: "*I came, I saw, I conquered*."
Sentences:	Alfred Lord Tennyson was the British poet who wrote lyrics in his early life and dramas in his closing years. Robert Browning was the British poet who wrote dramas in his early career and other forms of poetry in his later life.

As an effective test for true parallelism, draw lines under the parallel elements. Then draw a corresponding number of lines in parallel form and write the underlined words on these parallel lines. Examples from the illustrations above:

Every afternoon grandfather is at the barber shop

<u>telling yarns about his youth</u>

or

<u>hearing the yarns that his cronies tell.</u>

Julius Caesar's most famous statement was this: <u>I came</u>

<u>I saw</u>

<u>I conquered</u>

For clear and effective parallelism, apply the following principles:

45a. Sentence elements that are coordinate in rank should be parallel in structure.

An infinitive phrase should be coordinate with an infinitive phrase, a prepositional phrase with a prepositional phrase, a participial phrase with a participial phrase, a dependent clause with a similar dependent clause, an independent clause with an independent clause. The same general principle applies to other kinds of phrases and to similar kinds of words.

Wrong: He liked to row and playing tennis.
Right: He liked to row and to play tennis.
      or
      He liked rowing and playing tennis.

Wrong: Our Glee Club sings at many school functions, engagements in nearby towns, and concert tours.
Right: Our Glee Club sings at many school functions, has engagements in nearby towns, and makes other concert tours.

Wrong: An all-round student would like to make Phi Beta Kappa and that he might earn a varsity letter.
Right: An all-round student would like to make Phi Beta Kappa and to earn a varsity letter.
      or
      An all-round student has two ambitions: a Phi Beta Kappa key and a varsity letter.

Observe how a parallelism diagram helps to distinguish faulty parallelism from true parallelism:

He liked

to row	to row
and	and
playing tennis	to play tennis

Our Glee Club sings at

many school functions	sings at many school functions
engagements in near-by towns	has engagements in near-by towns
and	and
concert tours	makes other concert tours

An all-round student
would like

to make Phi Beta Kappa	to make Phi Beta Kappa
and	and
that he might earn a varsity letter	to earn a varsity letter

Absolute parallelism is naturally not always required. Although in the following the form is not parallel, the functions are. In the first example, the parallel elements are adverbial; in the second, three nouns (two proper and one common, with a modifier) are parallel.

> The second speaker talked *slowly* and *with a slight stammer.*
> I saw *John, Henry,* and *a man whom I have not met.*

45b. Sentence elements following correlative conjunctions should be parallel in form.

The four common pairs of correlative conjunctions are *both—and, either—or, neither—nor,* and *not only—but also* (see pp. 580 and 591, 592). Since these conjunctions coordinate and correlate similar ideas, each member of the pair should be followed *immediately* by exactly the same grammatical form—two similar words, two similar phrases, or two similar clauses.

Faulty: I *neither* have the time *nor* the inclination to play basketball.

Either you can cash your check at the bank *or* at the local bookstore.

The committee requests that you are *either* seated before the beginning of the concert *or* that you wait outside until the conclusion of the first number.

Improved: I have *neither* the time *nor* the inclination to play basketball.

You can cash your check *either* at the bank *or* at the local bookstore.

The committee requests *either* that you are seated before the beginning of the concert *or* that you wait outside until the conclusion of the first number.

Parallelism diagram:

```
I have neither the time
          nor   the inclination to play basketball
You can cash your check either at the bank
                          or     at the local bookstore
The committee requests either that you are seated before the beginning
                              of the concert
                       or     that you wait outside until the conclu-
                              sion of the first number
```

45c. Avoid ineffective partial parallelism.

In using the formula A, B, and C for a series of elements, make certain that the sentence elements are similar ideas and are parallel in form. If they are not, a faulty and unemphatic series will result.

Undesirable: The story is *vivid, interesting,* and *has a simple plot.*
Improved: The story is *vivid, interesting, simple in plot.*
                or
                The story is *simple, interesting,* and *vivid.*
Undesirable: Uncle James has worked *in the steel mills, ordnance plant, a factory,* and *kept a filling station.*
Improved: Uncle James has worked in *the steel mills, an ordnance plant,* and *a factory;* he has also kept a filling station.

Parallelism diagrams:

(Showing error)   The story is vivid
                                     interesting
                                     and
                                     has a simple plot

(Showing corrections)   Uncle James has worked in   the steel mills

                                                       an ordnance plant

                                                       and

                                                       a factory

                          he has also kept a filling station

45d. Avoid misleading parallelism.

Do not use the same structural form for sentence elements which
are not of equal value. Apparent parallelism misleads the reader in
two ways:

1. Certain ideas are arranged in parallel form, but only a little
study shows that they are neither parallel nor coordinate in content, that there is little logical relationship in the ideas expressed.
Example (second idea not related to first):

> We recently bought a radio with seven tubes and with a beautiful
> mahogany finish.

Example (third idea not parallel in thought with the first two
ideas):

> The speaker pointed out that college graduates have more earning
> power, enjoy a higher social status, and can be more accurately
> sampled in a survey of this kind than manual workers.

2. A series of elements may appear to modify the same element
when really not parallel. The fact that two phrases or two clauses
begin with the same words does not signify that they introduce
parallel elements or ideas. Apply the parallelism diagram as a test.

Wrong: *For your sake for 50 dollars* I will help you.
       It is important *that each of you bring along a prospective new
       member that you can whole-heartedly recommend.*
Clear: For your sake I will help you to the extent of 50 dollars.
       It is important that each of you bring along a prospective new
       member whom you can whole-heartedly recommend.

EXERCISES

A. Make parallelism diagrams for all parallel elements in the following passages, each of which is from the work of a master of English
prose:

1. The world will little note nor long remember what we say here, but it can never forget what they did here. It is for us, the living, rather, to be dedicated here to the unfinished work which they who fought here have thus far so nobly advanced. It is rather for us to be here dedicated to the great task remaining before us; that from these honored dead we take increased devotion to that cause for which they gave the last full measure of devotion; that we here highly resolve that these dead shall not have died in vain; that this nation, under God, shall have a new birth of freedom; and that government of the people, by the people, for the people, shall not perish from the earth.

—ABRAHAM LINCOLN, "Address at Gettysburg"

2. Studies serve for delight, for ornament, and for ability. Their chief use for delight, is in privateness and retiring; for ornament, is in discourse; and for ability, is in the judgment and disposition of business. For expert men can execute, and perhaps judge of particulars, one by one; but the general counsels, and the plots and marshalling of affairs, come best from those that are learned. To spend too much time in studies is sloth; to use them too much for ornament, is affectation; to make judgment wholly by their rules, is the humour of a scholar.

—FRANCIS BACON, "Of Studies"

3. It is the fate of those who toil at the lower employments of life to be rather driven by the fear of evil than attracted by the prospect of good; to be exposed to censure, without hope of praise; to be disgraced by miscarriage, or punished for neglect, where success would have been without applause, and diligence without reward. . . .

In this work, when it shall be found that much is omitted, let it not be forgotten that much likewise is performed, and, though no book was ever spared out of tenderness to the author, and the world is little solicitous to know whence proceeded the faults of that which it condemns, yet it may gratify curiosity to inform it, that the *English Dictionary* was written with little assistance of the learned, and without any patronage of the great; not in the soft obscurities of retirement, or under the shelter of academic bowers, but amidst inconvenience and distraction, in sickness and in sorrow. . . . I have protracted my work till most of those whom I wished to please have sunk into the grave, and success and miscarriage are empty sounds; I therefore dismiss it with frigid tranquillity, having little to fear or hope from censure or from praise.

—SAMUEL JOHNSON, "Preface to *A Dictionary of the English Language*"

B. Correct all errors in faulty parallelism in the following sentences by (a) changing the structure of the first element to agree with that of later ones, and then (b) changing the structure of later elements to agree with that of the first.

1. Making a living in a small town is easier than to make a living in a large city.
2. My youngest sister has blond hair, blue eyes, and a cute youngster.
3. At present I am a freshman in the College of Education, live in MacMillan Hall, and a member of the Future Teachers of America Club.
4. During vacation there was nothing to do but enjoy myself, have dates, parties, and just about everything that I did not have time for at college.
5. On Homecoming Day freshmen are on hand to help alumni with their luggage, their coats, and to show them around the dormitory.
6. I do not care to write home and having them criticize my poor writing habits.
7. Our dean of men and our dean of women are young, attractive, athletic, and can get along with parents and students.
8. A dog can be used for protection, for companionship, and to help with work.
9. Joe has been a coal miner, a waiter in a restaurant, a cab-driver in Chicago, and also has worked on the railroad.
10. Three of the more popular superstitions are, a black cat walking in a person's path, to break a mirror, and to walk under a ladder.
11. He told me to talk with the local city engineer and that he would give me all the help I needed.
12. During that summer I had the job of mowing the lawn and help with the garden.
13. I am 19 years of age, 5 feet 9 inches tall, weight 165 pounds, have grey eyes, and red hair.
14. In my senior year we wrote 16 themes, grammar usage, several class discussions, and had spelling.
15. I have marveled at the wonder of radio and that a person's voice could be transmitted from one place to another.
16. I appreciate the importance of attendance in class, and that it should be given preference over extracurricular activities.
17. The dictionary includes several general aids for spelling, grammar, and a list of common abbreviations.
18. Richard is planning on completing his education here at Atwater and then engage in farming.
19. I like to listen to music, play cards, dancing, camping, go sailing, and out with girls.
20. I'd better close now and hoping I'll hear from you very soon.

C. Correct all faulty parallelism in the construction of the sentence elements following the correlative conjunctions:

1. As a county agent, not only will I work with students, but also with adults.
2. Every summer the lake is filled with sailboats by people who are either sailing for pleasure or to get away from the heat.
3. This job was not only profitable to me in money, but also in experience.
4. Our tennis team has neither been state champions nor runners-up for the last 8 years.
5. When 11 o'clock comes, you are either too tired to do good work or you decide to go to bed and just forget it.
6. A good English background will both help you in your college English courses and in other courses.
7. Charleston is not only known for its industries, but also for its tourist trade.
8. After dinner we either play games, or we just sit and talk.
9. These terms not only concern the military field, but also chemistry, aeronautics, and medicine.
10. If you do not have a car, you will either find yourself walking or begging someone to give you a ride.
11. A careless driver both endangers his own life, and the life of others.
12. You not only live just for today, but also the future.
13. Our town not only has a large business district but also an extensive residential area.
14. We either go to the Youth Center or the Community House for our recreation.
15. With our many American and foreign students, this university is not only important to our country but also to many nations of the world.

CONSISTENCY

46. *Consistency* in the sentence means that the parts are in agreement, are similar, and must remain so unless there is good reason for shifting. In order to write appropriately and effectively, a writer should be consistent in the use of the following: tense, voice, and pronoun reference in number and person.

46a. Be consistent in the use of tense.

Tense (see Section 80), is the grammatical term meaning the time of the verb: present, past, future, present perfect, past perfect,

320

future perfect. Do not shift unnecessarily from one tense to another. The error is especially frequent in narrative and narrative exposition, when the writer shifts from past to present or from present to past, or back and forth between the two.

Inconsistent: My nearest approach to death came last summer. I was walking slowly down a little-traveled country road when an automobile came suddenly over the rise in the road. It dashes wildly down the road, careening and twisting as if its driver is crazy. I think he is going to strike me, and I jump across the ditch and over the fence. Thus, I saved my life.

Consistent: My nearest approach to death came last summer. I was walking slowly down a little-traveled country road when an automobile came suddenly over the rise in the road. It *dashed* wildly down the road, careening and twisting as if its driver *were* crazy. I *thought* he *was* going to strike me, and I *jumped* across the ditch and over the fence. Thus, I saved my life.

46b. Be consistent in the use of subject and voice in a sentence.

Voice is the grammatical term telling whether the subject of the sentence is acting (active voice) or is acted upon (passive voice). (See Section 81.) Writing is more effective if one voice, active or passive, is consistently used unless there is excellent reason for a shift. Consistency in voice also eliminates one of the major reasons for shifting from one subject to another in a compound or complex sentence.

Faulty: You should follow a budget, and much money will be saved. When a person approaches the Great Smoky Mountains, a blue haze can be seen in the distance.
Join the Navy and the world will be seen—through a porthole!
I asked a question but he made no reply.

Improved: You should follow a budget, and you will save much money. When a person approaches the Great Smoky Mountains, he can see a blue haze in the distance.
Join the Navy and see the world—through a porthole!
I asked a question but received no reply.

46c-d

In being consistent in the use of voice, consider also the application of the principles of effective coordination and subordination (Sections 37 and 38).

Effective: If you follow a budget, you will save much money.

46c.   Be consistent in the use of number.

Frequent errors in inconsistent use of number are shifts from singular nouns to plural nouns, or plural nouns to singular, or failure to make pronouns and antecedents agree in number (see Section 77).

Faulty: If *a college man* really works hard, *they* are bound to succeed.
Correct: If *a college man* really works hard, *he* is bound to succeed.
    If *college men* really work hard, *they* are bound to succeed.

46d.   Be consistent in the use of the class or person of pronouns.

The error here also involves a shift in pronoun reference and violates the general principle that pronouns and antecedents agree in person (see Section 77). The most frequent occurrence of the error is shifting from the third person to the inappropriate second person *you*.

Faulty: If *one* studies hard enough in high school, *you* will have no trouble with college subjects.
Correct: If *one* studies hard enough in high school, *he* will have no trouble with college subjects.

EXERCISES

Rewrite the following sentences, making them conform to the principles of consistency:

1. Many businessmen play golf because it is a game that takes your mind off your work.
2. You can enjoy beautiful country scenes and wild life in the country, and a lot more elbow room may be had. Pets may be more easily kept and taken care of, while privacy may be had, too.
3. A coach has to work only 9 months of the year, and the other 3 months can be spent fishing, hunting, or working in a boys' camp.
4. In Canada I hired a guide. They could neither read nor write.
5. If I flunked a test, I took the same test over until you passed it.

6. We wish to advise that we feel these chairs are quite wonderful. The writer is one of those who are blessed with an injured back and while other chairs have sent me home many times with a backache, we feel this model is the most comfortable chair that one has used. (From a testimonial letter)

7. I am glad to get a college education, for it will help you in your future life.

8. I was going to see my uncle in San Francisco, and he is going to take me to some interesting places there.

9. At most colleges and universities they have several requirements you must meet.

10. If you ever sleep in a dormitory, one has an experience that they will never forget.

11. As I approached the park, you could hear the band playing marching melodies.

12. A student must learn to take his adviser's advice. They will save both time and energy if they do.

13. Our city was once famous for dirt and grime; now it has smoke-abatement, and she has clean buildings and streets.

14. On the last day of our tour, most of us walked around and bought trinkets that would help them remember New York City.

15. The lecturer talked and talked until the bell rings and it is time for a change in classes.

16. If a student tries to engage in too many extracurricular activities, his assignments will be neglected.

17. Our class made a tour of Radio City, where the air-conditioning apparatus particularly amazed us.

18. Our dormitory adviser said we must study more; they will be giving you an examination in them soon.

19. Be careful to remove all rubbish from the cellar near the furnace, and the risk of fire will be greatly reduced.

20. Our fraternity was asked by the dean to have our attitude toward having so many dances explained.

CHOPPY SENTENCES

47. Avoid writing a series of short, jerky sentences.

An occasional short sentence is effective. A series of short sentences, however, conveys a sense of choppiness and jerkiness and violates principles of unity, clearness, and effectiveness. Such a series is monotonous; it gives undue emphasis to relatively unimportant ideas. To remove the error of short, choppy, jerky sentences, give careful thought to the relationship of ideas and then coordinate or subordinate them properly in one longer, unified sentence (Sections 37, 38, 39).

Faulty: As a boy I once found a pocketbook. I saw that it contained a large sum of money. Naturally I wanted to keep it.

Improved: When I was a small boy, I found a pocketbook which contained a large sum of money and which, naturally, I wanted to keep.

Faulty: Mulberry is a small town in Clinton County. It is in the northwestern part of Indiana. It is located 10 miles west of Frankfort and 15 miles east of Lafayette on State Road 38. It has a population of about 1,050. It is an incorporated town and is governed by a local town board. It boasts a city water works, a volunteer fire department, and a public library. It has its own newspaper, *The Reporter,* published weekly.

Improved: Mulberry, a small town in Clinton County in northwestern Indiana, is located 10 miles west of Frankfort and 15 miles east of Lafayette on State Road 38. With a population of about 1,050, it is an incorporated town, governed by a local town board. It boasts a city water works, a volunteer fire department, a public library, and its own newspaper, *The Reporter,* which is published weekly.

EXERCISES

A. Combine the following groups of sentences into complex or compound sentences:

1. I am preparing to become a doctor. Here in college I am enrolled in a course in biology. I am also taking chemistry. Both are valuable subjects. A doctor must know them well.
2. The ice broke up in the spring. We boys used to "hop cakes." We would ride downstream on the cakes. This kind of play was dangerous. We might have fallen off and drowned. The river was deep there. We received dire threats and warnings from our parents.
3. For weeks my buddy and I had planned a fishing trip. We finally set the day. Dawn had just begun to light up the east. Joe woke me up by throwing stones against my window. We had agreed upon this signal. We thought it the one least likely to wake my parents.

4. I went to the masquerade in a voluminous costume. The masquerade was held the night before Halloween. I went as a Hindu dancer. It took 3 yards of cloth to make the turban. The pantaloons had 6 yards of cloth in them, and my cape took 8 yards. A student from India drew the patterns for me.

5. The co-op houses have almost as many activities as the fraternities. The co-ops sponsor two dances each year. These are held in the University Union Building. The co-ops are active in the sports field too. Co-ops have basketball games, softball games, bowling, tennis, and even horseshoe contests. In these sports each co-op is given points for participation. They also receive extra points for winning games. At the end of the year the co-op house with the most points is given a trophy. This trophy is presented at the co-op banquet.

B. Rewrite the following paragraphs in order to eliminate the short, choppy, jerky sentences. Paragraph unity may also need attention.

1. My father's name is Victor Bright. Victor means the winner of a battle or a small person. He is about 5 feet 8 inches tall. He is not a large man. He is, however, a strong and well-muscled man. He is the son of Mildred and Noah Bright. He was the third of four children. He was born near Milltown, Jay County, Ohio. His parents were farmers. They lived on several farms while he was growing up.

2. My father is a prosperous farmer. Early in his life he was doing the work of a man. At the age of 8 he drove horses that the hired men were afraid of. He has always had a love for horses. Now on the farm all the work is done with tractors. My father is very considerate of other people. However, they must be fair with him. I think I have very fine parents. They are the finest parents any boy could have.

3. We have an 80-acre farm located in southern Virginia. Besides the 80 acres, we rent a neighbor's farm of 50 acres. Our farm is in the rolling country. We have to terrace our land. On our farm we have a small wood. This wood has a creek running through it. There are two hills on both sides of our farm. We therefore call our farm "Green Valley Farm." Our farm is shaped like the state of Texas. The creek we call the Little Rio Grande.

POSITION AND ARRANGEMENT

48. Clearness in a sentence depends partly upon right word order (see Section 40). Effectiveness can also be attained in sentences which have words arranged for maximum impressiveness. In addition to applying the suggestions for emphatic diction (Section 63), for correct, clear, and effective word arrangement (Sections 40–42, and 45), and for proper coordination and subordination (Sections 37, 38), you should give careful attention to the position and arrangement of words in sentences since these also contribute to effectiveness. Naturally, not all words or ideas in a sentence are of equal importance; consequently, you must attempt to place the elements of your thought so that relatively unimportant items will remain in the background and important ones will achieve prominence.

48a. Place strong and relatively important words and ideas at the beginning or end of a sentence.

The most conspicuous and emphatic parts of a sentence are the beginning and end. Like other first and last impressions, they are remembered. Sentences should usually be built with the most important idea at the beginning or end, the places of stress, the places where the attention of the reader is most keen. You should remember, also, that transitional words and phrases, although seemingly colorless, are really important and frequently deserve near-beginning positions (see Section 43). On the other hand, prepositions, pure conjunctions, and many other parenthetical expressions are usually not pivotal or important words and should usually not begin a sentence. When appropriate, they should be placed within the sentence although you should avoid artificiality and awkwardness in so placing them.

Ineffective: These are the dormitories which the women students live in.

Mrs. Browne is the only person here whom we haven't spoken to.

The operation was a long and delicate one. However, Mother will recover, the physician says.

Improved: These are the dormitories in which the women students live.

Mrs. Browne is the only person here to whom we haven't spoken.

The operation was a long and delicate one; however, the physician says that Mother will recover.

There is nothing grammatically wrong with placing prepositions at the end of sentences, nor is there any question of clearness. The problem is solely one of effectiveness—a weak word in a strong, emphatic sentence position. Hence, the joking rule which violates its suggestion:

> A preposition is a weak word to end a sentence with.
> Improved: A preposition is a weak word with which to end a sentence.

Remember, however, Winston Churchill's famous reply to those who objected to prepositions at the end of sentences:

> This is the kind of thing up with which I don't intend to put.

There is a moral also in the following, a newspaper columnist's reply to one who had criticized his ending a sentence with a preposition (from *Word Study,* April, 1949):

> What do you take me for? A chap who doesn't know how to make full use of all the easy variety the English language is capable of? Don't you know that ending a sentence with a preposition is an idiom many famous writers are very fond of? They realize it's a colloquialism a skillful writer can do a great deal with. Certainly it's a linguistic device you ought to read about.

48b. Use periodic sentences to secure emphasis.

A *periodic sentence* is so constructed that its full meaning is not apparent until the end; that is, the independent clause, the main verb, the direct object, the complement, or some other completion word or group of words is placed at or very near the end of the sentence. Such a sentence creates suspense; something is held back and the reader continues in a state of expectation. You should avoid a too frequent use of periodic sentences because an awkward and artificial style will inevitably result. Their occasional use, however, is fully justified by the effectiveness of the suspense they achieve. Note the following:

> Tired, hungry, bewildered, and sick at heart, the derelict stumbled into the warm and brightly lit restaurant. At first hesitantly, then eagerly, then almost fiercely, he seized and drank a cupful of steaming coffee.

> On men reprieved by its disdainful mercy, the immortal sea confers in its justice the full privilege of desired unrest.

When we are young and concerned with the overriding importance of the approaching football game, the class dance, the long summer vacation, with making an impression on the new employer, passing the C.P.A. or the Bar examinations, getting married—the importance of knowing a great deal fails to disturb us.

—Dean Paul A. McGhee

As these three examples show, sentences introduced by phrases or by dependent clauses are periodic; they are effective. In loose sentences—usually compound sentences or complex sentences with the dependent clause following the independent clause—complete meaning is possible before the end of the sentence. There is nothing wrong with loose sentences; they predominate in most writing. Because of this predominance, an occasional periodic sentence is especially effective.

48c. Arrange ideas in the order of their importance so as to secure climax.

Climax is attained when the ideas in a sentence are so arranged that each succeeding idea has greater force than its predecessor. The idea, implied or expressed by the phrase, "last and most important," is a fair statement of the order of climax. Consider the following:

Unemphatic: In this wreck, some died horrible deaths, some received serious injuries, and a few were barely scratched.

Better: A few were barely scratched in this wreck; but some received serious injuries; and some died horrible deaths.

Unemphatic: We were frightened by the noises: the crashing of the thunder, the pouring of the rain, and the steady blowing of the wind.

Better: We were frightened by the noises: the steady blowing of the wind, the pouring of the rain, and the crashing of the thunder.

48d. Use words out of their natural order, occasionally, as a method of emphasis.

The usual English word order is subject and modifiers, predicate and modifiers, object or complement and modifiers. Since the reader expects this usual word order, it may be clear, but it does not strike his attention. Putting the predicate or the object or the complement

328

or an adverbial modifier first is unusual; if not overdone and made monotonous, it is emphatic.

Normal: Thirty men have sleeping quarters in the dormitory of our fraternity.
The days of our life are swift and fleeting.
If any, speak; for I have offended him.

Inverted and
effective: In the dormitory of our fraternity 30 men have sleeping quarters.
Swift and fleeting are the days of our life.
If any, speak; for him I have offended. (SHAKESPEARE, *Julius Caesar*)

48e. Repeat important words to gain sentence emphasis.

Faulty repetition should be avoided (see Section **68**), but the effectiveness of many sentences can be increased by repetition of pivotal words. Thus the ideas are driven home, clinched. Notice, however, that effective repetition is not done or overdone in one sentence; it occurs in a series of sentences.

Study the effect of repetition in the following:

Give! Give money when you see that women and children are hungry. *Give* sympathy when you can cheer a beaten man. *Give* time to study conditions in your own community. *Give* your whole self in an attempt to change and better the life of all humanity.

48f. Avoid overfrequent use of the passive voice.

The use of the passive voice often detracts from the emphasis of a sentence because a subject being acted upon is rarely so effective as a subject acting. Many sentences require a passive verb, but the active voice normally gives sentences greater force and strength (see Section **81**).

Unemphatic: The lecture *is scheduled to be given* by Professor Browne on Wednesday.

Better: Professor Browne *will give* the lecture on Wednesday.

Don't avoid the use of the passive voice, however, if you wish to emphasize the subject in the sentence-beginning position (Section 48a).

329

Effective: A lecture on "Better Living at Less Cost" will be given on Wednesday by Professor Browne.

NOTE: The effectiveness of a sentence depends not entirely on the *position* of any single word or idea but on the arrangement of the whole sentence. The *sense* of the sentence must always be considered; the statement must be correct and clear. Effectiveness cannot be gained by a thoughtless or artificial attempt to employ the rules mentioned in this section. They will help to increase effectiveness only if their use does not destroy correctness, clearness, naturalness, and appropriateness.

Unemphatic: This essay was read by me four times before it was understood.
Better: I read this essay four times before I understood it.

Unemphatic: Many children are never really understood until they are given a heart-to-heart talk by their parents.
Better: Many children are never really understood until their parents give them a heart-to-heart talk.
In order really to understand their children, parents should have a heart-to-heart talk with them.

EXERCISES

A. Study sentence beginnings on any three pages of this handbook. How many begin with ineffective words? How can the sentences be improved? Write your suggestions to one of the authors in business letter form (see Business Letters, pp. 709–732).

B. Study sentence endings in any six paragraphs of your book of readings or in a current magazine. How many sentences end with ineffective words? How can the sentences be improved?

C. Make the following sentences more effective by changing them from loose to periodic:

1. I was awarded first prize after the judges had deliberated for a considerable time.
2. Bret Harte is still a favorite among short-story readers, since he portrayed the exciting life and conditions during the California gold rush.
3. Grandfather was known as a pioneer among pioneers, having crossed and recrossed the continent frequently during his lifetime.

4. We knew we had won the game when the kick sailed over the cross-bar in the last 3 seconds of play.
5. Edward FitzGerald meant that the past can never be called back when he wrote, "The Moving Finger writes, and having writ moves on."
6. Decisive action is to be taken at the meeting, and everyone is urged to be present.
7. You have been admitted to the university, your high school principal having written you an excellent recommendation.
8. John knew that he had turned in the winning answer; so he wasn't surprised when the results were announced.
9. We braced ourselves for the shock as the car swerved and started to skid.
10. To be awakened from a sound sleep is startling, even though you realize immediately that what awakened you is the alarm clock ringing.

VARIETY

49. A series of sentences monotonous in structure is not effective. The reader tires of a long succession of identical sentences, or nearly identical ones, just as he tires of sameness in anything. Variety is more than the spice of writing; it is a quality which accurately reflects the mature or immature processes of the writer's mind.

Monotony may be caused by a series of short, simple sentences (see Section 47); by a series of compound "seesaw" sentences (see Section 37b); by a series of sentences beginning with the same word (*this, that, it,* etc.), or same kind of phrase, or same kind of dependent clause; by a series of similarly constructed complex sentences; or by a series of sentences of approximately the same length.

Revise sentences to make sure that they have variety. Vary their length, and, occasionally, their normal word order. Avoid sentences which are similar in form. Use declarative, imperative, interrogative, and exclamatory sentences (see Section 50b) and use periodic sentences as well as loose sentences (see Sections 48b and 50c). Subordinate ideas and thus construct complex sentences (see Section 38) to take the place of too many simple and compound sentences.

You will find that even a series of simple sentences can be given variety by using various kinds of phrases as beginnings or endings.

49a. Do not begin a number of successive sentences with the same word or phrase or dependent clause.

Avoid, whenever possible, outworn beginnings such as *there is, there are, it is, this, that, the, he,* and *we.*

Awkward: It was just the kind of trip our high school class had planned. It was just the time of year for the trip. It was the consummation of our 4 years of planning.

Improved: It was just the kind of trip our high school class had planned and just the right time of year for the trip—the consummation of our 4 years of planning.

Do not begin every sentence with a phrase and do not overuse the same kind of phrases (prepositional, participial, preposition gerund, absolute, adverbial) as a beginning. Note the monotony of the following:

Having considered going to college, I wrote to various colleges about admission. Receiving their catalogues, I gave them careful study. Deciding that engineering was my major field of interest, I applied for admission at Kansas Tech. Being accepted, I made plans to be on the campus by mid-September. Having carried out these plans, I am now here, writing this orientation theme.

Do not begin every sentence with a dependent clause (a *when, while, if, since, because* clause, etc.). To begin with a series of dependent clauses is monotonous; to begin these clauses with the same subordinating conjunction is deadly.

Changing the phrases in the faulty example above to dependent clauses is merely changing the grammatical form of the monotony:

When I considered going to college, I wrote to various colleges about admission. After I received their catalogues, I gave them careful study. As soon as I had decided that engineering was my major field of interest, I applied for admission at Kansas Tech. After I was accepted, I made plans to be on the campus by mid-September. Since I have carried out these plans, I am now here, writing this orientation theme.

49b. Do not place the subject at the beginning of every sentence.

Occasionally change the word order of subject + verb + complement (direct object, object complement, predicate noun, or predicate adjective). A deviation from this order will avoid monotony and, if correctly done, will attract attention and be emphatic (see Section 48d).

Usual order:	I saw that play when I was in St. Louis.
	Those who can study with people about them are fortunate.
Position changed:	That play I saw when I was in St. Louis.
	Fortunate are those who can study with people about them.

49c. Vary the length of successive sentences.

Monotony results when every sentence in a series is of approximately the same length. If the sentences are all short, they read like the writing of a childish or immature person; at best, they give a choppy, jerky effect (see Section 47). The same number of words in a series of medium-long or long sentences is likewise undesirable. Consciously vary the length of your sentences. Twelve to 20 words may be a good average. For variety, use an occasional sentence of three or four, one of 30 or 40.

49d. Vary the form of successive sentences.

Not every sentence in a series should be simple, or complex, or compound, or compound-complex, or periodic, or loose. Sentences of the childish or immature person are likely to be predominantly simple or compound, whereas the work of the effective writer will abound in variety, a judicious mixture of sentences with their ideas effectively coordinated and subordinated (see Sections 37 and 38).

EXERCISES

A. Make a study of any three paragraphs in three essays in your book of readings or in three articles in a current magazine. Prepare a summary report for each three paragraphs, giving the following kinds of information:

1. Number of simple sentences.
   Number of complex sentences.
   Number of compound sentences.
   Number of compound-complex sentences.

2. Number of sentences.
   Number of words in each sentence.

Average length of sentences.
Number of words in longest sentence.
Number of words in shortest sentence.

3. Number of sentences beginning with subject or subject and modifiers.
Number of sentences beginning with inverted order (adverbial phrase, predicate, object, etc.).
Number of sentences beginning with phrases.
Number of sentences beginning with adverbial clauses.

4. Number of periodic sentences.
Number of loose sentences.

Write a paragraph of comment on each author's use of sentence variety.

B. Apply the methods of A to one of your recent themes. What are your conclusions?

APPROPRIATENESS

50. Appropriateness requires the use of the most suitable kinds of sentences to convey purpose and meaning correctly, clearly, and effectively. Sentences differ in grammatical classification, in meaning and purpose, in word order and arrangement of ideas, and in length. A judicious mixture of varying sentences results in both a clear and an effective style, if at all times full consideration is given to the reader.

50a. Use the appropriate kind of sentences according to grammatical classification.

Sentences are classified grammatically as simple, compound, compound-complex, and complex (see Section 74a).

1. Are your ideas best expressed in two sentences?
2. Are your ideas best expressed in a compound sentence?
3. Are your ideas best expressed in a compound-complex sentence?
4. Are your ideas best expressed in a complex sentence?
5. Are your ideas best expressed in a simple sentence? With numerous phrases and word-modifiers? With a minimum of modifiers?

50b. **Use sentences appropriate for the expression of meaning**
purpose.

Declarative, imperative, interrogative, and exclamatory sente
(see Section **74b**) have specific purposes.

1. Use declarative sentences for statements of fact or condi
They are appropriate for all kinds of narration, description,
position, and argument.

2. Use imperative sentences for giving directions, giving advice,
or addressing someone directly. When you are writing completely
from the reader's point of view, and using, as in this sentence, the
second person *you* when *you* mean, specifically and directly, *your*
reader, use imperative sentences.

3. Use interrogative sentences when you are asking direct questions or rhetorical questions (asked, for effect, of one person or
group, but to which direct answers are not expected). A paragraph
of such questions can only be monotonous, but one or two direct
questions in a paragraph of declarative or imperative sentences can
be appropriate and effective.

4. Use exclamatory sentences—such as "What a day!"—when they
serve for interest, emphasis, and effectiveness. Like a series of
interrogative sentences, a series of exclamatory sentences is monotonous and ineffective, but an occasional exclamatory sentence,
appropriately used, is an excellent means of achieving clearness, interest, and effectiveness.

50c. **Use the appropriate kind of sentences for the clear and**
effective arrangement of ideas in sentences.

There are loose, periodic, and balanced sentences (see Sections
74c and **48b**). For effective arrangement of ideas in sentences consider also word order (Section **40**), parallelism (Section **45**), position
and arrangement (Section **48**), and variety (Section **49**).

50d. **Use the most appropriate kind of sentences according to**
length.

Sentences can vary in length from long and medium-long sentences to short sentences of one word or of a few words only. A
judicious mixture makes for clearness, interest, emphasis, and effectiveness (see Section **49c**).

EXERCISES

A. In three paragraphs of an essay in your book of readings or in a current magazine, analyze each sentence according to its appropriateness for both subject and reader. Apply the tests suggested above for appropriateness.

B. Apply the directions given in A to one of your recent themes.

The Word

THE WORD is the smallest grammatical unit of speech or writing which can stand alone as an utterance, which has meaning by itself. Problems with words involve spelling and diction. Both are important and difficult.

Correct spelling is mandatory in all printed materials; even errors due only to faulty proofreading are inexcusable. Correct spelling should also be the aim in all longhand writing and typescript; even two or three misspelled words in an otherwise well-written paper are a source of irritation and distraction for the reader. Misspelling is therefore looked upon by teachers, employers, business and professional associates, and friends as a serious fault.

Diction is the choice of words for the expression of ideas. As thus defined, diction applies to both writing and speaking, although "diction" has additional meaning when applied to speech, since it involves enunciation, voice control, and voice expression. From the Latin, *dictio,* meaning "saying, word," consider how the root *dict* adds meaning to words like *dictaphone, dictate, dictator, dictionary, dictograph,* and *dictum.*

Words are the most important medium for communicating thought from one person to another. Compare, for example, word use with other communication media like painting, sculpture, architecture, music, and dancing. Because there are many different ideas to express in many different shades of meaning and emphasis, because there are many words to choose from, and because there are many errors in word choice to be avoided, students frequently maintain that the most difficult part of composition to master is diction.

Diction reveals the man even more clearly than dress or manners. A person's choice of words is not accidental but is an organic part of him—of his education, his environment, his background, his occupation. Listen to someone for a few minutes, or read something he has written, and you will learn much about the kind of person he is. Thus, we frequently say of someone, "He talks like a lawyer," or a physician, or a scientist, or a sailor. A novelist or a dramatist makes each of his characters use words that are suitable, "in character."

Since diction is basic in all writing, and since it is clearly indicative of what we are and what we wish to express, every one who puts words on paper, who even opens his mouth to speak, must keep in mind the necessity for regular effort to improve in the choice and use of words. He must make an earnest effort to choose painstakingly the basic materials which he puts into his themes. Improvement in diction is a constant challenge; you, as a college student, have an unusual opportunity to meet it.

Diction should be *correct, clear,* and *effective.* No standards of diction, however, can be absolute. There is only one worth-while test: *appropriateness.* As an analogy, consider table manners and how we vary these manners according to circumstances: camping, picnicking, at roadside tables, roadside restaurants, drive-ins, lunch counters, in cafeterias, middle-class restaurants, hotel dining rooms, at informal dinners, formal dinners, elaborate banquets. So, too, with diction. The words used in a discussion in your home are not precisely the words used in a classroom or church discussion group. The language used casually with your roommate is not exactly the language you would use in an interview with your dean or a prospective employer. Following the principles of the process of communication, you—the writer or speaker—should adapt your language to your subject, your reader or listener, and the occasion.

Any rule or prescription concerning word usage, therefore, must be modified by considerations of time, of place, and of situation. Word choice is not inflexibly "good" or "standard." A word or expression in "correct" or "clear" usage a generation or two ago may now be outmoded. A word appropriate in one section of the country ("localisms") or used before a particular group of hearers—technical expressions, for example—may not be correct, clear, or effective elsewhere. A local broadcast of interest only to the community, or a telecast closed-circuit presentation of some scientific process will use a number of words which would be changed if the same materials were adapted for a national hook-up for "general America" to listen to and see.

Nor can the use of this or that word be justified by saying that it is seen frequently in print. Advertisements, newspapers, magazines, and even well-considered books may exhibit poor diction. Several examples in print, several misuses by a famous speaker or writer, several mispronunciations in a national radio broadcast do not make a word, an expression, a pronunciation generally acceptable. If the purpose is *general* acceptance, you should use words that are understandable in all sections of the country at the present time, words that are used generally by reputable writers and speakers of the past and present. In short, correct, clear English is that which is in *present, national,* and *reputable* use, and the use of such English is, in *general,* our safest practice.

The best guide to present, national, and reputable diction is an adequate dictionary, since it records—*not* dictates—and labels words and expressions for its users; by observing carefully the information that the dictionary provides (see Section **51**), users learn what current practice is and can be guided accordingly.

Avoid *substandard* words and expressions, such as narrowly local dialect, ungrammatical expressions, illiterate words, slovenly vocabulary and constructions, mispronunciations, misspellings, excessive and unskillful use of slang, archaic and obsolete words, and unauthorized, newly coined words. Use all available means to assure yourself that your diction is *standard* diction used and understood by cultivated people over a wide area.

Such *standard* diction may be *formal,* i.e., used when we are on "our very best behavior," as in letters of application, platform speaking, technical and scientific papers and speeches, serious friendly letters (like condolence), petitions, research papers, and some of our themes. Or such diction may be *informal,* frequently termed *colloquial,* i.e., friendly, familiar, conversational, the usual writing and speaking of most educated people, as in friendly letters, letters home, friendly exchange of ideas, some forms of discussion, much of our speaking, familiar essays, and some of our themes. Note that *formal* and *informal* apply to both writing and speaking; further that, depending upon the occasion, there are degrees of *formality* and *informality* in language as in dress.

By way of summary, substandard, formal, and informal English is made graphic in the accompanying diagram. Worthy of particular notice is the fact that many words and expressions are in general use in two of and even all three groups.

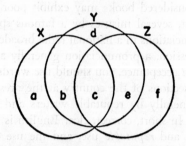

The three circles **X, Y, Z** represent the three sets of language habits indicated above.
X—formal literary English, the words, the expressions, and the structures one finds in serious books.
Y—colloquial English, the words, expressions, and the structures of the informal but polite conversation of cultivated people.
Z—illiterate English, the words, the expressions, and the structures of the language of the uneducated.
b, c, and **e** represent the overlappings of the three types of English.
c—that which is common to all three: formal literary English, colloquial English, and illiterate English.
b—that which is common to both formal literary English and colloquial English.
e—that which is common to both colloquial English and illiterate English.
a, d, and **f** represent those portions of each type of English that are peculiar to that particular set of language habits.

From Charles C. Fries, "Usage Levels and Dialect Distribution," *The American College Dictionary,* p. xxviii. Reprinted by courtesy of the publishers. Copyright, 1947–1956, by Random House, Inc. Text Edition by Harper & Brothers.

The following sections will help you improve your diction. Section **51** introduces you to, or reinforces your knowledge of, the dictionary; Section **70,** a "Glossary of Faulty Diction," contains a list of common errors in the use of specific words. The other sections deal with *correctness, clearness,* and *effectiveness.*

Correctness in the use of words
 Spelling—Section **52**
 Obsolete and archaic words—Section **53**

Localisms—Section **54**
Colloquialisms—Section **55**
Idiomatic English—Section **56**
Illiteracies—Section **57**
Improprieties—Section **58**
Slang and neologisms—Section **59**

Clearness in word choice
Precise diction—Section **60**
Technical words—Section **61**
Mixed figures—Section **62**

Effectiveness in word choice
Emphatic diction—Section **63**
Appropriateness—Section **64**
Triteness—Section **65**
Fine writing—Section **66**
Conciseness—Section **67**
Useless repetition—Section **68**
Euphony—Section **69**

Some of these sections simultaneously deal with correctness, clearness, and effectiveness. For example, incorrect idiomatic usage can be neither clear nor effective; mixed figures are incorrect, ineffective, and vague in meaning. But the outline above may be useful in keeping your attention focused on important principles.

USING THE DICTIONARY

51. A student beginning college study and expecting to be able to write and speak competently through all the years of his life needs on his desk at least two, and possibly three or four source books. One is a good handbook of composition or communication; another is a reliable dictionary; and, if the student expects to do much speaking or letter writing, good guides to public speaking and business and social correspondence.

If you haven't done so yet, now is the time to make the acquaintance of your dictionary. Better still, make it your friend; best of all, make it your constant companion. If we may paraphrase the advice of Samuel Johnson, the great lexicographer, about learning to write well, we would advise: "Give your days and nights to wise study of your dictionary."[1]

51a. Choose a reliable dictionary.

An appeal to *"the* dictionary" as an authority is as illogical as saying, "Don't buy me a book; I already have one," or "It must be so; I saw it in print." There are dictionaries and dictionaries. Some, like a pocket dictionary, are so small that they are virtually worthless except as a limited guide to spelling and pronunciation. Others, of fair size, may be so hastily and carelessly produced that they are unreliable. Even the name "Webster" in the title is no longer a guarantee of quality; as a label "Webster" is no longer copyrighted, and it appears alike in both reliable and unreliable dictionaries.

Choose and *buy* a dictionary which you, your bookstore, and your teachers can trust. The following test questions should receive satisfactory answers:

→1. Has this dictionary been recently published or recently revised?
→2. What are the qualifications of those who compiled and edited it?
→3. What is the reputation of the company that publishes it?
→4. Is it sufficiently large (approximately 100,000 entries)?

Here are some reliable dictionaries, comparable in size and price:

> *The American College Dictionary* (Random House, Inc.; Text Edition, Harper & Brothers, New York).
> *Webster's New Collegiate Dictionary* (G. & C. Merriam Co., Springfield, Massachusetts).
> *Webster's New World Dictionary* (The World Publishing Company, Cleveland, Ohio).

Slightly smaller, slightly less expensive, but suitable is *Thorndike-Barnhart Comprehensive Desk Dictionary* (Scott, Foresman and Company, Chicago, Illinois).

Excellent larger dictionaries provide more information but are expensive and are difficult to carry around. Such are *Webster's New*

---

[1] "Whoever wishes to attain an English style, familiar but not coarse, and elegant but not ostentatious, must give his days and nights to the volumes of Addison." Samuel Johnson, "Addison," in *Lives of the English Poets,* World's Classics Edn. (London, New York, and Toronto, Oxford University Press, 1906), I, 466.

International Dictionary, The Shorter Oxford Dictionary (2 vols.), Funk and Wagnalls' *New Standard Dictionary,* and the monumental twenty-volume *New English (Oxford) Dictionary.* These dictionaries are usually placed in classrooms, libraries, and offices for reference.

51b. Learn the general use of your dictionary.

A reliable dictionary is a guide to use of English. It tells us much about "standard English—the practice of the socially accepted, those who are carrying on the important affairs of English-speaking people."[2] It is an "authority" in the sense that it *records* and *interprets* English words and phrases. But it does not dictate or prescribe, except in a deductive sense. The dictionary indicates what is *general* language practice. When we have specific or particular problems about usage, we can apply in our own writing and speaking the general information which the dictionary has recorded and interpreted.

In initiating and developing your friendship with your dictionary, turn first to the table of contents to see what kinds of information and materials the editors have included. Examine the inside of the front and back covers. At least skim the prefatory pages as well as any supplementary materials at the back. Next read carefully any editorial sections that will enable you to use the book more effectively. These sections may have headings such as "general introduction," "guide to the use of the dictionary," "guide to pronunciation" or "pronunciation key," "etymology key," "explanatory notes," "symbols and abbreviations used in the work."

Each page in the body proper of your dictionary contains a wealth and variety of useful, valuable information. Examine the reproduction on pages 344, 345 for tangible guides to this wealth and variety.

51c. Master the variety of information given for word entries.

Many students use a dictionary merely to learn the spelling, pronunciation, or one definition of certain words. The attentive writer will *study* each word he looks up; that is, he will read carefully the entire entry and thus make the word a real part of his vocabulary. Time spent in thoroughly studying words will save time and

[2] Charles C. Fries, "Usage Levels and Dialect Distribution," *The American College Dictionary,* p. xxviii.

343

glad

glad (glăd), *adj.*, **gladder, gladdest. 1.** delighted or pleased (fol. by *of, at,* etc., or an infinitive or clause): *to be glad at the news, glad to go, glad that one has come.* **2.** characterized by or showing cheerfulness, joy, or pleasure, as looks, utterances, etc. **3.** attended with or causing joy or pleasure: *a glad occasion, glad tidings.* —*v.t.* **4.** *Archaic.* to make glad. [ME; OE *glæd,* c. Icel. *gladhr* bright, glad, D *glad* and G *glatt* smooth; akin to L *glaber* smooth] **—glad′ly,** *adv.* **—glad′ness,** *n.*

—Syn. 1. elated, delighted, gratified. **2.** merry, joyous, cheerful. **—Ant.** sad.

Gla·mor·gan·shire (glə môr′gən shĭr′, -shər), *n.* a county in SE Wales. 1,155,000 pop. (est. 1946); 816 sq. mi. *Co.* seat: Cardiff. Also, **Gla·mor′gan.**

glare[1] (glâr), *n., v.,* **glared, glaring.** —*n.* **1.** a strong, dazzling light; brilliant luster. **2.** dazzling or showy appearance; showiness. **3.** a fierce or piercing look. —*v.i.* **4.** to shine with a strong, dazzling light. **5.** to be too brilliantly ornamented. **6.** to be intensely bright in color. **7.** to be conspicuous. **8.** to look with a fierce or piercing stare. —*v.t.* **9.** to express with a glare. [ME *glaren,* c. MD and MLG *glaren;* akin to GLASS (cf. OE *glæren* glassy)]

—Syn. 4. See **shine. 8.** GLARE, GLOWER, GLOAT all have connotations of emotion which accompany an intense gaze. To GLARE is to look piercingly or angrily: *a tiger glares at its victims.* To GLOWER is to look fiercely and threateningly, as from wrath; it suggests a scowl along with a glare: *to glower at a persistently mischievous child.* To GLOAT meant originally to look with exultation, avaricious or malignant, on something or someone: *a tyrant gloating over the helplessness of his victim.* Today, however, it may imply simply inner exultation.

glare[2] (glâr), *n.* **1.** a bright, smooth surface, as of ice. —*adj.* **2.** bright and smooth; glassy: *glare ice.* [special uses of GLARE[1]]

G-man (jē′măn′), *n.* an agent for the FBI.

gnome[1] (nōm), *n.* one of a species of diminutive beings fabled to inhabit the interior of the earth and to act as guardians of its treasures, usually thought of as shriveled little old men; a troll. [t. F, t. NL (Paracelsus): m.s. *gnomus*] **—gnom′ish,** *adj.* **—Syn.** See **goblin, sylph.**

gnome[2] (nōm), *n.* a short, pithy expression of a general truth; aphorism. [t. Gk.: judgment, opinion, maxim]

gno·mic (nō′mĭk, nŏm′ĭk) *adj.* **1.** like or containing gnomes or aphorisms. **2.** of, pertaining to, or denoting a writer of aphorisms, esp. certain Greek poets. Also,

gno′mi·cal. [t. Gk.: m.s. *gnōmikós*] **—gno′mi·cal·ly,** *adv.*

go (gō), *v.,* **went, gone, going,** *n., pl.* **goes.** —*v.i.* **1.** to move or pass along; proceed. **2.** to move away or out; depart (opposed to *come* or *arrive*). **3.** to keep or be in motion; act, work, or run. **4.** to become; assume another state or condition: *to go mad.* **5.** to continue; be habitually: *to go in rags.* **6.** to move toward a point or a given result or in a given manner; proceed; advance. **7.** to be known: *to go by a name.* **8.** to reach or extend: *this road goes to the city.* **9.** (of time) to pass; elapse. **10.** to be awarded, transferred, or applied to a particular recipient or purpose. **11.** to be sold: *the property went for a song.* **12.** to conduce or tend: *this only goes to prove the point.* **13.** to turn out; result: *how did the game go?* **14.** to belong; have a place: *this book goes on the top shelf.*

15. (of colors, etc.) to harmonize; be compatible; be suited. **16.** to act or operate with sound, as a bell or a gun; make a certain sound: *the gun goes bang.* **17.** to be discharged, or explode. **18.** to be phrased:

how do the words go? **19.** to resort; have recourse: *to go to court.* **20.** to get the facts; find out (fol. by *behind*). **21.** to be given up; be worn-out; be lost or ended. **22.** to die. **23.** to fail; give way. **24.** to be overwhelmed; be ruined (fol. by *under*). **25.** to begin; come into action: *here goes!* **26.** to attack (fol. by *at*). **27.** to be contained (fol. by *into*): *4 goes into 12.* **28.** to

goût

contribute in amount or quantity; be requisite: *16 ounces go to the pound.* **29.** to share equally (fol. by a complementary substantive): *to go partners.* **30.** to contribute to a result: *the items which go to make up a total.* **31.** to be about, intending, or destined (used in the pres. part. fol. by an infinitive): *he is going to write.* **32.** to change course by tacking or wearing) fol. by *about).* —*v.t.* **33.** *Colloq.* to endure or tolerate: *I can't go his preaching.* **34.** *Colloq.* to risk or wager. **35.** Some special verb phrases are:

go around, 1. to move about; circulate. **2.** to be enough for all.
go back on, *Colloq.* **1.** to fail (someone); let (someone) down. **2.** to fail to keep (one's word, promise, etc.).
go by, 1. to pass. **2.** to be guided by.
go down, 1. to descend; slope down. **2.** to be defeated, **3.** *Brit.* to leave the University at the end of the term or permanently (according to context).
go in for, to make (a thing) one's particular interest.
go on, 1. to go ahead; proceed. **2.** to manage; do. **3.** to behave; act. **4.** to begin to operate.
go out, 1. to come to a stop; end: *the light went out.* **2.** to go to social affairs, etc.
go over, 1. to read or reread. **2.** to repeat. **3.** to look at; scan.
go through with, to complete; bring to a finish.
go up, 1. to rise or ascend; advance. **2.** *Brit.* to go to the University at the beginning of term.
go with, *Colloq.* **1.** to harmonize with. **2.** to frequent the society of.
—*n.* **36.** act of going: *the come and go of the seasons.* **37.** *Colloq.* energy, spirit, or animation: *to be full of go.* **38.** *Eng.* the first or preliminary examination at Cambridge University for the degree of A.B. **39.** *Colloq.* a try at something; attempt: *to have a go at something.* **40.** *Colloq.* something that goes well; a success: *to make a go of something.* **41.** *Colloq.* a bargain: *it's a go!* **42. on the go,** *Colloq.* constantly going; very active. [ME *go(n),* OE *gān;* akin to D *gaan,* MLG *gān,* OHG *gān, gēn,* G *gehen.* Cf. GANG², v.] —**Syn. 1.** walk, run, ride, travel, advance. —**Ant. 1.** stay.

G.O., general order.

Go·a (gō′ə), *n.* a district of Portuguese India, on the Arabian Sea, ab. 250 mi. S of Bombay. 624,177 pop. (1940); 1538 sq. mi. *Cap.:* Panjim.

Goe·thals (gō′thəlz), *n.* **George Washington,** 1858–1928, U.S. major general and army engineer, in charge of building the Panama Canal.

-gon, a suffix denoting geometrical figures having a certain number or kind of angles, as in *polygon, pentagon.* [t. Gk.: m. *-gōnos* (neut. *-gōnon*) -angled, -angular]

gor·mand (gôr′mənd), *n.* gourmand.

gos·pel (gŏs′pəl), *n.* **1.** the body of doctrine taught by Christ and the apostles; Christian revelation. **2.** glad tidings, esp. concerning salvation and the kingdom of God as announced to the world by Christ. **3.** the story of Christ's life and teachings, esp. as contained in the first four books of the New Testament. **4.** *(usually cap.)* one of these books. **5.** *(often cap.) Eccles.* an extract from one of the four Gospels, forming part of the Eucharistic service in certain churches. **6.** *Colloq.* something regarded as true and implicitly believed: *to take for gospel.* **7.** a doctrine regarded as of prime importance: *political gospel.* —*adj.* **8.** pertaining to the gospel. **9.** in accordance with the gospel; evangelical. [ME *go(d)spel,* OE *gōdspel,* f. *gōd* GOOD + *spell* tidings (SPELL²), trans. of L *ēvangelium.* See EVANGEL]

gour·mand (gŏŏr′mənd; *Fr.* gŏŏr män′), *n.* one fond of good eating. Also, **gormand.** [late ME, t. F: gluttonous, der. *gourmet* GOURMET]

goût (gŏŏ), *n.* French. taste; perception. [F, g. L *gustus* taste]

— Subject Label
— Usage Label
— Geographic Label
— Idiomatic Entries
— Synonyms
— Antonyms
— Abbreviation
— Place Name
— Biographical Entry
— Suffix
— Cross Reference
— Capitalization
— Etymology
— Foreign-word Label

345

errors later. This advice applies to English words fully as well as to foreign words. Who has not had to look up the same French, or German, or Latin, or Spanish word many times when translating, simply because he did not master the word at first? And who, for the same reason, has not gone back frequently to an English dictionary for information about words or expressions that he is meeting constantly in his reading and listening?

Here is the entry under the word *rival* in *The American College Dictionary:*

rî·val (rī′vəl), *n., adj., v.,* **-valed, -valing** or (*esp. Brit.*) **valled, -valling.** —*n.* **1.** one who is in pursuit of the same object as another, or strives to equal or outdo another; a competitor. **2.** one who or that which is in a position to dispute preëminence or superiority with another: *a stadium without a rival.* **3.** *Obs.* a companion in duty. —*adj.* **4.** being a rival; competing or standing in rivalry: *rival suitors, rival business houses.* —*v.t.* **5.** to compete with in rivalry; strive to equal or outdo. **6.** to prove to be a worthy rival of: *he soon rivaled the others in skill.* **7.** to equal (something) as if in rivalry. —*v.i.* **8.** *Archaic.* to engage in rivalry; compete (*with*) [t. L: s. *rīvālis,* orig., one living by or using the same stream as another] —**Syn. 1.** competitor, contestant, emulator, antagonist. See **opponent.** —**Ant. 1.** partner.

Reprinted by courtesy of the publishers from *The American College Dictionary.* Copyright, 1947–1956, by Random House, Inc. Text Edition by Harper & Brothers.

From such an example may be learned:

1. Vocabulary entry.
2. Spelling.
3. Syllabication.
4. Pronunciation.
5. Part(s) of speech.
6. Meanings.
7. Level(s) of usage.

8. Derivation (Origin).
9. List of synonyms and, frequently, definition of synonyms.
10. Antonyms.
11. Other information.

1. Vocabulary entry.

Ordinarily, the basic or "entry" word is given in black type. Associated with the main entry will be other words in black type indicating run-on entries (endings such as *-ly, -ness* added: *suddenly, suddenness*) and alternative entries or variant forms (*brigandage, brigandism*).

2. Spelling.

As indicated, the basic or "entry" word is ordinarily given in black type, this same form serving for the spelling. Also, in an attention-attracting type (blackface or capitals), the spelling of the word with its various endings may be given. Note especially:

a. The plurals of nouns are given, if the noun forms its plural other than by adding -s or -es.

b. The comparative and superlative degrees of adjectives and adverbs are given, if there is a spelling change in adding -er, -est.

c. The past tense, past participle, and present participle of verbs are given if these forms differ from the present tense form or if there is a spelling change in adding the ending.

d. Compound words spelled with a hyphen, as one word, or as two words, are so indicated.

When a word has two or more spellings, the preferred spelling form is usually given first. Sometimes the variant spelling is also placed separately as a vocabulary entry.

The spelling of proper names (people, places, etc.) is given either in the regular place in the alphabetical listing or in a special section or sections at the back of the dictionary, depending upon the dictionary that you own.

3. Syllabication.

Learn to distinguish between the light mark or dot (·) used to separate syllables (e·jac·u·late—written solid) and the hyphen (-) used to show that the word is a compound (*well-known*). All reliable dictionaries use the dot system of indicating syllabication; some may replace the dot in the vocabulary entry by an accent mark after the stressed syllable.

A knowledge of syllabication is important for two reasons: it helps in the pronunciation of words, which in turn helps in correct spelling, and it indicates where we divide words—between syllables—if we need to divide them at the ends of lines (see Section 93c).

4. Pronunciation.

Pronunciation depends upon accent or emphasized syllables and upon the sound given to alphabetical letters or letter combinations. Some dictionaries include both accent marks and syllabication dots in the entry word; other dictionaries include only the syllabication dots in the entry word and include the accent marks in the "pronunciation" word.

Learn to distinguish the accent marks: primary or heavy stress is indicated by a heavy mark (′) and secondary or less heavy stress by a light (′) or double (″) mark: *search′light′, search′light″*.

Pronunciation of sounds is more complicated than accent. That we need considerable help is evident from the fact that our 26 alphabetical letters are used in 250 common spellings of sounds. Linguists have successfully devised systems whereby between 40 and 60 symbols, depending upon the dictionary, are adequate to solve most pronunciation problems. The general method is the use of a "pronunciation" word, which is usually included in parentheses just after the entry word. It is a respelling of the word, giving the sounds of vowels and consonants by syllables and according to the pronouncing key which the dictionary has adopted. Look for and become acquainted with this pronouncing key in your dictionary; it may be inside the front or back cover or both, or it may be included at the bottom of each page or alternate pages.

Learn to interpret diacritical marks. These marks (¨ placed above the second of two consecutive vowels) are used when each vowel is separately pronounced. Sometimes or as a variant method hyphens are used instead. Examples: *naïve, coöperation* or *co-operation, coördination* or *co-ordination*. As such words become more common, the diacritical marks or the hyphen may be omitted, as in *cooperation*.

For foreign words or those recently adapted from a foreign language, your dictionary may contain a separate "foreign sounds" key.

When two or more pronunciations of a word are given, the more commonly used pronunciation is usually given first. Occasionally, a variant pronunciation may be labeled *British* or *Chiefly British, Brit.* or *Chiefly Brit.,* indicating that this pronunciation is the common one in Great Britain.

5. Part(s) of speech.

Since every word in English is a "part of speech," the part of speech of each entry is usually given. If the word can be properly used as more than one part of speech, such information is provided, with the particular meaning or meanings under each explained. Also indicated are the singular or plural of many nouns, the comparative and superlative degrees of many adjectives and adverbs, and the correct use of verbs as transitive or intransitive, or both.

Learn from the table of abbreviations or elsewhere in your dictionary the more common abbreviations: *act.* for *active, adj.* for *adjective, adv.* for *adverb, art.* for *article, auxil.* for *auxiliary, compar.* for *comparative, conj.* for *conjunction, def.* for *definite, fem.* for *feminine, fut.* for *future, indef.* for *indefinite, indic.* for *indicative, inf.* for *infinitive, intens.* for *intensive, interj.* for *interjection, masc.* for *masculine, n.* for *noun, neut.* for *neuter, nom.* for *nominative, obj.* for *objective, part.* for *participle, pass.* for *passive, perf.* for *perfect, pers.* for *person* or *personal, poss.* for *possessive, pp.* for *past participle, pred.* for *predicate, prep.* for *preposition, pres.* for *present, prin. pts.,* for *principal parts, pron.* for *pronoun, refl.* for *reflexive, rel.* for *relative, subj.* for *subjunctive, superl.* for *superlative, v.* for *verb, v. i.* for *verb intransitive, v. imp.* for *verb impersonal, v. t.* for *verb transitive.*

Such a list is a constant reminder that some knowledge of grammar and grammatical terms is necessary for intelligent and effective use of the dictionary (see sections in this handbook on "Grammar," especially Section **85,** pp. 586–608).

6. Meanings.

Words may have one or more of the following meanings: a historical meaning, a traditional meaning, a figurative meaning, a special meaning, or a new meaning. Note the various definitions giving both the usual and the specialized meanings. Learn the method used in the order of definitions—by parts of speech, for example, or by historical development of meanings, by frequency of occurrence, or by general to specialized meanings. Learn also the significance of definitions preceded by Arabic numbers (1, 2, 3, etc.) or by letters of the alphabet (a, b, c, etc.). Observe carefully the method of entry for capitalized and small-letter words, for words known as homographs and homonyms, and for words that have a superficial resemblance. Although all these may be spelled nearly alike, or pronounced alike, their meanings are quite different. Fit the meaning into the context where you have met the word in your reading and listening.

Hyphenated words and two or more words forming phrases which have an idiomatic, a specialized, or a figurative meaning are explained in the regular alphabetical listing, either entered separately or put under the main word. Most dictionaries, also, now include abbreviations and foreign words or phrases in their alphabetical position.

7. Level(s) of usage.

Remember that mere entry in a dictionary does not guarantee that a word is in good use or that special meanings of the word are appropriate in current English. Your dictionary enables you to judge the acceptability of a word by the absence or presence of a "restrictive label." Note that some words have no labels, and that others have labels applying only to certain meanings or to use as a certain part of speech. Any word not accompanied by a restrictive label may be regarded as appropriate in formal English. Any word labeled "colloquial" is generally acceptable in *all* informal speech and writing. All other labels are guides to special appropriateness of word use.

Four classifications of restrictive labels are common:

a. *geographical,* indicating a country or section of a country where the word is common: *Chiefly U.S., British, Scotch, New England, Southern, Southwest, Western U.S., dialect,* etc. It is not surprising that geographical labels are necessary, for English is the native language of 250 million people in various parts of the world.

b. *time,* indicating that the word is no longer used, is disappearing from use, is still used but has a quaint form or meaning: *obsolete, obsolescent, archaic.* Words bearing no "time" label are in current use.

c. *subject,* indicating that a specialized word or a specialized meaning belongs to a restricted department of knowledge such as science, technology, trade, profession, sport, and the like. As many as 50 such labels are in use, such as astronomy, biology, electrical engineering, carpentry, dentistry, painting, baseball.

d. *cultural,* indicating whether the word or a special use is substandard or acceptable as informal English: *illiterate, slang, dialect* (may be geographical also), *colloquial, poetic, literary.* Absence of any such label indicates that the word is suitable for use in formal and informal writing and speaking.

NOTE: There is no Supreme Court in language to which a final appeal can be made. Our lexicographers can only use their best judgment in compiling and interpreting language data. Do not be surprised, therefore, if dictionaries differ in the labels they attach to certain words or certain meanings. For example, the same word in several dictionaries may bear the label "obsolete," "archaic," "dialect," or even none at all.

8. Origin.

The origin of a word—linguistically speaking, its etymology—may be twofold: (a) less commonly, a narrative account of how a word was formed or received its meaning (see in your dictionary, for example, *derrick, burke, macadam, radar*), or (b) whenever known, the ancestral or foreign languages from or through which the word attained its English form. Old English, Latin, Greek, German, and French have been heavy contributors, but an amazing number of other languages have had a part in current English: Italian, Spanish, Scandinavian, etc.

These derivations, usually entered between brackets, may come near the beginning or at the end of the vocabulary entry. They are of value in helping to fix the meaning and spelling of words in your mind. Learn the more common abbreviations used by your dictionary to indicate them: *OE* (*Old English*), *L.* (*Latin*), *Gk.* (*Greek*), *Sp.* (*Spanish*), etc. Learn also the space-saving short cuts: *b.* (*blended of*), *f.* (*formed from*), *t.* (*taken from*), < derived from, etc. Every dictionary contains a table or tables of such abbreviations.

9. Synonyms.

Synonyms are words that in one or more of their definitions have the same or similar meanings. Study synonyms; frequently these approximate equivalents have significant differences in meaning which will enable you to choose more precise and emphatic words (see Sections **60, 63**). So necessary is this study that entire volumes have been compiled to aid speakers and writers: *Webster's Dictionary of Synonyms, Crabb's English Synonyms,* and *Roget's International Thesaurus of English Words.*

Your dictionary includes the listing and frequently a brief discussion of hundreds of synonyms, showing the differences in meaning of apparently similar words and indicating by a number which usage is part of synonymous meaning. For example, study this treatment of synonyms of the word *silent:*

> **si′lent** (sī′lĕnt), *adj.* [L. *silens, -entis,* pres. part. of *silere* to be silent.] **1.** Making no utterance: **a** Speechless; mute. **b** Taciturn; not loquacious. **2.** Free from noise; still. **3.** Performed or borne without utterance; as, *silent* prayer, grief. **4.** Making no mention; as, history is *silent* as to this; also, unmentioned. **5.** Performed without sound; as, the *silent* drama. **6.** Maintaining a state of inactivity; as, a *silent* volcano. — **si′lent·ly,** *adv.* — **si′lent·ness,** *n.*
> **Syn.** Silent, taciturn, reticent, reserved, secretive mean showing restraint in speaking to others. **Silent** implies a habit of saying no more than is absolutely necessary; taciturn, a temperamental disinclination to speech; reticent, a disposition to keep one's own counsel or to withhold much that could be said; reserved, a temperamental indisposition to the give and take of familiar intercourse; secretive, a displeasing reticence that gives the impression of concealing something. — **Ant.** Talkative.

By permission. From *Webster's New Collegiate Dictionary.* Copyright, 1949, 1951, 1953, 1956, by G. & C. Merriam Co.

10. Antonyms.

Antonyms are pairs of words that have opposite or negative meanings: *man—woman, man—boy, man—beast, man—God, holy—unholy,* etc. You will note that these opposite meanings are not all-inclusive: a word may be an antonym of another only in a certain limited meaning. One antonym of *man* concerns sex; another, age; another, biology; another, religion. Your dictionary suggests antonyms for many words. For example, see the antonym entry under *silent.*

11. Other information.

Other information included as part of an entry or as separate entries in the main part of your dictionary includes geographical names; biographical names; words spelled with both capitals and small letters; abbreviations; homographs and homonyms (words spelled alike but having different meanings, or words spelled differently but pronounced alike); cross references to other words listed elsewhere; examples of word use in phrases and sentences; foreign words and phrases (usually so labeled or given a special symbol); and, for appropriate words, pictorial or graphic illustrations.

51d. Become familiar with other miscellaneous information in your dictionary.

In addition to the wealth of information included under each vocabulary entry (see Section **51c**), reliable dictionaries contain additional materials in the front or back pages. Become familiar with this material. In addition to treating spelling (orthography), pronunciation, usage levels, etc., you may find sections giving guidance on punctuation, grammar, letter writing, proofreading, rhyming, a list of American colleges and universities, and other useful and interesting information.

51e. Use your dictionary to improve and increase your vocabulary.

For greater effectiveness in writing, speaking, reading, and listening, you should constantly improve and enlarge your vocabulary. Knowledge of a foreign language, listening to good speakers in person or via radio and television, carefully reading the works of good writers, and attention to the meanings of prefixes, suffixes, and root words, to synonyms and antonyms are effective aids.

Building an adequate vocabulary is not the work of a week or a month or even a year, but intelligent use of a good dictionary will accomplish much for you in a comparatively short time. These three suggestions will help:

1. Learn the meaning of as many prefixes and suffixes as you can. When these are attached to a word, notice how the meaning is changed. For similar study is the combination of two root words (*absent-minded, air-conditioned, masterpiece*). Here are representative examples:

ante- (before)	antedate anteroom	*poly-* (many)	polygon polysyllable
anti- (against, opposite)	antisocial antiwar	*post-* (after)	postwar postseason
auto- (self)	automobile autograph	*syn-* (with)	synthesis synonym
eu- (well)	eulogy euphony	*-graph* (writing)	geography orthography
hyper- (beyond the ordinary)	hypercritical hypersensitive	*-logos* (study)	biology geology
im-, in- (not)	impossible immature inaccurate indefinite	*-meter* (measure)	speedometer thermometer
		-phone (sound)	dictaphone homophone
peri- (all round)	perimeter periphery		

353

2. Either read with a dictionary at hand, examining words about which you need information, or, if that is not possible, make lists of unfamiliar words and look them up later.

3. List words which you hear in lectures or conversations, study them in a dictionary, and thus add them to your active vocabulary by using them in your conversation and in your writing.

An effective step toward building an active vocabulary is checking your list of words periodically (perhaps once a week) for words which appear twice or oftener. These are likely to be met over and over; they should become part of your speaking and writing vocabulary.

Following are 75 not uncommon words which any student, adopting this plan, can add to his vocabulary:

1. altruistic	26. gregarious	51. nocturnal
2. antithesis	27. hallucination	52. obsequious
3. apotheosis	28. immolation	53. omniscient
4. ascetic	29. impeccably	54. pedantic
5. atavistic	30. imperturbable	55. peremptory
6. autocratic	31. impotent	56. perfunctory
7. capricious	32. innocuous	57. petrified
8. circumambient	33. insatiable	58. precocious
9. conflagration	34. insidious	59. procrastinate
10. contamination	35. iridescent	60. propitiate
11. cynical	36. irrelevant	61. recantation
12. desiccate	37. lachrymose	62. resplendent
13. dogmatic	38. lassitude	63. restive
14. eccentric	39. loquacious	64. reticent
15. edification	40. lucrative	65. saturnine
16. efficacious	41. lugubrious	66. scintillating
17. enigmatic	42. malevolent	67. sententious
18. ephemeral	43. mellifluous	68. sinister
19. eradicate	44. mendacious	69. stertorous
20. eulogy	45. meretricious	70. superannuated
21. exotic	46. meticulous	71. surreptitious
22. extraneous	47. misanthropic	72. taciturn
23. facetious	48. mitigation	73. tenacious
24. futility	49. mollifying	74. vacillation
25. garrulous	50. monotonous	75. vindictive

EXERCISES: THE DICTIONARY

The purpose of the following exercises is to make you completely familiar with the resources of your dictionary.

A. Write a 400-word paper to be read by or to the members of your English class, on one of these subjects:

An Introduction to My Dictionary.
The Uses of a Dictionary.
Good and Bad Features of My Dictionary.
How to Use a Dictionary.
Why Everyone Should Own a Desk Dictionary.
How to Pronounce Words.
Special Features of My Dictionary.
Supplementary Information Supplied by My Dictionary.
The Dictionary as a Source for Synonyms and Antonyms.
Usage Labels as Illustrated in My Dictionary.

B. Read carefully every word on *one* page of your dictionary. Write a 400-word paper telling some of the interesting items you have found.

C. What does your dictionary say about the letters of the alphabet? For example, give a class report on the information given for two or three of the following (include capitals and small letters): A, I, O, Q, S, V, X, Y.

D. Of the 20 words on this "demon list," which are misspelled? *sargeant, temperment, exhilerate, naphtha, siege, morgage, perseverance, merangue, sieve, sacrilegious, questionaire, weird, mosquitos, rarefy, supercede, diphteria, villian, ecstacy, batallion, liquify.*

E. How should these words be written: as one word, with a hyphen, or as two words? *white wash, boom and bust, under dog, able bodied, pot boiler, will o' the wisp, soldier of fortune, table talk, young blood, cul de sac, twenty one, ante chamber, sell out, boll weevil, well nigh, hand made, court martial, base ball, post office, let up.*

F. Since each of the following words has two pronunciations, what does each pronunciation indicate about the part of speech and the meaning? *record, moderate, produce, subject, compound, appropriate, rebel, present, address, insert, transfer, progress, contest, insult, minute, protest, refuse, object, increase, contrast.*

G. Find out the pronunciation of the following words: *gnome, adult, amateur, egotist, data, beret, imperturbable, maraschino, subtle, superfluous, often, impugn, victuals, valet, advertisement, italics, suite, coupon, forehead, indefatigable.*

H. What is the pronunciation of, and what are, the following geographical names? *Sault Sainte Marie, Attu, Mandalay, Okinawa, Monadnock, Dunsinane, Austerlitz, Dolomites, Rotterdam, Oahu, Gibraltar, Cappadocia, Monaco, Assisi, Thames, Pompeii, Thermopylae, Mackinac, Riviera, Eire.*

I. For each of the following persons, give (1) the proper pronunciation of the name, (2) the given or Christian names, (3) dates of birth and death, (4) major occupation: *Tschaikovsky, Robespierre, Euripides, Lafayette, Daguerre, Phyfe, Audubon, Cortez, Vinci, Tagore, Oglethorpe, Galileo, Liszt, Tecumseh, Verdi, Puccini, Tennyson, Garibaldi, Lippi, Rousseau.*

J. The following names come from legend, mythology, or folklore. Identify each: *Damocles, Avalon, Bucephalus, Lilith, Oberon, Rosicrucian, lamia, Uther, Valkyrie, Cyclops, Nibelungs, Icarus, Arden, Robin Hood, Eblis, Elysium, Paul Bunyan, Rumpelstiltskin, troll, Lorelei.*

K. According to your dictionary, what are the plural forms of the following nouns: *erratum, moose, automaton, ax, seraph, ultimatum, virtuoso, salmon, cupful, candelabrum, duomo, basis, campus, bateau, ceramics, mongoose, poet laureate, stigma, tenderfoot, stratum.*

L. What are the past tense, the past participle, and the present participle of the following verbs? *speak, fall, flee, fling, sneak, strive, bear, swear, shake, bite, broadcast, free, grow, hurry, bivouac, drink, forbid, throw, forsake, spring.*

M. Answer the following questions with the aid of your dictionary. If your answer to any question is "yes," explain. Can (1) *cabbage* be used as a verb? (2) *perquisite* be a synonym for *prerequisite*? (3) *how* be used as a noun? a conjunction? (4) *author* be used as a verb? (5) the plural of *money* be spelled *monies*? (6) *daily* be an adjective? adverb? noun? (7) *propeller* be spelled also *propellor*? (8) *buy* be used as a noun? (9) *carry* be used as an intransitive verb? (10) *by* be used as an adjective? an adverb? a noun? (11) *data* be used in the singular? (12) *quahog* be used to refer to pork? (13) the past tense of *fly* be written *flied*? (14) *dieing* ever be a correct spelling? (15) *farewell* be an interjection? noun? adjective? verb? (16) *either* be an adjective? a conjunction? (17) *thank* be used as the past tense of *think*? (18) *loafs* be used correctly in a sentence? (19) *sacred* and *religion* be considered the root words of *sacrilegious*? (20) *merry* be considered an adjective or an adverb in the Christmas carol, "God rest you merry, gentlemen"?

N. The following common, everyday words have many meanings: *appeal, set, spring, point, go, fix, field, about, strike, stay, all, buck, do, sweep, go, free, up, take, top, work.* Prepare for class an oral or written

356

discussion of five of these words. (1) Which meanings seem to you most common? (2) Which meanings seem most unusual? (3) What idiomatic phrases do these words appear in?

O. Apply the directions of N to *break, send, short, stand, hand, run, fast, off, stock, boot, button, even, get, face, give, way, time, type, turn, style.*

P. From your dictionary give the origin (derivation) of the following words including the languages involved in the history of each word: *interregnum, anthropomorphic, banzai, safari, snorkel, cortisone, hasheesh, voodoo, gammadion, pagoda, coulee, succotash, cameo, chocolate, potato, dinghy, gingham, caravan, alpaca, indigo.*

Q. For each of the following words, give the current meaning and the "narrative" origin, i.e., the story behind the word: *bazooka, marathon, meander, chauvinism, Hobson's choice, gerrymander, quisling, loran, boycott, brummagem, macadam, boondoggle, willy-nilly, robot, strafe, milquetoast, poinsettia, bedlam, guillotine, realtor.*

R. With what is each of the following proper names associated (person, river, mountain, valley, island, etc.)? Also, how is each pronounced? *Antoinette, Axminster, Susquehanna, Waikiki, Colosseum, Simplon, Wimbledon, Balearic, Magellan, Adriatic, Saranac, Pribilof, Micman, Himalayas, Matterhorn, Esperanto, Frankenstein, Bayeux, Eiffel, Blarney.*

S. When the following words begin with a capital letter, they mean one thing; when they begin with a small letter, they mean another. For each of the following, distinguish both meanings: *derby, ham, revere, scotch, warren, utopia, renaissance, host, laud, meander, polish, chinook, seine, marathon, polo, ruth, sac, battery, husky, maud.*

T. The following words or phrases, of foreign origin, have been "naturalized" into English, i.e., used without underlining or italics. (1) What was their original language? (2) What do they mean? (3) How are they pronounced? *a la carte, carilloneur, chaise longue, potpourri, danseuse, a priori, précis, bête noire, anno Domine, ad infinitum, zwieback, hors d'oeuvre, debris, rendezvous, cañon, grand tour, au gratin, smörgåsbord, blitz, tête-à-tête.*

U. The following foreign words or phrases have not been "naturalized" into English, but appear frequently in an English context. (1) What language do they belong to? (2) What do they mean? (3) How are they pronounced? *amigo, annus mirabilis, risorgimento, entre nous, enfant terrible, auf Wiedersehen, tout le monde, garçon, sub rosa, adios, ad hoc, cum laude, au jus, Zeitgeist, faux pas, flâneur, Deo volente, bouleversement, ex libris, deus ex machina.*

V. Give the meaning of the following prefixes and list at least five common words containing each prefix: *non-, mono-, semi-, pseudo-, over-, micro-, bi-, cross-, hyper-, multi-, pre-, sub-, re-, intra-, un-.*

W. Give the meaning of the following suffixes and list at least five common words containing each suffix: *-ly, -ness, -less, -ine, -hood, -ship, -ish, -ment, -like, -ist, -able, -er, -y, -al, -est.*

X. What is the meaning of each of the following abbreviations? Which *must* have periods? Which *may* have periods? *AAA, ad lib, DDS, VFW, kw, ARC, RSVP, Mlle, AWOL, ie, bbls, qv, GOP, blvd, DSC, BPOE, circ, %, DNB, SPCA.*

Y. What restrictive label is attached to each of the following? Group these words and their labels under one of these classifications: geography, time, subject, culture (see Section **51c7**): *pesky, rodeo, caboose, dight, baloney, allegro, canny, renege, selectman, sashay, dado, pica, boughten, primp, corn pone, jiffy, rotenone, stymie, chaw, orb, lunkhead, colleen, nohow, pectin, dogie, benison, osmosis, bree, e'er, nubbin.*

Z. Prepare five groups of 10 words each which your dictionary marks with subject labels. After each word, indicate its "subject" and its specialized meaning. (If your dictionary has a list of abbreviations, you can easily compile a subject label list of at least 25 or thirty items from which to choose your five groups.)

EXERCISES: SYNONYMS AND ANTONYMS

A. List all the synonyms given in your dictionary for each of the following words, and prepare for class presentation (oral or written) a brief discussion of the likenesses and differences among the synonyms given for two of the words: *street, defame, trite, yield, opposite, magic, intolerant, know, blunt, avenge, beat, choice, building, colloquial, effort, kindle, grasp, frank, answer, blemish.*

B. Give one antonym for each of the following: *arrive, tempt, affirmative, arrogant, grave, taste, professional, climb, suave, refuse (v.), latent, sophisticated, temporary, repudiate, dark, huge, fine, draw, decrease, solitude.*

EXERCISES: VOCABULARY

A. The following words, although not too uncommon, have only one, two, or three meanings. On 3 x 5 cards to turn in, copy these words; check their spelling; give their syllabication, pronunciation, and meaning; and use each word properly in a sentence: *cacography, hegemony, innuendo, ubiquitous, capitulation, quondam, deify, procrastinate, erubescent, stalactite, nostalgia, lexicographer, fanfaronade, pulchritude, ornithology.*

B. Directions given in A: *apropos, valetudinarian, surreptitious, chiaroscuro, superannuated, cicerone, genuflection, rodomontade, pusillanimous, cosmogony, lugubrious, eleemosynary, culinary, immolate, hypothesis.*

C. In a selection in your book of readings, or in a current magazine article, underline or encircle all the words not in your active speaking or writing vocabulary. Copy 15 of these words on 3 x 5 cards and include with each several additional words to give the context. For each word, give its syllabication, pronunciation, meaning, and origin.

D. Prepare a vocabulary exercise or test, for class use, containing 25 items similar to the vocabulary tests given in E and F, below.

E. Select in each series the word or word group which is closest in meaning to the word italicized in the phrase. Put your list on a separate sheet. Check it with your dictionary.

1. *Propriety* of actions.	property/properness/standard/principle/behavior
2. I replied *glibly.*	fast/profoundly/slowly/loudly/fluently
3. Your reasoning is *erroneous.*	incorrect/convincing/right/pleasing/learned
4. *Edified* by the sermon.	pleased/disgusted/saddened/amused/uplifted
5. These fruits are *indigenous.*	common/expensive/sweet/native/nonexistent
6. *Harassed* by upperclassmen.	praised/ignored/loved/guided/tormented
7. Completely *exasperated.*	thoughtful/exalted/pleased/worn out/angered
8. A *sagacious* decision.	shrewd/foolish/unanimous/necessary/overdue
9. To eat *voraciously.*	rapidly/slowly/politely/indifferently/greedily
10. With much *vehemence.*	pettiness/violence/venom/expression/ease
11. Religious *intolerance.*	unwillingness/uneasiness/narrow-mindedness/faith/sincerity
12. *Ostensibly* confused.	much/unexpectedly/professedly/possibly/stupidly
13. An *antiquated* building.	rustic/outdated/magnificent/modern/haunted
14. To *dominate* a conversation.	improve/interrupt/participate in/rule/object to
15. A *boon* to mankind.	legacy/blessing/boost/friend/curse
16. A *lucrative* occupation.	dull/interesting/overcrowded/lucky/profitable
17. We *subjugated* the natives.	educated/clothed/conquered/harassed/victimized
18. The action was *deplorable.*	useless/desirable/regrettable/necessary/decisive
19. The child wept *copiously.*	little/abundantly/often/secretly/openly
20. Complete *annihilation.*	destruction/praise/anger/despair/victory
21. A *peculiarity* of manners.	politeness/quality/genuineness/change/oddity
22. Acting *flippantly.*	smartly/half-scared/half-apologetically/flinchingly/stupidly
23. A *beatific* smile.	silly/flashing/beaming/blissful/sincere
24. To *succumb* to a disease.	overcome/yield to/ignore/be immune to/be cured of
25. A *colossal* undertaking.	approved/amazing/huge/impossible/secret

F. Select in each series the word or word group which is closest in meaning to the word italicized in the phrase. Put your list on a separate sheet. Check it with your dictionary.

1. *Lucidity* of explanation. — vagueness/wordiness/fertility/brevity/clearness
2. An ugly *scowl*. — boat/look/nose/statement/skull
3. An *irrelevant* remark. — pertinent/cute/irreverent/unrelated/brilliant
4. Never *procrastinate!* — forget/delay/hurry/prophesy/overeat
5. *Exotic* perfumes. — excellent/ordinary/sweet/expensive/foreign
6. An *orthodox* belief. — ordinary/mistaken/religious/approved/pagan
7. To *obliterate* all traces. — witness/destroy/investigate/emphasize/ignore
8. An *incredulous* person. — insincere/kind/inefficient/unbelieving/skillful
9. To speak *monotonously*. — tiresomely/alone/vigorously/effectively/clearly
10. Financial *solvency*. — saving/transaction/debt/soundness/contract
11. Lost in a *maze*. — amazement/marsh/confusion/mirth/surprise
12. *Spontaneous* applause. — unpremeditated/forced/insincere/loud/pleasing
13. A *synonymous* word. — harsh/illiterate/difficult/easy/similar
14. To *tantalize* a child. — tease/please/titillate/adopt/caress
15. To *assimilate* food. — desire/need/buy/absorb/reject
16. A *somnolent* atmosphere. — sleepy/clear/warm/cloudy/healthful
17. To *concoct* an alibi. — destroy/prepare/ignore/insinuate/concentrate on
18. A *potent* medicine. — bitter/pleasant/patented/powerful/expensive
19. A *rendezvous* in New York. — friend/appointment/apartment/show/night club
20. Reached the *zenith*. — horizon/rim/top/zero point/goal
21. An unkind *allusion*. — act/reference/insult/illusion/admission
22. The *limpid* water. — cold/muddy/clear/obscure/purified
23. A *precarious* position. — desirable/premeditated/perilous/elevated/misunderstood
24. To be *arraigned* in court. — invited/acquitted/accused/presented/sentenced
25. All kinds of *vitality*. — victuals/drink/people/necessities/vigor

SPELLING

52. Misspelling is not a problem in word choice, but since it concerns word use, it is obviously an important initial phase of word study.

The spelling of English words *is* difficult. For centuries many words have been spelled "without rime or reason," and through this method, or lack of it, their spelling became "fixed" or permanent. Very likely, in past centuries enough people misspelled certain words that the misspelled forms became considered correct. Many words are not spelled as they sound; many which sound alike are spelled differently; many contain silent letters. Also, spelling by analogy is not a safe guide.

The first step in correct spelling is to have the *desire* to learn, really to want to become a competent speller. The second is to devote the necessary *time* to learn. The third is to use all available *means* to learn. If you are, chronically and consistently, a poor speller, you should obtain a special book which deals solely with spelling problems and which gives you many spelling exercises.[1]

As you study, remember these words of a spelling authority: "All the investigations indicate that any *child* of normal intelligence can learn to spell with very little difficulty in a reasonable length of time." Other spelling authorities assert that the common causes of poor spelling are *carelessness* and *laziness!*

Most college students are not, by birth and constitution, chronic misspellers, but many do have trouble with spelling. In addition to *desire, time,* and *means,* it should be comparatively easy to improve if such students will habitually do these seven things:

→1. Pronounce words correctly.

→2. Mentally *see* words as well as hear them.

→3. Use a dictionary to fix words in the memory.

→4. Use memory devices to help remember troublesome words.

→5. Learn a few simple rules for spelling.

→6. Write words carefully in order to avoid errors due not to ignorance but to carelessness.

→7. *List* the words most frequently misspelled.

52a. Pronounce words correctly.

Let us recognize at once that pronunciation is not a safe guide to spelling. It is possible to spell the sound of many simple words and yet not get a single letter right: by sound *coffee* can be spelled K A U P H Y. Another illustration—frequently cited—is that if you spell the sound of *f* as in *enough,* of *i* as the *o* in *women,* and of *sh* as the *ti* of *fiction,* you can spell *fish* as *ghoti.*

Aside from many fine distinctions in sound, let us remember that there are between 40 and 50 common sounds in English pronunciations. Our 26 vowels and consonants must represent these sounds, but to do so there are approximately 250 *spelling combinations!*

[1] Among such books—inexpensive, too—are the following: Patrick H. Hodgkin, *It's Easy to Spell,* The Culver Press, Culver, Indiana; Julia N. McCorkle, *Learning to Spell,* D. C. Heath and Co., Boston, Massachusetts; Thomas Clark Pollock and William D. Baker, *The University Spelling Book,* Prentice-Hall, Inc., New York; Harry Shefter, *Six Minutes a Day to Perfect Spelling,* Pocket Books, Inc., New York.

For example, the simple sound of long *e* is represented, inconsistently, by 11 spellings: *e* (evening), *ee* (need), *ea* (read), *ei* (receive), *eo* (people), *ey* (key), *ay* (quay), *i* (police), *ie* (piece), *oe* (amoeba), and *ui* (suite). Illogical? Yes. Hopeless? No!

Correct pronunciation may not help too much, but mispronunciation is a definite hindrance. It is responsible for a large number of misspelled words, for it is difficult to spell correctly a mispronounced word. Could anyone spell *Egypt* if it were pronounced *eggpit?* Or *garage* pronounced *gararge?* Or *corsage* if it were pronounced *corsarge?*

1. Do not add vowels in pronouncing such words as *disastrous, similar, remembrance, hindrance,* and *athletics,* and you will not misspell them as disasterous, similiar, rememberance, hinderance, and athaletics (or atheletics).

2. Do not omit consonants in pronouncing such words as *eighth, library, government, environment.*

3. Do not omit syllables in pronouncing such words as *miniature, sophomore, laboratory, accidentally, criticism, convenience.*

4. Do not mispronounce the prefixes of words such as *perfix* for *prefix, preform* for *perform, prehaps* for *perhaps, porprosal* for *proposal.* Remember the student who said:

When I wrote "preformance" for "performance" five times and "preformer" for "performer" seven times, my instructor commented: "An interesting perper but you percipitate too many prejuries in preversely misusing per and pre!"

5. Carefully examine words that contain silent letters. In a number of English words, the following letters are often silent: *c* (*scene*); *ch* (*yacht*); *e* (*come*); *g* (*sign, gnat*); *gh* (*bough*); *h* (*ghost, honest*); *k* (*knife*); *p* (*raspberry, psychology*); *t* (*often*); *u* (*guess*); *w* (*answer*).

6. Be suspicious of words containing lightly stressed syllables. The technical name, *schwa* (ə), is given to indicate the sound, a kind of "uh"; the vowel used may be any one of the six, *a, e, i, o, u, y: dollar, grammar, corner, model, nadir, peril, professor, sponsor, murmur, sulfur, martyr.* In such words, it may help to exaggerate the "trouble spots": *grammAr, sepArate, repEtition, mathEmatics, humOrous, existEnce, dEscribe.*

7. Cultivate the habit of spelling troublesome words aloud, writing them, and then spelling them aloud again in order to relate the sound to the spelling.

52b. Actually see words as well as hear them.

An important method of improving your spelling is to look at, or repeat, a word until you can really *see* it. Correct pronunciation will be of help to an "ear-minded" person in spelling correctly, but to visualize words is also important. Frequently we say of a word we have written, "That doesn't look right." But many students constantly misspell words because they have never really learned to observe a printed page; their errors in spelling come from an unwillingness or apparent inability to *see*. Pronounce, write, study, pronounce words until you can *see* them anywhere—a method particularly valuable when dealing with tricky words which add, drop, do not pronounce, transpose, or change letters for no apparent reason: *explain* but *explanation, proceed* but *procedure, pronounce* but *pronunciation, curious* but *curiosity, maintain* but *maintenance, fire* but *fiery.*

The most frequent error in visualizing words is mistaking one for another similar to it or pronounced alike but spelled differently (homonyms). Observe carefully the pairs or triplets in the following list. Those marked with an * are among the words most frequently misspelled in written work, although every student could probably spell such words correctly in a spelling test. Understand the meaning of each word and do not use one when you mean the other. (See also Section **58b.**)

*accept, except
*advice, advise
*affect, effect
an, and
angel, angle
are, our, or
biding, bidding
breath, breathe
capital, capitol
*choose, chose, choice
cite, sight, site
clothes, cloths

*coarse, course
conscience, conscious
counsel, council, consul
dairy, diary
decent, descent
desert, dessert
dining, dinning
due, do
ever, every
formally, formerly
*forth, fourth
freshman, freshmen

363

*hear, here
hoping, hopping
human, humane
*its, it's (never *its'*)
know, no
*later, latter
*lead, led
least, lest
lightening, lightning
*loose, lose
*lose, loss
medal, metal
of, off
on, one
passed, past
peace, piece
*personal, personnel
*precede, proceed

*principal, principle
*quiet, quite, quit
shone, shown
shudder, shutter
stationary, stationery
*than, then
*their, there, they're
therefor, therefore
*thorough, through
though, thought, through
*to, too, two
*want, wont, won't
weak, week
*weather, whether
*were, where
whose, who's
woman, women
*your, you're

Illustrations of correct use:

I can only *advise* you; you do not have to follow my *advice*.

The *effect* of the damp weather is that my sinuses are *affected*.

Breathe deeply before you dive, and then hold your *breath*.

When some of mother's *clothes* wear out, she uses them as *cloths* for dusting.

This laboratory *course* makes use of fine and *coarse* rocks.

He's a *decent* old gentleman of French *descent*.

Our high school *principal* is a man of high *principle*.

My talkative roommate has been unusually *quiet* for *quite* a time now.

There go the runners; *they're* on *their* last two laps now.

I was *then* a smaller boy *than* my playmate.

Two people are not *too* many *to* share a room of this size, especially since there are *two* doors leading *to* the hallway.

I *want* to buy a record-player, but I *won't* spend the money.

With such *weather,* we don't know *whether* to wear overcoats or not.

The handkerchiefs *were* in the bottom drawer, *where* I did not think of looking.

When *you're* down town tomorrow, you can buy *your* ticket.

52c. Use the dictionary to help in your spelling.

When you are suspicious of the spelling of any word, check its spelling immediately in the dictionary. If you can't find it, look up and down the column, since a silent letter may be causing the trouble: *aghast* will be there, but not *agast*. If the initial letters confuse you, ask someone for suggestions: you will never find *pneumonia* under *n*, *philosophy* under *f*, or *psychology* under *s*.

A knowledge of the etymology (origin, derivation) of a word may also help you to spell it correctly. For example, if you know that *preparation* is derived from the prefix *prae* plus *parare* (to make ready), you will not spell the word *prepEration*. If you know that *dormir* is the French word for sleep (from Latin *dormitorium*), you will not spell *dormitory* with an *a* for the *i*.

Similarly a study of prefixes and suffixes—noting their meaning and their spelling, and of course helping in vocabulary study—will enable you to spell correctly by grouping similar forms in a way which will emphasize their resemblance.

Common prefixes are: *a-, ac-, ad-, ante-, anti-, dis-, fore-, il-, in-, ir-, mis-, non-, over-, per-, pre-, pro-, re-, sub-, un-*.

Common suffixes are: *-cede, -er, -est, -ful, -hood, -ist, -less, -like, -ly, -ment, -ness, -ship, -some,* and *-y*.

In using prefix and suffix words, you can avoid many misspellings by applying the one-plus-one rule (see **52e4**).

Further assistance in the use of your dictionary for spelling is available if your dictionary has among its supplementary aids an article on orthography or correct spelling. Read carefully any such article.

52d. Use memory devices to help remember troublesome words.

Some of these devices apply to groups of words, such as the common spelling rules (**52e**) and the rhyme for the *ei-ie* words (**52e, 1**).

Others that you may devise apply to specific words. For example: *PrepAration* is from the basic word, *prepAre; infinIte* and *definIte* are from *finIte; relAtive* from *relAte*. Certain puzzlers to watch, however, are *explanation, maintenance, procedure, pronunciation, curiosity,* and the like (see Section **52b**).

PrincipLE means a *ruLE*, a theory, a standard; otherwise, *principAL* is used.

SIege literally means that an army *SIts* down before a city until it surrenders.

SuperSede begins its first and last syllables with *s*.

"Together" breaks into "to get her"; "piece" has "pie"; "tomatoes" and "potatoes" have "toes"; "pa" and "ma" appear in "se*pa*rate" and "gram*ma*r."

52e. Learn a few simple rules for spelling.

There are numerous rules for spelling certain words and classes of words, but it is doubtful that many of them are really helpful. Remember that the words came *first*, the rules *second*, and that the rules are generalized statements applicable to a fairly large number of words, but not all; consequently, there are exceptions to every rule.

For words ending in *-able* or *-ible*, *-ant* or *-ent*, *-ance* or *-ence*, *-ise*, *-ize*, or *-yze*, *-tion* or *-sion*, there is no safe guide except memory or constant reference to the dictionary, nor is there a safe guide for the addition of *s* or *es* to words ending in *o*. (See Section 71c4.)

The eight rules which follow, with their corollaries, are simple and easily learned; mastering them will eliminate a large number of recurring errors.

1. Words containing <u>ei</u> or <u>ie</u>.

> Write *i* before *e*
> Except after *c*,
> Or when sounded as *a*
> As in *neighbor* and *weigh*.

This rule or principle applies *only* when the pronunciation of *ei* or *ie* is a long *e* as in *he* or the *a* sound as in *pale: believe, chief, field, niece, piece, siege, yield, view, conceive, deceive, relieve: eight, freight, reign, veil.*

A simple memory device for remembering whether the *e* or *i* comes after the *c* or *l* is the key word *Celia* (or *Alice*, or *police*, or *lice*).

Exceptions often misspelled: *neither, leisure, seize, either.*

If the sound of *ei* or *ie* is other than long *e* or *a*, the principle does not apply: *science, conscience, conscientious, raciest, financier, omniscient, weird.*

2. Final y.

a. Words ending in *y* preceded by a consonant usually change *y* to *i* before any suffix except one beginning with *i* (such as *-ing, -ish, -ist*).

activity, activities	carry, carries, carrying
enemy, enemies	try, tried, trying
library, libraries	modify, modifying
strawberry, strawberries	study, studied, studying
lucky, luckily	lovely, loveliness
easy, easier	empty, emptiness
merry, merriment	lively, livelihood

Important common word exceptions: one-syllable adjectives adding *-ly* or *-ness: shy, shyly, shyness; wry, wryly, wryness;* and a few polysyllables adding *-ship, -like, -hood: ladyship, city-like, babyhood, busyness* (state of being busy).

Proper name exceptions: Proper names ending in *y,* especially family names, simply add *s* to form their plurals, regardless of whether a vowel or a consonant precedes the final *y:*

The *Murphys* and the *Kellys* will hold their annual reunion at Hudson River State Park.

b. Words ending in *y* preceded by a vowel do not change *y* to *i* before suffixes or endings.

valley, valleys	annoy, annoyed, annoying
monkey, monkeys	stay, stayed, staying
turkey, turkeys	array, arrayed, arraying

Important exceptions: *lay, laid* (but *allay, allayed*); *pay, paid; say, said; slay, slain; day, daily.*

The foregoing rule, the most commonly illustrated of all spelling principles, is especially helpful in forming plurals of nouns ending in *y* (see Section **71c**) or in forming the third person singular present tense, the past tense, and the past participle of verbs ending in *y.*

3. Doubling final consonant.

a. Monosyllables and words of more than one syllable accented on the last syllable, when ending in a single consonant (except *x*) preceded by a single vowel, double the consonant before adding an ending which begins with a vowel.

This rule is valuable in forming the past tense, past participle, and present participle of many regular verbs and in forming the comparative and superlative degrees of adjectives. Common endings beginning with a vowel are the following: *-ed, -ing, -er, -est, -able, -ible, -ance, -ence, -ish,* and *-y.*

drop, dropped, dropping
plan, planned, planning
refer, referred, referring
admit, admitted, admitting, admittance
overlap, overlapped, overlapping
acquit (qu equals kw), acquitted, acquitting, acquittal

run, running, runner
tax, taxes, taxable
forget, forgettable, unforgettable
red, redder, reddish, redden
man, mannish
clan, clannish
tin, tinny

Important exceptions: *transferable, transference, gaseous, humbugged, humbugging.*

b. If the accent is shifted to an *earlier* syllable when the ending is added, the final consonant is not doubled.

refer, referred, referring, *but* reference
prefer, preferred, preferring, *but* preference

Exception: *excellent, excellence.*

c. Derivatives from basic words that change pronunciation from a long vowel to a short vowel follow the doubling rule:

write, writing, *but* written
bite, biting, *but* bitten
inflame, inflamed, *but* inflammable

d. Words ending in a final consonant preceded by *two* vowels do not double the final consonant:

appear, appeared, appearing, appearance
need, needed, needing, needy
train, trained, training, trainee

e. Words ending in *two* consonants do not double the final consonant:

bend, bending (*not* bendding)
turn, turned, turning (*not* turnned, turnning)
insert, inserted, inserting (*not* insertted, insertting)

f. Words not accented on the *final* syllable do not ordinarily double the final consonant:

happen, happened, happening
murmur, murmured, murmuring
benefit, benefited, benefiting (*but* fit, fitted, fitting)

A good key word for this rule is *combat*. It can be pronounced with the accent on either syllable, but note the spelling:

combat′   combat′ted   combat′ting
com′bat   com′bated   com′bating

4. The "one-plus-one" rule.

When the prefix of a word ends in the same letter with which the main part of the word begins, or when the main part of the word ends in the same letter with which the suffix begins, be sure that both letters are included. Otherwise, do not double the letters.

The same rule applies when two main words are combined, the first ending with the same letter with which the second begins: *roommate, bookkeeping, glowworm, bathhouse.*

In your study of spelling, note especially how words are spelled when to the word bases are added prefixes like *dis-, il-, ir-, mis-, non-, over-, un-,* and *under-,* or suffixes like *-less, -ly, -ment, -ness,* and *-ship.*

dissatisfied	disappear	soulless	reckless
dissimilar	disappoint	accidentally	sadly
illiterate	discolor	coolly	severely
irresponsible	incomplete	cruelly	suddenly
misspell	misfit	occasionally	sadness
nonnavigable	nonsuccess	brownness	greatness
overrun	overdo	meanness	contentment
unnoticed	undecided	suddenness	wonderment
underrate	undertake	transshipment	craftsmanship

Exception: *eighteen,* not *eightteen.*

Naturally, three consonants are never written solidly together: cliff-face, not cli*fff*ace; shell-like, not she*lll*ike; still-life, not sti*lll*ife; cross-stitch, not cro*ss*stitch.

5. Final silent e.

A final silent *e* is an *e* ending a word but not pronounced; its function is to make the vowel of the syllable long; *rate* (but *rat*); *mete* (but *met*); *bite* (but *bit*); *note* (but *not*); *cute* (but *cut*).

a. Most words ending in silent *e* drop the *e* before a suffix beginning with a vowel but keep the *e* before a suffix beginning with a consonant.

believe, believing	sincere, sincerely
come, coming	amuse, amusement
live, livable	safe, safety
arrive, arrival	sure, surely
ice, icy	hope, hopeless
argue, arguing	bare, bareness

b. Words which end in *ce* or *ge* retain the *e* when *-able* and *-ous* are added, in order to prevent giving a hard sound (*k* or *ga*) to the *c* or *g:*

notice, noticeable	outrage, outrageous
service, serviceable	courage, courageous
marriage, marriageable	change, changeable

Compare the pronunciations of *cable* and *serviceable, gable* and *changeable.*

c. The few words ending in *ie,* in which the *e* is also silent, change *ie* to *y* before *-ing,* perhaps to prevent two *i*'s from coming together:

die, dying	hie, hying (*but also* hieing)
lie, lying	tie, tying (*but also* tieing)
vie, vying	

d. The silent *e* is retained in the *-ing* forms of *dye, singe, swinge,* and *tinge* (*dyeing, singeing, swingeing, tingeing*) to distinguish these words from *dying, singing, swinging,* and *tinging.*

370

6. The inserted -k- rule.

In the few words ending in *c* to which a suffix is added beginning with *e, i,* or *y, k* is usually inserted before the suffix in order to prevent mispronunciation. Note the different pronunciation, for example, between *picnicking* and *icing.*

picnic, picnicked, picnicking	shellac, shellacked, shellacking
panic, panicky	frolic, frolicked, frolicking
traffic, trafficked, trafficking	

7. The -ceed, -cede rule.

When words end in a *-ceed* sound, remember that only three words are spelled with a *-ceed* ending; only one ends in *-sede;* and all other words in this group end in *-cede:*

exceed	supersede	accede
proceed		intercede
succeed		precede
		recede
		retrocede
		secede

8. -s and -es endings.

When nouns end in an *s* sound (*ch, sh, j, s, x,* or *z*) and the plural requires an extra syllable to pronounce, *-es* is added. If there is no extra syllable or if the noun ends in silent *e,* only *-s* is added.

-es	-s	-s
church, churches	delight, delights	table, tables
ax, axes	boy, boys	noise, noises
bush, bushes	street, streets	edge, edges
box, boxes	room, rooms	ache, aches
adz, adzes	book, books	advice, advices

When verbs end in an *s* sound (*ch, sh, j, s, x,* or *z*) and the third personal singular requires an extra syllable to pronounce, *-es* is added. If there is no extra syllable or if the verb ends in silent *e,* only *-s* is added.

-es	-s	-s
rush, rushes	encounter, encounters	argue, argues
finish, finishes	rain, rains	raise, raises
tax, taxes	buy, buys	advise, advises
polish, polishes	mock, mocks	move, moves
filch, filches	walk, walks	notice, notices

52f. Do not carelessly misspell words.

Many spelling errors are caused by carelessness, not ignorance. Nearly everyone makes errors in writing, and the careful student, realizing this, will read and reread his written work to eliminate slips, sometimes rereading once or twice solely for the purpose of finding misspelled words.

Not the difficult words but the simple, easy ones cause most trouble in careless misspelling. The following words, which probably everyone could spell correctly in a test, are among the most frequently misspelled in student papers (see also Section 52b):

> *acquaint, against, all right, amount, appear, arise, around, basis, begin, before, careless, clothes, coming, consider, decide, extremely, field, finish, laid, likely, lonely, mere, noble, paid, passed, past, piece, prefer, prepare, sense, simple, stories, strict, therefore, those, tries, truly, until, whose, woman*

Do not omit letters, or carelessly transpose letters of words, or write two words as one when they should be written separately.

a lot, *not* alot	in spite, *not* inspite
Britain, *not* Britian	piano, *not* panio
collapse, *not* collaspe	radio, *not* raido
curl, *not* crul	research, *not* reaserch
doesn't, *not* does'nt	religion, *not* regilion
first, *not* frist	third, *not* thrid
frolic, *not* floric	thirty, *not* thrity
high school, *not* highschool	thoroughly, *not* throughly
in fact, *not* infact	wouldn't, *not* would'nt, etc.

52g. Keep a list of the words you most frequently misspell.

Learning to spell correctly seems a hopeless task because so many thousands of words must be mastered. But it is well to remember that no one is expected to be able to spell all words, on demand, and that only a comparatively few words are the most persistent troublemakers. For, curiously enough, words like *Mississippi, Tennessee, literature, excommunicate,* and *Canaan* are not frequently misspelled, even when frequently used; rather, words like *too, all right, it's, its, there, their* most often are the offenders (see 52b and 52f).

Keep a list of words which you misspell and study them (perhaps according to **52a, 52b, 52c, 52d,** and **52e**) until you thoroughly learn their spelling.

According to one estimate, a basic list of only 1,000 words appears in 90 percent of all writing, a basic list of only 2,000 words in 95 percent of all writing. Many of these words appear in the following group. About 10 percent of this list are the words most frequently used in English; about 75 percent are among the words most frequently misspelled;[2] the others appear here because they have been misspelled numerous times by college students.

Your own list will contain words not given here, but try to see that none of the following appears on your list or remains there very long. Master the spelling of these words, but do not try to do so all at once; rather, try to master five words a day.

1. absence	11. achievement	21. advantages
2. absolutely	12. acknowledge	22. advertisement
3. academic	13. acquaintance	23. advisable
4. accidentally	14. across	24. afraid
5. accommodations	15. activities	25. aggressive
6. accompanying	16. actually	26. allotting
7. accomplishment	17. address	27. allowance
8. according	18. adequate	28. almost
9. accumulation	19. admiration	29. already
10. accustomed	20. adolescent	30. although

[2] The list given has been checked against some of the major studies of frequency word use and frequency misspellings of the last 40 years, as follows:

William Niclaus Andersen, *Determination of a Spelling Vocabulary Based upon Written Correspondence,* University of Iowa Studies in Education, Vol. II (1917), No. 1.

Alfred Farrell, "Spelling as a College Subject," *Journal of Education,* 122 (January, 1939), 20, 21.

Arthur I. Gates, *Spelling Difficulties in 3876 Words.* (New York: Bureau of Publications, Teachers College, Columbia University, 1937).

John G. Gilmartin, *Gilmartin's Word Study,* rev. ed. (New York: Prentice-Hall, 1936).

Harry V. Masters, *A Study of Spelling Errors, University of Iowa Studies in Education,* Vol. IV (1927–1929), No. 4.

Thomas Clark Pollock, "Spelling Report," *College English,* 16 (November, 1954), 102–109.

Edward L. Thorndike and Irving Lorge, *The Teacher's Word Book of 30,000 Words* (New York: Bureau of Publications, Teachers College, Columbia University, 1944).

31. altogether
32. amateur
33. ambitious
34. American
35. amusement

36. analysis
37. announcement
38. answer
39. antecedent
40. anticipation

41. anxiety
42. apology
43. apparatus
44. apparently
45. appearance

46. applied
47. appointment
48. appreciation
49. approach
50. appropriate

51. approval
52. approximately
53. argument
54. aroused
55. arrangement

56. article
57. assistance
58. association
59. athletic
60. attack

61. attendance
62. attitude
63. attractiveness
64. authority
65. autobiography

66. auxiliary
67. available
68. awkward
69. bachelor
70. basically

71. beautiful
72. becoming
73. beginning
74. believing
75. benefited

76. boundary
77. business
78. calendar
79. campaign
80. candidate

81. capital
82. carrying
83. category
84. celebrate
85. certain

86. century
87. challenge
88. changeable
89. characteristic
90. cheerfulness

91. chiefly
92. chosen
93. circumstance
94. clothes
95. coincidence

96. comfortably
97. commission
98. committee
99. communication
100. community

101. companies
102. comparatively
103. comparison
104. compelled
105. competence

106. competition
107. completely
108. complexion
109. compliment
110. composition

111. comprehension
112. conceivable
113. concentrated
114. condemn
115. confidence

116. congratulations
117. conscious
118. conscientious
119. consequently
120. considerable

121. consistent
122. consolation
123. contemporary
124. contemptuous
125. continually

126. continuous
127. contribution
128. controversy
129. controlled
130. convenience

131. correspondence
132. counsellor
133. countries
134. courageous
135. courtesy

136. criticism
137. curiosity
138. curriculum
139. customer
140. dangerous

141. dealt
142. deceive
143. decidedly
144. decision
145. defenseless

146. deficient
147. definitely
148. definition
149. delinquent
150. demonstrated

151. depression
152. descendant
153. descent
154. description
155. desirability

156. despair
157. desperate
158. destruction
159. determination
160. devices

161. difference
162. difficulty
163. diminish
164. dining room
165. disastrous

166. disappear
167. disappoint
168. discipline
169. discoveries
170. disease

171. dissatisfied
172. distinguished
173. divide
174. divine
175. dominant

176. dormitories
177. edition
178. education
179. efficient
180. eighth

181. either
182. elementary
183. eligible
184. eliminate
185. eloquently

186. embarrass
187. emergency
188. emphasize
189. emptiness
190. encouragement

191. enemies
192. English
193. enormous
194. enough
195. entertainment

196. entrance
197. enthusiasm
198. environment
199. equally
200. equipment

201. equipped
202. equipment
203. especially
204. essential
205. eventually

206. everybody
207. evidently
208. exaggerating
209. excellent
210. exceptionally

211. excitable
212. exercise
213. exhausted
214. exhibit
215. existence

216. expectation
217. expenses
218. experience
219. experiment
220. explanation

221. extravagant
222. facilities
223. faithfulness
224. fallacy
225. familiar

226. fascinating
227. favorite
228. February
229. fictitious
230. finally

231. financially
232. foreign
233. forty
234. forward
235. fourth

236. fraternity
237. friendliness
238. fundamental
239. further
240. genius

241. gentleman
242. glorious
243. government
244. grammar
245. guarantee

246. guidance
247. handicapped
248. happening
249. happiness
250. haughtiness

251. healthy
252. heartily
253. heavier
254. height
255. helpful

256. heroes
257. hindrance
258. hopelessness
259. hoping
260. hospitality

261. humiliate
262. humorous
263. hungry
264. hurriedly
265. hypocrisy

266. ignorance
267. imaginary
268. immediately
269. important
270. impossible

271. inadequate
272. incidentally
273. indefinitely
274. independent
275. indispensable

276. individual
277. industrial
278. influential
279. initiative
280. innocence

281. insistence
282. installation
283. instructor
284. instrument
285. intellectual

286. intelligent
287. interesting
288. interference
289. interpretation
290. interruption

291. intolerance
292. introductory
293. invariable
294. involved
295. irrelevant

296. island
297. knowledge
298. labeled
299. laboratory
300. laboriously

301. language
302. leisurely
303. lengthening
304. libraries
305. license

306. lightning
307. likelihood
308. literature
309. livelihood
310. liveliness

311. loneliness
312. lovable
313. loyalty
314. luxuries
315. magazine

316. magnificent
317. maintenance
318. managing
319. manufacturing
320. marriageable

321. mathematics
322. meanness
323. meant
324. mechanics
325. medicine

326. mentality
327. merchandise
328. metropolitan
329. millionaire
330. miniature

331. miscellaneous
332. misspelled
333. modified
334. monotonous
335. month

336. morale
337. multiplication
338. mysterious
339. narrative
340. nationalities

341. naturally
342. necessary
343. negative
344. neighbor
345. neither

346. niece
347. nineteen
348. ninety
349. ninth
350. noticeable

351. numerous
352. obstacle
353. occasionally
354. occupying
355. occurred

356. occurrence
357. o'clock
358. omission
359. omitted
360. operation

361. opinion
362. opponent
363. opportunities
364. optimistic
365. organization

366. originally
367. overwhelming
368. pamphlet
369. parallel
370. paralyze

371. participated
372. particularly
373. pastime
374. peaceable
375. peculiarities

376. penniless
377. perceive
378. performance
379. permanent
380. permissible

381. perseverance
382. persistent
383. personalities
384. persuade
385. pertain

386. phase
387. philosophy
388. physical
389. physician
390. picnicking

391. planned
392. planning
393. pleasant
394. politician
395. portrayed

396. possessions
397. possibility
398. poverty
399. practically
400. precedent

401. preceding
402. predominant
403. preferable
404. preference
405. preferred

406. prejudice
407. preparation
408. prevalence
409. previous
410. primitive

411. privilege
412. probably
413. procedure
414. proceed
415. process

416. professor
417. prominent
418. pronunciation
419. propaganda
420. provisions

421. psychology
422. punctuation
423. pursue
424. qualities
425. quantity

426. quarter
427. questionnaire
428. realize
429. really
430. receipt

431. receive
432. recognition
433. recognize
434. recollection
435. recommendation

436. reference
437. referred
438. regard
439. refrigerator
440. regrettable

441. relative
442. relieve
443. religious
444. remembrance
445. reminisce

446. renowned
447. repentance
448. repetition
449. representative
450. requirements

451. research
452. resources
453. response
454. responsibility
455. restaurant

456. reverent
457. reviewing
458. rhythm
459. ridiculous
460. righteous

461. rivalry
462. roommate
463. sacrifice
464. safety
465. sandwich

466. satirical
467. satisfaction
468. satisfied
469. Saturday
470. scarcity

471. scenery
472. schedule
473. scholarship
474. shoulder
475. scientific

476. secretary
477. seize
478. selection
479. semester
480. sentences

481. separation
482. seriousness
483. several
484. severely
485. shining

486. siege
487. significance
488. similar
489. sincerely
490. situation

491. solution
492. sophomore
493. sorrowful
494. source
495. sovereignty

496. specialization
497. specifically
498. specimen
499. spectacle
500. speech

501. sponsor
502. statement
503. stationary
504. stopping
505. straighten

506. strength
507. strenuous
508. studied
509. studying
510. subscription

511. substantiate
512. substitute
513. subtle
514. succeeding
515. successful

516. sufficient
517. summarize
518. superintendent
519. supersede
520. superstitious

521. suppose
522. suppress
523. surprised
524. surrounded
525. suspense

526. suspicious
527. swimming
528. symbol
529. system
530. synonymous

531. tactfulness
532. technical
533. technique
534. temperament
535. temperate

536. temperature
537. temporarily
538. tendency
539. territory
540. theories

541. thirtieth
542. thirty
543. thoroughly
544. thought
545. thousand

546. together
547. tomorrow
548. tradition
549. tragedy
550. transferred

551. transportation
552. tremendously
553. truly
554. Tuesday
555. twelfth

556. typical
557. unbelievable
558. uncivilized
559. unconscious
560. uncontrollable

561. undesirable
562. undoubtedly
563. uneasiness
564. unforgettable
565. universities

566. unmanageable
567. unnecessary
568. until
569. unusual
570. usage

571. useful
572. unsuccessful
573. usually
574. vacuum
575. varieties

576. various
577. vengeance
578. versatile
579. veteran
580. vicinity

581. victim
582. view
583. village
584. villainous
585. virtuous

586. visible
587. volume
588. warranted
589. wealthiest
590. weather

591. Wednesday
592. weird
593. wherever
594. whether
595. wholly

596. witnessed
597. wonderful
598. writing
599. written
600. yield

EXERCISES

A. Pronunciation: Copy on a sheet of paper the following words with their pronunciation "re-spelling." Carefully pronounce them, and then mark the division into syllables (see Syllabication, Section **51c,** 3): *environment, government, incidentally, emperor, frantically, temperament, laboratory, mischievous, metropolitan, pronunciation, misspell, secretary, maintenance, villain, delicatessen, kindergarten, accommodate, extraordinary, conspicuous, opportunity.*

B. Rules:

1. Insert *ie* or *ei* in the following:

ach--ve	fr--ght	p--ces	gr--vance
br--f	c--ling	s--ge	n--ce
dec--ve	r--gn	n--ther	f--rce
s--ze	y--ld	w--rd	n--ghbor
rev--w	misch--f	bel--f	w--ld

2. Write the present participle (i.e., the *-ing* ending) of each of the following verbs: *strive, force, free, argue, singe, die, refuse, change, dye, string.*

3. *Study—studies—studied—studying.* Supply the same verb forms for the following: *carry, allay, cry, pray, reply, bury, modify, enjoy, envy, marry.*

4. Add suffixes beginning with vowels to the following words: *clan, gas, defer, bag, begin, hot, swim, split, concur, commit.*

C. Dictionary study: See if a study of the derivations of the following words will aid you in spelling them correctly: *atonement, bilingual, assignee, nasturtium, precedence, nickname, saxophone, coexist, bungalow, senile, precancel, necrology, orthography, ridiculous, sacrilegious.*

D. Some of the following words are misspelled; correct the misspellings: *beachead, ecstacy, excellent, retreive, irrelavant, transship, transfered, interrupted, unoticed, approximately, cleptomania, meddle-some, murmered, suddeness, roommate, existence, accomodation, independant, electrofy, grievious.*

E. Some of the following proper names are misspelled. Correct the errors:

Amercian	Floridia	Phillippines
Britian	Hawaiian	Saterday
Britannica	Louisiana	Southren
Christain	McBeth	Tennessee
Cincinnati	Massachusetts	Teusday
Conneticut	Minnesota	Wendesday
Febuary	Pennsylvania	Wisconson

F. Consult your dictionary to find the preferred or the variant spellings of *theatre, traveler, defense, esthetic, acknowledgment, enclose, fulfil, medieval, judgment, tranquillity, sextet, catalog, instalment, sulfur, canyon;* the preferred plurals of *appendix, stratum, index, medium, cherub.*

G. Find any carelessly misspelled words in the following sentences.

1. Those two weeks where the worse, I beleive, that I every spent.
2. Tribute was payed to my father by many friends.
3. The fog was so think that I bearly got back to land.
4. I believe their going to be some good acts in this student show.
5. A college education will be of great help to you in your latter years.
6. With the food we get here, I'll probably loose weight.
7. New York is America's principle exporting port.
8. Several dictionaries our adequate for general use.
9. The eggs of some birds are layed in nests on the ground.
10. If this method of studying dosen't work, try something else.
11. The boys my own age were much bigger then I.
12. Our park is a place of quite and solitude.

13. My feet are like led when I try to dance.
14. I wasn't recieving any monetary reward for my labors.
15. I am living in one of the freshmen residence halls.
16. My high school days passed far to swiftly.
17. During vacation their is a lot of studying to be done.
18. During the summer we road all the way to Quebec and back.
19. Let me here from you soon.
20. Some students were skeptical, but with my arguments I soon changed there minds.

H. Find any misspelled words in the following sentences.

1. Frankfort is the capitol of the state of Kentucky.
2. Our high school dean of women was a wonderful councillor for us girls.
3. When my parents suggested that I take another theme-writing coarse, I shuttered.
4. I thank you for the oppertunity of making up this work.
5. My best college prepatory subject was mathemetics.
6. Every night I write a few paragraphs in my dairy.
7. My brother joined the Marine Corp after he graduated from high school.
8. There are numberous reasons why I like football.
9. Every month I read the articles entitled "The Most Unforgetable Character I Have Met."
10. Every Sunday our church plays hymns over a loud speaker, the music issueing from the bell tower.
11. The sharp shrill of the offical's whistle kept our slim hopes alive.
12. My roommate is allmost a month younger than I am.
13. The old man's hands were chapped and course.
14. Because of the low wages I cannot except this job.
15. Fewer than 35 metals are in commerical use today.
16. Singing is one of my familie's favorite pastimes.
17. Certain courses needed in college should be made mandantory in high school.
18. I spent the morning choosing my colors, and I have been dying all afternoon.
19. The pitcher wound up and through the ball.
20. With a feeling of sadness, we said our farwells.

I. Correct any errors in spelling in the following sentences, errors caused by confusing two words of the same sound or of similar meaning (Section 52b).

1. This fall our freshmen class has about 800 students.
2. When I was a freshman, I got all sorts of advice from students that I new.
3. Bad luck can be the basis for the lose of thousands of dollars.
4. Service organizations do there part to make the program a success.
5. I do not no all of the last names of the students in my classes.
6. I couldn't decide weather to join the Army or to come to college.
7. It is less dangerous to hit a leather dashboard then one made of medal.
8. I past the objective test with a nearly perfect score.
9. Our high school principle was well liked by all of us.
10. At one time the calvary was an important part of the United States Army.
11. It is annoying to be interrupted in the mist of your studies.
12. There are several good golf coarses in the vicinity.
13. Thomas A. Edison has been an idle of mine since I was a small boy.
14. Father sent me to college so that I would not be a coal minor all my life.
15. It seemed a might strange to leave home so early in the morning.
16. There is an old mill in our vicinity where milestones are still used to grind corn.
17. Most of the city of Gary was planned and laid out before the populous moved in.
18. Two drive-inn movies have been built near the city.
19. My home town is located on the boarder line between Ohio and Pennsylvania.
20. Having decided what the trouble was, I preceded to tear down the motor.

J. In the following there are 50 words incorrectly spelled. List these words on a separate sheet of paper and opposite each give the correct spelling. If a word is incorrectly spelled more than once, list it only once.

Except for the fact that virtually every other word in my themes is mispelled, I am a fairly good writer. Whether this grievous fault is due to ignorance or negligance on my part, I am unable to say. I know it is a hinderance to my recieving high grades in all my subjects, and my perseverance in overcoming this fault is a joy to behold—at least, so my grandfather says. For Grandfather has given me four precepts which have benefitted me tremendously; the excellant results in my writing from a diligent following of these precepts have been so encourageing that I am going to pass them on to you.

Exercises

(1) Look well to your speach. For each time that we write, we speak from fourty to ninty times. If we are on our guard against errors in our speaking, we have a fair gaurantee that we will not make the same or similiar errors in writing. The errors common to both our speaking and our writing are errors in grammar and in the use of words (errors in pronounciation are limited to our speaking, and errors in punctuation are limited to our writing). If we are familar with the simpler rules of grammar and if we apply them constantly, not occcassionally, we shall rarely make any errors that will be especially noticable, and those that we do make we can easily eraddicate. But it is essential that we have a fundimental knowlege of grammar.

(2) Welcome every oppertunity for writing. It is an unusual student who does much writing. A reluctant letter home now and then (usually, a forcable plea for assistance, finacially), a few lecture notes, a labratory report now and then—these are, ordinarilly, the limits of our writing, and they occupy approximatly only an average of a few minutes a day. It is a melancholy truth that no one ever becomes proficient by such a proceedure. We must recognize the truth of the old saying that "practice makes perfect," and if we want to become even adaquate (not great) writers, we must make a concious effort to obtain this practice. Also, if we take the atitude that all our writing is important, we should be persistent in re-reading everything we write—even a problem in mathematics—looking for careless errors, for it is the little, mischievious, careless errors that lead us into errors much more serious.

(3) Remember the other person. For clearness in our communication, this third principle is of extreme helpfullness. In a buisness letter, and in a friendly one, too, we have some definate person in mind; and when we speak, the presence of our hearer is inevatable. But in much of our writing, this principle is often forgotten. But keep it in your remembrance. Make your writing representative of the person to whom you write. By keeping him always in mind, you will not fall into the fallicy of writing to your dean in the language of a six-year-old, or of addressing a child in a style of unecessary grandeur.

(4) Lean upon the subject. Some of us in our writing become so enthusastic that we ramble on and on, with the result that we have a very incoherent theme. We should always stick close to our subject, and organize our material in such a way that it is immediatly clear. Our writing should have a begining which should be direct; a middle which should discuss our most important topics; and an ending which should round out the subject. By using an outline, we can be sure that nothing has been ommitted and that everything has been included. Also, to the de-

velopment of each part of our outline, there should be alloted a certain number of words; thus, we shall not excede the limits we have been set and be guilty of wordiness, nor shall we be handicapped by having to put in an additional sentence here and there to make our quota of words. If we procede according to plan, we need not be affraid that we are bringing in unimportant information.

These are the laudible precepts that my grandfather taught me. They have been responsable for his own clear style, but he wants me and all others to understand that they did not have their origin with him; he freely admits that he aquired them from a former teacher of his, George Herbert Palmer, who, incidently, was at one time a very famous proffesor at Harvard University.

OBSOLETE AND ARCHAIC WORDS

53. One of the requirements of good usage is that words must be intelligible to readers and hearers of the present time. Words are constantly going out of use because our language is constantly growing and changing. Except for somewhat doubtful purposes of humor, we should guard against using expressions which, though antiquated, may persist in our vocabularies because of our seeing them in books written centuries ago.

Antiquated expressions are of two kinds: the actual words themselves which have disappeared from current English, or, much more common, certain meanings of words which in other meanings are frequently and acceptably used.

53a. Do not use obsolete words.

An *obsolete* word is one which has completely passed out of use—either in its form or in one or more of its meanings. An *obsolescent* word is one which is becoming obsolete. The status of such words is difficult to be sure of, and compilers of dictionaries usually label many seemingly obsolete or obsolescent words as "rare" or "archaic." Indeed, dictionaries differ, in that one may label a word "obsolete," another will label the same word "archaic," and a third may use no label at all, indicating that the word is currently used. (Look up *loblolly boy* and *murther* in several dictionaries.) Consequently, the number of words or word meanings labeled "obsolete" in a dictionary is surprisingly small. Examples:

In form: *infortune* for *misfortune; egal* for *equal; gaol* for *jail* (U.S.); *twifallow* (to plough a second time).

In meaning: *permit* for *give over, commit; and* for *if; anon* for *coming; hold* for *bear, endure; petrol* for *petroleum; garb* for *personal bearing.*

53b.   Avoid the use of archaic words.

An *archaic* word is old-fashioned, a word common in earlier speaking and writing. It may be retained in special contexts, such as legal and Biblical expressions, but has almost entirely passed from ordinary language. Like obsolete words, many so-called archaic words are archaic in only one or two meanings and in current use in others.

Do not use archaic words except to achieve some particular stylistic effect. Even then, be certain that this effect can be secured in no other way. Because archaic words are easier to recognize, a much larger number of words bear the dictionary label "archaic" than that of "obsolete." Examples: *enow* for *enough; eftsoon (eftsoons)* for *again;* to *glister* for to *glisten; gramercy* for *thank you; methinks* for *it seems to me;* to *jape* for to *jest (joke); lief* for *willing; whilom* for *formerly; wight* for *person; wot* for *know; y-clad* for *clothed; y-clept* for *named* or *called; silvern* for *like silver.*

"Poetic" words, sometimes so labeled in dictionaries, such as *ope,* are usually archaic words found in poetry written in or designed to create the atmosphere of a somewhat remote past. Examples are certain contractions such as *'tis, 'twas,* and the use of *-st, -est, -th, -eth* endings on present tense verbs: *dost, would'st, doth, leadeth.*

EXERCISES

A. Glance through several pages of your dictionary. Compile three short lists of words labeled "obsolete," "archaic," and "poetic."

B. Read several of the older English or Scottish popular ballads or Samuel Taylor Coleridge's "The Rime of the Ancient Mariner." Compile and explain a list of the archaic words.

C. Read one or more of the familiar essays by Charles Lamb. Compile and explain a list of the archaic words.

D. Read or reread one of Shakespeare's plays. From it can you compile a list of 20 archaic words? Of 20 obsolete words?

LOCALISMS

54. Avoid the inappropriate use of localisms.

A *localism* is a word or phrase used and understood in only a particular section or region of the country. It may therefore be called also a *regionalism* or a *provincialism* (apparently because, formerly, English used in London was "good English"; English used outside London in the "provinces" was not good English but "provincial").

In the United States, the northeastern (New England), southern, southwestern, and western areas, among others, are especially rich in colorful localisms which add flavor to speech but which may not be immediately intelligible in other areas. Such expressions are difficult to detect because a writer or speaker may have come to accept them as reputable and to assume that they are generally understood since he himself has known them from childhood. Also, combinations of words into phrases used locally as slang or idioms (see Sections **59, 56**) may not be explained in print anywhere. Dictionaries do label many words, however, according to the geographical area where they are common.

Examples: New England: *selectman* for *a town official*. Southern: *corn pone* for *corn bread; granny* for *a nurse; butternuts* for *a kind of brown overalls; hoecake* for *a cake of Indian meal.* Western: *dogie* for *a motherless calf; rustler* for *a cattle thief.*

Should localisms be used? The answer, again, is appropriateness. If you live in an area or address people in an area where localisms are common, they are certainly appropriate in your speaking and in your informal writing. But in formal writing for such a geographical area, and in speaking and writing to be understood in other sections of our country, avoid localisms in the interests of clearness. To be generally understood, words must be in national not merely sectional use.

Localisms can also include *dialect*—written or spoken expression used in a limited geographical area, or used by a certain social group in a limited area (like Pennsylvania Dutch), or used by a certain social group on a more extensive geographical scale, like Scotch dialect.

A further extension of localism is *nationalism,* a term describing expressions common in or limited to English used by one of the English-speaking nations. *Americanism* and *Briticism* refer to words or word meanings common in the United States and in the British Isles. Available and most interesting is *A Dictionary of Americanisms,* recording such American usage. Desk dictionaries also label many expressions *U.S., Chiefly U.S., British, Chiefly British,* or *Scotch.* Examples:

Americanisms: *calaboose* (prison, jail); *tote* (carry, or a load); *catchup* (tomato sauce); *stump* (travel to electioneer); *levee* (an embankment); *gangster; caboose; haberdasher; swat; gusher; bellhop.*

Briticisms: *croft* (small enclosed field); *gaol* (jail); *tube* (subway); *petrol* (gasoline); *solicitor* (lawyer); *accumulator* (storage battery); *kerb* (curb); *stay-in strike* (sit-down strike).

Scotch dialect: *bairn* (child); *minnie* (mother); *awee* (a little while); *bree* (broth); *sumph* (sulky person); *canty* (cheerful); *tawie* (tractable); *vera* (very); *chucky* (little chick); *auld* (old).

EXERCISES

A. Make a list of localisms heard in your neighborhood or vicinity.

B. Select some localisms from your dictionary. What is the label attached to each? Can you recall any of them from your reading?

C. Read a novel with a setting in a limited geographical area. List and explain about 20 of the localisms used. (Suggested authors: Zane Grey, George Washington Cable, Mark Twain, Jack London, Lafcadio Hearn, Marjorie Kinnan Rawlings, Mary Ellen Chase.)

D. What are the American equivalents for the following Briticisms? *dustman, treacle, barmy, bowler, fen, lift, tosh, biscuit, collier, barrister, petrol, airdrome, tram, suspender, lorry, poulterer, navvy, pram, draper, queue.*

COLLOQUIALISMS

55. A *colloquialism* is a word or phrase which is used in conversation and which is frequently indispensable to an easy informal style of writing and speaking. The origin of the word is Latin *colloquium* for "conversation," from Latin *col* plus *loqui,* "to speak." Note that the current word *colloquy* means "speaking together, a conversation, a conference," and *loquacious* means "given to talking, fond of talking." Coined words like "speakism" or "speechism" might well be synonyms for *colloquialism.*

Remember two important statements about colloquialisms. First, a colloquialism is never a localism—that is, a *provincialism* or regionalism (see Section **54**). Second, there is never any stigma attached to any word labeled "colloquial." Such words are not vulgar, bad, incorrect, substandard, or illiterate.

Dictionaries mark words as colloquial (*Colloq.*) when in the judgment of the editors they are more common in speech than in writing or more appropriate in informal than formal discourse. The number of words and phrases so labeled is, naturally, quite large. Because editors differ in the interpretations of their findings and because informal English has a far wider range than formerly, this label applies to many kinds of expressions. Many contractions—for example, *don't, shouldn't, won't*—are respectable colloquialisms, whereas some other kinds—*'tis, 'twas, 'twere*—should be guarded against in even very informal writing.

In other words, there are degrees or ranks of colloquialisms, ranging from a high, just below "formal," English to a low of just above "dialect," "slang," and "illiterate English." Dictionary editors are content with one general label, "colloquial," and do not try to indicate differences. Experimentally, you might think of "high level," "middle level," and "low level" as differentiating descriptions.

55a. Use colloquialisms appropriately and effectively.

In view of the wide range within which colloquial expressions come, the only test for their use is appropriateness and effectiveness. There is no objective test or exact rule to enable you to determine when they may be used. Certainly it is better to employ them and make your writing easy and fluent than to avoid them and make your writing artificial and awkward. In the various kinds of informal English—speaking and informal writing—mentioned on pages 338–340, colloquialisms not only are not objectionable but also are positively desirable for smoothness, ease, clarity, and power of communication. Some words are colloquial in all their meanings; others are colloquial only in one or more of various meanings.

Examples (avoiding as do dictionaries and linguists any attempt to indicate their comparative ranking): *angel* (financial backer), *brass* (impudence), *freeze* (stand motionless), *jinx, enthuse, phone, ad, gumption, cute, hasn't got any, brass tacks* (facts), *show up, try and, take a try at, alongside of.*

55b. Avoid colloquialisms in formal writing.

In formal, well-planned writing (see p. 339), colloquialisms should be avoided unless they are deliberately used to achieve some stylistic effect (see Section **64**). As an analogy with clothing, formal writing, without colloquialisms, corresponds to the evening gown, the dress suit, the tuxedo; informal writing, depending greatly for ease, clearness, and effectiveness on colloquial expressions, corresponds to the comfortable clothes of everyday wear. For guidance consult your dictionary to determine what words and expressions are colloquial. Remember that the absence of any label implies words or phrases acceptable in both formal and informal writing.

EXERCISES

A. From any two pages in your dictionary list all the words or word meanings labeled *Colloquial*. Can you make any general statements about the kinds of expressions on your list?

B. Make a list of colloquial expressions which you have heard used by educated speakers, in person, on the radio, on television, at the movies. Bring your list to class for discussion.

C. Make a list of colloquial expressions you have read in books—fiction or nonfiction—by reputable authors. Bring your list to class for discussion.

D. What are the colloquial meanings of the following words? *primp, bossy, jinx, middy, preachify, highfalutin, burg, fluke, lab, numbskull, buddy, fizzle, type, sleuth, catch* (n.), *grapevine, mum, rambunctious, uppish.*

E. What are the colloquial meanings of the following phrases? *war horse, small potatoes, blue streak, freeze out, salt away, yes man, walking papers, close call, make time, buck fever, yours truly, rubber stamp, play up to, fill the bill, Dutch treat, sweet tooth, pass the buck, cut a figure, square shooter, pitch in.*

F. What do the following colloquialisms mean? *bobbysocks, bobby-soxer, playboy, soap opera, standee, jiffy, flimflam, doodad, goner, flabbergast, nosy, get, fellows, take it easy, scoot, getaway, grand, frost, kibitzer, pop.*

G. Try to rank the expressions in D and F according to "high level," "middle level," and "low level."

IDIOMATIC ENGLISH

English *idiom* or *idiomatic* English concerns words not used alone but in combination with others. The key to an explanation of idiom and idiomatic is *particularity* or *peculiarity*. Of Greek origin, the word meant "a private citizen, something belonging to a private citizen, personal," and, by extension, something individual and peculiar. That is, for idiomatic expressions, there are no laws or principles describing their formation, comparable for example to principles describing tense formation or uses of punctuation marks. Each idiomatic expression is a law unto itself. Normally, it may violate grammar or logic, or both; yet it is an acceptable phrase, familiar, deep-rooted, widely used, easily understandable—for the native-born.

Not English alone but every language has its idioms, its peculiarities. French and German and Spanish idioms are difficult for us to understand and master, and many foreign expressions cannot be translated literally. In literal translation, the French say, "Here one speaks French" and "We have come from eating"; the English equivalent is, "French is spoken here" and "We have just eaten."

Likewise, idiomatic English is difficult not only for foreigners but for all who have not listened closely to the talk of acceptable speakers. For example, foreign students may have considerable trouble with *the,* using it where English-speaking people omit it, and omitting it where we use it, as "When I came to the America, thing that impressed me most was vast distance between the New York and the San Francisco." Or we may tell a foreign student not to misuse number or concord by saying "many man," "many man is," "a students," "10 foot," and then we confuse him by saying, correctly, "many a man is," "a few students," and "a 10-foot pole."

The many idiomatic expressions in English permit only a few

very generalized statements. One is that several words combined may lose their literal meaning and indicate something only remotely suggested by any one word: *lay up, heavy hand, toe the line, bed of roses, make out, dark horse, open house, birds of a feather, read between the lines, black list.*

An adaptation of the foregoing statement is that the parts of the human body and words expressing activity have suggested many idioms: *fly in the face of, burn one's fingers, stand on one's own feet, keep one's eyes open, keep body and soul together, all thumbs, make believe, do oneself well, let drive,* etc.

A third generalization is that hundreds of idiomatic phrases contain adverbs or prepositions with other parts of speech. There is no "rule" guiding their use; yet certain combinations are allowable and clear while others are not. Here are some examples (see also Section 56, just below):

run down, run in, run off, run out, walk off, walkover, walk-up, get nowhere, get through, get off. Also:

agree
- *to* a proposal
- *on* a plan
- *with* a person

contend
- *for* a principle
- *with* a person
- *against* an obstacle

differ
- *with* a person
- *from* something else
- *about* or *over* a question

impatient
- *for* something desired
- *with* someone else
- *of* restraint
- *at* someone's conduct

rewarded
- *for* something done
- *with* a gift
- *by* a person

56. Use acceptable idiomatic expressions.

Despite the fact that idiomatic English cannot be explained scientifically, you should never avoid using idiomatic expressions. They are necessary short cuts in our language and make writing and speech vigorous, imaginative, and effective. In fact, idioms are the essential material of which language is made: the widespread, everyday usage of people.

The careful writer and speaker will not assume, however, that he can create or adapt idioms as he pleases. His usage should conform to the word links generally acceptable. A good dictionary will contain a statement of idiomatic usage following words which need such explanation. It should be noted, however, that dictionaries differ and that some of the expressions cited below are in controversial use.

You should be especially careful to consult your dictionary when using certain word groups of *prepositions* with nouns, adjectives, or verbs. The following lists of idiomatic and unidiomatic expressions contain numerous examples of the use of troublesome prepositions:

Unidiomatic	*Idiomatic*
accord to	accord with
according with	according to
accuse with	accuse of
acquaint to	acquaint with
acquitted from	acquitted of
adverse against	adverse to
aim at proving	aim to prove
all the farther	as far as
among one another	among themselves
angry at (a person)	angry with
as regards to	as regards
authority about	authority on
blame it on me	blame me for it
cannot help but talk	cannot help talking
comply to	comply with
conform in	conform to, with
convince to	convince that
correspond with (a thing)	correspond to
desire of	desire to
desirous to	desirous of
die with (a disease)	die of
disdain of	disdain for
dissent with	dissent from
doubt if	doubt whether
enamored about	enamored of
feel of	feel
free of	free from
frightened of	frightened by, at

graduated (high school)	graduated from (high school)
have got to	must
identical to	identical with
in accordance to	in accordance with
in search for	in search of
jealous for	jealous of
kind of a	kind of
listen at	listen to
monopoly for, on	monopoly of
oblivious to	oblivious of
on line	in line
out loud	aloud
plan on going	plan to go
prefer (one) over (another)	prefer to
prior than	prior to
responsible on	responsible for (to)
sensitive about (a stimulus)	sensitive to
superior than	superior to
tend to	attend to
to home	at home
treat on (a subject)	treat of
unequal for	unequal to
unmindful about	unmindful of
vie against	vie with

EXERCISES

A. Correct the errors in idiom which occur in the following sentences:

1. Please listen at this music; it is superior than anything I've ever heard before.
2. He was initiated to our fraternity during his first year at college.
3. Oblivious to all sound, he concentrated on his studying.
4. She was enamored with the idea, but there was nothing she could do about it.
5. As I sat in the bench, I looked quietly about the room.
6. I become very bored of doing nothing but study all the time.
7. If you will wait on me for only 10 minutes, I'll be glad of an opportunity of going with you.
8. There was a 5,000-feet drop on the right of the road.
9. That is a trait which is peculiar with this race of people, but they seem to be unmindful to it.

10. If you don't plan on going with me, I shall be free of all future obligations to you.
11. My new dictionary cost $6, which to my estimation was money well spent.
12. Some students enjoy very much to go to the movies twice a week.
13. I hope of having my own business some day.
14. The school paper is an interesting activity to participate with.
15. It was the card catalog section, in which I was most impressed.

B. Make the following sentences idiomatically acceptable by listing the prepositions which would properly fill in the blanks:

1. This letter means that he will accede .... your request.
2. Contrast this idea .... that one.
3. She does not adhere .... that theory.
4. Mr. Bullock will compensate you .... the work.
5. In this instance, the boys don't agree .... the girls.
6. Sarah was then admitted .... the theater.
7. Are you really independent .... your father?
8. Your mother is apprehensive .... your safety.
9. Surely you can accommodate yourself .... any plan.
10. What do you infer .... that proposal?
11. She could not bear to part .... it.
12. Mrs. Smoak will be .... home this afternoon.
13. Do you know an antidote .... this poison?
14. That species is peculiar .... this vicinity.
15. Please don't meddle .... affairs not your own.
16. This drug is not a substitute .... that one.
17. She will prohibit you .... doing that.
18. Jack is now reconciled .... living on a small salary.
19. I didn't think him capable .... doing such a thing.
20. Jane is too careless .... her appearance.

C. Use correct prepositions with each of the following verbs: *acquaint, acquiesce, center, collide, engage, sympathize, wait, part, concentrate, listen.*

D. Use correct prepositions with each of the following words: *peculiar, prodigal, independent, unmindful, glad, sympathy, angry, repugnant, vexed, hatred, ambitious, sick, careful, obedient, worthy.*

E. In the following (1) what is the meaning of each word separately? (2) what is the meaning of the phrase? *oak leaf cluster, gentleman's agreement, scorched earth, second fiddle, far cry, day letter, blue laws, rabbit punch, automatic pilot, square dance, salad days, poor law, pilot plant, pidgin English, oxygen tent, olive branch, king's evil, match play, round robin, petty cash.*

ILLITERACIES

57. Avoid the use of illiterate words and phrases.

Illiteracies are words and phrases not accepted in either colloquial or formal language. Characteristic of uneducated speech, they are always to be avoided in writing unless you put them into the mouths of people you are characterizing or use them on exceedingly rare occasions for purposes of humor. Illiteracies are not necessarily coarse and are frequently effective; in fact, there are examples of eloquent writing and speaking by illiterate persons who were deeply sincere in what they said. But any one with a high school education or beyond should have no need of illiteracies to help him express his ideas.

Illiterate words and phrases are also referred to as *vulgarisms* (the language of the ill-bred, the uneducated), or *barbarisms*. The latter word is from the Greek word for "barbarian," once used slightingly of foreigners not included in Greek civilization, hence, linguistically, a word or phrase not accepted in the language.

Dictionary makers apply a label to indicate the foregoing words, but what may be marked *illiterate* in one dictionary may be termed *dialect* or even *colloquial* in another. Not many examples may appear because most dictionaries primarily record "standard" usage. The following words and phrases are representative of those that should be guarded against: *ain't, youse, to burgle, boughten, borned, losted, drownded, mistakened, disremember, irregardless, anywheres, nohow, nowheres, hisself, concertize, vacationize, kepted, hadn't ought, this here, couldn't of, being as, being as how, snuck* (past of *sneak*), *acrossed, fellers, ourn, brung, them there, drug* (past of *dragged*).

EXERCISES

A. Write a short paper summarizing what your dictionary tells you of these words applied to language: *barbarism, illiteracy, impropriety, solecism, vulgarism.*

B. From what is the word *vulgarism* derived? What is the difference between *vulgarism* and *vulgarity*?

C. Make a list of 20 illiteracies heard in the conversation of others or reported in books.

D. Below are 2 selections from narratives which include the speech of uneducated people. From each compile a list of words that are illiterate and another list which includes words common to informal and formal "good" English.

Tom broke in irritably, "Well, you ain't never gonna know. Casy tries to tell ya an' you jest ast the same thing over. I seen fellas like you before. You ain't askin' nothin'; you're jus' singin' a kinda song. 'What we comin' to?' You don't wanta know. Country's movin' aroun', goin' places. They's folks dyin' all aroun'. Maybe you'll die pretty soon, but you won't know nothin'. I seen too many fellas like you. You don't want to know nothin'. Just sing yourself to sleep with a song—'What we comin' to?' . . . I didn't mean to sound off at ya, mister. It's the heat. You ain't got nothin'. Pretty soon you'll be on the road yourse'f. And it ain't tractors'll put you there. It's them pretty yella stations in town. Folks is movin'," he said ashamedly. "An' you'll be movin', mister."

—John Steinbeck, *The Grapes of Wrath*

"It's the onluckiest place ennywhar nigh about," said Nathan White, as he sat one afternoon upon the porch of his log-cabin, on the summit of Old Rocky-Top, and gazed up at the heights of the T'other Mounting across the narrow valley. "I hev hearn tell all my days ez how, ef ye go up thar on the T'other Mounting, suthin' will happen ter ye afore ye kin git away. An' I knows myself ez how—'t war ten year ago an' better— I went up thar, one Jan'ry day, a-lookin' fur my cow, ez hed strayed off through not hevin' enny calf ter our house; an' I fund the cow, but jes' tuk an' slipped on a icy rock, an' bruk my ankle-bone. 'T war sech a job a-gittin' off'n that thar T'other Mounting an' back over hyar, it hev l'arned me ter stay away from thar."

—Charles E. Craddock, "Over on the T'other Mounting," *In the Tennessee Mountains*

E. Find acceptable words to replace the illiteracies in the following sentences:

1. I have been somewhat dissolutioned by campus politics.
2. My mother was borned 38 years ago in Akron, Ohio.
3. My car has always been kepted in first-class condition.
4. This course helped to make me awear of good writing.

5. On our way we passed through many little sleeply Mexican towns.
6. I am having no trouble here because I had an excellent college preparance course in high school.
7. I packed a few clothes and much junk into my newly boughten suitcase.
8. Many years ago this city was choosen as the state capital.
9. At the Thanksgiving dinner we stuffed ourselfs with turkey and all the trimmings.
10. My best friend has very smilly lips.
11. After that rugged game I found I had a busted lip and a swelled left eye.
12. The slides will give you different vues of the city.
13. Our teacher does his best to get his ideas acrossed to us.
14. A student living at home doesn't have much opportunity to get acquainted with other college fellas and gals.
15. We stayed home that day because of the inclimate weather.

F. Find acceptable replacements for the illiteracies in the following sentences:

1. Fish fries and square dancing are helded in the county park during the summer.
2. Disregardless of the signs, some people take curves too fast.
3. Joe was a star in football and basketball durning his last year in high school.
4. I hope sometime to travel extensibilitively.
5. Because of our disobedience we received several hard whippens that year.
6. I am very muchly interested in chemistry and mathematics.
7. The British seem to be calm and disconcerned with all that goes on.
8. When I do or say the wrong thing, I get flusterated quite easily.
9. Our town is completely residentual, except for a bank, a few stores, and two filling stations.
10. I am the misfortunate student who has 8 o'clock classes 6 days a week.
11. Our family has spent many pleasant summers among the hills and dills of Wisconsin.
12. Women have proven themselfs to be just as competent as men.
13. Joe made quite a schoolastic record in high school, standing at the top of a class of 200 students.
14. Our eyes never weavered from the speaker.
15. All of a sudden the motor klunked, and the car stopped.

IMPROPRIETIES

58. Unlike illiterate words, *improprieties* are recognized English words which are misused in function or meaning. The word that constitutes an impropriety is acceptable; it is its misuse which causes an error in diction.

58a. Avoid improprieties in grammatical function.

One classification of improprieties includes words which are acceptable as one part of speech but unacceptable as another: nouns for verbs, verbs for nouns, adjectives for nouns, adjectives for adverbs, adverbs for adjectives, prepositions for conjunctions, misuses of principal parts of verbs.

A word identified as more than one part of speech may be so used without question; otherwise, a careful writer will not transfer a word from one part of speech to another until this new function is sanctioned by good use. Examples of improprieties in grammatical function:

Verbs used as nouns: *eats, an invite, a think, a combine* (combination).

Nouns used as verbs: *matineeing, author* an article, *birthing* an idea, *biographying* Abraham Lincoln.

Adjectives used as adverbs: *real pretty, some tall,* etc. (See Section **83.**)

Other examples: *seen* for *saw; don't* for *doesn't; done* for *did; except* for *unless; being as* or *being that* for *because, since.*

For guidance, consult your dictionary, which labels every word according to the part or parts of speech that it is. Note also the "usage" label: *colloquial, dialect, slang,* etc., since the same word may be acceptable as one part of speech but not as another.

58b. Avoid improprieties in meaning.

A second classification of improprieties includes words similar or vaguely similar to other words and used inexactly or wrongly for them. Such words include homonyms and homographs. *Homonyms* are two words that have the same or close pronunciation, but are different in meaning, in origin, and, very often, in spelling; for example, *pale* and *pail; sew* and *so; hour, our,* and *are; bough* and *bow.* *Homographs* are two or more words that have the same spelling but are different in meaning, origin, and perhaps pronunciation. Examples: *row* (a straight line) and *row* (a noisy dispute); *air* (atmosphere) and *air* (melody), *hooky* (full of hooks) and *hooky* (truancy). Errors also arise in confusing words which are near-homonyms: *midst* for *mist, medal* for *metal, later* for *latter, latter* for *ladder, shutter* for *shudder.* (See also Section **52b.**)

> A mother with a large family has a difficult time keeping her children in *toe.*
> Some babies very early accomplish the *fete* of learning to walk.
> Children are likely to get distorted *fews* from reading comic books.

Perhaps such confusions are caused by the increasing emphasis put upon listening, upon hearing words (and hearing them inexactly) rather than seeing them in print and associating their meaning with their appearance as well as their sound.

In your writing, bear in mind the lack of clarity caused through confusing homonyms, homographs, near-homonyms, and near-homographs. Your aim should be the word that means *precisely* what you want to say, the word that conveys to the reader *exactly* the meaning that you intend. If you are in doubt about the meaning of a word, or of two similar words, the usual advice about dictionary use applies.

In addition to the list of homonyms given under spelling (Section **52b**), other pairs of words frequently confused in their meaning are the following:

accept, except	believe, feel, think
adverse, averse	casual, causal
affect, effect	climactic, climatic
aisle, isle	complement, compliment
aggravate, irritate	continual, continuous
all ready, already	convince, persuade
all together, altogether	council, counsel, consul
allude, elude	credible, creditable, credulous
allusion, illusion	decent, descent
alter, altar	disinterested, uninterested
amount, number	envelop, envelope
anxious, eager	expect, suspect
avenge, revenge	faint, feint

farther, further
fewer, less
formally, formerly
healthful, healthy
human, humane
imply, infer
ingenious, ingenuous
interest, intrigue (*v.*)
irrelevant, irreverent
later, latter
liable, likely
luxuriant, luxurious

marital, martial
moral, morale
noted, notorious, notable, noteworthy
official, officious
personal, personnel
practical, practicable
principal, principle
prophecy, prophesy
reputed, reputable
respectfully, respectively
stationary, stationery
statue, stature, statute

EXERCISES

A. Use correctly in sentences 10 of the pairs of words listed in Section 58b.

B. Use correctly in sentences 10 of the pairs of words listed in Section 52b.

C. Use each of the following words correctly in a sentence: *creditable, apt, vocation, consul, can, may, mad, counsellor, capitol, lightening, personnel, wont, exasperate, imply, noteworthy.*

D. From your dictionary, find the answers to the following questions. If the answer is "yes," explain. Can the following words be used as indicated? (1) *complected* as a variant for *complexioned?* (2) *contrariwise* as an adjective? (3) *rose* as a verb? (4) *conjugate* as an adjective? (5) *sure* as an adverb? (6) *ditto* as a verb? (7) *quarry* as a verb? (8) *manly* as an adjective? (9) *stratums* as a plural? (10) *cool* as a noun? (11) *appropriate* as an adverb? (12) *pshaw* as a verb? an interjection? (13) *throw* as a noun? (14) *wrought* as a past participle of *work?* (15) *quail* as a verb? (16) *mimicry* as a verb? (17) *holp, holpen* as past tense and past participle, respectively, of *help?* (18) *hardy* as a noun? (19) *equal* as a noun? (20) *corp* as the singular of *corps?*

E. Point out any improprieties in word use in the following selection:

From everywheres comes the cry to save white paper and in my letters only recently I all ready mentioned about the props. of all the big newspapers in the country held a meeting in New York City and disgust the shortage and promised they wouldn't use no more of it then was nessary but from all as I can see the papers is still comeing out daily and Sun. as big as life and all the paper they been saveing wouldn't make a night gown for a cigarette and a outsider might think they had give their promise as a practical joke and with no intentions of carrying them out. But a friend of mine that knows some of the big editors personly claims that they would be tickled to death to live up to the agreement only they haven't no idear in regards to how to go at it in other words they don't know what they could leave out of the papers without the subscribers getting sore.

—RING LARDNER, "A General Commentary: On Newspapers."

F. Correct any grammatical improprieties in the following sentences:

1. I have come to college because I do not wish to be a labor in the coal mines all my life.
2. The college superintendent businessed in Chicago last Friday.
3. Being as I live only 50 miles from college, I usually go home every week end.
4. When the car wouldn't run any farther, I had to let her set and try to hitchhike into town.
5. Those two points gave us a win in our final game.
6. My friend finally seen that something was wrong and drug me from the water.
7. Doing homework became to seem as natural as eating.
8. I like dancing, partying, and sports.
9. On the farm I would help chore in the mornings and evenings.
10. My parents suspicioned that I would soon forget about the gun or perhaps break it.
11. My father has supervisored the work of this plant for years.
12. Everybody oh and ah when they saw our new dormitory.
13. My sister and I are the only offsprings of our parents.
14. Driving on pasted the sign, we soon came to the park entrance.
15. Milwaukee is the town that homes the Milwaukee Braves.
16. This company supplies here and surrounding areas with all the canned goods needed.
17. Many magazines are kept in the library in a bounded form.
18. In some parts of the training program, I think I shall forever be a burst.
19. I am going to college to future my education.
20. We received word that some one in my roommate's family had deceased.

G. Correct any improprieties in meaning in the following sentences:

1. English can be taught just as affectively through other means as through grammar.

2. In college your studies should take precedent over activities.
3. If Friday comes on the 13th, I'm unusually beware of the fact.
4. On one ill-faded day of Friday, the 13th, a number of unfortunate things happened to me.
5. If you live in a private home, you don't have any social live at all.
6. In the course of time the adolescence grows older and reaches maturity.
7. Carrying too heavy a schedule of classes proposes numerous problems.
8. I want to insure you of my complete loyalty and cooperation.
9. We must make our streets a safety place to live on.
10. Several decisions that my family made last year have completely alternated my life.
11. All through high school I had a number of choirs to do around home.
12. When the first two races were walkaways, a feeling of conundrum ran through the crowd.
13. Police often use radium to catch traffic and speed violators.
14. My city is predominately an industrial city.
15. Grandmother was reverent all over the city as a grand old lady.
16. A bright affect resulted when the lights were turned on.
17. I like to engage in familiar conservation with a small group of friends.
18. A second visit will dislodge any allusions you might have about the place.
19. We interred the church for the morning service and were deeply impressed.
20. Our speech teacher was always watching for any errors in our annunciation.

H. Correct any improprieties in the following sentences:

1. I hate to say this, but your handwriting is quite ineligible.
2. It seems to us now that the Acadians of Longfellow's *Evangeline* lived in time immemoriam.
3. According to costume, every home is decorated with red and green at Christmas time.
4. I suppose I'm supercilious, since I believe that 13 is an unlucky number.
5. To be a mountain climber, you have to be a ragged individual.
6. Some nouns like *house, lawn,* and *road* belong to the neutral gender.

7. I wonder what they mean when you play bridge and they call you venerable.
8. This semester we are studying the ideas of some of the Old Testament profits.
9. I stood on the wall of the mighty Hoover Dam and thought, "What a tremendous farce there is here."
10. A proposition is one of the eight parts of speech.
11. I've been reading about the Middle Ages, and I'm sure glad I didn't live during the Futile System. I'd of probably been a surf, or at best a pedant.
12. An old saying is that you should let your conscientiousness be your guide.
13. Some students have trouble learning the active and passing voice of verbs.
14. Astronomy and gravitation obey the eternal and unchanging laws of our university.
15. You should always close a business letter to a superior with, "Respectably yours."
16. The dean's notice about absences has been tackled on every bulletin board.
17. On several recent occasions I have felt like deifying the university officials.
18. Because he failed a math course, Corzymanski was declared illegible for the team.
19. I attended a top-notch ballet last evening, and was impressed by the anaesthetic dancing.
20. Any one who can't read or write is said to be illegitimate.

SLANG AND NEOLOGISMS

59. *Slang* is a label for words and phrases ranging from just below acceptable colloquialisms (see Section 55) down to the lowest level of illiteracies (see Section 57).

Originally the term *slang* was applied to the cant of gypsies, beggars, and thieves—apparently used to keep outsiders from understanding their conversation—or to the jargon of any particular class of society. The characteristics of slang include flippant or eccentric humor; forced, fantastic, or grotesque meanings; novelty; attempts to be vivid, fresh, pungent, colorful. Such expressions may appeal to the popular fancy or to some segment of it (college slang, Army slang, Navy slang, baseball slang), but in general they are substandard. Even so, slang may for a time be used over a wide area, and a considerable number of words and phrases bear the *"slang"* label in our dictionaries. If such expressions persist, they may eventually receive the respectable label, *colloquial.*

Slang expressions appear as one of several forms:

1. Neologisms (newly coined words): *snafu, blurb, cop, prex, goofy, wacky, nix, oops, razz, bozo, geezer, mooch, jeepers, shindig, scram.*

2. Words in otherwise acceptable use given extended meanings: *jerk, crab, croak, lemon, brass, pip, snap, rat, swell, oyster, some, yellow, stuff, grind, rhubarb.*

3. Words formed by compounding or coalescing two or more words: *slanguage (slang* and *language), cinemactor (cinema* and *actor), sweedle (swindle* and *wheedle), attaboy (that's the boy), jyeetyit (did you eat yet?), high-hat, lowbrow, stash (store* and *cache), whodunit, brunch (breakfast* and *lunch).*

4. Phrases made up of one or more newly coined words (neologisms) or one or more acceptable ones: *stow the gab, get hep, brass hat, what the heck, make whoopee, bum steer, have a heart, juke box, hot rod, sob sister, dead beat, yackety-yak, stool pigeon, sound off.*

59a.   Avoid slang in formal and informal writing.

Slang is popular, but it has little place in formal writing or even in effective informal writing. There are sound reasons for avoiding it.

First, many slang words and phrases are ephemeral; they last for a brief time and then pass out of use, becoming unintelligible and violating the principle that words must be in current use (see Section 53). How many college students can explain clearly what these phrases—college slang of a generation or so ago—meant when applied to coeds: (a) *powder-house fluff,* (b) *fever frau,* (c) *hothouse bowwow,* (d) *pop-eyed pansy,* (e) *green peas,* (f) *butter-and-egg fly,* (g) *lolleos,* (h) *cloud,* (i) *wows,* (j) *tin pans.*[1] Numerous

---

[1] (a) sorority girl, (b) girl full of life and animation, (c) a dream girl, (d) and (e) young women lacking charm, (f) social queen, (g), (h), (i), and (j), women students.

currently popular slang expressions will likewise be outmoded in a short time.

Second, the use of slang expressions may keep you from searching for the exact words you need to express your meaning. Many slang expressions are only rubber stamps; to refer to a person as a "peach" hardly expresses exactly or fully any critical judgment or intelligent description. To argue that such a word conveys precisely the intended meaning is to reveal a poverty of vocabulary, or careless thinking, or laziness. The most serious charge against slang is that it becomes a substitute for thinking.

Third, slang does not serve the primary purpose of writing: conveying a clear message from writer to reader. This objection to slang is evident from the characteristics given above. Without explanatory parentheses, how understandable would the following paragraph be?

> I usually drop into the local beanery (restaurant) three or four times a day to fill my grub tank (stomach). For breakfast, I usually have a stack (wheat cakes) or maybe Adam and Eve on a raft (two poached eggs on toast) or Adam and Eve on a raft and wreck 'em (two scrambled eggs on toast). I like plenty of sand (sugar) in my draw one in the dark (black coffee). I don't eat much at noon, maybe one on the city (glass of water) with a cowboy (Western sandwich), a million on a platter (baked beans) with plenty of red lead (catchup), or graveyard stew (milk toast). For my evening meal I eat whatever I'm in the mood for: La Bullie Hibernian (corned beef and cabbage), Noah's boy, with Murphy carrying a wreath (ham, potato, and cabbage), yesterday, today, and forever (hash), or a chewed fine, with a breath (hamburg steak with onions). Just before going to bed I have a team of grays (two doughnuts) and cow (glass of milk).

Finally, slang is not appropriate in most formal writing because it is not in keeping with the context. Words should be appropriate to the audience, the occasion, and the subject matter (see Section **64**).

There are good arguments in favor of slang and places where it should be used. Slang does express feeling, although explosively and sometimes grotesquely. It also makes effective short cuts in expression and often prevents artificiality in writing. Furthermore, it should be used in reporting dialogue to give the flavor of the speech actually used. But you should avoid an excessive or injudicious use of slang expressions, for the reasons already mentioned.

59b. Use neologisms appropriately.

A *neologism* is a newly coined word or an established word with a new meaning. If the latter characteristic applies, your dictionary should include this meaning. If the former characteristic describes the word, dictionaries may or may not include it, depending upon its recency and the area of its use.

Many newly formed words are slang, like *lowbrow;* some have risen rapidly to colloquial status, like *highbrow;* some are like *motel,* coined by a Los Angeles architect, a common word among motor tourists; and some are still comparatively or completely unknown, despite creation by popular or literary speakers and writers: *clouder-puffs* (a sky full of round soft clouds), by Conrad Aiken; *cigarettiquette* (light the lady's first) and *popaganda* (Father's Day), by Edward Anthony; *looklister* or *listlooker* for TV audience-spectators; *globilitterate* (one ignorant of world affairs), by Norman Corbin; *Babbitt* (narrow-minded businessman), by Sinclair Lewis; *elephantasy* (heavy-handed or -footed writing), by Louis Untermeyer; *avoirduprose* (heavy language), *millionairess,* and *cinemactress,* from *Time* magazine.[2]

Still other new coinages are in the fields of the sciences and technology—terms needed to describe new inventions, discoveries, applications and occupations: *A-bomb, H-bomb, cyclotron, klystron, rhombatron, radar, loran, realtor, beautician,* and the like. Perhaps in this classification also are registered tradenames or trademarks: *Kodak, Nylon, Dacron, Simonize, Linotype, Technicolor.* Sometimes a major change in our national way of living, like a depression or a war, creates many new words; from World War II came these representative examples: *blitz, foxhole, jeep, kamikaze, tank trap, roadblock, flak, bazooka.*

If you use any of these various neologisms in your writing or speaking, be sure that they are appropriate, that is, that they will be easily understood by the people whom you are addressing (see Section 64). Or perhaps you will want to apply the advice of Seumas O'Brien: "I had such an extensive vocabulary as a young man I

---

[2] Examples taken from *Word Study,* published by G. & C. Merriam Co.

did not need to invent any words. I never read without a dictionary and was richer in words than in anything else."

EXERCISES

A. Write a brief paper comparing and contrasting the meanings given by your dictionary for the following: *slang, argot, cant, dialect, jargon, lingo, shoptalk, vernacular.*

B. Look up in your dictionary the meaning of the following slang words and phrases: *cahoot, gimmick, goo, shyster, jittery, nix, mooch, tizzy, kibosh, hooey, get one's goat, pork barrel, sad sack, on the make, long green, stool pigeon, stuffed shirt, sound off, on the loose, high-hat.*

C. Give a slang meaning and an acceptable meaning for each of the following: *applesauce, flame, guy, plug, salted, noodle, pinch, rat, sell, punch, oyster, stall, stuff, pony, ham, grind, yellow, show, sap, classy.*

D. Collect at least 25 examples of slang words and phrases from your dictionary. What does each mean?

E. Collect at least 25 examples of slang words and phrases heard around the campus. From your list, write a 400-word theme on the subject, College Slang, 19—.

F. Read several issues of *Time* magazine and bring to class a representative list of 20 neologisms that appear there.

G. Point out and correct any slang words or phrases in the following sentences:

1. I think now that I have brought too many clothes and junk to college.
2. The play put on by our senior class was certainly a crumby performance.
3. There seem to be some good-looking dames in this year's freshman class.
4. I felt a heck of a lot better when I had stowed a big dinner away.
5. I dislike bridge partners who louse up good hands.
6. Wow! Was that a test? The old bozo threw the book at us.
7. Our star halfback got plastered every time he carried the ball.
8. After a hard day of sightseeing, we were all pretty bushed.
9. Being a soda jerk is an easy way to earn money during college.
10. During the first few weeks I didn't study but just skinned by.
11. I have always liked to mess around with motors.
12. Among my boy friends, one or two are goons but the others are pretty smooth.

13. I like to wear sharp ties to class.
14. Every Monday night I pile my car full of guys and dolls, and we drive to an outdoor cinema; the whole bunch of us can get in for a buck.
15. Look at our quarterback tackle; he sure has guts.
16. I think I must have hit every grocery store in town.
17. My grandfather is a remarkable person; I always get a big kick out of him when I go for a visit.
18. The trouble with blind dates is that your date may turn out to be dumb.
19. I went wild when I received your letter.
20. John is a basketball forward that can fake the daylights out of you.

H. Point out and correct any slang words or phrases in the following sentences:

1. Although he has plenty of money, my roommate is a little on the tight side.
2. Joe was a fall guy all through high school.
3. I wrote an urgent letter home, for I had to kick in with my fraternity dues.
4. There are times when things get pretty tough here in college.
5. In high school most of his classmates considered him a jerk.
6. Thanks for the invite and the grub; I've had a whale of a time.
7. The old buzzard flunked me on this test.
8. After a long evening of studying, I am ready to hit the sack.
9. The retired people in our town are stinking rich and live in monstrous homes.
10. I should have studied harder, especially for the hourlies.
11. I'm in this job for the money, not the kicks.
12. Some teachers will blow their stacks on the slightest provocation.
13. There may be dumber bunnies than that guy but I'd sure hate to see them.
14. I am taking this course again because I goofed too much last semester.
15. The days of giving a kid a licking for every little thing are or ought to be past.
16. The best theme I have read was by a guy named John Thompson.
17. We were invited to a coffee blast last Friday afternoon.
18. Uncle William drives me crazy every week end.
19. Most of the boys on my floor are real swell guys.
20. Your grade depended a lot upon how much time you may, or may not have spent, polishing the teacher's apple, so to speak.

PRECISE DICTION

60. The primary purpose of writing is communication; therefore, it is important for you to use words which will express precisely what you wish to convey. These words must not be misused for or confused with words like or similar in sound and spelling to others, i.e., improprieties in meaning (see Sections **52b, 58b**). Even with a choice of several words approximating what you wish to say, there is for each idea a word or phrase which will express your meaning more precisely than all others. It is your task, your obligation, to find this word or phrase, and use it.

Preciseness in diction requires you to think clearly and carefully. Sometimes the first word which comes to mind is the most exact which can be used; more often it is not. The good writer always remembers that a word means to the reader what the reader thinks it means. Exact diction results not when the writer knows precisely what he means but only when the reader understands exactly what the writer intended to communicate.

60a. Use specific words.

Try to be definite in your word choice. Use a specific word rather than one which only approximates the idea. Such vague, general words may be illustrated by these examples:

> *Fine*—"a fine day," "a fine time."
> *Vital*—"a vital message," "a vital game."
> *Thing*—used for any idea or object, as "another thing to remember."

Other vague, ineffective words: *item, phase, element, feature, factor, instance, nature, case, character, condition, persuasion, degree, quality, asset, state, lot, job, personality, nice, cute, interesting, along the line of, with regard to, in respect of, in connection with, in the case of, according as to whether.*

The best way to avoid the use of vague words is to think *carefully* what you mean to say and to consider in saying it how ineffective are vague, general words. A study of the synonyms listed for an expression in a dictionary or thesaurus will enable you to choose a more precise term. For example, before allowing the word *jocular* to stand in one of your themes, find out whether one of the following adjectives will communicate your meaning more precisely: *blithe, joyful, joyous, jolly, jocose, jovial, jocund, gay, merry, sportive.*

Do not let the use of synonyms lead you into error. Two words may be synonymous in one of their meanings but not in another. Consider the following ludicrous uses of synonyms for *steal, vision,* and *face.*

> The moon is pilfering over the mountain-top.
> In her beautiful new evening gown my girl was a *sight* at the Junior Prom.
> In the poem Lancelot says that the Lady of Shalott had a lovely *map.*

What popular expression is conveyed through these synonyms: "Oh, you monstrously huge pulchritudinous puppet!"?

60b.   Avoid excessive exaggeration.

Hyperbole is a figure of speech which is sometimes effective. In fact, the word "effective" is part of the definition of hyperbole: "exaggeration, or a statement exaggerated imaginatively, for effect; not to be taken literally."

> An ancient man—as old as Methuselah, I'd say—tottered into the village square.
> The towering mountain peaks pierced the heavens.

Exaggeration, however, unless for deliberate effect, is misleading because of its inexactness and possible ludicrousness. "As a boy I used to die laughing at my grandfather's jokes." Do not inexactly use such words as *terrible, ghastly, horrible, thrilling, marvelous, gorgeous, amazing, awful, splendid,* and *phenomenal.* Each of these and similar words have their legitimate uses but have been used inexactly so often that they are rarely effective.

Another kind of exaggeration is substituting a "monumental" phrase for a word which a writer may not wish to repeat or find a synonym for. Joe Louis, when heavyweight boxing champion, was referred to as "The Brown Bomber," "The Detroit Menace," "The Tan Terror"; Babe Ruth, once the New York Yankees' star batter, was "The Home-Run King," "The Sultan of Swat." College athletic teams may be any kind of wild animals. A fleet track man or fast football backfield star (note use of *star*) is a "galloping ghost" or

"The Dan Patch of the cinder path (or gridiron)"; the football line is "a concrete wall" or "seven blocks of granite"; a girls' swimming team consists of "freshwater mermaids" or "Desert Pool Dolphins"; a popular radio singer is "the nightingale of the airways."

Such exaggeration in phrasing must receive careful consideration. When inappropriate, it should be avoided; when appropriate, it is picturesque and effective, as a poet's description of the German Obernkirchen Children's Choir, "angels in pigtails."

EXERCISES

A. Substitute better words in the following sentences which use most of the words mentioned above.

1. Having to go to an 8 o'clock class is a ghastly experience.
2. It's just terrible, terrible; my boy friend hasn't called me all afternoon.
3. I always put off doing my horrible old assignments as long as I can.
4. We're going to listen to TV tonight; won't it be thrilling?
5. That's an awful way to eat a piece of pie.
6. It's perfectly splendid that you are studying so hard for this test.
7. The way my roommate cuts classes is simply amazing.
8. No professor has ever commented on my gorgeous typing.
9. I had a marvelous time reading the newspaper last evening.
10. I'd say any one was phenomenal who attends class regularly.
11. One factor has completely changed my way of life here at college.
12. Our high school is one of the prettiest in the state.
13. By cramming, I figured I could pull my grades up.
14. I had a feeling that my freshman year was going to be just awful.
15. Two of the most important things in college life are the selection of studies and outside activities.

B. Distinguish among the meanings of the words in each of these groups:

    argue, debate, discuss, comment
    dislike, disgust, distaste, nauseate
    feature, characteristic, peculiarity, quality
    color, hue, tinge, shade
    walk, go, totter, stumble

C. In the following sentences, the writers obviously did not say what they intended to say. What did they mean to say?

1. I am sure that you will agree that my town is a good town to be from.
2. When I was in grammar school, I used to trade my friends for knives.
3. I always walk inside my mother when we go down town.
4. It is the duty of a bellhop to carry all the customers' gripes to their rooms.
5. Our dinner at the fraternity last week consisted of the deans and their wives.
6. My roommate, having had one date, is convinced that all girls are flirtatious little wrenches.
7. My sister has an excellent shape on the golf course.
8. When my biology teacher returned to the campus, students were present whom he had taught for 40 years.
9. My father was an officer in the Navy and kept all the enlisted men's money.
10. My oldest brother is 22 and I am 18; the middle-aged one is the bright one in our family.
11. I think that my father is the biggest man alive.
12. As I look back to my athletic activities, I see that I have always had a basketball on my brain.
13. I think I shall never forget a talk by the coke machine, before I left high school.
14. Our high school English teacher inspired her students to greater lengths.
15. He and his brother would take stomach aches from the green apples.

D. What did the writers intend to say in the following sentences?

1. It will be good to get away from bookies for two weeks at Christmas.
2. My grandpa is like grandma an ideal grandpa.
3. Miami, Florida, is a name that is surrounded by pictures of sunshine, sea, and people at play.
4. For an excellent method of transportation I would like to dwell upon the automobile.
5. In this accident only one person was injured, and she was killed outright.
6. Chicago is second in size in the United States with about four million population and is located in the Midwest at the bottom of Lake Michigan.

7. I have thought of getting married many times.
8. We are having my aunt and uncle for Christmas dinner, and I am sure we will enjoy them.
9. I stand solidly on the freshman learning to stand on his own feet.
10. Franklin D. Roosevelt was the longest president that this country has ever had.
11. My father is a barber who has really reached the top.
12. The Governor's mansion is embraced by beautiful flowers and trees.
13. Composition is a point that was never covered in my high school.
14. I kissed my parents off and they left for home.
15. I have had to work twice as hard as all the other students in order to make good grades.

TECHNICAL WORDS

Technical words are those that have special meanings for people in particular fields, professions, or occupations.

Special subject labels are attached by dictionaries to such words. Approximately 50 subject labels are used: Astronomy, Engineering, Entomology, Manufacturing, Marine, Naval, Psychology, etc. Examples of technical words are *lepidopterous* (zoology), *diastrophism* (geology), *broadside* (nautical), *monocotyledon* (botany), *sidereal* (astronomy), *coniferous* (botany), *stratus* (meteorology), *cuprous* (chemistry).

Not all the thousands of technical words are in general dictionaries, but the number is sufficiently large that the general reader need not be baffled by seeing them in print. When technical words are widely enough used or extend their meanings, their subject labels may be dropped. Some examples (made popular by special fields) are *broadcast* (from radio), *telescope* (from astronomy), *weld* (from engineering), *chisel* (from carpentry), *diagnose* (from medicine), *daub* (from painting), *mold* (from sculpture), *starry* (from astronomy), *arch* (from architecture), *virtuoso* (from music and art).

61. Use technical words and phrases appropriately.

A specialist writing for or speaking to other specialists uses many difficult technical terms. If he communicates with others in his general scientific field, he uses less difficult terms. If he addresses the nonspecialist, he should avoid all technical terms or use only those generally understood. These three approaches divide the style used into *technical, semitechnical,* and *nontechnical* or *popular.* For example, few of us could understand a technical treatment of a subject in the magazine, *Electronics.* More of us could understand its treatment in *Scientific American.* All of us could understand it if it were adapted for one of the general magazines on the newsstands.

Many students plan to specialize in one of the arts, sciences, or professions. In writing for your English and other courses on the campus and in later communications, let the kind of reader or listener you are addressing determine your vocabulary in treating technical subjects.

EXERCISE

Using your dictionary, tell what sports or games the following terms are associated with. Some may refer to more than one sport. *Rabbit-punch, spare, fall, javelin, foul, clay pigeon, K.O., dash, half-nelson, double dribble, lateral pass, baby split, fast break, mouse trap, double fault, deuce, Texas leaguer, goalie, ace, grand slam, bull's-eye, bank shot, ringer, break, birdie, love, frame, set-point, vulnerable, strike.*

MIXED FIGURES

Well-phrased similes and metaphors add clarity and effectiveness to writing (Section 63). The chief value of such figures of speech is that, if successful, they suggest attractive associations in the reader's mind. But they should not be considered as mere ornaments of style; they should not be used too frequently; they should not be confused or inappropriate. To violate these principles is to be guilty of one kind of "fine" writing (see Section 66).

62. Avoid the use of mixed and inappropriate figures of speech.

Literal speech, i.e., writing and speaking, is language that means more or less exactly what it says: "I *walked* downstairs to answer the telephone." Figurative language suggests images, imagination, a picture; it is not actually true, but we like the suggestion and find it effective: "I *flew* down the stairs to answer the telephone."

Figurative language, incidentally, has given us many of our idioms (see Section 56).

Verbs are common suggestion words for figurative language, as are nouns. When two words *express* a comparison, we call the "figure of speech" a simile: "She sings like an angel"; when the comparison is *implied,* and we use our imagination, it is a metaphor: "She is an angel when she sings."

Figurative language is, therefore, imaginative, picturesque, and effective. But there are several cautions. Do not shift suddenly from figurative language to literal speech. Do not confuse the images suggested by bringing in several which cannot possibly be related. Especially in the use of metaphor or simile, you should sustain one figure of speech and not shift to another. Finally, remember that direct, simple statement is usually preferable to a series of figures, always preferable when the figures are elaborate, artificial, or trite. Note these examples of inappropriate or mixed figures:

1. The road to dental school is straight, narrow, and strewn with rocks, but the diligent student must swim through it.
2. When she lost her job, she got into a rut and felt all at sea.
3. We stopped at the nearest garage, had the crankcase drained, and thus nipped our trouble in the bud.
4. Directly behind her and pushing her along is the powerful magnet of modern advertising with its fangs of generalities and vague references.
5. Although I can run like a frightened rabbit, the coach has thrown me off the team like an old shoe.

EXERCISES

A. Improve the wording of the five sentences above.

B. Point out any inconsistent figurative language in the following, and rewrite sentences containing it.

1. I was a "big wheel" on our high school campus, but I haven't done much trotting around here at college.
2. Later on, I hope to become a well-oiled cog in the beehive of industry.
3. The British prime minister dove into the sea of European politics

415

and soon stood on the top of the highest Alp of international diplomacy.

4. Come commencement time, I plan to set my sails, get up steam, take off, and make a real dent in the highway of Life.

5. Three of us boys were sure the kingpins on the roost in our high school.

6. Our commencement speaker gave us this advice: "Make hay while the sun shines, or you may find yourself out on a limb with your nose to the grindstone."

7. My father is always on his toes when he is driving a car.

8. After football season many a football player who was a tidal wave on the football field has to put his head to the grindstone and study.

9. At any party there is always a rotten apple that throws a monkey wrench in our food and drink.

10. My tour through Pennsylvania was my maiden voyage through the coal regions.

11. I shall not eat any of my companions' dust as we soar through the air and hit pay dirt across the goal line.

12. Some truck drivers are so skilful that they can turn around on a dime and give you 9 cents in change.

13. A self-made man is one who has looked into the future with a stiff upper lip, and has used his backbone as a spark in washing away difficulties.

14. This man was formerly a bum who was knocked to the floor by the vicissitudes of life, but he kept his head above water, finally hit the bull's-eye, and is now a success in business.

15. The very lifeblood of student government has been sapped because student senate members have refused to turn over a new leaf.

16. When I stood at the foul line in that crucial game, I was sure behind the eight-ball, but I heaved it in the air and with a sigh of relief fell through.

17. Northern Canada is full of virgin forests; the hand of man has never set foot there.

18. In learning to fly, a young air cadet may stub his toe in the air and have to come down in a hurry and land on water.

19. I was at that awkward age that whenever I opened my mouth, I put my foot in.

20. In the high tide of prosperity, our country went over the cliff in 1929, and, neither sinking nor swimming, wandered in the wilderness of depression for 10 years.

C. Note that the sentences above contain numerous *trite expressions* (see Section 65). Try to rewrite some of the sentences, substituting less worn phrases.

D. Make a list of 20 *effective* figures of speech which you have found in reading.

EMPHATIC DICTION

63. Words should be emphatic as well as clear. Certain words are correct and clear but do not have strength or force. Such expressions are abstract, or feeble, or worn out. Good writing is positive and vigorous; it shuns tame, colorless diction.

63a. Prefer specific and concrete to general and abstract words.

A specific word names a narrow concept; a general word names a broad concept. Thus *animal* and *land* are general words; *stallion* and *pasture* are specific. Notice the greater effectiveness of the second sentence following:

> It was a noisy stream as it came running down the mountain.
> Chestnut Creek felt its way down Mount Greybeard over smooth, greenish-white stones.

An abstract word suggests no very tangible picture or impression: *go, move, truth, envy, fast.* A concrete word suggests something tangible, something usually perceivable by the senses: *totter, mile-a-minute, incarnadine, jagged, lemony, rose-scented, drum-beats.*

The use of specific nouns and concrete phrases, and of specific verbs which tell of action (motion) or relate to the senses (emotion) will help make writing more forceful. The diction of the following passage is so emphatic and exact that the reader, with no further details supplied, can form a satisfactory picture of Ichabod Crane:

> The cognomen of Crane was not inapplicable to his person. He was tall, but exceedingly lank, with narrow shoulders, long arms and legs, hands that dangled a mile out of his sleeves, feet that might have served for shovels, and his whole frame most loosely hung together. His head was small, and flat at the top, with huge ears, large green glassy eyes, and a long snip nose, so that it looked like a weathercock perched upon his spindle neck to tell which way the wind blew. To see him striding

along the profile of a hill on a windy day, with his clothes bagging and fluttering about him, one might have mistaken him for the genius of Famine descending upon the earth or some scarecrow eloped from a cornfield.

—Washington Irving, *The Legend of Sleepy Hollow*

63b. Make occasional use of figurative language.

Effective writing frequently contains some figures of speech, usually metaphors or similes. A metaphor is a statement which implies a comparison between two ideas or objects; it is not literally true but it has a genuine effectiveness in driving home an abstract idea. A simile is essentially the same as a metaphor except that it expresses by means of such words as *like* and *as* a comparison which the metaphor only implies. The passage from Washington Irving quoted above suggests how apt and effective both metaphor and simile may be.

Effective as they are, you should not overload your work with figures of speech and, above all, you should not mix them (see Section 62). Many of the most trite phrases are worn-out similes: *brave as a lion, brown as a berry, busy as a bee, clear as crystal, cold as ice, mad as a wet hen.* Of course, similes such as these should not be used (see Section 65).

63c. Use words and phrases rich in suggestive values.

If your goal is writing exposition or argument (see Sections 16c, d), you will use words which are as exact and specific as possible. Clearness is a basic guiding principle. Even in such writing, however, as well as in narration and description, search for words which suggest more than they say, which stimulate the imagination. San Francisco is "a seaport city in California," but the name suggests such connotations as "Golden Gate," "The Gateway to the Orient," "Chinatown," and "earthquake of 1906." *Connotative* words are effective, for they have implied, suggestive, or associated meanings; *denotative* words are clear, for they are to be taken in their literal, explicit meaning. Contrast what *house* and *home, woman* and *mother, animal* and *dog* suggest to you. A dog is, according to denotative meaning, "a carnivorous, domesticated mammal," but to anyone who has ever owned or loved a dog, the word suggests a wealth of associated meanings.

418

No rule can be laid down for the choice and use of words rich in connotative meanings. Skilled writers sense the suggestive powers of words, and a study of the language of such writers will aid more than any mere reading of the dictionary can. But do not exaggerate unduly in your word choice; otherwise you will reduce effectiveness (see Section **60b**).

63d. Use direct and simple words.

The use of pretentious words is dealt with in Section **66,** but it should be noted here that simple, direct words add force to writing. Do not use *tonsorial parlor, purloiner, lubritorium, emporium, natatorium,* etc.; use the simpler words: *barber shop, thief, service station, store, swimming pool.*

Other means to attain emphasis in diction:

→1. Prefer words that fit the context (see Section **64**).
→2. Use fresh, unhackneyed words (see Section **65**).
→3. Be economical in using words (see Section **67**).

EXERCISES

A. With the aid of your dictionary, substitute more emphatic words for the following: *building, applause, task, utter* (verb), *sticky, flock* (noun), *loose* (adjective), *writer, vicinity, run* (verb), *say, walk* (noun), *thing, hastily, instrument, comfortable, good, bite* (verb), *tired, careful.*

B. Name several words which have the same general meaning as the word italicized but which are more exact and emphatic: (1) A *tall* building; (2) a *vital* story; (3) your *nice* child; (4) a *talkative* man; (5) his *grave* condition; (6) a *brief* statement; (7) a *kind* person; (8) a *loud* noise; (9) he *worked* hard; (10) on the *boat;* (11) she *walked* in; (12) an angry *speech;* (13) a *leading* merchant; (14) I was *surprised;* (15) it's a *pleasant* room; (16) a *dislike* of war; (17) a good *pattern* to follow; (18) the bird *flew* away; (19) a *good* mind; (20) he *got* on the carousel; (21) he *ran* quickly; (22) a *small* animal; (23) a dilapidated *conveyance;* (24) the doorbell *sounded;* (25) a miserable *house;* (26) Dr. Jonas is a *specialist;* (27) a *warm* day; (28) a *delightful* book; (29) an interesting *trip;* (30) an *intelligent* student.

C. The poetry of John Keats is noteworthy for its specific, concrete, sense-appealing terms. Discuss and point out the *specific* words in the first stanza given; point out and discuss the *concrete* words in the second. (Both stanzas are from "Ode to a Nightingale.")

My heart aches, and a drowsy numbness pains
　　My sense, as though of hemlock I had drunk,
Or emptied some dull opiate to the drains
　　One minute past, and Lethe-wards had sunk:
'Tis not through envy of thy happy lot,
　　But being too happy in thine happiness—
　　　　That thou, light-winged Dryad of the trees,
　　　　　　In some melodious plot
Of beechen green, and shadows numberless,
　　Singest of summer in full-throated ease.

I cannot see what flowers are at my feet,
　　Nor what soft incense hangs upon the boughs,
But, in embalmed darkness, guess each sweet
　　Wherewith the seasonable month endows
The grass, the thicket, and the fruit-tree wild;
　　White hawthorn, and the pastoral eglantine;
　　　　Fast fading violets cover'd up in leaves;
　　　　　　And mid-May's eldest child,
The coming musk-rose, full of dewy wine,
　　The murmurous haunt of flies on summer eves.

D. Review Section **53**, "Obsolete and Archaic Words." Then reread the stanzas above; make a list of all the terms that *seem* to you obsolete or archaic. Check your list against dictionary labels. Which of your words are labeled "poetic"?

APPROPRIATENESS

64. Choose words which are appropriate.

The first essentials of diction are that it should be *clear* and *exact*. But as is pointed out at various places in this book, diction can be clear and exact for one purpose and yet be neither for another. A word is wrongly chosen when it is out of harmony with either its context or the circumstances under which it is used.

You are not likely to use illiterate words (Section **57**) except, perhaps, in the most informal of informal conversations, and, even then, perhaps only for humorous purposes. Illiterate words do appear, frequently with good reason, in reports of conversation given in narrative and also in certain comic strips and radio or TV programs. If they aptly characterize or are used for other purposes, they are appropriate and hence may be said to "belong." Similarly much slang and shoptalk appear in these communication media, in the conversation of fellow workers or close friends, and in informal letters.

Informal writing and speech may use localisms (Section 54), colloquialisms (Section 55), and slang (Section 59). Purposefully used, they aid communication of thought from speaker or writer to hearer or reader and are not to be avoided.

For appropriate writing and speaking, the three general areas discussed briefly on pages 337–340—formal, informal or colloquial, and substandard—can be further subdivided.

As Professor Paul Roberts points out in *Understanding Grammar*,[1] there is no single "standard" English but several standards, or levels, of usage whose appropriateness depends upon the circumstances in which they are employed. Dictionaries themselves do not always agree on the names given to various levels. Professor Roberts writes:

> Some terms emphasize distinctions affected by the medium (written English, spoken English, newspaper English, radio English, stage English); some emphasize the situation (formal English, informal English, literary English, academic English, trade talk, colloquial English); some emphasize the taste or temperament or background of the user (conservative English, liberal English, provincial English, vulgate English). It seems best to choose main terms that will emphasize the medium and the background of the user rather than the situation. Grammar is, to be sure, affected also by circumstances; we vary some grammatical forms according to whether we are addressing an umpire or a bishop. But compared to vocabulary, grammar changes little with the situation, whereas it is very much affected by whether we are speaking or writing and by our social background. . . .
>
> Choice Written English: This is the writing found in carefully edited and copy-read books and magazines. These are published for the most part in the larger cities, but the writing of many people in all parts of the country would fall in this category. This is the usage described by most handbooks of English.

[1] *Understanding Grammar* (New York: Harper & Brothers, 1954). Much of the discussion in this section is based upon the comment on levels of usage in this book, pp. 13–15; the authors gladly acknowledge their indebtedness to Professor Roberts.

General Written English: This is exemplified by the ordinary run of newspapers the country over and by the scripts read by the average radio announcer. Newspaper and radio writing is necessarily hasty and is often produced by people who are ignorant of or unimpressed by the niceties of Choice Written. General Written English is probably the level attained by the average college graduate who takes pen in hand.

Choice Spoken English: This is the language heard in formal and serious speeches and addresses. It is used also, however, in much ordinary conversation, being for many people the native dialect learned in the nursery and for others the result of an effort to apply the precepts of Choice Written to the spoken language. Choice Spoken English is the language of many college graduates and of some others as well.

General Spoken English: This is the level used by most educated people in conversation. It is the level indicated by the label "colloquial" as this term is used in most dictionaries. General Spoken English is more easygoing than Choice Spoken, and it tends to employ newer and shorter forms, but it is not on that account "incorrect." Some people who are able to speak either, prefer General to Choice Spoken English.

Vulgate English: This is the term used for all expressions associated with the uneducated. (Words are powerful and likely to be invidious when they have social implications. It may not be superfluous to say that one who speaks Vulgate English is not necessarily vulgar, any more than one who speaks Choice English is necessarily snobbish or affected. Most of us simply speak the language of our fathers and our friends.)

These distinctions are more or less arbitrary; they are easily distinguishable at their centers, but they run together at the extremes. Indeed, it might be said that there are as many levels of usage as there are speakers of the language. Vulgate English has many well-marked subdivisions, and these would have to be specified in a grammar of substandard English. Since we, however, are primarily concerned with English acceptable among the educated, the blanket term *Vulgate* will serve.

We may also observe that most expressions in the language are identical on all levels. For example, no dialect deviation is likely in the sentence "I walked home." In this expression Choice Written English and Vulgate English coincide. On the other hand, there are numerous constructions that we recognize as common to some and not to others.

It is often difficult to label a construction apart from the whole context, but the five levels may be roughly illustrated as follows:

Choice Written:	I shall not return.
General Written:	I will not return.
Choice Spoken:	I'll not return.
General Spoken:	I'm not coming back.
Vulgate:	I ain't comin' back.

Inappropriateness in writing and speaking is often the result of incongruous associations. Remember that illiterate and slangy words and expressions, and some kinds of colloquialisms, are as out of place in formal writing as are learned and dignified words in an informal, humorous account of some campus activity, even though such sets of words may express exactly what the writer means. It is important that there be harmony between word and tone, between what you say and your attitude toward your material. Is your purpose a serious, whimsical, satiric, or humorous account? Is your aim a plain or an ornamental style? A formal or a conversational style? A green bow tie does not belong with a full-dress suit, nor is a tuxedo seen on the golf course. Words, too, must be appropriate.

As you plan, therefore, and as you write or speak, keep constantly in mind (1) your reader or listener, (2) the circumstances or occasion, (3) your purpose, and (4) the possibilities in your subject. Are your words appropriate for each? Effective communication is effective adaptation.

EXERCISES

A. Discuss the appropriateness and correctness of:

    nonsense, twaddle, buncombe, bunk
    money, financial resources, legal tender, swag
    talk, converse, chatter, gab
    skin, complexion, pelt, hide
    contemptible, shameful, unsatisfactory, lousy
    combat, scuffle, tussle, scrap
    osculation, caress, kiss, smack
    banquet, dinner, snack, bite
    automobile, car, jalopy, hot rod
    fascinate, entertain, please, wow

B. Choose some term from one of your science courses, a term that should have a more detailed definition than that given in the dictionary.

Write four definitions of the term, one each for an elementary school child, a high school freshman, a classmate not taking the science course, and a "pen pal" in a foreign country.

TRITENESS

Trite or hackneyed expressions, or clichés, are words which have lost their force through overuse. The origins of the words *triteness, hackneyed,* and *cliché* are illuminating: the first comes from the Latin word *tritus,* the past participle of *terere,* which means *to rub, to wear out; hackneyed* is derived from the idea of a horse, or carriage, let out for hire, devoted to common use, and thus worn out in service; *cliché* comes from the French word *clicher,* meaning to *stereotype,* "to cast from a mold, to use over and over."

Thus trite words and phrases are but rubber stamps or stereotyped plates of thought and expression. They may be tags from common speech, or overworked quotations, or outworn phrases from newspapers. They save the writer the trouble of thinking exactly what he means, but their use results in writing which is stale and ineffective. Such words and phrases inevitably seem humorous; they are, indeed, regularly used for humor or irony by fiction writers and columnists. Used seriously, they are signs that the speaker, or writer, is naïve.

65. Avoid trite language.

Our familiarity with trite words and expressions is likely to cause them to occur to us more readily than others which are more effective. We should therefore look with suspicion upon each word or phrase which leaps to mind until we can assure ourselves that the expression is exact, fresh, and unhackneyed. We should be on our guard especially against overused similes. It is also well for us to remember that words and phrases which do not seem trite to us may be clichés to any reader more familiar than we with overworked expressions.

Note this list of clichés:

a bolt from the blue	acid test
abreast of the times	after all is said and done
aching void	a long-felt want

all in all
along these lines
and like that
arms of Morpheus
artistic temperament
as luck would have it
at a loss for words
at one fell swoop
bathed in tears
beggars description
believe me
bitter end
blood is thicker than water
brilliant performance
budding genius
busy as a bee
by and large
by leaps and bounds
captain of industry
center of attraction
checkered career
clinging vine
close to nature
conspicuous by its absence
Dame Fortune
deadly earnest
depend upon it
depths of despair
doomed to disappointment
drastic action
dull thud
each and every
epic struggle
equal to the occasion
eyes like stars
fair sex
familiar landmark
favor with a selection
few and far between
fiber of his (my) being
filthy lucre

first and foremost
flower of the Old South
fools rush in
footprints on the sands of time
force of circumstances
free as the air
goes without saying
golden locks (tresses)
goodly number
green as grass
green with envy
gridiron heroes (warriors)
heartfelt thanks
heart's content
heated argument
he-man
holy bonds of wedlock
holy estate of matrimony
in great profusion
in the last analysis
In the spring a young man's
    fancy . . .
iron constitution
irony of fate
it stands to reason
last but not least
last straw
last white line
like an old shoe
limped into port
looking for all the world like
mantle of snow
meets the eye
method in his madness
monarch of all I survey
more in sorrow than in anger
Mother Nature
motley throng
myriad lights
needs no introduction
nipped in the bud

no thinking man
none the worse for wear
of the earth earthy
paramount issue
pending merger
picturesque scene
pleasing prospect
powers that be
promising future
proud possessor
psychological moment
race, creed, or color (substitute: race, belief, or national origin)
red as a rose
reigns supreme
riot of color
ruling passion
sad to relate
sadder but wiser
safe to say
sea of faces
(seething) mass of humanity
self-made man
shadow of the goal posts
sigh of relief
simple life
skeleton in the closet
sleep the sleep of the just
snow-capped mountains
soul of honor
strong as an ox

strong, silent man
struggle for existence
sturdy as an oak
take my word for it
take pen in hand
taken into custody
the happy pair
the plot thickens
the time of my life
the weaker sex
the worse for wear
thereby hangs a tale
thunderous applause
time marches on
tired but happy
too full for utterance
too funny for words
venture a suggestion
walk of life
wends his way
wheel of fortune
where angels fear to tread
where ignorance is bliss
with bated breath
words fail me
words fail to express
work like a Trojan (or a beaver)
wrapped in mystery
wreathed in smiles
wrought havoc
wry countenance

EXERCISES

A. Compare and summarize the meanings given in your dictionary for *banal, cliché, commonplace, hackneyed, stereotyped, trite.*

B. Criticize the following piece of doggerel:

> When will we cease to write in books
> Of murmuring, gurgling, twisting brooks,
> Of winds that sigh and moan and beat,

Of the beautiful maiden's dainty feet,
Of crowds that surge and wagons that clatter,
Of waters that swirl and birds that chatter,
Of his firm jaw and his modest ties,
Of her sunlit hair and her heavenly eyes,
Of fleeting clouds that fleck the sky,
Of loves that wait but never die,
Of lips that tremble and quiver and curl,
Of bosoms that heave, and teeth like pearl,
Of engines that puff and throb and groan,
Of the villain's hiss, and his low, tense tone,
Of the dying sun's last flickering beam,
Of the pale moon's mellow, tender gleam?
 When, my friend? When the universe is dead,
When the brooks are dry, or gone instead,
When the sun doesn't shine, and the moon doesn't show,
There you have it, my friend—and now you know.

C. Rephrase 10 of the clichés in this doggerel, above, so that the phrasing has an air of freshness.

D. Make a list of 20 trite expressions which you have used in recent themes or conversations, or which you have overheard.

FINE WRITING

"Fine writing" is writing which is mistakenly thought to be free from all impurities because it has been elevated and brought to perfection; actually, it is writing which is affected or overcareful.

66. Avoid "fine writing."

The use of direct and simple words to gain effectiveness in writing is mentioned in Section **63.** You should avoid pretentiousness, artificiality, and affectation if you wish to be clear, exact, and emphatic.

1. Polysyllabication.

The use of pompous and flowery words of several syllables is fine writing. To use the short word rather than the long, if it will serve as well, is sound practice. Short words are usually more understandable and less self-conscious than polysyllabic words. Someone has said, "Short words are words of might"—good advice for effective writing.

This advice does not mean that polysyllables should never be used; it means that they should not be used if they cause writing to sound high-flown, ostentatious, or pedantic. Note these examples: *auriferous teeth; savory repast* for *meal; retire* for *go to bed; prevaricate* for *lie; ratiocinate* for *think; pulchritude* for *beauty; inebriated, intoxicated* for *drunk; comestibles* for *food; devouring element* for *fire; obsequies* for *funeral; peregrinations* for *travel*.

2. The Use of Too Many Modifiers.

Be careful to give your reader a clear, full understanding of your meaning but avoid piling on descriptive words. Use adjectives and adverbs intelligently, not lavishly.

3. The Use of Foreign Words and Briticisms.

The inexperienced writer may be tempted to adopt a pretentious style of writing because he is overwhelmed by the seriousness of his purpose. Frequently he will make the mistake of interlarding his work with foreign expressions or Briticisms (British expressions rather than American) in a desire to convince the reader of his erudition and dignity. Examples: *chef d'oeuvre, magnum opus, à bon marché, à propos de rien, dum vivimus vivamus, exempli gratia, garçon, morceau, robe-de-chambre, lift* for *elevator, petrol* for *gasoline*. (See also Exercise D, p. 387.)

Do not hesitate to use the foreign word if it has been generally accepted through naturalization or if there is no exact English equivalent. But do not use such words too frequently or merely to show your erudition.

EXERCISES

A. Improve the wording of the following sentences:

1. I am an enthusiast for erudition in the nidification of ornithology.
2. Ah, how invigorating to quaff the immaculate waters of a frigidized mountain spring!
3. My teacher says that I am having serious trouble with my orthography and some slight trouble with my calligraphy.
4. The charabancs between New York and Chicago use hundreds of liters of petrol.
5. Some men are so penurious that they make amanuenses out of their wives.

6. Your name's fair escutcheon has been tarnished beyond redemption.
7. His vitriolic discourse exacerbated the overweening students.
8. *Mirabile dictu,* he soon became convalescent and finally regained his strength, *peu à peu.*
9. He entered the sudatorium and, after leaving that, he plunged into the gelid natatorium.
10. He presaged the *Anschluss* because of an insidious *Weltschmerz* which had suffused his whole spirit.

B. Improve the wording of the following:

1. Every morning I imbibe deep inhalations of uncontaminated ozone.
2. Our family's improved financial status has eliminated our former eleemosynary situation.
3. My cogitations about osculation are that it is the mutual approximation of oral zones.
4. As a child, Grandmother perambulated 12 miles every day to a little bucolic edifice of erudition.
5. A superfluity of gastronomical tidbits contributed to the *bon vivant's* demise.
6. My prognostication for any student who doesn't participate in activities is that he will soon sink from inanition into nonentity.
7. If the ineptitude of the professorial artists on this campus does not increase the multiplicity of my erudition, I shall migrate to a more circumambient center of learning.
8. I deprecate the obfuscation of my last semester's instructor; the semanticistic terminology he used in his peculiar calligraphy kept me in a perpetual state of intrepidation.
9. A British prime minister, in the apotheosis of his linguistic abilities, once asseverated that his opponent was "a sophistical rhetorician, inebriated with the exuberance of his own verbosity."
10. Prime Minister Winston Churchill, under obligation to make a retraction of an asseveration that a fellow-Parliamentarian was a prevaricator, did so by saying that he was responsible for a terminological inexactitude.

CONCISENESS

Diction, to be effective, must be as economical as possible. This does not mean that writing should be sketchy or that necessary words may be omitted (see Sections **35, 31**). On the other hand, wordiness weakens the force of expression.

In forceful writing, the ratio of ideas to words is high. In poetry, which consists of "words in their best possible use," "each word must carry 20 other words upon its back." Conciseness alone does not achieve effective writing, but it is difficult for you to write forcefully if you use two or three words to convey the idea which one word would express.

Two types of wordiness which apply particularly to sentence structure—the useless repetition of an idea and the useless piling up of unnecessary details—are discussed in Section **44.** For some writers it may be easier to consider such wordiness as problems in word use rather than as problems in sentence construction. They are therefore discussed here as applicable to your diction when you are using more words to express your meaning than are needed.

67. Avoid wordiness.

1. Eliminate words which are superfluous. Study these examples, noting that in each example one word of the two or three expresses the idea, and the other words add nothing:

more perfect	four-cornered square
more paramount	from whence
unusually (most) unique	fellow classmates
many in number	complete monopoly
round in form (shape)	each and everyone
perfect circle	individual person

2. Repeating a pronoun after a noun and overuse of *there is, there are, there was,* etc., are other examples of superfluous use of words:

Wordy: The coach *he* has a difficult job.
Concise: The coach has a difficult job.

Wordy: My mother *she* writes me letters three times a week.
Concise: My mother writes me letters three times a week.

Wordy: *There were* three books lying open on the table.
Concise: Three books lay open on the table.

Wordy: In the library *there are* many reference books to help you.
Concise: The library has many reference books to help you.

3. Do not use two or three words where one will serve.

Wordy: You will find the reference librarian *in back of* the desk.
Concise: You will find the reference librarian *behind* the desk.

Wordy: Give your directions *very definitely and precisely.*
Concise: Give *definite* directions.

Wordy: John *is going to plan to* write you tomorrow.
Concise: John *will* write you tomorrow.

Wordy: My absence was *due to the fact that* I had an attack of influenza.
Concise: My absence was due to an attack of influenza.

4. Use direct words instead of circumlocutions and euphemisms. A circumlocution is literally "a roundabout way of speaking": *tame, villatic fowl* for *chicken, lowing herd* for *cattle.* Euphemisms are mild, inoffensive expressions for blunter, less pleasant, and perhaps more effective words: *to pass away* for *to die, remains* for *corpse, perspire* for *sweat.*

Wordy: He has pursued his course of studies along the lines of mechanical engineering.
Concise: He has studied mechanical engineering.

Wordy: Grandfather was called home and passed to the Great Beyond in 1937.
Concise: Grandfather died in 1937.

Wordy: Students who disobey regulations will be separated from the university.
Concise: Students who disobey regulations will be expelled.

5. Avoid too many modifiers (especially adjectives and adverbs), which result in wordiness (see Section **66**, part 2). Example:

It was a cold, bleak, gray day. John walked home nimbly and briskly. He felt full of life, keenly alert, and far from sluggish, despite the gloominess and cloudiness of his immediate surroundings.

EXERCISES

A. If you have not done so yet, do Exercise B on page 311 (end of Section 44).

B. Apply the principles of conciseness to the following sentences:

1. To many questions, I always answer in the complete negative.
2. Benjamin Franklin succeeded because he pursued his various tasks with great diligence.
3. Father and Mother have been in a continual state of blessed matrimony for 25 years.
4. There are three sports that are played during the summer and that are popular.
5. The Red Cross is in constant and necessary need for donors to give of their precious life-giving fluid.
6. I am going to make a fresh start, and begin anew on my term paper by starting from scratch.
7. In the summers we enjoy the rural life of the country, but in the fall we are glad to return to the urban life of the city.
8. Gerald's height is not very tall for playing basketball.
9. Each and everyone of the teachers in high school tried to help us.
10. I worked hard, and finally my grades began rising toward the top.
11. I have found it very easy to maintain average grades.
12. I do not wish a paper weight which is square in shape; I want one oval in form.
13. The end of the corridor comes to a conclusion at a small green door.
14. The desire to express oneself well is a universal craving which is common to all people.
15. It is undeniably true that once you start to study in earnest that your troubles will be lessened and mitigated.

C. To attain conciseness, improve the wording of the following sentences:

1. Our local ne'er-do-well has long been notorious for his being a complete stranger to the truth.
2. There are times when one is justified in yielding to the temptation of indulging in the pleasant little practice of telling little albescent prevarications.
3. According as to whether there is any precipitation of humidity tomorrow, we plan to spend the day using our wiles in angling for the finny prey.
4. To be perfectly honest and not to tell a lie, this is the plain, unvarnished, denuded truth.
5. My girl friend has an unconcealed dislike for any boy who shows significant tendencies toward gulosity.
6. Our representative of the local press announces that last evening a

little bundle from heaven arrived at the domicile of Mr. and Mrs. Harry Butler.

7. As your eye travels over the vast expanse of ocean, you are impressed to the deepest and highest degree by the fact that man is a creature of little importance on the terrestrial part of this cosmic universe.

8. From the time he was 5 years old, and he is now 18, Stephen has suffered during the months of August, September, and October from the malady known as hay fever.

9. The Dean has been in communication with my parents to the effect that I have been receiving considerably below passing grades in two of my subjects.

10. The greatest factor in his success was that he had reached a man's estate in a healthy physical condition.

11. With great diligence the student pursued his studies along the lines of medicine.

12. In this instance, his answer in the affirmative was a distinct asset to our business.

13. He was a serious type of student: he wished to major in the chemical field.

14. Illumination is required to be extinguished before this building is closed for the night.

15. In cashing checks, balance on deposit must cover checks to be cashed.

USELESS REPETITION

68. Some repetition is effective, particularly in sentence structure (see Sections **35, 45**). But faulty repetition of words, phrases, or sentence structure is always objectionable. (See Sections **48, 50** for comment on monotonous sentence structure.) Ineffective repetition of words or phrases is caused by an unwillingness to search for a substitute, by a limited vocabulary, or by careless re-use of the same word.

68a. Avoid objectionable repetition of words and phrases.

Repetition is faulty unless a word or phrase is repeated for effectiveness or for clarity. Faulty repetition may be corrected by using pronouns more liberally, by substituting equivalent expressions (synonyms), or by recasting the sentence. Note the following examples of objectionable repetition:

1. *Since* several weeks have elapsed *since* you wrote, I have decided not to repeat the offer.

2. He *thought* everyone would *think* his act to be generous.
3. Each of you must *study* hard in order to finish your *studies* by noon.
4. He *said that* you *said that* we should apply promptly.
5. She *placed* the box in another *place*.

NOTE: Repetition, however, even if faulty, is preferable to artificial and awkward avoidance of it.

Artificial: Some newspapers publish news; other organs of the press issue material which frequently has only an approximate degree of timeliness.

Improved: Some newspapers publish news; others publish material which has only an apparent timeliness.

Especially faulty repetition results when a conjunction or a preposition already used is repeated, such as *that* or *in;* the necessary grammatical relationship or meaning needs only the one word, not both.

Bad: I hope *that* after I graduate *that* I will be able to go into business for myself.

Don't think *that* because you have never had an accident *that* you can't easily have one.

Characteristic of my cousin is the high degree of honesty *in* which he believes *in.*

At what place are you living *at* now?

The Reference Room, *in* which we went *through* quickly, seemed to be the most interesting.

68b. Avoid useless repetition of ideas already expressed by a word or phrase.

When meaning is expressed or implied in a particular word or phrase, repeating the idea by additional words is useless. Common examples are using *again* with many verbs beginning with *re:* less frequent is the use of *more* or *most* with adjectives and adverbs already ending in *-er, -est.* Examples:

most unkindest	to meet up with
more older	connect up with
more better	rise up
repeat it again	the sunset in the west
return back	cooperate together
recur again	join together

resume again	long length
loquacious talker	first beginnings
Christmas Eve evening	this afternoon at 3 P.M.
endorse on the back	visible to the eye
necessary need	audible to the ear

EXERCISES

A. Correct the objectionable repetition in the five illustrative sentences in Section 68a.

B. Correct the faulty repetition in the following sentences:

1. In autumn the leaves are all colored red, yellow, brown, and etc.
2. Please note that in November all football games will begin at 1:30 P.M. on Saturday afternoons.
3. In this modern age of today, most people are too highly educated to believe in superstitions.
4. I have no real cause to dislike the number "13," but, nevertheless, I do.
5. In a department store you will see many new novelties.
6. The main thought that should be kept in mind is that people are at college to learn, so therefore studies must have first place.
7. Long ago in past centuries people were prone to believe in superstitions.
8. I think that with an English class once a day that the teacher learns to know each student better.
9. Before too many years roll by, I hope to roll up and down the world.
10. You will soon find it will not be difficult to find ways to avoid repetition.
11. For days I was unable to pay for it, for my allowance was a few days late.
12. The depth of the pool at that end is about 12 feet deep.
13. My room that I now have in the new dormitory has much more room than the room I had in the old dormitory where I lived.
14. He had but 10 dollars, but he was determined to go since no one but him had volunteered.
15. The cover of my dictionary is covered with a blue cover.
16. All of Shakespeare's plays have been dramatized for the stage.
17. Weeds in a lawn or a garden are a nuisance, but, nevertheless, they can be controlled.
18. Tired but happy, we arrived here yesterday morning at 2 A.M.

19. The end of the lecture was concluded with the speaker's closing remarks.
20. As a freshman in college, my future glows bright in the future.

C. Correct the faulty repetition in the following sentences:

1. In this book there is a conclusion at the end of each chapter.
2. We got up at 4 A.M. in the morning to begin our 600-mile drive.
3. The height of the highest mountain in my state is over 4,000 feet high.
4. The opening of this essay begins with a quotation from Shakespeare.
5. We must look for certain desirable qualities when we choose a future companion for the years to come.
6. Sometimes strategy demands that an army retreat back.
7. Older automobiles had windshield wipers which were hand-operated by hand.
8. To introduce myself to you, I am writing this autobiography of myself.
9. We all pitched in and did the work rapidly fast.
10. To reiterate what I have said in the preceding paragraphs, I wish to say it again.
11. The depth of the water in this lake must be three hundred feet deep.
12. In the future years to come that lie ahead, I hope to be a successful business executive.
13. In many ways my roommate and I are similarly alike.
14. I have since changed my mind since then.
15. Mark Twain has written an autobiography of his life.
16. Our school didn't have a large number of students, so consequently all grades from one to 12 were in the same building.
17. The articles in our book of readings are quite long in length.
18. An atomic scientist is one who knows all about the atomic structure of atoms.
19. The first few days I felt sort of alone and lonely.
20. In order to avoid repeated repetition, I usually try to find synonymous words of nearly the same meaning.

EUPHONY

69. Euphony means "pleasing sound." Its antonym is cacophony, "harsh, ugly sound." Say each word aloud several times, and notice the difference. To be effective, diction should be euphonious, pleasant to the ear.

Euphony

Most of us obtain meaning from the written or printed page through our eyes. The words we see are wriggly black figures spread across the page and can seldom be called beautiful. As we read, however, we are forming—subconsciously, semiconsciously, or even consciously—conceptions of how this writing would sound if read aloud. Even in silent reading the sense conveyed is lessened and our attention is distracted by disagreeable combinations of cacophonous words.

Writing which is beautiful, therefore, symbolizes sounds which please the ear, not the eye. Of course, the *sense* of words is more important than their *sound,* but really good prose contains words whose sound and sense are harmonious. Reading aloud is a good method of detecting uneuphonious sounds in our own writing and in that of others.

69a. Avoid awkward and harsh combinations of sounds.

Euphonious prose rarely contains *rhyme* or *alliteration;* it also shuns the frequent repetition of *unpleasant sounds.*

1. *Rhyme* means similarity of sound of vowels and consonants: *sound, found; bubble, trouble; fair, wear.* In poetry, it is an added adornment; in prose it is a general source of annoyance to the reader.

> Don't worry about me; I'll hurry to be on time.
> I start studying at seven so that I can be in bed by 11.
> I'm writing you this letter to tell you that my health is considerably better.

2. *Alliteration* is the using of a number of words in the same sentence beginning with the same consonant sound or using in fairly close succession words beginning with the same consonant sound. Common examples are the so-called tongue-twisters:

> Peter Piper picked to pickle pints of pickling peppers; did Peter Piper pickle the pints of pickling peppers that he picked?
> Summer swallows, swiftly skimming, sail serenely summer's skies.
> The statistics of this strange situation surely seem simple.
> The balmy winds blew warmly over the bay.

3. Unpleasant sounds are conveyed through overuse of words containing *k, ck* sounds (*flak, clack, black*), hissing sounds of *s*

(*hiss, miss*), nasal sounds of *m, n* (*wrangle, climb*), guttural sounds of *g* (*gutter, gaseous, go*). Pleasant sounds are suggested by words containing, for example, letters like *z* or the *z-sound* of *s*, and *l*, and *r*.

> Joe's a go-getter; backed against the wall and with bleak and black prospects, he'll get going and never let the gutter get him down.
> Roses are flinging their perfumes through the air.

69b. Avoid overuse of the same or similar-sounding words.

Overuse of the same or similar-sounding words distracts a hearer's attention, and, subconsciously or half-consciously, also distracts the reader.

1. Overuse, through repetition of the same words:

> My coming to college was made possible by some money which was made possible by a job I had last summer.
> The use of crop rotation is used on many farms.
> Organized charitable organizations carry on charitable work in my community.

2. Overuse of *homographs:* words with the same spelling but of different origin and meaning.

> I was pleased to see so many fair ladies in attendance at our county fair.
> The last archer to wield bow and arrow was wearing an Arrow bow tie.
> Mr. Robinson will now lead us in a discussion of the poisons possible through the use of lead.
> The sole reason for using these soles to half-sole shoes is their inexpensiveness.

3. Overuse of *homonyms:* words with the same pronunciation but different in origin, meaning, and, very often, spelling.

> The bare facts will bear me out in my assertion.
> My date at the dance was an unmitigated bore, but I patiently bore with him for the entire evening.
> I shall meet you at the butcher's to buy our meat for the picnic.

4. Overuse of a series of words having endings which are alike or nearly alike. Exaggerated example:

Driven oxen aren't seen moving many times ridden by many singing citizens.

5. Ending a sentence with a phrase and beginning the next sentence with the same or nearly the same phrase:

During this semester I had to learn to study with people about me. Studying with people about me has many disadvantages.

A good example of an historical novel is Charles Dickens' *A Tale of Two Cities*. *A Tale of Two Cities* is a story of the French Revolution.

EXERCISES

A. Rewrite the sentences used as illustrations in 69a and 69b, to make them euphonious.

B. In accordance with the principles of euphony, rewrite the following sentences:

1. Bill could not pay the bill until he opened the till.
2. These apples the boys packed into boxes for the railroads to carry away.
3. Analytics is the science of analysis.
4. The job of building the display was a big one, but we built it in a big way, fast.
5. Frank fearlessly faced the fiendish foe, and foremost fighting fell.
6. In organizing this organization, we hoped to organize a group that would become prominent among campus organizations.
7. Because the Grand Canyon is so deep, one cannot help being deeply impressed by it.
8. For the past 20 years or more, critics have been very critical in criticizing radio programs.
9. Civil Engineering has two main divisions. These two main divisions are Sanitary Engineering and Structural Engineering.
10. As a serviceable organization, the local drug store serves the counter style of service.

C. Improve the sound and sense of the following:

1. The sense of these sentences is such that some of them make nothing but nonsense.
2. Some wise pioneers used food wisely by the wise use of such wild animals as wild rabbits, squirrels, and raccoons.
3. Christmas is a big affair in our family. The shopping and mailing

greeting cards are some of the big tasks. The turkey dinner is another big feast, and a big family celebration ends the big Christmas celebration.

4. The first place that we saw in Chicago was "The Loop." "The Loop" is the main business section in Chicago.
5. The order of definitions in my dictionary is of the historical order.
6. Getting up tired, doctors say, is the worst way to start the day.
7. Our neighbor tells us that his niece is having a nice time on the beach at Nice, France, where the weather has been very nice this winter.
8. With prices what they are, Carl doesn't care if he never cuts his hair.
9. Scenes such as these are best seen at sunset from some lofty parapet.
10. At college there is usually someone always studying in the same room with some one. Most of the people around one are interested in one person, themselves, and it is necessary for one to be able to study in noise and confusion.

D. Which of these words are pleasing to your ear? Which are harsh-sounding? *Spinach, tintinnabulation, cacophony, clackety-clack, vermilion, melody, parsnips, jazz, nevermore, diaphanous, luxuriant, lyrical, autocratic, cabbage, cranberry, moonlight, shrimp, sap, cuspidor, roundelay.*

GLOSSARY OF FAULTY DICTION

70. The following glossary, alphabetically arranged and numbered for easy reference, contains words and expressions often misused. The list is not all-embracing, but it is a short-cut discussion to some of the most common violations of good usage. If the material given below does not apply to your problem or if you do not find listed the word or phrase you are seeking, consult your dictionary.

A few of these expressions are always to be avoided, but many are inappropriate only in formal English. Apply the advice of Section **64,** page 420, as you interpret the comments provided for these words and phrases. Remember especially that no stigma attaches to the label "colloquial"; it indicates that a given expression is more appropriate in conversation and in informal discourse generally than it is in formal writing (see pp. 337–340; 421–423).

Usage is so constantly changing that expressions which are now restricted in some way may later be considered standard. Furthermore, because no dictionary or grammar is a final authority, some usages are disputed. Probably no two linguists would agree on all the comments which follow. But this illustrative list of 150 items should be serviceable as a starter; to it you may add from time to time other words and expressions.

1. **A, an.** *An* should be used before an initial vowel sound, *a* before a word beginning with a consonant sound: *an* adult, *a* problem; *an* honor, *a* hopeful sign.

2. **Accept, except.** *Accept* means "to receive," "say yes to"; *except* as verb means to "exclude"; as preposition, "other than."

    He *accepted* the invitation.
    I agree to the conditions if I may *except* the fourth in the list.
    No one *except* me knew the answer.

3. **Accidently.** An illiteracy (see Section **57**). Use *accidentally.*

4. **Ad.** Colloquial abbreviation for *advertisement.* In formal writing avoid such abbreviations as *ad, auto, exam, lab, phone,* and *prof.*

5. **Advise.** Used incorrectly and ineffectively in business letters for "inform," "tell."

    I am happy to *tell* (not *advise*) you that your remittance has been received.
    Please be *informed* (not *advised*) that your order is being shipped today.

6. **Affect, effect.** *Affect,* as verb, means "to influence" or "assume"; *effect* as verb means "to cause" and, as noun, means "result."

    This essay has *affected* student thinking.
    Though nervous, he *affected* nonchalance.
    This testimony *effected* a political scandal.
    What *effect* has low temperature on iron?

7. **Ain't.** This contraction of *am not* is considered illiterate or dialectal and is cautioned against in standard English, both written and spoken. Virtually every other contraction is in good use in informal English: *isn't, aren't, wasn't, weren't, haven't, hasn't, hadn't, doesn't, don't* (see No. 43), *didn't, won't, shan't,* etc.

8. **Alibi.** Used colloquially to mean an excuse or any kind of defense. Precisely, "a plea or fact of having been elsewhere when an offense was committed."

9. **All right, alright.** *All right* is overworked to mean "satisfactory," "very well." *Alright* is not an acceptable word.

10. **All the farther, all the faster.** These and similar expressions are

considered objectionable when the meaning is "as far as," "as fast as," etc.

> This is *as far as* we are going (Not "This is *all the farther* we are going.")
>
> Is this *as fast as* your car will go? (Not "Is this *all the faster* your car will go?")

11. **All together, altogether.** The former means "everybody (or everything) in one place"; *altogether* means "wholly," "completely."

12. **Allusion, illusion.** The former means "an indirect reference," "a hint"; *illusion* means "a misleading image or vision."

> The speaker made an *allusion* to the strike.
>
> "Your security," he said, "is but an *illusion.*"

13. **Already, all ready.** *Already* means "previously," "by this time"; *all ready* (two words) means "everything (or everyone) is ready."

14. **Also, then.** Each word is frequently ineffective and improper when used as a conjunction to join words.

> He asked his question, *then* sat down.
>
> For dessert we are having apple pie, *also* ice cream.
>
> Improved: After asking his question, he sat down.
>
> For dessert we are having apple pie and ice cream.

15. **A.M. or a.m.** (midnight to noon); **P.M. or p.m.** (noon to midnight). Both are clear indicators of time. Do not add, "in the morning," "in the afternoon," etc. (See Section **68.**) Figures, not words, are conventionally used:

> We leave here at 8 *a.m.* and arrive in Detroit at 3 *p.m.*

16. **Among, between.** The former shows the relation of more than two objects; *between* refers to only two, or to more than two when each object is considered in relation to the others.

> He distributed the prizes *among* the five winners.
>
> He divided the prize *between* Jack and Joe.
>
> This water-level route runs *between* New York, Albany, Cleveland, and Chicago.
>
> Concord *between* nations is desirable.

17. **Amount, number.** *Amount* is used with a unified mass; *number,* with separate units.

> What is the *amount* of your cash?
>
> I have a *number* of quarters and half-dollars.
>
> The *amount* of traffic depends upon the *number* of cars on the road.

18. And etc. Redundant. *Etc.* is the abbreviation for Latin *et cetera,* meaning "and so forth."

19. Anxious, eager. In precise use, *anxious* implies "anxiety," "worry," "uneasiness"; *eager* means "keenly desirous," "wanting to," not "worried about."

> I am *anxious* about Father's health.
> I am *anxious* about the outcome of the examination.
> I am *eager* to hear all the news from home.

20. Anywheres, nowheres, somewheres. Illiteracies. Omit the *s* from these words.

> I cannot find my pen *anywhere.*
> The kitten is *nowhere* to be found.
> There is a class schedule here *somewhere.*

21. Apt, liable, likely. *Apt* suggests "fitness" or "tendency"; *liable* implies "openness or exposure to something burdensome or disadvantageous"; *likely* means "expected," "probable." *Apt* and *likely* are sometimes interchangeable but not in the meaning of "probability."

> She is *apt* in mathematics.
> You are *liable* for damages.
> It is *likely* to rain. (Not: "It is *apt* to rain" or "It is *liable* to rain.")

22. As. (1) Overworked as a conjunction for *since, because, when,* etc.

> *As* it was raining, we decided . . . (Use *since.*)

(2) Misused as a substitute for *that* or *whether:*

> I doubt as I can. (Use *that.*)

(3) In affirmative comparisons, *as . . . as* is used:

> I am *as* tall *as* my father.

In negative comparisons, some writers prefer *so . . . as*—"I am not *so* tall *as* my brother"—but *Webster's New International Dictionary* reports *as . . . as* and *so . . . as* are now generally used interchangeably.

23. As good as, if not better than. A mixed comparison, correctly phrased, but awkward. The statement is more effective when the "if not better than" is put at the end.

> Awkward: My record is *as good as if not better than* your record.
> Improved: My record is *as good as* yours, *if not better.*

24. Auto. See Ad.

25. **Awful, awfully, abominable, abominably, terrible, terrific, terribly,** etc. Loose overworked intensives for *very,* etc.

26. **Awhile, a while.** *Awhile* is an adverb; in *a while, while* is a noun.

> Wait *awhile,* and I'll go with you.
> I cannot go for *a while.*

27. **Believe, feel.** Precisely, *believe* suggests "think," "judge," "have convictions about"; *feel* suggests "feeling," "emotions," not "reason."

> I *feel* cheerful when I read your letters, for I *believe* you have the right attitude toward life.

28. **Beside, besides.** *Beside* is usually a preposition meaning "by the side of"; *besides* is a preposition meaning "except," and, more commonly, an adverb meaning "moreover."

29. **Bursted, bust, busted.** *Bursted* is an illiteracy; *bust* or *busted* slang or dubiously colloquial for *burst.* Principal parts: *burst—burst—burst,* and *bursting.*

30. **Can, may, might.** *Can* suggests "ability," physical and mental:

> He *can* make good grades if he tries hard enough.

> *May* implies permission or sanction:

> The teacher says that you *may* leave.

> In colloquial and informal expression, *can* and *may* are both used in the sense of permission or sanction; formally, the distinction between *can* and *may* ("ability" vs. "permission") is illustrated in this sentence:

> I doubt that you *can,* but you *may* try if you wish.

> *May* also expresses "possibility" and "wish" (desire):

> It *may* rain today. (Possibility)
> *May* you have a pleasant trip! (Wish, desire)

> *Might* is used after a governing verb in the past tense, *may* after a governing verb in the present tense:

> He says that you *may* go.
> He said that you *might* go.

31. **Cannot help but.** An illogical double negative (*cannot help + can but*). Omit *but.* Preferable:

> I *cannot help* writing you about this matter. (See Section 36f.)

32. **Can't hardly.** An illogical double negative. Omit the contraction of *not.*

> I *can* hardly hear you. (See Section 36f.)

33. **Case.** Overused as a word having little specific meaning: similar words are *phase, factor, instance, nature, thing,* etc. (See Section **60a.**)

34. **Complected.** Dialectal or colloquial for "complexioned." Preferable:

> He was *dark-complexioned.*
> He was a man *of dark complexion.*

35. **Contact, contacted.** Overworked business terms. Possible replacements: *communicate, call, call upon, telephone, get in touch with.*

36. **Continual, continuous.** In some uses, synonymous. A subtle distinction is that *continual* implies "a close recurrence in time, rapid succession"; *continuous* implies "without interruption."

> The *continual* ringing of the telephone annoys me.
> The ticking of the clock was *continuous.*
> Some alarm clocks ring *continually;* others ring *continuously.*

37. **Credible, creditable, credulous.** *Credible* means "believable"; *creditable* means "praiseworthy"; *credulous* means "gullible."

> The story is *credible.*
> This is a *creditable* theme.
> You are too *credulous.*

38. **Cute.** An overworked colloquialism for *attractive, pleasing,* etc.

39. **Data.** Plural form of a naturalized Latin word, *datum,* "something known." The intriguing question of whether *data* can be used in the singular is ignored by some dictionaries. According to *Webster's New Collegiate:* "Though plural in form, *data* is often used as a singular"; and according to the *Thorndike-Barnhart Comprehensive Desk Dictionary:* "Strictly, *data* is a plural, with a little-used singular *datum.* Its meaning is actually collective and may sometimes stress a group of facts as a unit and so be used with a singular verb. Sometimes, referring to individual facts, *data* is used with a plural. . . . The singular verb can be safely used in any but the most formal writing."

40. **Disinterested, uninterested.** *Disinterested* means "unbiased," "not influenced by personal reasons"; *uninterested* means "having no interest in," "not paying attention." As a colloquialism, *disinterested* means *uninterested, indifferent.*

41. **Disregardless.** See **Irregardless.**

42. **Different than, different to, different from.** *Different than* and *different to* are considered colloquial by some authorities, improper and incorrect by others. These idioms have long literary usage to

support them. *Different from* has no objectors to its formal and informal use.

43. **Don't, done.** *Don't* is used incorrectly as a contraction in the third person singular, present tense. The correct form is *doesn't. Done* is incorrectly used as the past tense of *do*. Principal parts: *do—did —done*.

> It *doesn't* make any difference.
> He *doesn't* know any better.
> We *did* our studying this morning.

44. **Drug, drugged.** Illiteracies when used as parts of the verb *drag*. Principal parts: *drag—dragged—dragged*, and *dragging*.

> We *dragged* (not *drugged*) the initiate to the shower.

45. **Due to.** As compound prepositions, *due to* (from the adjective *due*), *owing to* (from the participle *owing*), and *caused by* (from the participle *caused*) originally were adjective phrases; adverbial meanings were expressed by *because of, on account of*. The grammatical status of the last three remains unchanged. *Owing to* has literary support as an adverbial phrase. The *New World Dictionary* labels *due to* as colloquial for *because of*—"widely so used despite purists' objections." Whatever you and your teacher decide, remember that, in many uses, *due to the fact that* is a wordy way of saying *since*.

46. **Each . . . are.** An error in grammar. *Each*, if not followed by *one*, implies *one*, and any plural words used in modifying phrases do not change the number.

> Wrong: *Each* of the students *are* expected to be present at each
>   class meeting.
> Right: *Each* of the students *is* expected to be . . .
> Wrong: *Each one* of you *are* invited.
> Right: *Each one* of you *is* invited.

47. **Eager.** See **Anxious.**

48. **Either . . . or, neither . . . nor.** The former means "one of two"; *neither* means "not one of two." The statements about "each . . . are" (above) apply if "one" is understood:

> *Either* (one) of you is a desirable candidate.

But

> *Neither* New Englanders *nor* Southerners speak like Midwesterners.

Or is used with *either, nor* with *neither*. The use of *either . . . or, neither . . . nor,* coordinating more than two words, phrases, or clauses, is sanctioned by some dictionaries but not by others.

49. **Enthuse.** A colloquialism. For formal writing, prefer "be enthusiastic," "become enthusiastic."

50. **Etc.** An abbreviation of the Latin phrase, *et cetera,* "and so forth." Preferably, *etc.* should be avoided; too often it is a confession that the writer can think of nothing further to add to a list; if he can, he might justify *etc.* See also *And etc.,* above.

51. **Exam.** See **Ad.**

52. **Except.** See **Accept.**

53. **Farther, further.** Interchangeable, but many writers prefer *farther* to indicate "space," "a measurable distance," and *further* to indicate "greater in degree, quantity, or time," and also "moreover," "in addition to."

> Let us drive ten miles *farther.*
> Next week we shall discuss this matter *further.*

54. **Feel.** See **Believe.**

55. **Fellow.** A word of many meanings, ranging from low to high, socially. Colloquial for "individual," "person," "one," "man," "boy," "student." *Fella* and *feller* are slang, dialectal, or illiteracies.

56. **Fewer, less.** Both imply a comparison with something larger in number or amount. *Fewer* applies only to number:

> *Fewer* houses are now unpainted on this street.

Less is used in various ways: applied to material in bulk in reference to amount (*less* money in the bank); with abstractions (*less* courage); with attributes such as degree and value (a nickel is *less* than a quarter).

> The *less* clay we have, the *fewer* bricks we can make.
> The *fewer* members we have, the *less* our income will be.

57. **Fine.** A much overused word in the general sense of approval. Try to find a more specific, concrete word. (See Section **60.**)

58. **Fix.** A word of many meanings. Colloquial: as a verb, "to arrange matters," "to get revenge"; as a noun, for "predicament," "difficulty." Dialectal or colloquial as a verb, "to prepare, get ready." Fill in these meanings:

> I can *fix* a date for Saturday night.
> A tough gangster always *fixes* his enemies.
> With my car locked and the keys inside, I certainly was in a *fix.*
> I was *fixing* to go home.

59. **Folks.** Colloquial for "relatives," "one's family."

60. **Formally, formerly.** *Formally* means "in a formal manner"; *formerly* means "in the past."

61. **Funny.** Colloquial for "strange," "queer," "odd," "remarkable."

62. **Get, got.** Colloquial in these meanings: "must," "ought," "puzzle," "irritate," "understand," "hit," "own," "possess." *Get* and *got* are also used in many idiomatic phrases. (See Section **56.**) Examples:

> I've *got* to go home next week.
> Have you *got* your book with you?
> I'm sorry, but I don't quite *get* you.

63. **Good, well.** *Good* is an adjective: "to have a good time," "to give a good performance." *Well* functions as either adjective or adverb, but with different meanings: as adjective, "in good health," and as adverb, "ably."

> After my illness, I have felt *well* all summer.
> The team played *well* during the first half.

64. **Had.** An illiteracy when used for *have* after auxiliary verbs in such expressions as would *had,* could *had,* might *had,* should *had,* etc.

65. **Had better, had best.** Idiomatic phrases meaning "ought to," "would be wise to."

66. **Healthful, healthy.** Often used interchangeably. Precisely, *healthful* means "conducive to health"; *healthy* means "possessing health."

> He is a *healthy* person.
> We live in a *healthful* climate.

67. **Help but.** See **Cannot help but.**

68. **Home, homey.** Do not loosely use *home* for *house.* Do not omit the preposition in such an expression as "He was *at home.*" *Homey* is a colloquialism meaning "homelike."

69. **I, me.** The former is nominative case, the latter objective. Watch especially in a compound phrase after a verb or preposition.

> This matter concerns only *you* and *I.* (Use *you* and *me.*)
> The way he raved in front of *you* and *I* made me ashamed. (Use *you* and *me.*)

70. **Illusion.** See **Allusion.**

71. **Imply, infer.** To *infer* is "to draw a conclusion from statements, circumstances, or evidence." To *imply* is "to suggest a meaning hinted at, not explicitly stated."

> The detective *inferred* from the position of the fingerprints that the man who fired the shot was left-handed.
> What you say *implies* that I am not telling the truth.

72. In, into. Verbs indicating motion to a place are generally followed by *into:*

When he walked *into* the room, he found the meeting in progress.

In is used to indicate motion within relatively narrow limits:

She paced up and down *in* the classroom for the whole period.

In is used when the place is not mentioned.

He came *in* after we finished the discussion.
The train came *in.*

73. In back of. Colloquial for *behind. In the back of* and *in front of* are proper in both formal and informal usage.

In the back of the building are seven windows.
The car is parked *in front of* the house.
There is a hole in the wall *in back of* the mirror. (Colloquial)
There is a hole in the wall *behind* the mirror. (Formal)

74. Individual. See **Party, person.**

75. Ingenious, ingenuous. The former means "talented," "inventive," "resourceful"; *ingenuous* means "frank" or "naïve."

76. Inside of, off of, outside of. As prepositional phrases, the *of* is superfluous.

Inside the house, the fire is burning brightly.
The boy fell *off* his bicycle.
You will need a passport to travel *outside* the United States and its possessions.

NOTE:

The *outside of* our house needs a coat of paint.
We are getting new upholstering for the *inside of* our car.

77. Irregardless, disregardless. Both words are illiteracies, substandard. The prefixes *ir-* and *dis-* are superfluous.

78. Is when, is where. Misuse of adverbial clauses for noun clauses and, more important, inexact phrasing in definitions. (See Section **39.**)

Bad: A "comma splice" *is where* you use a comma between independent clauses with no pure conjunction.
Passive voice *is when* the subject is acted upon.

Better: A "comma splice" is the *joining* of two independent clauses by only a comma, when no pure conjunction is used.
In the passive voice, the subject is not the actor but is acted upon.

79. **Its, it's, its'.** *Its* is the possessive form of "it"; *it's* is a contraction for "it is"; *its'* is an illiteracy, nonexistent in correct writing.

80. **Job.** Frequently and inexactly used in the sense of achievement. The chief objection to the word is its overuse to cover many general and inexact meanings. Find a more specific, concrete word (see Section **60**).

> The coach has done a good *job* with his material.
> Hemingway does a splendid *job* in his short stories.
> My roommate is doing a good *job* in chemistry.

81. **Kind of a, sort of a, type of a.** The *a* is superfluous. Logically, the last word should indicate a class, not one thing.

> What *kind of* book is this?
> He is the *sort of* person you like to associate with.
> What *type of* flower is suitable for this soil?

82. **Kind of, sort of.** Colloquial when used to mean "almost," "rather," "somewhat."

> Father looks *kind of* tired.
> I am *sort of* disgusted with myself.

83. **Leave, let.** Each word has various meanings, but *leave* in the sense of "go away from" is often confused with *let* in the sense of "allow," "permit," "cause."

> Wrong: *Leave* me speak to Marjorie Jones, please.
> The Dean *let* my roommate and me alone to talk the matter over.

84. **Less.** See **Fewer.**

85. **Liable, likely.** See **Apt.**

86. **Lie, lay.** The former, meaning "to recline," is intransitive, takes no object. The latter, meaning "to place," is transitive, requires an object. Notice especially the principal parts of each verb and do not confuse the past tense, past participle, and present participle of *lie* with the forms of *lay*.

> *Lie—lay—lain, lying*
> *Lay—laid—laid, laying*
> I shall *lie* down.
> Please *lay* the book on the desk.
> I was *lying* down when you telephoned.
> College freshmen are *laying* the foundations for success in life.

87. **Like.** A word of many meanings and with uses as suffix, adjective, noun, adverb, preposition, transitive verb, intransitive verb, and conjunction. As conjunction, its use is colloquial for *as, as if*.

Colloquial: The naval battle turned out *like* the Admiral predicted.

It seems *like* it might snow all day.

Formal: The naval battle turned out *as* the Admiral predicted.

It seems *as if* it might snow all day.

88. **Locate.** A colloquialism when used to mean "settle."

I am now *located* in Pittsburgh.

89. **Lots of, a lot of, whole lot.** Colloquial for "many," "much," "great deal." But the chief objection is overuse of a vague, general word. Try to find a more specific, concrete way of saying what you mean. (See Section **60.**)

90. **Luxuriant, luxurious.** *Luxuriant* refers to "abundant growth"; *luxurious* pertains to luxury.

The undergrowth was *luxuriant*.

The hotel was *luxurious*.

91. **Mad.** With a number of meanings such as "insane," "frantic," "frenzied," *mad* is colloquial when used to mean "angry," "furious."

92. **May, might.** See **Can.**

93. **Muchly.** An illiteracy. Substitute *much, very, greatly*.

94. **Nice.** A word with various meanings, including "agreeable," "pleasant," "attractive," "pretty," "delightful." Its overuse indicates the need for more specific, concrete substitutes. (See Section **60.**)

95. **Notorious, noteworthy, notable.** *Notorious* means "infamous"; *noteworthy* and *notable* mean "remarkable," "worthy of note."

96. **Nowheres.** See **Anywheres.**

97. **Number.** See **Amount.**

98. **Of.** An impropriety when used for *have* after auxiliary verbs in such expressions as *would of, could of, might of, should of,* etc. These should be *would have, could have,* etc.

99. **Off of.** See **Inside of.**

100. **O, oh.** The former is usually part of a vocative, always capitalized, and is rarely followed by a mark of punctuation:

O Richard! Come here, please.

Oh is an interjection, may be followed by a comma or an exclamation point, and follows the usual rules for capitalization.

Oh! What a pity!

But, *oh,* what trust we placed in him!

101. **Outside of.** See **Inside of.**

102. **Party, person, individual.** *Party* implies a group, and, except in legal and telephonic language, should not be used to refer to one person except in a slang or colloquial sense. *Individual* refers to a particular or single person. *Individual,* as an adjective, means "single," "separate," "particular"; it is therefore repetitious and unnecessary when used to modify *person,* as "individual person," or when "each" has been used, as "each individual member." As nouns, *individual* and *person* are synonyms.

103. **Pass out.** Slang in the sense of "faint," "become completely unconscious."

104. **Pep, peppy.** Slang. Use *zest, vigor, energy, vivacity, animation,* etc., and corresponding adjectives.

105. **Phase.** See **Case.**

106. **Phone.** See **Ad.**

107. **Plenty.** As an adverb, colloquial for "very," "fully."

> The weather is *plenty* hot this summer.

108. **Plus.** Not a synonym for *and* or *with.* Unacceptable:

> My roommate and I, *plus* the two boys across the hall, are attending a lecture tonight.

109. **Practicable, practical.** *Practicable* means "capable of being put into practice"; *practical* means "concerned with practice rather than theory."

> Let's quit dreaming and be *practical* about this.
> The proposal is not *practicable.*

110. **Pretty.** Colloquial when used for "rather," "moderately," "somewhat."

> This is a *pretty* large assignment.
> I did *pretty* well on the last test.

111. **Principal, principle.** *Principal* is a noun meaning "sum of money" or "a chief person," and an adjective meaning "chief" or "main." *Principle* is always a noun meaning "a doctrine," "a governing rule or truth."

112. **Proposition.** Colloquial for a *proposal, undertaking, offer, affair, project,* etc.

113. **Proven.** Although an illogical formation (*moved, moved,* but not *moven*) "proven" is accepted as one of the two past participles of *prove.* Principal parts: *prove—proved—proved* or *proven.*

114. **Provided, provided that, providing.** *Provided* and *providing* are in good use as conjunctions, with the meaning "if," "on condition,"

"in case," "it being understood." They are often followed by *that,* but *that* seems an unnecessary word.

> *Provided* I am asked, I shall join your organization.
> We are driving home next week, *provided* there is no snow on the roads.
> I plan to pay my tuition next week, *providing* Father sends me the money.

115. **Quite a.** Colloquial in phrases meaning "more than," as *quite a* few, *quite a* bit, *quite a* lot.

116. **Raise, rise.** The former requires an object, as a transitive verb; the latter, as an intransitive verb, does not require an object. Keep in mind also the principal parts and present participle:

> *Raise—raised—raised, raising*
> *Rise—rose—risen, rising*

With neither of these verbs is *up* needed. (See **Up,** below.)

> Please *rise* when you recite.
> I *raised* my right hand in greeting.

117. **Real.** An impropriety as an adverb meaning "very" or "really." "Are you *real* sure of what you say?"

118. **Reason is because . . .** The construction has a long history of usage behind it, and it is found in the writing and speaking of many people, literary and otherwise. Those who object do so because the expression is illogical (not that there aren't many other acceptable illogical expressions in English—idioms, for example). Since we do not say "The cause is because . . . ," why say "The reason is because . . ."? Logically we should give, not the *cause for the reason,* but the reason or cause itself, phrased as a noun or noun clause. (See also Section **39.**)

> Illogical: The *reason* for my absence *is because* of illness.
> The *reason* why I went *was because* I had no classes that afternoon.
> Logical: The *reason* for my absence *is sickness.*
> The *reason* why I went *was that* I had no classes that afternoon.

119. **Respectfully, respectively.** *Respectfully* means "in a respectful manner," and is the proper conventional closing for certain business letters; *respectively* means "severally," "each in the order given."

> Farewell, *au revoir, auf Wiedersehen* are ways of saying "goodbye" in, *respectively,* English, French, and German.

120. Refer back. Refer means "to direct attention" or "to make reference"; *back* is therefore superfluous. The same kind of faulty diction is evident in *repeat again* and other tautological expressions. (See Section **68.**)

121. Right along, right away, right then, etc. Colloquialisms. In formal writing, substitute *directly, immediately,* etc.

122. Seen, saw. The principal parts of *see* are *see—saw—seen. Saw* is improperly used as a past participle; *seen* is improperly used as the past tense.

> Right: I *saw* him yesterday.
> We have *seen* the exhibit.

123. Shall, will. (1) The distinctions in the use of *shall* and *will* to express simple future time have broken down, but some careful speakers and writers still observe them: *shall* in the first person and *will* in the second and third persons, "I *shall* go," "you (he) *will* go." For other ways to express future time, see page 554.

(2) For expressing determination or command, use *will* in the first person and *shall* in the second and third persons. "I *will* speak, no matter what the result may be." "You *shall* speak" (meaning "you must speak").

(3) To express intention, willingness, promise, use *will* (same verb, different meaning) with all personal pronouns: "I *will* help you." "You *will* be a candidate?"

124. Should, would. In general, use *should* and *would* according to the recommendations for *shall* and *will,* above. These words also have specialized meanings: *should* in the senses of "ought" or "expectation"; *would* in the senses of "habitual action" or "desire." (See p. 536.)

125. Sit, set. *Sit,* predominantly an intransitive verb, not requiring an object, has the meaning of "place oneself"; *set,* predominantly a transitive verb, requiring an object, means to "put" or "place."

> Let me *sit* on this bench; come and *sit* beside me.
> Please *set* the box under the table.

"Set" used for "sit" in the meanings above is dialectal or an impropriety. But both words have many special meanings, for example, an intransitive use of *set,* as in "The sun *sets*" (moon, stars).

126. So. *So* has various uses as adverb, conjunction, pronoun, interjection, and in combinations like *so as, so that.* Two objectionable uses of *so,* on the basis of ineffectiveness, are

(1) Overuse of *so* as a conjunction between independent clauses,

sometimes found three or four times on a single page of student writing. Use more exact connectives. If a clause shows purpose, use *so that;* if the relationship is "consequence," use *therefore, consequently, thus.* (See Section **37c.**)

> Martha went with Fred *so that* she could be sure to catch the bus.
> I need money for my tuition; *therefore,* I'm going to work this summer.

(2) Overuse of *so* as an intensive—a general substitute for *extremely, indeed, very;* these, too, are overused and might often be omitted. (See **Very,** below.)

> Dubious: You are *so* kind to let me borrow your typewriter.
>   Her gown is *so* beautiful.
> Approved: You are kind to let me. . . .
>   Her gown is beautiful.

127. **So . . . as.** See **As** (3), above.
128. **Somewheres.** See **Anywheres.**
129. **Sort of a, Sort of.** See **Kind of a, Kind of.**
130. **Sure.** Both adjective and adverb, but colloquial in the latter use for *surely, certainly, indeed.*
131. **Suspicion.** Used as a verb colloquially or in dialect for *suspect.*

> Approved: I *suspected* that he was lying.

132. **Terrible, terrific.** See **Awful.**
133. **That.** Colloquial as an adverb modifying an adjective or another adverb.

> I didn't realize that you were *that* good.
> In your explanation you shouldn't go *that* far.
> I am *that* angry I could shout.
> Formal: I did not realize *that* you were as good as you say.
>   I am *so* angry *that* I could shout.

134. **Then.** See **Also.**
135. **These kind, those kind, these sort, those sort.** *Kind* and *sort* are singular nouns, *these* and *those* are plural modifiers. Use *this kind, this sort, those kinds, those sorts.*
136. **Thusly.** An illiteracy for *thus.*
137. **To, too, two.** Correct usage here is mainly a matter of careful spelling. *To* is a preposition, *"to* the library," or the sign of the infinitive, *"to* study." *Too* is an adverb meaning "also" or "overabundance of." "I, *too,* am going, but John is *too* sick to go." *Two* is the number: *"two* girls," "the *two* of us."

138. Too. Overused as an intensive or as a replacement for *very* and consequently ineffective. (See **Very,** below.)

> I suppose I'm just *too* optimistic.
> I haven't read *too* much about this subject.

139. Try and. A colloquialism for *try to.*

140. Type. See **Kind of.** Not acceptable as a substitute for *type of.* We do not say "what kind insect," "what sort insect." Why say, "what type insect"? For comment on **Type of a,** see **Kind of a,** above.

141. Uninterested. See **Disinterested.**

142. Unique. Unique means "having no like or equal" and expresses absoluteness along with words like *round, square,* etc. Logically, with no comparison possible, these should not be used in the comparative and superlative degrees or with *most,* etc., unless there is a qualifying word like *nearly.*

> Illogical: This is the *most unique* painting on display.
>   I've never seen a *rounder* table.
>
> Logical: Of many strange flowers, this is the *most nearly unique* one we grow.
>   This table seems *more nearly square* than that one.

143. Up. Redundant when used with verbs which already include the idea, as in *rise up, stand up, end up,* etc. But *up* is needed in many idiomatic expressions, like *let up, sit up, move up,* etc.

144. Very. (1) *Very,* like *so, surely, too, extremely, indeed,* has been so overused that it has lost much of its value as an intensive. Use these words sparingly and thoughtfully; consider whether your meaning isn't just as emphatic without them: "You are *very* positive about the matter."

(2) *Very* is used colloquially to qualify participles; formal use has adverbs like *much* or *greatly:*

> Colloquial: I was *very disgusted* with myself.
> Formal: I was *very much disgusted* with myself.
> Colloquial: I am *very torn* between the desire to go and the desire to stay.
> Formal: I am *greatly torn* between . . .

145. Well. See **Good.**

146. Where at. As two words, redundant for *where.* Avoid such a statement as "He did not know *where* he was *at.*"

147. While. Colloquial when used in the sense of "although" or "whereas."

While sick, I kept attending classes.

You thought I was lying, *while* I was telling the truth all the time.

148. Who, whom. The former is nominative case, the latter objective. When in doubt, try as a memory device the substituting of *he* for *who* and *him* for *whom,* since proper use of these is more easily recognized.

I wonder *who* I should invite ("I should invite *him,*" i.e., "I wonder *whom* I should invite.")

149. Will, would. See **Shall, should.**

150. Worst kind, worst sort, worst way. Slang for *very much, greatly.*

EXERCISES

A. Point out and correct any errors in diction in the following sentences:

1. A large amount of firms do a thriving business during the summer.
2. No more food, please; I am plenty satisfied.
3. I always except any good advice that is given me.
4. A beginner's permit enables you to drive a car while accompanied by a experienced driver.
5. Other important sections deal with punctuation, compounds, capitals, and etc.
6. When evening comes, you are ready to try and find a camping site.
7. John stopped suddenly; he must of forgotten what he was going to say.
8. The team seemed sort of mixed up in the third quarter.
9. Every child anxiously waits for Christmas to come.
10. Our farm home isn't real modern, but we do have many conveniences.
11. We won the game, and I'm so glad.
12. I accidently attended the wrong class yesterday morning.
13. There are many common words which most everyone knows.
14. These few points, plus some others, are the concern of education in high school.
15. The thought of reading a book outside of class startled me.
16. The amount of trees to be taken out each year is limited by the United States Government.
17. My roommate is good at fixing people up with blind dates.
18. I want a camera that will take most all types of action scenes.

19. I had never been anyplace before where there was such a huge crowd.
20. This letter had the affect of making me change my plans about vacation.

B. Point out and correct any errors in diction in the following sentences:

1. Our town is rather unique in many ways.
2. I couldn't imagine what kind of a job it was, so she told me.
3. Our town has a large amount of retired people in it.
4. I feel I am not qualified to make any suggestions.
5. I never understood how some classmates got by with the little studying they done.
6. Where there are that many boys together, there is bound to be noise.
7. With more careful drivers there would be less accidents.
8. Waiting around with nothing to do gives me kind of a helpless feeling.
9. For awhile I thought of quitting school and going to work.
10. Each of these study habits have great possibilities for better grades.
11. The only reason I took math and drafting was because I liked them.
12. I feel that the writing laboratory has helped me a lot.
13. Sometimes I stayed up all night to pass a real hard test.
14. The band members assembled in back of the Hall of Music.
15. The lecturer's monotone made it difficult for us to get enthused.
16. Many businessmen play golf because it is a game that takes their minds off of their work.
17. My experience was quite different than that.
18. I am taking the normal amount of courses for a freshman student.
19. I am writing concerning matters in high school that have effected my studies here in college.
20. Take your time in your preparations, and you will do a good job.

C. Point out and correct any errors in diction in the following sentences:

1. Sarah's excitement, when I tried to teach her to drive a car, made me kind of nervous.
2. Your plans are alright, but they will never work out.
3. You should never say that anything busted; instead, you should say that it bursted.
4. I was anxiously looking forward to the good time that I would have.
5. Irregardless of what the book says, I think I'm right.

6. Today less people are as economical as they were a century ago.
7. Can you fix me up with a date for the Sophomore Hop?
8. I have received two letters that I feel are very good.
9. Grandfather laid there an hour before any one noticed the wreck.
10. My high school teachers did a wonderful job in preparing us for college.
11. For good fishing it is necessary to get up a hour before sunrise.
12. I have never been effected by superstitions.
13. The library is a large place to try and find anything you want.
14. On Sunday morning it is sort of hard to get up.
15. Our college gym is the nicest gym in the East.
16. Once in a while my parents get a little mad.
17. The main reason I do poorly in English is due to the fact that my high school training was poor.
18. As children my brother and I used to set on the floor listening to the radio.
19. In high school I would never leave anything go until the last minute.
20. My father is 45 years old and real sweet.

D. Point out and correct any errors in diction in the following sentences:

1. The painter had a bucket of paint setting on the top step of the ladder.
2. Next semester I'm going to try and work out a much better plan for studying.
3. All her life she dressed like a old lady.
4. It rained real hard the morning we left for the campus.
5. These other kind of fruits will be better.
6. In spite of the snow, the road was alright for driving.
7. My sister is dark complected and I am light complected.
8. By your going to college, your salary will be much higher than it would of been.
9. English is taken for granted by the greater amount of students in high school.
10. Many people were gathered inside of the auditorium.
11. It takes a lot of time to do a lot of studying, but it's a lot of fun and you get a lot of satisfaction out of it.
12. I feel that my problems are not as complex as they were.
13. I was hungry enough to eat any place.
14. The guide did a fine job of pointing out interesting features.
15. Canada has a great amount of natural resources.

16. My girl and I, plus another couple, planned to attend the high school basketball tournament.
17. We are usually present at most any athletic event.
18. Even when we win nobody gets real excited.
19. This man is a different kind of leader than those we have had.
20. The Golden Gate Bridge in San Francisco is one of the most unique bridges in the world.

E. Point out and correct any errors in diction in the following sentences:

1. Comic books are said to have bad affects on children.
2. In high school I took part in most all of the sports.
3. The reason for my low grade is due to the fact that I don't give the subject much effort.
4. All my friends are so friendly and understanding.
5. The average theme is not real demanding, if you approach it right.
6. Mother has done most of the cooking, housework, etc.
7. The products all ready discovered in chemistry make an amazing number.
8. In such an emergency we done the only thing we could do.
9. If more persons traveled, there would be less problems.
10. When I have a lot of studying to do, I get to it at once.
11. I should like to go someplace for the spring vacation.
12. If I had of known then that I was going to college, I would of taken different subjects.
13. No matter what kind of a dictionary a person has, the important thing is that he use it frequently.
14. I hope that I can improve some in English during this semester.
15. We wrote only a small amount of themes in my 4 years of high school.
16. Mom always fixes hot coffee and orange juice for breakfast.
17. Then the worst thing that could of happened did happen.
18. You won't learn much copying off of some one else.
19. As a transfer student, I have had only half my college credit excepted.
20. Enclosed is an account of my education, activities, and etc.

Grammar

A Useful Review

You as a college student may reasonably be expected to employ language as do others with your educational and social advantages. In carrying on your affairs in college and in later life, you should have pride in knowing and being able to use words and forms of words and word combinations appropriate to English as it is spoken and written by educated people.

There is also a practical reason for studying grammar. A knowledge of many grammatical terms does not guarantee good writing —it is even possible, although unlikely, that some gifted person may not know a single grammatical term and yet write decently and competently. On the other hand, most of us need some guidance in writing and speaking, and we obtain that guidance most easily and efficiently through some grammatical vocabulary.

Certain grammatical knowledge can help us to write correctly.[1] If we write correctly, grammar can help us write clearly: if we write correctly and clearly, grammar can help us write effectively and even appropriately.

What, then, is grammar? The *American College Dictionary* gives the simplest dictionary definition: "the features of a language (sounds, words, formation and arrangement of words, etc.) considered systematically as a whole, especially with reference to their mutual contrasts and relations."

Grammar is the science that deals with words and their relationships to each other; it is a descriptive statement of the way a lan-

---

[1] *Correct, correctly*—used throughout this book, not in an absolute sense but in the meaning permitted by every standard dictionary: "in accordance with an acknowledged or accepted standard; according to recognized usage."

guage works. Grammar includes a discussion of the forms of words, their use in phrases, clauses, and sentences, their tenses, cases, or other changes in form. It is the scientific record of a series of observed language phenomena and is subject to constant fluctuations. Many grammatical essentials may seem definite and unchangeable, but this fixity is more apparent than real. A useful review concentrates on those words, their changes, and their relationships that can assist in making writing and speaking correct, clear, effective, and appropriate.

A study of grammar is *descriptive,* its application is *prescriptive.* Grammar is descriptive in that it records the actual and changing status of words and their relationships, descriptive in showing how words are said or written, not how they should be said or written. Grammar is not properly considered as a list of rules, imposed by authorities, a rigid set of *do's, do not's, avoid's.* Yet there must be a certain amount of prescription if our speaking and writing are to conform to principles generalized from description. For example, description shows us that pronouns following prepositions are in the objective case. If our own usage is to conform to the description, we follow the prescription: *Use the objective case of pronouns following a preposition.*

The following sections are a review of the useful principles of grammar. Master them and make them serve you in your writing and your speaking.

Definitions of grammatical terms used are listed alphabetically in the glossary, Section **85,** page 586. Refer to this glossary whenever necessary as you study the following pages.

WORDS

71.   A *word* is a letter or a combination of letters, a sound or a combination of sounds, forming a unit of thought capable of standing alone as an utterance.

71a.   Learn to identify each word as a part of speech.

Words are classified according to their use in larger units of thought—in phrases, clauses, and sentences. This functional classification results in *parts of speech,* a descriptive phrase applied to words used in speaking and writing. A part of speech, therefore, is a word—sometimes a combination of words serving the purpose of one word—used to express a definite idea, such use becoming clear only in relation to surrounding words. Every word must be one of the eight parts of speech: *noun, pronoun, adjective, verb, adverb, preposition, conjunction, interjection.* Every word bears at least one such label in your dictionary.

Many words are always used in one certain way, as one unchanging part of speech, but since our language is constantly changing and since words also change in meaning, the function of words reflects such change. The word *iron,* at first thought, seems to be a noun only, as in *made of iron;* yet in *an iron bar* it is an adjective and in *to iron a shirt* it is a verb.

Unless your dictionary permits, do not use nouns for verbs, nouns for adjectives, nouns for adverbs, adjectives for nouns, adjectives for adverbs or adverbs for adjectives (Section **83**), adjectives for verbs, verbs for nouns (but see Section **71g**). Notice, however, that often a slight change in a word, such as a change of ending, can change a word from one part of speech to another: *arrive* (verb), *arrival* (noun). To determine what part of speech a given word is, see how the word is used in the sentence or clause or phrase of which it is a part.

71b. Distinguish carefully the purposes that words serve.

Although words are classified according to one of the eight parts of speech, they can be classified also according to the purpose that they serve:

Naming words:	nouns and pronouns
Asserting words:	verbs
Modifying words:	adjectives and adverbs
Joining words:	prepositions and conjunctions

NAMING WORDS: NOUNS AND PRONOUNS

A *noun* (from a Latin word, *nomen,* meaning *name*) denotes or "names" a person, place, or thing, a quality, idea, or action. Common nouns name all members of a common group: *man, officer, city, building, state.* Proper nouns name particular members of a group and are capitalized: *Mr. Ward, Jefferson Davis, Dallas, Rose*

Bowl, Arkansas. Some common nouns are concrete: *book, candy, hammer, sweater*—names of objects which can be perceived by the senses of touch, sight, taste, hearing, or smell. Some are abstract nouns: *honesty, intelligence, grace, strength*—names of abstractions which cannot be perceived by the senses. Some are collective nouns: *crew, family, assembly, union*—names used for groups considered as units.

Nouns have certain characteristics:

1. Nouns can be, and usually are, preceded by such words as *the, a, my, his, this, some, each.*

2. Certain groups of nouns have typical endings—*tion, ness, ment, ure*—which distinguish them from corresponding verbs (e.g., *determination, determine*) or from corresponding adjectives (e.g., *goodness, good*).

3. Nouns are frequently distinguished from similarly spelled verbs by accent: *sub'ject, subject', per'fect, perfect'.*

4. Nouns are marked as nouns by their occurrence in a complicated but well-ordered set of positions, e.g., usually before the verb in statements, after prepositions.

5. Nouns are, or may be, marked by other characteristics: number, gender, case.

Nouns have *number:* singular (one) or plural (more than one); *gender:* masculine, feminine, neuter, common; and *case,* a common form for both nominative and objective, and a special form for the possessive (genitive).

71c. Do not carelessly use the singular form of a noun for the plural, or a plural form for the singular.

Wrong: I go home every week end, since my home town is only 80 mile from here.

A good student has many favorable characteristic.

Becky, being a very scheming women, could twist most people around her fingers.

There were over 800 freshman assembled in the chapel.

I am the freshmen who sits in Seat No. 1 on the front row.

Plurals of nouns are formed as follows:

1. Most nouns form the plural by adding *s* to the singular: *dog, dogs.*

2. Nouns ending in a sibilant or *s* sound (*ch, sh, s, x, z*) add *es: church, churches; fox, foxes.*

3. Nouns ending in *y* preceded by a consonant ordinarily change *y* to *i* before adding *es: library, libraries; sky, skies.* When the final *y* is preceded by a vowel, the *y* usually remains unchanged and only *s* is added: *valley, valleys; key, keys.* (See Section **52e2** for the spelling of words ending in *y*.)

Note that final *y* also remains unchanged in the plurals of proper names: *Percys, Tracys.*

4. Nouns ending in *o* preceded by a vowel add *s: radio, radios.* Some nouns ending in *o* preceded by a consonant form their plurals with *s: piano, pianos; zero, zeros;* others with *es: echo, echoes; potato, potatoes.*

5. Nouns ending in *f* are so variable that a dictionary should be consulted: *chief, chiefs; loaf, loaves.* Nouns ending in *ff* add *s: sheriff, sheriffs.* Most nouns ending in *fe* change *fe* to *ve* and add *s: wife, wives.*

NOTE: normal use, *leaf, leaves;* nickname of baseball and hockey teams, Maple *Leafs.*

6. Irregular plurals are numerous: *man, men; child, children; foot, feet; sheep, sheep.*

7. Compound nouns ordinarily form the plural by adding *s* or *es* to the important word in the compound: *sons-in-law, passers-by.* If the word elements are so closely related as to be considered a single word, the *end* of the word is pluralized: *handfuls.*

8. Certain nouns of foreign origin retain the plural of the language from which they were borrowed: *alumnus, alumni; datum, data; hypothesis, hypotheses.* Some have two plural forms: *index, indices, indexes.* Many borrowed words, however, have gradually assumed plurals with *s* or *es: area, areas; campus, campuses.*

When in doubt concerning the spelling or the specific form of the singular or plural, consult your dictionary.

71d. Use the correct form of a particular noun in the possessive (genitive) case.

Misuse of nouns in the possessive case is usually due to carelessness. Many students write the plurals of nouns when these should be showing possession, either singular or plural. Possessive case is a grammatical term, but in English the possessive case of nouns is formed by a punctuation mark, the apostrophe, according to the principles stated in Section **94a, b, c, d, e.**

For variety, for avoiding awkwardness, and for showing possession of inanimate objects, possession is expressed by an *of* phrase:

the home *of my parents* (my *parents'* home)
the activities *of any student* (any *student's* activities)
the arm *of the chair* (preferable to the *chair's* arm)
the leaves *of the trees* (not the *trees'* leaves)

The use of the possessive case is further discussed in Section **75j, k,** and **l.**

Although it is sometimes called the *genitive* case, the usual word in English is *possessive*. In other languages, such as German and Latin, the genitive case has various uses, including the expression of possession. In English the possessive case does what its name indicates, with one exception—the measurement of time or space (see Section **75l**).

EXERCISES

A. Correct all errors in the use of number (singular and plural) in the following sentences:

1. Being a women myself, I have similar ideas.
2. One of the most skillful and clever use of words is the development of a mood.
3. A strange phenomena appeared in the northern sky last evening.
4. The upper-class students seem to have a grudge against us freshman.
5. Before I was admitted to the university, I had to take several test.
6. My brother stands 6 foot 4 in his stocking feet.
7. The Methodist and Presbyterian Church's are the two largest in town.
8. We buy in one of the largest department store in the city.
9. An elderly gentlemen sitting next to me asked me where I was going.
10. In these paragraph I have described my father and told a few reason why he is the best friend I have.
11. In the valley there are a few small farm.
12. Homecoming is the time of year nearly all alumnus looks forward to.
13. That bass must have weighed at least 10 pound.

14. There were many preparation to be made for the parade.
15. Joseph Greene is one of the best sportsman in our country.
16. Nearly all the summer employees are college student.
17. Mother was the first women graduate in the School of Engineering.
18. As a youngster on my uncle's farm, I was given a nickel for each mice that I killed.
19. I became an alumni of our high school last June.
20. There are some wonderful artist in the world.

B. Study the principles of possessive case formation of nouns in Section **94a, b, c, d, e.** Then correct all errors in the use of possessive case of nouns in the following sentences:

1. Some fraternitys' treatment of freshman pledges leaves much to be desired.
2. I shall try to live up to the doctors code of medical ethics.
3. I am living in the Womens' Residence Halls.
4. The word "Fort" has been dropped from our citie's name.
5. In automobile manufacturing, Michigan is the nations top industrial state.
6. The Dean's office takes care of most of the students housing problems.
7. I have sold many magazines to farmer's wives.
8. The loneliest time of a mans life is Christmas time away from home.
9. I am enclosing a guide for your roommates use.
10. We frequently cannot have much effect on societies attitude toward us.
11. Both boy's and girl's themes are selected for our freshman magazine.
12. We are all proud of our universities' great football stadium.
13. Our candy kitchen can hardly supply our customers demand for candy.
14. Stores in large cities feature by mail a personal shoppers service.
15. My next theme is to be an account of a dogs life.
16. Our families reunion last August was a great success.
17. The initial T for my middle name was my mothers' idea.
18. This is the story of a young girls first visit to a circus.
19. The making of plastics is one of the newer industrie's in my town.
20. This article would hold anybodies attention.

71e. Distinguish carefully the different kinds of pronouns and the purposes that they serve.

A *pronoun* (*pro,* literally *for* or *instead of*) substitutes for a noun or, sometimes, another pronoun. Every pronoun refers directly or by clear implication to a noun or another pronoun—called the *antecedent* of the pronoun—and it agrees with that antecedent in person, number and gender: "Each *man* present will please raise *his* hand." "Does every *girl* here have *her* luncheon ticket?"

Pronouns, which are used in all the grammatical functions of nouns (as subjects of sentences or clauses, in apposition, as direct or indirect objects of verbs, etc.) are of eight kinds: *personal, relative, demonstrative, interrogative, reflexive, intensive, indefinite,* and *reciprocal.*

1. *Personal* pronouns are those referring to an individual or individuals. Of all the kinds of pronouns, personal pronouns cause the most trouble; they have 30 different forms. Some of these include all genders, and some have special forms for masculine, feminine, or neuter.

Personal pronouns also bear the labels of 1st person, 2nd person, 3rd person:

First person pronouns indicate the speaker or writer—as singular (*I, my, mine, me*) or as plural (*we, our, ours, us*). Second person pronouns indicate the person or persons spoken to or written to, with the same forms for both singular and plural: *you, your, yours, you.* Gender or sex is the same for all 1st and 2nd person pronouns. Third person pronouns indicate the person or persons spoken or written about—and here sex raises its head for consideration. Singular masculine: *he, his, him;* singular feminine: *she, her, hers, her;* neuter: *it, its, it.* Plural, all genders: *they, their, theirs, them.* For a table of these pronouns and their use, see Section **75a.**

2. A *relative* pronoun relates or connects an adjective clause to the antecedent. It has no gender or number; the same forms serve for all. However, the choice of a relative pronoun is determined in part by its antecedent: *who, whose,* and *whom* are used to refer only to persons; *which* is used in reference to things (inanimate objects, animals) and may be used for a group of persons; *that* may refer to either things or persons. The same forms—*who, whose, whom, which, that*—are considered singular or plural depending upon whether the antecedent is singular or plural.

> The flyer *who* served in World War II is now an important airline official. (Singular)

The flyers *who* served in World War II have formed an official organization of their own. (Plural)

This company owns only one small ship, *which* is used for river traffic. (Singular)

A New York company owns seven large freighters, *which* ply between Europe and America. (Plural)

The *man* that I mean was named Mortimer Taylor. (Singular)

The men *that* I like have the same interests as I do. (Plural)

That and *which* have no changes in form (compare with *who, whose, whom*), The possessive case of the pronoun *which* is indicated by *of which*. A possessive, *of that,* is never used.

Who, which, and *that* are the most frequently used relative pronouns. *Whoever, whomever, whichever,* and *whatever* are less frequently employed compound forms; *whosoever, whichsoever,* and *whatsoever* have almost entirely gone out of current use.

3. A *demonstrative* pronoun points out and identifies. It has different forms for number but not for gender or case. The most important demonstrative pronouns are *this* (singular), *that* (singular), *these* (plural), *those* (plural), *such* (singular or plural).

This is the book that I have recommended.
That is the record I have just bought.
These are your books; *those* on the desk are mine.
Such are the magazines that our teacher recommends.

These five words can also be used as adjectives: *this* and *that* modify only singular nouns, *these* and *those* only plural nouns, and *such* either singular or plural.

This magazine is interesting, *that* book is dull.
These magazines are interesting, *those* books are dull.
Such a book and *such* magazines are worth reading.

4. An *interrogative* pronoun (*who, which, what,* occasionally *whoever, whichever, whatever*) introduces a question.

Who will read his book report on Wednesday?
Which is the best road to take to Louisville?
What do you think about extracurricular activities?
For *whom* are you writing this theme?

Whose, as possessive, can of course accompany a noun. *Which* and *what* are frequently used as adjectives also.

> *Whose* tie are you wearing today?
> *Which* book do you recommend as an exciting novel?
> *What* road should I take to Louisville?

5. A *reflexive* pronoun is used for simple reference to the subject; it usually follows the verb or a preposition and directs or *reflects* its action back to the subject. It is composed of one of the personal pronoun forms with *self* or *selves.* Most frequently employed reflexive pronouns are *myself, yourself, himself, herself, itself, ourselves, yourselves, themselves* (and the indefinite *oneself*).

6. *Intensive* pronouns have exactly the same forms as the reflexive pronouns, but they appear in an appositive position and are used to emphasize or *intensify* a noun or other pronoun. Use of commas depends upon whether the apposition is considered close or parenthetical.

> Yesterday my roommate hurt *himself* playing basketball. (Reflexive use)
> He *himself* decided to go out for basketball. (Intensive use)
> Some students consider *themselves* lucky to be here. (Reflexive use)
> The seniors *themselves* chose the day for their commencement. (Intensive use)
> Mary asked *herself* the question many times. (Reflexive use)
> Sometimes she talked aloud to *herself.* (Reflexive use)
> She *herself* finally reached a satisfactory decision. (Intensive use)

7. *Indefinite* pronouns are somewhat less exact in meaning than other pronouns. They are *pronouns* because they refer to antecedents; they are *indefinite* because the antecedents are not specifically named persons or things. Among the more frequently used indefinite pronouns are the following: *another, any, anybody, anyone, anything, all, everybody, everyone, everything, few, many, nobody, no one, none, one, oneself* (as indefinite reflexive), *several, some, somebody, someone.* Compound forms built upon the pronoun *one* or the element *body* have a possessive form ending *'s,* like *anyone's, everybody's, one's.* Indefinite pronouns involve grammatical problems of agreement which are discussed in Section **76c** and Section **77a.**

470

8. A *reciprocal* pronoun indicates an interchange of action suggested by the verb. This interchange may be seen in the following sentences involving the only two reciprocal pronouns in English:

My roommate and I always confide in *each other.* (Two only)
The members of the party exploring the cave shouted to *one another.* (Three or more)

ASSERTING WORDS: VERBS AND VERBALS

71f. Understand clearly the functions and uses of verbs.

A *verb* is a part of speech that asserts something, says something, expresses action, expresses a state of being or a condition. It may make a positive statement, make a conditional statement or statement of probability, give a command, ask a question, make an exclamation.

Today *is* Friday, the 13th. (Positive statement)
If your grades *are* high, you will receive a scholarship. (Condition)
We *may have* to have another meeting this month. (Probability)
Be prepared to come to this meeting. (Command)
Will you please *let* us *know* about your plans? (Question)
You *were* really *surprised!* (Exclamation)

Frequently, auxiliary or helping verbs (see Section **78**) add particular shades of meaning—usually of time (see Section **80**) or tone (see Section **80**) or voice (see Section **81**) to what is called the main verb (see Section **79**). Such combinations are usually called *verb phrases.*

I *have written* 10 themes this semester. (Time or tense)
I *do believe* in thorough proofreading. (Tone)
This theme *was revised* four times. (Voice)

Various uses of verbs—the main verb alone or an auxiliary and the main verb—are the following:

1. To express *time* (tense): present, past, future, present perfect, past perfect, future perfect. See Section **80** for full discussion.

2. To express *tone:* simple, progressive, emphatic. See Section **80** for full discussion.

3. To express *agreement with subject in number and person*. See Section 76 and Section 80 for full discussion.

4. To express *active* or *passive voice*. See Section 81 for full discussion.

5. To express *mood* or *mode*: indicative, imperative, subjunctive. See Section 82 for full discussion.

71g. Distinguish between predicate verbs and verbals.

A *predicate verb* is a *verb* or *verb phrase* used in the predicate of a clause or a sentence where it makes a statement about the subject. The italicized verbs or verb phrases in the examples in Section 71f are predicate verbs. Nearly every clause or sentence contains them. Predicate verbs agree (are in concord) with their subjects in number and person (see Section 76).

Verbals are *verb forms* that cannot serve as predicates; the verbals are *participles, gerunds,* and *infinitives*. Understanding the differences between predicate verbs and verbals will help you avoid a serious error in writing, the use of unjustifiable sentence fragments (see Section 31). Ordinarily, for clearness and effectiveness verbals or verbal phrases should not stand alone. If a group of words contains a verbal, it should include with it or elsewhere in the sentence the kind of verb or verb phrase which serves as the predicate of the clause or sentence.

A *participle* is a word which has the function of both verb and adjective. The *present participle* always ends in *ing* (*speaking, singing*). The *past participle* has various forms (*spoken, sung, walked, sat*). The *perfect participle* consists of *having* or *having been* followed by the past participle (*having sung, having been asked*). (See Section 79.) The participle as a verb form can take an object and be modified by an adverb; the participle as adjective can be modified by an adverb and can itself modify a noun or pronoun.

Coming events cast their shadows before. (Adjective)

Expertly *driving* the car in traffic, Harry has no fear of cities.

(As adjective, *driving* modifies *Harry;* as verb, it is modified by the adverb *expertly* and it takes a direct object, *car.*)

This brightly *polished* silver is beautiful. (As adjective, *polished* modifies *silver,* is modified by the adverb *brightly.*)

The *gerund* is a verbal noun usually ending in *ing* (*speaking, singing*). Because the gerund usually has the same form as the present participle, you must be careful to note the difference in their use: the participle is a *verbal adjective,* the gerund is a *verbal noun.* The gerund as a verb form can take an object and be modified by an adverb; the gerund as a noun can be modified by an adjective and can be the subject or object of a verb or the object of a preposition.

> *Playing* tennis is good exercise. (Gerund is subject of sentence, but as verb form it takes a direct object, *tennis.*)
> Steady *running* won the race for Henry. (As noun, the gerund is subject and is modified by the adjective *steady.*)
> Henry won the race through his *having run* steadily. (As noun, the gerund is object of the preposition *through;* as verb, it is modified by the adverb *steadily.*)

An *infinitive* is a word which has the function of both verb and noun and which may also be employed as an adjective or an adverb. The infinitive is usually introduced by the "sign" *to* (*to speak, to sing*).

> *To work* intelligently is sometimes difficult. (Infinitive as noun is subject of sentence; as verb form it is modified by an adverb, *intelligently.*)
> *To win* a scholarship means constant study. (Infinitive as noun is subject of sentence; as verb form it has a direct object, *scholarship.*)
> The best time *to study* is early in the morning. (Infinitive serves as adjective.)
> I came *to inquire* about your vacation. (Infinitive serves as adverb.)

71h. Do not use a transitive verb for an intransitive verb, or an intransitive verb for a transitive verb.

Verbs are classified as either *transitive* or *intransitive. Transitive* literally means *passing over, crossing over, building a bridge across.* A *transitive* verb is followed by a direct object which completes the meaning of the verb. In other words, a transitive verb is a bridge, a means of crossing over from subject to object. "The teacher *accepted* my excuse." An *intransitive verb* requires no direct object to complete its meaning; there is no passing over, no crossing over. It may of course have word, phrase, or clause modifiers. "I *am going;* I *am going* very soon; in fact, I *am going* just as soon as I can."

Whether a verb is transitive or intransitive—the same verb very frequently may be either, and be so labeled in your dictionary— depends upon meaning, upon the idea the writer wishes to show.

I *obeyed* the traffic officer's instructions. (Transitive)
He gave me instructions; I *obeyed*. (Intransitive)

For almost all practical purposes in writing, being able to distinguish transitive and intransitive verbs is useless information. There are three pairs of verbs, however, concerning which the information is useful, unless you memorize these verbs, their principal parts, and their uses, and forget about the transitive-intransitive distinctions:

Transitive: *lay, laid, laid, laying*
Intransitive: *lie, lay, lain, lying*
Transitive: *raise, raised, raised, raising*
Intransitive: *rise, rose, risen, rising*
Transitive: *set, set, set, setting*
Intransitive: *sit, sat, sat, sitting*

NOTE: *lie* in the meaning of "tell a falsehood" and *set* in the sense of "go down" (the sun *sets*) are verbs that cause no trouble.

I *laid* your books on your desk. (From *lay*)
As I was *laying* your books there, the telephone rang. (From *lay*)
Harry *lay* down for a short time. (From *lie*)
The books are now *lying* on your desk. (From *lie*)
I spent the afternoon *setting* the boxes on the top shelf. (From *set*)
Then I began to rest, and have been *sitting* here for an hour. (From *sit*)
The speaker *raised* the microphone six inches higher. (From *raise*)
The preceding speaker had *raised* it only two inches. (From *raise*)
Tired of resting, I *rose* and went for a walk. (From *rise*)
The waters have *risen* two feet since yesterday. (From *rise*)

EXERCISES

A. From the following sentences, make a list of verbals and after each write an identifying letter: **P**—participle, **G**—gerund, **I**—infinitive.

1. I try to study and to make high grades, but studying seems to get neglected when someone tempts me with swimming, bowling, or golfing.

474

2. A smiling face is better than a discontented one; to smile is one way of winning friends.

3. The college has no objection to our cutting classes, but it does object to our complaining about low grades on tests covering the work that we have missed.

4. Having written with more than usual care, I was surprised when the instructor said that my writing was illegible.

5. To know more about a subject than other people know is a worthy ambition; not to make a parade of one's learning is an even more worthy ambition.

6. William liked to swim and dance with me, but I always felt that he would rather read than do either.

7. He is constantly striving to better himself by taking courses in adult education.

8. Bathing, shaving, and dressing are necessary preliminaries to eating breakfast.

9. The man buying his ticket is a local merchant going to Chicago.

10. The game already having been won, we decided to leave soon after the intermission.

11. Joe's tackling and running are excellent, but I don't believe that he will ever learn to punt or catch passes.

12. He was a person who had enjoyed rowing for years—since reaching his sixth birthday, in fact—but now in this moment of peril to move an oar seemed impossible.

13. Spoken words are naturally kept in mind with much more difficulty than those one reads, but a well-trained person can retain amazing amounts of conversation that he has heard.

14. As it flowed down the gray rock wall, the swiftly falling water seemed to have lost its liquid quality; it looked like a smooth and solidified pillar of green.

15. For a skater to fall occasionally is no more of a calamity than occurs to a speeding hurdler when he topples over a hurdle, but I fell times past counting.

B. Make a list of numbers from 1 to 20. Opposite each, write from the following sentences the correct forms of *lay—lie, raise—rise, set—sit* (see Section 71h):

1. Did you say I'd find your fountain pen *laying lying* on your desk?

2. Now all we had to do was *set sit* back and wait.

3. John's anger had been *raised risen* by the remarks made about his dog.

4. When there are good coals, you can *lay lie* the steaks on the grill.
5. Many of us just *laid lay* on the beach, absorbing the sunshine.
6. The plane was *setting sitting* on a small lake just outside of town.
7. Because he had done so well, the king had *raised risen* him to a knighthood.
8. The day before I left, I gathered together all my clothes that had been *laying lying* around my home.
9. I like to go to the lake for a few days and *lay lie* around and fish.
10. Since we are not allowed to have cars, those of us who have autos have left them *setting sitting* at home in the garage.
11. As I *laid lay* in bed that night, I thought of what a pleasant day my birthday had been.
12. We all know that the sun *raises rises* in the east and *sets sits* in the west.
13. We *sat set* card tables up for those who wanted to play bridge.
14. Here they expect you to *set sit* down and write a good theme without a lot of grammatical errors.
15. Columns of smoke are continually *raising rising* from the blast furnaces.
16. Whenever a storm comes, we take care of all the materials of value *laying lying* around the house.
17. It was some months later that I *sat set* foot on the island.
18. Japan is in the land of the *raising rising* sun.
19. I would dream that I was *laying lying* on some land that no other white man had ever seen.
20. Any summer evening you will find my uncle *setting sitting* on the front porch and reading the evening paper.

MODIFYING WORDS: ADJECTIVES AND ADVERBS

71i. For correct and exact meaning, understand the functions of adjectives.

An *adjective* modifies a noun or pronoun by describing, limiting, or in some other closely related way making meaning more nearly exact. An adjective may indicate quality or quantity, may identify or set limits. Specifically, therefore, adjectives tell *what kind of, how many, which one*. Adjectives are of two general types: *descriptive:* a *black* dress, an *easy* lesson, a *smashed* thumb; *limiting:* the *sixth* period, her *former* home, *several* times. Another classification includes *common* adjectives and *proper* adjectives (from proper nouns), important only because proper adjectives begin with a capital letter: an *American* play; *Italian* olives.

Some adjectives—indeed, most—have endings which mark them as adjectives. The more important of these include:

y:	muddy, stony, funny, dreamy, seedy
ful:	beautiful, faithful, hurtful, sinful
less:	faithless, timeless, lawless, guileless
en:	rotten, golden, wooden, molten
able (ible):	payable, desirable, likable, permissible
ive:	permissive, constructive, excessive, decisive
ous:	vigorous, nervous, marvelous, advantageous
ish:	mannish, selfish, Danish, dwarfish
al:	cordial, promotional, optional, musical
ic:	metric, carbonic, Byronic, artistic
ary:	elementary, visionary, contrary, secondary
some:	lonesome, tiresome, handsome, bothersome
ly:	lonely, queenly, manly, friendly

The words *a, an, the* are classed as adjectives because they always accompany a noun or, infrequently, a pronoun. They certainly have no descriptive power, but in a limited sense they limit. Compare

man	*a* man	*the* man
deer	*a* deer	*the* deer

A and *an* are *indefinite articles: the* is the *definitive article: a* physician, *the* physician; *an* orange, *the* orange. The initial sound of the following word determines the choice of *a* or *an: an* is used before words beginning with a vowel sound (including silent *h*); *a* is used before consonant sounds (except silent *h*) and before initial vowels that have consonant sounds:

an apple	an hour	a hero	a European visitor

An adjective may modify a noun by preceding it, as do usually single adjectives or a series of single adjectives:

A *merry* laugh greeted us.
Red, green, and *yellow* lights are traffic signals.
The *tired, hungry,* and *emaciated* survivors moved feebly toward the ship.

Certain adjectives or adjective combinations may either precede or follow the noun; others, like restrictive adjective phrases and clauses (see Section **88m**), must follow:

One student *only* is needed to represent your dormitory.
Our delegate *alone* will travel to Washington.
Food *enough* has been provided for everyone.
The traffic lights, *red, green,* and *yellow,* were visible for blocks ahead.
The survivors, *tired, hungry,* and *emaciated,* moved feebly toward the ship.
The boy *in the brown suit* is my brother.
The girl *who is rising to speak* is the valedictorian.

Another position of the adjectives in sentences is after certain verbs:

The corn is *green.*
The water felt *warm.*
The children have grown *taller.*

Such adjectives are related to the subject, the word they modify. The verbs are called linking or joining or coupling verbs because they link subject and adjective, and the adjectives in this use are called predicate adjectives or complements. For fuller discussion, see Sections **78a** and **b, 83c.**

71j. For correct and exact meaning, understand the functions of adverbs.

An *adverb* modifies a verb, an adjective, or another adverb by describing, limiting, or in some other closely related way making meaning more nearly exact. Adverbs usually tell *how, how much, how often, when, where, why.*

A distant bugle sang *faintly.* (Adverb modifies verb *sang*)
We heard it *only once.* (Adverb *once* modifies verb *heard;* adverb *only* modifies adverb *once*)
Then the bugle sang *again.* (Both adverbs, *then* and *again,* modify verb *sang*)
I do *not* see my hat *anywhere.* (Both adverbs, *not* and *anywhere,* modify verb *see*)
We were *almost* ready to start. (Adverb modifies the adjective *ready*)

Close the door *very slowly*. (Adverb *very* modifies the adverb *slowly*, which modifies the verb *close*)

Adverbs have the following characteristics:

1. Adverbs are commonly distinguished from corresponding adjectives by the suffix *ly*.

2. Certain adverbs are distinguished from corresponding nouns by the suffixes *wise* and *ways: lengthwise, sideways*.

3. Certain adverbs are distinguished from similarly spelled prepositions in not being connected to a following noun:

Adverb: He came *up*.
Preposition: He came *up* the street.

4. Like adjectives, but unlike nouns and verbs, adverbs may be preceded by words of the "very" group (intensifiers):

The *very beautifully* dressed girl is the class queen.
He went *right* by.

Adverbs modifying adjectives and other adverbs are usually placed just before the words they modify. Adverbs modifying verbs can be placed almost anywhere in the sentence, smoothness and euphony (or good sound) permitting.

Both adjectives and adverbs have changes in form to indicate three degrees of *comparison—positive, comparative, superlative: good, better, best; great, greater, greatest; slowly, more slowly, most slowly*. For discussion, illustration, and application, see Section **83e, f, g, h.**

Errors in the use of adjectives and adverbs are discussed in Section **83.**

JOINING WORDS: PREPOSITIONS AND CONJUNCTIONS

71k. Distinguish between the functions of prepositions and conjunctions.

A *preposition* (note its literal meaning: *pre—before*, plus *position*) is a linking word used before a noun or pronoun to show its relationship to some other word in the sentence. The following list contains most of the prepositions used in English:

about	beside	in	since
above	besides	inside	through
across	between	into	throughout
after	beyond	like	till
against	but	near	to
along	by	notwithstanding	toward
alongside	concerning	of	until
amid	despite	off	under
among	down	on	underneath
around	during	onto	unto
at	ere	outside	up
before	except	over	upon
behind	excepting	per	with
below	for	regarding	within
beneath	from	save	without

Each of these prepositions is of course followed by its object (see Section **75d**)—noun, pronoun, noun phrase, or noun clause. In some word combinations the preposition may, paradoxically, follow its object:

> *In which house* do you live?
> *Which house* do you live *in?*
> The man *for whom* I am working . . .
> The man *whom* I am working *for* . . .

There are also compound prepositions, two or more words serving the purpose of a single one-word preposition. The most common of these in English are the following:

as for	for fear of	in view of
as to	for the sake of	on account of
aside from	in accordance with	owing to
because of	in addition to	pertaining to
by means of	in behalf of	regardless of
by reason of	in case of	with a view to
by way of	in company with	with reference to
contrary to	in favor of	with regard to
due to	in regard to	with respect to
exclusive of	in spite of	with the exception of

In common usage, certain prepositions are used with other parts of speech, such as verbs, adjectives, adverbs, to form idiomatic combinations:

480

comply with	entertain at
independent of	plan on going
blame you for it	different from

These are only a few of hundreds of such idioms in English using prepositions. Most of them are discussed in your dictionary; there is also a fuller discussion of them in Section **56**, pages 391–393.

A *conjunction* is a linking word used to connect words or groups of words in a sentence, or even to connect sentences. In some detail, conjunctions and their use are discussed in Section **84**.

These seven kinds of words—nouns, pronouns, verbs, adjectives, adverbs, prepositions, and conjunctions—are the principal parts of speech.

The eighth part of speech, the *interjection,* is an exclamatory or parenthetic word which has little connection with the remainder of the sentence; in fact, it frequently serves alone as a sentence: *Whoops! Ouch!* "*Oh,* must you go?" "And here, *alas,* our good fortune came to an abrupt end."

The following list contains most of the interjections found in English:

ah	bravo	hurrah	so
aha	encore	hush	tush
ahoy	gosh	indeed	tut
alas	halloo	lo	what
amen	hello	mum	whist
ay	hem	O	why
bah	hey	off	whoa
behold	hist	oh	whoopee
boo	ho	ouch	whoops
botheration	huh	pshaw	woe

Overuse of interjections gives the effect of a strained or immature style.

EXERCISES

A. Copy the following sentences. Put one each on a page of paper, and put one word only on a line, in column form, beginning at the extreme left margin. After each word write the part of speech that it is: noun, pronoun, adjective, verb, adverb, preposition, conjunction, interjection.

1. Many students attend football games every week during the season, whereas we notice that some work busily in the library even while the games are in progress.
2. A Canadian humorist and professor of economics once said that for a great university only three things are needed: a library, a body of interested students, and a scholarly faculty; what do you think of that statement?
3. Ah, if only more of our students would put their studies above their activities, this college would become a great center of learning; will you be the student who will first set the example?

B. From the following sentences, copy in column form the italicized words; after each, write the part of speech that each italicized word is.

1. It was a *very* warm day.
2. Susan was a most *intelligent* child.
3. He *caught* the book as it fell.
4. The *suit* will cost *too* much money.
5. He is sitting *by* a roaring fire.
6. They cannot go *because* it has rained.
7. This is the magazine of *which* you spoke.
8. He bought his books and *a* writing tablet.
9. *"Pshaw!"* she said; "I'm an hour late already."
10. It seems to me that he *talks* too *much*.
11. Carnations *and roses* make a *beautiful* bouquet.
12. *What!* six *hot* dogs in *one* afternoon!
13. The edge of the *razor* blade *resembled* a saw.
14. The tide *crept* imperceptibly *but relentlessly* on.
15. The rusty, *worn* old *chain* snapped in an instant.
16. The extent of the storm is *difficult* to *estimate*.
17. *Her* slant on life *is* a hard one to explain.
18. *Who* wrote the note is *his* problem, not *mine*.
19. *Come,* Thomas, can't you hurry up *quietly*?
20. *For* the life of *me,* I could *not* solve the problem.

PHRASES   Read This.

72. Identify phrases correctly, both for clearness and effectiveness in writing and for avoiding unjustifiable "sentence fragments."

A *phrase* is a group of related words not containing both a subject and a predicate.

Phrases classified according to use.

A phrase is used as a part of speech, fulfilling the functions of a single noun, adjective, verb, or adverb. Phrases containing adjectives modifying nouns or containing adverbs modifying verbs are labeled according to their stronger words, that is, noun phrases or verb phrases.

> Our city is proud of *its wide, well-paved, shady streets and boulevards.* (Noun phrase)
> Many a river *runs swiftly and silently to the sea.* (Verb phrase)

A phrase can be used in a sentence as a noun is used—as subject, object, etc. It is called a *noun phrase.*

> *Freshmen and sophomores* are known as lowerclassmen. (Noun phrase as subject)
> *Playing on a major football team* was his special ambition. (Noun phrase as subject)

A phrase may modify a noun or pronoun—may function, that is, exactly as a single adjective functions; such a phrase is called an *adjective* (or adjectival) *phrase.*

> Our city is proud of *its wide, well-paved, shady* streets.
> The farmers *in the West* (cf. the *western* farmers) need rain.

A phrase may modify a verb, adjective, or adverb—may function, that is, exactly as a single adverb functions; such a phrase is called an *adverb* (or adverbial) *phrase.*

> Many a river runs *swiftly and silently to the sea.*
> Our fullback fumbled *on the 2-yard line.*

If a modifying phrase is essential to explain or identify the word to which it is attached or refers, the phrase is called *restrictive.* If the phrase is not absolutely necessary, it is called *nonrestrictive.* Proper identification is necessary for clear punctuation. Restrictive and nonrestrictive phrases are discussed in Section **88m-R** and **88m-N,** with examples of punctuation given.

A *verb phrase* consists of a group of words serving the function of a verb, such as an auxiliary verb with its main verb, or a verb with its modifiers. A *verb phrase* is not the same as a *verbal phrase* —participial, gerundial, infinitive, defined below.

> By June your first college year *will have been completed.*
> Every student *should write correctly, clearly, effectively, and appropriately.*

Phrases classified according to form.

important

Phrases may also be classified according to form; such phrases usually receive their name from their initial or more important word. Six common divisions are the following:

Prepositional (used as adjectives or adverbs):
> The house *on the corner* is the home of Mayor Williams.
> The road winds *through the mountains* and down *into a valley.*

Participial: ~verb
> *Having completed my assignments,* I went to bed.
> *Puffing like steam engines,* we reached the top of the tower.

Gerundial: ~noun
> *Playing on a major football team* was his special ambition.
> The audience enjoyed *his playing of the Viennese waltzes.*

Prepositional gerundial (a phrase introduced by a preposition which is followed by the gerund as noun):
> *After graduating from college,* I plan to go on to medical school.
> We won *by having a superior line and a faster backfield.*

Infinitive:
> *To win games* is the aim of every team.
> He has worked hard *to achieve success.*

Absolute:
> *Night coming,* we ceased our work.
> *My theme written,* I signed my name to it and turned it in.
> John went to bed, *his work being finished.*

The *absolute phrase* is a peculiar kind of phrase, consisting usually of a noun followed and modified by a participle or participial phrase. It is a phrase because it cannot stand alone as a sentence; absolute, because it modifies no single word in the sentence of which it is a part, although it has a close thought relationship to the sentence or some word or phrase in it. (See also Section **88p.**)

484

EXERCISES

A. From the following sentences compile a list of phrases and classify them under these headings: prepositional, participial, gerundial, prepositional gerundial, infinitive, and absolute.

1. Through the night the train roared on to its destination.
2. To get along well with people, you must learn to share their interests.
3. In the spring, according to the poet, a young man's fancy lightly turns to thoughts of love.
4. Having reached the age of 19, I have no desire ever to fall in love again.
5. A motion for adjournment having been made, the meeting disbanded.
6. Traveling by airplane is our swiftest mode of travel; traveling by oxcart is the slowest.
7. Your teacher has no objection to your turning in well-written themes.
8. John wrote to a friend in Chicago to inquire about obtaining employment for the summer.
9. Smith being pretty well battered, the coach sent in Jones to replace him at tackle.
10. Seen from a distance, the night train, creeping up the mountain grade, looked like an animated glowworm.
11. A motion was made to close the nominations, no other names being proposed.
12. After opening and reading your letter, I understood your not receiving my invitation in time to accept.
13. To get experience and not to make money was his goal in seeking a summer job.
14. Having been unanimously elected president, I expressed my gratitude for the honor bestowed upon me.
15. In catching 15 trout, we had a good day of fishing, the legal limit being 20.

B. After each phrase in the list you compiled according to A, indicate how the phrase was used: noun, adjective, adverb, or verb.

CLAUSES ReAd

73. A clause is a group of words which has both subject and predicate and which forms part of a sentence. Clauses are of two kinds: *independent* (or *main,* or *principal*) and *dependent* (or *subordinate*).

73a. Identify independent clauses carefully for effectiveness in writing and for correctness of punctuation.

An *independent clause* makes a complete grammatical statement and may stand alone; that is, it makes reasonable sense if the remainder of the sentence is omitted. It could stand as a sentence. Context, of course, is usually necessary for completely clear meaning.

> Although I should have studied last evening, *I listened to the radio.*
> (Independent clause)
> *I listened to the radio.* (Sentence)

There may be more than one independent clause in a sentence.

> *My roommate studied,* but *I listened to the radio.*

73b. Identify dependent clauses carefully, as a safeguard against writing unjustifiable sentence fragments and against incorrect punctuation.

A *dependent clause,* or *subordinate clause,* is not capable of standing alone; it depends upon the remainder of the sentence for its meaning. Dependent clauses function as nouns, adjectives, or adverbs. Like an independent clause, a dependent clause contains a subject and predicate; it shows that it is dependent, usually, by the linking word which joins it to the independent clause.

Noun clauses.

In the following examples the dependent clause is used as a noun; each italicized clause functions exactly as would a single noun.

> *What you paid* was too much. (Noun clause used as subject. Compare: The *price* was too much.)
> He promised *that he would lend me the money.* (Noun clause used as object of verb *promised.*)
> I am not aware of *what he has in mind.* (Noun clause used as the object of the preposition *of.*)
> Your remark *that you hate college* surprises me. (Noun clause used as an *appositive;* see **Appositive,** in glossary, Section **85.**)
> His remarks usually were *whatever came to his mind first.* (Noun

clause used as a *predicate complement;* see **Complement,** in glossary, Section **85.**)

Adjective clauses.

In the following examples the dependent clause is used as an adjective; each italicized clause functions exactly as would a single adjective.

> The farmers *who live in the West* need rain. (Compare: The *western* farmers need rain.)
> The price *which he paid* was too much. (Clause modifies *price.*)
> People *who rarely think* should say little. (Clause modifies *people.*)
> You are the very person *whom I wanted.* (Clause modifies *person.*)
> He is a boy *I never admired.* (Clause modifies *boy; whom* after *boy* is understood.)

Adverbial clauses.

Dependent clauses function as adverbs in the following sentences; each italicized clause functions exactly as might a single adverb.

> I shall pay the bill *when you send it.* (Clause modifies the verb *shall pay;* compare: I shall pay the bill *later.*)
> You study more efficiently *than I do.* (Clause modifies the adverb *more efficiently.*)
> As a residential town, West Liberty is more desirable *than East Liberty is.* (Clause modifies the adjective *more desirable.*)

If a dependent clause—usually adjective, sometimes adverb—is essential in order to explain or identify the word on which it depends or to which it refers, the clause is called restrictive. If the dependent clause is not necessary, if it is in the nature of a parenthetical remark which could be removed from the sentence, leaving the essential meaning intact, it is called nonrestrictive. Proper identification is necessary for clear punctuation. Restrictive and nonrestrictive clauses are discussed in Section **88m-R** and **88m-N,** with examples of punctuation given.

Elliptical clauses.

A special kind of clause is the *elliptical clause.* For practical purposes, it is a dependent clause; its subject and frequently part of its predicate are omitted because they are understood from the main clause. In the following pairs, the first example contains complete clauses, the second contains an elliptical clause. (See Section **41b**.)

Although I was ill, I insisted on attending class.
Although ill, I insisted on attending class.
When he was in New York, John went to the theater every night.
When in New York, John went to the theater every night.
While she was sewing, Mary listened to the radio.
While sewing, Mary listened to the radio.

Trouble arises when the omitted, understood parts are *not* those of the main clause.

When driving a car, the emergency brakes should be released.
When six years old, my mother married my stepfather.

EXERCISES

Copy the following sentences, leaving a blank line between each two lines. Underline each clause in the sentences. Above each clause indicate by these abbreviations its function in the sentence: **N**—noun, **Adv.**—adverb, **Adj.**—adjective, **Ind.**—independent.

1. As it was getting late, we began looking for a place where we might land and camp for the night.
2. During the night we heard strange noises, which frightened us considerably, but they finally stopped, and we soon went back to sleep.
3. When school was out on Friday afternoons, a few of us stayed behind to take special instructions in learning how to typewrite.
4. Among other kinds of men we can single out these two: those who think and those who act.
5. I have often heard it said that people are funny, and I am sorry to have to admit that the statement is true.
6. I recommend a visit to Chicago, but when you go, remember that your impressions will be determined by where you get off the train.
7. Not all people in the library are scholars: across the table from me a boy is enjoying himself looking at the cartoons in a magazine; sitting farther away in a quiet corner are a boy and a girl having a library date.
8. The high light of my childhood summers was a visit to Grandfather's farm; letting a boy do everything under the sun, it seemed, was Grandfather's idea of showing me a good time.

9. I have now been on the campus for eight weeks, and I have long since overcome my fears of meeting new people.
10. The people in that section have been marketing a great quantity of vegetables in the city this summer.
11. The task which he has set himself is too heavy for his limited ability. He has been trying to recover his health, catch up with the class, and do the current assignments all at the same time.
12. Now that he has made a fortune, he is expected to start for Europe within the month.
13. He jumped up and down, he shouted and yelled; and yet, for some strange reason, no one paid him the slightest attention.
14. The men who have been working in the experiment station are trying to develop a plant that will grow in any kind of soil.
15. Whenever my high school friends assembled, we listened to the new records in anyone's collection.

SENTENCES Read

74. "Grammatically defined, a sentence consists of a subject and predicate and expresses a complete thought. Yet various kinds of statements express a complete thought without an expressed or implied subject or predicate."

This quotation, attempting a usable definition of a sentence for college students of writing, is discussed, expanded, and qualified in Section 31, where are included statements giving complete meaning without either or both a subject and predicate and where, in addition, justifiable and unjustifiable sentence fragments are considered and illustrated.

Most statements giving complete meaning contain a *subject* and a *predicate*. The subject is the name of the person (persons) or thing (things) about which the verb makes a statement. The predicate is that which is said of the subject; it must contain a verb which, with the subject, makes a complete, independent statement. Obviously, subjects and predicates have to be defined in terms of one another: a statement without a subject has no predicate; a statement without a predicate has no subject. It is worth remembering, in writing clearly and effectively, that participles, infinitives, and gerunds cannot serve as predicates.

74a. Understand the grammatical classification of sentences to obtain variety in your expression of the relation of ideas.

Sentences may be classified—according to the number of clauses they contain—as *simple, compound, complex,* or *compound-complex.*

A *simple sentence* contains only one subject and one predicate and expresses only one thought, although part of the thought can contain several related ideas. It *could* serve as an independent clause if other clauses were added to it. In addition to one simple subject and one simple predicate, the simple sentence may contain a compound subject (two or more nouns or pronouns joined by the proper conjunction) or a compound predicate (two or more verbs joined by the proper conjunction), or both. The simple sentence is excellent for the expression of one or two simple, uncomplicated ideas.

> Our campus has paved roads. (Simple subject, simple predicate)
> Oaks, maples, and elms line the campus roads. (Compound subject, simple predicate)
> The speaker arose and bowed. (Simple subject, compound predicate)
> My father and mother discuss and settle every important family matter. (Compound subject, compound predicate)
> Alumni, faculty, and students attended the game, cheered the team, and celebrated the victory. (Compound subject, compound predicate)

A *compound sentence* contains two or more independent clauses. Each clause of a compound sentence is grammatically capable of standing alone. The compound sentence is excellent for expressing two equally related parts of one main idea.

> In Arizona the days are warm, but the nights are cool.
> On our vacation Mother read, and I wrote letters.
> A team may not always win; nevertheless, it should try.

A *complex sentence* contains one independent clause and one or more dependent (subordinate) clauses. The complex sentence is excellent for expressing two ideas, one of which is not so important as the other.

490

Leonard is a student who puts his studies above his activities.
If the weather is fair, we shall go to the lake for the weekend.
Helen said that she had spent four hours writing her theme.

A *compound-complex sentence* contains two or more independent clauses and one or more dependent clauses. The compound-complex sentence is excellent for expressing two equally related parts of one larger idea and one or more ideas not so important as either of the two main ideas.

Since the day was unpleasant, we spent Sunday indoors; John studied mathematics, and I wrote the first draft of my theme, which is due on Tuesday.

74b. Understand the classification of sentences for the expression of meaning and purpose in clear and effective writing.

Sentences are also classified according to *meaning* and *purpose,* that is, according to the kind of statement that each makes.

A *declarative sentence* makes an assertion or states a fact, a possibility, or a condition.

This dormitory houses 120 students.
It may rain before tomorrow.
If it rains, we must change our plans for tomorrow.

An *imperative sentence* expresses a request, an entreaty, or a command.

Fill out the enclosed application blank and send it in immediately.
Please ask your friends to attend this important meeting.
Attend every class before and after the vacation period, or be prepared to suffer the consequences.

An *exclamatory sentence,* which may even consist of a word, a phrase, or a dependent clause, expresses strong feeling.

Ouch!
Attention, please! Danger ahead!
Oh, if only you had telephoned!
Thank goodness, you are here at last!

Frequently the exclamatory sentence consists of an exclamatory word + complement + subject + predicate:

> How lovely these roses are!
> What a brilliant student you have become!
> What a busy day we have had!

An *interrogative sentence* asks a question, makes a direct inquiry. An interrogative sentence can be written in several different ways:

By placing the subject after the auxiliary verb: *Are* you going? *Have* you bought any oranges? *Did* you study last night?

By using an interrogative pronoun or adverb: *Who* is it? *Which* is my book? *Where* did you find it? *How* are you?

By adding an interrogative statement to a declarative sentence: You have many visitors here, *haven't you?* You did study, *didn't you?*

By a question mark after a declarative statement: You're going home? You've been to the theater?

74c. Understand the arrangement of ideas in sentences for effectiveness of expression.

Sentences are also classified according to the *arrangement* of their content. Depending upon this arrangement, sentences are classified as *periodic, loose,* and *balanced,* a variety of either the periodic or the loose sentence.

A *periodic* sentence is one in which the words are so arranged that the meaning is not completed until the end or near the end.

A *loose* sentence is one in which a full or moderate completeness of meaning is obtained long before the end of the sentence.

Our conversation and informal writing contain many more loose sentences than periodic, because a loose sentence is, probably, a more natural means of expression. Yet a periodic sentence does provide suspense and variety; it holds the interest and attention of reader or listener and thus contributes to effectiveness of expression. Although a natural form of expression also, the periodic sentence is less common—hence, its effectiveness—but its overuse makes for monotony.

> Act quickly, or you will be too late to secure the bargain you want. (Loose)
> He liked to play baseball and tennis but more than either he enjoyed dancing and ice skating. (Loose)
> If you do not wish to go, please say so. (Periodic)

According to a former college president, to be at home in all lands and ages; to count Nature a familiar acquaintance and Art a familiar friend; to gain a standard for the appreciation of other men's work and the criticism of one's own; to make friends among men and women of one's own age who are to be the leaders in all walks of life; to lose one's self in generous enthusiasm and to cooperate with others for common ends; to learn manners from students who are gentlemen and gentlewomen, and to form character under professors who are dedicated—these are the returns of a college for the best four years of one's life. (Periodic)

A *balanced sentence* is so written that similar or opposing thoughts have similar grammatical phrasing. One part *balances* another: independent clause and independent clause, dependent clause and dependent clause, phrase and phrase (see Parallelism, Section 45); most effective, however, is the use of independent clauses to make statements especially emphatic through comparisons and contrasts.

Spring is planting time; summer is growing time; autumn is harvest time.
In the morning I attend classes; in the afternoon I study; in the evening I work.
A wise man changes his mind, a fool never.
You can take a man out of the country; you can't take the "country" out of a man.

For further discussion of the sentence, see "The Sentence," Sections 31 to 50.

EXERCISES

A. On a blank sheet of paper, make a column of figures, 1 to 15. After each number, write for the corresponding number of the following sentences whether each sentence is a simple sentence, compound sentence, complex sentence, or compound-complex sentence.

1. Every street in the village is paved with wood blocks.
2. Whenever the postman rings twice, my sister knows that he has a letter for her from Jack.
3. The snow covered the roads to a depth of eight inches, but we had no difficulty in rolling right along.

4. If the gun jams easily, you should notify the corporal, and he will provide you with a new one.
5. Twelve hours is a long while to sleep, but our bodies need such a rest occasionally because we regularly overwork them.
6. Joan and Patricia, eager to make a real contribution to the bazaar, worked from early morning until after midnight.
7. Cheap cars soon begin to consume a great deal of oil, and I know of no inexpensive way to remedy the fault.
8. Literature is often difficult for engineers, it seems to me, because they have spent their youth working with gadgets instead of reading books.
9. Since red-shouldered hawks rarely utter a call, the bird you heard screaming must have been a red-tailed hawk.
10. I will go because you have invited me, but if the orchestra is poor and the girls are stupid, I won't stay late.
11. Why don't we get all the interested men, women, and children of the towns around Midvale to contribute toward the pool?
12. The folly of such wild spending ought to be patent enough, even to people of little education.
13. When I told about my plans, she agreed at once, and so did he.
14. A tornado is a cyclone which has small diameter but great intensity.
15. Hard work seems to have more than personal or social advantages.

B. On a blank sheet of paper, make a column of figures, 1 to 15. After each number, write for the corresponding number of the following sentences whether each sentence is a loose or periodic sentence.

1. Sometimes when we sit down to think things over, we somehow approach a detached attitude as we compose our thoughts.
2. At 5:30 in the evening Fred stepped off the bus about two blocks from his home; then he walked down the street to where his family awaited him.
3. Anyone interested will find that the University of Illinois is located in the twin cities of Urbana and Champaign.
4. As I walked down the east side of the street, I noticed numerous neon signs announcing that I was approaching the town's business district.
5. I put on my skis and started tracking up the side of the hill, in fear and trepidation of what was to come later.
6. Because I get very sleepy right after lunch, I usually take a nap just before my first afternoon class.

7. I recall vividly the little village in the southern part of Missouri, where I lived as a little girl.
8. When I started to write my outline for my research paper, I discovered that I had not investigated my subject very thoroughly.
9. Horse racing, once the so-called sport of kings, has long since become the sport of the common man.
10. Why, I often wonder, aren't parents compelled to lock up mean children just as owners are required to confine vicious dogs?
11. I never liked Uncle Anthony, because to me he represented the terrors of sarcasm and repression, epitomizing a generation as cold and brittle as ice.
12. Student government plays an important part in training young people to be responsible, well-informed citizens of tomorrow.
13. Even though it is customary for a bridge game to cease when the players leave the card table, bridge fanatics insist on a heated post-mortem of every hand played.
14. People of the West, that is, people who have grown up in the culture of Western Civilization, have developed a biased view of history.
15. Our train was now coming into Washington, D.C., and I caught a glimpse of the famous Washington Monument.

C. Copy the following sentences with spaces between the lines. Then underline all simple subjects, all simple predicates, all compound subjects, and all compound predicates. Above each indicate what kind of subject (simple or compound) and what kind of predicate (simple or compound).

1. At our Homecoming exercises there have been honored in past years five women and seven men.
2. Nobody knows or cares about my troubles.
3. Our club is having a small party and is inviting a few friends; come early and stay late.
4. My father and my mother have been the best parents that any child could deserve.
5. Father has lent me money for my college education but says that he not only expects but believes that I can repay it and will repay it.
6. All during vacation we swam, played golf, hiked, played tennis, and, in general, just had a wonderful time.
7. A college preparatory course, a commercial course, and a vocational course are the three major courses that our high school offers its students.

8. When Father called and told me the bad news, I hurriedly packed my clothes, called a taxicab, rushed to the airport, and took the first plane home.
9. Unless you now speak forth or forever after hold your peace, the class will never vote for you as their president.
10. Football, basketball, and baseball are major sports on our campus; track, wrestling, fencing, swimming, and golf are minor sports.
11. I stood on the lawn, watched the stars, and wondered what kind of life might be lived there.
12. Suddenly, from every building on the campus, poured the freshmen, sophomores, juniors, seniors, and even the faculty; lunch hour had arrived!
13. There stands the Statue of Liberty, I proudly said to myself.
14. Chicago and New York are hundreds of miles apart but compete in all forms of friendly rivalry.
15. Every morning local delivery men and long-distance truck drivers come in, pick up their assignments, check their cargo, and set out for their destinations.

CASE

75. Case is a grammatical term referring to one of the forms that a noun or pronoun takes to indicate its relation to other words in a sentence. There are only three cases in English: subjective or nominative; possessive or genitive; objective or accusative.

In English, case and case endings are less important grammatically than in other languages you may be studying, such as German, Spanish, Italian, Latin, or Greek. For example, English nouns are not inflected—i.e., they have no distinguishing endings—to show the difference between nominative and objective case; in German and Latin, nouns are declined to show endings for the nominative, possessive, dative (indirect object), and objective cases. In addition, Latin nouns have another case called the ablative case, with appropriate endings. In these two languages also, German and Latin, adjectives are fully declined, but English adjectives in general take no endings.

The following rules for the use of the nominative and objective cases rarely apply to nouns but are a guide for the use of pronoun forms (See Section **71e.**) The most difficulty comes from the case forms of the personal pronouns and the relative or interrogative pronoun, *who*. The grammatical problems arise because these pronouns, unlike nouns, have different forms for the nominative and objective cases.

75a. Learn the different forms of personal, relative, and interrogative pronouns.

Singular

NOMINATIVE	POSSESSIVE	OBJECTIVE
1st person: I	my, mine	me
2nd person: you	your, yours	you
3rd person		
masculine: he	his	him
feminine: she	her, hers	her
neuter: it	its	it

Plural

NOMINATIVE	POSSESSIVE	OBJECTIVE
1st person: we	our, ours	us
2nd person: you	your, yours	you
3rd person		
all genders: they	their, theirs	them

When there are two possessive forms of the personal pronoun, the first one given in the list above is followed by the noun it qualifies; the second is used alone.

My book is on the desk; *yours* is on the shelf.
The book on the desk is *mine*.
His appointment is at nine; *hers* is at ten o'clock.

Singular and Plural

NOMINATIVE	POSSESSIVE	OBJECTIVE
who	whose	whom

75b. The subject of a sentence or a clause is in the nominative case.

If the subject is a noun, forget about it. Only the most illiterate American could get its form wrong. If the subject is a pronoun, used as the first or even the second member of a compound subject, again only the most poorly prepared college freshman would write sentences like the following:

497

Incorrect: Myself was the first freshman pledged to Iota Nu Nu this semester.

My father and me have gone on many a successful fishing trip.

Himself has been the most desirable roommate that any freshman could ask for.

As for my mother, Father and her have always encouraged me to do my best.

Whom is speaking, please?

Correct: I was the first freshman pledged to Iota Nu Nu this semester.

My father and I have gone on many a successful fishing trip.

He has been the most desirable roommate that any freshman could ask for.

As for my mother, Father and she have always encouraged me to do my best.

Who is speaking, please?

75c. A predicate complement is in the nominative case (see Complement, Section 85).

Remember that a predicate complement means a noun (no problem), a pronoun (nominative case, essentially), or a predicate adjective (not an adverb) used after a linking or copulative (coupling) verb. Not nouns, but only pronouns have different forms for nominative and objective. After a coupling or copulative verb, only the nominative, or subject case, of pronouns is used, not the objective case.

> This is *he* (not *him*) speaking.
> That is *she* (not *her*) there at the desk.
> It was *they* (not *them*) who made the decision.

The foregoing principle applies to second and third person pronouns, singular and plural, *she, her, he, him, we, us, they, them.* Controversy exists over "This is *I*" or "It is *I*" versus "This is *me*" or "It is *me*." In one opinion poll among competent judges, 59 percent labeled the *me* use acceptable. Curiously enough, studies have shown that *both "It is I" and "It is me" are avoided by careful speakers and writers.*

75d. The object of a verb or preposition is in the objective case.

Again nouns, or *it* or *you,* cause no trouble. Only the pronouns —*who* vs. *whom, I* vs. *me, she* vs. *her, he* vs. *him, we* vs. *us, they* vs. *them*—must be carefully observed. Pay especial attention to the cases of pronouns which are used as the second member of a compound object.

> The teacher blamed *her*.
> This was good news for *us*.
> A committee of *us* students is assisting in the planning.
> We are inviting both *him* and *her* to go along with *us*.
> There has never been any disagreement between my roommate and *me*.

75e. The indirect object of a verb is in the objective case.

The indirect object, like the direct object, is a source of trouble only with the pronouns mentioned in **75d**. The indirect object is the noun or pronoun before which *to* or *for* is understood.

> Give (to) *us* our daily bread.
> Write (to) *me* a letter about your plans.
> If you do (for) *him* a favor, he will never forget it.
> Tell *whom* my story? John? I should say not.

75f. The subject, object, or objective complement of an infinitive is in the objective case.

Infinitives are certain verb forms preceded by an expressed or implied *to*. As in the application of the other principles in this section, it is pronouns, not nouns, that cause trouble.

> The fraternity made *him* do that. (Subject of *to do*)
> The fraternity caused *him* to do that. (Subject of *to do*)
> The class has named *me* to serve as treasurer. (Subject of *to serve*)
> *Whom* did you take *her* to be? (I.e., did you take *her* to be *whom*?) (*Her* is the subject of *to be*; *whom* is an objective complement.)

If the grammar in the four preceding examples seems unduly complicated, just pretend that the pronoun is the object of the preceding verb and is modified by the infinitive. Your writing will turn out to be just as correct. If you write constructions like the foregoing and are puzzled about correcting them, revise and recast the sentence.

> My desire to please *her* was great. (Object)
> Did you think her to be *me*? (Objective complement)

NOMINATIVE OR OBJECTIVE CASE

75g. An appositive should be in the same case as the noun or pronoun it explains or identifies.

We, *you* and *I,* are the only candidates with a chance to win. (Nominative)
The dean gave friendly advice to both of us, James and *me.* (Objective)
Last evening the club pledged two additional men, my roommate and *me.* (Objective)

75h. An elliptical clause of comparison, preceded by <u>than or as,</u> requires the case called for by the expanded <u>construction.</u>

An elliptical clause is one with a word or more missing; the omitted word or words are understood from other parts of the sentence.

I am as strong as *he* (is). (Nominative)
You are much taller than *I* (am). (Nominative)
Mother does not drive a car as well as *I* (do). (Nominative)
I do not like her as much as (I like) *him.* (Objective)
I do not like her as much as *he* (likes her). (Nominative)
This TV program amused you much more than (it amused) *me.* (Objective)
This TV program amused you much more than *I* (amused you). (Nominative)

75i. <u>Who</u> and <u>whoever</u> are used as subjects of verbs or predicate <u>pronouns;</u> <u>whom</u> and <u>whomever</u> are used as objects of verbs and <u>prepositions.</u>

Many grammatical errors arise from a misunderstanding of the function of the pronoun, particularly the pronoun forms *who* or *whom* and *whoever* or *whomever.* The following discussion supplements and expands that given above, Sections **75a-h.**

1. The following sentences illustrate proper use of *who* and *whoever,* nominative forms serving as subjects of the verbs in the dependent clauses:

I demand membership for *whoever* wishes it! (*Whoever* is the subject of the verb *wishes;* the whole dependent clause is the object of the preposition *for.*)

500

The question of *who* can ask for membership should not arise. (*Who* is the subject of *can ask;* the whole dependent clause is the object of the preposition *of.*)

This book tells *who* is *who* in America, and that one tells *who* was *who.* (Each *who* before *is* and *was* is the subject; each *who* after *is* and *was* is a predicate pronoun.)

2. The following sentences illustrate proper use of *whom* and *whomever,* objective forms serving as objects in the dependent clauses:

This is the same man *whom* I saw at Oak Bluffs last summer. (Direct object of *saw.*)

The letter began, "To *whom* it may concern." (Direct object of *concern;* the dependent clause is the object of the preposition *to.*)

Ask *whomever* you desire. (Direct object of *desire;* the dependent clause is the object of *ask.*)

Grandfather tells the same yarns to *whomever* he meets. (Direct object of *meets;* the dependent clause is the object of the preposition *to.*)

3. The nominative and objective cases are frequently confused because of intervening words. The case of a pronoun depends upon its use in the sentence and must not be influenced by words which come between the pronoun and its antecedent.

He asked me *who* I thought would be chosen. (Check by omitting *I thought.*)

Who do you suppose drew up these plans? (Check by omitting *do you suppose.*)

I danced with the girl *whom* no one suspected we had chosen "Beauty Queen." (Check by omitting *no one suspected.*)

4. Whenever you are in doubt about *who* or *whom,* substitute *he* or *him,* and see which makes sense:

Who/whom are you writing to? (To *who/whom* are you writing?)

He, him are you writing to? (To *he, him* are you writing?)

This is the kind of student *who/whom* we need.

. . . . we need *who/whom.*

. . . . we need *he/him.*

NOTE: Current usage studies indicate that the distinction between *who* and *whom* is breaking down, partly because keeping them straight is difficult and partly because many people start a sentence or clause with *who,* not knowing how they are going to end. One dictionary says of *whom:* "the objective case of *who:* in colloquial usage, now often replaced by *who"* (*Webster's New World Dictionary*). The Thorndike-Barnhart *Comprehensive Desk Dictionary* says: "In formal English *whom* is always used as the accusative [objective] form. In informal English when the *who* stands before a verb or preposition of which it is the object, *who* is the generally accepted form."

POSSESSIVE (GENITIVE) CASE

75j. A noun or pronoun linked immediately with a gerund should preferably be in the possessive case.

> He resents *your* being more popular than he is.
> Most of the members paid their dues without *my* asking them.
> We objected to the *girl's* being at the football banquet.

This principle is not invariably followed, but the possessive case with a gerund is usually clear, whereas the objective case with the gerund may not be.

Awkward: Most of the members paid their dues without *me* asking them.

Similarly, when the use of a possessive with a gerund causes awkwardness, for example, other words coming between the two, recast the sentence.

> There are no rules against anyone's saying what he thinks.
> There are no rules against anyone in this class saying what he thinks.
> We objected to the girl from the Women's Athletic Association being at the football banquet.

Do not confuse the possessive with gerund and noun-or-pronoun-with-participle constructions.

> The student body heard *the coach appealing* for more spirit. (Participle)
> The student body responded to *the coach's appealing* for more spirit. (Gerund)

I like to see *you wearing* brown. (Participle)
I am proud of *your wearing* beautiful clothes. (Gerund)

75k. **Avoid using the possessive case of an inanimate object; use an of phrase.**

Awkward: The *house's* roof was on fire.
             We pledges had to wax and polish *the dining room's* floor.
Better: The roof *of the house* was on fire.
             We pledges had to wax and polish the floor *of the dining room*.

75l. **Use the possessive case in accordance with good English idiom.**

The principle stated in Section **75k** should not be followed implicitly if it produces awkwardness or violates good idiomatic usage. Although inanimate objects are rarely put in the possessive case, good English idiom prefers the possessive case of certain nouns of measure, time, and the like. It is not a question of ownership or possession; it is simply an effective expression of measure, extent of time, etc. Instead of the awkward "of" phrase, the following expressions are preferable and desirable:

a day's work   a dollar's worth
a moment's notice   a stone's throw
ten minutes' walk   at his wit's end
three years' experience   the law's delay
one summer's work   tomorrow's weather report
two semesters' study   four inches' space

For some of these ideas, of course, hyphenated expressions are perfectly acceptable and sometimes preferable alternatives: *a 10-minute walk, a 5-mile drive, a two-semester course, a 95-yard run* (vs. *a 95 yards' run*).

EXERCISES

A. On a separate page, write a list of numbers 1 to 20. Opposite each number, write the correct form of italicized words in the following sentences.

1. I received permission from my grandmother, *who whom* I was staying with at the time.

whom

75 Exercises

2. Napoleon was the emperor *who whom* was constantly saving Europe.
3. The actual giving of gifts is less of a problem than *who whom* to give them to.
4. The author chose 12 people from history *who whom* he believed fitted his definition of heroes.
5. Andrew Connolly is a man *who whom* I believe should be considered the greatest benefactor of our college.
6. Avoiding accidents often depends on *who whom* drives the car.
7. I shall write about a person *who whom* was a hero in the Spanish-American War.
8. Albert is looking for a girl *who whom* he thinks will be suitable for a wife.
9. It is sometimes a problem *who whom* to give gifts to.
10. Next month's issue will answer these football questions: *Who whom* will our team beat? *Who whom* might they lose to? *Who'll whom'll* be the top players?
11. Americans admire people *who whom* they see as benefactors to America.
12. The person *who whom* I picked as being the most unforgettable is my grandfather.
13. At the fraternity were many important men *who whom* I would never have met otherwise.
14. I can't remember now *who whom* I was employed by.
15. The first question is: "What shall we build for *who whom*?"
16. We asked the boy's father *who whom* we could get to cook the turtle.
17. I want you to forget all about Jane, *who whom* I am afraid is socially inferior to you.
18. My first airplane ride was with an old Navy pilot, *who whom* was one of the best in the service.
19. I made friends with a man *who whom* was Mr. Gray's son.
20. There have been some great high school players *who whom* will be eligible for college football next fall.

B. Directions given in A.

1. I didn't know *who whom* to help first.
2. You never know *who whom* you'll see at a dance.
3. *Who whom* do we play next Saturday?
4. When you attend school in another state, it is a problem *who whom* to "root" for.

504

5. My roommate is a very nice girl *who whom* I'm sure I'll become very close friends with.
6. The person *who whom* I would consider my best friend is Ned Forester.
7. I have two younger brothers *who whom* I feel like disowning every once in a while.
8. Introduced early in the novel is a gentleman *who whom* Elizabeth, after being snubbed at the first meeting, considers arrogant and unlikeable.
9. I went through the stage of playing "cops and robbers," "doctor," "soldier," and all the other men *who whom* boys worship.
10. My first name came from a boy *who whom* my father helped through college.
11. I shall write about the girl *who whom* I hope to marry.
12. The boy *who whom* I rode with was a good driver.
13. He introduced me to many men, some of *who whom* had been idols of mine since childhood.
14. It was always a race between *we us* boys to see *who whom* could get to Grandfather's barn first.
15. Just *who whom* is the Homecoming for?
16. There were two good candidates and a poor one, and *who whom* did the class choose?
17. My brother was named after a lawyer *who whom,* I suspected, was my mother's childhood sweetheart.
18. Senator Brown objects to the presence of lawyers, lobbyists, and publicity men *who whom* he says are hired to influence legislation.
19. I don't care *who whom* is going to speak; I won't go to the lecture.
20. The part should be given to *whoever whomever* is the best actor.

C. Copy the following sentences, correcting all errors in the use of case. Specify each kind of error.

1. I like him better than her.
2. Some people expect the possession of a rabbits foot or a four-leaf clover to bring them good luck.
3. In the last of the six rooms that are occupied live me and my roommate.
4. He was almost a month younger than me.
5. We love our little house which to us, my parents and I, is really and truly home.
6. Each summer since my mother's marriage, my father and her have taken a summer vacation.

7. Those boys were so much bigger than me.
8. Mary has led a more active life than many of those older than her.
9. In the fall of my senior year in high school his parents and him had my brother and I sold on going to college.
10. My brother was born in 1942 which makes him two years older than me.
11. Two girls and another boy and me planned to attend the first dance in honor of the freshmen.
12. Mother, my little brother, and me spent the last week before school at one of the state parks.
13. Me and Bill will do our best to represent this group at the convention.
14. I had only had 3 hours sleep the night before.
15. My little brother likes to go fishing with my Dad and I.
16. This conversation actually took place between my grandmother and I.
17. Our singing often brought my brother and I before the student assembly for a program.
18. Love of nature was always a tie between he and his sister.
19. I returned to college this semester after a 4 months illness.
20. The dictionarys principal use is still that of supplying definitions of words.

D. Directions given in C.

1. This 9-room house is occupied by only two people, my grandmother and I.
2. Sunday my parents came and took my roommate and I for a 50-mile ride and an appetizing picnic-dinner.
3. We have the greatest admiration for she and her mother.
4. The striking similarity between my new roommate and I insures our getting along well together.
5. One of my instructors in high school was only several years older than me.
6. Another boy and me were closely matched in our basketball ability, but I beat him out for the position.
7. I can remember how my father took us, my brother and I, to the river to swim.
8. There has been a contest on grades between he and I, since we started to school.
9. Father has always made a comfortable living for my mother, brother, and I.

10. To someone like I, a vocabulary course would be not only fascinating but beneficial.
11. The marriage between he and one of the girls would insure the property's remaining in the family.
12. A fast friendship grew up between Jerry and I.
13. I watched one listener; my gestures made he feel that I meant every word.
14. During vacation some of we boys got together and formed a basketball team.
15. It takes several hours for my brother and I to string the lights.
16. Like you and I, she is a former member of the 4-H.
17. The Glider Club is the main interest of my roommate and I.
18. The contests among we boys always ended in a friendly manner.
19. My mother is 5 years younger than him.
20. My sister constantly reminds my parents and I what she wants for her birthday.

E. Directions given in C.

1. The waiter accidentally spilled coffee on one of the girls dress.
2. Thanksgiving Friday found very few of we students left in town.
3. Our being the same age made my cousin and I like brother and sister.
4. William thought very highly of he and his paintings.
5. My roommate is two sizes smaller than me, and so I can't wear her clothes.
6. As the old proverb says, all things come to he who waits.
7. At that time, in the raising of vegetables, I thought there was no one bigger or better than me.
8. Since Father traveled a great deal, Mother had the responsibility of my sister and I.
9. These pictures were colored by he and his sister.
10. The dummies that Edgar Bergen has molded are as real as you or me.
11. My best friend is about 4 years older than me.
12. Jack, who is the brother between Bruce and I, now owns a poultry business in Somerset.
13. My twin brother is about one inch taller than me.
14. There is one major difference between my roommate and I.
15. My youngest aunt is just twice as old as me.
16. I was hoping that Mother would forget about me going to school that day.

17. The 4-H class was invited to visit one of the speakers farm.
18. We stopped at some of our friends home to watch television.
19. We had a vacation reunion at one of the boys home.
20. We must learn the "how" and "why" of a machines operation before we can use it.

AGREEMENT OF SUBJECT AND PREDICATE

76. Grammatical agreement means *unison* or *oneness* or *concord* or *harmony* of parts of a sentence. Thus when a subject agrees with its predicate, both subject and the verb in the predicate are alike in having the same *person* (first, second, or third) and *number* (singular or plural).

76a. A predicate normally agrees with its subject in person and number.

Few problems in agreement arise because English verbs (except *to be*—see p. 532) have one form for singular and plural and for *all* persons except the third person singular present tense. Most nouns and verbs form their plurals in directly opposite ways. Except for special groups, nouns form their *plurals* by adding *s* or *es: desk, desks; glass, glasses; lady, ladies.* (See Section **71c.**) Most verbs add an *s* in the third person singular. Do not be misled by an *s* sound in the verb. Examine carefully the following forms, 1st, 2nd, and 3rd person singular, present tense:

I do	go	ask	possess	exist	suppose
You do	go	ask	possess	exist	suppose
He does	goes	asks	possesses	exists	supposes
The man does	goes	asks	possesses	exists	supposes

In the plural, with *we, you, they,* the *men,* etc., there is only one plural form: *do, go, ask, possess, exist, suppose,* etc.

Errors in agreement which do occur are serious; they are usually subtle and make sound deceptively easy the principle that subjects and predicates agree in number; usually they appear when a writer or speaker is confused over the number of the subject because of other words intervening or when he uses a verb to agree not with the grammatical form of a subject but with its meaning—as is sometimes logical and acceptable. In short, you need to know what the subject is, whether it is singular or plural, and what its true meaning is.

Section 76a states the general rule; however, study the following sections in order to avoid serious errors and to understand variations.

76b. A verb should not agree with a noun which intervenes between it and the subject, when such noun is an appositive or the object in a phrase.

Correct: The *cause* for all the requests and demands *was* not apparent.
I, the delegate, *am* the one to determine that.
I, together with John and Mary, *am* going.
The *boy,* as well as all the members of his family, *was* determined to stay.

76c. Singular pronouns require singular verbs. These pronouns are singular: <u>each</u>, <u>everyone</u>, <u>everybody</u>, <u>anyone</u>, <u>anybody</u>, <u>someone</u>, <u>somebody</u>, <u>no one</u>, <u>nobody</u>, <u>one</u>, <u>many a one</u>, <u>another</u>, <u>anything</u>, <u>either</u>, <u>neither</u>.

Each *has* his own money.
Someone *is* speaking now.
One of you *has* made a mistake.
No one *skates* better than Thomas.

76d. Certain nouns or pronouns are considered singular or plural according to the singular or plural number of the key word in a modifying phrase.

Examples are *some, all, half, none* (*no one* or *not any*), *what.*

Some of my *money has* been lost.
Some of our *students have* been awarded scholarships.
There is no food left; *all* of *it has* been eaten.
No students are left on the campus; *all* of *them have* gone home for vacation.
Half of this *building is* to be completed by autumn.
Half of the *buildings* on our campus *are* of red-brick construction.

None (literally *no one,* but frequently meaning *not any*) may be followed by either a singular or a plural verb. Studies of the use of *none* have revealed that it is as frequently followed by a plural as

509

by a singular verb, especially when the phrase which modifies *none* contains a plural noun.

> *None* (no one) of the students in our dormitory is a candidate for a class office.
>
> *None* (not any) of our students have recently disobeyed any college regulations.

A tricky subject-predicate combination is one beginning with *what,* a pronoun used in both the singular and plural. When it is used in the sense of *that which,* it has a singular predicate. When it is used in the sense of *those (persons) who* or *those (things) which,* it has a plural predicate.

76e. For nouns plural in form but singular in meaning, use a singular verb.

The following are nearly always used with singular verbs: *physics, economics, mathematics, news, politics, whereabouts, mechanics, ethics,* and *stamina. Athletics,* on the other hand, is usually used with a plural verb. When in doubt about any particular word, turn to your dictionary for guidance.

> There *is* good news tonight.
> Politics *has* always been one of Father's major interests.

Subjects plural in form, which describe a quantity or number, require a singular verb when the subject is regarded as a unit.

> Ten miles *is* too far to walk.
> Two from five *leaves* three.
> Five dollars *was* asked for the lamp.
> Three-fourths of a bushel *does* not seem enough.

76f. Use a plural verb, ordinarily, with two or more nouns or pronouns joined by <u>and</u>.

> The house and the automobile *were* both painted green.
> Behind the wall *stand* a house and the garage.
> Both the secretary and the treasurer *have* agreed to be present.

When the two nouns or pronouns form a single thought or have a closely related meaning or mean one thing or one person, a singular verb is used.

The secretary and treasurer of our club *is* Harrison Thompson.
My oldest pal and best friend *was* my roommate this year.
The sum and substance of the speaker's remarks *has* caused much comment.
My house and home *is* at 1707 Maryland Drive.

76g. **Two or more singular subjects joined by or or nor or two singular subjects joined by either . . . or, neither . . . nor require a singular verb.**

Father or Mother *is* to represent our family at the meeting.
Neither John nor Henry *makes* very high grades.
Either economics or history *is* the course I shall elect next semester.

76h. **When the parts of the subject differ in number or person and are joined by or, nor, either . . . or, neither . . . nor, the verb agrees with the nearer subject member.**

There *isn't* a history course or any English courses that I like.
Neither the teacher nor the students *want* to meet at 7 o'clock.
Either my classmates or I *am* willing to write the petition.

76i. **Relative pronouns referring to plural antecedents require plural verbs; relative pronouns referring to singular antecedents require singular verbs.**

Each house has its own elected *officers, who conduct* the business of the house.
Our city has an excellent *beach, which attracts* many of our residents each summer.
My dictionary concludes with some *pages that contain* a list of American universities.

1. A troublesome application of this principle concerns *one of those who* or *one of those which*.

My English teacher was one of those high school *teachers who were* always getting off the subject.
This is one of the most important *events that have* ever occurred to me.
I happen to be one of those *people who like* to travel.
I hope to get a ride from *one* of my friends *who is* driving to Philadelphia.

511

In sentences like these, check carefully to see which is the *true* antecedent of the relative pronoun. Sometimes putting the *of* phrase first will help.

> Of the important sporting *events that take* place each year, the Indiana High School Basketball Tournament is one.
> Of those *people who like* to travel, I happen to be one.

2. If *the only* or some similar qualifying words precede *one*, the relative pronoun and the verb are singular:

> He is *the only one* of those present *who plays* well.
> My English teacher was *the only one* of my high school teachers *who was* always getting off the subject.

3. Sometimes you can determine the antecedent by the proper use of *who* or *which*:

> This is a *list* of students *which has* been prepared.
> This is a list of *students who have* been invited.

76j. A verb does not agree with a predicate noun; it agrees with the subject.

In some constructions, between two nouns or pronouns comes some form of the verb *to be: am, is, are, was, were, have been, has been.* The noun or pronoun coming first is considered the subject.

> The best part of the meal *is* the coffee and cookies.
> Coffee and cookies *are* the best part of the meal.

76k. After expressions like <u>there is, there are, there was, there were, there has, there have,</u> and other verbs, the verb is singular or plural according to the number of the subject that follows.

> There *seem* (not *seems*) to be one book and three magazines missing.
> Fortunately, there *exist* (not *exists*) people who can help us.
> There *have been* (not *has been*) many exciting games this fall.
> At camp there *were* (not *was*) baseball, softball, tennis, and swimming.

The same principle applies when *there* is replaced by other words and the subject still follows the predicate:

> In front of our Administration Building *stands* (not *stand*) a towering oak.
> In front of our Union Building *stand* (not *stands*) an elm, two maples, and an oak.

761. A collective noun takes a singular verb when the group is regarded as a unit, a plural verb when the individuals of the group are regarded separately.

Common collective nouns are nouns like the following: *army, clergy, committee, company, couple, crowd, family, flock, group, herd, jury, mob, multitude, orchestra, pair, squad, team*. These nouns can be plurals: *company, companies; crowd, crowds; team, teams.* Without the *s*, they are considered singular and take a singular verb and singular pronouns when the collection of individuals is thought of as a unit, as a whole; they are considered plural and take a plural verb and plural pronouns when the members of the group are thought of as individuals, acting separately. (For collective nouns as antecedents of pronouns, see Section **77c.**)

> Our crew [a unit] *is* going to compete this afternoon.
> Our crew [members] *have* been on shore leave and *are* coming aboard in a few hours.
> The team *has* elected Robbins captain.
> The team *have* been unable to agree on a man for captain.
> The family next door *is* named Browne.
> The family *were* seated in armchairs on the lawn.

EXERCISES

A. Make a list of numbers from 1 to 20. Opposite each, write the correct form of the verb from the italicized forms in the following sentences.

1. Henry turned out to be one of those students who *says say* that activities are more important than studies.
2. On our campus the best teacher is considered to be the one who always *draw draws* the largest number of students to his classes.
3. Commencement is one of the biggest events that *take takes* place on our campus.

4. Our college now has five buildings that *is are* used to house women students.
5. I expect to solve the few problems which *confronts confront* me.
6. My university is the only one of the large universities that *has have* no connection with any association of universities, like the Ivy League or the Big Ten.
7. There are three professional sports that *happen happens* to be in season now.
8. Inland Steel Company has three main plants, which *employs employ* about 60,000 men.
9. I judged this letter on the criteria that *was were* set up in the classroom.
10. Correct English, someone has said, is the only one of various languages which *is are* used correctly and properly by everyone except the native-born American!
11. A railroad runs through our town that *connect connects* it with the state capital.
12. The museum is visited daily by thousands of tourists like us, who *was were* told not to miss it under any conditions.
13. This section is only part of the material that *makes make* up the supplementary information in my dictionary.
14. I was amazed at all the color and energy which *was were* put forth to make the exhibits a success.
15. My dictionary has a large number of illustrations which *makes make* it look better and *adds add* information for the reader.
16. Our city is the home of a large university which *helps help* our local merchants and *makes make* the city a prosperous one.
17. There are 20 different factories which *include includes* ceramic plants, tool-making plants, and bakeries.
18. The campus has various kinds of trees and shrubs which *help helps* to beautify it.
19. One of the largest sporting events that *takes take* place each year is the nationally known Kentucky Derby.
20. Seaborsky is one of those unusual football players who *puts put* his scholarship above his football; in fact, his coaches have been quoted as saying that Seaborsky is the only player on the squad who *has have* the wrong attitude toward college life.

B. Directions given in A.

1. Neither the professor nor his wife *were was* at home.
2. Each of you *is are* to be congratulated.

3. The most exciting part of a football game *is are* the long runs.

4. Some students think a college instructor *don't doesn't* care whether his students learn anything or not.

5. There *wasn't weren't* many cars parked in front of University Hall that day.

6. A combination of teaching and farming *seem seems* to be a good idea.

7. Of the new employees, John is the only one who *show shows* any initiative.

8. Your chances of getting a job during Christmas vacation *isn't aren't* very good.

9. Ellen, along with two or three of her friends, *plan plans* to tour the Southwest this summer.

10. Every one of these books *is are* well worth reading.

11. Neither the other students nor the instructor *was were* surprised when I came in late.

12. Elmwood is one of the few towns that *does do* not have a chamber of commerce.

13. Charles Dickens' greatest achievement *is are* the novels that he wrote.

14. The weakest section in student themes *is are* the conclusion.

15. Five years *is are* certainly a long time to wait for a girl.

16. The sprinter, with two half-milers, *was were* warming up.

17. The reason for these superstitions *is are* not known.

18. A good activity *help helps* a student to gain recognition in college.

19. Almost everyone of my classmates *was were* in some kind of activity.

20. As basketball players neither one of us *were was* very good, and we spent most of our time on the bench.

C. Rewrite the following sentences, correcting the lack of agreement between subject and predicate.

1. The supplements, the third section of my dictionary, contains a large assortment of facts and special features.

2. A magazine containing 15 to 20 outstanding freshman themes are published each semester.

3. This company hires 375 employees and manufacture approximately 400,000,000 cans a year.

4. The everyday life in foreign countries seem impressive to the American tourist.

5. The origin of the words precede the definition.

6. John was above reproach where loyalty to his friends were concerned.

7. In athletics, our high school has always had good football and basketball teams but have not finished first in the city championships.
8. One of the rooms in the building have been reserved for meetings of hobby clubs.
9. After breakfast comes lectures, classes, and laboratories.
10. Synonyms often clarifies the meaning of the word and sharpens it.
11. In the stores in a large city the choice of items you may want are large.
12. The talk of all these safety devices are fine, but it is not enough.
13. The qualifications of a home economics teacher enables her to direct community activities.
14. On one side of the town is swamps, and on the other are a big bay.
15. About 50 percent of the cars on the roads today does not have good brakes.
16. Every one of my classes are at the far end of the campus.
17. The shopping center in the downtown area include four large department stores.
18. The price of automobiles have increased almost half again above what they were 15 years ago.
19. One of the finest things about Chicago are its many parks.
20. To the onlooker the game of basketball seem easy.

D. Directions given in C.

1. The few days that steak are served, the supply always seem to run out before I arrive.
2. On our farm is a few dairy cows and many chickens.
3. The grade school student, the high school student, and the college student all has definite need of a dictionary.
4. A survey of the dormitories and private rooming houses have been made.
5. Hunting and fishing are one of the ways our people of the United States spends their vacations.
6. My high school education as well as my part-time employment were obtained in Buffalo.
7. There is only three members in my family: my mother, brother, and me.
8. Frankfort has won the state basketball championship four times and have come close several other times.
9. Driving on icy roads are very dangerous to everyone who drives.
10. Radio and television plays an important part in bringing the world together.

11. The complicated mathematical formulae is difficult for the average student.
12. In this experiment there has been no definite results.
13. Every week end my brother and I was to help cultivate the corn.
14. Gas and oil adds up to a lot of money when you have a car.
15. The main character and hero of the story are David Copperfield.
16. Near our farm there is a feed mill, two hatcheries, and an orchard.
17. The story tells how these people after a while becomes reconciled to their fate.
18. One of the amazing things in Yellowstone Park were the animals.
19. The stars around the moon hasn't anything to do with a coming rain.
20. In the chain companies there exists a few jobs as managers or assistant managers.

E. Directions given in C.

1. One in every eight people are employed in merchandising.
2. When either of us have a problem, we talk it over together.
3. We must learn to thrive under the conditions that science impose.
4. Gerald and I was the most inexperienced hunters that you could find.
5. Valley City has four grade schools now and have a new one being built.
6. A knowledge of drugs and first aid are essential for a pharmacist.
7. Each of these words are defined and examples are given.
8. The alumni from each fraternity and sorority is welcomed back to the campus.
9. In such work, food purchasing, quantity food preparation, and quantity cookery is put to use.
10. Everyone as they enter a new class are a stranger.
11. These various industries provides employment for many of our citizens.
12. The day I left, every one in our household were up at daybreak.
13. The only street improvements I've seen for three years is some sloppy filling in of chuck holes.
14. The floods of our rivers each year was due to lack of forests.
15. The etymologies of words is one of the main features of my dictionary.
16. The operation of our two farms keep my father busy.
17. Each of these terms are explained in the back of the dictionary.
18. Row after row of buildings are visible across the fields.

19. Another idea that impresses me very much are the dialects of our country.
20. All day Friday and part of Saturday is spent in decorating the hall.

F. Directions given in C.

1. When you add up all the bills, living in a co-op house cost less than a fraternity or residence hall.
2. In high school the only thing that interested me were sports.
3. The two subjects that I have the weakest background in is English and Math.
4. Included in my plans for the summer is plans to have a lot of fun.
5. In high school one of my instructors were only several years older than I.
6. Patience, skill, and foresight is all that is required.
7. There is next two or three sentences describing the use of the word.
8. On Easter the fragrance of Easter lilies fill the church.
9. Our industries is what makes America the world power she is today.
10. Fishing, boating, and swimming is our major activity at that summer resort.
11. Purdue, along with nine other Midwest universities, make up the Western Conference, known better as the Big Ten.
12. There is a few more jobs I shall try to do during the vacation.
13. Good study habits gives one more time for recreation.
14. Turkey or ham are to be served at the class banquet.
15. Good looks isn't necessarily required in a mate.
16. Almost every program on radio and television are planned to help entertain people.
17. I was amused by the children; neither Joe nor his two friends was willing to begin the fight.
18. Last month Jim along with his Marine company were sent to Southern Spain.
19. Another unique attraction of Yellowstone National Park are the boiling mud pots.
20. On Saturday, there is a parade, contests, and stage acts.

PRONOUN AND ANTECEDENT

77. A pronoun does not necessarily agree with its antecedent in case (its use in the sentence determines the correct case—see Section 75), but it does agree in gender, number, and person. Since a pronoun (*pro-* means *for*) is a word used instead of a noun or a group of words serving as a noun, such noun or noun group—called the *antecedent* of the pronoun—must be unmistakably clear if your reader is not to be misled or confused.

The *woman* put on *her* hat. (Singular antecedent, feminine)
The *women* put on *their* hats. (Plural antecedent, feminine)
The *boy* misplaced *his* tickets. (Singular antecedent, masculine)
The *boys* misplaced *their* tickets. (Plural antecedent, masculine)

77a. Singular pronouns refer to singular antecedents. (See also Section **76c.**)

Has anyone here forgotten *his* dictionary?
The student was lucky to find the dictionary that *he* had lost.
In the new dormitory, each girl will have a room to *herself.*
Every person in favor will please raise *his* right hand.
Everybody is expected to do *his* share.

Since or when the sense of *everybody, anyone,* etc., is *many* or *all,* the plural personal pronoun referring to these indefinite pronouns is frequently found in both formal and informal English: "Everybody is expected to do *their* share of the work." Such use is preferable to the somewhat artificial and even awkward "Everybody is expected to do *his* or *her* share of the work." Notice, however, that a singular, not a plural verb form is used.

77b. A pronoun agrees with the nearer of two antecedents.

Occasionally in a sentence there are two antecedents, different in gender or in number. When these appear, and only one pronoun is used, the pronoun refers to the antecedent nearer to it.

He loves anything and everybody *who* is connected with his work.
He loves anybody and anything *which* is connected with his work.
Either the plant or the flowers will lose *their* freshness.

77c. A collective noun used as an antecedent takes either a singular or plural pronoun depending upon whether the collective noun is considered as a unified group or a group of individuals acting separately. (See Section **76l.**)

The crowd of men took off *their* hats. (The *crowd* acted as individuals.)

The crowd shouted *its* approval. (The *crowd* acted as a unit.)

Be consistent in the use of collective nouns with singular or plural predicates and with singular or plural pronouns.

Inconsistent: The class *was* unanimous in *their* choice of a president.
Consistent: The class *was* unanimous in *its* choice of a president.
Inconsistent: The team *were* unable to agree on whom *it* considered *their* most valuable player.
Consistent: The team *were* unable to agree on whom *they* considered *their* most valuable player.
The team *was* almost immediately ready with *its* choice of *its* most valuable player—Harry Brown, the center.

77d. Do not confuse the relative pronouns <u>who,</u> <u>which,</u> and <u>that.</u>

1. *Who* usually refers only to persons; *which* usually refers only to things; and *that* refers to persons or things.

Wrong: The horse *who* stands there is a thoroughbred.
The person *which* you mentioned is away from the city.

2. Distinguish among *that, which,* and *who,* in restrictive and nonrestrictive adjective clauses: *that,* as a relative pronoun, invariably introduces a restrictive clause, *who* and *which* introduce either restrictive or nonrestrictive clauses, according to the meaning. (See Section **88m.**)

77e. In the use of "I" in a compound subject, politeness suggests that the "I" come last.

The same politeness applies to *we* in a compound subject and to *me* and *us* in a compound object.

Dubious: *I* and my roommate are both studying engineering.
Last spring the fraternity pledged *me* and six other boys.
We and our neighbors have a community picnic each fall.
Preferable: My roommate and *I* are both studying engineering.
Last spring the fraternity pledged six other boys and *me.*
Our neighbors and *we* have a community picnic each fall.

77f. Do not use <u>myself,</u> <u>himself,</u> etc., unless an intensive or reflexive idea is present. (See Section 71e.)

Incorrect: John and myself can carry it.
Correct: John and I can carry it.

Incorrect: This is a matter that concerns only you and myself.
             This is a matter that concerns only you and himself.
Correct: This is a matter that concerns only you and me.
             This is a matter that concerns only you and him.

In correcting the error just discussed, do not make a "frying pan" error (a worse error than the original one) by using the wrong case of the personal pronoun.

Wrong: John and me can carry it.
         This is a matter that concerns only you and I.
         This is a matter that concerns only you and he.

77g.   Do not use illiterate forms for reflexive or intensive pronouns.

Such illiterate forms are *meself, mineself, youself, hisself, itsself, ourself* (see dictionary), *theyself, theyselves, theirself, theirselves, themself.*

The correct forms are the following: *myself, yourself, himself, itself, ourselves, yourselves, themselves.* (See Section **71e,** 5 and 6.)

77h.   Avoid using personal pronouns directly after nouns and referring to them.

Such repetition is useless for both clearness and effectiveness. To be avoided are sentences like these:

My friends *they* expect me to go with them everywhere.
Father *he* thinks that sometimes I spend too much money.
Our high school English teacher *she* did more for us than she will ever realize.

77i.   Avoid implied reference for a pronoun.

The relation of a pronoun to its antecedent (the noun or other pronoun to which it refers) must be clear and unmistakable. The reference word should generally be placed as close as possible to its antecedent in order that no intervening words may cause confusion. A *relative* pronoun must be in the same sentence as its antecedent, but *personal* or *demonstrative* pronouns may be placed some distance away, frequently in other sentences, if there is no intervening noun or pronoun to cause confusion.

Implied reference occurs when the antecedent of a pronoun is not actually expressed but must be inferred from the context. One of the most common forms of implied reference is the use of the pronouns *it, which, this, that,* etc., to refer to an entire preceding statement rather than to some noun or pronoun in that statement. The same confusion arises when *this, that,* and *such* are used as demonstrative adjectives.

The writer must decide whether such words refer to an implied antecedent or whether their antecedent is contained, paradoxically, in a statement which follows. Frequent occurrence of implied reference is found in the work of many reputable writers, and when there is no possibility of confusion, the use is effective, but remember that there *should* be no possibility of confusion.

Faults in the implied reference of *this, that, which, the,* etc., may be corrected by (1) summing up the idea of the preceding statement in a noun which acts as the antecedent; (2) rephrasing the sentence so as to make ideas coordinate or subordinate, according to meaning and appropriateness.

Doubtful: The Dean's attitude gave me *that* sinking feeling.

Improved: The Dean's attitude gave me a sinking feeling.

                  The Dean's attitude depressed me.

                  or

                  The Dean's attitude gave me that sinking feeling which accompanies frustration.

Doubtful: My father is a dentist. *That* is the profession I intend to enter.

Improved: My father is a dentist, and I too plan to enter the profession of dentistry.

                  or

                  My father has practiced dentistry for many years, and I too plan to enter that profession.

Doubtful: I mislaid your address, *which* was the reason why I did not write you sooner.

Improved: I mislaid your address, a fact which kept me from writing to you sooner.

                  or

                  I mislaid your address and therefore could not write to you until I found it.

Doubtful: I won two first places and one third place, *which* pleased my English teacher very much.

Improved: I won two first places and one third place, an achievement which pleased my English teacher very much.

Acceptable: I could also tell you of my experiences in Alaska, but *that* is another *story*.

Even the definite article *the* is sometimes misused as a demonstrative pronoun. This use is vague and ineffective; either avoid it or amplify it to clearness.

Vague: These island people were evidently in *the* early stage of cultural development.

Improved: These island people were evidently in *an* early stage of cultural development.

or

These island people were evidently in *that* early stage of cultural development which precedes any use of complex machines and mechanisms.

77j. Avoid the indefinite use of <u>you</u>.

In some kinds of informal and colloquial writing, an expression such as "*You* can see the importance of money" is permissible, even though *you* may refer to no particular person or group. In general, however, when using *you,* be sure that you mean the person or persons whom you are addressing. For example, the following is inappropriate in a paper designed for reading by an adult: "When you become a Boy Scout, *you* learn many useful things." (See Section **4b.**) If you wish to refer to a number of people in general and to no one in particular, use indefinite pronouns like *one, anyone, a person.*

Dubious: In high school you should be compelled to do more theme writing.

Preferable: In high school the student should have to do more theme writing.

When a youngster becomes a Boy Scout, he learns many useful things.

For the use of *you* as an appropriate or inappropriate theme beginning, see Section **8f, 5.**

77k. Avoid the indefinite use of <u>it</u>.

It as a third person singular pronoun, neuter, should usually have an appropriate antecedent. When *it* is used impersonally (*it* seems, *it* is possible, *it* is raining, etc.), another *it* should not be used in the same sentence referring to a definite antecedent.

Dubious: In this picture *it* showed some of the dark side of city life.

Better: This picture showed some of the dark side of city life.

Dubious: In this magazine article *it* states that not all wars are victories for the victors.

Better: This magazine article states that not all wars are victories for the victors.

Dubious: Bar Harbor is a beautiful summer resort; we liked *it* very much and *it* is possible that we shall go there again.

Better: We liked Bar Harbor very much as a summer resort, and *it* is possible that we shall go there again.

Dubious: Our roof needs patching, and when *it* rains *it* leaks badly.

Better: Our roof needs patching, and *it* leaks badly in rainy weather.

77l. Avoid the indefinite use of they.

They, their, theirs, them, as plural forms of the third person personal pronoun, should have definite antecedents: plural nouns or other pronouns in the plural. Otherwise, these pronouns should not be used.

Dubious: *They* have good roads in Texas.

Better: Texas has good roads.

Dubious: *They* said that Mexico is becoming very popular among tourists.

Better: Many people are saying that Mexico is becoming popular among tourists.

Dubious: We do our shopping in Chicago, for we like *their* large department stores.

Better: We do our shopping in Chicago, for we like the city's large department stores.

Dubious: In my high school *they* had excellent courses in English and mathematics.

Better: My high school had excellent courses in English and mathematics.

77m. Avoid double reference for a pronoun.

Double reference occurs when there are two possible antecedents

524

for a single pronoun. The pronoun reference is therefore ambiguous; the antecedent of every pronoun should be clear and definite.

Ambiguous reference can be corrected by (1) repeating the antecedent, (2) using a synonym for the antecedent, (3) changing the wording of the sentence so that the antecedent of each pronoun is unmistakable.

Dubious: When a salesman hands over an article to a customer, *he* is not always certain of its worth.

Better: A salesman is not always certain of the worth of an article when he hands it over to a customer.

Dubious: The professor told George that *he* should vote in the next election. (Who should vote: *George?* the *professor?*)

Better: The professor said, "I shall vote in the next election." (The *professor* will vote.)

The professor told George that he (the professor) should vote in the next election. (The *professor* will vote.)

The professor advised George to vote in the next election. (*George* should vote.)

The professor told George that he, as a mature student, should vote in the next election. (*George* should vote.)

EXERCISES

A. Correct all errors of disagreement between pronoun and antecedent.

1. In a few more weeks we shall have another vacation. They really are something to look forward to.
2. The two towns of West Newton and East Newton consolidated its schools into one.
3. The alumni himself prove that they have spirit.
4. Many boys think that mathematics and shop work will do him more good than English and economics.
5. A train gives you fast service at reasonable prices. The only trouble with them is that they do not always run at convenient times.
6. As a county agent I shall visit farmers and find out what he thinks of new ideas and improvements.
7. English is difficult for me for two reasons; I will try to explain it in this theme.
8. My instructors do not care whether I do all of my assignments. However, I am supposed to know it when I have a test.

9. I feel very sorry for any person who doesn't attend college, because they'll never know what they're missing.

10. This method helps a person find when and where they are making mistakes in their writing.

11. No doctor will tell a person to smoke because they know it is harmful.

12. If one is lucky enough to kill a bear, they make very nice rugs.

13. Ever since that first sports event, I have been going to them quite regularly.

14. After all my articles were laid about on beds and chairs, the problem of packing it arose.

15. A black cat! What are the superstitions about them?

16. The Red Cross will give swimming instructions to those who want it.

17. I stopped there for a sandwich and found they were the best I had ever eaten.

18. Being from the city, I was a college freshman before I saw a cow; he was in a field alongside the highway.

19. Although I have never had many voice lessons, I enjoy it very much.

20. No one in the camp could believe their eyes.

    B. With numbers corresponding to the sentences, make a list of the pronoun forms which are correct in each sentence.

1. Joe's grandfather was one of those Gloucester fishermen of *which who whom* we hear so many tales.

2. *Myself me I,* like many other students, am working my way through college.

3. In our family are ten children, all of *which whom who* are still living.

4. On our campus there are many foreign students, *which who* give the college a cosmopolitan atmosphere.

5. *Yourself you* and *I me myself* should be able to put this project over in a big way.

6. The dark spot was formed by the diminutive microbes *who which that* tended to collect in that area.

7. The girl *which who whom that* I marry will have to be attractive, intelligent, and capable.

8. I have seen a team *who which that* was well trained in fundamentals but *who which that* lost every game.

9. Two other fellows and *myself me I mineself* were discussing our religions just yesterday.

10. A person can drive at high speed on an icy road, and *they he* can end up in a ditch.
11. On busy week ends rooms must be found for all the guests *which who* are arriving.
12. I have two brothers and two sisters *that who which* are all younger than *myself me I.*
13. My brother's hobbies are the same as mine; *this is these are* sports of any kind.
14. My twin brother is about an inch taller than *me myself I.*
15. Most of the college professors have received a doctor's degree in *his their* particular field.
16. You should select a major study and a minor or two; *this these* will give you a good deal of knowledge in a given area.
17. Many cars have safety belts now, and if *this does these do* not break, *you have one has* a good chance of surviving a crash.
18. Tomorrow we start classes, and I don't have a very good idea of what *it they* will be like.
19. Since many of our words are derived from older languages, *it has these have* a bearing on the language we use today.
20. Every student should take such a course; *it they* will help *him them* to speak clearly and correctly.

C. Correct all errors in pronoun use in the following:

1. I asked the doctor to give me some medicine, which he did.
2. In Rocky Mountain National Park, if it is winter, it is probably snowing, and if it is summer, it might also be snowing.
3. When I serve my time in the Army, I hope they send me to Hawaii.
4. Our city is in the process of building several new schools, and this will help to relieve the pressure on the school system.
5. Everyone there takes it easy, which makes it a delightful vacation spot.
6. In my English literature course I learned how to read Shakespeare, and now I enjoy it.
7. I and my immediate family live on a farm.
8. In the wind tunnel they can simulate all kinds of weather conditions.
9. When Mother fainted, I threw some cold water in her face which was handed to me by my sister.
10. There are always new people with which to become acquainted.
11. When I entered high school, I had the idea that when you finished eighth grade you were on top of the world.

12. Many businessmen play golf because it is a game that takes your mind off your work.
13. You may like to learn what progress myself and others of your former students are making.
14. Grandfather had four broken ribs which developed into pneumonia.
15. Father had to be rushed to the hospital which was a strain on my mother.
16. The last day at camp they gave us all the watermelon we wanted to eat.
17. When I was home for the Christmas vacation, there was nothing for you to do but enjoy yourself.
18. The place that I and my father farm contains 80 acres.
19. Since I had practically no training writing in high school, it made it very difficult for me in college English.
20. I went to the court house and told them I wanted to apply for a driver's license.

D. Directions given in C.

1. I showed the policeman my driver's license, and he gave them one look and said they were no good.
2. When a person rides a horse, they are facing a challenge because here is an animal much bigger than a human being.
3. In college classes the students are treated as adults, as it should be.
4. Mother told Mary that she was devoted to her, and she cried.
5. Some people have little knowledge of their own cars; they don't know how fast it will turn, how fast it will stop, and how fast it will accelerate.
6. This first seven weeks of college have been the greatest, and I wouldn't trade it for anything in the world.
7. Dental schools require that students have at least two years of college training before he is admitted to a four-year course in dentistry.
8. Myself, I like to watch good golfers play all the time.
9. I had to wear my older sister's dresses until I grew out of it.
10. The chorus sang in Italian and English, and mixed it up some.
11. Students who study all the time are smart. He will know the answer to any question the teacher asks.
12. In this dictionary they have included a number of special features.
13. She was careful not to speak to girls to which she had not been introduced.
14. On Saturday nights my aunt, uncle, and myself have dinner in an expensive restaurant.

15. Before we know it, Christmas dinner is ready and you are eating it.
16. My sister does not sulk or pout, but gets it off her mind in a mild explosion.
17. When the plane finally got me in the air, it was more beautiful than I imagined.
18. My room in the dormitory has a big closet where you can hang your clothes.
19. My mother always has time to help you with your problems.
20. I remember when I and several other boys on our street built a fort.

E. Directions given in C.

1. Last year a truck with bad brakes went down that hill, and as a result he ended up in the hospital.
2. A good student will study and learn equally in any subject whether he has a liking for them or not.
3. Several hundred students are enrolled in our electrical engineering curricula. His average day is a most interesting one.
4. The boy next to me spent 90 dollars before they let him out of the bookstore.
5. Friday the 13th is a common superstition; even if you don't believe in it, it makes you stop and think.
6. I learned that a drug store needed a boy to drive their delivery truck.
7. It isn't good for one to stay in their room all the time and not spend some of their time in college activities.
8. In the last of the six rooms that are occupied live myself and my roommate.
9. The card catalog system is easy to learn. They are uniform in all libraries.
10. A good example of a careful driver is a race driver. When they are on the track racing, they are anticipating what the other drivers might do.
11. Names of available jobs are given the student, but it is entirely up to him to secure it for himself.
12. This house is a private home in which myself and six other students are living.
13. When I went home at Thanksgiving, my town had that same look.
14. He became embittered toward society and hated the thought of facing them.
15. The Northern Paper Company has an interesting factory, and they will take visitors through at any time.

16. I was given a new shotgun for my birthday, with which you can go hunting any time.
17. I have never lived in a dormitory but I have always been interested in them.
18. In my high school, they offered English for four years. I wish now that I had taken them.
19. Women are often considered foolish, but many times it is only a means to an end.
20. After Mayor Brown had seen the lion perform, he was taken to Main Street and fed 25 pounds of raw meat in front of the Imperial Hotel.

LINKING AND AUXILIARY VERBS

78. In order to write correctly, clearly, effectively, even appropriately, as well as to read satisfactorily, we all need an adequate understanding of linking and auxiliary verbs. Such verbs are basic in many foreign languages; they are also basic in English.

LINKING VERBS

Most verbs assert action but a few express a static condition or state of being (no action). Most, not all, of these "inactive" verbs are *linking* (or *joining* or *copulative*) verbs. They serve the purpose of coming between, or *coupling,* two substantives or a substantive and an adjective. See list, just below. Examples:

> *This* is my *roommate.*
> *Mr. Browne* was my English *instructor* last semester.
> My *roommate* is *dark-complexioned.*
> *Mr. Browne* will be *busy* tomorrow.

The substantive following the linking verb is a *predicate noun* or *predicate pronoun* (never a direct object). Nouns cause no trouble, pronouns do (see Section **75c**). An adjective following the linking verb is a *predicate adjective,* for it modifies the subject, not the predicate (see Section **83c**).

The most common linking verb is *to be,* in its various forms of number, person, tense, and mood (for a table of these forms, see pp. 532, 533; for the meaning of tense, see p. 549; for the meaning of mood, see p. 567). Other common linking verbs are *seem, appear, taste, smell, sound, look, feel, become, grow, prove, turn, remain, stand*. Some of these may also imply or express action occasionally; you can tell when they are linking verbs if you can substitute some form of *to be* (*are, is, was, were,* especially) for them. Not expressing action but not considered linking verbs are verbs such as *endure, exist, wait, sit, lie,* etc. Examples of linking verbs:

> My name *is* John.
> That *was* he who just spoke.
> The weather *seems* (*is*) cold today; tomorrow it may *turn* (*grow, become, be*) colder.
> The excitement *became* (*seemed, grew, was*) greater as the game progressed.
> These clouds *appear* (*look, seem, are*) salmon-colored.

78a. Do not confuse a linking verb with a verb expressing action.

Distinguish carefully between the meanings of the same verb word when it asserts action of the subject in one meaning and does not assert action in another; in the latter sense only is it a linking verb, followed by an adjective not by an adverb (see Section **83c.**) Observe differences in the following:

> The river *looks* muddy this morning. (Linking)
> John *looked* steadily at the scene before him. (Action)
> Oranges *taste* sweet. (Linking)
> Mary carefully *tasted* the salad. (Action)
> We do not *feel* bad about our defeat. (Linking)
> In the dark John stumbled against the furniture and *felt* his way carefully across the room. (Action)

78b. Use correct grammatical agreement in a linking verb, the correct pronoun case after it, and, as predicate complement, an adjective, not an adverb.

For correct agreement, see Section **76**; for correct case, see Section **75**; for adjective-adverb use, see Section **83**. Remember that when the linking verb is specifically described, an adverb is used; when the subject is described, an adjective is used.

AUXILIARY VERBS

78c. Use the correct form of the auxiliary verb with a main verb.

An auxiliary verb is one that "helps out" a main verb; that is, it

TABLE I. LINKING AND AUXILIARY VERBS

	TO BE		TO HAVE		TO DO	
Principal Parts	be, was, been		have, had, had		do, did, done	
	Singular	Plural	Singular	Plural	Singular	Plural

INDICATIVE MOOD

Present Tense

	Singular	Plural	Singular	Plural	Singular	Plural
1st person	I am	we are	I have	we have	I do	we do
2nd person	you are	you are	you have	you have	you do	you do
3rd person	he is (she, it)	they are	he has (she, it)	they have	he does (she, it)	they do

Past Tense

	Singular	Plural	Singular	Plural	Singular	Plural
1st person	I was	we were	I had	we had	I did	we did
2nd person	you were	you were	you had	you had	you did	you did
3rd person	he was	they were	he had	they had	he did	they did

Future Tense

	Singular	Plural	Singular	Plural
1st person	I shall be	we shall be	I shall have	we shall have
2nd person	you will be	you will be	you will have	you will have
3rd person	he will be	they will be	he will have	they will have

Present Perfect Tense

	Singular	Plural
1st person	I have been	we have been
2nd person	you have been	you have been
3rd person	he has been	they have been

Past Perfect Tense

	Singular	Plural
1st person	I had been	we had been
2nd person	you had been	you had been
3rd person	he had been	they had been

NOTE: The present perfect, past perfect, and future perfect tenses of *have* and *do* are rarely, if ever, used as *auxiliary* verb forms. As *main* verbs, they form these tenses as does any other main verb. See pp. 539–559.

Future Perfect Tense

	Singular	Plural
1st person	I shall have been	we shall have been
2nd person	you will have been	you will have been
3rd person	he will have been	they will have been

SUBJUNCTIVE MOOD

Present Tense

Singular	Plural	Singular	Plural	Singular	Plural
(if) I	(if) we	(if) I	(if) we	(if) I	(if) we
(if) you } be	(if) you } be	(if) you } have	(if) you } have	(if) you } do	(if) you } do
(if) he (she, it)	(if) they	(if) he (he, she)	(if) they	(if) he (he, she)	(if) they

Past Tense

Singular	Plural
(if) I	(if) we
(if) you } were	(if) you } were
(if) he	(if) they

NOTE: The other tense forms, in the subjunctive mood, of *to be, to have, to do* are identical to the corresponding tense forms of the indicative mood.

Verbals (Non-finite Verb Forms)

Present infinitive:	to be	to have
Perfect infinitive:	to have been	to have had
Present participle:	being	having
Past participle:	been	had
Perfect participle:	having been	having had
Present gerund:	being	having
Perfect gerund:	having been	having had

NOTE: Gerunds have the same form as participles, except that there is no past gerund.

helps to form some of the tenses and the tone (see Section 80), the mood (see Section 82), and the voice (see Section 81) of the main verb. Sometimes it has little meaning of its own; sometimes it changes the meaning of the main verb, which of course contains the central or "key" meaning of the verb phrase. In the following sentences, the italicized form is an auxiliary verb, the black-type form is the main verb.

> John *has* **gone** home.
> The furniture *will be* **shipped** by express.
> As we *were* **coming** home, we *were* **stopped** by a policeman.
> I *did* **mail** your letters.

The most common auxiliary verbs are forms of *to be, to have,* and *to do.* A table showing the various forms of these as auxiliary verbs is given on pp. 532, 533. The other common auxiliary verbs are *shall, should, will, would, may, might, can, could, must,* and *ought.* Also used, less frequently, are *let, need, used,* and *dare.*

78d. Never use of as a substitute for the auxiliary have.

The error is frequently made after *shall, will, should, would, may, might, could,* and *must.* The reason is *sound,* not *grammar:* unless we are careful, we pronounce *have* (as infinitive) and *of* alike, and then we confuse them in our writing—another example of how careful speech helps in correct writing.

Wrong: You should *of* informed me sooner.
          I would *of* lent you the money if you had asked me.
          It might *of* been much worse.
          I could *of* gone yesterday.
          Mother must *of* paid this bill, for she has a receipt.

78e. Use the correct form of the main verb with the auxiliary verb.

Given the principal parts of the main verb (see Section 79) and knowing the auxiliaries, you can form any desired tense, tone, mood, and voice, if such exist in good English usage. The present infinitive (with or without the sign *to*), the past participle, and the present participle ending in *-ing* are the parts of the main verb used with auxiliaries. (See Sections 71g and 85, and tables on pp. 550, 551, 562, 563.)

78f. **Distinguish between a verb form used as an auxiliary and a verb form used as a main verb.**

At least three specific verbs, dependent upon purpose, may be either auxiliary verbs or main verbs. *To be* may be a linking (and therefore main) verb, or it may help to express the progressive tone or the passive voice; *to have* (the auxiliary in the perfect tenses) and *to do* (expressing emphasis in the present and past tenses) are also used as main verbs. Notice the differences in the following:

His name *was* John. (Main verb)
He *was* named John. (Auxiliary verb)
He *was* telephoning when I came. (Auxiliary verb)
I *have* no money. (Main verb)
I *have* lost my money. (Auxiliary verb)
She *does* her work well. (Main verb)
She *does* spend her money foolishly. (Auxiliary verb)

For the various meanings of *have* and *do* as main verbs, see your dictionary.

78g. **Do not use the same verb form to serve as both auxiliary verb and main verb.**

Incorrect: His name was John and given him by his grandfather.
            She does her work well but spend money foolishly.
Correct: His name was John, and it was given him by his grand-
            father.
            She does her work well, but she does spend foolishly the
            money that she earns.

78h. **Use the correct auxiliary verb.**

For the meanings of the commonly used auxiliary verbs, see your dictionary. Common auxiliary verbs and their uses are as follows:
1. *to be*—
    used in all tenses in forming the progressive tone and the pas-
    sive voice. (See Sections **80b** and **81a**.)
2. *to have*—
    used in the present perfect, past perfect, and future perfect
    tenses; also in the perfect infinitive and the perfect participle.
    (See Section **80a**.)

3. *to do*—
   used to express emphasis (emphatic tone) in the present and past tenses. (See Section **80b.**)
   used to avoid repetition of a verb or full verb expression: "John slept as soundly as I *did*." "I shall go when you *do*."

4. *shall*—
   used as the precise auxiliary for the first person, future and future perfect tenses (but see p. 554).
   used in the second and third persons to express command or determination: "You *shall* not fool me again."

5. *will*—
   used as the precise auxiliary for the second and third persons, future and future perfect tenses (but see p. 554).
   used in all three persons to express willingness or consent: "I *will* write you tomorrow."
   used in the first person to indicate determination or resolution: "We *will* rush your order immediately."

6. *should*—
   used as a kind of "past" tense of *shall,* in the first person, but weaker in emphasis: "I *should* prefer not to come." "I *should* not judge him harshly."
   used frequently in a conditional meaning: "If I *should* decide, I shall let you know." "If John *should* call, tell him to leave a message."
   used in all three persons to express duty or propriety or necessity: "You *should* attend class regularly." "He *should* be ashamed of himself."
   used in all three persons to express expectation: "By dusk we *should* be halfway to St. Louis." "Mary *should* arrive home by noon if she left early this morning."

7. *would*—
   used as a kind of "past" tense of *will,* in the second and third persons, but less strong in meaning: "You *would* not recognize him."

NOTE: If the verb in the independent clause is in the past tense, use *would* to express futurity in the dependent clause; if the verb in the independent clause is in the present tense, use *will* in the dependent clause: "Henry *said* that he *would* go." "Henry *says* that he *will* go."

    used frequently in a conditional meaning, or after a conditional clause: "If you *would* consent, everyone would be happy." "If the weather were good, he *would* walk in the park."

    used to express determination: "He *would* do it, no matter how much we protested."

    used in all three persons to express repeated or habitual action: "Last summer I *would* read three books every week."

    used to express wish or desire: "*Would* that I had gone with you!"

8. *may*—

    used to express permission: "*May* I borrow your book?" "You *may* have it until tomorrow." "If I *may* say so, the idea is absurd."

    used to express probability or a wish: "It *may* rain tomorrow." "*May* your college years be happy ones!"

9. *might*—

    used as a kind of "past" tense of *may* to express the same ideas of possibility or probability in a weaker manner: "You *might* find the address in the telephone directory."

10. *can*—

    used to express ability or power or the idea of "being able to": "I *can* come at 6 o'clock." "He *can* do anything that you *can*."

11. *could*—

    used as a kind of "past" tense of *can* to express the same ideas in a weaker manner: "John *could* not do all the assigned work."

12. *must*—

    used to express obligation or compulsion: "Every man *must* do his part." "You *must* have your report in by next week."

    used to express reasonable certainty: "John left for Louisville this morning, and he *must* be there by now." "It *must* be about ten o'clock."

13. *ought*—

    used to express duty or obligation, one of the few auxiliary verbs followed by the sign of the infinitive (*to*) with the main verb. "You *ought* to write letters to your friends more frequently." "Everyone *ought* to pay his bills promptly."

NOTE: *Have* and *had* are never used before *ought* or *must*.

Wrong: I *had ought* to start studying.
Right: I *ought to have started* studying an hour ago.

14. *let*—

used to express the ideas of "allowing" or "permitting," "suggesting," "ordering": *"Let* me think a minute." *"Let* me call you tomorrow." *"Let's* go to the movies." *"Let* the man have his money."

15. *need*—

used to express necessity or obligation: "I *need* not tell you the reasons." "You *need* bring only your pen and theme paper."

NOTE: 3rd person singular form is also *need*: "He *need* not doubt my word."

16. *used*—

in the past tense only, *used* expresses custom or habitual action: "On my vacation I *used* to lie in the sun for hours." "It *used* to rain every day in the mountains."

17. *dare*—

used, usually with *say,* to express probability: "I *dare* say it will be a good game." "I *dare* say you're right."

EXERCISES

A. In the following sentences, indicate which verbs are linking verbs and which express action:

1. Everyone was glad that the sea remained calm during our voyage.
2. The sentry, standing silently at attention, appeared statuesque.
3. On a bright Sunday morning, church bells sound peaceful and beautiful.
4. Farmers have never seen crops grow so rapidly.
5. If the water turns rough, we shall turn around rapidly and head for shore.
6. The runner seemed stronger at the finish than at the beginning.
7. The dog smelled the bone indifferently.

8. When you have a cold, you certainly feel bad.
9. You have misspelled five words; you are becoming careless.
10. As a good chef Henry tasted the unsavory mess wryly.
11. You surely look good to me.
12. When you lose an argument, you feel certain that you are miserable.
13. Put the dog outside; he smells.
14. The fighter looked sure of himself after the first round.
15. On a cold day a cup of hot coffee smells good and tastes better.

B. From the following sentences, list all the linking and auxiliary verbs. If the verb is an auxiliary verb, indicate the purpose that it serves or the meaning that it expresses.

1. Let everyone express an opinion; it will do us all good.
2. If the Dean does not hear about this, no one need worry about excuses, I dare say.
3. I ought to go now; I should have gone an hour ago, don't you think?
4. Harry used to think he was a good golfer; now he is not so sure.
5. I did write carefully and my writing was legible, but I must have forgotten to proofread.
6. Must you go? You have not been here long.
7. We should have won the relay race; in fact, we might have won it if our anchor man had not stumbled on the last lap.
8. You may borrow my car, but can you drive it?
9. The roses are fresh and fragrant today, but by next week they will be wilted.
10. I will never permit a friend of mine to be without money.
11. Some people should buy a book of etiquette; they could certainly profit by reading it.
12. When I was a boy, Mother would serve us fried chicken at least once a week.
13. Have you tried hot lemonade? It might help you.
14. I shall be bowling this evening, but I can help you with your chemistry tomorrow morning.
15. One ought to obey traffic regulations; otherwise, he may find himself involved with an officer of the law.

PRINCIPAL PARTS OF VERBS

79. Knowing the principal parts of verbs and using proper auxiliary verbs (see pp. 531–538) with them when necessary, you can express a great variety of meaning and can also indicate precise shades of meaning. This variety is possible through the proper use of tense (Section **80**) and the proper use of active and passive voice (Section **81**). Errors in tense and voice are often due to insufficient knowledge of the principal parts of verbs.

In every language, verbs have principal parts, sometimes three as in German, sometimes five, as in French and Spanish. The English verb has three principal parts: the *present tense* (present infinitive), the *past tense,* and the *past participle.* Example: *see, saw, seen.* An excellent way to recall the principal parts of a verb is to substitute those of any verb for the following:

I *see* today.	I *work* today.
I *saw* yesterday.	I *worked* yesterday.
I *have seen* every day this week.	I *have worked* every day this week.

Almost a principal part and a most necessary verb form is the present participle, formed by adding *ing* to the present infinitive form. This "fourth" part, if it is in any way irregular, is given in your dictionary. Examples: *seeing, working, doing, beginning, choosing, raising.* The present participial form has constant use both as part of the predicate and as an adjective (see Section **71g**, p. 472).

79a. Add the proper endings, <u>d</u>, <u>ed</u>, or <u>t</u>, to form the past tense and past participle of regular verbs.

The past tense and past participle of *most* English verbs are formed by adding the endings *d, ed,* or *t* to the present infinitive: *move, moved, moved; walk, walked, walked; mean, meant, meant.* Any comparatively recent verb added to our language also forms its principal parts with these endings: *telegraph, telegraphed, telegraphed; telephone, telephoned, telephoned; radio, radioed, radioed.*

Verbs which form their principal parts by adding the endings *d, ed,* or *t,* are called *regular* verbs (or *weak* verbs). Notice that the past tense and past participle forms are alike. When in doubt, look up the verb in your dictionary. If no additional forms follow the main entry, the past tense and past participle are formed with the endings *d, ed,* or *t.* Otherwise, the past tense and past participle, and even the present participle, will be given immediately after the verb.

540

79b. Do not carelessly omit the ending of a regular verb, <u>d</u>, <u>ed</u>, or <u>t</u>, in the past tense or past participle.

Remember that regular verbs form the past tense and past participle by adding the endings *d, ed,* or *t.* Omitting these endings from these forms is a serious error in grammar.

Wrong: We are *suppose* to get our work in on time.
  Last week I *ask* for permission to miss one class.
  These children *use* to swim every day; now they are completely *use* to the water.
  We should not be *prejudice* against those who don't agree with us.

Right: We are *supposed* to get our work in on time.
  Last week I *asked* for permission to miss one class.
  These children *used* to swim every day; now they are completely *used* to the water.
  We should not be *prejudiced* against those who don't agree with us.

79c. Use your dictionary to find the principal parts of irregular verbs.

Irregular verbs, sometimes called *strong* verbs, are verbs which form their past tense and past participle by a vowel change within the verb as well as by the occasional addition of an ending: *see, saw, seen; do, did, done; give, gave, given; throw, threw, thrown; sleep, slept, slept.* A few have the same form for all three parts: *cut, cut, cut; burst, burst, burst; hurt, hurt, hurt; put, put, put.* All told, there are about 200 irregular verbs in English.

The principal parts of any verb are given in your dictionary, your safest guide. For all irregular verbs, the dictionary gives immediately after the entry word the past tense, the part participle, and the present participle; if there are alternative forms, these are given also.

79d. Check carefully to see that you are using correctly the principal parts of regular and irregular verbs.

The following verbs—some regular, most of them irregular—are especially troublesome. Study them carefully; put them into the three expressions mentioned above on page 540; memorize them. If other regular or irregular verbs cause you trouble, copy their principal parts from your dictionary and memorize them also.

1. ask	asked	asked
2. arise	arose	arisen
3. bear	bore	borne (born—given birth to)
4. beat	beat	beaten
5. become	became	become
6. begin	began	begun
7. bid	bid	bid (as in an auction)
8. bid	bade, bid	bidden, bid (as in a command)
9. bite	bit	bitten
10. blow	blew	blown
11. break	broke	broken
12. bring	brought	brought
13. build	built	built
14. burn	burned or burnt	burned or burnt
15. burst	burst	burst
16. cast	cast	cast
17. catch	caught	caught
18. choose	chose	chosen
19. climb	climbed	climbed
20. come	came	come
21. cut	cut	cut
22. deal	dealt	dealt
23. dig	dug	dug
24. dive	dived, dove	dived
25. do	did	done
26. drag	dragged	dragged
27. draw	drew	drawn
28. drink	drank	drunk, drunken (see your dictionary)
29. drive	drove	driven
30. drown	drowned	drowned
31. drug	drugged	drugged
32. eat	ate	eaten
33. fall	fell	fallen
34. feel	felt	felt
35. find	found	found
36. flee	fled	fled
37. flow	flowed	flowed
38. fly	flew	flown

39. fly (baseball)	flied	flied
40. forecast	forecast, forecasted	forecast, forecasted
41. forget	forgot	forgotten, forgot
42. freeze	froze	frozen
43. get	got	got, gotten
44. give	gave	given
45. go	went	gone
46. grow	grew	grown
47. hang (object)	hung	hung
48. hang (person)	hanged	hanged
49. happen	happened	happened
50. hear	heard	heard
51. help	helped	helped
52. know	knew	known
53. lay	laid	laid
54. lead	led	led
55. lend	lent	lent
56. let	let	let
57. lie (falsehood)	lied	lied
58. lie (recline)	lay	lain
59. loose	loosed	loosed
60. lose	lost	lost
61. mean	meant	meant
62. meet	met	met
63. pass	passed	passed, past (see dictionary)
64. pay	paid	paid
65. prove	proved	proved, proven
66. put	put	put
67. raise	raised	raised
68. rise	rose	risen
69. ride	rode	ridden
70. ring	rang	rung
71. run	ran	run
72. say	said	said
73. see	saw	seen
74. set	set	set
75. sit	sat	sat
76. shine	shone	shone
77. show	showed	shown, showed
78. shrink	shrank, shrunk	shrunk

79. sing	sang	sung
80. sink	sank, sunk	sunk (see your dictionary)
81. sleep	slept	slept
82. speak	spoke	spoken
83. spend	spent	spent
84. spring	sprang, sprung	sprung
85. stand	stood	stood
86. steal	stole	stolen
87. suppose	supposed	supposed
88. swim	swam	swum
89. swing	swung	swung
90. take	took	taken
91. tear	tore	torn
92. think	thought	thought
93. throw	threw	thrown
94. use	used	used
95. wake	waked, woke	waked, woken
96. wear	wore	worn
97. win	won	won
98. wind	wound	wound
99. wring	wrung	wrung
100. write	wrote	written

79e.   Do not confuse an irregular with a regular verb.

For many centuries, most strong and weak verbs in English have kept the principal parts that they now have. Only in a few isolated instances has a strong or irregular verb changed to weak or regular (*help, holp, holpen* to *help, helped, helped*) or has a weak verb added an alternative strong-verb ending (*prove, proved, proved* or *proven*).

Confusion or carelessness may cause you to add regular-verb endings to irregular verbs or to treat an occasional regular verb like an irregular verb.

Wrong: I was *borned* on a small farm in Ohio.
All my early years were *pasted* there, and these *pasted* years were the happiest I have lived.
Once I was *losted* in downtown Atlanta.
In our drawing class we *drawed* plans for several new buildings.

The trouble with these shirts is that they have *shrinked* too much.

These are errors in verb forms; they can also be considered as illiteracies—errors in diction or word choice (see Section **57**).

Right: I was *born* on a small farm in Ohio.

All my early years were *passed* there, and these *past* years were the happiest I have lived.

Once I was *lost* in downtown Atlanta.

In our drawing class we *drew* plans for several new buildings.

The trouble with these shirts is that they have *shrunk* too much.

79f. Do not misuse the past tense for the past participle, or the past participle for the past tense.

The confusion of the past tense with the past participle is a serious grammatical error. You can avoid it by memorizing the principal parts of all verbs used or, when in doubt, by consulting a dictionary.

Past tense wrongly used for past participle:

We have *did* the best we could.

We can skate tomorrow; the lake has *froze* over.

Our second semester has already *began*.

Past participle wrongly used for past tense:

I *seen* my duty and I *done* it.

That night our Glee Club *sung* like angels.

I *drunk* two cups of strong coffee to keep awake.

You may be helped by remembering that in predicates and other verb phrases, past tense forms are not preceded by auxiliary verbs and that past participle verb forms are preceded by auxiliary verbs.

Right: The Army is *to attack;* the city is *to be attacked*.

Mother and Father *use* good English; I *am used* to hearing good English.

Three Boy Scouts *swam* across the river today; three others *had swum* across it last week.

EXERCISES

A. From each of the following sentences, make a list of the correct forms of the verb.

1. He was very much embarrassed because his trousers were *tore torn*.
2. Our team was *beaten beat* badly last Saturday.
3. The bread was *cast casted* to the fish.
4. Before the teacher had *spoken spoke* a word, he drank a glass of water.
5. The man was sentenced to be *hung hanged* on October 15.
6. Clark pulled off his clothes and *dived dove* into the icy water.
7. The teacher saw immediately that I had *brung brought* the book.
8. I have *swum swam* across the lake nine times this summer.
9. She was so exhausted that she *laid lay* down to rest.
10. After a little while it *began begun* to rain.
11. The bell for assembly has already *rang rung* twice.
12. He *sprung sprang* into the saddle and galloped away.
13. Our captain has *drawn drew* the pole position.
14. He struck a blow that would have *felled fallen* a heavyweight boxer.
15. *Set sit* the book on the table and *set sit* down.

    B. Give the correct forms of the verbs that appear in parentheses in the following sentences.

1. I refuse to have that book (bite) by your puppy.
2. He wasn't sure when he should have (sow) the wheat.
3. He (lead) me a dog's life.
4. The teacher should have (know) the answer.
5. It is not easy to remember just when one has (give) money to people who have (come) to the door.
6. No one wants to be (catch) in his company.
7. Let's forget that he (steal) that loaf of bread.
8. In my youth I could have (spring) to my saddle easily.
9. The twins were (bear) last Sunday at 10 o'clock.
10. Children like to have lots of pictures (hang) on the walls of their rooms.
11. His suit had (shrink) to the point of being almost unwearable.
12. She never (bear) her share of the responsibilities.
13. Crowds used to come to watch a man get (hang).
14. He knew then that he had (dive) too deep.
15. I don't care if you (lend) him all you had yesterday afternoon.

    C. Correct all errors in the use of regular verbs in the following sentences:

1. Most accidents are cause by carelessness.
2. Three years of high school English are require of each student.
3. People do not realized the danger of driving on icy roads.

4. I am still wondering why this happen to me.
5. Last week a policeman stop me and gave me a lecture on driving.
6. It is hard to get use to not going home every week end.
7. My name was suppose to be Patricia, but my father had me christen Rosemarie.
8. Variety shows and dances are include among the week end's activities.
9. The flickering light was cause by the reflection of the moon.
10. Our school has recently build a new gymnasium.
11. Knocking on wood is suppose to ward off bad luck.
12. I had never work putting in windows before.
13. That was the most pleasant Thanksgiving that I have ever spend.
14. We would like to see the time of the meeting change by an hour.
15. If I had done what I was ask to do, I'd be much better in English now.
16. I think too much emphasis is place on grades.
17. My summer's work has help me in many ways.
18. At least an hour and a half should be spend in preparing each assignment.
19. The air was fill with the planes of the flying farmers.
20. The remaining cattle were place in another barn.

D. Correct all errors in the use of irregular verbs in the following sentences:

1. My parents have gave me every advantage.
2. Enterprising citizens have built new homes, tore down trees, and made a beautiful residential section.
3. We drove out to the _____ Inn and seen a lot of old schoolmates.
4. The team we had beat the week before scored an upset in the tournament.
5. John is my best friend and the finest person I have ever know.
6. I was glad to be at home, but I would have turned right around and went back to St. Louis if I could have.
7. In the battle the fish got worned down first, and I landed him.
8. When my mother seen my wet hair, she knew I had been swimming.
9. The rain had began to fall by 9 o'clock.
10. It seems we seen a lot of each other after that because we both went to the same school.
11. We have went through many an experience together.
12. Once my speech is began, I lose all fear of the audience.

13. I have founded trapping to be more exciting than hunting or fishing.
14. My clothes were soaked from the rain, and I wrang them out thoroughly.
15. As I approached my first vaccination, I wouldn't have gave a penny for getting out of there alive.
16. No one has ever went broke following the policy of regular saving.
17. In his reckless driving Tom has came quite close to many a serious accident.
18. When you have clumb to the top of the tower, you can see beautiful scenery for miles.
19. I begun driving the tractor as if I had drove it for years.
20. With a flourish the next contestant doved off into the deep end of the pool.

E. Directions given in D.

1. In my field I shall have a large variety of jobs to chose from.
2. For the past 10 years my parents have went traveling for a month each summer.
3. While stationed in California, he meet a girl whom he later married.
4. This lunch stand serves the best milk shakes that I have ever drank.
5. If I ever seen a person with patience, my math teacher is that person.
6. In high school we never gave book reports or done any outside reading.
7. A daydreamer isn't any better than a student who hasn't did anything but loaf.
8. By the end of the picnic I had drank five cups of coffee.
9. I had drove to school early that icy morning.
10. My mother would have lose everything she had if I was involved in a bad auto accident.
11. What he done is none of my business.
12. After everyone had said his piece or sang his song, the party ended.
13. A specialist usually knowns more than any other person in his field.
14. The sermon concluded with a poem which the minister had wrote himself.
15. The ball was down the middle, and I swang with all my might.
16. The door must have blowed shut during the night.
17. If our luck had ran out, we'd be laying in a cemetery right now.
18. When a word has began to be obsolete, it is removed from the dictionary.
19. As you suggested, I have completely rewrote this paper.
20. No sooner did I sat down than some usher told me I was in the wrong seat.

TENSE AND TONE

80. Tense indicates the time of the action or static condition expressed by a verb. The three divisions of time—*past, present,* and *future*—are shown by six tenses in English: *present tense, past tense, future tense, present perfect tense, past perfect tense, future perfect tense.*

Within some tenses, verbs also have certain "tones" which express precisely what the writer wishes to say: *simple tone, progressive tone,* and *emphatic tone.*

English, unlike a highly inflected language such as German or Latin, has few distinctive tense *forms,* verbs with change of endings to indicate time. Instead, these English tenses are revealed mainly through auxiliary verbs, only occasionally by a verb ending.

Students frequently have difficulty in using tenses but such difficulty is caused by ignorance of the functions of the six tenses, by the writer's not having thought out carefully the *time* expressed in his ideas, and by his failure to spend the small amount of effort necessary to learn how in English the various tenses and tones are formed.

Study carefully the following comments on the meaning of time in each tense and on the formation of tenses and tones. Study also Table II, pages 550, 551.

80a. Use the correct tense to express precise time.

The three primary tenses are the *present tense,* the *past tense,* and the *future tense.*

1. *Present tense* indicates that the action or condition is going on or exists *now.*

> A careful driver *watches* the road constantly.
> Our team *is playing* in Philadelphia today.
> Mary *does make* a nice appearance.

2. *Past tense* indicates that an action or condition took place or existed at some definite time in the past—before *now.*

> As we *drove,* we *watched* the road constantly.
> Our team *was playing* in Cleveland yesterday.
> Mary *did appreciate* the compliment.

TABLE II. **To See, INDICATIVE MOOD, ACTIVE VOICE**

Principal Parts: see saw seen

	Singular			Plural	
	Simple	Progressive	Simple	Progressive	

Present Tense

	Simple	Progressive		Simple	Progressive
1st person	I see	am seeing	we ⎫		are seeing
2nd person	you see	are seeing	you ⎬ see		are seeing
3rd person	he sees (she, it)	is seeing	they ⎭		are seeing

Past Tense

	Simple	Progressive		Simple	Progressive
1st person	I ⎫	was seeing	we ⎫		were seeing
2nd person	you ⎬ saw	were seeing	you ⎬ saw		were seeing
3rd person	he ⎭	was seeing	they ⎭		were seeing

Future Tense

	Simple	Progressive		Simple	Progressive
1st person	I shall see	shall be seeing	we shall see		shall be seeing
2nd person	you will see	will be seeing	you will see		will be seeing
3rd person	he will see	will be seeing	they will see		will be seeing

Present Perfect Tense

	Simple	Progressive		Simple	Progressive
1st person	I have seen	have been seeing	we ⎫		have been seeing
2nd person	you have seen	have been seeing	you ⎬ have seen		have been seeing
3rd person	he has seen	has been seeing	they ⎭		have been seeing

Past Perfect Tense

	had seen	had been seeing		had seen	had been seeing
1st person	I ⎫		1st person	we ⎫	
2nd person	you ⎬ had seen	had been seeing	2nd person	you ⎬ had seen	had been seeing
3rd person	he ⎭		3rd person	they ⎭	

Future Perfect Tense

	Singular		Plural
1st person	I shall have seen	shall have been seeing	we shall have seen · shall have been seeing
2nd person	you will have seen	will have been seeing	you will have seen · will have been seeing
3rd person	he will have seen	will have been seeing	they will have seen · will have been seeing

Verbals (Non-finite Verb Forms)

	Simple	Progressive
Present infinitive:	to see	to be seeing
Perfect infinitive:	to have seen	to have been seeing
Present participle:	seeing	(none)
Past participle:	seen	(none)
Perfect participle:	having seen	having been seeing
Present gerund:	seeing	(none)
Perfect gerund:	having seen	having been seeing

NOTE: Gerunds have the same form as participles, except that use of a past gerund is rare: "The battlefield was filled with *the injured* and *the slain*."

3. *Future tense* indicates that action will take place, or that a certain condition will exist, in the future—after the present, after *now*.

> We *shall arrive* in Pittsburgh tomorrow.
> Our team *will be playing* in Pittsburgh on Tuesday.
> The weather *will be* warmer by mid-July.

The other three tenses—*present perfect, past perfect,* and *future perfect*—are called *secondary* or *perfect* tenses. The key word is *perfect* or *perfected,* in the sense of *completed.* In these tenses

> The action or condition has begun.
> The action or condition begins.
> The action or condition has continued.
> The action or condition continues.
> The action or condition will continue.
> **and**
> The action or condition has just been completed.
> The action or condition is being completed.
> The action or condition will be completed by a certain stated or implied period.

4. *Present perfect tense* is used to indicate that an action or condition was begun in the past and has just been completed or is still going on. The present perfect tense presupposes some relationship with the present.

> You *have been* very ill. (Illness has just ended.)
> The ice on the lake *has melted.* (The melting has just been completed.)
> The class *has been writing* steadily for an hour. (The writing began an hour ago and is still going on.)

5. *Past perfect tense* is used to indicate that an action or condition was begun at some point in the past, and was completed at some point in the past, or has just been completed. It presupposes some action or condition expressed in the past tense, to which it is related.

> The roads were impassable because the snow *had fallen* so fast. (The falling of the snow *began* in the *past* and *ended* in the *past.*)
> Henry worked in a drug store; he *had been* there a year when he resigned. (His work there *began* in the *past* and *ended* in the *past.*)

6. *Future perfect tense* is used to indicate that an action or condition began in the past or begins in the present and will be completed at some future time, stated or implied.

> I *shall have spent* all my money by June. (Spending *began* in the *past, will be finished* by June.)
> The snow *will have melted* before you arrive. (Melting of snow *has begun, is continuing,* and *will soon be completed.*)
> One year from now my father *will have been working* for his present employer exactly 20 years. (Work *began 19 years ago, is continuing,* and *will be completed* one year from now.)

HOW TO FORM TENSES AND TONES

80b. Use the correct tense form and tone form to express precise meaning.

In the *active* voice, tense and tone are formed according to the directions given below (for a discussion of *voice* and of the *passive* voice, see Section 81).

Within certain tenses, verbs also have certain tones which express precisely what the writer wishes to say. These are the *simple* tone, the *progressive* tone, and the *emphatic* tone. For example, consider the differences in the following:

> I *study* my assignments every day. (Simple tone)
> Right now I *am studying* my history assignment. (Progressive tone)
> I *do study* each of my assignments two or three times. (Emphatic tone)

The *simple* tone is a concise statement, a kind of snapshot picture. The *progressive* tone indicates, in general, a kind of moving picture, a continuing action or state of being within a tense limit. The *emphatic* tone serves both to emphasize a statement and—by use of inverted order—commonly to ask a question.

Simple Tone

Present tense.

The present tense is the first principal part of the verb. All forms in the singular and plural are alike, *except* the third person singular, which varies from all the other forms by adding *s* or *es:*

I *go*	I *do*	I *come*	I *speak*
he *goes*	he *does*	she *comes*	she *speaks*

Past tense.

The past tense of the verb is the second principal part, given in your dictionary (see *regular* and *irregular* verbs in the glossary). Except for *was* and *were,* all singular and plural forms are alike: *had, did, came, spoke, went.*

Future tense.

The future tense, as *future* tense, is formed by the auxiliary verb *shall* in the first person and the auxiliary verb *will* in the second and third persons preceding the present infinitive.

I *shall* come.	We *shall* come.
You *will* come.	You *will* come.
He *will* come.	They *will* come.

Careful writers and speakers still observe these distinctions between *shall* and *will* as auxiliaries in the future tense; but the distinction is breaking down in current use, partly because it does not seem important, partly because *will* suggests the idea of willingness, as in *I will speak* (i.e., *am willing to speak*) *before your group.* However, *shall* in the second and third persons is used only to express determination on the part of the speaker: "You *shall* not borrow my clothes, and your friends *shall* not play that trick on me again." So, too, *will* in the first person can express determination or emphasis: "I *will* speak."

Even careful and precise speakers and writers, however, have other perfectly acceptable and idiomatic ways of expressing future time. These include using the present tense accompanied by an adverb or adverbial phrase of time or using expressions like "going to" or "plan to." Expressions like the following express future time:

The new students arrive tomorrow.
I am taking my entrance examinations next week.
This Saturday the team leaves for University Park to play Penn State.
I am going to pay my tuition fees tomorrow.
We plan to attend the convention in Detroit in March.

Present perfect tense.

The present perfect tense is formed by using the auxiliary verb *have* (*has*) with the past participle. It expresses action or state of being which began in the past and has just been completed or is still continuing in the present.

> I *have* just *completed* writing my theme.
> We *have had* a wonderful time here.
> John *has been* studying for over two hours.

Past perfect tense.

The past perfect tense is formed by using the auxiliary verb *had* with the past participle. It expresses action or state of being which began in the past and was completed at some point or time in the past.

> By last June I *had finished* my first two years of college.
> I *had never read* a Hardy novel until I read *The Return of the Native.*
> Our family *had* never *seen* a living president until we saw President Eisenhower.

Future perfect tense.

The future perfect tense is formed by using the future of the auxiliary verb *have* (*shall have, will have*) with the past participle. It expresses action or state of being which began in the past or begins in the present and which will not be completed until some specified or implied time in the future.

> Three years from now I *shall have graduated* from this university.
> By July 4, 1975, this country *will have celebrated* the 200th anniversary of its independence.

For *verbals,* or non-finite verb forms, the formation is as follows:

Present infinitive, usually without the sign *to,* is given as the first principal part of the verb: *to be, to do, to have, to see.*

Perfect infinitive of any verb is formed by using the present infinitive of the auxiliary verb, *to have,* followed by the past participle: *to have been, to have done, to have had, to have seen, to have come.*

Present participle is formed by adding *ing* to the present infinitive or the present tense form: *being, doing, having, seeing, coming.*

Past participle is the third principal part of any verb. When in doubt about its formation, see your dictionary.

Perfect participle is formed by using the present participle of the auxiliary verb, *having,* followed by the past participle: *having been, having done, having had, having seen, having come.*

Progressive Tone

The progressive-tone forms in each tense are built by using the proper tense forms of the auxiliary verb *to be* (pp. 532, 533) followed by the present participle of the main verb: *am coming, were coming, will be coming, have been coming, had been coming, will have been coming.* (See Table II, on pp. 550, 551.)

Emphatic Tone

The emphatic tone is used only in the present and past tenses, indicative mood, active voice, and it is formed by the auxiliary verb forms of *do* with the present infinitive of the main verb. The emphatic tone has two common uses: (1) to emphasize and (2) to ask a question: I *do* study. I *did* study. *Do* you plan to come? *Did* you know the answers?

Present		Past	
SINGULAR	PLURAL	SINGULAR	PLURAL
I do see	we do see	I did see	we did see
you do see	you do see	you did see	you did see
he does see	they do see	he did see	they did see

With the foregoing information mastered, you should have little difficulty in using the correct tense and tone form for any given time of action or state of being.

CONSISTENCY OF TENSE USE

When a verb is used alone in a sentence, the tense should express the precise time. When there are two or more verbs in a sentence: (1) two or more members of a compound predicate expressing the same time should have the same tense; (2) verbs in the clauses of a compound sentence should be clear and consistent in their tenses; (3) the tense of the verb in a dependent clause is determined by the tense of the verb in the main clause.

80c. Use the present tense to express a timeless or universal truth or, in a dependent clause, a general truth.

Iron, copper, and tin *are* metals.
The power of logical thinking *distinguishes* man from the animals.
In the Middle Ages some people did not believe that the earth *is* round.
In high school I learned that the speed of light *is* 186,000 miles a second.

80d. Avoid shifting needlessly from one tense to another.

In sustained prose, consecutive sentences developing ideas and thoughts, do not needlessly shift tenses, as from present to past, or past to present. (See also Section **46a.**)

Last summer we spent a few weeks at Bar Harbor, Maine. We fish nearly every day, but sometimes we drive around and enjoy the beautiful scenery. On rainy days we wrote letters or read.

Do not allow the tense of a verb to be attracted into the past when it should be present tense: "On our way home, we visited Gloucester, Massachusetts. The houses there were old and picturesque." Does the writer mean that the houses are no longer there?

80e. Use the appropriate tense of participles.

Your use of one of the participial forms—present participle, past participle, or perfect participle—depends upon the ideas you are expressing. Ordinarily, however, a present participle indicates action at the time expressed by the main verb (present or present perfect tense); a past or perfect participle indicates action previous to that of the time expressed by the main verb (past or past perfect tense). Notice the participles and main verbs in the following:

Traveling constantly from coast to coast, my parents *see* much of this country.
Traveling from coast to coast, my parents *have seen* much of this country.

Having traveled from coast to coast, my parents *saw* much of this country.

Making a good academic record, Henry *expects* to get excellent letters of recommendation.

Having made a good academic record, Henry *obtained* many excellent letters of recommendation.

80f. Use the appropriate tense of infinitives.

Your use of one of the infinitive tenses—present infinitive or perfect infinitive—likewise depends upon the ideas you are expressing.

Ordinarily the *present infinitive* expresses action occurring or state of being existing at the same time as the main verb or supposed to occur or exist at a time future to the main verb:

Mr. Browne, I am happy *to meet* you.
I have been asked *to invite* you to your meeting.
Will you come Friday evening *to speak* to us?

The perfect infinitive ordinarily indicates action which has occurred or state of being which has existed prior to the time of the main verb:

Mr. Browne, I am happy *to have met* you.
Every member is pleased *to have listened* to you as our speaker.

80g. Be consistent in the use of tense in dependent and independent clauses.

Consistency demands the correct "sequence of tenses." Sequence is the order of events in time and the proper expression of that order. Note these principles:

1. When the tense in the independent clause is the *present,* the *future,* the *present perfect,* or the *future perfect,* any tense can be used in the dependent clause which will adequately express the thought.

Henry *tells* me that he *will visit* Niagara Falls.
Henry *will* also *tell* you that he *will visit* Niagara Falls.
John *tells* me that he *has seen* Niagara Falls.
I *have told* you that I *have* not *seen* Niagara Falls.

2. When the tense in the independent clause is *past* or *past perfect,* a past tense or past perfect tense should be used in the depend-

558

ent clause (except to express a timeless or universal truth or general truth, Section 80c).

> John *told* me that he *saw* Niagara Falls yesterday.
> John *told* Henry that he *had seen* Niagara Falls a year ago.
> Our instructor *told* us yesterday that our themes *would be* due tomorrow.

3. In conditions and contrary-to-fact statements (see Section 82c), the *past* tense or *past perfect* tense in the dependent clause is followed by *should, would, could,* or *might* in the independent clause:

> If you *were* I, you *would* do exactly the same thing.
> If it *had* not *rained* yesterday, we *might have seen* two ball games.

Note that ordinarily *should, would, could,* or *might* do not appear in both clauses:

Dubious: If you *should* go to Chicago, you *would* see Lakeshore Drive.
           If John *would* reconsider, I *would* offer him the position.
Better: If you *should* go to Chicago, you *will* see Lakeshore Drive.
        If John reconsiders, I *would* offer him the position.

EXERCISES

A. Make a list of all the verbs and verb phrases in the following sentences; after each write the tense and the tone.

1. When I have finished writing my theme, I shall begin to prepare my history assignment.
2. Father and Mother will celebrate their silver wedding anniversary next month; they do not plan a celebration.
3. Mary has been sending out letters of application, but by last evening she had not received any replies.
4. Our leaders said that they saw that war was inevitably coming.
5. You do believe, don't you, that to see a football game is better than to read about it in the Sunday newspaper?
6. Whenever John leaves me, he always says, "I'll be seeing you."
7. Having flown on numerous trips, I am wondering whether I shall have the patience ever to travel by automobile again.
8. Henry had never heard of our product before I mentioned it to him; now he is using it continuously.
9. I heard a new radio program last evening; I had never heard it before and I most certainly shall not listen again.

10. My family is going to travel abroad this summer, and when my summer school is over, I am flying over to join them.
11. If you live until January 1, 2000, you will have seen the birth of a new century.
12. Did you wonder what had happened to us when we did not meet you as we had planned?
13. Professor Jones does not know why Mary failed; she did study, she said, and he believes her.
14. When you reach the top of the hill, you will see an abandoned building on the left.
15. The outfielder ran back to the fence and caught the ball, but he did succeed only after a hard run.

B. Correct all errors in tense in the following sentences:

1. James and Marie corresponded with each other ever since the latter went to Omaha.
2. The credit manager explained to her that he already wrote her twice.
3. I accepted the invitation because I knew that Shirley would have wished me to have been there.
4. Did you get the check your father was to send yet?
5. Walking slowly up the stairs, he was entering the room quietly.
6. She wouldn't have dreaded to have gone to the dance if she had not been afraid no one asked her to dance.
7. The speaker was so vigorously applauded that he seems to be liked.
8. He lives in New Mexico now; he was there for nearly 2 years.
9. Frank did not intend to have been rude, but he forgot his manners.
10. The novel revealed clearly the scenes about which the author is writing.
11. The old dog lay on his grave for days because it knew its master would have wanted it to have stayed there.
12. He lengthened his stride to the point where he has to take only three steps between hurdles instead of four.
13. Her book lays bare the many tragedies that occurred in her family in the four generations since her ancestor had landed in Boston.
14. If Gertrude would have put on less lipstick, her face will have seemed less tough looking.
15. Did Bill Omwake get his football letter yet?
16. How could you ever forget that salt was soluble in water?
17. Since my 12th birthday I was able to save an average of four dollars a month.
18. Finishing the tower on the first of last June, the contractors were able to have had the chimes rung on the Fourth of July.

19. My trip to the circus was exciting, but it may have been forgotten if I did not bring home those souvenirs.
20. Having seen the broken rail, the little girl runs to the station and tells the agent.

VOICE (ACTIVE AND PASSIVE)

81. In the study of grammar, when you hear or use *voice,* think of verbs and of A and P (active and passive). Voice is the grammatical term indicating whether the subject of the sentence or clause is acting or being acted upon. In the *active voice* of verbs expressing action, the subject (person or thing) is literally the actor, the doer; in the *passive voice,* the subject does nothing, is literally passive or inactive, and has something done to it. Study these examples:

John *wrote* a short story. (Active voice)
A short story *was written* by John. (Passive voice)

Every day I *ride* my horse, Bulger. (Active voice)
My horse, Bulger, *is ridden* every day. (Passive voice)

Father *has changed* his place of residence three times in five years. (Active voice)
His place of residence *has been changed* by Father three times in five years. (Passive voice)

81a. Use correct forms of the auxiliary and main verbs in forming the passive voice.

Like verbs in the active voice, verbs in the passive also have tense (time) and tone. To form the passive voice, use the auxiliary verb *to be* in its various forms and the past participle of the main verb. Study the forms of this auxiliary verb (Table I, pp. 532, 533), and then study Table III (pp. 562, 563), noting how auxiliary forms are applied.

Note also that in tone the passive voice has all the forms in the simple tone; it has none in the emphatic tone; and it uses, commonly, in the progressive tone the present, past, and future tenses only. The compound tenses (present perfect, past perfect, future perfect) in the progressive can be formed, but they are cumbersome, awkward, and uneuphonious. The ideas in the perfect progressive tenses (*have been being seen, had been being seen, shall have been being seen*) are more easily and effectively expressed by the

TABLE III. **To See, INDICATIVE MOOD, PASSIVE VOICE**

Principal Parts: see saw seen

	Singular			Plural	
	Simple	Progressive		Simple	Progressive

Present Tense

	Simple	Progressive
1st person	I am seen	am being seen
2nd person	you are seen	are being seen
3rd person	he is seen (she, it)	is being seen

	Simple	Progressive
1st person	we	
2nd person	you } are seen	are being seen
3rd person	they	

Past Tense

	Simple	Progressive
1st person	I was seen	was being seen
2nd person	you were seen	were being seen
3rd person	he was seen	was being seen

	Simple	Progressive
1st person	we	
2nd person	you } were seen	were being seen
3rd person	they	

Future Tense

	Simple	Progressive
1st person	I shall be seen	shall be being seen
2nd person	you will be seen	will be being seen
3rd person	he will be seen	will be being seen

	Simple	Progressive
1st person	we shall be seen	
2nd person	you will be seen	
3rd person	they will be seen	

Present Perfect Tense

	Simple
1st person	I have been seen
2nd person	you have been seen
3rd person	he has been seen

	Simple
1st person	we	
2nd person	you } have been seen
3rd person	they	

Past Perfect Tense

1st person I
2nd person you } had been seen
3rd person he

we
you } had been seen
they

Future Perfect Tense

1st person I shall have been seen
2nd person you will have been seen
3rd person he will have been seen

we shall have been seen
you will have been seen
they will have been seen

Verbals (Non-finite Verb Forms)

Simple

Present infinitive:	to be seen
Perfect infinitive:	to have been seen
Present participle:	being seen
Past participle:	(none)
Perfect participle:	having been seen
Present gerund:	being seen
Perfect gerund:	having been seen

NOTE: Gerunds have the same form as participles, except that there is no past gerund.

simple tone of these tenses (*have been seen, had been seen, shall have been seen*).

81b. Do not use intransitive verb forms in a passive-voice construction.

With a transitive verb, you recall (see p. 473), there is a direct object which receives the action of the verb; with an intransitive verb there is no such object. Only transitive verbs, therefore, can be used in the passive voice. In this process, the direct object of the transitive verb is shifted in front of the verb and becomes the subject, and the subject of the transitive active verb becomes the expressed agent (preceded by the preposition *by*) or the implied agent.

> John Brown writes novels. (Active voice, transitive verb)
> Novels are written by John Brown. (Passive voice)
> Our class has performed many experiments dealing with moisture condensation. (Active voice, transitive verb)
> Many experiments dealing with moisture condensation have been performed. (Passive voice; "by our class," the agent, is implied)

A passive-voice construction is sometimes used when an indirect object in one sentence is made the "passive" subject in a rephrased sentence.

> Father gave me some money. (Active voice)
> I was given some money by Father. (Passive voice)
> or
> Some money was given me by Father.

> His company granted John a month's vacation. (Active voice)
> John was granted a month's vacation by his company. (Passive voice)
> or
> A month's vacation was granted John by his company.

Verbs with an intransitive meaning cannot be used in the passive voice.

Incorrect: The river has been risen because of the recent rains.
Correct: The river has risen because of the recent rains.

Incorrect: The dog was sat on the chair.
Correct: The dog was made to sit on the chair.

Incorrect: Your letters have been lain on your desk.
Correct: Your letters have been laid on your desk.

NOTE: Idiomatic usage permits an *apparent* passive construction of a few intransitive verbs: Jesus is risen; Mary is gone; I am come to tell you the plans.

81c. Do not shift needlessly from active voice to passive voice.

Use the passive voice when it is effectively appropriate, that is, when the point of your writing is to represent the subject of the sentence as acted upon. Use verbs in the active voice wherever you express or imply action, mental or physical.

Do not, however, shift needlessly from active to passive voice, or from passive to active, since such a shift becomes annoying and troublesome to the reader. Clear, effective, appropriate use of voice is mainly a matter of being consistent. For discussion of consistency in the use of subject and voice in a sentence, see Section **46b**.

81d. Use the passive voice in impersonal writing.

Writing is impersonal when it avoids use of personal pronouns; it is completely impersonal when it avoids even the use of the indefinite pronouns, *one, someone, everybody,* and the like. In certain kinds of writing, as in the recording of experiments, completely impersonal expression may be desirable and is obtained by using the passive voice (See also Section **48f**). The agent or doer is usually not expressed, only implied.

The experiment was performed in order to . . .
The following facts were obtained . . .
The results were tabulated, and from them the following conclusions were reached . . .
On the basis of these conclusions, the following changes are recommended . . .

EXERCISES

A. Copy from the following sentences all the verbs or verb phrases in the passive voice. Make a list of these. After each, write also the tense or tone that each illustrates.

1. The cause of the accident was not determined until a thorough investigation had been completed.

2. The purse was lost on Main Street; if it is found, please telephone 92–2668.
3. This draft of the theme has been thoroughly revised; now the final draft must be written.
4. The contest will be closed Saturday night; all entries must be sent in by midnight, and winners will be announced on Monday.
5. When candidates are considered for class offices, it is an honor to be asked to be included among the nominees.
6. The work will be done, even if one hundred men are needed for the job.
7. I am being considered as a candidate for class president.
8. Heavy-duty trucks are used in long-distance hauling; light trucks are utilized for local deliveries.
9. The subject of the address was not announced until the guests of honor had been ushered to their seats.
10. Five recommendations were proposed on the basis of the facts that had been established.
11. A famous movie star in person will be being seen all next week at the Acme Theater.
12. My having been elected vice-president last year was a stepping stone to my being chosen president this year.
13. To be forced from your home by floods is as tragic as to be driven from your home by fire.
14. Although the fact was not known to you, you were being heard on the radio by thousands of unseen listeners.
15. Old jokes have been told so often that script writers are hard pressed for material.

   B. Change all passive-voice verb forms in the following sentences to the active voice.

1. The student was asked by the instructor to read the theme which had been written.
2. Freshmen will be invited by the college dormitories to the open house which is being held.
3. Because of the noise, doors and windows were closed by the students.
4. The dog was tied up by its master, because several holes in lawns had been dug by it.
5. The roof was blown off by the storm, and the furniture was badly damaged by the rain.
6. The letter was written by me to Mother.
7. When the question was asked by Mary, it was considered too difficult to be answered by the lecturer.

8. The chair was sprung from by the woman, and a piercing shriek was uttered by her.

9. The vegetables are being cooked by the women, and the dessert is being bought by the men.

10. Over a hundred speeches will have been given by the candidate before the ballots are cast by the voters.

11. The grass has been mowed by John, but the hedge has been trimmed by Henry.

12. Being seen in public for the first time in weeks, John was asked by us how his illness had been overcome.

13. "Aye" was shouted by the majority, and a few "No's" were uttered by the minority.

14. When your theme has been finished, your paper is to be folded and handed in.

15. The house will be painted by George, if he can be persuaded by me that the job should be undertaken by him.

MOOD (MODE)

82. *Mood*, literally, is a state or temper of mind; *mode*, literally, is a prevailing fashion or manner. In grammar, the *mood* or *mode* of a verb indicates the state of mind or the manner in which a statement is made: a fact, a request or command, a condition or probability. English has three moods: *indicative, imperative,* and *subjunctive.* Other "states of mind" or "prevailing manners"—such as willingness, duty, propriety, necessity, expectation, permission, ability, obligation, compulsion, duty, custom—are expressed by auxiliary verbs (see Section **78h**).

82a. Use the indicative mood to express a fact or what seems to be a fact, or to ask a question of fact.

Verb forms in the indicative mood are the most frequently used verb forms in English. An outline of the indicative mood of the auxiliary verbs *to be, to have, to do* and of the main verb *to see,* active and passive voice, is given in Tables I (pp. 532, 533), II (pp. 550, 551), and III (pp. 562, 563). Examples:

When *are* the term papers due? (Question of fact)
They *are* due on the second Friday in January. (Statement of fact)
Oak trees *are* taller than maple trees. (Statement of fact)

82b. Use the imperative mood to express a command, a polite request, a strong request, an order.

The imperative mood of the verb has only one form, the same form as the present infinitive without the sign *to*. It is both singular and plural. Examples: *come, go, speak, do, be.*

> Forward, *march!* Company, *halt!* (Commands)
> *Line up* in a column of twos. (Command)
> *Come* to the meeting and *bring* a friend with you. (Polite request)
> This class will begin promptly at 8 A.M. *Be* here. (Strong request)
> Please *deliver* these flowers this afternoon. (Order)

82c. Use the subjunctive mood to express (a) a condition contrary to fact, (b) a supposition, (c) a highly improbable condition, (d) doubt or uncertainty, (e) necessity, (f) parliamentary motions, (g) a desire.

The use of distinctive subjunctive verb forms in current English has disappeared in favor of more commonly used indicative verb forms.

Former use: If it *be* possible, I shall come.
              A student, if he *write* well, will receive a high grade.
Current use: If it *is* possible, I shall come.
              A student, if he *writes* well, will receive a high grade.

The verb *to be* (both as linking and as auxiliary verb) has only two distinct subjunctive forms now in occasional use: the form *be* for all persons in the singular and plural, present tense, and the form *were* for all persons in the singular and plural, past tense. See Table I, "Subjunctive Mood," on page 533. The same table gives any currently used subjunctive forms of the verbs *have* and *do.*

For all other verb forms except *be,* and including *have* and *do,* the only subjunctive form different from the indicative in any tense is the third person singular present, which, by dropping the *s* ending, becomes exactly like the other forms:

(if) I do	(if) I have	(if) I see	(if) I come
(if) you do	(if) you have	(if) you see	(if) you come
(if) he do	(if) he have	(if) he see	(if) he come

Only rarely, however, can you find such main-verb subjunctive forms, third person singular present tense, in current writing. Instead, both subjunctive and other non-indicative mood and non-imperative mood ideas are expressed by the use of auxiliary verbs: *should, would, can, could, may, might, must, ought, let, dare, need, used* (see Section **78h**).

Rare: If she *come*, it will be a pleasure.
            If he *write* me, I shall reply.
Common: If she *can come*, it will be a pleasure.
            If he *should write* me, I shall reply.

Our language still retains a number of subjunctive forms in sayings handed down from times when this mood was more widely used: *Heaven forbid, Thy Kingdom come, if need be, he need not speak, suffice it to say, come what may,* etc. Also, careful speakers and writers employ the subjunctive mood to express the precise manner in which they make their statements, when the indicative mood would not serve.

As indicated in the general principle introducing this section, current English uses subjunctive verb forms to express

a. A condition contrary to fact, something that is not true, that could not be true

> If I *were* the king, I would have you decorated.
> If she *were* I, would she succeed in doing better?
> If it *were* not so cold, we could go swimming.

b. A supposition

> Suppose he *were* to ask you that question!
> Let's assume that she *were* to be chosen campus queen.

c. A highly improbable condition, even though not completely contrary to fact

> He worked as if he *were* never going to have another chance.
> If I *be* too talkative at the meeting, please inform me at once.

d. Doubt or uncertainty

> He talks as if he *were* the only intelligent person in the group.
> As though he *were* any smarter himself!

e. Necessity

> It is necessary that she *pass* this course in order to be initiated.
> It is essential that Henry *appear* in person for the honor.
> The Dean of Women insisted that Jane *come* to her office.
> It is expected that every man *pay* his own way.

f. A parliamentary motion

> I move that the chairman *be authorized* to proceed.
> The motion is that the remark of the last speaker *be expunged* from the record.
> Resolved, that Henry *be made* an honorary member of this organization.

g. A wish, a desire, volition

> She wishes that she *were* going to go along.
> Our officers desire that you *be* rewarded.
> "The Kingdom *come,* Thy Will *be done."*

82d. In parallel constructions, do not shift the mood of verbs.

Be consistent in the use of the subjunctive mood, or the indicative, or the imperative.

Inconsistent: If I *were* in your position and *was* not prevented, I should certainly go.

Consistent: If I *were* in your position and *were* not prevented, I should certainly go.

EXERCISES

A. Choose between the subjunctive and indicative forms in the following sentences and give reasons for your choice:

1. I move that the chairman (be, is) appointed our delegate to the state convention.
2. Write your friend that he (needs, need) not worry about the money he owes me.
3. If anyone here (have, has) a desire to speak, now (is, be) the time.
4. Resolved, that Jeremiah Wilson (be, is) given public recognition for his contribution to the Society for Kindness to Coeds.
5. You speak as though it (was, were) an easy matter to preside at such meetings.

6. I wish that I (were, was) you!
7. If this (were, was) December, I could pay you what I owe.
8. If she (were, was) pretty, he might love her more.
9. I wonder if the doctor (be, is) willing to operate.
10. If only he (were, was) in Detroit, and I (were, was) at Ann Arbor!
11. If I (were, was) going, I should begin to make preparations.
12. I wondered whether this (were, was) an intentional error.
13. Although every precaution (be, is) taken, the expedition will be hazardous.
14. If this (be, is) what you mean, you are in error.
15. If you (were, was) to meet him, what would you say?

B. From the following sentences make a list containing the italicized forms that you prefer. If you choose the subjunctive form, state which of the subdivisions under 82c you are following.

1. Assume, now, that she *was were* to be our official delegate.
2. If she *be is* chosen our delegate and *was were* sent to Chicago, would we be well represented?
3. To put this campaign over, it *be is* necessary that the class president *be is* here Tuesday to make final plans.
4. My only hope is that John *receive receives* full recognition for his work.
5. Heaven *grant grants* that he *be is* not seriously injured.
6. It made no difference to me if he *were was* coming or not.
7. If I *was were* thirty instead of twenty, I'd know what to do.
8. I strongly advocate that a vote of censure *be is* ordered.
9. It is imperative that there *is be* not the slightest delay.
10. We shall all suffer if the country *be is* invaded.
11. Even though extreme measures for our safety *are be* taken, the consequences are dubious.
12. My, how he wished he *was were* a few inches taller.
13. If the President were given a free hand and *were was* sent to negotiate, we would see some action.
14. It hardly seems possible that the doctor *is would be* willing to give that anesthetic to a baby.
15. You can be sure the corporal wished he *was were* miles away.

C. Rewrite the following sentences, correcting all errors in the use of verbs: principal parts, tense, tone, mood, or voice:

1. I would have liked to have stayed in Bermuda longer.
2. The total distance that we hike last Saturday was approximately eight miles.

3. After studying the plan of the dictionary, a student would have a better idea of how to use the book.
4. If I would have had more composition in high school, I would have been better prepared for college English.
5. If I would have taken chemistry, I would not have so much trouble with it now.
6. Until last November I maintain average grades very easily.
7. The hardest thing this past semester is learning to study.
8. I had hoped you could have come down for our commencement week end, but you must have had gone elsewhere.
9. In high school my brother seem to be interest in mathematics and science.
10. I have always like arithmetic, algebra, geometry, and such.
11. I often wonder whether my grandfather truly believe the tales he told.
12. In high school I would have taken four years of English instead of the three I did take.
13. A big deer jumps right across the road in front of us.
14. If I would have studied harder, I would have made some decent grades this semester.
15. If I could turn back the clock, I know I would have made better use of my high school days.
16. When I look back to my high school days, I realize that I would have participated in one or two more activities.
17. If one would look up the name *Karl* in the dictionary, he would find it to be a German name for *Charles*.
18. If only we would have beaten Michigan, we would have gone to the Rose Bowl.
19. Many a person may not have been dead today if they would have use safety devices in their cars.
20. Some people can tell of some incidents that would never have happen if they would have sought advice.

ADJECTIVES AND ADVERBS

83. Ordinarily it is not difficult to determine when an adjective or adverb should be used. An *adjective* modifies only a noun or pronoun; an *adverb* modifies only a verb, adjective, or another adverb, or, infrequently, the general idea of a sentence. This rule is simple enough, and yet misuse of adjectives and adverbs is common. Part of the confusion is caused by the fact that after linking or coupling verbs, the adjective is used, since it really modifies the subject noun or pronoun, and after certain other verbs the adjective *or* adverb is used depending upon the meaning of the verb.

Still more confusion comes from the fact that the form of a word does not always reveal whether it is an adjective or adverb. Most words ending in *ly* are adverbs, but some are not, *womanly* and *holy*, for example. Many adverbs do not end in *ly*. Again, some adjectives and adverbs have identical forms (*quick, little, early*), but these cause no trouble until you are called on to tell which is which, in order to use them correctly. A few adverbs, also, have two forms which differ in meaning, like *sharp, sharply,* or *late, lately*.

In general, remember that if the word or phrase about which you are in doubt modifies sensibly a noun or pronoun, the chances are that it should be an adjective. If it modifies or even loosely applies to the verb, it should be an adverb. (For additional discussion, see pp. 476–479.)

83a. Do not use an adjective to modify a verb.

Wrong: Our chemistry teacher talks too *rapid*.
        Some people take themselves too *serious*.
        On every occasion my sister always dresses *neat*.

Correct: Our chemistry teacher talks too *rapidly*.
         Some people take themselves too *seriously*.
         On every occasion my sister always dresses *neatly*.

83b. Do not use an adjective to modify another adjective or an adverb.

Wrong: Joe is a *real* good boxer.
        This is a *strong* made box.

Dubious: Small auto racers are *plenty* fast.

Correct: Joe is a *really* good boxer.
         This is a *strongly* made box.
         Small auto racers are *very* fast.

83c. After such verbs as appear, be, become, feel, look, seem, smell, taste, grow, the modifier should be an adjective if it refers to the subject, an adverb if it describes or defines the verb. (See Section **78**.)

Correct: The cake tastes *good*. (Adjective)
         The girl looked *beautiful*. (Adjective)

> She looked at him *angrily*. (Adverb)
> She feels *strongly* that she was cheated. (Adverb)

The first two italicized modifiers are adjectives because they refer to the *subjects* of the sentences. The last two are adverbs because they modify *verbs*. (See Sections 78a, 78b.)

> He looks *careful*. (Adjective: he appears to be a person who is careful.)
> He looks *carefully*. (Adverb: describes the way in which he *looks*.)

83d. Be accurate in the use of words that may be either adjectives or adverbs, and of adjectives that end in <u>ly</u>.

Cheap, deep, far, fast, wrong, sure, and many others are both adjectives and adverbs. Further, *cheap, deep, wrong,* and many others have *ly* forms, also. Words such as *lovely, timely, manly, kindly, goodly* are adjectives, normally. Consult your dictionary when you are in doubt; it will tell you which words are adjectives only, which are adverbs only, which may be either, and what their label is—colloquial, informal, formal.

Correct: This is a *fast* color. (Adjective)
           The miler ran very *fast*. (Adverb)
           He ran the mile in *fast* time. (Adjective)
           Cleopatra, though a queen, was still *womanly*. (Adjective)
Dubious: Cleopatra, though a queen, ruled *womanly*.

83e. Use the correct forms of adjectives and adverbs to indicate the three degrees of comparison.

Both adjectives and adverbs have changes in form or added modifiers to indicate *comparison,* to show a greater or lesser degree of the quality they indicate. If there is no comparison, the degree is *positive: tall, competent, violently.* If two are compared, the degree is *comparative: taller, more competent, less violently.* If three or more are compared, the degree is *superlative: tallest, most competent, least violently.*

The comparative and superlative degrees are formed by adding *er* and *est* to adjectives and adverbs of one syllable and to some of two syllables. The words *more* and *most* (upward comparison) and *less* and *least* (downward comparison) are used to form the comparative and superlative degrees of two-syllable adjectives and adverbs which would be made awkward by the addition of *er* and *est*. *More, most, less,* and *least* are also used to show degree with adjectives and adverbs of three or more syllables. (For further discussion, see the Glossary, pp. 589, 590.)

> Smith is a *tall* [*competent*] man. (Adjective, positive degree)
> Smith is a *taller* [*more competent*] man than I am. (Adjective, comparative degree)
> Smith is the *tallest* [*most competent*] man in our society. (Adjective, superlative degree)
> The Wabash River flows *fast* [*violently*] during the rainy season. (Adverb, positive degree)
> The Wabash River flows *faster* [*more violently*] in spring than in fall. (Adverb, comparative degree)
> The Wabash River flows *fastest* [*most violently*] in April, *least violently* in the winter months. (Adverbs, superlative degree)

83f. Use the <u>comparative</u> degree for comparison between two things, the <u>superlative</u> degree for more than two.

Both adjectives and adverbs may be changed in form (or word, sometimes) to show a greater or lesser degree of the quality they indicate: *positive degree,* no comparison; *comparative degree,* two compared; *superlative degree,* three or more compared—*large, larger, largest; good, better, best; magnificent, more magnificent, most magnificent; slowly, less slowly, least slowly.* (For additional discussion, see p. 479 and the Glossary, pp. 589, 590.)

In incorrect and sometimes informal usage we hear such statements as "In the Army-Navy series, Navy's team has been the best," or in a boxing match "May the best man win." In such statements, only *two,* not three or more, are being compared. Accurate speakers and writers would use *better* in such sentences.

> Let us vote for the *better* of the two candidates. (Only two are concerned.)
> Let us vote for the *best* of these five candidates. (More than two are concerned.)

In informal, colloquial, or idiomatic English, the superlative qualifying adverb *most* is sometimes used when no particular comparison is intended: "You are *most* generous." In such a meaning, *most* is used as an intensive or a substitute for *very:* "You are very generous."

(For unjustifiable omissions in making clear comparisons, see Section 35c; for mixed and illogical comparisons, see Section 36c, d, e.)

83g. Avoid the trap of the double comparative or double superlative.

When the comparative and superlative forms of adjectives and adverbs are formed by adding *er* and *est* endings, the adverbs *more* and *most* should never be used, even though such a model as Shakespeare slipped with "This was the *most unkindest* cut of all" (*Julius Caesar*, III. ii). Such expressions are currently not permissible even in informal usage.

Wrong: This test was much *more longer* than the one last month.

Our senior high school queen was the *most prettiest* of any we had chosen during my four years of high school.

83h. Do not compare adjectives and adverbs that are in meaning logically incapable of comparison.

Adjectives and adverbs are logically incapable of comparison when their meaning is absolute; what they say is said once and for all. Such words are *perpendicular, horizontal, parallel, unique, excellent, perfect, accurate, absolute, round, square, final, fatal, impossible.*

More nearly accurate writing (not *more* accurate) uses qualifying adverbs: *nearly impossible,* not *completely impossible* or *more impossible; almost fatal,* not *completely fatal; almost square* or *more nearly square,* not *squarer; the most nearly round,* not *the roundest.*

EXERCISES

A. Rewrite the following sentences correcting all errors in the misuse of adjectives and adverbs.

1. My aunt is remarkably gracefully for a lady of 50.
2. I didn't realize I would need near as many textbooks as the bookstore sold to me.
3. The first day on the campus went along uneventful.
4. People do not watch careful when they drive.

5. Of the animals, muskrat, mink, and raccoon, the mink is the smarter of the three.
6. When there is a lot of studying to be done, you grow more tired easier.
7. If you are a good reader, you will find that your studies will come much more easier.
8. The counselor is very important, particular to the beginning freshman.
9. Education helps to make people more equal.
10. These directions will make the book easily to find.
11. I still believe in fraternities as strong as the day I was pledged.
12. To become a psychologist I must delve a little more deeper into the subject.
13. I could be no more happier, if I had twice as much money.
14. I think I can make friends just as quick as any one can.
15. As a child, Jane never acted selfish.
16. We rented a couple of bicycles and thus made our trip more pleasanter.
17. My training in grammar and literature is more superior than my training in composition.
18. Things ran along very smooth for the first few months.
19. In my years of driving I have seen only one real bad accident.
20. Of those tasks, the first turned out to be the easier of the three.

B. Directions given in A.

1. When a driver is sleepy, he doesn't watch the road as careful as he should.
2. Animals can outsmart you just as quick as you can outsmart them.
3. No one ever heard Mary speak bad about her friends.
4. Larry is a little shorter than I, but heavier built.
5. One boy was hurt bad when the car overturned.
6. Time passed so fast and furious that I didn't finish more than half the test.
7. It is near impossible to find a satisfactory solution.
8. Our Homecoming this year started out rather awkward; however, it ended all right except for the score of the football game.
9. There could possible be other ways of solving the problem.
10. My brothers all graduated fairly good in their classes.
11. There is nobody closer related to you than your own family.
12. Trained workers could do the job easier, better, and quicker.
13. We sang as loud and plain as we could.

14. In every post-season bowl game, I'm sure that the best team always wins.
15. One of the most unique displays was prepared by the local yacht club.
16. As a child, I was a great trial to my parents, but my father was always the angriest of the two.
17. We have been through many parts of the United States and through most of Canada. Canada has impressed me the most.
18. Can you give me a more simpler explanation?
19. Central High is the largest of our city's two high schools.
20. Several times I have acted very foolish in driving a car.

C. Directions given in A.

1. As a boy I wanted to be a frontiersman very bad.
2. As members of the glee club we sing as loud and plain as we can.
3. I now like my English course real good.
4. When the motor finally started, it was running terrible.
5. To prevent recoil, I squeezed the trigger slow.
6. I am particular interested in an easy course in chemistry.
7. At the age of 14 my brother could drive quite good.
8. Every one should learn to meet new friends easy.
9. In an accident 5 years ago my father was injured very bad.
10. The Empire State Building is easy reached from any point in New York City.
11. In driving, women panic quicker under pressure than men.
12. Rain was falling heavy long before we arrived in Louisville.
13. I was scared so bad that I lost half a year's growth.
14. One of the most favorite pastimes of the American people is looking at television programs.
15. Of the three kinds of farming we do, I like grain farming the better of the three.
16. My alarm clock rings loud every morning at 7; being electric, it is the most loudest alarm that I have ever had.
17. Wrestling and swimming are two of the more better known indoor winter sports.
18. I have never seen a student work so slow and so careless.
19. I never did get along too good with my English.
20. These two faults are primary responsible for my trouble.

D. From each of the following sentences, list the italicized form which is correct:

1. Going home for my first vacation, I couldn't get there *quick quickly* enough.
2. Everything went *smooth smoothly* in the laboratory today.
3. The *heavier more heavier* benches are reserved for the *more beefier beefier* members of the football team.
4. Many auto drivers wonder why they should drive *careful carefully*.
5. In that accident, Jim fortunately wasn't hurt very *bad badly*.
6. At the fairs in the past we have done very *good well* with our cattle and sheep.
7. There are a written test and a driving test; the actual driving test is the *worse worst* of the two.
8. A mispronunciation of a word can make a person feel *bad badly*.
9. Doris Day fit into her role *perfect perfectly,* for she can dance, sing, and act.
10. I'm glad to say I'm doing *excellent excellently* in all my subjects.
11. For pleasure you *sure surely* can't beat a good baseball game on a Saturday afternoon.
12. Mother's health has improved *some somewhat* since you last saw her.
13. My high school years went by almost *uneventful uneventfully*.
14. *Different differently* positions on the football team are played *different differently*.
15. My father was the *older oldest* of two boys.
16. Eddie and I always got along *good well* together.
17. It is *remarkable remarkably* to see operations in this college function so *smooth smoothly*.
18. In rainy weather your brakes don't work as *efficient efficiently* as on dry roads.
19. It takes more than money to make a person *real really* happy.
20. An owl sees much *clearer more clearly* at night than a hawk does.

CONJUNCTIONS

84. A *conjunction* is a word—sometimes several words—used to join words, phrases, clauses, and, occasionally, sentences. It is a *joining* or *linking* or *connecting* or *relating* word and has no other function than to couple two or more elements.

A writer must know the various kinds of conjunctions in order to write clearly and effectively. Conjunctions are divided into two main groups: (1) *coordinating* and (2) *subordinating*.

A *coordinating conjunction* joins words, phrases, clauses, or sentences of equal rank, that is, elements not dependent grammatically upon one another, although they may be in meaning. Three kinds of conjunctions are classified as coordinate:

a. *Pure* or *Simple conjunctions*—*and, but, or, nor, neither, yet,* and some teachers add *for* and *so.* In their most common uses, these join two or more words or phrases or clauses or even sentences of equal rank.

b. *Correlative conjunctions*—words used in pairs and serving to emphasize the relationship between two ideas. The most frequently used of these pairs are *both . . . and, either . . . or, neither . . . nor,* and *not only . . . but also.* Sometimes other pairs get listed, but careful study reveals that they do not coordinate, but subordinate. For example, *whether . . . or* really means that there are two *whether* statements joined by *or,* even though the second *whether* is understood: "*Whether* you attend *or* (*whether* you) don't attend the football games is of no concern to your English instructor."

c. *Conjunctive adverbs*—ordinarily, adverbs used parenthetically in a sentence but frequently used to relate two independent clauses or two sentences: words or phrases like *however, thus, besides, still, then, in fact, for example* (see also Section 89b).

A *subordinating conjunction* serves only one purpose: to relate a noun clause or an adverbial clause to its independent clause (the adjective clause is related to its noun or pronoun by a relative pronoun). Examples: *if, since, because, as, while, so that, although, unless, before.*

Conjunctions, particularly when they join clauses, must be chosen with care, for they should always show clear and appropriate relationships of ideas. Often, a careless writer will use *and* where the relationship of clauses needs to be more accurately expressed, probably by use of subordination.

Study Table IV, pages 582, 583. It classifies all the commonly used conjunctions according to whether they are *pure* or *simple, correlative, conjunctive adverb,* or *subordinating;* this table also clearly shows their meaning and exactly how this meaning can be expressed through either coordinating or subordinating relationships.

The following suggestions deal both with the right or appropriate conjunction as a matter of diction and with the right or appropriate conjunction to indicate proper relationship of ideas.

84a. Distinguish among the meanings of simple coordinating conjunctions. (See Table IV, pp. 582, 583.)

Wrong: I had hoped you would go, *but* you did.
             The book may have been excellent in your opinion, *and* it was not in mine.

Right: I had hoped you would go, *and* you did.
             The book may have been excellent in your opinion, *but* it was not in mine.

84b. Use correlative conjunctions to correlate only two ideas.

Since by definition correlative conjunctions are used in pairs, their clear and logical use is to relate two ideas, not more than two.

Wrong: *Both* my father, my mother, *and* my oldest sister are graduates of this university.
             Neither rain, snow, hail, ice, *nor* tornado could have kept me from our high school Junior Prom.
             At this early date it looks as if *either* Michigan, Ohio State, Illinois, Wisconsin, *or* Iowa will represent the Big Ten in the Rose Bowl.

Note: *Neither . . . nor* go together, not *neither . . . or.*

Wrong: Williamsport is *neither* the biggest *or* the most beautiful city in the state.

NOTE: As indicated in the "Glossary of Faulty Diction," Item 48, page 446, the use of *either . . . or, neither . . . nor* to coordinate more than two words, phrases, or clauses is sanctioned by some dictionaries but not by others. Logic and clearness suggest that they relate two only.

84c. Avoid using conjunctive adverbs to join words or phrases or dependent clauses. (See Section **89b**.)

The adverbs which can also serve as conjunctions relate only two independent clauses or two sentences.

Wrong: Mother's favorite colors are blue and yellow, *also* pink.
             John, *also* Henry, will be at the meeting.
             I worked on my theme for 2 hours, *then* revised it and went to bed.

TABLE IV. CONJUNCTIONS

This table contains all the more commonly used conjunctions: pure or simple coordinating conjunctions, correlative conjunctions, conjunctive adverbs, and subordinating conjunctions. The various kinds of relationships, through meaning, are suggested in parallel columns. Note that, depending upon the writer's purpose, the same ideas may be made coordinate in one of several ways or one idea may be subordinated to the other. Some of the conjunctions have overlapping, double, or additional meanings. When you are in doubt about their use, consult your dictionary.

	COORDINATING CONJUNCTIONS		CONJUNCTIVE ADVERBS	SUBORDINATE CONJUNCTION
	Pure or Simple	Correlative		
Along the same line or in the same direction of thought	and	both . . . and not only . . . but also	also besides likewise furthermore moreover indeed	whereupon
Contrast	but yet	not only . . . but also	however nevertheless still notwith- standing	whereas although
Affirmative alternation	or	either . . . or	still moreover anyhow	whether else whereas
Negative alternation	nor neither	neither . . . nor	however nevertheless otherwise	only except that whereas
Reason, result, purpose, cause	for (?) so		therefore thus so consequently hence as a result	for so that in order that since because as that why whereas inasmuch as

TABLE IV. **CONJUNCTIONS** (Continued)

	COORDINATING CONJUNCTIONS		CONJUNCTIVE ADVERBS	SUBORDINATING CONJUNCTIONS
	Pure or Simple	**Correlative**		
ample			in fact indeed namely for example	
mparison			moreover indeed in fact	than as . . . as so . . . as
me			then meanwhile henceforth	since when whenever while till until as long as as soon as before after
ce				where wherever whither whence
ndition				if as if though although as though unless provided providing lest
ncession				unless though although notwithstand- ing the fact that while in so far as

At last reports the channel swimmer had swum for 12 hours; *still* was going strong.

In sentences such as these, a pure coordinating conjunction should be used before the adverb, which becomes weakly parenthetical.

Right: Mother's favorite colors are blue, yellow, and also pink.
John, and also Henry, will be at the meeting.
I worked on my theme for 2 hours and then revised it and went to bed.
At last reports the channel swimmer had swum for 12 hours and was still going strong.

84d. Use the proper subordinating conjunction to express subordinate relationships.

Faulty diction: *Being as how* I was small, I did not make the football team.
I do not know *as how* I trust such a person.
Father wrote me *how that* he had gone fishing.
I read *where* Joe had broken another track record.
He was so fond of mathematics *until* he didn't want to talk of anything else.
Expenses became so unbearable *until* I sold my car.

Right: *Because* I was small, I did not make the football team.
I do not know *how* I could trust such a person.
Father wrote me *that* he had gone fishing.
I read *that* Joe had broken another track record.
He was so fond of mathematics *that* he didn't want to talk of anything else.
Expenses became so unbearable *that* I sold my car.

84e. Be sparing in the use of <u>like</u> as a subordinating conjunction.

In recent years *like* (for *as* or *as if*) has been increasingly employed as a subordinating conjunction and has reached the respectable status of having dictionaries give it a "colloquial" label as a subordinating conjunction. Perhaps the chief objection to *like* in this meaning is not its use but its overuse (as with *so,* see Section 37c). Discuss the following sentences:

1. Blood was running from my nose *like* a red river had been undammed.

2. My face felt *like* it had been baking in a kiln for a week.
3. College teachers don't keep after you to do an assignment *like* the teachers do in high school.
4. As a veteran I'm trying to make up for lost time *like* the rest of the veterans are doing.
5. Some students try to live *like* they were millionaires.
6. I felt *like* I had been tied to the bottom of the lake.
7. My overcoat felt *like* it weighed a ton.
8. With everything going *like* I had hoped, the summer was a profitable one.
9. I was not named after my father *like* many sons are.
10. Do you go to classes at West Point *like* we do here?

Don't you, too, wish that the writers of these sentences had used an occasional *as, as if, though, as though,* just for the sake of effective variety?

EXERCISES

A. Rewrite the sentences given in Section **84e,** giving them greater variety and effectiveness.

B. Correct all the errors in the use of conjunctions in the following sentences:

1. I had knocked over a fence post, then stopped in the middle of a field.
2. Dad looked at the car when I returned, also drove out to where the accident had happened.
3. At our first football game all our seniors wear their new yellow skirts and corduroy trousers.
4. There are other superstitions about Friday the 13th, and I don't remember them well enough to repeat them here.
5. Being that I am a sociable person, I speak to many people to whom I have not been regularly introduced.
6. He cannot pitch well except he warms up thoroughly.
7. You may have thought it an excellent program, and it was not.
8. John overslept his 8-o'clock class, so had no good excuse.
9. He acts like he knew exactly what to do under all circumstances.
10. He never answers without he first knows what Louise is going to say.
11. I read my day's assignments carefully, then made notes on my reading.

12. I don't know as they have any right to enforce this regulation.
13. I read where another swimming record was broken at a recent meet.
14. Mary's luncheon consists mainly of salads, also light desserts.
15. I went to my room early that evening, but I had much work to do.
16. Did you have my suit cleaned like I told you to?
17. Father telegraphed that he had missed the last train; therefore will come home tomorrow.
18. The grass was very wet; nevertheless, it had rained hard during the night.
19. Fred engaged in all types of athletics, although Bill went to dances almost every afternoon and night.
20. Henry received the majority of the votes; thus was declared elected.

GRAMMATICAL TERMS DEFINED

85. Many writers have partially or entirely forgotten the definitions of most grammatical terms. Some of these can well be forgotten. A knowledge of others is necessary if a writer wishes to phrase his ideas correctly, clearly, effectively, and appropriately.

The following list defines briefly and illustrates some of the elements of grammar which you will have most need for and have possibly forgotten. Refer to this glossary whenever you are in doubt about the definition of a grammatical term as you study the sections on grammar (**71–85**), punctuation (**86–100**), and the sentence (**31–50**). Cross-references will guide you to other pages where important matters are discussed in some detail.

1. **Absolute phrase** or **Absolute expression,** sometimes called **Nominative absolute.** An absolute phrase or expression usually consists of a noun or pronoun followed by a participle modifying it. The participle is usually expressed; it may be understood. The expression is "absolute" because it modifies no special word in the sentence; yet it rarely stands alone as a sentence. (See pp. 252 and 484.)

   My work finished, I left on my vacation with a clear conscience.
   The meeting adjourned, *no one having anything else to say.*
   The game (being) over, we started a victory parade.

2. **Abstract noun.** The name of a thing not evident to one of the senses, like a quality: *beauty, honor, duty, sadness.*

3. **Accusative.** A *case* name meaning the same as the *objective* (which see). The word is rare in English, common in a study of some foreign languages like German and Latin.

4. **Active voice.** The form of an action-expressing verb which tells that the subject does or performs the action. (See **Voice,** below.)

5. **Adjective.** A part of speech modifying a noun or pronoun by limiting or describing: *red* shoes, *happy* children, *six* eggs. See Section **83** for discussion of right and wrong use of adjectives.

6. **Adjective clause.** A dependent clause used to modify a noun or pronoun. (See pp. 487 and 627.)

> The book *which you borrowed* from the library is overdue.
> Go to see Mr. Wells, *who will advise you about future courses of study.*

7. **Adverb.** A part of speech modifying a verb (he runs *swiftly*), an adjective (an *extremely* good dinner), or another adverb (she spoke *very* rapidly). Some adverbs, especially when used for transition, modify the whole statement (We are, *however,* planning to spend the vacation in Florida). See Section 83 for discussion of right and wrong use of adverbs.

8. **Adverbial clause.** A dependent clause used to modify a verb, an adjective, or an adverb.

> John works part-time *because he needs the money.* (Modifies verb *works.*)
> This is better *than I usually do.* (Modifies adjective *better.*)
> Do you work more rapidly *than your brother does.* (Modifies adverb *more rapidly.*)

9. **Agreement.** Correspondence or sameness in number, gender, and person—between subject and predicate, and between pronoun and antecedent. Subjects and predicates *agree* in number (both are singular or both are plural):

> *John is* my brother. (Subject and predicate are singular.)
> *John and Harry are* my brothers. (Subject and predicate are plural.)

Pronouns agree with their antecedents in having the same gender, person, and number:

A *man* hopes to attain *his* goal in life.
Many *men* attain *their* goal in life.
Sue is one of those *girls who* are always pleasant and gracious.

10. **Antecedent** (meaning, literally, *placed before*). The substantive (noun or pronoun) to which a pronoun refers. See Section **77**.

> The *girl* has lost *her* gloves. (*Girl* is the antecedent of *her*.)
> A *man* hopes to attain *his* goal in life. (*Man* is the antecedent of *his*.)
> Many *men* attain *their* goal in life. (*Men* is the antecedent of *their*.)

Although by definition the antecedent is placed before the pronoun, it is sometimes illogically, yet clearly, placed, after:

> When *he* finally arrived, *Father* explained why he was late.

11. **Appositive.** A substantive, usually a noun, added to or following another substantive to identify or explain it. The appositive signifies the same thing, and the second substantive is said to be in *apposition.*

> One important product, *rubber*, this country had to import.
> (*Rubber* is in apposition with *product*.)
> More hardy than wheat are these grains—*rye, oats*, and *barley*.
> (*Rye, oats*, and *barley* are in apposition with *grains*.)

An appositive agrees with its substantive in number and case; it is set off by commas if its relationship is loose (nonrestrictive) and is used without punctuation if the relationship is close (restrictive). See page 632.

12. **Articles.** The *indefinite* articles *a* and *an*, and the *definite* article *the* are adjectives since they always accompany nouns. There is no description, however, and not much limiting; but *the book* is somewhat more definite, for example, than *a book*.

13. **Auxiliary.** A verb used to "help" another verb in the formation of tenses, voice, mood, and certain precise ideas. *Be* (*am, is, are, was, were, been*), *have* (*has, had*), *do* (*does*), *can, could, may, might, shall, should, will, would, must, ought, let, dare, need, used* are examples. See Section 78.

> Mother *has* gone to Cleveland for a visit.
> *Will* you please turn out the light?
> We *should have been* studying an hour ago.

14. **Balanced sentence.** A sentence so written that certain thoughts or ideas have similar phrasing for purposes of comparison, contrast, or emphasis. See Section **74c** and Section **45**.

> Diligently to seek advice is wise; blindly to follow it is foolish. We fought our enemy in the streets; they fought us from the housetops.

15. **Case.** A term referring to the forms that nouns or pronouns have (nominative, possessive, objective) to indicate their relation to other words in the sentence. See Section **75**.

16. **Clause.** A group of words containing a subject and predicate and forming part of a sentence. An *imperative* (which see), with the understood subject *you,* can of course serve as an independent clause.

> Knowledge is wisdom, and wisdom is power. (Two independent clauses)
> Come early and stay late. (Two independent clauses)
> When I arrive, I shall telephone you. (One dependent clause, one independent)
> Those who strive usually succeed. (One dependent clause, one independent)

17. **Collective noun.** The name of a group composed of individuals but considered as a unit: *team, class, audience, jury.*

18. **Common noun.** A noun naming a member or members of a common or general group: *street, coat, automobile.*

19. **Comparative degree.** The form of an adjective or adverb comparing two objects, two persons, etc. See **Comparison,** below.

20. **Comparison.** The change in the form of an *adjective* or *adverb* to indicate greater or smaller degrees of quantity, quality, or manner. The change is indicated by endings *er, est,* or by the use of adverbial modifiers, *more, most, less, least.* The three degrees of comparison are *positive, comparative* and *superlative:*

small	smaller	smallest
little	less	least
wisely	more wisely	most wisely
quickly	less quickly	least quickly

Positive degree—the first or simple form of an adjective or adverb—shows no comparison:

Fred is *tall*.
The Ohio River flows *swiftly*.

Comparative degree is used to show relationship between two persons, objects, or ideas:

An oak tree is *taller* than a maple.
Harry is a *less skilful* tennis player than Leonard.

Superlative degree is used to show relationships among three or more.

Alan is the *tallest* one in his family.
Of all the rivers in our area, the Ohio River flows *most swiftly*.

For further discussion of *comparison,* see pages 574–576.

21. **Complement.** A word or expression used to *complete* the idea indicated or implied by a verb. A *predicate complement* (sometimes called *subjective complement*) may be a noun, a pronoun, or an adjective which follows a linking verb and describes or identifies the subject of the linking verb.

This book is *a novel*.
The leaves of this tree are *red*.

An *objective complement* may be a noun or adjective which follows the direct object of a verb and completes the necessary meaning:

We are painting our house *gray*.
Our neighbors named their baby *Maryann*.
His teammates elected Schmidt *captain*.

22. **Complex sentence.** A sentence containing one independent clause and one or more dependent clauses.

When I arrived, the first person I saw was my father, who had come to the station to meet me.

23. **Compound object.** See **Object,** below.

24. **Compound sentence.** A sentence containing two or more independent clauses.

We planned to spend the day at the beach, but rain spoiled our plans.
Give willingly; give promptly; give abundantly.

25. **Compound-complex sentence.** A sentence containing two or more independent clauses and one or more dependent clauses.

> Since I am not skilful with my hands, I like to read, but my brother, who is mechanically inclined, rarely opens a book.

26. **Compound predicate.** See **Predicate,** below.

27. **Compound subject.** See **Subject,** below.

28. **Concord.** In grammar, *concord* is a term meaning the same as **Agreement** (which see).

29. **Concrete noun.** A noun naming an object evident to one of the senses of sight, hearing, touch, taste, smell: *shoe, song, velvet, coffee, perfume.*

30. **Conjugation.** The changes in the form or uses of a verb to show tense, mood, voice, number, and person. See these terms in this glossary and see also Sections **79, 80, 81, 82.**

31. **Conjunction.** A part of speech which serves as a linking or joining word to connect words or groups of words like phrases, dependent clauses, independent clauses, or sentences: *and, or, if, when, nevertheless, moreover,* etc. See Section **84.**

32. **Conjunctive adverb.** A certain kind of adverb which can also be used as a conjunction coordinating two independent clauses: *also, furthermore, nevertheless, besides, however, therefore, thus, so, consequently, hence, likewise, still, then, moreover,* etc. See pages 582, 583 and also Section **89b.**

33. **Construction.** A somewhat vague word, meaning the *arrangement* and *connection* or *relation* of two or more words in a phrase, clause, or sentence. Poor or bad or faulty or awkward construction therefore means poor arrangement, bad arrangement, faulty arrangement, awkward arrangement of words; or poor connection, bad connection, faulty connection, or awkward connection between words.

34. **Coordinating conjunction.** A *conjunction* (which see) relating words or phrases or clauses of equal grammatical value or importance (*coordinate* literally means *of equal rank*).

35. **Copula.** See **Linking verb,** below.

36. **Correlative conjunctions.** Coordinating conjunctions used in pairs. The most common are: *neither . . . nor, either . . . or, both . . . and, not only . . . but also.* Each member of the pair is followed by the same grammatical word or phrasing. See also Section **45b.**

Both Father *and* Mother are natives of Kansas. (Nouns co-related)

My books were *neither* at home *nor* at school. (Prepositional phrases co-related)

37. **Declarative sentence.** A sentence which states a fact, a possibility, a condition.

> Abraham Lincoln was born February 12, 1809.
> If more money is needed, there may be another campaign for funds later.

38. **Declension.** The changes in the form or use of a noun or pronoun to indicate case, number, and person. "To decline" means to give these grammatical changes.
Examples:

	Singular				Plural	
Nominative	man	I	who	men	we	who
Possessive	man's	my, mine	whose	men's	our, ours	whose
Objective	man	me	whom	men	us	whom

39. **Decline.** See **Declension.**

40. **Demonstrative pronoun.** A pronoun identifying, pointing to, pointing out, calling attention to: *this, that, these, those, such.*

41. **Dependent clause** (or subordinate clause). A *clause* (which see) that does not provide complete meaning in itself, that "depends" on an independent clause. There are three kinds of dependent clauses: *noun clause, adjective clause,* and *adverbial clause* (which see).

42. **Direct address.** The noun or pronoun showing to whom speech is addressed (also called the *vocative*):

> *John,* where are you?
> When we finish rolling the court, *Fred,* we'll still have time for two sets of tennis.

43. **Direct quotation.** Giving the exact words as written or spoken by someone.

> Father wrote, "I'll be there on Friday."
> "Please use your dictionary more often," the instructor said.

44. **Elliptical clause.** From ellipsis, the omission of a word or words from a clause or sentence; not needed because understood from

other words or from context. An elliptical clause is occasionally an independent clause; usually it is a dependent clause with its subject and part of its predicate omitted, since these are clearly understood from the main clause. In the following examples, the words shown in brackets are often omitted in speaking and writing.

> Some of the patriots carried guns, others [carried] swords, still others [carried] clubs and sticks.
> While [we were] drifting downstream, we grounded on a sand bar.
> He was 18 years of age, his brother [was] 12 [years of age].
> Although [he is] in New York frequently, Father rarely goes to the theatre.

45. **Emphatic verb form.** Present or past tenses using the auxiliary verb forms, *do, does, did,* for emphasis.

> Though I *did* work and still *do* work, I make no progress.

46. **Exclamatory sentence.** A sentence or sentence fragment expressing surprise or strong feeling: *What a time! We're there!*

47. **Expletive.** Frequently when a writer is at a loss as to how to begin a sentence or independent clause, he resorts to an *expletive*—a word or words not needed for the sense but used merely to fill out a sentence. The most common expletive is *there;* the most common expletive phrases are *there is, there are, there was, there were.* Usually, *there is* no weaker or more ineffective way to begin a sentence; occasionally, however, such expletives are desirable or even necessary. As a general principle they should be avoided whenever *there is* a better, more effective way of beginning a statement. (See Section **67.**) Compare for effectiveness the following:

> There stands a castle on the hill.
> On the hill stands a castle.
> There are three students sharing this room.
> Three students share this room.

48. **Finite verb.** A verb form or verb phrase that serves as a predicate; it has number and person. Opposed to the finite verb is the non-finite verb form, which cannot serve as a predicate—such non-finite forms are participles, gerunds, and infinitives.

49. **Future perfect tense.** The time of the action of a verb beginning in the present and ending at some time in the future.

In 1975 Father will have finished 40 years of medical practice.

See page 553 also.

50. **Future tense.** The time of a verb expressing "after now" or after the present."

In 1975 Father will be 75 years old.

See page 552 also.

51. **Gender.** The classification of nouns or pronouns according to sex. There are four genders: masculine, feminine, neuter, and common (either masculine or feminine): *boy, girl, it, individual.* In modern English nearly all traces of grammatical gender, as these are indicated by endings, have disappeared: *poetess* is an obsolete word, *actress* is still in good use. Gender, when indicated, is clear from the noun or pronoun, and no one pays any attention to endings as such: *actor, actress, he, she, it.*

52. **Genitive.** A *case* name meaning the same as *possessive* (which see). The word is rare in English, common in a study of foreign languages such as German and Latin.

53. **Gerund.** A verbal noun ending in *ing,* that is, a noun formed from and based on a verb. A gerund has the same form as the present or perfect participle: "Your *speaking* is appreciated"; "Your *having spoken* to us is greatly appreciated." See also pages 472, 473.

54. **Gerundial phrase.** A phrase introduced by a gerund. If begun by a preposition, the phrase is a prepositional gerundial phrase.

> *Memorizing poetry* is a pleasant pastime. (Gerundial phrase)
> *Upon achieving my first goal,* I aimed *at achieving my second.*
> (Prepositional gerundial phrases)

55. **Grammar.** The science which deals with words and their relationships to each other. *Rhetoric* deals with the art of expressive speech and writing, and with the principles of clear, effective writing. *Grammar,* a descriptive statement of the way language works, includes a discussion of the forms of words, their use in phrases, clauses, and sentences, their tenses, cases, or other changes in form according to their relationships with one another. See pages 461–584.

56. **Imperative.** The mood, or mode, of a verb expressing a command or a request. See **Mood,** below, and pages 567–570.

57. Imperative sentence. A sentence expressing a command or a request.

> Please reply by return mail.
> Send the enclosed card immediately.
> Give generously if you can.

58. Impersonal construction. A method of phrasing in which neither personal pronoun nor a person as noun is stated as the actor. The passive voice is used, or words like *it* or *there*.

> I have three reasons for my choice. (Personal)
> There are three reasons for this choice. (Impersonal)

> We must consider three proposals. (Personal)
> It is necessary to consider three proposals. (Impersonal)

> or

> There are three proposals to be considered.

> or

> Three proposals must be considered.

59. Indefinite pronoun. A pronoun implying an antecedent but referring to no specific person, place, or thing: *one, someone, everyone, everybody, somebody, each, none, no one, nobody, everything, nothing,* etc.

60. Independent clause. A clause (which see) that is complete grammatically by having a subject and predicate, that makes complete sense in the light of its context, that could if necessary stand as a complete sentence.

> Harry plans to be a chemist, but Roger will become a doctor.
> (Each clause here makes a complete statement.)
> If he is admitted, Roger will enter medical school this September.
> (The first clause is dependent; the second one is independent.)

61. Indicative. The mood, or mode, of the verb expressing a fact or what seems to be a fact. See **Mood,** below, and pages 567–570.

> We sell books here.
> I think that today is Tuesday.

62. **Indirect object.** A noun or pronoun preceding the direct object of a verb, and before which the word *to* or *for* is understood. When such an object follows the direct object, the preposition *to* or *for* is used.

> Yesterday I sent *him* a telegram.
> (Yesterday I sent a telegram *to him*.)
>
> Will you lend *her* $10.00 until Monday?
> (Will you lend $10.00 *to her* until Monday?)
>
> Do *me* a favor, please.
> (Do a favor *for me*, please.)

63. **Indirect question.** Restatement by one person of a direct question asked by another (see **Interrogative sentence,** below).

> Direct: When will you arrive?
> Indirect: Jane asked when I would arrive.

64. **Indirect quotation.** Restatement by one person in his words of the exact words written or spoken by some one else.

> Direct: Father wrote, "I'll be there on Friday."
> Indirect: Father wrote that he will be here on Friday.

65. **Infinitive.** A verb form which is the first of the three principal parts of a verb; the infinitive has the function of a verb (as part of the predicate), but it is also commonly used as a verbal or in a verbal phrase, like a noun, adjective, or adverb. In these last three uses—as verbal—it is usually preceded by the sign of the infinitive, the word *to*.

> I must *study* tonight. (Infinitive as part of predicate)
> Will you please *reply* by return mail? (Infinitive as part of predicate)
> *To succeed* in life is my ambition. (Infinitive as noun)
> The candidate *to elect* is the present president. (Infinitive as adjective)
> John is going *to tell* us of his trip to Mexico. (Infinitive as adverb)

66. **Infinitive phrase.** A phrase introduced by an infinitive: *to study mathematics*. For other examples, see **Infinitive,** above.

67. **Inflection.** A change in the form of a word to show a change in use or meaning. *Comparison* (see p. 589) is the inflection of adjectives and adverbs; *declension* (see p. 592) is the inflection of nouns

and pronouns; and *conjugation* (see p. 591) is the inflection of verbs.

68. Intensive pronoun. A pronoun having the same form as the *reflexive pronoun* (which see) and usually used immediately after its antecedent for emphasis.

> My sister *herself* baked this cake.
> I *myself* will see that you are invited.
> Students *themselves* are responsible for their attendance at classes.

69. Interjection. A part of speech—an exclamatory word—expressing strong feeling or surprise, which has little connection with the remainder of the sentence.

> *Oh,* so that's how it was.
> *Hurrah!* We've finally won a game.

70. Interrogative adverb. An adverb used in asking a question: *where, when, how, why,* and, less commonly, *whence, whither.*

> *Where* is University Hall? *When* was it built? *How* large is it?
> *Why* is it called University Hall?

71. Interrogative pronoun. A pronoun used in asking a question: *who, which, what,* and, less commonly, *whoever, whatever.* (Note: *which* and *what* sometimes combine two duties: pronoun and adjective.)

> *Who* is arriving tonight? On *which* train? *Which* is the hotel where he will stay? *What* is he coming for? *Whoever* had the bright idea of inviting him?

72. Interrogative sentence. A sentence asking a question and followed by a question mark. See Section 74b. In addition to the examples under **Interrogative adverb** and **Interrogative pronoun,** just above, note:

> Have you received your semester grades yet?
> You're planning to go tonight, aren't you?
> You're not going to accept this invitation?

73. Intransitive verb. A verb that does not require a direct object to complete its meaning; the meaning ends with itself and the verb therefore may have adverbial modifiers but not an object.

> The night plane *has arrived.* It *flew* in just before midnight.
> The speaker *paused* for a few minutes before he *replied.*

74. **Irregular verbs.** Sometimes called *strong* verbs, irregular verbs do not follow a regular system or pattern in forming their principal parts. Instead, these principal parts are usually formed by a change in the vowel: *see, saw, seen; drive, drove, driven; choose, chose, chosen; lose, lost, lost.* Your dictionary is your guide. See Section 79c also.

75. **Linking verb.** (Also called a *joining verb*, a *copula*, a *copulative verb*, a *coupling verb*). A verb which does not express action but only a state of being or a static condition. It serves to link the subject with another noun (predicate noun) or pronoun (predicate pronoun) or with an adjective (predicate adjective). These words following the linking verb are predicate complements (which see) or subjective complements. Common linking verbs are the forms of *to be, look, seem, smell, sound, appear, feel, become, grow, prove, turn, remain, stand,* etc. See Section **78**.

> This man *is* my uncle.
> This is *he* speaking.
> I *feel* happy this morning.
> This price *seems* expensive.

76. **Loose sentence.** A sentence with its parts arranged so that its meaning is clear before the end of the sentence.

> I shall be in Chicago early next month, and I shall hope to see you then.

77. **Mode.** A term meaning the same as **Mood** (which see).

78. **Modify.** To describe or limit. Adjectives are used with nouns or pronouns, and adverbs are used with verbs, adjectives, or other adverbs to describe, limit, or make meaning more definite in some other closely related way. Descriptive: *blue* skies, *tall* buildings. Limiting: *seven* books, the *only* woman.

79. **Mood.** A characteristic of verbs, revealing how action or expression is thought of: as a fact (*indicative mood*), as a possibility or something desired (*subjunctive mood*), or as a command or request (*imperative mood*). See Section **82**. Other kinds of expression are possible through use of certain auxiliary verbs. See Section **78**.

80. **Nominative.** The *case* form of nouns or pronouns used as grammatical subject or predicate complement. See Section **75**.

81. **Nominative absolute.** See **Absolute phrase**, above.

82. Non-finite verb. A verb form which cannot serve as predicate, since it shows neither person nor grammatical number. Non-finite verb forms—the verbals—are *gerunds, participles, infinitives* (which see).

83. Nonrestrictive. A modifier that does not limit but describes or adds information. The term is ordinarily used with phrases and dependent clauses. See Section **88m.**

> Professor Brown, *having given out the test questions,* told us to begin.
> This hat, *which I borrowed from my roommate,* does not fit me.

84. Noun. A part of speech naming a person, place, thing, quality, idea, or action: *John, meadow, paper, beauty, realism, walking.* See page 463.

85. Noun clause. A dependent clause serving the purpose of a single noun.

> *What I achieve* will depend upon me. (Noun clause as subject of sentence)
> My mother wrote *that she would come here for Mother's Day.* (Noun clause as object of verb)

86. Number. The change in the form of a noun, pronoun, or verb to show whether one or more than one is indicated. The formation of the plural of *nouns* is discussed on page 464; the few *pronouns* that have plural forms are listed on page 497.

Plurals of *verbs* are relatively simple. Main verbs have the same form for singular and plural except in the third person singular, present tense, which ends in *s* (*sees, moves, thinks,* etc.) or occasionally *es* (*goes*).

Of the verb *to be:* in the present tense, *am* (1st person) and *is* (3rd person) are singular, *are* is 2nd person singular and 1st, 2nd, 3rd person plural; in the past tense, *was* is 1st and 3rd person singular, *were* is 2nd person singular and 1st, 2nd, 3rd person plural.

Of the verb *to have, has* is the third person singular, present tense form. Of the verb *to do, does* is the third person singular, present tense form.

Use your dictionary when you are in doubt concerning the singular or plural form of a noun, pronoun, or verb.

87. Object. The noun, pronoun, or noun clause following a preposition or following a transitive verb.

Your book is on the *table*. (Object of preposition)
I have written many *themes*. (Object of verb)
I am sending *what you have ordered*. (Object of verb)

A *simple object* is the noun or pronoun or noun clause alone. A *complete object* is a simple object together with its modifiers. A *compound object* consists of two or more nouns or pronouns or noun clauses.

88. **Object complement.** A word—usually a noun or adjective—used after a direct object of certain verbs to complete the meaning.

We have elected Mary *secretary*.
Let me try to make this picture *clear*.

89. **Objective.** The *case* form of nouns or pronouns used as objects of prepositions or as direct or indirect objects of verbs. See above, **Object** and **Indirect object.**

90. **Participial phrase.** A phrase introduced by a participle or an adverbial modifier + participle.

Writing steadily, I soon finished my theme.
Having finished my theme, I signed my name and turned in my paper.
Carefully *watching the numbers,* we had no trouble following Route 303.

91. **Participle.** A verb form having the function either of a verb used as part of the predicate or of an adjective. See page 472. There are three forms: *present participle, past participle, perfect participle* (all of which, see).

I am *writing* my theme now. (Present participle, part of predicate)
I have *finished* my theme. (Past participle, part of predicate)
A *driving* rain delayed our progress. (Present participle, used as adjective)
Heard melodies are sweet. (Past participle, used as adjective)
Having finished my theme, I turned it in. (Perfect participle, used as adjective)

92. **Parts of speech.** The classifications to one of which every word must belong: *noun, pronoun, adjective, verb, adverb, preposition, conjunction, interjection.* See each of these terms in this glossary; see also pages 462, 463.

93. **Passive voice.** The form of an action-expressing verb which tells that the subject does not act but is acted upon. Literally and actually, the subject is *passive*. See **Voice,** below.

94. **Past participle.** The third principal part of a verb (see Section **79**) used as part of the predicate or as an adjective. Unless it is formed simply by adding *d* or *ed* or *t,* you will find the correct form given in your dictionary. See **Participle,** above.

95. **Past perfect tense.** The time of the action of a verb beginning at a point in the past and ending at a later point in the past. See page 552.

By last September I *had earned* over 300 dollars.

96. **Past tense.** The second principal part of a verb (see Section **79**), and the time of a verb which expresses a before-now action. Unless the past tense is formed simply by adding *d* or *ed* or *t,* you will find the correct form given in your dictionary.

97. **Perfect infinitive.** Formed by the auxiliary *to have* followed by the past participle: *to have seen, to have worked.*

98. **Perfect participle.** Formed by the auxiliary verb *having* followed by the past participle: *having seen, having worked.* See **Participle,** above.

99. **Periodic sentence.** A sentence with its parts arranged so that its meaning is not complete or clear until the end is reached or nearly reached. See page 492.

When I received the telegram, I knew that I had won.

100. **Person.** The change in the form of a pronoun or verb—sometimes, merely a change in use as with verbs—to indicate whether the "person" used is the person speaking (*first person*) the person spoken to (*second person*), or the person or thing spoken about (*third person*): *I* read, *you* read, *he* reads, *she* reads, *we* read, *you* read, *they* read, *it* plays.

101. **Personal pronoun** (see **Person,** above). A pronoun referring to the speaker or person writing (first person, *I, we*), the person spoken or written to (second person, *you*), or the person spoken of or written of (third person, *he, she, it, they, them*). See page 468.

102. **Phrase.** A group of related words not containing a subject and a predicate. See pages 482–484.

103. **Plural.** A classification of nouns, pronouns, subjects, and predicates, to indicate two or more units or members. Note that two or more singulars joined by *and* become a plural.

104. **Positive degree.** The simple form of an adjective or adverb in which no comparison is expressed: *red, tall, rapid, beautiful, swiftly.* See **Comparison,** above.

105. **Possessive.** The *case* form of nouns or pronouns indicating, usually, ownership or some idiomatic use, like extent of space or time: *the man's hat, my job, the people's choice, children's activities, a week's vacation, two years' experience.* See pages 502, 503.

106. **Predicate.** The verb or verb phrase in a sentence which makes a statement—an assertion, an action, a condition, a state of being— about the subject. A *simple predicate* is a verb or a verb phrase alone, without an object or modifiers; a *complete predicate* consists of the verb with its object and all its modifiers; a *compound predicate* consists of two or more verbs or verb phrases.

> Mr. Tyler drove the ball nearly two hundred yards. (*Drove* is the simple predicate; *drove the ball nearly two hundred yards* is the complete predicate.)
> I *wrote* the letter that night *and mailed* it this morning. (Compound predicate)

107. **Predicate adjective.** An adjective used in the predicate after a linking or joining or coupling verb; this adjective modifies or qualifies the subject. See **Complement,** above.

> This task is *difficult.*
> Today seems *colder* than yesterday.
> The team appears *ready* for the game.

108. **Predicate complement,** also called **Subjective complement.** A *predicate noun* or *pronoun,* or a *predicate adjective.* See these terms in this glossary.

109. **Predicate noun or pronoun.** A noun or pronoun used in the predicate after a linking or joining or coupling verb and identifying the subject. See **Complement,** above.

> She was *the best teacher* I ever had.
> This is *he* speaking.

110. **Preposition** (literally, *placed before: pre-position*). A part of speech showing the relationship of a noun or pronoun (the object of the

preposition) to some other word: *at* home, *to* school, *from* a book, *through* the tunnel, *across* the street.

111. Prepositional phrase. A phrase introduced by a preposition. For examples, see **Preposition.** Sometimes the preposition *follows* its object: *Which car* did you ride *in?*

112. Present participle. A verb form (verbal) ending in *ing* and used as part of the predicate or as an adjective. See **Participle,** above.

> I am *working* every afternoon. (Part of predicate)
> This restaurant does a *thriving* business. (Adjective use)

113. Present perfect tense. The time of the action or state of being of a verb, beginning in the past and just ending or still going on in the present. See page 552.

> I *have studied* until I am tired.
> I *have been studying* since early this morning.

114. Present tense. The "now" time of the verb, including the *simple present,* the *progressive present,* the *emphatic present* (which see): I *study,* I *am studying,* I *do study.*

115. Principal parts. The three parts of a verb (*present infinitive, past tense,* and *past participle*) from which all other forms and uses of verbs (tense, mood, tone, voice) can be expressed, sometimes without but most frequently with the necessary auxiliary verbs. In learning the principal parts of unfamiliar verbs, consult your dictionary. See **Regular verbs** and **Irregular verbs;** see also Section **79.**

116. Progressive verb form. A statement of continuing action or state of being within a tense, formed by the proper forms of the auxiliary *to be* followed by present participle. See page 556.

> We *are writing* our themes today.
> John *was playing* golf when I arrived.
> *Are* you *coming* early? We *shall be leaving* before six o'clock.

117. Pronoun (literally, *pro,* for, plus *noun,* name). A part of speech which is used instead of a noun, primarily to prevent overuse and repetition of the noun: *I, you, he, she, they, it, who, whom, which,* etc. See pages 467–471.

118. Proper noun. A noun naming a particular or individual member of a group: *Harry, Mrs. Jane Wilson, Mexico, Methodist.* Note that proper nouns are capitalized.

119. Pure conjunction. A short or simple commonly used coordinating conjunction, to connect words, phrases, clauses, or even sentences: *and, but, or, nor, neither, yet,* etc. See Section **88d.**

120. Quotation. Words written or said by someone. If these are given exactly as written or spoken, the quotation is *direct;* if they are restated and given in the words of another person, the quotation is *indirect.* Note the differences in punctuation.

> Direct: Henry said, "I have finished my work."
> Indirect: Henry said that he had finished his work.

121. Reciprocal pronoun. A pronoun indicating interchange of action. There are only two reciprocal pronouns in English: *each other, one another.*

> Father and Mother consult *each other* before they make an important decision.
> In our family we have the greatest confidence in *one another.*

122. Reference. A word used with pronouns and their antecedents to indicate the relationship between them. The pronoun *refers* to the antecedent, the antecedent is indicated or *referred* to by the pronoun.

123. Reflexive pronoun. A combination of *self* or *selves* with one of the forms of personal pronouns, usually placed after a verb or preposition and referring or reflecting back to the subject: *myself, yourself, himself, herself, itself, ourselves, yourselves, themselves, oneself.*

> We asked *ourselves* these questions.
> He sometimes whispers nonsense to *himself.*

124. Regular verbs. Also called weak verbs, these are the most common verbs in English because they usually form their past tense and past participle by adding *d, ed,* or *t* to the present infinitive form: *move, moved, moved; walk, walked, walked; mean, meant, meant.* See Section **79a,** also.

125. Relative pronoun. A pronoun *relating* or connecting an adjective clause to its antecedent, a noun or pronoun: *who, whom, which, that.* The relative pronoun has a double function: to connect the clauses and to serve as a substantive in the dependent clause.

The man *whom* we met lives in the house *that* we just passed. A teacher *who* likes reading will recommend books *which* his students will enjoy.

126. **Restrictive.** A modifier that limits or identifies the word modified. The term is ordinarily used with phrases and dependent clauses. See Section **88m.**

> A man *who works hard* should succeed. (Restrictive adjective clause)
> The books *on the top shelf* belong to the college library. (Restrictive adjective phrase)
> He works well *when you watch him.* (Restrictive adverbial clause)

127. **Sentence.** A word or group of words which convey completeness of meaning from writer to reader or from speaker to listener. For fuller discussion, see Sections **31** and **74.**

128. **Sentence fragment.** A word or group of words, usually a phrase or a dependent clause, not expressing completeness of meaning. Exclamatory sentences, answers to questions, and broken conversation are allowable and frequently used sentence fragments. For discussion of justifiable and unjustifiable sentence fragments, see Section **31a** and **b.**

129. **Sequence of tenses.** When independent and dependent clauses occur in a sentence, there should be a clear statement of the tense or time relationship in these clauses. Hence, sequence of tenses: the clear order of time in verb forms. For fuller discussion, see pages **558, 559.**

130. **Sign of the infinitive.** The word *to* accompanying the infinitive form of the verb: *to* go, *to* see, *to* arrive. "I plan *to* go." "I hope *to* arrive next week." In certain expressions, especially with certain auxiliary verbs, the *to* is not used: "He can *go.*" "I do *see.*"

131. **Simple sentence.** A sentence containing one subject (simple or compound) and one predicate (simple or compound). See page **490.**

> Weather conditions were perfect for flying.
> Books and magazines are read by some and are studied by others.

132. **Simple verb form.** Usually a statement of a "snapshot" or instanteous action of a verb. Compare with **Emphatic verb form** and **Progressive verb form,** and see comparative table on pages **550, 551.**

You *win*, but I *won* yesterday and I *shall win* tomorrow.
We *have read* seven books this semester.

133. Singular. The number classification of nouns, pronouns, subjects, and predicates to indicate *one: Boy, student, woman, I, he, she, it, is, has, was, goes, studies.* See **Number,** above.

134. Strong verbs. See **Irregular verbs,** above.

135. Subject. The person or thing (noun, pronoun, noun phrase, noun clause) about which a statement or assertion is made in a sentence or clause. *A simple subject* is the noun or pronoun alone. A *complete subject* is a simple subject together with its modifiers. A *compound subject* consists of two or more nouns, pronouns, noun phrases, noun clauses.

> The green *house* is for sale. (Simple subject)
> *The green house on the hill* is for sale. (Complete subject)
> *The green house and two acres of land* are for sale. (Compound subject)
> *What you say and what you do* are no concern of mine. (Compound subject)

136. Subjective complement. See **Predicate complement,** above.

137. Subjunctive. The mood, or mode, of a verb expressing possibility, desire, or a condition contrary to fact. See Section **82.**

> I wish I *were* in New York right now.
> If I *had gone,* I should have regretted it.

138. Subordinate clause. Another name for **Dependent clause** (which see.)

139. Subordinating conjunction. A conjunction joining a dependent clause (noun or adverbial) to its independent clause: *when, if, since, because, that,* etc. For fuller list of subordinating conjunctions, see pages 582, 583.

> Dues were increased *because* there was no money in the treasury.
> He thinks *that* he will come.
> *If* I had gone, I should have regretted it.

140. Substantive. An inclusive term for noun, pronoun, verbal noun (gerund, infinitive), or a phrase or a clause used like a noun. The practical value of the word *substantive* is that it saves repeating all the words which are included in this definition. The following italicized words are examples of substantives:

My *dog* is three years old.
They will arrive tomorrow; in fact *everyone* is arriving tomorrow.
Your *coming* is looked forward to.
To improve myself is my *aim.*
From Chicago to San Francisco is a long distance.
What you say is no *concern* of *mine.*
Do *you* know *that he was here yesterday?*

141. Superlative degree. The form of an adjective or adverb comparing three or more objects, persons, etc. See **Comparison,** above.

Of the three brothers, Alan is the *tallest.*
In our family, Mother is the one who drives *most carefully.*

142. Syntax. For all practical purposes, not a very useful word. Compare these three dictionary definitions of *syntax:*

"The patterns of formation of sentences and phrases from words in a particular language; the study and description thereof."—*American College Dictionary.*

"Sentence structure; the due arrangement of word forms to show their mutual relations in the sentence; that part of grammar which treats of the expression of predicative, qualifying, and other word relations, according to established usage in the language under study."—*Webster's New Collegiate Dictionary.*

"In grammar, the arrangement of words as elements in a sentence to show their relationship; sentence structure; the branch of grammar dealing with this."—*Webster's New World Dictionary.*

Let's use, then, the words *grammar* and *grammatical.*

143. Tense. The time of the action or of the state of being expressed by the verb: *present, past, future, present perfect, past perfect, future perfect.* See these terms in this glossary. The first three of these six are sometimes named the *simple* or *primary* tenses; the last three are sometimes named the *compound* or *secondary* or *perfect* tenses. See pages 549–559.

144. Tone. A word used in this handbook to distinguish a characteristic of tenses of verbs, indicating within any one tense or time limit *emphasis* or *progress* or just *simple* time. See **Emphatic verb form, Progressive verb form, Simple verb form,** above.

145. Transitive verb. A verb accompanied or followed by a direct object which completes its meaning. See pages 473, 474.

> The batter *hit* the ball.
> We have carefully *studied* the assignment.

146. Verb. A part of speech expressing action or a state of being (static condition).

> The river *flows* slowly.
> My name *is* John.
> Yesterday *seemed* warm.

147. Verb phrase. A verb together with an auxiliary or auxiliaries, or with its object or its modifiers: *is going, was finished, shall take, shall have taken, will have been taken, studied the assignment, flows slowly, whispers nonsense to himself.* Distinguish between a *verb phrase* and a *verbal* (participle, infinitive, gerund).

148. Verbals. The verb forms—*participles, gerunds, infinitives* (which see). One or more of these serve at times as adjectives, adverbs, nouns, parts of the predicate—but *never* as the predicate alone.

149. Voice. The change in the form or use of a verb—a transitive verb only—to indicate whether the subject is the performer of the action (*active* voice) or is acted upon (*passive* voice). In the formation of the passive voice, some form of the auxiliary verb *to be* is used with the past participle. See Section 81.

> Leonard Brown *wrote* the theme that I *have* just *read*. (Active voice)
> The theme *was written* by Leonard Brown. (Passive voice)

150. Weak verbs. See **Regular verbs,** above.

Punctuation and Mechanics

Punctuation is a system or method by which, through the use of certain mechanical marks, the meaning of written or printed communication is made clear.

Mechanics, a somewhat vague word, here simply means: When do we use capital letters, when small letters? When do we use italics or underlining? When do we use abbreviations, when do we spell out certain words? When do we use figures for numbers, when do we use words instead?

Proper punctuation is an indispensable aid to correct, clear, effective, appropriate writing because it helps to express thoughts and to make clear the relationships of thoughts to a reader. Punctuation developed originally because, without it, written language was unable to indicate or reproduce certain qualities of speech. In speech, a pause or a rising inflection, for example, conveys meaning. These and other qualities of speech are reproduced in writing by certain marks of punctuation. Similarly, the relationship between parts in a sentence is revealed by word order, but since modern English is not a highly inflected language, word order is flexible. In written English, therefore, the various marks of punctuation suggest and indicate the grouping, relationship, and kind of expression needed to convey meaning clearly.

With only a few words—even one word—punctuation marks change meaning. Note the differences conveyed in the following:

See!	What a pity.	I'm not shouting.
See?	What a pity!	I'm not shouting!
	What? a pity?	I'm not shouting?

What do you think? I'm giving you this automobile for a song.
What! Do you think I'm giving you this automobile for a song?

Punctuation is thus an *organic* part of writing; it is neither mechanical nor arbitrary. Usage does vary with individual writers but fundamental principles remain the same. These fundamental principles, or descriptive "rules," are drawn from thousands of examples of punctuation as applied in writing and printing by authors, printers, editors, and others whose knowledge and practice we respect. When there are enough examples of one use of a certain punctuation mark, we state this as a general principle or rule, beginning it thus: "Use the . . ." or *"Always* use the . . . ." When most of our examples agree: "The [mark] is *usually* used . . ."; when there are not enough examples to make a generalization: "The [mark] is *occasionally* used. . . ." Correct punctuation permits individuality only to the extent that communication of ideas from writer to reader is aided, not impeded.

The most important marks of punctuation are:

. Period	— Dash
? Question mark	- Hyphen
! Exclamation point	' Apostrophe
, Comma	" " Double quotation marks
; Semicolon	' ' Single quotation marks
: Colon	( ) Parentheses

Less commonly used marks of punctuation are:

[ ] Brackets	∧ Caret
. . . Ellipsis periods	¨ Dieresis marks
*** Asterisks	´ ` ^ Accent marks

The Four Purposes of Punctuation

Ordinarily you will apply a principle or specific "rule" of punctuation to a specific instance or sentence element. You may be helped in such application by remembering that punctuation usually serves one of four general purposes:

1. To *end* or *terminate* a statement—use period, question mark, or exclamation point.

Punctuation and Mechanics

Little progress was reported.
Are you going home?
What an occasion!

2. To *introduce*—use comma, colon, or dash.

Only one quality is needed, perseverance.
My purpose is simple: to succeed in life.
My goal in life is simple—success.

3. To *separate* parts of a sentence or word—use comma, semicolon, dash, hyphen, or apostrophe.

If you have any influence at all, try to have me excused.
Some people prefer dinner at noon; others prefer it in the evening.
Commas, periods, semicolons, and colons—these are common marks of punctuation.
Mr. Brown was elected secretary-treasurer.
It isn't nine o'clock yet.

4. To *enclose* parts of a sentence or a whole sentence—use commas, dashes, quotation marks, single quotation marks, parentheses, brackets. *Enclosure marks are used in pairs, except when the capital letter at the beginning of a sentence takes the place of the first or when a terminating mark at the end takes the place of the second.*

An elderly lady, Miss Eleanor Moorson, was my favorite high school teacher.
Miss Eleanor Moorson, an elderly lady, was my favorite high school teacher.
My favorite high school teacher was Miss Eleanor Moorson, an elderly lady.

You are not—and everyone knows this—a very careful driver.
You are not a careful driver—and every one knows this.

"The word 'lousy' is not in reputable use as a term in literary criticism," said the lecturer.

You are referred to the United States Constitution (see especially Article VIII).

Different marks indicating these four principal purposes of punctuation are, obviously, not necessarily interchangeable. The comma and the dash, for example, can serve three of the purposes, but the writer must choose the appropriate mark which will best serve overall clearness and effectiveness.

Also, there can be a progression in the strength of the punctuation marks as they indicate strength of ideas. For example:

> Very weak parenthetic material—no commas; weak—commas; strong—dashes; strongest—(possibly) parenthesis marks.
>
> Very weak separation—no comma; normal separation—comma; stronger separation—semicolon; strongest (between sentences) —period, question mark, or exclamation point.

A more specific approach to punctuation is a study of each punctuation mark and its use. Many of the principles make use of grammatical terms; if you are in doubt about their meaning, study their definitions on pages 586–608. If you know what kinds of words, phrases, clauses, or sentences you have but are in doubt about the punctuation marks to use, consult the Glossary of Applied Punctuation, pages 701–706.

THE PERIOD

The period (.) is usually a mark of termination, although it has a special use after abbreviations and, in series, a special use to indicate separation.

86a.   Use a period at the end of a declarative sentence.

> When autumn comes, birds begin flying south.
> Some people read two or three newspapers a day.
> Grandfather spends his winter vacations in Florida; Father spends his in Maine.

86b.   Use a period after a mildly imperative sentence (a command or a polite request).

> Drive carefully and avoid accidents.
> Come over this evening and watch TV.
> Write all your business letters on business stationery.

86c.   Use a period after an indirect question (see Section **87c**).

> Mr. Brown asked when I could report for work.
> Tell me what he said.

86d. Use a period after a standard abbreviation.

Mr. and Mrs. James Brown.
Henry Smith, M.D. (b. 1900; d. 1950)
Sept. 15; lbs.; n. b.; ff.; q.v.; a. m.; p. m.; i.e.
(See Section 98c for exceptions.)

If a declarative sentence ends with an abbreviation, one period only is used. If the sentence is interrogative or exclamatory, a question mark or exclamation point follows the abbreviation period. Inside the sentence, the period is followed by any logical punctuation which would have been used regardless of the period.

86e. Use periods properly in an outline.

A period is conventionally used after each symbol in the outline—Roman and Arabic numbers and capital and small or lower-case letters. See illustrations in Section **6a.**

A period usually is *not* used at the ends of lines in the topic outline; it *is* used at the ends of lines in sentence and paragraph outlines. See illustrations in Section **6a.**

86f. Use a period before a decimal, to separate dollars and cents, and to precede cents written alone.

4.25 percent $5.75 $.52

86g. Use ellipsis periods (three) to indicate an intentional omission from a sentence or quotation.

This device is especially helpful when only part of a sentence or line of poetry is quoted. Thus:

". . . nothing walks with aimless feet."
—TENNYSON
"Your eyes smile peace . . ."
—ROSSETTI

When ellipsis periods follow a complete sentence, the end-of-sentence period is also used.

> The game was filled with dramatic moments. . . . No one will ever forget the long, spine-tingling, game-winning shot in the last second, just as the gun fired.

1. A question mark or exclamation point may follow ellipsis periods.

2. Do not use ellipsis periods as a substitute for the dash. See Section **91f**.

3. Do not use ellipsis periods purely as a stylistic device. Students occasionally use them to indicate that much more could be said. Generally, they have nothing in mind.

4. Asterisks (***), three in number, serve the same purpose as ellipsis periods but are not frequently used to indicate omissions within a sentence. They are more likely to indicate omissions of paragraphs or long passages.

86h. Use no period at the end of a title or after a centered or side subhead in the body of a manuscript.

86i. Use no period after a quotation mark that is preceded by a period.

Wrong: He said, "Stop at the next corner.".
Right: He said, "Stop at the next corner."

86j. Do not punctuate sentence fragments as complete units of thought unless they obviously qualify as complete expressions.

Correct: *"Hello,* Joe."
            "Hello."
            "Where have you been?"
            "At the library."
            "What were you doing?"
            "Reading a magazine."
Incorrect: I spend part of every afternoon at the library. *Reading a magazine or anything else that looks interesting.*
            We sat in the first balcony. *Although there were still a few seats available downstairs.*

For full discussion of the Sentence Fragment ("Period Fault"), see Section **31**.

EXCLAMATION POINTS AND QUESTION MARKS

87. The exclamation point (!) and the question mark (?), like the period, are usually marks of termination.

Exclamation Points and Question Marks　**87a-c**

87a. **Use the exclamation point to terminate a forceful interjection, or to express surprise, emphasis, strong emotion, or command (i.e., a vigorously imperative sentence).**

> Ouch! That hurt!
> Oh, what a remark to make!
> Help! Help!
> What wonderful news!
> Come at once!
> Here's to Smithson, the Man of the Year!

An exclamation point also may be used after a phrase or sentence to express irony. Often the exclamation used for this purpose is put in parentheses.

> You're a fine friend!
> She said that she might possibly condescend (!) to write.

Do not overuse the exclamation point. The emotion must be strong, the surprise genuine, the command really imperative to call for this punctuation. Too frequent use of the exclamation point weakens its effectiveness. Notice that a comma, not an exclamation point, is used after the mild interjection, *oh,* in the second illustration above.

87b. **Use a question mark at the end of every direct question.**

For various ways of asking questions in English, i.e., of stating ideas in interrogative sentences, see Section **74b.**

> Do you really know?
> You really do know?
> Why are you so eager to go?
> Where is the Administration Building?
> Which student left his dictionary in the classroom?
> You're going home next week, aren't you?
> Who said, "What is Man?" (Note use of single question mark.)

87c. **Do not use a question mark after an indirect question.**

An indirect question is a question repeated in different words by the same speaker or by another person. The usual mark is a period (Section **86c**).

615

87d-f   Exclamation Points and Question Marks

Wrong: I asked myself whether I had heard the announcement correctly?

Right: I asked myself whether I had heard the announcement correctly.

Wrong: John inquired whether Joyce had a date for the Prom?

Right: John inquired whether Joyce had a date for the Prom.

87d. Use question marks to indicate a series of queries in the same sentence.

> Will you be there? or your brother? or your parents?
> Who will be there from your house? You? Your brother? Your parents?
> Also: Will you be there—or your brother—or your parents?
> Will you be there, or your brother, or your parents?

Notice also the different possibilities of capitalization.

87e. Use a question mark, enclosed in parentheses, to express doubt or uncertainty.

> This is a genuine (?) leather bag.
> The University of Socomber was founded in 1350 (?).
> Shakespeare was born on April 23 (?), 1564.

Do not overuse the question mark to express doubt or uncertainty. If it is impossible for you to find the exact information needed, use the question mark, but do not use it as an excuse for not trying to find out exact information.

87f. Do not use a question mark in parentheses to indicate an ironical or humorous meaning.

Undesirable: The ambitious candidate sang his own praises in a modest (?) way and never raised his voice above a gentle (?) roar.

EXERCISES (Sections 86, 87)

A. Copy a paragraph of 100–300 words from an article in your book of readings or from a magazine, omitting all terminal punctuation marks and changing all sentence beginnings to small letters. Exchange your paper for a similar one prepared by a classmate. Each of you should recapitalize and reinsert all terminal marks in the other's paper.

B. Underline all the periods, question marks, and exclamation points on a page in your book of readings or in a current magazine. Account for the use of each mark by careful reference to one of the principles cited in Sections **86, 87.**

C. Use the period, exclamation point, and question mark correctly in the following sentences, or if any of these marks are misused, make the necessary corrections.

1. In Barton, Nev, one of the best lawyers is Milton Johnson.
2. Isn't it strange that both Prof and Mrs Browne were born on Nov 11, 1898.
3. The first two speakers argued that final exams. should be abolished.
4. T Woodrow Wilson, 28th president of the U S (b 1856; d 1924) served from 1913 to 1921
5. If only I could relive my high school days How differently I would act
6. We wrote only one theme a week in Miss. Douglas's class.
7. We did finally obtain one dog, and what a dog.
8. I should like to inquire what the monthly dues are in this club?
9. Our initiation was over at nine, and how we did celebrate that night.
10. My mother finally helped me to pack. What a relief.
11. Who would think that people would stand in line to pay their bills.
12. How shall we come to the dance. In formal dress.
13. Not everything in this story may be fiction; who knows.
14. Is courtesy to women a custom of the past.
15. There were Mother and Father. What a pleasant surprise.
16. Are today's high school graduates adequately prepared for college.
17. There isn't a girl alive who wouldn't like to have Mrs in front of her name.
18. What would we do today without all our modern conveniences.
19. Every student asks himself at some time just why he is going to college?
20. If you study medicine, you will become an M D, and if you study dentistry, you will become a D D S.

THE COMMA

88. The comma (,) serves the purpose of introducing, separating, or, with another comma, enclosing. Because it has varied and distinct uses and is the most frequently seen mark of punctuation, it is the most troublesome of all the punctuation marks. Always used within the sentence, it differs from terminal marks—the period, question mark, exclamation point—in *degree*. It shows a brief pause, less separation than the full stops.

Note also that the comma, the semicolon, and the period form a series in which the members have a relative and increasing strength. The *comma* is the weakest mark of the three, for it separates short groups within the sentence and indicates comparatively close connection. The *semicolon* is used between longer and more important groups within the sentence, or between those which have a comparatively remote connection in thought. The *period* is the strongest mark of the three: it points out the most important division of thought, the sentence; it also indicates the greatest remoteness in thought.

Remoteness is, of course, relative. Independent clauses in a sentence are closely related since they are parts of one sentence. A series of sentences can be closely related since they make up a unified paragraph. *Remoteness,* as here used, therefore, means that one phase—whether minor or fairly important—of a subject has been completed; another phase begins with the next independent clause or sentence.

NOTE: Mastery of the comma depends upon the individual. Some teachers in reading themes prefer to give students a specific reference discussing and illustrating comma use—the plan followed in this handbook. Other teachers find satisfactory the assigning and use of five broad principles dealing with comma use. These are as follows (with some parenthetic references to more detailed sections):

88/1. Use a comma to separate long independent clauses of compound sentences (Section **88d**).

88/2. Use a comma to set off long introductory subordinate elements, usually adverbial or participial (Section **88f** and **g**).

88/3. Use commas to set off parenthetical word groups, including nonrestrictive elements, whether words, phrases, or clauses (Section **88m, n, o, p, q, r, s, t**).

88/4. Use commas to divide elements in series (Section **88h, i**, and **j**).

88/5. Use commas in the conventional uses of setting off or enclosing dates, initials, numbers, letter salutations, etc. (Section **88b, c, q, r, s,** and **t**).

COMMAS TO INTRODUCE

88a. Use a comma to introduce a word, a phrase, or, occasionally, a clause.

My aim in this course is easily stated, a high grade.
There is only one other possibility, to travel by air.
I had an important decision to make, whether I should drop out of school or borrow the money and continue.
I have need of only two things, money and more money.

This principle of the introducing comma applies to asking a mental question or expressing a thought or musing aloud:

I wondered, should I tell Father the whole story?
I thought, you're in real trouble now.
I told myself, you can do this as well as anyone.
Our next problem is, where do we go from here?

88b. Use a comma to introduce, or separate, a short quotation.

Henry said, "I'll never do that again."

1. If the "he said" or its equivalent follows the quotation, it is separated from it by a comma, provided a question mark or exclamation point is not demanded.

"I'll never do that again," said Henry.

2. If the "he said" or its equivalent is inserted between the parts of a quotation, it is enclosed by commas.

"I'll never do that again," said Henry, "unless I lose my temper."

3. When the quotation being introduced is long or formal, the colon replaces the comma. (See Section **90d**.)

4. Make a careful distinction between quotations which are really quotations of speaking or writing and quoted material which is the subject or object of a verb, or material stressed by quotation marks

619

such as titles, slang, and special word use. As examples of such special uses, observe the following:

> The usual remark is "May the better man win."
> "Make haste slowly" is the motto that came to my mind.
> When Patrick Henry thundered "Give me liberty or give me death," he contributed a great catch phrase to the world.
> If the "he said" comes between parts of a quotation, it is enclosed by commas.
> "Itty-bitty" is not the exact phrase to use for "very small."

88c. Use a comma after the salutation to introduce a friendly or social letter. (See Section **90e**.)

> Dear John, Dear Mary, Dear Father, Dear Mr. Browne,

COMMAS TO SEPARATE

88d. Use a comma to separate independent clauses joined by one of the pure or simple coordinating conjunctions: <u>and</u>, <u>but</u>, <u>nor</u>, <u>or</u>, <u>neither</u>, <u>yet</u>.

To this list, *for* (see Section **88e** for discussion of *for*) and *so* are sometimes added. *So* is a short word and is a conjunction; its meaning is *therefore* or *thus*. It is assuredly coordinate, but the chief objection to it is its constant overuse (see Section **37c**).

> I have not seen John recently, nor has anyone else seen him.
> Commas are important marks of punctuation, and you will do well to master their use.
> I tried to show him the error of his argument, but he would not be convinced.
> The Dean had no specific objections, yet he would not approve our proposal.

The principle stated in Section **88d** is one of the most frequently used and illustrated in English writing. This frequency accounts for considerable flexibility in application, as follows:

1. If the independent clauses are short, the comma may be omitted before the pure conjunction. This statement, however, immediately brings up the question, "How short is short?" If the independent clauses consist of only subject and predicate, or of three

620

or four words each, then they are obviously short and the comma may be omitted, except perhaps before *neither* and *yet.* Examples:

> The rains came and the rivers rose.
> I made a motion but no one heard me.
> In the final judging, Mary did not win nor did Jane.

Sometimes lack of punctuation between short clauses may cause momentary misreading, and a comma is necessary for clearness.

Misleading: We ate *bacon and the Brownes* ate eggs.
Clear: We ate bacon, and the Brownes ate eggs.

2. Fairly long clauses are sometimes written without a comma between them if their connection is particularly close. The comma, for example, is frequently omitted before the pure conjunction when the subjects of both clauses are the same (same noun or noun and pronoun).

> I read for an hour or two and then I studied.
> Henry read the assignment over hurriedly and then he began a more careful rereading of it.

When the subject of the second clause is omitted, the sentence has merely a compound predicate and does not contain a comma before the conjunction, unless the members are unusually long. Use of a compound sentence or a simple sentence with a compound predicate depends upon a writer's view of which is more effective for a particular purpose.

> Henry came into the house and called excitedly to his mother.
> The last person spoke clearly and made a favorable impression upon the audience.

3. Use commas between clauses to which you wish to give special emphasis.

> You must pay promptly, or you will be penalized.
> I did not expect to win, but I did.

4. Long independent clauses—but be sure they are *long*—which contain complicated internal punctuation (a sprinkling of three, four, or five commas) should be separated by a semicolon before the pure conjunction (see Section 89c).

88e-f

88e. Use a comma before the conjunction for.

The word *for* is used either as a conjunction or as a preposition. A comma before it is a fairly sure sign that the word is a conjunction, no comma that it is a preposition. Of course, a prepositional phrase beginning with *for* and used parenthetically is enclosed by commas.

Conjunction: I went home early last evening, *for* my parents did not wish to be alone.

                    We cannot pay a bill as large as this, *for* we do not have the money in our treasury.

Preposition: I went home early last evening *for the purpose* of getting a good night's sleep.

                    One convincing argument, *for example,* concerns our pocketbook.

                    My high school, *for that matter,* has always had excellent teachers in English and mathematics.

Because of its smallness, *for* is frequently listed with the other pure coordinating conjunctions (**88d**), even though its meaning is *because, as, since.* If you apply **88e,** the grammatical classification of *for* is of little importance.

88f. Use a comma to separate an introductory adverbial clause from the independent clause.

When you have finished the examination, sign your name and turn in your paper.

Before John started on his trip, he made a careful plan of his itinerary.

If I arrive first, I'll wait for you in the library.

The foregoing applies *only* to adverbial clauses. An introductory noun clause is not set off by a comma.

What you say is true.

That your theme was turned in late is unfortunate.

Many introductory adverbial clauses are simply transposed elements. Inserted in their natural order, they may or may not have commas, depending upon meaning. Inserted elsewhere, they are enclosed by commas.

After you arrive on the campus, various meetings will be held to help orient you.

Various meetings, after you arrive on the campus, will be held to help orient you.

Various meetings will be held to help orient you after you arrive on the campus.

When the adverbial clause follows the independent clause:

1. Omit the comma if the adverbial clause is necessary to complete (i.e., if it restricts) the meaning of the sentence.

The accident occurred as I turned into Tenth Street.
John works because he has no other way to live.

2. Use a comma if the clauses are fairly long, or if a slight pause is desired; omit it if the clauses are short.

I'm quite willing to be a delegate to the convention, although there are others more capable than I.
I'll go, if I have to go.
I'll go if I have to go.

88g. Use a comma to set off an introductory modifying phrase containing a verb form.

Not universally applied, this principle is so commonly illustrated that it is still recommended for the student-writer. The introductory phrase may be participial or prepositional, adjective or adverb. If an adjective phrase, it is very likely nonrestrictive (see Section **88m**).

Half-concealed in the bushes, the dog watched us go by.
In order to play a vigorous game, you should be in good physical condition.
By studying slowly and carefully, John mastered the subject.
Because of his hidden fear of water, he refused to go swimming.

1. Neither an introductory gerund phrase nor an introductory infinitive phrase used as subject is a modifying phrase; therefore, neither one is set off by a comma unless for other reasons. Frequently even a short modifying infinitive phrase is not set off.

Playing on a championship basketball team is a thrilling experience. (Gerund phrase as subject)
Playing on a championship basketball team, according to my room-

mate, is a thrilling experience. (Gerund phrase as subject, followed
by parenthetic element)
To be a successful fisherman is not easy. (Infinitive phrase as subject)
To be a successful fisherman I use only the best equipment. (Introductory modifying infinitive phrase)

2. An introductory modifying phrase without a verb form, unless it is fairly long, is not set off by a comma.

> Without fail I'll be there.
> Because of lack of money some students have to drop out of school.
> After careful consideration of the matter for a week or ten days, we decided that the trip was too long to justify the expense.

NOTE: Many phrases containing verb forms do not come at the beginning of sentences, and they may be usually considered as some kind of parenthetic element, such as absolute phrases (Section **88p**) or nonrestrictive phrases (Section **88m**).

88h. Use commas to separate words, phrases, or clauses in a series.

1. One kind of series is represented by A, B, and C—three or more words, phrases, or clauses, with an appropriate pure conjunction joining the last two members.

> I have brought my textbook, my notebook, and some theme paper with me.
> You will find Henry around somewhere: in the living room, in the basement, or out in the garden.
> He whispered, he muttered, but finally he shouted.

Some writers omit the comma before the conjunction and use A, B and C. Since greater clearness is frequently obtained by the use of the comma before the conjunction, present practice favors the comma there—a practice advocated by the United States Government Printing Office *Style Manual,* the University of Chicago's *A Manual of Style,* and The Modern Language Association *Style Sheet.*

2. Another kind of series is represented by A, B, C—three or more words, phrases, clauses, with no conjunctions. Commas are used after each member except *after* the last, unless the clauses are all independent (see Section **89a, 32b**).

This store sells newspapers, magazines, books.
Joe believes in good sportsmanship on the football field, on the basketball court, in the swimming pool, on the golf course.

3. Do not use commas separating members of a series—unless emphasis is desired—when a conjunction is used to join each pair.

I have read nothing by Swift or Milton or Wordsworth.
Billy says he is going to have ice cream and cake and pie and chocolate pudding for his dessert.
At times I have no energy, or enthusiasm, or skill. (Emphasis)

88i. Use a comma to separate two or more adjectives when they modify, equally and coordinately, the same noun.

I bought an old, dilapidated chair and a new, ugly, badly faded rug.
Our Administration Building is surmounted by a tall, stately, ivy-covered tower.

When the adjectives are not coordinate, commas are omitted.

A heavy steel cable spans the rugged green ravine.
The old oaken bucket was covered with green wet moss.

Notice that a comma is *never* used to separate the last adjective from the noun.

Sometimes there may be doubt as in "an old, dilapidated chair" above; then you must use your judgment in deciding.

Admittedly, it is sometimes difficult to determine whether the adjectives are coordinate or not. One or more of several tests, although not infallible, may help. One way of testing is to insert the coordinate conjunction *and* between the adjectives; if the *and* fits naturally, use a comma when it is omitted, otherwise not. Another test: if the position of the adjectives can be reversed, the adjectives are coordinate. Another test: does the first adjective modify the idea of the second adjective and the noun? If so, the adjectives are not coordinate. Also, if one of the adjectives describes shape or material or color, the adjectives likely are not coordinate.

88j. Use a comma to separate contrasted coordinate elements.

1. Such contrasted elements may be words or phrases:

Psmith begins his name with a *P,* not an *S.*
Your misspelling is due to carelessness, not ignorance.

The pitcher threw slowly, but effectively.
This garden spray is effective, yet safe.

2. Two dependent clauses may contrast. There is in good use a special kind of contrasting dependent clauses: neither makes sense alone, but taken together the two form a complete sentence.

The higher we go into the air, the more rarefied the atmosphere becomes.
The more tired the team became, the better it played.
The less haste some people make, the more progress they achieve.

3. Two independent clauses contrast when the first is a declarative statement and the second an interrogative one—a common way of asking a question:

You did telephone, didn't you?
We should have longer vacations at Thanksgiving, shouldn't we?
You believe I was justified, don't you?

88k. Use a comma to separate words or other sentence elements that might be misread.

Misleading: The day after a salesman called with the same product.
Outside the house needs a coat of paint; inside the walls need replastering.
Instead of a hundred thousands came.
In 1956 800 freshmen appeared on our campus.
Last week I was in bed with a cold and my mother took care of me.

Improved: The day after, a salesman called with the same product.
Outside, the house needs a coat of paint; inside, the walls need replastering.
Instead of a hundred, thousands came.
In 1956, 800 freshmen appeared on our campus.
Last week I was in bed with a cold, and my mother took care of me.

Constructions in which commas are needed to prevent misreading are usually questionable or faulty. If it is possible, rephrase such sentences to eliminate awkwardness and to increase clearness.

Instead of the hundred people expected, thousands came.
Last week, when I was in bed with a cold, my mother took care of me.

88l. Use the comma to separate thousands, millions, etc. (i.e., numbers of four or more digits except numbers indicating years, telephone numbers, and house numbers).

In the fall of 1956 our freshman class numbered exactly 1,956 students.

In this contest 5,612 entries have been received.

If you telephone Prospect 1452, you will learn that the population of our city is now 312,456.

The government deficit may reach $5,565,000,000 this year.

The Blacks have sold their home at 2455 Jefferson Street and have moved to 8634 Avondale Avenue.

COMMAS TO ENCLOSE

88m-N. Use commas to enclose nonrestrictive clauses and phrases within the sentence.

88m-R. Do not use commas to enclose restrictive clauses and phrases.

1. Clauses and phrases are *nonrestrictive* when they do not limit or restrict the meaning of the sentence. Clauses and phrases are *restrictive* when they limit the word or words modified. Usually such clauses and phrases serve as adjectives and limit (one meaning of an adjective) or describe (another meaning of an adjective) the noun or pronoun they modify. Observe what the same clause does in each of the following sentences:

The *Queen Mary, which arrived yesterday,* is a large passenger liner.

The ship *which arrived yesterday* is named the *Queen Mary.*

In the first sentence above, the omission of the adjective clause, *which arrived yesterday,* does not materially change the meaning of the sentence; its purpose is to give added information. In the second sentence, the adjective clause, *which arrived yesterday,* is necessary for the complete expression of the idea; that is, it identifies, it tells which ship *is* the *Queen Mary.* The clause in the first sentence is *nonrestrictive,* and it is thus enclosed, or set off from the remainder of the sentence, by commas; the clause in the second sentence is *restrictive* and is not enclosed by commas. Adjective clauses usually begin with the expressed or understood relative pronouns, *who, which, that.* A *that* adjective clause is invariably restrictive; a *who* or *which* adjective clause may be either restrictive or nonrestrictive, depending on meaning.

Note the labels attached to the following:

> Chapter 10, *which tells of the rescue,* is well written. (Nonrestrictive or nonlimiting clause)
> The chapter *which tells of the rescue* is well written. (Restrictive or limiting clause)
> The car *that you saw* was a sports model. (Restrictive or limiting clause)
> The books *that I own* are all by American authors. (Restrictive or limiting clause)
> The man *my brother met in Chicago* has traveled widely. (Restrictive or limiting clause)
> Arthur Johnson, *whom my brother met in Chicago,* has traveled widely. (Nonrestrictive or nonlimiting clause)

The foregoing examples show that the adjective clause immediately follows the noun it modifies.

2. When an adjective phrase, not a series of adjectives, precedes its modifier, it is usually nonrestrictive; when it immediately follows, it may be restrictive or nonrestrictive; when it follows a few words farther on, with no sacrifice of clearness, it is usually nonrestrictive. Examples:

> *Living very simply and economically,* Father and Mother have saved enough money to put me through college. (Nonrestrictive)
> *Having won the regional championship,* our basketball team moved into the semifinals. (Nonrestrictive)
> The book *lying on the living-room table* is dog-eared and dirty. (Restrictive)
> *Encyclopedia Britannica,* Volume II, *lying on the living-room table,* is dog-eared and dirty. (Nonrestrictive)
> World War II exploded, *shattering my dreams.* (Nonrestrictive)
> I thought only of the moment, *not realizing that the next few minutes would have a lasting effect on me.* (Nonrestrictive)
> Occasionally a student walks into a building, *leaving his companion outside to open the door for herself.* (Nonrestrictive)

3. Preceding sentences show that the modifier (clause or phrase) may be either restrictive or nonrestrictive, depending upon the in-

tended purpose. Restrictive phrases and clauses may therefore be explained as those necessary to identify the word or words they modify. They answer such questions about the word or words as *who? which one?* Each of the restrictive modifiers above serves to identify the word it modifies.

The *context* sometimes determines whether a clause or phrase is restrictive or nonrestrictive. If the word or words are already identified by a phrase or clause, an additional modifier is likely to be nonrestrictive.

> The man who sharpens our lawn mower every summer is a genius.

> We were fortunate in finding a little shop full of all kinds of mechanical gadgets and kept by a thin, undersized little old man. We have no doubt that the man, who sharpens our lawn mower every summer, is a genius.

In the first example, *who sharpens our lawn mower every summer* is restrictive, for it identifies. In the second example, the man is identified in the sentence discussing the shop, and the clause *who sharpens our lawn mower every summer* is nonrestrictive. Similarly:

> The man *sitting across the aisle from us* was going to Cincinnati. (Restrictive)
> The man in the blue serge suit and wearing a brown straw hat, *sitting across the aisle from us,* was going to Cincinnati. (Nonrestrictive)

4. Usually proper names, being already limited and identified, are modified by nonrestrictive phrases or clauses. But occasionally they, too, need identification.

> The John Jones *who is our postman* is not the John Jones *who lives on University Avenue.* (Restrictive)
> The President Roosevelt *who initiated the New Deal* was not the President Roosevelt *who served as vice-president under William McKinley.*

5. Avoid the error of double restriction:

> This is *my* new suit *that I bought last week.*

Both italicized elements are restrictive; the latter is the important limiting statement:

> This is the new suit *that I bought last week*.

88n. Use commas to enclose parenthetical words, phrases, or clauses.

A fairly adequate test is this: an expression is parenthetical if it may be omitted without materially affecting the meaning of the sentence; frequently, although not always, its position in the sentence may be shifted without any change in meaning.

> *However,* we do not disagree too much.
> We do not, *however,* disagree too much.
> We do not disagree too much, *however.*
> We must, *on the other hand,* discuss every aspect of the problem.
> I believe, *if anyone should ask my opinion,* that action should be postponed.

Parenthetic elements vary in intensity, and a writer shows by punctuation their relative strength.

1. Many words and phrases are so weak that they require no punctuation.

> I *also* believe in progress.
> *In fact* I am inclined to agree.

2. Other words, like *oh, well, yes, no, too, etc., i.e.,* when used parenthetically, are enclosed by commas.

> *Oh,* what a game!
> *Oh, yes,* I agree completely.
> *Well,* that was the remark that closed the discussion.
> *Then, too,* other problems need consideration.
> Am I going? *No,* I believe not.
> Dictionaries, paper, pencils, pens, erasers, *etc.,* are used in the writing laboratory.

The letter-combination *i.e.* (Latin, *id est—that is*) is a parenthetical element always followed by a comma and preceded by a comma or a semicolon (see Section **89a**).

> Please report to Room 217, *i.e.,* the Writing Laboratory.
> Your work has been satisfactory; *i.e.,* it has been accurate and it has been turned in promptly.

3. Other phrases or dependent clauses have enough parenthetic strength to require commas.

> Consider, *for example,* the benefits of extracurricular activities.
> Those activities, *as I said,* may require considerable time.

4. Independent clauses—as well as some phrases and dependent clauses used emphatically—are so strong, parenthetically, that the enclosure marks should be dashes or parentheses. (See Sections **91e** and **92a.**)

> There is no reason—*no good reason, that is*—for spending so much money now.
> The lovely little town of Kickapoo Falls—*I was born there, you know*—hasn't changed much since I was a boy.
> My father has been a physician (*he received his training at the University of Louisville*) in Kickapoo Falls for 30 years.

88o. Use commas to enclose inserted sentence elements.

Inserted sentence elements—emphatic, suspending, or transposed expressions—are somewhat similar to parenthetical words, phrases, and clauses. *Emphatic* expressions are those set off because the writer wishes to indicate that he considers them emphatic. *Suspending* expressions are those which interrupt or retard the movement of the sentence, holding important information until near the end of the sentence. *Transposed* expressions—*I believe, I think, it seems to me, I suppose, you see*—are out of their normal order and require punctuation that would not be used in normal word order. Such inserted expressions are frequently more essential to the thought of the sentence than purely parenthetical material, but they are nonrestrictive in function.

Emphatic insertion:	He did not make that statement, *as you will see if you read more carefully,* and I am certain that he did not mean it.
Suspending:	This is a good novel, *not only because it contains plenty of action,* but because it fully develops three characters.
	Another secret for successful study, *and not many students know this,* is the preparation and use of a study schedule.
Transposed:	Action, *I believe,* should be postponed.
	On that night, *it seems,* there is to be a full moon.

Not transposed: *I believe* action should be postponed.

                    It seems on that night there is to be a full moon.

88p.   Use commas to enclose absolute phrases.

An absolute phrase is a group of words that has no grammatical relation to any word in the sentence; it consists of a noun and a participial modifier, the latter being sometimes omitted but understood.

NOTE: The last seven words in the preceding sentence form an absolute phrase, which can come at the beginning, in the middle, or at the end of a sentence.

> *The game (being) over,* the crowd soon scattered.
> *The task having been finished,* we started on our return trip.
> I went to the first desk, *my application (held) in hand,* and asked for Mr. Brown.
> We needed a fourth member for our bridge club, *Mary Ellen having moved to another town.*

An absolute phrase should not be punctuated as a sentence.

Wrong: We needed a fourth member for our bridge club. Mary Ellen having moved to another town.

88q.   Use commas to enclose words in apposition.

A word in *apposition* is a noun or pronoun (word or phrase) identifying in different words a preceding noun or pronoun. (See Section **85**.)

> My father, a physician, has just retired from active practice.
> This is Mr. Browne, our newly elected president.
> My task, to compose a short story, seemed hopeless.

1. Omit the commas when the appositive is restrictive, or part of a proper name, or closely related to the preceding word.

> The river Ohio is beloved of song writers.
> We have recently seen an excellent performance of the play *Julius Caesar*.
> Richard the Lion-Hearted was a famous English king.
> My brother James is a senior in high school.

2. Omit the commas, usually, when the appositive is a noun clause.

> The fact that I was ill caused my absence.

3. Frequently words in apposition are introduced by *namely, for example, for instance, i.e., such as,* etc. These words and phrases are enclosed by commas, as parenthetical expressions, except that *such as* is *not* followed by a comma or a colon. If these and the apposition are fairly strong—that is, long and emphatic—dashes should enclose them. (See Section **91e, 1.**)

Two of the candidates, *namely,* John Smith and William Browne, are my friends.

Any difficult subject, *for example,* chemistry, needs careful study.

Some of our cities, *such as* New York, Chicago, and San Francisco, are thriving centers of commerce.

The various seasonal sports—*for example,* football in the fall, basketball in the winter, and baseball in the summer—attract thousands of spectators.

88r. Use commas to enclose nouns or pronouns or a noun phrase in direct address (vocatives).

Mr. Brown, will you speak next?

I am proud, *Father,* of what you have accomplished.

We are assembled, *ladies and gentlemen,* to discuss an important problem.

Will you please, *sir,* speak more distinctly?

Never doubt that you will be rewarded, *George.*

88s. Use commas to enclose places and dates explaining preceding places and dates.

Henry left on June 20, *1956,* to go to Cincinnati, *Ohio,* for an interview. (But note: Henry left on June 20th to go to . . .)

In *October, 1956,* he was transferred to Albany, N.Y.
or
In *October 1956* he was transferred to Albany, N.Y.

He told us to send his mail to him at 147 Prospect Avenue, *Albany 21, N.Y.,* his new address.

1. The state and the year following both month and day are enclosed by commas—the second comma must be used. When only month and year are used, the use of commas around the year is optional: use two or don't use any.

2. No comma is used before the postal-delivery zone number: Chicago 16; Philadelphia 27.

88t. Use commas to enclose initials or titles following a person's name.

Abbett, H. M., Abner, T. W., and Adams, R. B., head the list of names.

James Norman, M.D., and Frank Hale, D.D., are the featured speakers on the program.

The son of William McAdams, Sr., is listed as William McAdams, Jr., on our records.

88u. Use no unnecessary commas; i.e., use commas only where needed and justifiable.

Comma usage varies with different writers, but the fact that a reputable writer may vary occasionally from conventional practice does not establish a new principle. When practice varies so widely that no principle of punctuation can be stated, remember that every comma used must be needed for sense construction, clearness, or effectiveness. Modern punctuation usage omits more commas than formerly; therefore, be able to account for each comma you use. Do not needlessly separate closely related sentence elements.

Some of the more common misuses or overuses of the comma are discussed in the following series of "do not use" statements.

1. Do not use a comma to separate a subject from its predicate or a verb from its object or its complement. Remember that noun phrases and clauses act as the subjects, objects, or complements of verbs and should not be separated by commas without logical reason.

Wrong: What you say, is true. (Noun clause as subject)
To do satisfactory work, is my aim. (Infinitive phrase as subject)
We asked, to hear the motion reread. (Infinitive phrase as object)
The reason is, that I have been ill. (Noun clause as predicate nominative)

2. Do not use a comma before the indirect part of a quotation. Frequently the indirect quotation is a noun clause used as the object of the verb.

Wrong: The letter informed me, that I should report for an interview.
John told me definitely, that he would come.
The speaker asserted, that he stood squarely for progress.

3. Do not use a comma indiscriminately to replace a word omitted. The word *that* in indirect discourse, the word *that* in introducing other noun clauses as objects, and the relative pronouns *who, whom, which, that* are frequently omitted in informal writing; they should not be replaced by commas.

Wrong: John replied, he would return next week. (Comma incorrectly substituted for *that* in an indirect quotation)
Joe never realized, he could learn to write so easily. (Comma replaces, wrongly, *that* in introducing a noun clause as object of a verb)
The man, I met was a friend of a friend of mine. (Comma incorrectly substituted for the relative pronoun *whom*)
The last house, we lived in was just the right size for our family. (Comma incorrectly substituted for the relative pronoun *which*)

4. Do not use a comma, ordinarily, to separate two words or two phrases joined by a pure coordinating conjunction. (For contrasting elements, see 88j.)

Wrong: He has dignity, and integrity.
The leader has strength of body, and firmness of purpose.

5. Do not use a comma indiscriminately after a pure or simple conjunction. The use of other parenthetical or inserted elements may justify a comma after the conjunction.

Wrong: But, I shall never make that mistake again.
We are leaving early, and, I shall expect to receive your check before I go.
Right: But, as a lesson learned from experience, I shall never make that mistake again.
We are leaving early, and, to save trouble all around, I shall expect to receive your check before I go.

6. Do not use a comma before the first or after the last member of a series.

Wrong: Avoid a mixture of, red, yellow, green, blue, and brown paints.
We went swimming in a cool, clear, smooth-flowing, river.

7. Do not use a comma to set off quoted words which are not direct quotations but which use quotation marks to call attention to the words. For examples, see **88b.**

88v. Avoid the comma splice: Do not use a comma to separate independent clauses not joined by one of the pure or simple conjunctions, <u>and</u>, <u>but</u>, <u>or</u>, <u>nor</u>, <u>neither</u>, <u>yet</u> (for, so).

The comma splice—a common and serious error also named "comma blunder" and "comma fault"—is the joining or *splicing* of two separate, complete statements by a comma. This punctuation is confusing to the reader, who expects a sharper break between such clauses. For full discussion of this error and methods of correcting it, see Section 32.

EXERCISES

A. Choose a page from your book of readings or from a current magazine. Underline or encircle every comma. Give a reason for each comma, or each pair of commas, according to the principles stated in Section 88. Do not be surprised if a few of the commas are unconventionally used, unnecessary, or incorrectly placed.

B. Buy one of the larger popular magazines. Read at least three full pages. Underline all the A, B, and C series, the A, B, C series, and the coordinate adjectives (Section **88h** and **i**). What are your conclusions about the use of commas?

C. Read at least two full pages in the same magazine (Exercise B). Underline or encircle all restrictive and nonrestrictive adjective clauses and phrases (see Section **88m**). What are your conclusions about the use of commas?

D. Coordinate adjectives, the A, B, C series, and the A, B, and C series need commas (see Sections **88h** and **i**). In the following sentences, some commas are misused, and some are omitted. Where should commas be properly used? For what reasons?

1. Dick's wardrobe consists of many suits ties shirts sports coats shoes and all the latest apparel for men.
2. We spent the last 2 weeks of August in a small, lake town.
3. I like to fish swim hunt play basketball and pitch horseshoes.

4. I'm glad to be back at the dear, old University of M_____.
5. Joe always wears a plain white tie shirt and slacks.
6. One of my favorite, summer sports is swimming.
7. We usually hunted in the large, timber areas near our farm.
8. A person susceptible to colds should avoid exposure to cold wet or snowy weather.
9. Let's use as examples winter spring and summer.
10. The outstanding landmark of the town is the huge old brick water tower.
11. Our town is filled with real, estate agents.
12. I was born on a cold wintry day in early January.
13. All of a sudden the left, rear tire blew out.
14. Smoking is a very harmful, and dirty habit.
15. A tall good-looking boy sits next to me in class.

E. Where are commas needed, for clearness, in the following sentences? (See Section 88k.) Why?

1. Needless to say the extra spending money was put to good use.
2. When she was asked why Mary gave three or four good reasons.
3. As you can see my father has been successful in his field.
4. Mother is always doing something to help me and my little sister usually tries to help Mother.
5. Our city supports a Class D baseball team; other than this local sport fans must support the high school teams.
6. If the industries aren't producing the workers aren't buying in the stores.
7. As you can see I still have the interesting hobby of meeting people.
8. Besides working our family took time out for summer vacations.
9. Ever since I can remember our family has been very much interested in music.
10. I was in bed with a cold and my dog kept me company.
11. As you probably know Dizzy Dean was a great pitcher in his time.
12. During the 8 days of the holiday gifts are given to friends and relatives.
13. I'll always remember the old proverb saying "You get out of a thing just what you put into it."
14. After eating and picking my girl up, I came back to school as fast as I could.
15. After reading this one should begin to realize the value of a dictionary.

16. Just before leaving Grandma called and asked me to write her.
17. While I was bathing our kitten jumped on the edge of the tub and then landed squarely on my chest.
18. Whenever we are eating the child next door invariably rings our doorbell.
19. Whenever I am deeply studying my roommate interrupts with some inane remark.
20. Whenever you have time to kill the boys on this floor will help you kill it.

F. The following sentences contain restrictive or nonrestrictive clauses or phrases (see Section **88m**). Indicate by your use of commas which are restrictive and which are nonrestrictive.

1. A dance which I attended last Saturday night was the best one held this semester.
2. I expect to talk with our Dean of Boys who is coming here to interview his high school's graduates.
3. My oldest sister Evelyn is married and has two children: Corinne who is four and Christine who will be two in February.
4. Our town has a population of 18,000 people most of whom commute to New York City which is just 20 miles away.
5. I picked up my first dog on my way to a new school that I was attending.
6. Donaldson Cave is named after Mr. Harry Donaldson who previously owned part of the park and the land in the area.
7. Mother being a shrewd woman knows how to get Father to do things for her.
8. Our teacher realized what the students who were going to college would be up against.
9. Everyone started arriving for Saturday's game which was against Pennsylvania.
10. The Pennsylvania Turnpike has many tunnels each of which is about a mile long.
11. His latest hobby is parachuting which he says is thrilling and exciting.
12. The next day we arrived at Lookout Mountain where we visited Point Park and Rock City Gardens.
13. I went to see my high school principal who promised to write a recommendation for me.
14. Henry exhausted from the race fell from the saddle.
15. My grandfather who is a real character is now 92 years old.

16. I am planning on joining the Hoof and Horn Club which is a club for students interested in animal husbandry.
17. My brother Richard who is now in the Air Force is 22 years old.
18. My improvement was due to our editor who rewrote every story that I wrote.
19. The teacher whom I like best is the one who is patient and understanding.
20. Mr. Lynn having no children left his property for a recreation center.

G. Directions given in F.

1. Wolf Cave located at one end of the park is an outstanding natural attraction.
2. Most of the people who are occupants of our city came from foreign countries.
3. Safety belts which will be made mandatory on all cars are an old thing on racing cars.
4. I was named after my father's mother whose name was Ida Mae.
5. Memorial Park which is on the east edge of town is open during May through September.
6. It was in an English class that I was introduced to a magazine which was of great interest to me.
7. Edward Burr Smith whom I know rather well was 18 years old last May.
8. In this issue there are several articles that look extremely interesting.
9. Marjorie is an intelligent person who has received a good education.
10. Students who are just out of high school find summer employment at this factory.
11. That morning I walked under a ladder which was leaning against our house.
12. One humorous superstition that comes to my mind concerns the belief in an evil spirit.
13. Fort St. John which once stood here has long since disappeared.
14. Two other disadvantages that I had to learn to study against were loud radios and loud record-players.
15. This book should give students who are planning to attend college a good idea of what to expect.
16. Amanda married Fred Hoyes who was an explorer.
17. The best theme was written by a Navy veteran who was on a destroyer for three years.

18. Most of the themes which we write in this class are considered for publication in our freshman magazine.
19. All of the students from my high school that I have talked to are having trouble with chemistry.
20. I hope to get a responsible job that will pay me in part for the time and money I spent in college.

H. In the following sentences, various parenthetic or inserted sentence elements (see Sections **88n, o, p, q, r, s, t**) need commas. Where should the commas go, and why, specifically?

1. One major cause and probably the chief cause of accidents is speeding.
2. This being our first day we didn't know where the different classrooms were.
3. The town I am writing about is Gilman Illinois.
4. The town has one railroad the Chicago and Eastern Illinois.
5. The next week to our disappointment we learned that the plans had been changed.
6. The decision is on the other hand not an easy one to make.
7. I spend too much time watching television I'm afraid.
8. I am ready to accept the responsibility that goes with college life and believe me there really is responsibility.
9. In Amarillo Texas we stopped at the house of one of my friends.
10. Many men as a result of difficult obstacles lose their desire to succeed.
11. The best known and most popular building however is the Union Building.
12. After my two weeks are over at the Navy base I will fly to Clearwater Florida where I will meet my parents.
13. My name by the way is Wally Schmidt.
14. Take for example the slow or Sunday driver.
15. Well as I said a few moments ago I am indefinite about my future plans.
16. Located on the Potomac River a few miles from Washington D.C. is the home of our first President George Washington.
17. Although my father's business card reads "Theodore J. Smith D.D.S." mine simply says "Theodore J. Smith Jr."
18. Whiting known as the "Oil City" is located in northern Indiana.
19. Let's take my home town Georgetown Kentucky a typical small American city.
20. I first met Dick as he has always been known in 1954.

Exercises

I. Directions given in H.

1. The great Mississippi longest river in North America twists and turns its way to the Gulf of Mexico.
2. An expository composition whether it is a written or an oral theme requires skill to develop.
3. Much to my surprise though I have found all my professors young and interesting.
4. I Harry N. Wilson reside at 821 North Ferry Street Cincinnati Ohio.
5. I couldn't see any future in English much to my regret.
6. Needless to say I received a low grade.
7. St. Louis deserved its title "Gateway to the West."
8. Let us say for instance that some one breaks a mirror.
9. I remember going to Washington D.C. when I was quite young.
10. Of course this was only coincidental I figured.
11. What can they the people do to reduce auto accidents?
12. Americans abroad seldom meet the same class of people that they themselves are.
13. This scholarship was made possible by J. H. Robbins a Utopia University alumnus.
14. This book like most books contains a table of contents.
15. I want you to meet Sharon my younger sister.
16. Two weeks ago I drove to Newport Rhode Island to see some relatives.
17. I attended grade school in Glen Park a small suburb of Lincoln.
18. Grandfather a silver-haired old gentleman wears gold-rimmed glasses.
19. We the students of Ashland University are proud of our Observatory.
20. America has Hollywood movie capital of the world and Louisville home of the famous Kentucky Derby.

J. Commas are misused or not used in the following sentences containing parenthetical or inserted elements (see Sections 88n, o, p, q, r, s, t). Correct all errors in the use of commas. Give a specific reason for every correction.

1. The main event, of the evening, is a parade.
2. Barry resided in Montclair, New Jersey where he attended Bradford School.
3. September 18, 1955 was a big day. I entered Walton College as a freshman.
4. Perhaps, I can illustrate the point from my own experience.

5. The people of Vicksburg, Mississippi are very hospitable to visitors.
6. Friday, the 13th does not come very often during the year.
7. The first theme, "Public Enemy Number One," was one in a set of four that won a prize.
8. The other factory, the General Packing Company is comparatively famous.
9. Pasadena, California is the setting for the Tournament of Roses.
10. I was graduated from Greenwater High School and on the whole, did very well with my grades.
11. Early one morning, after I finished breakfast, I started on my first job.
12. Detroit, Michigan, a city of 1,900,000 people is located near the southeastern border of Michigan.
13. I believe however, that smoking is an undesirable habit.
14. My goal, therefore is to become an outstanding dentist.
15. I graduated from West Township a small country school.

K. Directions given in J.

1. Home economics, as an area of study offers young men and women opportunities in everyday living.
2. This summer, being very interesting to the boy, time went by quickly.
3. At our centennial, one of the highlights was the pageant "Down Through the Years" put on by the citizens of the town.
4. Your time will not be wasted in my opinion if you attend the concert.
5. Needless to say no one else has such a record in the Olympics.
6. We, here in the United States, have the greatest amateur athletic system in the world.
7. I should like to tell you in general, what happened during our Homecoming.
8. If you have any random scraps, of information, I should like to be told of them.
9. We should not depend too much on first impressions because, nine times out of ten they are wrong.
10. My father was married, as soon as he graduated from college to my mother.
11. Another restaurant that is very good in my opinion, is Browning's Cafeteria in Pittsburgh.
12. I have, what I believe to be, three interesting hobbies.

13. I was lost to say the least, when I first entered the chemistry laboratory.
14. My eldest brother is now, I believe 31 years old.
15. I am writing you about my home town Chicago.

L. Certain clauses and phrases need to be separated or enclosed by commas (see Section **88d, e, f, g, j**). In the following sentences, where should the commas go? For what reasons?

1. As far as I am concerned that was the most exciting moment in our high school life.
2. Florida is visited all the year round but the busy season starts in December and lasts through March.
3. The oftener we hear certain stories the more we want to hear them again.
4. After wandering through the woods all afternoon I found enough mushrooms for our supper.
5. Such courses are needed to develop good study habits and some concentration is required to master them.
6. To demonstrate what I mean by a mean trick I'll relate an experience that happened to me.
7. Soon after arriving in New York my parents moved westward to St. Louis.
8. The atmosphere is of the old world and all the charm of old Italy can be found there.
9. The more education a person has the more capable he is of facing the problems of life.
10. Now that I have entered college the bad study habits I formed in high school are evident.
11. Our farm home isn't very modern but we do have many conveniences.
12. Because the football stadium is not centrally located it is an inconvenience to most of the fans.
13. If I were a high school student again I would do many things differently.
14. I wish that I had studied harder in high school for it would be easier for me now in college.
15. Before Grandfather became a marine engineer the family lived in Springfield.
16. Whenever a holiday comes the whole town moves to the beach.
17. The smaller the car is the easier it is to handle.

18. Although he is 65 years old Grandfather hasn't a single gray hair.
19. After everyone has eaten a big dinner we return to the living room.
20. Since our town is quite small there are not many recreational facilities available.

M. The commas in the following sentences are misused (see Section 88m-N, 88m-R). Why?

1. Writers, who do not use commas properly, may leave their readers in a coma.
2. Any boy, who is interested in a 4-H project, will learn many things of value to himself and his community.
3. The biggest responsibility, I ever had, was to drive a truck to California.
4. The boy, who is undecided about going to college, should go if he possibly can.
5. The parade floats, that I saw, were very clever.
6. Those themes, reaching the finals in the competition, are published in our college newspaper.
7. I continued to think of things, which I had forgotten to include.
8. A nice girl, with a pleasing disposition, greeted us at the library.
9. One town, I will always remember, was in southern Tennessee.
10. On the new golf course there is hardly a hole, which does not have a few sand traps about it.
11. I would describe my grandfather as a man, who looks very much like Abraham Lincoln.
12. The pictures, that we saw at the art exhibit, were done by old masters.
13. A man, who is a graduate of a school of business, should be able to get a good job in the business world.
14. One of the boys, that I know very well, is an honor student in the College of Commerce.
15. An inventor is a man, who finds new and easier ways of doing things.
16. A copy, of the article, is enclosed for your reading.
17. All the themes, that each student writes, are kept on file for ready reference.
18. The best themes are chosen by the staff, of the Department of English.
19. One advantage, that we had as children, was that we had no prejudices.
20. Has any student, of your class, written anything outstanding?

Exercises 88

N. In the following sentences, commas are misused. Make the necessary corrections and give good reasons.

1. James Browning, is from southern Virginia.
2. I was so proud, that I ran and told all my playmates.
3. My father received, "Greetings from the President of the United States."
4. You will agree with me, that the author has a vivid imagination.
5. Each week at this college, students compose one theme apiece.
6. I must close now. So, long until I see you again.
7. Our state has been called, "The Land of Lincoln."
8. In autumn the leaves are all colored, red, yellow, orange, and brown.
9. While working there, I met a girl named, Amelia Bright.
10. Gary is, and always will be, "The Steel City."
11. The title of my best theme was, "How I Learned to Ski."
12. I might add, that most of the time, we were pretty successful in our fishing.
13. The author points out the fact, that all races can live in harmony together.
14. If I tell you the background, you will be more interested, in what I have to say.
15. I doubt very much, that I will be able to surpass my brother's record.
16. The loss of this first game was a great disappointment, because, our ambition was to be the champions of the tournament.
17. I am proud of the fact, that out of 40 students I received the highest grade.
18. But, very few people can drive a car skillfully on icy roads.
19. The most famous New Year's game is the one called, "The Rose Bowl."
20. My brother and his family will return, to this country, at the end of the year.

O. Directions given in N.

1. I resented the, "come little children," attitude that seemed to prevail.
2. I participated in English 101 under the instruction of, Mr. Moyer.
3. It seems, that family never had a dull moment.
4. But, the greatest spectator sport of all time is basketball.
5. For three years I went to Washington, Elementary School.
6. The most interesting thing of all, is that the principal remembers me, and calls me by my first name.

7. Some of the largest falls in the world are in Yosemite National Park, as well as, the largest redwood trees.
8. In high school I studied nothing, but grammar and some literature.
9. I do not have too much time to study at nights, because, I am working from 8 P.M. to midnight.
10. He said, that he would call me the following Monday.
11. I talk with my roommate a lot but, our conversation is mostly about school.
12. We had a wonderful time visiting relatives, some of whom, I had not seen for months.
13. I have never played la crosse before, but, I am willing to try anything once.
14. Mother prepared a delicious meal, of which, the part I liked best was the oyster dressing.
15. My city is sometimes called, "The City of Bridges."
16. In Indianapolis probably the greatest single attraction, is the Motor Speedway.
17. In that play I took the part of a, "dumb farmer."
18. I have found, that driver's training is the best way to learn to drive a car.
19. I received a pamphlet entitled, "Safe Driving Rules and Laws."
20. The main reason I think I am a careful driver, is the fact that I had a good driver-training course.

THE SEMICOLON

89. The semicolon (;) is a mark of separation only, a stronger mark of punctuation than the comma, signifying a greater break or a longer pause between sentence elements. It is not, however, so forceful as the terminal marks of punctuation; its use indicates that two or more statements are not closely enough related to justify commas, yet they are too closely related to justify being put in separate sentences. In all its uses, it is entirely a mark of coordination.

89a. Use the semicolon to separate independent clauses not joined by a pure or simple conjunction, such as <u>and</u>, <u>but</u>, <u>or</u>, <u>nor</u>, <u>neither</u>, <u>yet</u>. (See Section **88d**.)

Phrased slightly differently, this principle is that the semicolon is used between two independent clauses with *no* conjunction between them.

I am certain you will like this dress; it will suit you perfectly.
Please close the window; the room is too cold.
You have only ten more minutes; please stop writing and revise what you have written.

89b. Use the semicolon to separate coordinate independent clauses joined by a conjunctive adverb or a phrase which serves as a conjunctive adverb (besides, however, nevertheless, therefore, thus, so, also, consequently, hence, likewise, furthermore, still, also, then, moreover, indeed, otherwise, meanwhile, in addition, in fact, as a result, etc.)

I tried for two hours to solve the problem; *then* I gave up and worked on my English assignment.
There are many sharp curves in this road; *however,* a careful driver will have no difficulty.
Mr. Greene is a busy man; *in fact,* he seems busier than he really is.

To apply correctly and effectively the foregoing principle, keep in mind the following explanatory statements:

1. Note that the semicolon is used immediately before the conjunctive adverb when the conjunctive adverb comes *between* the two independent clauses. If the conjunctive adverb is shifted to a position within the second clause, the semicolon separates the two clauses (see Section **89a**), and the adverb, depending upon its parenthetic strength, is, or is not, enclosed by commas.

I tried for two hours to solve the problem; I *then* gave up and worked on my English assignment.
There are many sharp curves in this road; a careful driver, *however,* will have no difficulty.
Mr. Greene is a busy man; he seems busier, *in fact,* than he really is.

2. When the conjunctive adverb comes between the clauses, should there be a comma after it? There is no unvarying principle. As a guide: decide upon the weakness or strength of the word or phrase, parenthetically, in relation to the second clause. If it is weak, omit the comma; if it is strong, use a comma; if it is mildly strong (like *therefore,* for example), use or omit, depending upon your desire to indicate a pause. Another guide: commas follow long conjunctive adverbs and phrases (*nevertheless, in fact, for example,* etc.), rarely follow shorter ones (*thus, hence, then,* etc.).

647

I have trained myself to read rapidly and carefully; *thus* I save myself many hours a week.

I did not favor spending the money; *nevertheless,* I did not vote against the proposal.

This climate is subject to sudden weather changes; *therefore* (or *therefore,*) you should bring a variety of clothing.

3. Distinguish between a conjunctive adverb and a simple conjunction. A conjunctive adverb is both conjunction and adverb; as such it has an adverbial function which no simple conjunction possesses. Furthermore, it is used only between independent clauses, or sentences, whereas a simple conjunction may join words, phrases, dependent clauses, independent clauses, or even sentences.

4. Distinguish also between conjunctive adverbs placed between independent clauses and subordinating conjunctions (*although, because, since, whereas, inasmuch as*) introducing a dependent clause coming between the two independent clauses. The subordinating conjunctions are preceded by a semicolon in such uses only when there is no pure coordinating conjunction joining the independent clauses (see Sections **89a, 89d**).

I shall attend the lecture this evening, *although I can ill afford the time.* (Dependent clause follows independent clause)

I shall attend the lecture this evening; *although I can ill afford the time,* I believe that I shall learn something of profit. (Two independent clauses separated, second being introduced by a dependent clause)

I am having trouble with English and chemistry, *because my high school training in these subjects was inadequate.* (Dependent clause follows independent clause)

I am having trouble with English and chemistry; *because my high school training in these subjects was inadequate,* I have been assigned to non-credit sections in these subjects. (Two independent clauses separated, second being introduced by a dependent clause)

89c. **Use the semicolon to separate independent clauses joined by a pure conjunction if the clauses are long or contain much internal punctuation.** (See Section **88d**, 4.)

In applying this principle do not overuse the semicolon. The longer a sentence becomes, and the more involved its punctuation, the less likely it is to be clear. One, two, or even three commas in a sentence are scarcely enough to justify a semicolon before a pure conjunction.

> Success in college, so some maintain, requires intelligence, industry, and honesty; but others, fewer in number, assert that only personality is important.
>
> Many books, particularly very cheap ones, are slapped together so hastily that they have little durability and cannot withstand the wear and tear a student must subject them to; but, with proper care such as the true lover of books would bestow, even these books can be made to serve during a student's college years, or even longer.

Use semicolons also to separate phrases of great length, as well as dependent clauses, and series of words in which clearness might not otherwise be attained.

> The nominations for class president include the following: Adams, J. B., of New Richmond, member of Skull and Bones; Davis, H. M., of Belleville, formerly secretary of the Camera Club; and Wilson, M. L., of Newtown, captain of the football team.

89d. Do not use the semicolon to set off a phrase or a dependent clause.

Ordinarily the semicolon serves the same purpose as the period: to indicate the end of one complete thought and the beginning of another; it is this break in thought that your reader expects when he sees a semicolon. *One fairly safe guide is this: no period, no semicolon.* Setting off dependent clauses or phrases with semicolons leads to the same confusion in your reader's mind as is caused by the *unjustifiable sentence fragment* (see Section 31).

Frequent misuses of semicolons concern dependent clauses and participial or absolute phrases:

> Inasmuch as Joe has a fiery temper; we have to be careful what we say to him. (Dependent clause)
>
> The next meeting of the club has been postponed two weeks; because most of the membership are on an inspection trip to Detroit. (Dependent clause)
>
> Olson has a good position waiting for him; as soon as he finishes college. (Dependent clause)
>
> If I were you; I should ask for a recount of the ballots. (Dependent clause)

Being careful to observe all traffic regulations; I am considered a good driver. (Participial phrase)

The excitement of our mock political campaign having died down; we once again turned our attention to our studies and the approaching final examinations. (Absolute phrase)

To correct semicolon errors like these, use no punctuation or the comma for the semicolon.

89e. Do not use a semicolon for a colon as a mark of introduction.

Wrong: My purpose is simple; to succeed in life.

Yesterday the bookstores sold me the following; textbooks, theme paper, drawing instruments, and laboratory equipment. (in business letters) Dear Sir; Dear Mr. Woods; Gentlemen;

To correct semicolon errors like the foregoing, substitute colons for the semicolons.

89f. Do not use the semicolon for the dash as a summarizing mark. (See also Section **91d**.)

Wrong: Class plays, debates, a newspaper, and the yearbook; these were the major non-athletic activities in our high school.

Mathematics, chemistry, English; these give me more trouble than any other subjects.

Right: Class plays, debates, a newspaper, and the yearbook—these were the major non-athletic activities in our high school.

Mathematics, chemistry, English—these give me more trouble than any other subjects.

EXERCISES

A. The following sentences contain conjunctive adverbs as part of the second independent clause. Where should the semicolons and commas go?

1. I have little money therefore I shall stay here over the holiday.
2. Our star miler has a very sore leg consequently he will not run on Saturday.
3. We must leave for the Stadium early otherwise we'll miss the exciting moment of the kick-off.
4. Bob spent the larger part of his naval career at Great Lakes he was sent overseas however on special duty twice during that time.

5. Education is considered very desirable every student therefore should try to get at least a little while he is in college.

6. Not every trout fisherman has the time to tie his own flies besides the materials are very expensive.

7. You should give that chair at least two coats of flat paint then in addition you should put on one coat of varnish.

8. If you travel by air you should make reservations in advance otherwise you may not be able to go when you want to.

9. He said the quotation was from Shakespeare nevertheless I was certain that it was from the Bible.

10. I disliked everything that went with English I never did learn much therefore about writing and reading.

B. Semicolons are misused in the following sentences. Why?

1. I knitted a lot while I was home; but when I came back to college, I could not find enough time in which to knit.

2. His immediate aim in life is centered in two things; becoming an engineer and learning to fly an airplane.

3. A freshman must set a goal for himself; a goal that he can reach through hard work.

4. Included in our curriculum are many of the physical sciences; such as engineering, biology, and chemistry.

5. The first week of camping was wonderful; living in cabins instead of tents.

6. One funny thing; you never seem to remember what the point of the story is.

7. My roommate also likes sports; particularly football, basketball, and baseball.

8. Now that the football season is over; basketball is the sport most talked of.

9. I cannot say that I like one state better than another; as each state is entirely different.

10. The big difference between college and high school is; you have to study on your own time.

11. Some students drop out of school after one semester and say it was a good experience; a very expensive one at that.

12. The English before my senior year in high school was mostly grammar; as I wrote only seven or eight themes during the entire period.

13. About five minutes before the program went on the air; we were invited to participate.

14. I never seem to notice the clouds, the green grass, and the trees in the summer time; or the fallen leaves and bare limbs of the fall.
15. Interruptions at home are something I have to contend with; such as the radio or television blaring out in another room.
16. Like all students in the past; I wish I'd spent more time on English.
17. College has more people for activities; all of whom have different talents.
18. We were shown the various rooms of the library; and we were told also how to use the books in them.
19. Believe me; at that moment I saw visions of being a great movie star.
20. The content consists of; the vocabulary entry, spelling, accents, and syllabic division.

C. Directions given in B.

1. Grandfather met some friends in New York; and then decided to come west to Illinois.
2. If the instructor can't help you; you may have to hire a tutor.
3. My roommate and I have similar habits, such as; studying, eating, sleeping, talking, and reasoning processes.
4. Although I like baseball best; I shall also try out for the basketball team.
5. We should have some objective in mind; at least the acquiring of a good foundation in mathematics.
6. Our high school stressed mathematics and English; which are the two courses most necessary for college-bound students.
7. I do most of the operating of our farm; when I am home, at least.
8. Dear Mr. Brown; (salutation of a letter)
9. The noise of the band exploded in her ears; and the bright lights hurt her eyes.
10. In conclusion; I believe the colleges should put more pressure on the high schools to improve their English teaching.
11. There are several reasons for this; mainly, no time, no money, no energy.
12. Just as we were ready to leave; the prize winners were announced.
13. During his freshman year; my brother played in the orchestra.
14. All plans of study have one aim; to prepare the student to live a happy, prosperous life.
15. My first salary was four dollars a week; payable on Thursdays.
16. You see; I have to buy my own license plates and insurance for my car.
17. If the title of this theme seems sarcastic; I meant it to be that way.

18. I shall divide blind dates into three classes; although I imagine there are more kinds.
19. We began making cotton dresses; then finally wool dresses, suits, and coats.
20. A safe driver should know the traffic laws of his state; and should be able to apply them if he has to.

   D. Directions given in B.

1. There seems; however, no line to be drawn between fact and fiction.
2. This fits an old saying; an hour before 12 is worth three in the morning.
3. The first stone struck Goliath on the forehead; knocking him to the ground unconscious.
4. For instance, my Animal Husbandry class is held in the Livestock Pavilion; a distance of seven or eight blocks from my house.
5. For lunch there is a choice of vegetables; corn, peas, carrots, beets, and a few others.
6. Since my brother is only two years older than I; our influence on each other has been great.
7. There are many interesting stories, such as; Moses guiding his people through the Red Sea.
8. When you have bought the polish and are ready to do the work; the first thing is to clean the car.
9. So we decided; Mother, Tom my brother, and I to spend Christmas vacation in Florida.
10. There are always things that have to be done; like mowing the lawn or working in a garden.
11. Located in Indianapolis is the 500-mile race; where people from all over the world gather.
12. I think our city is a very good location for a home; because it is large enough for a person to buy about anything.
13. There, too, is the well-known city of Avalon; the Chicago Cubs' spring training field and the home of Wrigley.
14. The reason for this change is because; in the south there is year-round pasture for grazing.
15. The Derby is truly the meeting place for all kinds of people; "rich man, poor man, beggar man, thief."

THE COLON

90. The colon (:) is usually a mark of introduction, sometimes a mark of separation. Unlike the semicolon, which is a mark for *separating* coordinate sentence elements, the colon is primarily a mark for introducing lists, series, and quotations.

90a. Use the colon to introduce a word, phrase, or, occasionally, dependent clause when emphasis is desired.

For a comparison of the colon, as a more emphatic mark, with the comma in such uses, see page 611 and Section **88a.**

> My aim in this course is easily stated: a high grade.
> There is only one other possibility: to travel by air.
> This is our next problem: where do we go from here?
> I am positive there is one appeal which you cannot overlook: money.
> These two things he loved: an honest man and a beautiful woman.

90b. Use the colon after an introductory statement which clearly shows that something is to follow: an enumeration, tabulation, list, etc.

> You will need the following equipment for the trip: a change of clothes, a few toilet articles, and a supply of money.
> There were three reasons for his success: integrity, industry, and a good personality.
> Everything will be arranged: the paper provided, the pencils sharpened, the chairs placed.

There must be a break between the introduction and what follows, and the best indication of this break is the use of words such as *the following* or *as follows*. Like commas (see Section **88u**), colons do not separate verbs from complements or objects, or prepositions from their objects.

Note especially that the expression *such as* is *never* followed by a colon (see Section **88q**, 3).

Wrong: I am fond of: books, newspapers, and magazines.
            I like to read: novels, detective stories, and biographies.
            The three Ohio cities Marvin visited were: Toledo, Cleveland, and Dayton.
            In our community there are a number of popular sports, such as: basketball, tennis, and bowling.

Right: I am fond of the following: books, newspapers, and magazines.
            I like to read the following: novels, detective stories, and biographies.

The three Ohio cities Marvin visited were as follows: Toledo, Cleveland, and Dayton.

In our community there are a number of popular sports, such as the following: basketball, tennis, and bowling.

or

In our community there are a number of popular sports, such as basketball, tennis, and bowling.

90c. Use a colon to introduce a clause that summarizes or gives an example of or carries on the thought of a preceding clause.

Only skillful and infrequent use of the colon for this purpose is effective. Its overuse is ineffective and misleading, because the reader expects the conventional mark between such clauses to be the semicolon, not an introducing but a separating mark.

The purpose of reading is not alone recreation: it is also information. Many a man succeeds through sheer attention to industry: Benjamin Franklin was such a man.

I went to the fair for two reasons: first, I wanted to visit the various 4-H exhibits, and, second, I wanted to see about a job for the summer.

90d. Use the colon to separate the introductory words from a quotation which follows, if the quotation is formal, long, or paragraphed separately. (See also Section **88b**.)

General Robert E. Lee once said: *"Duty* is the sublimest word in the English language; no man should do more, nor should any man be expected to do less."

The actor then stated: "I would rather be able adequately to play the part of Hamlet than to perform a miraculous operation, deliver a great lecture, or build a magnificent skyscraper."

The mayor arose, wiped his spectacles, cleared his throat, and said: "It seems inevitable that we should have differences of opinion about this important community problem."

The most important suggestion was made by William Furniss, who spoke as follows: ". . ." (one or more paragraphs of the speech)

90e. Use the colon after the formal salutation of a letter.

Dear Sir:
Dear Mr. Brown:

Gentlemen:
My dear Mr. Burns:

The usual practice is to place a colon after the salutation of a formal or business letter and a comma after the salutation of an informal, friendly letter. (Section **88c.**)

90f. **The colon also has the following uses: to separate hour and minute figures in writing time, the title of a book from the subtitle, the scene from the act of a play, the chapter from a verse in the Bible.**

By my watch it is exactly 10:25 A.M.
Lew Wallace is the author of *Ben Hur: A Tale of the Christ.*
The passage quoted occurs in Shakespeare's *Macbeth,* III:ii.
John iii:16 is my best loved Bible verse.

For the last two examples above, and similar uses, the Modern Language Association *Style Sheet* suggests periods without spacing, and, for the books and chapter numbers of the Bible no italics and small Roman numerals: *Macbeth,* III.ii; I Chron. xxv.8; Luke, xiv.5.

90g. **Do not use the colon for the dash as a summarizing mark.** (See Section **91d**).

The colon looks ahead; the summarizing dash tells the reader what has preceded.

Wrong: Class plays, debates, a newspaper, and the yearbook: these were the major non-athletic activities in our high school.
Mathematics, chemistry, English: these gave me more trouble than any other subjects.

To correct sentences like these, replace the colon by the dash.

EXERCISES

Some of the following sentences need colons and some already have them. Check each sentence carefully and make each one correct in its use of the colon.

1. There are three parts to the chemistry course lecture, recitation, and laboratory.
2. Four dyes were used in coloring the eggs red, green, blue, and yellow.

3. All my high school teachers said one thing in particular college is going to be difficult.
4. It all adds up to this every one should be compelled to carry auto insurance.
5. There is one major difference between my roommate and me we are of different religious beliefs.
6. I want these people: my mother, my father, and the rest of my family, to be proud of me.
7. The dictionary gives other pertinent information such as: population, natural resources, and political status.
8. I would like you to meet my family my father, my mother, and my brother Bill.
9. First of all, I'll give you a little of my background where I was born, attended school, etc.
10. The high school I attended was: old, centrally located, and small.
11. There are two courses offered in forestry one is the care and conservation of forests, and the other is wood utilization and technology.
12. I always say to my younger brother "You don't know how lucky you are."
13. Our daily schedule consisted of: getting up at seven o'clock, preparing breakfast, and then ice-skating all day long.
14. The second superstition is this one if you break a mirror, you are supposed to have as many years of bad luck as there are broken pieces.
15. Included in our curriculum are many of the physical sciences such as: engineering, biology, and chemistry.
16. Three courses of study are offered in the high school I attended academic, general, and commercial.
17. The list is long and includes: trays, thermometers, and chemicals.
18. What I am trying to say is this I am now about 20 dollars poorer.
19. Bob has taken intense interest in all scouting activities such as: jamborees, hikes, camping trips, and service projects.
20. I definitely agree with the statement in the newspaper "When Santa Claus comes to town, the shoppers do too."

THE DASH

91. The dash (—) serves the purposes of introduction, termination, separation, or, with another dash, enclosure.

The dash is a mark of punctuation most characteristically used to denote a sudden break or shift in thought. Although a stronger mark, it is approximately equivalent to a comma: both may be used in pairs or alone, and between expressions of coordinate or unequal rank. Logically, some other mark can usually be substituted for the dash, but its occasional use provides emphasis or surprise.

For those who type: the dash is the only common mark of punctuation not on the standard keyboard of the typewriter. To type a dash, use two hyphens together; no space precedes or follows the two hyphens. Example:

```
The dash--one of the important but less
frequently used marks of punctuation--adds
variety and emphasis to writing.
```

Only on the typewriter is the dash equal to two hyphens; the printed hyphen is somewhat smaller than half a dash. The double dash or long dash also finds occasional use in writing.

91a. Use the dash to introduce a word, a phrase, or, occasionally, a clause when emphasis is desired.

For some of these purposes the comma or the colon is used. Compare the following illustrations with those in Sections 88a and 90a.

My aim in this course is easily stated—a high grade.
There is only one other possibility—to travel by air.
Our next problem is—where do we go from here?
There is only one thing he needs for his complete success and happiness—love.

91b. Use the dash, or double dash, to indicate an interruption, an unfinished statement, or an unfinished word (usually in dialogue).

George began, "May I ask—"
"You may not," snapped the judge.

"I hardly know how to express—" and then the speaker blushed, and sat down.

He is the most despicable—but I should not say any more.
When John Smith comes in—oh, here you are now, John.
"I can't spell the word 'erysipe—'"

The double dash is usually used at the end of the statement, the ordinary dash within the line. Omit the period when such statement terminates with a dash.

658

91c. Use the dash to indicate a break, shift, or turn in thought.

Here is a fuller explanation—but perhaps your class will not be interested.

Do we—can we—propose such action to the trustees?

He was aware—he must have known—that the proposed solution was impossible.

91d. Use a dash to separate a final clause summarizing a series of ideas that precede it.

The usual summarizing words are *these, those, such.*

Mathematics, chemistry, English—these give me more trouble than any other subjects.
The meek, the kind, the gentle, the pure in heart—such are of the Kingdom of Heaven.
Food to eat, a place to sleep, a pleasant occupation, a congenial companion—what more can anyone ask from life?

Note that no other marks of punctuation, such as the comma, semicolon, or colon, are used with the dash in this summarizing use; note also that the semicolon or colon cannot be used in place of the summarizing dash (see Sections **89f, 90g**).

91e. Use dashes to enclose sharply distinguished parenthetical matter in order to secure emphasis or suspense.

We are in favor—completely in favor, we repeat—of the proposal.
I was surprised—in fact, pleasantly astonished—to hear of your splendid record.
My advice—if you will pardon my impertinence—is that you apologize to your friend.
My father is not afraid—he is a surgeon, you know—of performing the most delicate operation.

Note the following special applications of the foregoing principle:
1. Long appositional phrases are likely to be enclosed by dashes.

Three candidates for public office—Wilson of New York, Matthews of Illinois, and Adams of Colorado—are in favor of larger old-age pensions.

For commas with shorter appositional phrases, see Section 88q.

2. When the parenthetical material set off by dashes requires an exclamation point or question mark, such punctuation should precede the second dash:

> If I should fail this course—heaven forbid!—I shall have to attend summer school.

91f. Use the dash to indicate the omission of words or letters (other than contractions), or to connect combinations of letters and figures.

> General B— was an excellent soldier.
> The First World War, 1914—1918, was fought to end all wars.
> John Kline is a pilot on the Chicago—New York run.
> Monday—Friday classes will have one meeting more next week than Tuesday—Thursday classes.
> Please study pages 3—14 for tomorrow's assignment.

If a student types his work, hyphens could be justifiably used in all the examples above, except the first.

91g. Use the dash sparingly.

Overuse of the dash is inadvisable. It is legitimately used in the instances cited in this section, but other marks of punctuation have their functions, too, and are usually more commonly used. Frequent use of the dash detracts from its effectiveness.

91h. Never use the dash as a substitute for the period.

Except for the use of the dash to mark unfinished statements or interrupted dialogue (Section **91b**), the dash is never used for the period at the end of a sentence. Any writer who has the habit of using dashes for this purpose should immediately break the habit.

EXERCISES

A. Encircle all the dashes on two pages of a textbook, book of readings, or magazine. Account for the use of each.

B. Where should dashes be placed in the following sentences? Why?

1. Lake Philip is on the Michigan Indiana border line.
2. Walking under a ladder, breaking a mirror, having a black cat cross in front of you these are some of the superstitions I once believed in.

3. Another childhood experience this one I dreaded very much was going to school.
4. When we walked up to our new home did I say home it turned out to be a 20-room ramshackle house.
5. Robert I call him Bob joined the Navy in 1954.
6. The Municipal Opera, St. Louis Zoo, the Jewel Box, lakes, museums, fountains all these are located in Forest Park.
7. Carl said that he bought his dictionary I'd like to have a copy too at the College Book Store.
8. We were all tired from hiking, and the bed in my case a sleeping bag was like heaven.
9. The students here are fine, but the teachers.
10. The door was narrow, and sometimes Dave that's the fat one had a hard time coming in.
11. The owner of the airport I would hang around there every day finally began taking me for rides.
12. A cat I have long since forgotten her name was the first animal I owned.
13. You cannot get advantages from college this applies to every student just by being there; to make it pay you must apply yourself.
14. In typing, leave generous margins of at least one inch on each side of the page.
15. In certain types of manuscript for example, literary criticism you may want to single-space long quotations.
16. Colonel John H from Kansas lived behind enemy lines in Italy and Germany 1943 1945.
17. Some of our students maybe you're one of them are too indifferent to give full support to our athletic teams.
18. This character was a large man who wore a straw hat and a topcoat a very odd sight, I assure you.
19. From 1942 to 1945 perhaps it was 1941 to 1945 Father held various assignments with the Department of State.
20. Take Route 29 for the shortest way to oh, oh, I forgot that that road is closed for repairs.

PARENTHESES, BRACKETS, AND LESS FREQUENTLY USED MARKS

92. Parentheses ( ), sometimes called "curves," and brackets [ ] are marks of enclosure. The former find occasional use. The latter are infrequently used; in fact, they are not included on the regular keyboard of standard typewriters.

92a. **Use parentheses to enclose parenthetical material which is remotely connected with the context.**

> This punctuation (I am convinced it is important) should be carefully studied.
> If you find any holly berries (surely they must be numerous now), please bring me some.

To justify parenthesis marks, the writer must be sure that his material is strongly parenthetic, usually long phrases, perhaps dependent clauses, or independent clauses—not words or most phrases or most dependent clauses. In such constructions the parenthetic material merely amplifies the thought. Thus many writers prefer dashes to parentheses (see Section **91e**). These marks may frequently be used interchangeably, although parentheses are more commonly used when the strong parenthetic material is not quite so closely related to the main statement.

92b. **Use parentheses to enclose amplifying references, directions, and numbering figures.**

> Study carefully the assignment on credits. (See Chapter V.)
> Gulliver among the Lilliputians (see Book I) had some exciting experiences.
> Shakespeare was born on April 23 (?), 1564.
> I am studying medicine for three reasons: (1) I like the subject; (2) my father and grandfather are doctors; and (3) our town needs additional doctors.

92c. **Use parentheses to enclose figures repeated to insure accuracy.**

> He paid ten dollars ($10.00) for the shoes.
> There were thirty (30) claims for damages.

Repetition of figures after words is *rare* or *nonexistent* in formal and informal writing. Students often have an idea that a number written out must be followed by numerals. This is a mistaken notion; except in commercial writing, words alone are sufficient.

92d. Do not use parentheses to cancel parts of your writing. Erase or draw lines through the words you wish to delete.

92e. Use brackets to enclose a comment of the writer inserted or interpolated in a quoted passage.

"On the first float rode the Queen of the Tournament [Miss Emily Miller] and her attendants."

"In April of that year [1942] Johnson took out his first patent."

"Milton portrays Satan as a fallen angle [*sic*] of tremendous size."

92f. Do not confuse brackets and parentheses.

Brackets are used to set off inserted matter remotely related or merely incidental to the context, especially editorial interpolations and comments not by the author of the text. These interpolations may be corrections, comments, or explanations. Brackets are used to set apart the writer's addition to *quoted* material; parentheses are used to enclose the writer's *own words,* according to Section **92a.**

EXERCISES

Copy the following sentences, inserting parentheses or brackets where they belong.

1. It was in March I think it was in March that I was notified of my admission to Springfield University.
2. I have a friend I shall call him Bill who did not believe the warning about icy roads.
3. Not long ago Happy Hollow that was the name of the place before it became a park was bought by the city as a place of recreation for our citizens.
4. Stealing clothes and food materials from the poorer people in this case they were peasant-farmers kept them alive.
5. The magazine article began: "People these days are to *sic* busy to care about anyone but themselves."
6. This article by James Jones you remember him? has been widely quoted.
7. The letter reads: "John the boy I met at the dance has been asking about you every day since you left."
8. *Plain Sense* was published early in the 19th century 1836 by an English firm.

9. Totalitarianism see Chapter 10 was eagerly discussed.
10. This book the one I referred to earlier is an excellent example of 16th-century thought.

LESS FREQUENTLY USED MARKS

The miscellaneous marks discussed in this section (in addition to ellipsis periods and asterisks, Section 86g) are not strictly punctuation marks. They are symbols serving a purpose in writing; except for the caret, this purpose concerns a mechanical method of indicating pronunciation.

92g. Use a caret (ʌ) to insert an omitted expression or letter.

Place the caret below the line at the place of omission and write the inserted expression or letter directly above or in the margin.

92h. Use a dieresis (˙˙) to show that the second of two vowels is pronounced in the following syllable.

With such words as *zoölogy, coöperation,* and *aërate,* there is a growing tendency not to use this sign. It is useful, however, in words like *reënforce* and *naïve,* in order to prevent momentary confusion or mispronunciation. A hyphen may also be used to indicate this separation of vowels in a word like *re-enlist.*

92i. Use an accent or other mark, usually with words of foreign origin, where the spelling requires it.

Acute accent (´): *passé*
Grave (`): *à la mode*
Circumflex (^): *hôtel de ville*
Cedilla (¸): *façade*
Tilde (˜): *cañon*

Let your dictionary be your guide.

THE HYPHEN

93. The hyphen (-) is a mark of separation used only between parts of a word. Paradoxically, its most frequent use is unification, bringing together two or more separate words into a *compound* word which serves the purpose of a single part of speech.

The hyphen, therefore, is more a mark of *spelling* than of *punctuation,* to indicate that two or more words or two or more parts of one word belong together. It is a mechanical device necessary for correct, clear writing.

No longer is the hyphen used—as it once was in older dictionaries—to indicate division of words into syllables. That purpose is now served by the dot: re·sist, ad·vo·cate, ir·re·sis·ti·ble (see Section **51c,** 3). Hyphens presently used between syllables are an integral part of the word.

93a. **Use your dictionary to determine whether certain word combinations are written as two words, as one word written solid, or as compound words with a hyphen between parts.**

→1. Do not write as one word two or more words that should be completely separated.
→2. Do not write as two separate words any two words which should be written solid.
→3. Do not write as two or more words any word-combinations which should be hyphenated. (See expanded discussion, Section **93b,** below.)

There are no rules covering all combinations, and the combinations are so numerous that many such are not in your dictionary. Fortunately, many are.

The use of a hyphen in joining compound words—two or more words used as a unit—varies greatly. When in doubt, consult a standard dictionary. Dictionaries differ among themselves, but if you own a good dictionary (see p. 342), let it be your guide in hyphenating and compounding.

The general principle of word joining derives, of course, from usage. When two or more words first become associated with a single meaning, they are written separately; as they grow to be more of a unit in common thought and writing, they are hyphenated; finally they are written together as one word. This evolution is seen in the following, the third word in each series now being the accepted form: base ball, base-ball, baseball; basket ball, basket-ball, basketball; rail road, rail-road, railroad.

Many common expressions are still in the first stage; *mother tongue, boy friend, girl scout, girl friend, a lot, in fact, in spite, high school.* The one-word combination, *highschool,* for example, although used by a prominent educational magazine, has not yet been accepted by dictionaries.

93b. Use a hyphen to separate the parts of many compound words.

Many compounds are always written solid, many are written with a hyphen, and many are written either with a hyphen or as two words, depending upon meaning (numerous examples are given below). Note the difference in these:

> After three years of service, Joe was a hardened, *battle-scarred* veteran.

> The *battle scarred* the bodies and souls of all who took part.

> The *above-mentioned* principles are frequently illustrated in writing.

> The poem *above, mentioned* several times by the speaker, has been one of my favorites.

> In the quarrel between Ellen and Sue, Jean served as a *go-between.*

> The ball must *go between* the goal posts if the score is to be seven points instead of six.

Hyphens are generally used:

1. Between two or more words modifying a substantive and used as a single adjective, especially when placed before the substantive. These combinations may consist of
   a. an adjective or noun united with a present or past participle: *sad-looking, able-bodied, absent-minded, soft-spoken, battle-scarred, bell-shaped, wind-blown.*
   b. two adjectives, or an adjective and a noun, or a noun and an adjective: *Latin-American, ocean-blue, midnight-black, ten-foot, six-room.*
   c. a prefix or combining form attached to a capitalized word: *un-American, trans-Andean.*
   Note: Prefixes and suffixes attached to common words usually become part of the word, written solid; dictionaries often have

long lists of these—see, for example, combining words like *non, over, under* in your dictionary.

  d. an adverb and a present or past participle (unless the adverb ends in *-ly*): *fast-moving, above-mentioned, swiftly moving.*

2. Between words of a compound noun:

  a. three or more words: *mother-in-law, jack-of-all-trades.*

  b. an adverb or a preposition as the second element: *go-between, looker-on, leveling-off.*

  c. compounds when *fellow, father, mother, brother, sister, daughter,* or a similar word is the first element in a created compound: *fellow-citizen, brother-classmates, sister-nations.*

3. Between compound words when, usually, *self, ex, half,* or *quarter* is the first element: *self-control, self-respect, ex-president, half-asleep, half-truth, quarter-share.*

4. Between a single capital letter joined to a noun or participle: *A-flat, F-sharp, S-curve, T-shaped, U-turn.*

5. Between elements of an improvised compound: *make-believe, know-it-all, never-say-die, never-to-be-forgotten.*

6. Between the parts of compound numerals (from twenty-one to ninety-nine): *forty-three, sixty-seven, eighty-two.*

7. Between the numerator and denominator of a fraction: *two-thirds, four-fifths, one-thousandth* (but omitted when the hyphen already appears in either numerator or denominator: *twenty-four thirty-fifths; three ten-thousandths*).

93c. **Use a hyphen to indicate the division of a word broken at the end of a line.**

The rambling old house, it is true, would have looked considerably better if it had been freshly painted.

Occasionally, at the end of a longhand or typewritten line, a long word must be divided. Avoid such division if you possibly can, and never divide it if it is the last word on the page. When division is necessary, follow these directions:

1. Place the hyphen at the end of the first line, *never at the beginning of the second.*

2. Never divide a monosyllable. Such long one-syllable words as

curse, through, thought, though, ground, death, grace, quick, and *breadth* cannot be divided. The same suggestion applies to *ed* endings in one-syllable pronunciations: *asked, dressed.* Write the entire monosyllable on the first line; if this is not possible, carry the whole word over to the next line.

3. Divide words of more than one syllable between syllables, but avoid dividing one-letter syllables from the remainder of the word, as well as any unpronounced *ed.* Undesirable: a·bout; i·talics; man·y; attack·ed.

4. When in doubt about correct syllabication, consult your dictionary in order to divide words properly. Several simple suggestions, however, apply to many words:

Prefixes and suffixes can be divided from the main words (but see 3, just above).

Compound words are divided between their main parts.

Two consonants are usually divided.

93d. **Do not use a hyphen in place of a dash or a dash in place of a hyphen.**

In longhand, make the hyphen and the dash distinct. Remember that in typing, a dash consists of two hyphens, and that, in typing also, the hyphen may substitute for the dash in several uses (see Section **91f).**

EXERCISES

A. Encircle all the hyphens on one page of your book of readings, another textbook, or a magazine. Give the reason for each.

B. With the aid of your dictionary, determine which of the following words are compounds and should be written with hyphens: *johnnycake, chickenhearted, helterskelter, schoolboy, downstairs, drawbridge, textbook, pitchdark, fatherinlaw, bull'seye, laborsaving, airtight, selfstarter, runin, hangeron, thirtynine, offstage, blowout, quietspoken, campfire.*

C. Copy the following words in a list, and make a list of the same words without the hyphens. What is the difference in meaning when the same word is hyphenated or written solid? *re-treat, re-creation, re-view, re-claim, re-dress, re-lay, re-search, re-turn, re-tread, re-cover, re-act, re-collect, re-pose, re-tire, re-count, re-sign, re-prove, re-sound, re-solve, re-sort.*

D. Indicate where hyphens should be inserted in words in the following sentences:

1. An autobiography is a self written account of a person's life.
2. As a child I had trouble distinguishing sixtysix from ninetynine.
3. When I become a newspaper reporter, I shall observe the rules about off the record remarks.
4. Power driven machines are the basis of American industry.
5. Mother is a brown eyed, brown haired, dark complexioned lady in her late thirties.
6. Many made by hand products are superior to machine made ones.
7. When my twin sisters were married in a double wedding ceremony, I acquired two brothersinlaw simultaneously.
8. Nobody likes loudmouthed, selfish acting people.
9. In basketball the two on one situation is not uncommon, especially on a long down the floor pass.
10. Our undermanned team went on the field with a never say die and a we'll do it or die attitude.
11. On some campuses coop houses are very popular as places to live.
12. It is more expensive to make a person to person telephone call than a station to station call.
13. We were going sixtyfive miles in a forty miles per hour zone.
14. When I became a college freshman, I ceased being a fun loving, care free, irresponsible teen ager.
15. After a five minute recess we resumed giving our ten minute speeches.
16. It is a two hundred mile drive from the university to my home.
17. The ivy covered walls and the tree lined walks make our college unusually attractive.
18. Since Henry was an air minded individual, his father gave him for his 21st birthday a twin motored airplane.
19. Through self interest alone Anglo American relations should always be friendly.
20. Next Friday the president elect will become the new president, and the present president will become an expresident.

THE APOSTROPHE

94. The apostrophe (') as a mark of separation is used to indicate the possessive case of nouns and of indefinite pronouns (*another, everybody, no one,* etc.). It is also used to mark omissions in contracted words and numerals and to indicate the plurals of letters and numbers. Since the apostrophe is used only as part of a word, its use is not so much a matter of *spelling* as of *punctuation*.

94a. Use an apostrophe and <u>s</u> to form the possessive of a noun (singular or plural) not ending in <u>s</u>.

> The *doctor's* car is waiting at the door.
> Our fire department is ready for service at a *second's* notice.
> This store sells *men's, women's,* and *children's* shoes.
> Mr. *Smith's* office is on the second floor.

94b. Use an apostrophe alone to form the possessive of a plural noun ending in <u>s</u>.

The principle applies to both common and proper names: boys', dogs', doctors', days', weeks', the Smiths'.

> *Students'* attitude toward activities is not quite the same as their *professors'* attitude.
> During my two *weeks'* vacation I worked in a store selling *boys'* clothing.
> The *Smiths'* vacation was one that we all envied.

94c. Use the apostrophe alone, or the apostrophe with <u>s</u>, to form the possessive of singular nouns ending in <u>s</u>.

This principle applies usually to proper names. Most common nouns ending their singular in *s* are the names of nonhuman objects and form their possessive with an *of* phrase (see Section 75k).

> On *the cover of my atlas* (not *the atlas' cover*) was a drawing of the world.

One-syllable proper names ending in an *s* sound add an apostrophe and *s:*

> *Keats's* sonnets are among my favorites, but I've never cared much for Karl *Marx's* books.
> Robert *Burns's* cottage is a shrine in Scotland.

In words of more than one syllable ending in *s*, add the apostrophe only:

> Every student of Greek knows *Aristophanes'* comedies and *Demosthenes'* orations.

Some words not ending in *s* but having an *s*-sound ending also add only the apostrophe:

Let's sing "Auld Lang Syne" for old *acquaintance'* sake.
or
For the sake *of old acquaintance* let's sing "Auld Lang Syne."
Note: *Horace's* name is a somewhat unusual one.

94d. **In compound nouns add the apostrophe and <u>s</u> to the element nearest the object possessed.**

John borrowed his *brother-in-law's* car.
I could not afford that *attorney-at-law's* fee.
Charge these goods to *John Brown, Jr.'s,* account.
I left the restaurant wearing *somebody else's* hat.

94e. **Add the apostrophe and <u>s</u> to the last member of a group to indicate joint possession.**

I always use *Mason and Brown's* sporting equipment.
Let's get a soda at *Johnson and Stover's* drug store.

NOTE: Indicate individual possession by using the possessive case of each element of the series.

I am interested in the *Army's* and *Navy's* recruiting campaigns.
Mary is a baby-sitter for *Mrs. Brown's* and *Mrs. Wilson's* children.

94f. **Use an apostrophe to indicate that letters or figures have been omitted.**

Father was a member of the class of *'34;* I'm a member of the class of *'59.*
I myself never met a body *comin'* through the rye.

Contractions—usually the word *not* combined with certain verbs or pronouns or nouns combined with certain verbs—provide common examples of this principle: *isn't, aren't, wasn't, weren't, hasn't, don't, doesn't, won't, he's, it's, they're, that's,* etc.

John's in New York now; Joe is coming next week.
When *you're* careful, you *shouldn't* have any trouble in catching your serious errors in writing.
Come now; you *don't* have to say, *"What's o'clock?" That's* a stilted way of saying *"What's* the time?"

94g.   Use an apostrophe and s to indicate the plurals of figures, letters, and words considered as words.

I have trouble making legible *8's*.
Uncrossed *t's* look like *l's;* undotted *i's* are read as *e's*.
Don't overuse *and's, but's,* and *for's* in your writing.
My father spent the first half of the *1940's* in uniform.

94h.   Do not use the apostrophe in forming the plural of nouns.

Wrong: The *Smith's* are playing bridge with us tonight.
Right: The *Smiths* are playing bridge with us tonight.

Wrong: There have been more *boys'* than *girls'* among our freshman *student's* the past few *year's*.
Right: There have been more *boys* than *girls* among our freshman *students* the past few *years*.

94i.   Do not use the apostrophe to form the possessive case of the personal and relative pronouns.

Wrong:		Right:	
	our's		ours
	ours'		ours
	your's		yours
	yours'		yours
	his'		his
	her's		hers
	hers'		hers
	it's		its
	their's		theirs
	theirs'		theirs
	who's		whose

NOTE: *Never* use the apostrophe with the possessive *its*—one of the most common errors in student writing. *Its* is the possessive form of *it; it's* is the contraction for *it is*.

When a dog wags *its* tail, that's a sign *it's* happy.

94j.   Use the apostrophe and s to form the possessive case of indefinite pronouns.

The possessive case of such indefinite pronouns is illustrated as follows:

one's	another's
someone's	other's (plural, others')
anyone's	either's
no one's	neither's
each's	neither one's

You must have your father or mother sign this application; *either one's* (or *either's*) signature is satisfactory.
Everybody's business is usually *nobody's* business.

EXERCISES

A. Encircle all the apostrophes on a page of selected prose and give the reason for each.

B. Where are apostrophes needed in the following sentences? Why?

1. Tonights paper says that cooler weather is forecast for tomorrow.
2. The typical college students social life is of an informal kind.
3. One of the Queens Court was my sisters roommate.
4. Some people carry a rabbits foot for good luck.
5. An engineer and a mechanic are no good at doing each others jobs.
6. I am not exactly stingy, but I do like to get my moneys worth.
7. My best friends name is most unusual.
8. Since my parents marriage they have been saving steadily to buy their own home.
9. If you break a mirror, you will have seven years bad luck.
10. I hope sometime to be a buyer in the womens department.
11. Occasionally a comet passes through the earths orbit.
12. One must learn to put some trust in ones own judgment.
13. Sometimes my car has acted like a "buckin broncho."
14. After last years game we went home for the week end.
15. Now lets examine the other side of the question.
16. I wont let my parents down if I can help it.
17. In 1 or 2 days time you are able to meet people easily.
18. I begin studying every night at 7 oclock.
19. "Get up, Bill, were going hunting."
20. Will you make good in college? Its up to you.

C. Apostrophes are misused in the following sentences. Make the necessary corrections and tell why.

1. In college do not neglect your study's for activities.
2. Quebec, with it's French culture and beautiful scenery, is extremely charming.

673

3. Our students range from those who's parents are factory workers or farm laborers to those who's parents own the factories and farms.
4. Our's is one of the newer consolidated high schools.
5. My sister, who is 5 year's old, is usually the life of the party.
6. My thought's would wander to baseball during the class hour.
7. Our city has lost its' friendliness, and rolls up its' sidewalks at 10 o'clock at night.
8. This magazine is very attractive with its' clear print and beautiful illustrations.
9. I am not an authority on the actions of instructors' in their classrooms.
10. Those are the reason's why Stafford has such good teams.
11. My dictionary is the most used book I own, and I'm sure everyone has used their's many times.
12. Occupations in our town range from steel mill employee's to farmers.
13. I believe that the tour of the library served it's purpose.
14. One of the more interesting points in the Easter Parade is the womens' hats.
15. Attached to this letter are a few samples of the companys' labels.
16. I am certainly thankful that I am a farmers' son.
17. My father is a teacher in one of our local high school's.
18. On Friday a report of each students' class standing will be made.
19. A typed letter always shows the secretarys' initials.
20. After 2 day's fishing, I returned tired, happy, fish-laden.

QUOTATION MARKS

95. Quotation marks, double (". . .") and single ('. . .'), are solely marks of enclosure for words, phrases, clauses, sentences, and paragraphs. By definition, *quotation* is repeating what someone has said or written, but the marks themselves have several specialized uses.

In some books, magazines, and newspapers either no quotation marks at all or single quotation marks are printed where, according to rule, double ones would be used. Neither of these practices is any criterion because, in this country at least, they are usually experiments in typography or a kind of affectation.

The following principles explain and illustrate the conventional uses of quotation marks.

95a. Use quotation marks to enclose every complete direct quotation.

A direct quotation is the exact words of the person quoted, the original speaker or writer.

> John asked, "What time shall I come?"
> "Dinner will be served at 7," replied Mary.

95b. Use quotation marks to enclose each part of an interrupted direct quotation.

> "Father," I said, "I need 10 dollars."
> "You do," said Father, "and just why do you need 10 dollars?"

The *he said* or *said he* part, or its equivalent, inserted within a quotation is preceded by a comma, unless a question mark or exclamation point is required. It is followed by a comma, unless a stronger mark—period or semicolon—is demanded by the grammatical elements. The test: What mark would be used if the *he said* were omitted? Use that mark after the inserted part indicating the speaker.

> Joe Smith is a friend of mine, but I haven't seen him for 5 years.
> "Joe Smith is a friend of mine," I said, "but I haven't seen him for 5 years."

> There is no vacancy at present; however, we will keep your name on file.
> "There is no vacancy at present," the employment director said; "however, we will keep your name on file."

> I bought my hat at Johnson's Stores. It was on sale.
> "I bought my hat at Johnson's Stores," Henry told us. "It was on sale."

95c. In dialogue, use a separate paragraph for every change of speaker. (See also Section 29a.)

> "Oh, this isn't a final farewell! You must come in ten years' time and we'll compare notes . . ."
> She laughed.
> "I shall always see your movements chronicled in the newspapers, so we shall not be quite sundered; and you will hear of me perhaps."

"Yes, I hope you will be very successful."
She was looking at him, with her eyes wide open, from head to foot. He turned to the chair where his coat hung.
"Can't I help you put it on?"
"Oh, no, thank you."
He put it on.
"Button the throat," she said; "the room is warm."
—OLIVER SCHREINER, "The Buddhist Priest's Wife"

95d. **If a direct quotation extends for several paragraphs, use quotation marks at the beginning of each paragraph but at the end of <u>only</u> the last paragraph.**

95e. **In formal writing or in good informal writing use quotation marks to enclose words which suggest a widely different level of usage.**

If a word is appropriate, no quotation marks should be used as a form of apology. If it is not appropriate, the expression can usually be altered. In some instances, however, you may wish to shift to an expression having a specific, limited usage or usage label in order to communicate meaning realistically, exactly, or emphatically. Such expressions may be illiteracies, slang, difficult technical words, or common words with a technical meaning (see Sections, 54, 57, 58, 59, 61).

The recommendation that seemed most "cockeyed" came from the college president himself.
The conductor of the symphony was, in my opinion, a "stuffed shirt."

Do not rely upon this use of quotation marks as an excuse for inexact choice of words. Find the word that means exactly what you wish to say (see Section **60**). Also do not sprinkle your writing with quotation marks around words or expressions; enclose only those that would puzzle or mislead your reader. Words labeled *colloquial* in your dictionary are in good informal use and are not enclosed in quotation marks.

When words or expressions are enclosed in quotation marks in accordance with Section **95e**, commas are *not* used around them unless required for other reasons. Note the examples above and see also Section **88b**.

676

95f. Use quotation marks to enclose chapter headings, titles of articles, titles of short stories, and the like, when used in a body of prose.

When both chapter heading and book are mentioned, or title and magazine, the latter should be indicated by italics (see Section **96a**).

> For such information consult the chapter, "Private Preparatory Schools," in the *American Educational Directory.*
> John B. Martin's article, "There Goes Upper Michigan," in a recent issue of *Harper's Magazine,* deals with the passing of an era in the realm of vacation lands.

If there is no chance of confusion, quotation marks may be used instead of italics to indicate the names of ships, trains, airplanes, and the like, but the use of italics is preferred (see Section **96a**).

> "The City of Los Angeles" leaves the Union Station at nine o'clock.
> We have booked passage to England on the "Queen Mary."

95g. Use single quotation marks to enclose a quotation within a quotation.

> "Tell me," Father asked Mother after the wedding, "whether the bride said, 'I promise to obey.'"
> Our instructor said, "When you say, 'I'll turn in my theme tomorrow,' I expect it to be turned in tomorrow, not next week."

On the very rare occasions when it is necessary to punctuate a quotation within a quotation within a quotation, the order is double marks, single marks, double marks: ". . . . '. . . ". . . ." . . .' . . . ."

> The speaker said: "I shall quote from a letter of a Civil War veteran: 'When I was on sentry duty in Washington, a tall gaunt man stopped one day and said, "Good morning, soldier. How goes it?" It was Abraham Lincoln who thus greeted me.'"

95h. Use quotation marks always in pairs.

Since quotation marks are marks of enclosure, they are used in pairs. Be sure that they come at both the beginning and the end of the quotation.

Wrong: "I like football better than baseball, he said, and I like tennis better than either."

Right: "I like football better than baseball," he said, "and I like tennis better than either."

Remember also that quotation marks come at the beginning of each new paragraph of a speech or extended quotation, but the concluding quotation marks, closing the quotation, do not come until the end of the last quoted paragraph.

95i.   Place quotation marks correctly with reference to other marks.

1. The comma and the period come *inside* the quotation marks. This principle applies even when only the last word before the comma or the period is enclosed.

> "I need your help now," she said. "I need it more than ever."
> Some praised the performance as "excellent," and others thought it was only "fair."

2. Every question mark, exclamation point, or dash comes *outside* the quotation marks unless it is part of the quotation.

> Did she say, "I have enough money"?
> She asked, "Have I enough money?"
> "Have I enough money?" she asked.
> What is meant by "dog eat dog"?
> That is demonstrably a "pip"!
> "It's a 'pip'!" he stated firmly.

The question mark—one question mark—comes inside the quotation marks when both the nonquoted and the quoted elements are questions:

Wrong: Did Father ask, "Have you enough money?"?
Right: Did Father ask, "Have you enough money?"

3. Semicolon and colon come *outside* the quotation marks.

> Read E. B. White's "Walden"; it is, I think, his best essay.
> Look up the following in "A Glossary of Famous People": Theodore Roosevelt, Woodrow Wilson, Charles E. Hughes.

95j.   Do not put quotation marks around an indirect quotation.

In an indirect quotation, a writer or speaker puts into his own words the words of some one else or, at a later time, his own words.

Wrong:	The Employment Manager said that "I should report for work on Monday."
Right (indirect):	The Employment Manager said that I should report for work on Monday.
Right (direct):	The Employment Manager said, "Report for work on Monday."
Right (indirect):	I replied that I should be happy to attend the dinner.
Right (direct):	I replied, "I shall be happy to attend the dinner."

Note that the following are or can serve as indirect quotations:

> He answered yes.
> To a question of that kind I shall have to say no.

Direct: He answered, "Yes."
> To a question of that kind I say, "No."

95k. Do not confuse in one sentence a direct and an indirect quotation.

The confusion arises from a blending of direct and indirect questions (see Section **36b,** also).

Confused:	I asked him what grade did he receive in the course.
Indirect:	I asked him what grade he had received in the course.
Direct:	I asked him, "What grade did you receive in the course?"

Confused:	Mary asked her adviser hadn't she already obtained credit for History 12.
Indirect:	Mary asked her adviser whether she had not already obtained credit for History 12.
Direct:	Mary asked her adviser, "Haven't I already obtained credit for History 12?"

95l. Do not enclose in quotation marks the title at the beginning of a theme.

The only exception to this principle is the use of a quotation as the theme title.

Usual title:	The Dangers of Too Little Learning
Quotation as title:	"A Little Learning Is a Dangerous Thing"

EXERCISES

A. Study several pages of a short story or novel using dialogue. Examine the use of quotation marks and their position with other marks of punctuation. Discuss any uses which are not in accord with the principles given in Section **95**.

B. In the following sentences make quotation marks, capitals, and commas conform to commonly accepted principles:

1. Can this really be happening to me? I said to myself.
2. When I was "small" and our family lived in Boston, we bought a "summer house" at Bar Harbor.
3. Her lips said no, but her eyes said "yes."
4. There are three answers: yes, sir, no, sir, and no excuse, sir.
5. The soldier replied, the president is dead.
6. Who am I? and Why was I born? and How are other people thinking and living? are sample questions that literature should suggest.
7. Coach Smith said, "that he could not have asked for better officiating."
8. I think that the theme, "Prejudice", makes an important point.
9. Why, I never have caught poison ivy and I never will I said to John Woods.
10. The home of 600 happy people and a few soreheads—this is the sign that the traveler sees as he enters my town.
11. Our room was cool, and we slept like "logs."
12. Three outstanding themes were The Courtship of John, by Mary Consel; Christmas in the Loop, by Harry Whitesell; and Sea Trip, by Joseph Thompson.
13. There is no time for parley said the orator there is no time for deliberation and soft words.
14. I have read Keats' The Eve of St. Agnes and I think I have never come across a better poem.
15. After you leave college and obtain a job the adviser told Henry you will find that coming in late and not appearing once or twice a week will have serious consequences.

ITALICS

96. Indicate words that you wish to italicize, i.e., in print, slanting letters, by underlining them once, whether you typewrite or write in longhand. Quotation marks may also be used to set off words that would be italicized in print, but since these marks have various other uses (see Section **95**), the system of underlining is preferable.

96a. Use italics (underlining) to indicate titles of magazines, newspapers, books, long poems, plays, motion pictures, and the names of ships, trains, and airplanes.

I came from California to New York on the streamlined trains, the *City of Denver* and the *City of Philadelphia,* and sailed for England on the *Queen Mary.* From the ship's library I borrowed a copy of of *Newsweek,* The New York *Times,* and Thomas Hardy's novel, *The Return of the Native.* As I was reading, I saw *Lucky Lady III* fly overhead on the first leg of her world flight. Every night some famous movie was shown, like *The Birth of a Nation, Duel in the Sun,* and *It Happened One Night.*

1. When you use both the title of an article or story and the magazine in which it appears, in order to distinguish them use quotation marks to enclose the former and italicize the latter; apply the same principle to the chapter title of a book and the book. But do not italicize the title of your theme used in the position of the title. Note that the titles of articles and short stories are not italicized, in their position as titles.

Be sure to read Wilbur Carter's article, "Non-Military Uses of Atomic Energy," in *Harper's Magazine.*

Your parents will enjoy reading Chapter 17, "How to Stretch Dollars," in Allen Brown's book, *The Quest for Security.*

2. Do not italicize the name of the city in the title of a newspaper: the Philadelphia *World-Bugle.*

3. Do not omit an article which forms part of the title: *The Merchant of Venice* (not *Merchant of Venice*); *A Fable for Critics* (not *Fable for Critics*).

4. Do not add an article to a title if none appears in the original work: Shakespeare's *Two Gentlemen of Verona* (not *The Two Gentlemen of Verona*).

5. According to convention, the names of the books of the Bible are not italicized: Matthew 14:12.

96b. Use italics (underlining) to indicate foreign words or phrases.

There is a *je ne sais quoi* quality about this painting.
The foreign student in America must work out a *modus vivendi.*
A vicious cartoon of that kind has no *raison d'etre.*

Foreign words which have not been naturalized in English should be either italicized (underlined) or enclosed in quotation marks. Your dictionary will tell you whether foreign words and phrases are naturalized, i.e., are in good English use, or whether they are still considered distinctly foreign.

96c. Use italics (underlining) to refer to a word, letter, or number spoken of as such.

> Your undotted *i*'s look exactly like *e*'s.
> You have written *6* every time that you meant to write *9*.
> I stupidly wrote *Rode* 39 when I had meant to write *Road* 39.
> The four most frequently misused pairs of words in English are the following: *to* and *too*, *it's* and *its*, *their* and *there*, and *your* and *you're*.

96d. Use italics (underlining) to emphasize a word, a phrase, or a statement.

> *Always* sign your name to a letter.
> Never, *under any conditions*, keep poisonous substances in your medicine cabinet.

Used sparingly, italics for emphasis are effective. Overused, they become monotonous and ineffective.

EXERCISES

Recopy the following sentences, underlining the words that should be italicized. What are your reasons?

1. A good example of a historical novel is Charles Dickens' A Tale of Two Cities. A Tale of Two Cities is a story of the French Revolution.
2. I should like to become a reporter on some large city newspaper like the St. Louis Post-Dispatch.
3. On our campus the title of the magazine of freshman themes is Trial Flight; at the University of Illinois the title of the magazine is The Green Caldron.
4. In her music my sister was an élève of the celebrated Maestro Divani.
5. Everybody in our town reads the Daily Mining Gazette.

6. The New York Times is kept in our library on microfilm.

7. The American College Dictionary, Webster's New Collegiate Dictionary, and the New World Dictionary are sold in our college bookstore.

8. The once well-known magazine, Collier's, was published in my home town, Springfield, Ohio.

9. Off Marseilles, France, lies the island bastion, Chateau d'If, part of the setting of Dumas' The Count of Monte Cristo.

10. Mason Pryor, the columnist on the Richmond Clarion, says that Escape isn't as good a motion picture as its advance publicity predicted.

11. Some people say au revoir and some say auf Wiedersehen; I'll stick with the plain, old-fashioned American good-by.

12. Hollywood changes the titles of many movies, but the movie, Wuthering Heights, bore the same title as the novel, Wuthering Heights.

13. Among the news items in the New York Herald Tribune was one that the river tug John Henry Mason was rammed by the Cunard liner, the Queen Elizabeth.

14. Railroads are using novel expressions; for example, the City of San Francisco sails from Union Station in Chicago every evening at 5 o'clock.

15. Careful proofreading will prevent such errors as writing here for hear, know for no, and women for woman.

CAPITALS

97. The applications of capitalization are so numerous that rules or principles cannot be given to apply to every possible example. Stylebooks of various publishing firms usually contain from 20 to 40 pages dealing with capitals. For the student-writer a few underlying principles may be helpful.

97a. Capitalize each important word in titles of themes, articles, books, plays, motion pictures, poems, magazines, newspapers, musical compositions, songs, etc.

Capitalized in accordance with this principle are the first and each important word in titles, but within the titles do not capitalize articles, prepositions, and conjunctions, unless they consist of five or more letters.

Autumn Days on the Farm

The Manufacture of Cosmetics

The Value of the Liberal Arts

A Journey Through Louisiana

Caught Between Storms

The Stars Pass By

Steinbeck's *The Grapes of Wrath*

Hardy's *The Return of the Native*

A Midsummer Night's Dream

Gray's *Elegy Written in a Country*
Churchyard

The Saturday Evening Post

The Moonlight Sonata

If you were to write an essay on "The Value of the Liberal Arts" for *The Journal of Engineering Education,* you might well include a critical discussion of Sheridan's play, *The School for Scandal,* Rossini's opera, *The Barber of Seville,* and the Steinbeck motion picture, *The Grapes of Wrath.*

97b. Capitalize the first word of every sentence and the first word of every quoted sentence.

The first part of this rule is illustrated on every printed page.

Can you attend the meeting tonight?

Walter said, "Don't miss seeing that movie."

When only a part of a direct quotation is included within a sentence, it is usually not begun with a capital letter.

The press secretary, after a talk with Dr. Snyder, said that the President was "fine," and added that the doctor "just didn't want to take any chances with the flu."

97c. Capitalize the first word of every line of poetry.

My favorite simile occurs in the second stanza of Wordsworth's "She Dwelt Among the Untrodden Ways":
A violet by a mossy stone
Half hidden from the eye!
—Fair as a star, when only one
Is shining in the sky.

The foregoing illustrates traditional poetry. Some modern poetry is written without capital letters. If and when you quote poetry, use the capitalization that is used in the poem.

97d. Capitalize proper nouns.

These include:

1. Names of people and titles used in place of specific persons:

William Shakespeare, Theodore Roosevelt, the President, the Senator, the Treasurer, the General, Mr. Chairman, Father, Mother.

2. Names of countries, states, regions, localities, other geographic areas, and the like: United States, England, Pennsylvania, the Far East, the Dust Bowl, the Midwest, the Solid South, the Rocky Mountains, the Sahara Desert, the Mississippi River, Lake Michigan.

3. Names of streets: Michigan Boulevard, Fifth Avenue, Ross Street, Ravinia Road.

4. Names of the Deity and personal pronouns referring to Him: God, Heavenly Father, Son of God, Jesus Christ, Savior, His, Him, Thy, Thine.

5. Names for the Bible and other sacred writings: Bible, the Scriptures, Book of Genesis, Revelations, Koran.

6. Names of religions and religious groups: Protestantism, Catholicism, Presbyterian, Jesuit, Unitarian.

7. Names of the days and the months (but *not* the seasons) Monday, Tuesday, etc.; January, February, etc.; summer, winter, autumn, fall, spring.

8. Names of schools, colleges, universities: Hill School, Morton Grade School, Horace Mann High School, Kentucky Military Institute, Wabash College, Cornell University.

9. Names of historic events, eras, and holidays: Revolutionary War, Christian Era, Middle Ages, Renaissance, the Fourth of July, Labor Day, Thanksgiving.

10. Names of races, organizations, and members of each: Indian, Negro, Malay, League of Women Voters, American Academy of Science, National League, New York Giants, Big Ten Conference, an Elk, a Shriner, a Socialist.

11. Vivid personifications: Fate, Star of Fortune, Destiny, the power of Nature, the paths of Glory, the chronicles of Time.

12. Trade names: Studebaker Commander, Fordor sedan, Bon Ami, Ry-Krisp, Wheaties.

13. All names similar or comparable to those in the foregoing 12 groups.

97e. Capitalize a common noun or adjective when it is a part of or helps to make a proper name.

> Missouri River, Rocky Mountains, Wall Street, Fifth Avenue, Blackstone Theater, Washington High School, Swarthmore College, New York University, Roosevelt Dam, Yosemite National Park, Lake Erie, U.S. Highway 40, Route 33, Room 117, Chapter 26.

Common nouns and adjectives used alone are not capitalized: river, mountain, street, avenue, theater, high school, college, university, dam, park, lake, etc.

> He is not a professor.
> This is Professor Smith.

> My father is a dean in a college.
> My father is Dean Williams of Seneca University.

> These students attend the local high school.
> John is a graduate of Rocktown High School.

> The street in front of our house needs paving.
> There are vacant houses on Forest Street.

> The Brenta River is a well-known river in northern Italy, just outside Venice.
> I have explored many of the rivers in our country.
> The Holland Tunnel runs under the Hudson River.

> The Great Smoky Mountains are well worth a visit.
> The mountains in eastern Tennessee are known as the Great Smokies.

97f. Capitalize words derived from proper nouns.

> Shakespearian, American, Episcopalian, Biblical, Scriptural, Italian, Pennsylvanian, British.

Note two important specific applications and a list of exceptions.
1. The word *English* is always capitalized in reference to language and literature as well as its geographical application.
2. The first personal pronoun "I" is *always* capitalized.
3. Some proper nouns and derivatives of proper nouns (the number is approaching 200) have been used so frequently that they are

now considered common and are not capitalized. When in doubt, consult your dictionary. A fair sampling of such a list includes:

anglicize	macadam roads
bessemer steel	mentor
brazil nut	oxford shoes
brussels sprouts	pasteurize
castile soap	plaster of paris
chinaware	platonic friend
derby hat	quisling
english (spin imparted to	quixotic
ball)	scotch plaid
french dressing	turkish towel
german silver	venetian blind
india ink and rubber	vienna bread
italicize	watt (electric unit)

97g. Avoid careless use of capitals.

Do not carelessly write small (lower-case) letters so large that they resemble capitals (upper-case letters). Your reader is disconcerted and confused by this carelessness.

97h. Avoid unnecessary use of capitals.

1. Do not capitalize names of points of the compass unless they refer to a specific section.

Correct: My home is in the East.
John lives west of the Allegheny Mountains.
I should like to live in the southern part of California.
Walk two blocks west; then turn north.

2. Do not capitalize nouns of kinship unless they are used as a substitute for a proper name. When preceded by an article or a possessive, they are common nouns.

Correct: My father is a dean.
At Seneca College, Father (i.e., Mr. Smith) is Dean of Men.
My sister thinks I am quiet, but Grandma and Mother say that I talk too much.
Every autumn my cousin Harry and I go hunting.
Every autumn Cousin Harry and I go hunting.

3. Do not capitalize a noun or adjective if the reference is to any one of a class of persons or things rather than a specific person or

thing. For example, do not capitalize names of professions or occupations.

Wrong: My roommate is studying Engineering and expects to become a Teacher; I hope to become either a Doctor or a Dentist.

In capitalizing names of classes or college class members as members, follow the principle of consistency. One suggestion is that you do not capitalize the noun or adjective indicating college class members but that you do capitalize the name of a specific class.

Four of us are sharing a double room; Joe is a freshman, I am a sophomore, Bill is a junior, and Mike is a senior. On the floor below us every resident is a member of the Senior class and on the floor above us every one is a member of the Freshman class.

4. Do not capitalize names of general college subjects unless they are proper names, but titles of specific courses are capitalized:

Next year I shall have courses in history, Spanish, and journalism, and although I do not like science courses, I shall be required to take Mathematics 2 and Biology 12.

5. Do not capitalize unimportant words in titles (Section **97a**), or the first word of part of a direct quotation (Section **97b**), or common nouns and adjectives not part of or helping to make a proper name (Section **97e**).

EXERCISES

A. Encircle all the capitals on a page of prose selected from a textbook or magazine. Explain the reason for each capital.

B. Rewrite the following sentences, making the misuse or nonuse of capitals conform to the principles stated in Section **97**.

1. My sister has a good position as a private secretary in an Insurance firm.
2. Our city is located at the junction of U.S. route 40 and state highway 29.
3. I have had 4 years of english in high school.
4. There are many fine beaches along the shores of lake Michigan.
5. I completed the life-saving course given by the red cross.
6. In high school we studied poems, short Stories, a few plays, Essays, and a classic story.

7. The careless driver usually says, "my car let me down; it wasn't my fault."
8. I studied Reading, Spelling, and Writing all through Grade School and High School.
9. As we sit down to dinner, my 5-year-old Sister usually creates a problem.
10. In our city, the streets running North and South have numbers, and the East and West streets have names.
11. I always gave the answer, "sorry, I'm too busy."
12. My family consists of my Mother, my Father, and my Brother, Grant.
13. In Winter, Summer, Fall, or Spring, the Great Smoky Mountains are rich in atmosphere.
14. In High School, I won my letter in Football, Basketball, Baseball, and Tennis.
15. People will say, "that's the place I'd like to live."
16. Frankfort is located in the center of Clinton county, about 45 miles North-West of Indianapolis and 30 miles South-East of this University.
17. All the Sororities and Fraternities have open house during homecoming.
18. When I saw the magazine, I said, "these stories will be interesting."
19. I shall see you at the game on saturday.
20. Many Churches and Cathedrals are decorated for Good Friday and Easter.

C. Directions given in B.

1. Both my Father and my Mother were born in New Jersey.
2. My Education thus far in the college of pharmacy has not been too extensive.
3. I began to wonder, "why is it necessary to go to college?"
4. For the past 2½ years I have worked in a Drug Store.
5. I have chosen Architecture as my major Field.
6. My present courses consist of english, zoology, algebra, chemistry, and dairy science.
7. I hope to spend a few days of my Spring vacation in Washington, D.C.
8. For a period of years I had a perfect record of attendance at sunday school.
9. My mother's ancestors came down the Ohio river on a flatboat and settled a few miles from the Mississippi river.

10. Three blocks North of the town square is our railroad station.
11. Ferries are still used to carry passengers across the Hudson river.
12. I was 18 years old last may.
13. We walked down Chicago's state street and then over to michigan boulevard, comparable to fifth avenue in New York City.
14. I pretended that there were always indians around to fight.
15. Our college publishes a little magazine of themes written by freshman english students.
16. In reading the bible, I turn to the new testament more often than I turn to the old testament.
17. On easter sunday, easter lilies are in many homes and their fragrance fills the room.
18. My Brother and I, being twins, always hunted together.
19. My dictionary has a section on Orthography and one on Punctuation.
20. There are over 5,000 Biographical names and 7,000 Geographical names in the two lists.

ABBREVIATIONS

98a. Use only acceptable abbreviations in formal writing or in informal writing.

In all writing intended for the information and convenience of a reader, avoid all abbreviations that would be puzzling or unusual to him; write out words and expressions in full, unless condensation seems necessary or the spelled-out words are unconventional like *Mister* for *Mr.* or *Missus* for *Mrs.*

In the following examples, exaggerated for illustration, puzzling and unusual abbreviations occur:

Incorrect: A new sec. is to be elected to replace the sec.-treas. who has resigned.

Many a chem. prof. grades too severely; many a lit. prof. grades too easily.

Meet me in the Penn. Station Wed. p.m.

Chicago, Ill., lies n.e. of the Miss. R.

1. Themes and other college written work are or should be formal writing or good idiomatic informal writing. Usually, use abbreviations only in footnotes and bibliographies of term and research papers. Specifically and as a general rule, avoid in continuous prose the abbreviations for:

a. Names of states, rivers, mountains, etc.: Ala., Pa., Ill. R., Appalach. Mtns.

b. Parts of geographic names: Ft. Wayne (for Fort Wayne), N. Dakota (for North Dakota), Pt. Arthur (for Port Arthur). (*Saint* is abbreviated before a place name: St. Louis, St. Bonaventure.)

c. Christian names: Jos. (for Joseph), Benj. (for Benjamin), Thos. (for Thomas).

d. Names of months and days: Jan., Feb., Sun., Mon.

e. Most titles: Prof., Gen., Lieut., Pres.

f. Names of school and college subjects: chem., math., ed., P.E.

g. Words denoting length, time, weight, or capacity: in., ft., yd., sec., min., hr., mo., yr., oz., lb., pt., qt., gal., pk., bu., bbl.

h. Miscellaneous words like st. for street, ave. for avenue, blvd. for boulevard, dr. for drive, pl. for place, r. for river, mt. for mountain; a.m. and p.m. (as substitutes for *morning* and *afternoon:* "this a.m. and p.m."); & for *and*.

2. Certain very common abbreviations are permissible and should be used instead of the full word. These are usually conventional titles invariably used before names of people and the letters after the names indicating educational degrees:

Mr. William Brown; Mrs. John Smith; Messrs. William Brown and John Smith; Dr. Albert Jones; Hon. James E. Mason; Rev. Gordon Graham (but note: *The Honorable* James E. Mason, *The Reverend* Gordon Graham, but *never* Rev. Smith).

William Brown, A.B., A.M.; John Smith, Ph.D., LL.D.; Rev. Gordon Graham, D.D.

Harry Jones, M.D., and his brother, Henry Jones, D.D.S., share an office.
William Brown, Sr., and William Brown, Jr., were elected delegates.

Other necessary abbreviations include the following: a.m. and p.m. or A.M. and P.M., with numbers (7 a.m., 8:25 a.m., 2.10 p.m.); F. (for Fahrenheit); C. (for Centigrade), B.C. (before Christ); A.D. (anno Domini, i.e., in the year of our Lord).

NOTE: B.C. follows the year, A.D. precedes it: 73 B.C., A.D. 1956.

98b. Do not use contractions in formal writing.

A contraction is a form of abbreviation: a word written with an apostrophe to indicate the omission of a letter. Usually considered as colloquial expressions (proper in speech but questionable in writing), such contractions as *won't, don't, can't, shouldn't, wasn't,* and the like, seem out of place in formal writing. See Sections **55, 64.**

In reporting dialogue or conversation, however, a writer uses contractions correctly to convey the exact words of the speaker. Do not avoid the use of contractions and other colloquialisms to the extent of making your reports of conversation seem artificial and forced.

98c. Use a period after every abbreviation.

There are only a few exceptions to this rule. *No abbreviating period* is used after:

1. Contractions such as *don't, won't, isn't, haven't,* etc.
2. The ordinal numbers when written *1st, 2nd, 35th,* etc.
3. Shortened forms like *ad, phone, exam, lab* (see Section **70**).
4. Nicknames such as Bill, Joe, Al, etc.
5. A few specialized abbreviations, including broadcasting companies and stations: per cent or percent (but not %), TV, ABC, NBC, CBS, WEND, WBBM, WILL, KDAD, etc.
6. Certain unions, associations, and government divisions and agencies: AAF, AEC, AMVETS, FBI, FTC, NAM, TVA, UNESCO, VA, etc.

For similar abbreviations, the use or omission of periods is optional; for others, periods are required. When in doubt, follow the punctuation given in your dictionary.

EXERCISES

Correct all errors in the use of abbreviations in the following sentences:

1. I tho't you might like to read some of the themes in our freshman magazine.
2. My classes include English, Math., Psyc., Zoology, Soc., and P.E.
3. The snow last winter was at one time 4 ft. deep.
4. We will not be able to move into our apt. before the a.m.

5. Our high school had a good college prep. course.
6. Every spring people from all over the country visit D.C. to see the cherry blossoms.
7. Tom, Henry, & I drive home every other Saturday.
8. I have a room on College Ave. about three blocks east of the Union Bldg.
9. My one brother, Bobby, is 7 yrs. old.
10. I like our gym, and if I paid more attention to P.E., I'd be in better physical condition.
11. Since I have not lived in the state of Pa. very long, I do not have an official residence there.
12. The assignments in our English comp. book deal with all phases of writing.
13. Our president will be away from the campus in late Jan. and early Feb.
14. Some families have the same M.D. and the same D.D.S. for years.
15. My older brother is in his 4th yr. at the Univ. of Minn., but he is still not quite certain whether, after college, he will join the FBI or work on his M.S.
16. The parade down Penn. Ave. was something to behold; I should like to be in Wash., D.C., and see another.
17. I was born in Elwood, Mich., 19 years ago, but grew up in Lakeside, O.
18. I am glad that I have Mister Davis for my English teacher; my roommate is just as glad that he has Missus Wilson.
19. Our various homes have been in Evanston, Ill., Gary, Ind., St. Louis, Mo., and New Orleans, La.
20. Manufacturers of household appliances rely on women in the home ec field to test their products.

NUMBERS

99. The practice of writing words for numbers or of using figures is not a matter of correctness or incorrectness; it is one of convention and custom. The following suggestions are adapted from the United States Government Printing Office *Style Manual,* which follows this policy: "Most rules for the use of numerals are based on the general principle that numerals are more readily comprehended by the reader, particularly in technical, scientific, or statistical matter. However, for special reasons numbers are spelled out in indicated instances." (For the use of commas with four or more figures, see Section 88l.)

99a. Use words to represent numbers in special uses:

1. Isolated numbers less than 10.

> At least three men should be nominated for secretary.
> We can choose one of six magazines to use in this class.

2. Indefinite expressions or round numbers. (Figures are also acceptable, however.)

> This theater will seat two or three thousand persons.
> or
> This theater will seat 2 or 3,000 persons.

> The mid-fifties will probably be known as the atomic fifties.
> or
> The mid-50's will probably be known as the atomic 50's.

> Right now I could use a hundred dollars.
> or
> Right now I could use $100.

> We have some forty cows and about six hundred chickens on our farm.
> or
> We have some 40 cows and about 600 chickens on our farm.

3. One number or related numbers at the beginning of a sentence.

> Three of our class officers are from the College of Engineering.
> Twenty to thirty students will be absent on an inspection trip to Detroit.

4. Numbers preceding a compound modifier containing a figure.

> To line this wall we need twelve ½-inch pieces of plywood.
> Our tent is supported by two 8-foot poles.

5. Fractions standing alone.

> Be sure that the plywood is one-half inch thick.
> I live about one-fourth of a mile from the campus.

6. Numbers used with serious and dignified subjects.

Pennsylvania is proud to be listed among the Thirteen Original Colonies.

This bill was given serious consideration in the Seventy-eighth Congress.

99b. Use figures to represent numbers in special uses:

1. Isolated numbers of 10 or more.

Only 45 ballots were cast in the class election.

The university is 10 times as large as it was in 1900.

2. Dates, including the day or the day and the year.

Please return the blank by June 1.

My parents were married on June 28, 1934.

I worked on a farm from July 1 to September 1, 1956.

The proper date-line for a letter is

February 1, 1956

or

1 February 1956 (no comma)

never 2/1/56

3. House, room, telephone, and postal zone numbers.

I live at 1607 Ravinia Road, Columbus 14, Ohio; my telephone number is Lawndale 82–2784.

Tomorrow this class will meet in Room 212, University Hall.

We are staying at the Greenbriar Hotel, Room 712.

4. Highway or comparable numbers.

Take U.S. Highway 40 into Columbus and turn north on Route 33.

Our best TV reception comes in over Channel 6.

Trains for Chicago leave on Track 3.

5. Measurements.

Standard stationery is 8½ by 11 inches in size.

Father is 42 years old, Mother is 39, and my baby sister is 6.

The white lines on a football field are 5 yards apart.

The parcel post package weighed 6 pounds 9 ounces.

¾-inch pipe   1-inch margin   5-foot pole

6. Time.

    8:00 a.m.   3:25 p.m.   half past 3
    10 o'clock (not: 10 o'clock a.m., or 10 a.m. in the morning)
    7 hours 9 minutes 19 seconds
    8 years 4 months 27 days
    6 days   3 minutes   2 months   9-hour day   5-day week

7. Percentage.

    10 percent   one-half of 1 percent   4¼ percent bonds
    Many students waste 15 to 20 percent of their time just fooling
    around.

8. Money.

    $4.55 $0.60   60 cents $6 per bushel   35 cents apiece

9. Chapters and page numbers.

    Chapter 12   See p. 144   pp. 312–15

Sometimes these numbers are represented by Roman numerals (see Section **99d** below).

99c. Use figure-and-letter combinations appropriately.

Occasionally, a writer needs to use figures and letters in combination, especially in expressing the ordinal numbers: first, 1st; second, 2nd or 2d; third, 3rd or 3d; fourth through twentieth, 4th, 9th, 12th, 18th, 20th; others as they apply, 21st, 33rd or 33d, 99th, etc.

Such combinations are appropriately used in tables, sometimes in numbering ideas in a paragraph or a succession of paragraphs, sometimes in dates—but not when the year follows immediately, and usually in expressing a numbered street from 10th on.

    Your May 15th letter (or your letter of May 15th) has been re-
    ceived.
    Your letter of May 15, 1956, has been received.
    121 North First Avenue
    Corner of Fifth Avenue and 10th Street
    49 East 33d Street   South 199th Street

    Please note that after June 1st my address will no longer be 12
    West Second Street; it will be 833 East 24th Street.

Notice, 1st, that *no* period follows the figure-and-letter combinations, and 2nd, that the principles about figures versus words (Sections **99a, b**) apply usually to figure-and-letter combinations.

99d. Use Roman numerals correctly.

Our numbers were once Roman letters used as numerals until the 10th century. Our present figures came to us from the Arabs and are called Arabic numerals. Although these Arabic numbers are generally preferable, Roman numerals still find occasional use in current writing, as in preparing outlines (Section **6**), numbering the preliminary pages of a book, occasionally marking the date for a year, and frequently indicating acts and scenes of plays, volume numbers of books and magazines, and chapter numbers of books.

Lower-case letters (sometimes small capitals) are used for preliminary pages and play scenes; capitals for book, volume, act, part, or an individual in a series.

> The preliminary pages in my textbook are numbered from v through xi.
>
> The article, "Grecian Architecture," is printed in Volume XII of the *Universal Encyclopedia.*
>
> George I, George II, and George III reigned in the 18th century, George V and George VI in the 20th.
>
> Prince Hal and Falstaff first appear in Act I, Scene ii, of Shakespeare's *Henry IV,* Part I.
>
> This imposing building bears the date when it was constructed— MDCCCLXXIV.

Notice in Table V, below, how Roman numerals are formed: "a repeated letter repeats its value; a letter placed after one of greater value adds to it; a letter placed before one of greater value subtracts from it; a dashline over a letter denotes multiplied by 1,000." (From United States Government Printing Office *Style Manual,* 1953 Edition, from which the "Roman Numerals" table is also taken.)

TABLE v. ROMAN NUMERALS

I	1	V	5
II	2	VI	6
III	3	VII	7
IV	4	VIII	8

TABLE V. **ROMAN NUMERALS**—(*Continued*)

IX	9	LXXXV	85
X	10	LXXXIX	89
XV	15	XC	90
XIX	19	XCV	95
XX	20	XCIX	99
XXV	25	C	100
XXIX	29	CL	150
XXX	30	CC	200
XXXV	35	CCC	300
XXXIX	39	CD	400
XL	40	D	500
XLV	45	DC	600
XLIX	49	DCC	700
L	50	DCCC	800
LV	55	CM	900
LIX	59	M	1,000
LX	60	MD	1,500
LXV	65	MM	2,000
LXIX	69	MMM	3,000
LXX	70	MMMM	4,000
LXXV	75	$\overline{\text{V}}$	5,000
LXXIX	79	$\overline{\text{M}}$	1,000,000
LXXX	80		

Dates

MDC	1600	MCMXX	1920
MDCC	1700	MCMXXX	1930
MDCCC	1800	MCMXL	1940
MCM or MDCCCC	1900	MCML	1950
MCMX	1910	MCMLX	1960

EXERCISES

Correct any errors in the use of numbers in the following sentences:

1. 113 University Street is my local address.
2. Father was born in France 43 years ago, and at the age of 21 came to this country.
3. During the depression my father worked for 35 cents an hour.
4. St. Louis, Missouri, is two hundred and sixty-five miles from my home.

5. I received my highest grades on my 3rd and 7th themes.
6. 5′ 4″, brown eyes, brown hair, and one hundred and six pounds—that's me.
7. My fraternity was too noisy, and I have moved to a private residence on 2nd street.
8. In our high school there were approximately seven hundred and forty-five students.
9. 8 of my summers have been spent in 4-H club work.
10. The worst flood in our community occurred in fifty-five.
11. I am dating this letter 4/14/57.
12. In this course we wrote 15 themes of approximately 350 words each. 350 words is the normal length of the themes written.
13. I live at twenty-seven seventeen Medford Street in Kansas City.
14. On November twenty-second nineteen hundred and thirty-nine I was born.
15. This house is a private home in which 6 other students and I are living.
16. Our city's population has grown from 45 thousand to 65 thousand.
17. The town of Tefft is located in Northern Indiana, 60 miles north of Lafayette and 40 miles south of Gary.
18. This year Father's business will celebrate its 25th anniversary.
19. 2 per cent of the citizens opposed the paving of Main Street.
20. The population of my town is about twenty-five hundred souls. The town lies about 25 miles south of Huntingdon on Highway Thirty-seven.

GENERAL EXERCISES

A. Choose any two pages from your book of readings or from a current magazine. Underline or encircle every mark of punctuation. Give a reason for each separate mark, or pair of marks, according to principles stated in the preceding sections. If any mark or pair of marks cannot be explained by those principles, copy the sentence, give its full documentation (author, title of article, title of magazine or book of readings, volume and/or page number), and send it to one of the handbook authors in a business letter (see pp. 709–732).

B. Punctuated in one way, the following sentences have one meaning; punctuated in another way, they have a different meaning. Punctuate each sentence in at least two ways.

1. I was so confused I thought I was going to flunk both chemistry and algebra.

2. Attention please Smith the director has a few words to say.
3. Whatever other people do or say or believe we do we say and we believe.
4. Mother said Father is always hopelessly late.
5. Look out behind Henry there's another car coming.
6. While we are preparing to eat Henry will you see that the tables are properly arranged?
7. At the last filling station we stopped asking where County Road 5 is.
8. Mother told me to call you Father.
9. The alibi he told us was foolproof.
10. The driver in the first car said the policeman did not yield the right of way.
11. My soul is a light house keeper.
12. Woman was made by God to be the helpmeet of man.
13. Mary said June is a good pianist.
14. Why did you ever marry Mother?
15. Some of the students I know have already gone home.
16. My intention to be perfectly honest was not carried out.
17. Merle my little brother is nine years old.
18. Today we are honoring Mrs. Wilson the mother of General Wilson and two gold-star mothers from Pennsylvania.
19. The statement he told us has never been questioned.
20. You should have asked Henry when the directions became involved.

C. Give two clear meanings, through punctuation, for each of the following sentences:

1. Henry has six year old rabbits for sale.
2. As you know I am attending Atwater University I am having a wonderful time here.
3. I have three hour lectures and four hour laboratory periods every week.
4. I think every one should follow the basic rule that is the Golden Rule on the highways.
5. The man eating lion at the circus fascinated me.
6. Why didn't you know there was a meeting of our committee last evening?
7. I'm never going to leave you honey.
8. Most people I know are in a hurry.
9. There are twenty odd students in this class.
10. I have always been a small town boy.

11. I bought some second-hand boats which were in good condition.
12. Tess usually took her baby to the field to help with the harvesting.
13. Every day occurrences of this kind get noticed in the newspapers.
14. On the way home I stopped believing that I had another errand to do.
15. Did you say Tom my roommate has been arrested for speeding?

GLOSSARY OF APPLIED PUNCTUATION

100. In applying to your writing the general and specific punctuation principles reviewed in the preceding pages, answer the following questions when you have a problem about punctuation:

1. Exactly what is here that requires punctuation? That is, what kinds of sentences? What kinds of elements within sentences? What kinds of relations between elements?

2. What purpose do I want my punctuation to serve? Termination? Introduction? Separation? Enclosure? Correctness? Clearness? Effectiveness?

3. What punctuation mark or marks will best accomplish that purpose?

When you are sure of the answer to the first question—"Exactly what is here that requires punctuation?"—use the following as a guide in answering the second and third questions. Figures in parentheses refer to sections providing detailed discussion and illustration.

1. **Abbreviations.** Use a period after a standard abbreviation. **(86d)**
2. **Absolute phrase** (nominative absolute). Use commas. **(88p)**
3. **Act—scene.** Separate by a colon. **(90f)**
4. **Adjectives.** Two or more adjectives modifying, coordinately, the same noun, separate by commas. See also **Series,** below. **(88i)**
5. **Adjective clauses.** See **Clauses, dependent,** below.
6. **Adverbial clauses.** See **Clauses, dependent,** below.
7. **Although.** Never preceded by a semicolon, unless other conditions warrant. See **Conjunctions, subordinating,** below.
8. **Apposition.** Use commas. For long or emphatic appositional phrases, use dashes. **(88q, 91e)**
9. **Because.** Never preceded by a semicolon, unless other conditions warrant. See **Conjunctions, subordinating,** below.
10. **Break or shift in thought.** Use a dash. **(91c)**

11. **Cancellation.** Do not use parenthesis marks to cancel. Erase or draw a line through the material. **(92d)**
12. **Chapter headings.** In a body of prose, enclose in quotation marks. As the heading of a chapter, use no punctuation. **(95f)**
13. **Clauses.**
    Independent clauses. (1) Joined by pure coordinating conjunction, use a comma. If the clauses are long with complicated internal punctuation, use a semicolon. **(88d, 89c)** (2) Not joined by any conjunction, use a semicolon. **(89a)** (3) Joined by a conjunctive adverb, use a semicolon. **(89b)** (4) Used parenthetically, enclose in dashes or parentheses. **(91e, 92a)** (5) Between contrasting independent clauses, use a comma. **(88j)**
    Dependent clause. (1) Adverbial clause preceding independent clause, use a comma. **(88f)** (2) Adverbial clause following independent clause: if restrictive, use no punctuation; otherwise, use commas if adverbial clause is nonrestrictive or fairly long. **(88f)** (3) Adjective clause: if nonrestrictive, use commas; if restrictive, omit punctuation. **(88m)** (4) Noun clauses: used as subject or object or complement, no punctuation. **(88u)** (5) Dependent contrasting clauses, use a comma. **(88j)**
14. **Complex sentence.** See **Clauses, dependent,** above.
15. **Compound predicate.** With two members only, usually no commas; with three or more, commas. See **Series,** below.
16. **Compound sentence.** See **Clauses, independent,** above.
17. **Compound words.** Separate the parts by a hyphen or hyphens. **(93a, b)**
18. **Conjunctions, coordinating.** (1) Pure conjunctions joining independent clauses, use a comma before, but not after. **(88d)** (2) Pure conjunctions joining two words or two phrases, no punctuation; joining three or more, commas. **(88h)** (3) Conjunctive adverb (see **Conjunctive adverb,** below). (4) Correlative conjunctions: apply same principle as for pure conjunctions. **(88d, h)**
19. **Conjunctions, subordinating.** Never place a comma or a semicolon after, unless for other reasons; place a comma before if the clause is adverbial, is nonrestrictive, and follows the independent clause. **(88f, 88u, 89b)**
20. **Conjunctive adverb.** Use a semicolon before when placed between two independent clauses. Use a comma or no mark after, depending upon parenthetic strength. **(89b)**
21. **Contractions.** Use an apostrophe. **(94f)**
22. **Contrasted coordinate elements.** Use a comma. **(88j)**

23. **Coordinate adjectives.** See **Adjectives**, above.
24. **Correlative conjunctions.** See **Conjunctions, coordinating**, above.
25. **Dates and places.** Enclose in commas when they explain preceding dates and places. **(88s)**
26. **Decimal.** Use a period preceding. **(86f)**
27. **Declarative sentence.** See **Sentence**, below.
28. **Dependent clause.** See **Clauses**, above.
29. **Dialogue.** Use quotation marks and commas. **(88b, 95a, b, c)**
30. **Diction.** Provincialisms, slang expressions, misnomers, and unusual technical terms, use quotation marks. **(95e)**
31. **Direct address (Vocative).** Use commas. **(88r)**
32. **Dollars and cents.** Use a period between. **(86f)**
33. **Doubt or uncertainty.** Use a question mark in parentheses. **(87e)**
34. **Emphasis.** Italicize. **(96d)** Also see **Surprise**, below.
35. **Exclamatory sentence.** See **Sentence**, below.
36. **Figures.** Four or more figures, use comma in front of each three numbers. **(88l)**
37. **For.** As a conjunction, use a comma preceding. As a preposition, use no punctuation. **(88e)**
38. **For example, for instance, namely, etc.** Used parenthetically, enclose in commas, unless they are followed by an independent clause; then use a colon or semicolon before, a comma after. **(88n, 88q)**
39. **Fractions.** Use a hyphen between the numerator and the denominator. **(93b)**
40. **Hour—minute.** Separate by a colon. **(90f)**
41. **Imperative sentence.** See **Sentence**, below.
42. **Independent clauses.** See **Clauses**, above.
43. **Indirect question.** Use a period, *not* a question mark. **(86c, 87c)**
44. **Indirect quotation.** Use neither commas nor quotation marks. **(88u, 95j)**
45. **Inserted material.** (1) Inserted sentence elements, use comma or commas. **(88o)** (2) Omitted material inserted later, indicate by a caret ($_\wedge$). **(92g)**
46. **Interjections.** Mild, use a comma; strong or fairly strong, use an exclamation point! **(87a, 88n)**
47. **Interpolated material.** Use brackets. **(92e)**
48. **Interrogative sentence.** See **Sentence**, below.
49. **Interruption in dialogue.** Use a dash. **(91b)**
50. **Introduction.** Before a word, phrase, or clause being introduced, use a comma, colon, or dash. **(88a, 90a, b, 91a)**

51. **Irony.** Occasionally, indicate by an exclamation point within parentheses. **(87a)**
52. **Misreading.** Between words and elements that may be misread, use a comma, or recast. **(88k)**
53. **Namely.** See **For Example,** above.
54. **Names of ships, trains, airplanes.** Use quotation marks or italics. **(95f, 96a)**
55. **Nominative absolute.** See **Absolute phrase,** above.
56. **Nonrestrictive clause.** See **Clauses, dependent,** above.
    Nonrestrictive phrase. See **Phrases,** below.
57. **Noun clause.** See **Clauses, dependent,** above.
58. **Numbers.** See **Figures** above.
59. **Numerals.** Use a hyphen between the parts (from twenty-one to ninety-nine). **(93b)**
60. **Object.** Use no comma between a verb and its object or a preposition and its object (except for additional reasons). **(88u)**
61. **Oh.** As a mild interjection, use a comma following; as a strong interjection, use an exclamation point. Before a vocative, O (spelled thus) is followed by no punctuation. **(87a, 88n)**
62. **Omission of letters.** In a word, use a dash. In a contraction, use an apostrophe. **(91f, 94f)**
63. **Omission of words.** Use ellipsis periods or asterisks. **(86g)**
64. **Outline symbols.** Use a period after each. **(86e)**
65. **Parenthetic words, phrases, clauses.** Weak, no punctuation; fairly to moderately strong, use commas; strong, use dashes or parentheses. **(88n, 91e, 92a)**
66. **Phrases.** (1) An introductory modifying phrase containing a verb form, use a comma; not containing a verb form, use no punctuation, unless fairly long and then use a comma. **(88g)** (2) Nonrestrictive phrases, use commas; restrictive phrases, use no punctuation. **(88m)**
67. **Places.** See **Dates and places,** above.
68. **Plurals.** Formed by adding *s, es,* or change in form. *Never* use an apostrophe, except to form the plurals of words as words, of letters, and of figures. **(94g)**
69. **Possessive case.** Use the apostrophe in forming the possessive case of nouns and indefinite pronouns. Do *not* use the apostrophe in forming the possessive case of other classes of pronouns. **(94a–e, i, j)**
70. **Predicate.** See **Compound predicate,** above.
71. **Preposition and object.** Use no comma or colon between. **(88u)**
72. **Provincialisms.** See **Diction,** above.
73. **Pure conjunctions.** See **Conjunctions,** above.

74. **Queries, series of.** Use question marks. (87d)
75. **Question.** After a direct question, use a question mark; after an indirect question, use a period. (87b, 86c)
76. **Quotation.** (1) Enclose a direct quotation in quotation marks; use no quotation marks with an indirect quotation. (95a, b, c, j) (2) A short direct quotation is set off by a comma; an indirect quotation is not set off by a comma. (88b) (3) A long formal quotation is introduced by a colon. (90d)
77. **Quotation extending over one paragraph.** Use quotation marks at the beginning of each paragraph, but at the end of only the last paragraph. (95d)
78. **Quotation marks with other marks of punctuation.** See Section 95i.
79. **Quotation within a quotation.** Use single quotation marks. (95g)
80. **References and directions.** When these amplify, enclose in parentheses. (92b)
81. **Restrictive clause.** See **Clauses, dependent,** above.
    Restrictive phrase. See **Phrases,** above.
82. **Salutation.** In a business letter, use a colon after; in a friendly letter, use a comma. (88c, 90e)
83. **Sentence.** (1) After a declarative sentence, use a period. (86a) (2) After a mildly imperative sentence, use a period; if it is vigorous, an exclamation point. (86b, 87a) (3) After an interrogative sentence, use a question mark. (87b) (4) After an exclamatory sentence, use an exclamation point. (87a)
84. **Series.** Three or more words or phrases or clauses, separate by commas, including one before but not after the conjunction. (88h) When the conjunction joins each two members of the series, use no punctuation. (88h) But see **Clauses,** above.
85. **Slang.** See **Diction,** above.
86. **Subheads.** Use no period following. (86h)
87. **Subject—predicate.** Use no comma to separate. (88u)
88. **Subordinating conjunctions.** See **Conjunctions, subordinating,** above.
89. **Such as.** Use a comma or no punctuation preceding; use no punctuation following. (88q, 90b)
90. **Summarizing final clause.** Use a dash preceding. (91d)
91. **Surprise, emphasis, strong emotion.** Use an exclamation point. (87a)
92. **Suspended elements.** Use commas, usually. (88o)
93. **Technical words.** See **Diction,** above.
94. **Title—subtitle.** Separate by a colon. (90f)

95. **Titles.** (1) Titles of books, magazines, newspapers, motion pictures, use italics, or, less preferably, quotation marks. **(95f, 96a)** (2) Titles at the beginning of a theme or paper or chapter, use neither quotation marks around nor a period following. **(95l, 86h)** (3) Titles (personal) and initials following a name, use comma preceding. **(88t)**

96. **Transposed elements.** Use commas, usually. **(88o)**

97. **Unfinished statement or word.** Use a dash. **(91b)**

98. **Verb—object and verb—complement.** Use no comma or colon to separate. **(88u, 90b)**

99. **Vocative.** See **Direct address,** above.

100. **Word division.** Use a hyphen at the end of the line, between syllables, when the word is continued on the next line. Never use a hyphen at the beginning of a line. **(93c)**

APPENDICES

Appendix A

WRITING LETTERS

The letter is the most widely used of all forms of written communication. Each of you, during your college years, probably will write several times as many letters as formal themes. And after graduation you will perhaps find it necessary to write even more letters than you did in college. Surely so widely used a form of writing deserves attention; from the standpoint of utility only, training in no other form is so important. For the ability to write a good letter indicates much more than we are likely to realize. You will find that important businessmen and firms waste little time, for example, on applications written in slipshod style; friends frequently drift away from us when we persist in writing them hurried notes instead of sincere, attractive, detailed letters; only too often our social contacts are affected by our ignorance of proper forms and conventions.

It must be remembered that the letters we write are an unfailing reflection and representation of ourselves. What we say and how we say it, the paper and ink we use, even the way in which we address the envelope and affix the stamp reflect our personalities just as do our diction, our smiles, our gestures.

This universally used, important, and highly personal form of communication which we call the letter is, in a sense, a theme which is governed by the same rules and principles as other kinds of composition. A letter should be *correct, clear,* and *effective.* Good letters are rarely dashed off; usually they are the result of careful planning, writing, and rewriting.

There are two main kinds of letters: business letters and informal, friendly letters. A third kind is formal invitations and replies, but the conventional patterns of formal correspondence may be

709

found in any standard book of etiquette. Business letters and informal letters, however, are more variable. Each deserves attention, and each illustrates admirably the process of communication: you, *the writer,* send some specific question or information, *the subject,* to some specifically named person or company, *the reader.*

Business Letters

The business letter is largely utilitarian: its object is to convey information by precise exposition. The writer of business letters is primarily concerned with *presentation*—the way in which what one has to say is arranged and expressed, and *content*—the subject matter that is to be included. Later in your college years you may take one or more courses in general business correspondence. Since, however, less than one-fifth of our colleges and universities offer even one such basic course, the following material introduces you to some general principles for use now or later in business correspondence.

1. Presentation

A good business letter creates a pleasing impression the moment it is taken from its envelope. Physical appearance—quality of paper, neatness of typing or writing, arrangement of letter parts—is almost as important as content to the total effect. Correctness and attractiveness in form reflect a courteous attitude toward the reader.

STATIONERY

Business letters should be written on good-quality white unruled paper, preferably of the standard $8\frac{1}{2}$ x 11-inch size, although the half-size sheet ($8\frac{1}{2}$ x $5\frac{1}{2}$) is acceptable, using either the longer or the shorter measurement for the horizontal lines. Colored and unusual-sized sheets are in doubtful taste for business correspondence, as is fraternity, club, and hotel stationery.

TYPING

Letters should be typewritten if possible, but neat longhand, in black or blue-black ink, is permissible. For typing, a black ribbon fresh enough to insure legibility should be used. The letter must be neat in every detail. Never strike over or leave a visible erasure.

Writing Letters

FORM

Good business letters are arranged in a form which has now become so standardized that it is easy to follow. It consists of six parts:

1. The Heading
2. The Inside Address
3. The Greeting, or Salutation
4. The Body
5. The Complimentary Close
6. The Signature

Each part has certain set forms which must not be ignored or altered if your letter is to be attractive and easy to read. Study the letters on pages 717–728, not only for observing the position of the parts but also as an illustration of the correct use and balanced arrangement of these conventionalized forms.

The Heading. The heading contains the sender's full address—street, city, postal zone, state—and the date of writing. It is usually placed in the upper right-hand part of the sheet (but see p. 717), several spaces below the top edge, and flush with the right margin of the letter. It is single spaced. Abbreviations should be avoided, and *st, nd, rd,* or *d* should not follow the day of the month. On stationery with a letterhead, the writer need add only the date, which he places flush with the right-hand margin of the letter or centers directly beneath the letterhead. For position of lines and punctuation, see "Indented and Block Systems" and "Open and Closed Systems," pages 716, 717, and the letters on pages 717–720.

The Inside Address. The address of the person or company that the letter is written to should appear at least four spaces below the heading and flush with the left-hand margin of the letter. It is usually single spaced, and harmonizes with the heading in that it conforms to it in having either block or indented form and in being punctuated according to the open or closed system.

Some title should always precede the name of the person addressed: *Mr., Mrs., Miss, Messrs.,* etc. A business title should never precede the name, but a person of professional standing may be addressed as *Dr., The Reverend, President* (of a college), *Dean, Professor, General,* etc. The title *Honorable,* preceded by *The,* is widely used for a person holding an important government position.

If you know only the last name of the person to whom you are writing, direct your letter to the firm, adding *Attention: Mr.—*or *Attention of Mr.—*. The attention line usually appears directly above the greeting or flush with the right-hand margin; it has no bearing on the greeting itself, which is always determined from the first line of the inside address.

The following list indicates proper forms for addressing various persons:

	INSIDE ADDRESS	GREETING
One man	Mr. James T. Wilcox 49 Nottingham Road Silver Spring, Utah	Dear Mr. Wilcox:
One woman	Mrs. Robert Fitch Two Park Place Troy 65, Ohio	Dear Mrs. Fitch:
Partnership	Messrs. Herd and Tims 1350 Sumter Boulevard Tallahassee, Florida	Gentlemen:
Company	Cobblestone Paving Co. 569 West Shore Drive Chicago 25, Illinois	Gentlemen:
Firm of women	The Dora Dress Shop 14 Wilton Boulevard Portland, Maine	Ladies:
One man in a firm	Mr. Victor C. Woll Art Printing Company 332 Aiken Building Nashville 10, Florida	Dear Mr. Woll:
An officer in a firm	Mr. Lee Fox, Treasurer The Mayo Corporation West Falls, Montana or Mr. Walter Stephens Treasurer, Lea & Sons, Inc. 1659 Glenham Street Oak Park 4, Illinois	Dear Mr. Fox: Dear Mr. Stephens:
A college official (with professional standing)	President Roy G. Wild Charlotte College Jackson, Arizona	Dear President Wild:

Writing Letters

An officer in an organization, when individual name is unknown	The Registrar Polk University Brighton, New York	**Dear Sir:**
A clergyman	The Reverend Samuel **Clark** (or, if he has a doctor's degree, The Rev. Dr. Samuel Clark) Park Street Methodist Church 223 Park Street Buffalo 19, New York	Dear Sir: or Dear Mr. Clark: or Dear Dr. Clark:
A priest	The Rev. Father Smith or The Rev. Leo L. Smith 919 Euclid Avenue Pershingville, New York	Dear Father Smith: or Dear Reverend Father: or Dear Father:
Member of a sisterhood	Sister Mary Agnes Riverview Academy Riverview, Pennsylvania	Dear Sister: or Dear Sister Agnes:
Rabbi	Rabbi Joseph Simon or The Rev. Joseph Simon Temple of Israel North Ninth Avenue Cincinnati 12, Ohio	Dear Sir: or Dear Rabbi Simon:
Public Officials		
The President	The President The White House Washington, D.C.	Mr. President: or My dear Mr. President:
Cabinet member	The Secretary of — Washington, D.C. or The Honorable John Foy Secretary of — Washington, D.C.	Dear Sir: or My dear Mr. Secretary:
Senator	The Honorable John Rae The United States Senate Washington, D.C.	Dear Sir: or Dear Senator: or Dear Senator Rae:
Representative	The Honorable R. B. Burns The House of Representatives Washington, D.C.	Dear Sir: or Dear Mr. Burns:

713

Governor	The Honorable Paul Key Governor of Colorado Denver, Colorado	Dear Sir: or Dear Governor Key:
Mayor	His Honor, the Mayor City Hall Bangor, Maine	My dear Mr. Mayor: or Dear Mayor Woods:

The Greeting, or Salutation. The greeting, or salutation, should be placed two spaces below the inside address and flush with the left-hand margin. It is punctuated by a colon only, never a comma, semicolon, dash, or colon and dash. The following forms of salutation, arranged in decreasing formality, are correct. Select the one which corresponds to the first line of the inside address and to the general tone of your letter. However, for most business correspondence, the last form listed in each group is preferable (see also greetings shown above with the list of inside addresses). Notice the "dear" is capitalized only when it is the first word.

<table>
<tr><td align="center">To a Man</td><td align="center">To a Woman</td></tr>
<tr><td>My dear Sir:
Dear Sir:
My dear Mr. Pollock:
Dear Dr. Bard:</td><td>Dear Madam:
My dear Mrs. Lord:
Dear Mrs. Lord:</td></tr>
<tr><td align="center">To a Firm of Men</td><td align="center">To a Group or Firm of Women</td></tr>
<tr><td>Dear Sirs:
Gentlemen:</td><td>Mesdames:
Ladies:</td></tr>
</table>

NOTE: The more personal form using the name of the person addressed is now preferred to the older, more formal *My dear Sir, Dear Sir(s),* or *Dear Madam.* Use the person's name if it is known to you. However, *Dear Sir* and *Dear Madam* are commonly used for addressing officials.

The Body. The body of the letter contains the message and begins two spaces below the greeting. Most business letters are single spaced, although an extremely short message may be double spaced for attractive arrangement on a large page. Single-spaced letters require two spaces between each paragraph. Paragraphs may be in block form (if the heading and inside address correspond in form) or indented. They *should be* indented when the indented

Writing Letters

system is used. They *may be* indented, for clearness and effectiveness, even when the block system is used in the other parts. If double spacing is used in the body of the letter, paragraphs are more clearly separated by double spacing and indentation. On the typewriter, indentation may be five or ten spaces, or one space beyond the length of the greeting line.

Messages which are too long for one page should be continued on a second page; never write on the back of a sheet. However, the second page must contain at least two lines, preferably more, in addition to the complimentary close and signature. A paragraph may be continued from one page to another, but at least two lines of the paragraph should appear on the page on which it begins. Each additional page should carry a top line containing some sort of identification, such as the addressee's initials or name, the page number, and the date: H. M. Brown, 9/12/56. Page 2.

The Complimentary Close. The close is placed slightly to the right of the middle of the page, two or three spaces below the last line of the body of the letter. Only the first word is capitalized. The punctuation mark is a comma, even though open punctuation is used in the heading and inside address. Correct forms, arranged in groups of decreasing formality and used to harmonize with the formality or semi-informality of the greeting, are as follows:

Yours truly,	Sincerely yours,
Very truly yours,	Yours sincerely,
Yours very truly,	
Yours very sincerely,	Cordially yours,
Very sincerely yours,	Yours cordially,

Respectfully yours (never *Respectively yours*) is commonly used in letters to public officials, to clergy and others in religious orders, and to those ranking above us in academic circles, like a college president or dean. *Cordially yours* is frequently used among business friends or by older people writing to younger.

The close should be independent of the last paragraph of the letter. Do not link the last paragraph and the close by a participial phrase such as *Thanking you in advance, I remain,* or *Hoping for an early reply, I am.* Avoid "clever" or "original" forms such as

715

Enthusiastically yours, Apologetically yours, Yours for lower taxes, Yours for a cheery Homecoming.

The Signature. The signature is placed directly below the complimentary close. If the signature (name) is typewritten, leave four spaces for the insertion of the handwritten signature. Unless a letter is mimeographed or is plainly a circular letter, it should always have, in ink, a legible handwritten signature.

A married woman should sign her own full name, followed by her married name:

> Anne Marie Shelton
> (Mrs. Paul R. Shelton)

An unmarried woman places the title *Miss* in parentheses before her name:

> (Miss) Elizabeth West

Academic degrees and courtesy or professional titles—*Mr., Dr., Rev., Litt.D.,* etc.—should not be used with a signature, but the writer's title is often given—*General Manager, Superintendent, Vice-President,* etc. Letter convention opposes putting the writer's address under the signature; its proper place is in the heading.

MARGINS

Balanced layout of the letter on the page is determined by the length of the message. The entire letter, including heading, inside address, complimentary close, and signature, should have the appearance of a rectangle, with top and bottom margins slightly wider than those at the side. Side margins should be at least an inch wide, and particular care must be taken to maintain as even a right margin as possible. If necessary, long words should be divided, always according to their proper syllables. Short letters should be approximately centered, with wide margins.

INDENTED AND BLOCK SYSTEMS

Arrangement of the lines of the heading, as well as those of the inside address and the outside address on the envelope (see below), may follow the *indented* or the *block* system. In the first of these methods, each line is indented a few spaces to the right of the preceding line. In the block form, which is now more widely used,

Writing Letters

the lines begin at the same margin. The block form may be one of two kinds: In the "modified block" form, the lines of each part are blocked, and the various parts of the letter are placed in the positions indicated above. In the "full block" form, all the parts of the letter, including the heading, the complimentary close, and the signature, begin at the left-hand margin. For examples, see below. Because of ease and time-saving in typing, block systems are preferred.

OPEN AND CLOSED SYSTEMS

Punctuation of the heading and inside and outside addresses may follow the *open* or the *closed* system. In the open system, no commas or final periods, except after abbreviations, are used after the separate lines. In the closed system, commas are used after each line except the last; a period is used after the last line. Both methods are acceptable, although the open system is now more widely used.

```
1934 Travis Street
Louisville 8, Kentucky
February 3, 19—

Miss Lucy Irwin
Secretary, Society of Commerce
375 East Boone Street
Arlington, Kentucky

My dear Miss Irwin:

This letter is an illustration of the "full
block" or the "modified military" form, since
all the parts of the letter, including the
heading, complimentary close, and signature,
begin flush with the left-hand margin. Where
there are two or more lines in a part, each
line begins directly under the line just above.
Note also the space between the various parts
of the letter.

The paragraphs illustrate block form; that is,
each paragraph begins flush with the left-hand
```

margin. Division between paragraphs is indicated by double spaces. Within the paragraphs and within each part of the letter, single spacing is used.

No punctuation marks are used after the lines in the heading, inside address, and signature. This system, called open punctuation, does not apply, however, to the greeting and the complimentary close, which are followed by a colon and a comma, respectively.

This letter form—full block and open punctuation—is becoming increasingly popular among business men, secretaries, and stenographers, for it saves considerable time and trouble by its elimination of indentions and some of the end-punctuation marks.

Yours very truly,

Wilson F. Johnson

Wilson F. Johnson
Correspondence Consultant
Louisville Mercantile Corporation

"Full Block" Form

516 Tudor Place,
Detroit 22, Michigan,
November 2, 19—.

Rinebeck & Company,
1224 East Denver Avenue,
Chicago 12, Illinois.

Gentlemen:

This letter is an example of "modified block" or "semi-block" form; that is, the

718

Writing Letters

heading, complimentary close, and signature are on the right side of the letter, the other parts on the left. But within the parts the block form is used.

The paragraphs are indented here, but they could be block form. In fact, blocked paragraphs are optional: indented paragraphs can be used, if the writer so desires, with any type of letter, including even the full-block form.

Closed punctuation is used here: commas at the end of each line in the heading and the inside address except the last, which has a period. Such punctuation, too, is optional, for open punctuation could be used.

These three letters—this one, the one preceding, and the one following—also illustrate variety in the use of the greeting and the complimentary close. The tone of the complimentary close likewise is in harmony with the tone of the greeting, in each of the letters.

Very truly yours,

Rodney R. Rhodes

Rodney R. Rhodes

"MODIFIED BLOCK" FORM

125 South Fourth Street,
East Waltham, Illinois,
September 15, 19--.

Mr. Harrison McWilliams,
Supervisor of Correspondence,
Washington High School,
Clearwater, Indiana.

Dear Mr. McWilliams:

This letter illustrates "indented" form,
both in the various parts and in the paragraph
beginning. Such indentation is somewhat
troublesome, although preferred by some letter-
writers. Closed punctuation is used in the
heading and inside address, but open punctuation could be used. Since this is a one-paragraph letter, notice that it has larger margins
at left and right, and more white space at top
and bottom.

Sincerely yours,

Jane Ferguson

(Miss) Jane Ferguson

"Indented" Form

THE ENVELOPE

The envelope carries the sender's return address in the upper
left-hand corner and the addressee's name slightly below center and
to the right. The full address should be used in harmony with the
inside address on the letter, although double spacing of a three-line
address on the envelope is helpful to the Post Office Department,
which prefers indented lines regardless of the system used in the
inside address, as well as the placing of the state on a separate line.

Folding of the letter depends upon the size of the envelope.
When the large No. 10 (9½ x 4⅛) envelope is used, the lower
third of the sheet should be folded over the message, the upper

Writing Letters

part folded down to within a half inch, and the upper folded edge should be put in the envelope first.

For a No. 6¾ (6½ x 3⅝) envelope, fold the lower part of the letter page over the message to within approximately one-half inch of the top of the page. Next, fold from the right slightly more than one third, then from the left, leaving the left flap edge slightly short of the right folded edge. Insert the left folded edge in the envelope first.

The reason for these folds is obvious—courtesy to the reader. If he opens your letter in the conventional way, the letter comes out of the envelope literally half-unfolding itself, top edge and written face up, ready to be read. The conventional way for a right-handed person is as follows: the envelope is held in the left hand, with the address side face down, and the envelope flap at the top; the envelope is slit along the top long edge, and the letter is withdrawn by the right hand.

2. Content

In addition to adhering to general principles of effective writing, business letters should always be clear, concise, complete, and courteous, four important C-words in relation to letter-writing. As has been noted, the object of a business letter is to convey information by precise exposition. Since the writer hopes to secure the reader's careful attention, every letter should be carefully planned and phrased with its reader in mind.

OPENING SENTENCE

Open the letter with a statement of its subject or its purpose, a courteous request, a direct question, a simple direct important statement, or several of these in combination. Avoid such opening abbreviations, terms of jargon, and rubber-stamp expressions as *enclosed please find, your recent favor to hand and in reply would state, I beg to advise, yours of the 8th inst. recd*. Include briefly in the opening sentences or paragraph any pertinent "background" information which will clarify your message. Make the purpose of your letter evident, and arrange your thoughts in logical, easy-to-follow units. Separate ideas require separate paragraphs and should be developed according to the principles discussed on pages 193–195.

721

PARAGRAPHING

Business-letter paragraphs are shorter than paragraphs in most other kinds of prose. They usually vary in length from two to six lines. Longer paragraphs are rare; not infrequently one-line paragraphs are used. The reason for such paragraphing is to enable the reader to get the message of each paragraph, and of the letter, easily, quickly, clearly, and effectively.

CLOSING SENTENCE

Your letter should close strongly and effectively. As indicated above under "The Complimentary Close," avoid weak participial or prepositional phrases. Make your last group of words a complete sentence: an invitation, a direct question, a courteous request, a restatement of the subject of the letter, or a significant and important statement.

LANGUAGE

Remember your reader: avoid using too formal English, but at the other extreme avoid using trite, outworn, "business" expressions, such as *recent date, contents noted, as per, past favors, wish to advise, in receipt of, valued wishes, according to my records, attached hereto, enclosed herewith, under separate cover, beg to acknowledge, your kind indulgence, we trust, permit us, at your earliest convenience, as soon as possible, thank you in advance.*

Use instead an informal and soundly idiomatic style. Colloquialisms are permissible, but avoid using a telegraphic style. Someone has said that effective business letters use the same courteous and friendly language that is used in a business conversation over the telephone.

TYPES OF BUSINESS LETTERS

There are numerous kinds of business letters, classified according to their content, or message. The most common of these are

1. Order letters and acknowledgments of orders.
2. Inquiries and replies.
3. Sales letters.
4. Credit letters (designed to encourage buying now and paying later).

722

Writing Letters

5. Collection letters (designed to encourage paying, *now*).
6. Claims and adjustments.
7. Letters of application.
8. Letters of introduction or recommendation.

The four types you are most likely to use, now and later, are represented below. For more detailed discussion of all the various types of letters used in the transaction of business, you are referred to recent books which you will find listed in the card catalogue of your library under "Business Letters" or "Letter-Writing—Business."

ORDER LETTERS

Make your order letter (if you do not have a printed order blank available) brief, clear, and exact. Give a full description of the goods which you wish to buy, including quantity, size, color, price, and any other available identifying data such as catalogue number and trade name. Two or more items ordered in the same letter should be listed separately to facilitate reading. Always specify methods of shipment and payment, and remember to mention any special wish (delivery of the order by a certain date, etc.).

In the lower left-hand corner, several spaces under the last line of the body, write "Encl." (i.e., enclosure) if something is to be sent with the letter (check, sample, etc.). Whenever this is done, it serves to remind you, or whoever folds the letter, to be sure that the enclosure mentioned in the body of the letter is made; it is also a further indication, to the reader, of the enclosure.

240 King Street,
Maryville, Delaware,
June 9, 19—.

White Garment Company,
8639 West Street,
New York 17, New York.

Gentlemen:

Please send me, by parcel post, six pairs of ladies' nylon hose, 15 Denier, size 9, medium length, suntan color. In payment I enclose a money order for nine dollars ($9.00).

Yours very truly,
(Miss) Jane Smith

Encl.

INQUIRIES

Most inquiry letters are written to obtain information about the products or services of a business firm. Some may be written to an individual for information concerning a subject on which he is an authority. Always make your request understandable; avoid vague and general questions. Supply any information the reader may need in order to answer your questions definitely.

Routine requests for catalogues, price lists, or other prepared data may be limited to a one-sentence letter clearly identifying the desired material. If your letter is phrased as a question (*Will you please send me . . .*), it should close with a period instead of a question mark.

Nonroutine inquiries require more detailed letters. For example, a letter asking about an organization's policies must explain the use to which the information will be put. A request stemming from a personal problem must give a clear explanation of the problem and an indication of the type of help needed.

The general plan for the inquiry letter (usually from two to four paragraphs) is as follows: (1) reason for the inquiry, (2) the inquiry, (3) expression of appreciation (*never* a "thank you in

Writing Letters

advance"). Sometimes material may be included to show the reader how he will benefit by replying. If the inquiry includes several questions, these are more effective when numbered and paragraphed separately.

If the person or firm addressed will eventually profit, no postage should be enclosed. Otherwise, apply this principle: When you ask for that which is of benefit only or primarily to you, enclose a self-addressed stamped envelope.

Study the example below.

919 Fowler Avenue
Athens 12, Indiana
September 25, 19—

Secretary-Treasurer
American Institute of Electrical Engineers
33 West 38th Street
New York 18, New York

Dear Sir:

    As a student in the College of Electrical Engineering at Athens University, I am interested in eventually obtaining full membership in the American Institute of Electrical Engineers.

    Will you please answer the following questions:

(1) Is it possible for an undergraduate student of electrical engineering to obtain a junior membership in the A. I. E. E.?
(2) What is the cost of such membership?
(3) Is such junior membership transferable to full membership upon the student's graduation from college?
(4) Does the junior membership fee include a year's subscription to the official magazine, _Electrical Engineering?_

Your sending me this information will be greatly appreciated.

Very truly yours,

Wilson Hargrove

Wilson Hargrove

CLAIMS AND ADJUSTMENTS

The claims, or complaint, letter, is written not to accuse, blame, or threaten but to point out an error, such as shipment of wrong goods, damaged goods, failure to ship goods, an overcharge in a bill, and the like. Clarity is essential, brevity is desirable, and courtesy is diplomatic. Present the necessary facts fairly; identify the unsatisfactory article or service, explain how it is unsatisfactory, and suggest or give the reader an opportunity to suggest adjustment. The letter that the reader writes to you is the adjustment letter.

If you have to write an angry letter, by all means write it, but lay it aside for a day; then destroy it, and write the kind of letter you would like to receive if your position were that of the reader.

Usually your claims letter will consist of two to four paragraphs containing (1) a specific explanation of what is wrong, (2) the course of action you desire the reader to take, (3) sometimes, the inconvenience resulting to the writer, and (4) sometimes, the gains to be won by the reader's making prompt adjustment. Circumstances will determine the order in which these paragraphs come.

Writing Letters

R.F.D. 6,
Lansom, Pennsylvania,
November 15, 19—.

The Tryco Department Store,
49 East Tenth Street,
New York 10, New York.

Gentlemen:

On November 9 I purchased in your
radio department a Vinson radio, table model
R–350, with brown plastic case. The radio
arrived promptly, but I am disappointed to find
that it does not operate on DC. It was my
understanding that the Model R–350 is designed to operate on either AC or DC, but I
find that the accompanying instructions indicate only AC. I am returning the radio at once
in the hope that it can be exchanged for a set
suitable for DC wiring.

If there has been a misunderstanding
and the R–350 does not operate on DC, I shall
have to choose another model. In that case I
hope that I may have a refund, since I shall
not be in New York again for several months. I
hope, however, that you will be able to supply
an R–350 model which will fill my needs.

Very truly yours,

Edward J. Ryan, Jr.

Edward J. Ryan, Jr.

(2)

240 King Street,
Maryville, Delaware,
June 23, 19—.

White Garment Company,
8639 West Street,
New York 17, New York.

Gentlemen:

On June 9 I ordered from you six pairs of
ladies' nylon hose, 15 Denier, size 9, medium
length, suntan color, total price $9.00. I de-
sired to give these hose to a friend who was
leaving on June 20 for a trip abroad.

The hose arrived on June 18, and I was
greatly disappointed to find several mistakes
in the order: they were size 10, short length,
gunmetal in color.

As it is too late to have the error corrected, I am returning the hose to you parcel-
post insured and am asking that you return to
me the purchase money of $9.00.

Yours very truly,

(Miss) Jane Smith

(Miss) Jane Smith

LETTERS OF APPLICATION

An effective letter of application stresses, throughout, the applicant's desire and ability to be of benefit to the prospective employer.
Always emphasize what you, the applicant with your qualifications, can do for the employer, not what the latter can do for you.
The letter must be courteous, straightforward, and sincere in tone,
offering services without pleading or demanding.

Open your letter by applying for a specific position and indicating how you learned of the opening: from a friend, an agency, a classified advertisement, etc. Give your special reason for applying, if the application is unsolicited. Present qualifications—education, interest, aptitude—and experience honestly, emphasizing those which will be particularly useful to the employer's firm. Devote a brief paragraph to personal information: age, health, and any other pertinent details. Include two or three references, listing them separately, either in the body of the letter or immediately after the close, with full names, titles, and addresses. Close your letter by requesting an interview at the employer's convenience. If you are in the same city, indicate where you may be reached by telephone. An example of a letter of application is given below.

NOTE: Always secure permission from the persons whom you wish to suggest as references and remember that it is courteous to write letters thanking them for their help.

Letters Accompanying Data Sheets. Many applicants prepare a separate data sheet which should be labeled *Information Record Concerning* . . . , listing education, experience, personal information, and references. Such a record can be a full page, or even more, of information pertinent to the position desired; it will also have room, preferably in the upper right-hand corner, for the pasting of a good photograph. Subheadings should be used for ready reading. The letter accompanying such a sheet should not repeat information. It is usually in three paragraphs. The first applies for the position; the second points out the information on the data sheet which especially qualifies the applicant for the position; the third requests an interview.

Letters Replying to Newspaper or Magazine Advertisements. In responding to "Help Wanted" advertisements in newspapers or in certain professional magazines, the applicant must first analyze the information given to determine the required qualifications. *Blind advertisements* give neither name nor address of the advertiser and often provide scant information about the opening. The applicant must judge as best he can the qualifications needed and offer in his letter whatever details seem pertinent.

Here is an example of a blind advertisement:

Stenographer: Good beginner considered. 5 day week. Opp. for advancement. M4089 Tribune.

The applicant has no way of knowing the name of the firm, the kind of business, or exactly what "advancement" is suggested. It is likely that the work does not require knowledge of technical terminology since a beginner will be considered. In replying, the applicant can only express interest in a position which offers further opportunity and give details about her stenographic skill. She should of course include past experience in stenography, usually without referring to employers by name.

Classified advertisements ordinarily include the name of the firm and more detailed information about the position. The following advertisement clearly outlines the employer's needs:

Wanted: Young man to check reports of public accountants, prove figures, check references, etc. Prefer accounting education and background, ability to assist in preparing reports. Excellent opportunity young man studying for CPA. Reply in detail. Brown, Merrill and Scott, CPA, 35 National Bank Building.

The applicant analyzes the advertisement by listing in detail the qualifications desired; his letter, if he expects it to gain him an interview, must show precisely how he meets these qualifications. For the position just quoted, an applicant must indicate (1) strong interest in an accounting career; (2) experience, if any, in checking reports, etc.; (3) education; (4) ability to compile data and write reports.

Unusual Letters of Application. The purpose of the letter of application is to gain for its writer an interview; rarely is a position obtained solely through the letter. Therefore, to make your letters of application effective and to assure yourself of an interview, make your letters unusual; make them secure the favorable attention of the prospective employer.

Do not be vain, assertive, overconfident, but try to convey routine information in an unusual way. For example, you can use subheads: centered, or in the left margin, or on the left third of the page with the material developing the subheads filling the right two-thirds. One attention-getting letter of application had the applicant's picture centered at the top, with position desired at the left and date available at the right; a three-paragraph letter occupied the center of the page, enclosed by ruled lines; surrounding the letter

730

Writing Letters

were statements of the applicant's attainments and qualifications: educational background, campus activities, business experience, personal data, and references. Your own ingenuity may suggest other unusual letters of application.

LETTER OF APPLICATION

```
                        961 Boulder Drive
                        Atlanta 21, Georgia
                        October 21, 19—
```

```
Mr. David Carr, Office Manager
Textile Products, Inc.
16 Whicher Street
Nashville 8, Tennessee
```

```
Dear Mr. Carr:
```

        Through the courtesy of Professor A. D. Dwyer, I have learned that you are considering employing an office assistant. I should like to apply for this position.

        Under Professor Dwyer, I took several courses in office management at Black University. In addition to the usual classroom work, I had an opportunity to analyze various problems of office management as a part of my senior research work. This study was carried on in the model business office conducted by the University's College of Commerce and also in the offices of the Alliance Chemical Corporation.

        As background for my major studies, I have taken courses in business law, accounting, stenography, and typing. I can take dictation rapidly and am an accurate, though not rapid, typist.

        For the past four summers I have been employed as a "relief" secretary at the

Dow Smelting Company of this city, substituting for other girls while they were on vacation. At present, I am working as a typist with this same company, but I believe that my college training and practical background of experience have fitted me for duties of greater responsibility.

My age is twenty-two; I am in excellent health. My parents are native-born Americans. You can depend upon my working intelligently and diligently.

I shall arrange to come to Nashville for an interview at any time agreeable to you. When would be most convenient?

Very truly yours,

(Miss) Frances Whirter

(Miss) Frances Whirter

References:

Professor A. D. Dwyer, Black University, Columbus, Georgia.

Mr. James Ragsland, Personnel Manager, The Alliance Chemical Corporation, Columbus, Georgia.

Dr. Rufus J. Smythe, Plant Director, Dow Smelting Company, Atlanta, Georgia.

Informal, Friendly Letters

There is an old saying: "The best way to have a friend is to be one." This adage applies particularly to the writing and receiving of friendly letters. All of us are prone to say, "I love to get letters but, oh, how I hate to write them!" It is unfortunately true that good informal letters require careful planning and writing; they can no more be dashed off than can effective business letters. Writ-

Writing Letters

ing letters is not exactly an art, but many of us can approximate artistry in our personal correspondence *provided* we take the time and pains to plan and write our letters thoughtfully. They should, however, never seem or sound labored, strained, or artificial.

Conversation is no more a lost art than is friendly letter writing. We tend to live so hurriedly these days that we feel we have actually written a letter when all that we have done is to dash off a few hastily scrawled notes on a half-dozen random subjects. We can somewhat restore the lost art of friendly letter writing by practicing the following suggestions:

1. *Give details.* The full, clear description of one person or one place is likely to prove far more interesting than a series of choppy notes on numerous people or places. The detailed account of one interesting conversation which you have had will be far more revealing and entertaining than a kaleidoscopic series of random comments quoted from a dozen people whom you have met. The vivid narration of a single experience which you have had will prove more readable than scrappy accounts of several incidents. Try to write letters made up of unified details, not random notes which really are only topic sentences needing expansion. Think of each letter as a *theme* with a central purpose. Keep your central purpose in mind, reject all irrelevant details, and focus attention upon one primary incident or one piece of conversation, upon description of one person or place, or exposition of one idea. Of course, a letter may contain more than one topic, but the topics should be clearly related and each should be fully developed. In writing informal letters follow the principles of paragraph development mentioned on pages 203 ff.

2. *Vary your letters.* Our friends differ somewhat in their tastes and interests. An incident Sue would enjoy reading about might not be particularly interesting to George. Jack is a music lover: he will enjoy full details of that concert which you attended; Henry is not especially interested in music, but he will read avidly an account of the last fraternity dance that you went to. Friendship implies many obligations, one of which is to detect and respect individual differences. Rarely is it possible to give all our friends the same Christmas present. It should be equally obvious that the recipients of our letters have a right to expect individual treatment.

733

In other words, adapt each letter and its content to your specific reader.

3. *Take time.* No one can write a long, interesting letter in five or ten minutes. The best friendly letters are usually written by people who plan their letters before attempting to write them. They don't sit down to write a letter, saying, "Well, I owe Bill a letter and I can't put it off any longer. What can I tell him?" They sit down to write Bill about people, places, and events in which they know he will be interested and about which they have made mental notes for the very purpose of using in a letter to him. Nor do good letter writers try to write six or eight letters at a sitting. They write only one or two, and thus give each letter all the freshness, spontaneity, and chattiness which they can. Few of us can write good letters when we consider the task tiresome and laborious. Each of us can write letters with charm if we don't stint the care which we lavish upon them. Friendships, often kept alive necessarily through the medium of correspondence, are too precious for us to throw away for the lack of a little time. Each of us is occasionally irritated at receiving a long-expected letter which begins "I am sorry that this letter will be brief for I am in a great rush" or ends with a "Hastily yours." We may expect that those who receive from us letters beginning or ending in the same manner will be similarly nettled.

4. *Don't write illegibly or sloppily.* The friendly letter is different in form and purpose from business and formal correspondence. It is more intimate, much more informal. But hastily scrawled notes on odd pieces of paper do not show much interest in or respect for the persons to whom we are writing. Informality is not only permissible but desirable in friendly letters, but liberty must not become license. The illegibility and general carelessness which fairly scream "I haven't time to write you a good letter—take this or leave it" are not permissible.

It is now conventional and proper to type many friendly letters. Only intimately personal letters, such as those of condolence, should always be written in longhand.

Use letter paper of good quality and in good taste. White or cream or pale gray paper is preferable to that of other colors. Avoid the use of heavily perfumed paper. Don't use violet or red or green

734

Writing Letters

ink. Your letters, even in their paper, ink, and handwriting, reflect your possession or lack of good taste and refinement.

Types of Friendly Letters

Each of us is called upon to write various kinds of friendly letters. There is the "thank you" letter in which we express our appreciation for a favor, a gift, or hospitality. There is the informal invitation to attend, let us say, a house party, and the informal reply to that invitation. Letters of congratulation, of sympathy, letters to the family, "travel" letters, "bread and butter" letters are other types.

These types are so varied that no single rule or suggestion can be offered to cover them all. But for each of them, follow the directions given above; for each, make mental or written notes of the details you plan to include and the order in which you will treat them.

Remember also that the *form* of friendly letters is not nearly so important as their *content*. It should be noted, however, that a comma, not a colon, usually follows the greeting. It is suggested, too, that the writer's address and the actual date (not just the day of the week) be given in the usual place for the heading or in the lower left-hand corner of the last page of the letter. No inside address is necessary, but the outside address on the envelope of the friendly letter must be as accurate and full as that on a business letter.

The letters that follow may be helpful to you in suggesting solutions to some letter-writing problems, but do not follow any models slavishly. You may wish to comment on the appropriateness of the language in these letters.

A "THANK YOU" NOTE

Dear Uncle Jim,

I know that I wasn't the prettiest girl at the dance (although Jack, who took me, said I was); and I didn't get the biggest rush either, but then again I wasn't exactly a wallflower. And yet I'm positive about one thing—I was the happiest girl there. No one else was wearing such beautiful costume jewelry, and I could just see the looks of envy on the others girls' faces. I have always known that you knew the way to a girl's heart, but what I didn't know was that you thought enough of me to take the time and trouble to select and send me such an exquisite gift. I'm very grateful and the next time that I see you I'll tell you in person just how happy you have made me.

Your devoted niece,
Louise

923 Athens St.
New Orleans 6, La.
January 20, 19—

A Note of Congratulation

Jonas J. Franklyn Hall
McWhorter College
McWhorter, Texas
December 5, 19—

Dear Hank,

Dad's last letter contained a clipping from the home-town paper that you were one of three State U. freshmen chosen to be soph assistant football managers next fall.

That's mighty fine, Hank, and I'm glad to see that one of our high school classmates is making a big dent in college activities.

The three of us here at McWhorter from old Morton High keep struggling, but we haven't got very far yet. Bill Smead is still on the freshman basketball squad after the first cut. Harry Nicolson has a straight A average, I'm told, but I can't get him to admit it. As for "yours truly," meaning me, I'm still following my hobby and attend the meetings of the Camera Club regularly. Sometimes I even get to act as "secretary" when the regular sec. can't come. Ain't that sompin?

But with the example you've set, I'm going after bigger and better game. I hope we can get together with all the old gang for a big gabfest during Christmas vacation. What say?

Sincerely,
Joe

A Note of Sympathy

Dear Barbara,

As I sat in the church today, a whole host of memories came crowding about me. I remember so well when I met your mother; she received me, as your friend, with her arms literally open. And for all the months that I have been privileged to know her, she has always been graciously hospitable to me. I recall dozens of good times which she made possible for us; I remember especially how she helped me with that fancy dress

736

Writing Letters

costume when I was almost in tears because I couldn't get it to hang just exactly right.

Nothing that I can say will lessen either the shock of her passing or your grief. But I want you to know that as I paid her my last respects this afternoon, my own heart was heavy with a sense of personal loss. Her kindliness, thoughtfulness, and complete integrity will serve as a constant challenge to you and to me.

With sincere sympathy,
Alice

Hamilton Hall
Lake College
October 9, 19—

AN INFORMAL INVITATION

Blake University
130 Haven Hall
April 2, 19—

Dear Jane,

I haven't forgotten your interest in our annual Campus Carnival, and now that the big day is rolling around, I want very much to have you come for a visit. Then you can see for yourself how much fun the Carnival is.

The date is to be April 23, a Saturday, and I hope that you can spend the entire week end as my guest in the dormitory (special privileges for Carnival week end!). Please do plan to come on Friday afternoon or early Friday evening so that we can go to the informal Paddy dance. There's a handsome law student who's heard about you and thinks that's a wonderful idea.

If you'll just let me know which bus or train you'll arrive on, I'll be waiting for you at the station. And I'll be looking forward eagerly to seeing you again. It's been much too long now.

Sincerely,
Sarah

A "BREAD AND BUTTER" LETTER

26 Burton Place
Chicago, Ill.
July 21, 19—

Dear Helen,

I want to tell you again how very much I enjoyed spending these past four days with you. The train arrived in the city about ten minutes late, but Dad was waiting for me and brought me home in the car.

Mother was glad to see me, for my sister, Marion, is giving a party for the neighborhood gang this afternoon; you can imagine that Mother is doing most of the work!

Tell your brother that I'm going to plan on three or four tennis matches this week, so that next time I play him I may be able to win *two* games!

Thank you for such a good time, Helen. Let me know when you come to town on your next buying spree; perhaps we can arrange to get together for lunch and our usual window-shopping afternoon.

Sincerely,
Martha

EXERCISES

1. Collect and bring to class at least ten examples of business letters. (Perhaps you can supply these from your own correspondence; or a relative or business acquaintance may lend you some letters from his files.) Study the letterheads used; note especially both the usual and unusual features about the six parts of the letters (heading, inside address, greeting, body, complimentary close, signature). Notice the stock of paper used, the spacing and length of the paragraphs, the tone of the letters.

2. Classify the letters in your collection (Exercise 1) according to the types of business letters listed on pages 722, 723. For one example of each type that you find, make a paragraph outline of the content. Compare this outline with the plan of organization given for the order letter, inquiry letter, claims letter, and application letter (see pp. 723–732).

3. Write a letter answering an advertisement in a magazine, in which you request a catalogue.

4. From a magazine advertisement, write a letter ordering the item or items advertised.

5. Look through the advertisements of a magazine until you find some article or articles in which you are interested. Write for further specific information about the product.

6. You notice the announcement of an essay contest for college students being sponsored by a national publisher. Write a letter asking for details.

7. Write a letter to your dean asking permission to leave college before the close of the college year in order that you may accept a good summer position starting on June 1.

Exercises

8. Assume that you are preparing a paper or a speech on the history of your home town. Write a letter to the state historical society asking for information on the early shops and industries in the town.

9. Write a letter asking an entertainer or a guest speaker to appear on a program sponsored by your class or some organization of which you are a member. Then assume that the entertainment has been given; write the speaker a "thank you" letter.

10. Write a formal letter to the editor of your local newspaper, calling attention to some matter which you believe will interest your fellow-townsmen or fellow-students.

11. Write a letter to a railroad or bus company asking for a refund on an unused ticket.

12. Assume that some of your luggage has been lost on your way to or from college. Write a claims letter to the railroad or the express company.

13. Write a letter applying for a summer job on a cruise boat or for some kind of summer employment other than that mentioned in No. 14 and No. 15.

14. Answer the following "Want Ad": WANTED: Counselors and leaders for boys' and girls' camps, June through August. Youngsters are from 8 to 12. Give full details concerning qualifications. Acme Summer Camp Chain, Lake Onestoga Village, New York.

15. Answer the following "Want Ad": WANTED: Male college students to serve as lifeguards at public beaches, park pools, and summer camps. Three months' summer employment. Excellent salary and working conditions for those properly qualified. Lifeguard Agency, Inc., 412 North Wyoming Avenue, Indianapolis, Indiana.

16. Answer the following "Want Ad": WANTED: Student to be night cashier in local restaurant. Hours 8 to 12. Time for study during work. Give references and previous experience. Dept. S-7, *Citizen*, Columbus, Ohio.

17. Write a letter of application in answer to an advertisement in the "Help Wanted" section of a newspaper or magazine. Choose an advertisement giving a reasonable amount of information.

18. With a specific position in mind, prepare a record sheet giving pertinent information about yourself. Write a letter of application to accompany the record.

19. Write a completely self-contained letter of application (i.e., without use of a record sheet). Use one or two unique or unusual devices to make your letter distinctive.

20. Write a letter to a high school teacher or former college instructor, asking permission to use his name as reference in your application for a position.
21. Write an informal invitation to a friend, asking him to join you and your family on a week's automobile tour.
22. Write a "bread and butter" letter to a friend who has entertained you for a week end in his (her) home. Write a letter also to your friend's mother.
23. Write a letter to a friend who is in the hospital for a long stay following a serious operation.
24. Assume that you are spending some time in a foreign country or in a section of the country considerably removed from your home. Write a "travel" letter to a friend at home.
25. Write a "thank you" note to a friend's parents who have given you a "going-away-to-college" present.
26. Write a letter of advice to a friend who is a high school senior and who plans coming in the fall to the college which you are attending.
27. Write a letter to a friend attending another college, inviting him (or her) to one of the important social functions of your college.
28. Write a letter to a relative, asking him (her) to be your guest at some college activity in which you know that he (she) is greatly interested.
29. Send a letter of information to your high school principal, or your favorite high school teacher, giving your impressions of some phase of college life.
30. Write a letter to a former high school friend reminding him of, or suggesting, a reunion of your class or some other organization during the next vacation period.

Appendix B

SENTENCE ANALYSIS AND DIAGRAMING

Theoretically, one who knows grammar should be able to analyze a sentence both by words and by groups of words (phrases and clauses).

Consider the following sentence:

> *The little old lady across the street is carefully knitting a sweater for her grandson, who is a freshman.*

A grammatical analysis of this sentence is as follows:

The is a definite article modifying the noun *lady.*

little and *old* are adjectives modifying the noun *lady.*

lady is a noun used as *subject of the sentence.*

across is a preposition introducing the prepositional phrase; *the,* a definite article modifying the noun *street; street,* a noun used as object of the preposition *across.* The entire prepositional phrase, *across the street,* is used as an adjective modifying *lady.*

is is an auxiliary verb which with the present participle *knitting* forms the present progressive tense, active voice, and is the *predicate of the sentence.*

carefully is an adverb modifying the verb phrase *is knitting.*

a is an indefinite article modifying *sweater,* which is a noun used as direct object of the verb phrase *is knitting.*

for is a preposition; *her,* the possessive pronoun, third person singular feminine, referring to *lady* and modifying *grandson; grandson,* a noun, the object of the preposition *for.* The entire prepositional phrase, *for her grandson,* is used as an adverb, modifying *is knitting,* if we think of the phrase as being closely associated with and tied to the verb phrase *is knitting;* if, however, we think of *for her grandson* as closely associated with *sweater,* then both by logic and common sense we can call it a prepositional phrase used as an adjective, modifying *sweater.*

who is a relative pronoun, nominative case, referring to *grandson* and used as the subject of *is; is* is a linking verb; *a* is an indefinite article modifying *freshman;* and *freshman* is a predicate noun after a linking verb. The group of words, *who is a freshman,* is an adjective clause modifying *grandson.*

Lacking the skill (or knowledge) needed to analyze sentences as indicated above, many students find diagraming of value. This is a mechanical device by which you are aided in identifying words as parts of speech, in identifying phrases and clauses, and in indicating the uses or functions in a sentence of these words, phrases, or clauses. These purposes of diagraming are accomplished through the use of lines: horizontal lines, perpendicular lines, slanting lines, curved lines, and dotted lines.

But remember that diagraming, although it seems like a game, is only a *means* to an end, not an *end* in itself; it is simply a device to help you identify and see the relationships between various parts of a sentence.

The important parts of the sentence are put on lines in the positions indicated in the following skeleton diagram.

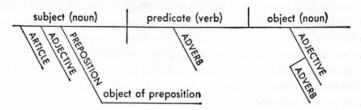

Filled in, such a diagramed sentence might read:

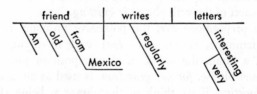

The simple subject, the simple predicate, the direct object, the object complement, the predicate noun (or pronoun), and the pred-

Sentence Analysis and Diagraming

icate adjective are written on the main long horizontal line. Subject and predicate are separated by a perpendicular line intersecting the horizontal line. The direct object is separated from the verb by a short perpendicular line extending up from the horizontal line. The object complement, the predicate noun or pronoun, or the predicate adjective is separated by a short slanting line extending leftward from the horizontal line.

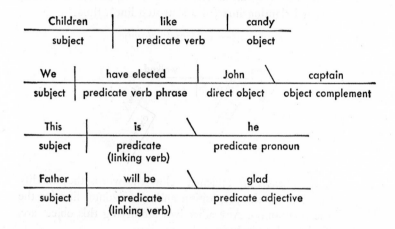

Dashes or dotted lines (usually perpendicular) are used to join, and the conjunction is written along or across such a line. In the following sentence, notice the compound subject, the compound predicate, and the compound object.

Freshmen and sophomores read or write stories and essays.

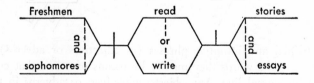

Slanting lines below the horizontal line are used for adjective and adverbial modifiers. Each adjective or adverb is on a separate slanting line.

The old man slowly but carefully signed his name.

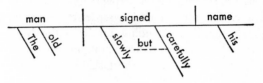

An adverb modifying an adjective or another adverb is written on an additional slanting line (or a stair-step line), thus:

The very old man walked extremely slowly.

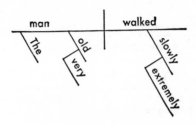

Prepositional phrases are attached below the words they modify by a slanting line for the preposition and a horizontal line for the object of the preposition. Any adjectives modifying this object are, as already indicated, written on a slanting line.

A friend of my father gave me the book with the red cover. (Note how *me*—the indirect object—is diagramed.)

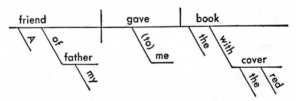

Participial and infinitive phrases (as adjectives or adverbs) are attached to the words they modify by means of a line that curves into a horizontal line. Any objects, adjectives, or adverbs in these phrases are placed as indicated above.

The man wearing the brown hat is the man to be nominated for president.

744

Sentence Analysis and Diagraming

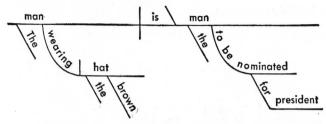

A gerund phrase or an infinitive phrase used as a noun is put on a horizontal line supported by a vertical line placed to indicate whether such phrase is the subject, object, predicate noun, etc. A noun clause or an infinitive "clause" is similarly supported. Within these phrases or clauses, objects, adjectives, adverbs, and the like, are placed as indicated above.

Gerund phrase as subject of a verb:

Occasionally reading a good book is a worthy achievement.

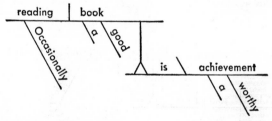

Infinitive phrase as predicate noun:

A precept worthy to be followed by everyone is freely to forgive your enemies.

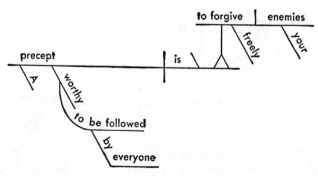

An infinitive "clause":

Henry asked me to lend him my dictionary.

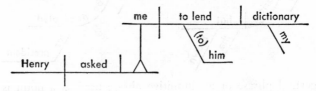

Noun clause as subject:

What you say has convinced me.

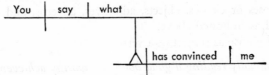

Noun clause as object:

John said that he had studied his lesson faithfully.

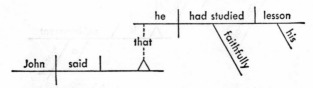

Absolute phrases are similarly placed on a vertically supported line but are enclosed in brackets:

The tire being repaired, we continued our journey.

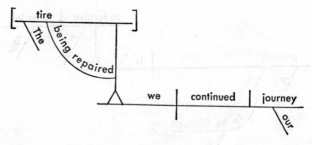

A vertical dotted line serves to link adjective clauses to the noun modified; adverbial clauses to the proper word in the independent

746

Sentence Analysis and Diagraming

clause; and one independent clause to another. Any conjunction expressed is written across the dotted line.

Adjective clauses:

Men who work diligently usually succeed.

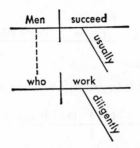

I met a friend whom I like.

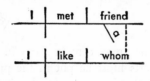

Adverbial clauses:

We won the game because we had the better team.

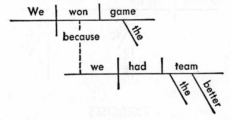

Mary is taller than her mother is.

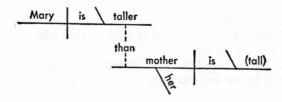

John drives faster than he should drive.

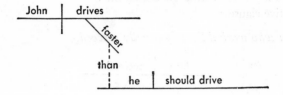

Compound sentence:

I like movies, but John prefers radio dramas.

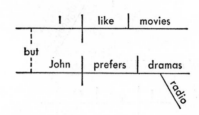

Sometimes a sentence may contain parts in inverted or transposed order; these parts must be put in the proper places in the diagram according to the directions already given.

Never again will John see so exciting a game.

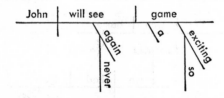

EXERCISES

A. Diagram the following sentences:

1. You may borrow my pen.
2. The Smiths saw many interesting sights on their trip.
3. I am painting my car green.
4. Father has appointed Mary his secretary.
5. You will be our next treasurer.

Exercises

6. An athletic victory is usually a joyful occasion.
7. The day is becoming colder and more gloomy.
8. Edison has been famous for a long time.
9. Books, magazines, and newspapers are available in the library.
10. Busy people receive and send many letters.

B. Diagram the following sentences:

1. Henry has worked faithfully to achieve his ambition.
2. Your winning the election so easily surprised everyone.
3. Tomorrow I shall begin taking regular exercise.
4. To recognize one's errors is to take the first step toward improvement.
5. The host invited us to come early and to stay late.
6. That I might have the pleasure of your company is my desire.
7. Father wrote that he would arrive on Friday.
8. We returned to college yesterday, our vacation having ended.
9. The college which I am attending is a small one.
10. To thoughts of love, in the springtime, often turns the fancy of a young man—and that of some old ones, too.

C. Diagram the following sentences:

1. I am looking forward to your coming to the university in September.
2. John wrote to Mr. Brown, who had promised him a job for the summer.
3. Driving carefully on icy roads is necessary in order to prevent accidents.
4. On this wintry day the weather outside is frightful but the weather inside is delightful.
5. Our first item of business today is to call the roll.
6. I am telephoning what I have to say and then am confirming it by letter.
7. People who make no provision for the morrow are like the five foolish virgins who are mentioned in the Bible.
8. Charles claims to be a better golfer than I am, but I dare him to prove it.
9. When I received your telegram, I dropped everything and came at once.
10. Always to be remembered is that traffic regulations are devised and enforced for the safety of drivers, passengers, and pedestrians.

Index

A, an, 441, 477
Abbreviations, 690–692; contractions, 692; footnotes, 173–174; period, 613, 692
Abominable, abominably, 444
Absolute expression, 586; diagraming, 746; phrase, 484, 586; punctuation, 632
Abstract noun, 464, 586
Accent marks, 347–348, 664
Accept, except, 441
Accidently, 441
Accusative, 587
Act, scene, 656
Active voice, 553, 561–565, 587; effectiveness, 102–103; table of forms, 550–551
Ad, 441, 692
Ad hominem argument, 87
Address, business envelope, 720–721; direct, 592, 633; forms of, 711–714; inside, 711–714
Adjective clause, 487, 587; diagraming, 746–747
Adjective phrase, 483
Adjectives, 476–478, 572–576, 587; absolute, 576; and adverbs, 572–574; capitalization, 686; common, 477; comparison, 574–576, 589–590; coordinate, 625; definition, 476; descriptive, 476; diagraming, 743–744; endings, 477, 573–574; kinds, 476–477; limiting, 476; linking verbs, 573–574; misuse, 573; position, 477–478; predicate, 530, 573–574, 602; proper, 477; punctuation, 625
Adjustment letters, 726–728

Adverbial clause, 487, 587; diagraming, 746–748; misuse, 288–290; punctuation, 622–623
Adverbial phrase, 483
Adverbs, 478–479, 572–576, 587; absolute, 576; and adjectives, 572–574; characteristics, 479; comparison, 574–576, 589–590; conjunctive, 580, 581–584, 591, 647–648; diagraming, 743–744; ending, 573–574; interrogative, 597; misused, 573–574
Advertisements, blind, 729–730; classified, 730
Advise, 441
Affect, effect, 441
Agreement, 508–513, 587–588; collective nouns, 513, 519–520; pronoun and antecedent, 518–525; relative pronouns, 511–512; singular pronouns, 509; subject and predicate, 508–513; subject and predicate noun, 512; *there is, there are,* etc., 512–513; words joined by *and, either . . . or, neither . . . nor,* 510–511
Aïda, as mnemonic device, 99
Ain't, 441
Airplane names, 681
Alcaro, Marion Walker, quoted, 68
Alibi, 441
All the farther, all the faster, 441–442
Allen, Agnes Rogers, quoted, 73
Allen, Frederick Lewis, quoted, 66
Alliteration, 437
Allusion, 442
Already, 442
Alright, 441
Also, 442
Although, punctuation with, 648

751

Index

Altogether, 442

A.M., a.m., 442

Americanisms, 387

Among, between, 442

Amount, number, 442

Amplifying references, 662

Analogy, and contrast, 119; faulty, 87–88

Analysis, central purpose, 42–44; of sentences, 741–742; theme subjects, 40–46; tone, 44–46

And etc., 443

And which, and who construction, 283–284

Anecdote, 115

Antecedent, 518–525, 588

Antonyms, 352

Anybody, anyone, 519

Anxious, eager, 443

Anywheres, 443

Apostrophe, 669–673; contractions and omissions, 671; indefinite pronouns, 672–673; joint possession, 671; misuse, 672; plurals of letters, figures, words, 672; possessive case, 669–671

Application, letter of, 728–732; accompanying data sheet, 729; illustration, 731–732; replying to advertisement, 729–730; unusual, 730–731

Applied punctuation, glossary of, 701–706

Appositive, 588; case, 500; punctuation, 632–633, 659–660

Appropriateness, colloquialisms, 388–389; diction, 420–423; neologisms, 406–407; paragraphing, 231–232, 237–243; sentences, 334–335; slang, 405–406; technical words, 413–414; tense of participles and infinitives, 557–558; theme, 32–33; word use, 420–423

Apt, liable, likely, 443

Archaic words, 385

Argument, 121–122

Arrangement, sentence, 325–329

Article (formal essay), *see* Essay

Articles, definite and indefinite, 477, 588; as part of title, 681

As, 443

As good as, if not better than, 443

Asterisks, 614

Auto, 443

Autobiographical writing, 116

Auxiliary verb, 471–472, 531–538, 588; correct use, 535–538; definition, 531, 534; with main verb, 531–535

Awful, awfully, 444

Awhile, a while, 444

Bacon, Sir Francis, quoted, 98

Balanced sentences, 492–493, 589

Baldwin, Hanson W., quoted, 73

Barbarisms, 395

Be as auxiliary verb, 531–534, 535, 598; as linking verb, 530; table of forms, 532–533

Beard, Charles A., quoted, 208–209

"Because" clause, misused, 288–289; punctuation, 648

Begging the question, 86–87

Beginning, business letters, 721–722; direct, 65–66; effective, 66–71; ineffective, 64–65; methods, 66–71; paragraph, 226; sentences, 326–327, 332–333; theme, 63–71; "you," 68–69

Believe, feel, 444

Bell, Bernard Iddings, quoted, 71

Bendiner, Robert, quoted, 70

Bennett, Arnold, quoted, 199

Beside, besides, 444

Between, among, 442

Biased evidence, 85–86

Bible, books, 681; chapter and verse, 656

Bibliographies, 175–177; arrangement of items, 175–176; card illustration, 167; descriptive, 176; illustration, 177, 184–187, 191–192; position, 177; punctuation, 176; special, 144, 146

Biography, reference works, 145

"Black Magic," research paper, 187–192

Blended sentences, 263–264

"Blends," direct and indirect quotation, 679; mixed, confusing, 275

Blind advertisements, 729–730

Block system, business letters, 716–717

Body, business letters, 714–715

Book reviewing, 120

Books, in bibliography, 175–177; in footnotes, 170–172, 174; italics, 681; numbers for chapters, 696; quotation marks, 677; titles, 681

Bosse, Diane, quoted, 210–211

Brackets, 663; misuse, 28

Bradford, Gamaliel, quoted, 204

"Bread and butter" letter, 737–738

Index

Brennan, Alys L., quoted, 116
Briticisms, 348, 387, 428
Brooks, Van Wyck, quoted, 70
Brown, Ivor, quoted, 75
Buck, Pearl, quoted, 75
Burroughs, John, quoted, 204–205, 208
Bursted, bust, busted, 444
Business letters, 709–732; adjustment, 726–728; application, 728–732; body, 714–715; claims and adjustments, 726–728; closing sentence, 722; complaint, 726–728; complimentary close, 715–716; content, 721–732; envelope, 720–721; folding, 720–721; form, 711–716; full block, 717–718; greeting, 714; heading, 711; illustrations, 717–720, 724–728, 731–732; indented and block systems, 716–720; inquiry, 724–726; inside address, 711–714; language, 722; margins, 716; modified block, 718–719; open and closed punctuation, 717–720; opening sentence, 721; order, 723–724; paragraphing, 239, 722; presentation, 710–721; salutation, 655–656, 714; second page, 715; signature, 716; stationery, 710; types of, 722–732; typing, 710

Cacophony, 436–439
Can, auxiliary verb, 537; *may, might,* 444
Cancellations, 28, 663
Cannot help but, 444
Can't hardly, 444
Capitalization, 683–688; direct quotation, 684; first word, 684; misuse, 687–688; proper nouns and adjectives, 684–687; titles, 683–684
Card catalog, 151–157
Caret, 664
Carhart, Arthur H., quoted, 242–243
Carson, Rachel L., quoted, 209
Case, 445
Case, 496–503, 589; accusative, 587; defined, 496–497; genitive, 502, 594; in elliptical clauses, 500; nominative, 496–498, 500–502, 598; objective, 498–502, 500–502, 600; possessive, 502–503, 602; pronoun forms, 497
Cause, paragraph development by, 209
Cedilla, 664
Central purpose, 42–44

Chafee, Zechariah, Jr., quoted, 69
Chapter and verse, Bible, 656
Chapters, book, 677
Chicago, University of, *A Manual for Writers of Term Papers, Theses, and Dissertations,* cited, 175–176; *A Manual of Style,* cited, 624
Choppy sentences, 323–324
Chronological order, 115, 225
Churchill, Winston, quoted, 327
Circumlocutions, 431
Claims letters, 726–728
Classification, 119
Classified advertisements, 730
Clauses, 485–488, 589; adjective, 487, 587; adverbial, 487, 587, 622–623; dangling elliptical, 297–298; dependent, 251–252, 486–488, 592, 626, 649–650; elliptical, 487–488, 592–593; falsely coordinated, 283–284; independent, 485–486, 595, 618, 620–622, 626, 646–649; introductory, 618–619; misplaced, 292–293; nonrestrictive, 487, 627–630; noun, 486–487, 599, 632; parenthetic, 630–631; restrictive, 487, 627–630; subordinate, 606, *and see also* Dependent clause; summarizing, 655, 659
See also Colon; Comma; Dash; Semicolon; Sentence
Clearness, definitions of terms, 81–82; diction, 409–411, 413–415; language, 81; themes, 80–89; thinking, 82–89
Clichés, list of, 424–426
Climactic order, 226–227
Climax, paragraph, 226–227; sentence, 328
Close, complimentary, 715–716
Closed punctuation, business letters, 717–720
Coherence, themes, 78–80; transitional devices, 79–80
Collective nouns, 464, 589; agreement, 513; antecedent, 519–520
Colloquialisms, 387–389; appropriateness, 388–389; in formal writing, 389
Colon, 653–656; clauses, 654; introductory, 653–655; miscellaneous uses, 656; misuse, 656; quotation, 655; quotation marks, 678; salutation of letter, 655–656; to separate, 655–656; vs. dash, 656

753

Index

Comma, 617–636; absolute phrases, 632; appositive, 632–633; broad principles, 617–619; comma splice (or "blunder" or "fault"), 20–21, 257–260, 264, 636; compound predicate, 621; contrasted coordinate elements, 625–626; coordinate adjectives, 625; dates, 619, 633; direct address, 633; emphatic expressions, 631–632; independent clauses, 618, 620–622; initials, 619, 634; inserted sentence elements, 631–632; introductory clause or phrase, 618–619, 622–624; misreading, 621, 626; *namely,* 633; nonrestrictive phrases and clauses, 627–630; numbers, 619, 627; parenthetical expressions, 618, 630–631, 633; places, 633–634; quotation marks, 678; quotations, 619–620; restrictive, 627–630; salutation of friendly letters, 620; series, 618, 624–625; *such as,* 633; summary of use, 617–619; suspended elements, 631–632; titles, 634; to enclose, 627–634; to introduce, 619–620; to separate, 620–627; transposed elements, 631–632; unnecessary use, 625, 634–636

Comma splice, 20–21, 257–260, 264, 636; correction, 258–260; definition, 257; justifiable, 260; unjustifiable, 257–260

Common nouns, 463, 589; part of proper name, 686

Communication, process of, 3–13

Comparative degree, 479, 574–576, 589

Comparison, 574–576, 589–590; adjective and adverb, 574–576; double, 576; elliptical clause, 500; incomplete, 269–270; mixed, 275–276; positive, comparative, superlative degrees, 574–576; use of "other," 276

Comparison and contrast, paragraph development by, 207

Complaint letters, 726–728

Complected, 445

Complement, 590; objective, 590, 600; predicate, 498, 590, 602; subjective, 590, 602

Complete object, 600

Complete predicate, 602

Complete subject, 606

Complex sentence, 334, 490–491, 590

Complimentary close, 715–716

Compound nouns, possessive, 671

Compound object, 600; diagraming, 743

Compound possession, 671

Compound predicate, 591, 602; diagraming, 743

Compound prepositions, 480

Compound sentence, 334, 490, 590; diagraming, 748

Compound subject, 606; diagraming, 743

Compound tenses, 607

Compound words, 664

Compound-complex sentence, 334, 491, 591

Conciseness, defined, 309; diction, 429–431; methods, 309–311; sentence, 309–311, 429–431; unnecessary details, 311; word use, 428, 429–431

Conclusion, *see* Ending

Conclusions, paragraphing of, 240–243

Concord, 508, 591

   See also Agreement

Concrete diction, 417–418

Concrete noun, 464, 591

Condition, improbable, 569; statements contrary to fact, 559, 569

Congratulation, letter of 736

Conjugation, 591; imperative mood, 568; indicative mood, 532–533, 550–551, 562–563, 567; subjunctive mood, 533, 568–570

Conjunctions, 481, 579–585, 591; and comma, 620–622; and semicolon, 646–649; conjunctive adverb, 580, 581–584, 591; coordinating, 579–581, 591; correlative, 580–581, 591–592; kinds, 579–580; misuse, 282–284, 581, 584–585; pure, 580, 582–584, 604, 620–621; simple, 580; subordinating, 580, 582–584, 606; table of, 582–583

   See also Conjunctive adverb; Coordinating conjunction; Correlative conjunctions; Subordinating conjunction

Conjunctive adverb, and semicolon, 647–648; defined, 580, 591; misused, 581, 584; test for use, 647–648

Connotation, 418–419

Consistency, dependent and independent clauses, 558; mental point of view, 96–97; mood, 97–98; number, 322; personal point of view, 95; physical point of view, 96; pronouns, 322; style, 98;

Index

subjective or objective, 95–96; tense, 320–321, 556–559; theme, 94–98; use of subject, 321–322; voice, 321–322

Construction, 273–275, 591

Constructions, impersonal, 595; incomplete, 273–275; mixed and illogical, 273–277; split, 301–303

Contact, contacted, 445

Content of themes, *see* Substance

Continual, continuous, 445

Contractions, 692; apostrophe, 671

Contrary to fact statements, 559, 569

Contrast, paragraph development by, 207–208

Contrasted elements, 625–626

Conversation, *see* Dialogue

Cooper, Duff, quoted, 129

Coordinate adjectives, 625

Coordinate clause, and comma, 620–622; and semicolon, 646–648

Coordinating conjunction, 579–581, 591; and comma, 620–622; and semicolon, 646–648; misuse, 282–284, 581

Coordination, false, 283–284; faulty, 280–284; inaccurate, 284; in subordinate form, 286–287

Copula, *see* Linking verb

Correction sheet, 18–19; 105, 108

Correctness, diction, 340–407; meaning of, applied to writing, 461 n

Correlative conjunctions, 580–582, 591–592; parallelism, 315–316

Could as auxiliary verb, 537, 559

Credible, creditable, credulous, 445

Criticism, 120

Cute, 445

Dangling elliptical clauses, 297–298; phrases, 295–297

Dare, auxiliary verb, 538

Dash, 631, 657–660, 678; interruption, break, or shift in thought, 658–659; misuse, 660; omission of words or letters, 660; overuse, 660; summarizing, 659; to enclose, 659–660; to introduce, 658; typewritten, 658; unfinished statement, 658–659; with other marks, 660

Data, 445

Data sheet with application letter, 729

Dates, 695; punctuation, 619, 633

Dean, Gordon, quoted, 73

Decimal and period, 613

Declarative sentence, 335, 491, 592, punctuation, 612

Declension, 592

Decline, 592

Deductive order, 119

Deductive thinking, 83–84

Definite article, 477, 588

Definition, exposition by, 119–120; for clearness, 81–82; paragraph development by, 211–212

Degrees of comparison, 574–575, 589–590, 602, 607

    See also Comparative; Positive; Superlative degrees

Deletions, 28

Demonstrative pronouns, 469, 592

Denotative words, 418

Dependent clause, 486–488, 592; misused, 288–290; punctuation, 619, 626–630, 649–650, 654, 658

De Quincey, Thomas, quoted, 71

Derivation, word, 351

Description, 118–119; mood, 118; paragraph development, 204–205; plan, 118; point of view, 118; purpose, 118; sketch, 118–119; space order, 118

Descriptive exposition, 120

Desire, 570

Details and particulars, paragraph development by, 203–205

Development, theme, 44; topic sentences, 196–200

Dewey Decimal Classification, 154–156

Diacritical marks, 348

Diagraming of sentences, 741–748

Dialect, 386

Dialogue, paragraphing, 238; quotation marks, 676–677

Diction, 337–341

    See also Words

Dictionaries as reference books, 141–144

Dictionary, and spelling, 347, 365; and vocabulary, 346, 353–354; choice, 342–343; compound words, 665; definitions, 349–350; general use, 343; information in, 343–353; lists, 141–144, 342; resources illustrated, 344–345; use of, 343–353; verb forms, 541

Dieresis, 664

Different than, 445–446

Direct address, 592; punctuation, 633

755

Index

Direct question, punctuation, 615

Direct quotation, 592; capitalization, 684; punctuation, 675–678

Directions, giving of, 120; paragraphing, 241–243; parentheses and, 662

Discussion and conversation, for theme content, 48

Disinterested, 445

Disregardless, 449

Division, paragraph development by, 208–209

Do as auxiliary verb, 531–534, 536, 556, 599

Documentation, bibliographies, 175–177; footnotes, 169–175

Dollars and cents, 613

Done, 446

Don't, 446

Double comparison, 576; double negatives, 277; double reference, 524–525; double sentences, 263–264; double superlative, 576

Doubt or uncertainty, 569; punctuation, 616

Drug, drugged, 446

Due to, 446

Durant, Will, quoted, 66–67, 209–210, 239

Each, 446

Eager, 443

Edman, Irwin, quoted, 75

Effect, paragraph development by, 209–210

Effect, affect, 441

Effectiveness, active voice, 102–103; by actual sense of fact, 99–100; diction, 102, 417–439; paragraph, 225–227; parallel structure, 100–101; repetition, 101–102; sentence, 309–335; themes, 99–103; variety of sentences and paragraphs, 100

See also Emphasis

Either . . . or, 446–447

Eliot, T. S., quoted, 66

Ellipsis, marks of, 613–614; sentences, 250

Elliptical clause, 487–488, 592–593; of comparison, 500; dangling, 297–298

Emphasis, climax, 328; italics, 682; order of words, 328–329; periodic sentences, 327–328; punctuation, 631–632, 654, 658; repetition, 329

Emphatic diction, 417–419

Emphatic verb form, 556, 593

Encyclopedias, 141–144

Ending, business letters, 722; effective, 72–75; ineffective, 71–72; methods, 72–75; paragraph, 226; sentences, 326–327, 439; theme, 71–75

Endorsement of themes, 29

English, capitalized, 686

Enthuse, 447

Enumeration, colon, 654

Envelope, business letters, 720–721

Errors, serious, to be avoided, 19–22

Essay, formal, 121; informal, 121; titles in bibliographies, 175–177; titles in footnotes, 171–172, 174

Etc., 447, 630

Euphemisms, 431

Euphony, 436–439

Evading the issue, 87

Evans, Bergen, quoted, 67, 69

Everybody, 519

Evidence, insufficient, biased, or suppressed, 85–86

Exaggeration, 410–411

Exam, 441, 692

Example, paragraph development, 205–206

Except, accept, 441

Exclamation point, 614–615, 678

Exclamatory sentence, 335, 491–492, 593; punctuation, 615

Explanation of a process, 120

Expletive, 593; agreement, 512–513

Exposition, 44, 119–121; criticism, 120; definition, 119–120; descriptive, 120; essay, formal and informal, 121; explanation of process, 120; forms, 119–121; giving directions, 120; narrative, 120; paragraph development, 205; types of order, 119

See also Essay

Fact and opinion, 84–85

Fact-finding, 84–85

Fadiman, Clifton, quoted, 68, 70, 74

Fairchild, Henry Pratt, quoted, 225

Farther, further, 447

Faulty analogy, 87–88

Faulty diction, glossary of, 440–457

756

Index

Faulty repetition, 311, 429-431, 433-435
Feel, 444
Fellow, 447
Fewer, less, 447
Figurative language, 418
Figures, *see* Numbers
Figures of speech, metaphor, 415, 418; mixed, 414-415; simile, 415, 418
Fine, 447
Fine writing, 427-428
Finite verb, 593
First person, 95, 468, 497
Fix, 447
Folding letters, 720-721
Folks, 447
Following, follows, use of colon, 654-655
Footnotes, 169-175; abbreviations, 173-174; form, 170-174; illustrations, 171-172, 174, 179-184, 187-191; italics, 170-174; numbering, 175; position, 174-175; punctuation, 170-174
For, 620, 622
Foreign words, 348, 428; accent mark, 664; italics, 681-682; plural, 465
Form, sentences, 333
Formal essay (article), *see* Essay
Formal writing, colloquialisms, 389
Formally, formerly, 448
Forster, E. M., quoted, 72
Fractions, 694
Fragments, sentence, 249-254, 605; justifiable, 249-250; punctuation, 614; unjustifiable, 250-254
French, Sidney J., quoted, 72
"Freshman English," 14
Friendly letters, 709-710, 732-738; "bread and butter" letter, 737-738; congratulation, 736; illustrations, 735-738; informal invitation, 737; salutation, 620; stationery, 734-735; suggestions for writing, 733-735; sympathy, 736-737; "thank you" note, 735-736; types, 735-738
Fries, Charles C., quoted, 340, 343
"Frying-pan" error, 260, 521
"Full block" form, business letters, 717-718
Funny, 448
Further, farther, 447
Fused sentences, 20, 263-264
Future perfect tense, 553, 555, 593-594
Future tense, 552, 554, 594

Gaps in thought, 79; transition, 236-237
Gender, 468, 594
Generalization, hasty, 85, 213-214
Genitive, 466, 594
Gerund, 472-473, 594; diagraming, 745; with possessive, 502-503
Gerundial phrase, 484, 594
Get, got, 448
Glossaries, applied punctuation, 701-706; faulty diction, 440-457; grammatical terms, 586-608
Good, well, 448
Good English, 337-341; aids in attaining, 17-19; standards, how to attain, 14-15
Grammar, 461-608; adjectives and adverbs, 476-479, 572-576; agreement of subject and verb, 508-513; asserting words, 471-474; case, 465-466, 496-503; clauses, 485-488; conjunctions, 481, 579-585; defined, 461-462, 594; descriptive, 462; gender, 468, 594; glossary of terms, 586-608; interjection, 481; joining words, 479-481; modifying words, 476-479; mood, 472, 567-570; naming words, 463-471; nouns, 463-466; number, 464-465, 468, 599; parts of speech, 462-481; phrases, 482-484; plural, 464-465, 468, 599; possessive case, 465-466; prepositions, 479-481; prescriptive, 462; principal parts of verbs, 539-545; pronouns, 467-471, 518-525; reason for study, 461; sentences, 489-493; serious errors in, 21-22; tense, 471, 549-559; tone, 471, 549, 553-556; value of, 461; verbs and verbals, 471-474, 530-565; voice, 472, 561-565
Grammatical terms defined, 586-608
Greeley, William B., quoted, 74
Greeting, *see* Business letters

Hackneyed language, 424-426
Had, had better, had best, 448
Hahn, Emily, quoted, 71
Hahn, Phyllis, quoted, 207
Handwriting, legibility, 29
Hasty generalization, 85
Have as auxiliary verb, 531-535, 568, 599
Heading, business letters, 711; theme outline, 55-59

757

Index

Healthful, healthy, 448

Help but, 448

Hieronymous, Nancy, quoted, 206

Highway numbers, 695

Himself, 520

Hitt, Mortimer, quoted, 178–187

Hoffer, Erich, quoted, 73

Home, homey, 448

Homographs and homonyms, 363–364, 398–400; overuse, 438

Hope, Anthony, quoted, 80

Hour and minute, 656

House and room numbers, 695

Huff, Darrell, quoted, 68

Hummel, William, quoted, 66

Huntress, Keith, quoted, 66

Huxley, Aldous, quoted, 212–213

Huxley, Thomas Henry, quoted, 65, 306

Hyperbole, 410–411

Hyphen, 664–668; compound words, 664–667; end of line, 667–668; misuse, 668; word division, 667–668

I, me, 448, 498, 520, 686

Ibid., 173, 174

Idiomatic English, 390–393, 480–481; defined, 390–391; lists of expressions, 391–393; possessive, 503

Illiteracies, 395, 422

Illogical constructions, 273–277

Illusion, 442

Illustration, paragraph development by, 205–206

Imperative mood, 568, 594

Imperative sentence, 335, 491, 595; punctuation, 612, 615

Impersonal construction, 595; impersonal point of view, 95; impersonal writing, 565

Imply, infer, 448

Improprieties, 398–400; in grammatical function, 398; in meaning, 398–400; list of, 399–400

In, into, 449

In back of, 449

Inanimate objects, possessive, 503

Incident, 115–116

Incompleteness, construction, 273–275; sentence fragments, 249–254; sentence meaning, 268–271, 273–275

Indefinite articles, 477, 588

Indefinite pronouns, 470, 595; possessive, 672–673

Indentation, business letters, 716–717, 720; outlines, 56; paragraph, 28, 195–196

Indented form, business letters, 720

Independent clause, 485–486, 595; and comma, 620–623; and semicolon, 646–649

Independent paragraph, 239–240

Indicative mood, 532–533, 550–551, 562–563, 567, 595

Indirect object, 499, 596, 744; indirect question, 596, 612, 615; indirect quotation, 596, and punctuation, 634–635, 678–679

Individual, 452

Inductive order, 119

Inductive thinking, 83–84

Infer, imply, 448

Inferences, paragraph development by, 210–211

Infinitive, 473, 555, 558, 596; case of subject, object, objective complement, 499; object of, 499; perfect, 601; sign of, 605; split, 303; subject of, 499

Infinitive phrase, 484, 596; dangling, 295–297; diagraming, 744–746

Inflection, 596–597

Informal essay, *see* Essay

Informal letters, *see* Friendly letters

Ingenious, ingenuous, 449

Initials, punctuation, 619, 634

Inquiry letter, 48, 724–726

Insertions, 28

Inside address, business letters, 711–714

Inside of, 449

Intensive pronouns, 470, 520–521, 597

Interjections, 481, 597; list of, 481

Interpolations, brackets and, 663

Interrogation point, *see* Question mark

Interrogative, adverb, 597; pronoun, 469–470, 497, 597; sentence, 335, 491–492, 597

Interviews, 48, 116–117

Intransitive verbs, 473–474, 564–565, 597

Introduction, *see* Beginning

Introductory statement, punctuation, 619, 654

Investigative paper or theme, *see* Research paper

758

Index

Invitation, informal letter of, 737
Irregardless, 449
Irregular verbs, 541–544, 598
Irving, Washington, quoted, 417–418
Is because, 288–289, 453
Is when, is where, 288–289, 449
Issue-evading, 87
It, indefinite use, 523–524
Italics, 680–682; emphasis, 682; footnotes, 170–174; foreign words or phrases, 681–682; misuse, 681; or quotation marks, 681; reference to word, letter or number, 682; titles, 175–177, 681
Its, it's, its', 450, 672

Jackson, Allen, quoted, 226–227
James, William, quoted, 70
Jerky sentences, 323–324
Job, 450
Johnson, Samuel, quoted, 342 n
Joining verb, *see* Linking verb; words, 664–667
Jones, Stacy V., quoted, 75

Keats, John, quoted, 132
Kennan, George F., quoted, 74–75
Kind of, sort of, 450
Kind of a, sort of a, 450
Klein, Alexander, quoted, 74
Known to unknown order, 119

Lab, 441, 692
Language, business letters, 722; misuse of, in thinking, 86–87
Lay, lie, 450, 474
Leave, let, 450
Legibility, manuscript, 29; friendly letters, 734–735
Length, paragraph, 230–232; sentences, 333, 335
Less, 447
Let, 450; as auxiliary verb, 538
Letter salutation, 712–714; punctuation, 620, 655–656
Letter writing, 114
    See also Business letters; Friendly letters
Letters, forming of, 29; plural of, 672; use of italics, 682
Levels of usage, 339–340, 350–351, 421–423; punctuation, 676

Lewis, C. S., quoted, 69
Liable, likely, 443
Library, 139–157; card, 152, 153; card catalog, 151–156; guide to use, 139–140, 151–157; main book collection, 151–157; periodical material, 148–151; reference books, 140–148; special bibliographies, 144, 146
Library of Congress Classification, 156–157
Lie, lay, 450, 474
Like, 450–451, 584–585
Likely, 443
"Lincoln the Soldier," research paper, 178–187
Linking verbs, 478, 530–531, 598; adjectives, 573–574
List, colon, 654–655
Listening, as communication, 10–13; directions for, 10–13; lectures, 10–11; movies, radio, and television, 12–13; speeches, 11–12
Literature, reference works, 146–149
Loc. cit., 173
Localisms, 386–387
Locate, 451
Logic, order of, 225
    See also Thinking
Loose sentences, 492–493, 598
Lots of, a lot of, 451
Luxuriant, luxurious, 451
Lynes, Russell, quoted, 67

McGhee, Paul A., quoted, 328
Mad, 451
Magazines, titles, 681; use of quotation marks, 677
Main verb, 531–535; clause, 485–486
Manuscript form, 27–30; beginning, 28; cancellations, 28; endorsement, 29; indentation, 28; insertions, 28; legibility, 29; margins, 28; page order, 28–29; paper, 27–28; proofreading, 30, 103–109; title, 28; typewriting, 29–30
Margins, business letters, 716; themes, 28
Mather, Kirtley F., quoted, 210
May, as auxiliary verb, 537
May, can, 444
Mayer, Marvin E., quoted, 187–192
Meanings, word, dictionary use, 349–350
Measurements, figures, 695

Index

Mechanics, abbreviations, 690–692; capitals, 683–688; defined, 609; italics, 680–682; manuscript, 27–30; numbers, 693–698; outlines, 50–59; paragraph, 195–196; punctuation, *see* individual marks of punctuation; theme, 27–30

Melville, Herman, quoted, 33

Mencken, H. L., quoted, 68

Metaphor, 415, 418

Metaphrase, 130

Might, 444; auxiliary verb, 537, 559

Misplaced clauses, phrases, words, 291–293

Misreading, commas, 626

Misspelling, 22, 360–373

Mixed constructions, 273–277; figures of speech, 414–415

Mode, *see* Mood

Modern Language Association *Style Sheet,* quoted, 170–171, 231–232, 624, 656

"Modified block" form, business letters, 718–719

Modifiers, dangling, 294–298; nonrestrictive, 599; overuse of, 428; restrictive, 605; "squinting," 293

Modify, 598

Money, figures for, 696

Mood as impression, 97–98; description, 118

Mood, verbs, 567–570, 598; imperative, 568, 594; indicative, 567–568, 595; subjunctive, 568–569, 606; unnecessary shifting, 570

Motion picture titles, 681

Movie listening, 12–13

Muchly, 451

Mudge, Isadore G., quoted, 140

Mullinix, Nancy L., quoted, 211–212

Musical compositions, capitalization, 683–684

Must as auxiliary verb, 537

Myself, 520

Name-calling, 86–87

Namely, punctuation, 633

Narration, 44, 115–118, 204; anecdote, 115; autobiography, 116; incident, 115–116; interview, 116–117; paragraph development, 204; point of view, 115; profile, 117–118; types, 115–118

Narrative exposition, 120

Nationalism, 387

Necessity, 570

Need as auxiliary verb, 538

Negative, double, 277

Neither . . . nor, 446–447

Neologisms, 404, 406–407

Newspapers, titles, 681, 683

Nice, 451

No, 630

Nominative absolute, 586

Nominative case, 497–498, 500–502, 598

Non-finite verb, 599

Nonrestrictive modifier, 599; clauses, 487; phrases, 483, 627–630
    See also Comma

Non sequitur error, 86

None, 509–510

Note taking, 160–163; lectures, 10–11; materials, 161; methods, 161–163; reading, 160–163; research paper, 167–168; speeches, 11–12

Notorious, noteworthy, notable, 451

Noun clause, 486–487, 599; apposition, 632; diagraming, 746; phrase, 483; subject or complement, 290

Nouns, 463–466, 599; abstract, 464, 586–587; capitalization, 684–687; case, 589; characteristics, 464; collective, 464, 519–520, 589; common, 463, 589; concrete, 464, 591; declension, 592; defined, 463–464; number, 464–465, 509–511, 599; plurals, 464–465, 599, 602; possessive case formation, 465–466, 669–671; predicate, 530, 602; proper, 463–464, 603, 684–686

Nowheres, 443

Number, 599; consistency in use, 322; plural, 602; plural of nouns, 464–465; plural of pronouns, 468, 497; relative pronouns, 511; shift in, 322; singular, 606

Number, amount, 442

Numbers, 693–698; book chapters, dates, highway, measurements, money, percentage, postal zone, streets, telephone, time, 695–696; commas, 619, 627; fractions, 694; italics, 682; parentheses, 662; plurals, 672; punctuation, 627; Roman, 697–698; words or figures, 694–696

760

Index

O, oh, 451, 615, 630

Object, 599–600; and predicate, 634; complement, 590, 600; compound, 600; direct, 498–499, 500–502, 599–600; indirect, 499, 596

Object complement, 499, 590, 600

Objective case, 497–502, 600

Objectivity, 95–96

O'Brien, Seumas, quoted, 406–407

Obsolete and obsolescent words, 384–385

O'Connor, Frank, quoted, 103

Odiorne, George S., quoted, 70–71, 74

Of, used for *have,* 451, 534

Off of, 449

Omissions, apostrophe, 671; asterisks, 614; caret, 664; ellipsis periods, 613–614; in sentences, 268–271; use of dash for, 660; wrong, 268–271

One of those who, which, 511–512

Oneness, *see* Unity

Only, position of, 291–292

Op. cit., 173–174

Open punctuation, business letters, 717–720

Opinion and fact, 84–85

Order, climax, 328; exposition, 119; paragraph, 224–227; phrases and clauses, 292–293; themes, 50–55; words, 291–292

Order letters, 723–724

Origin of words, dictionary use, 351

Orwell, George, quoted, 71

"Other," use in comparisons, 276

Ought as auxiliary verb, 537–538

Outlines, 50–60; aid to proportion, 59–60; correct form, 55–56; division and wording, 57–59; kinds, 50; logical division, 57–59; mechanics, 55–56; paragraph, 53–55; parallel phrasing, 57; punctuation, 56; research paper, 168; sentence, 52–53; subheads, 55–59; symbols, 56; theme, 50–60; thesis sentence, 60; topic, 51–52

Outside of, 449

Pages, order of, 28–29

Paper, for themes, 27–28

Paragraph, 193–246; appropriateness, 231–232, 237–243; as theme, 239–240; business letters, 239, 722; characteristics, 193–195; concluding, 238; conclusions, 240–242; defined, 193–195; development, 203–213; dialogue, 238, 675–676; directions, 240–243; effectiveness, 225–227; faulty, 196, 213–215; importance, 193; improper, 20; indentation, 195–196; introductory, 238; isolated statements, 242–243; length, 230–232, 238–239; mechanics, 194–196; order, 224–227; outline, 53–55, 56; proportion, 228–230; purpose, 193; quotation marks, 676; recommendations, 240–242; revision, 243–246; short paragraph overuse, 230–231; substance, 201–215; summary, 240–242; topic sentences, 196–200; transition, 233–237, 238–239; unity, 219–222

Paragraph outline, 53–55

Parallelism, 312–317; correlative conjunctions, 315–316; defined, 312–314; effectiveness, 100–101; illustrated, 313–317; ineffective, 316–317; misleading, 317; outlines, 57; partial, 316–317; structure, 100–101; tests, 313–314; verb use, 570

Paraphrase, 114, 129–132; example, 132; suggestions, 130–132; uses, 130

Parentheses, 616, 661–662; misuse, 28, 663

Parenthetical material, 630–631, 662; punctuation, 618, 630–631, 659–663

Parliamentary motions, 570

Participial phrase, 484, 600; dangling, 295–297; diagraming, 744–745; punctuation, 618

Participles, 472, 600; dangling, 295–297; past, 472, 601; past participle for past tense, 545; perfect, 472, 601; present, 472, 603; tense, 556–558

Particulars and details, paragraph development, 203–205

Parts of speech, 348–349, 462–481, 600; adjective, 476–478, 587; adverb, 478–479, 587; conjunction, 481, 579–585, 591; dictionary reference, 348–349; interjection, 481, 597; noun, 463–466, 599; preposition, 479–481, 602–603; pronoun, 467–471, 603; verb, 471–474, 608

Parts, principal, of verbs, 603

Party, person, individual, 452

Pass out, 452

Passim, 174

Index

Passive voice, 472, 561–565, 601; formation, 561–565; impersonal writing, 565; ineffective, 102–103; needless shifting, 565; overuse, 102–103, 329–330; table of forms, 562–563

Past participle, 540–541, 601; and past tense, 545

Past perfect tense, 552, 555, 601

Past tense, 549, 554, 601

Pep, peppy, 452

Percentage, figures, 696

Perfect infinitive, 555, 601

Perfect participle, 556, 601

Perfect tenses, 607

Period, 612–614; abbreviations, 613, 692; act and scene, 656; chapter and verse, 656; decimal, 613; declarative sentence, 612; dollars and cents, 613; ellipsis, 613–614; imperative sentence, 612; indirect question, 612–613, 615–616; misuse, 614; outline, 613; "period fault," 250–254; quotation marks, 678; sentence ending, 612; sentence fragment, 249–254; titles, 614

Periodic sentences, 492–493, 601; emphasis, 327–328

Periodical indexes, 148–151

Perkins, Milo, quoted, 73

Person, 452; person, 601

Personal point of view, 95

Personal pronouns, 468, 601; after nouns, 521; case forms, 497

Personification. capitalization, 685

Phase, 445

Phone, 441, 692

Phrases, 482–484, 601; absolute, 484, 586, 632; adjective, 483; adverbial, 483, 618; appositional, 588, 632–633; as sentence, 252–254; classified by use and form, 483–484; dangling, 295–297; gerundial, 484, 594; infinitive, 484, 596; introductory, 618–619, 623–624; misplaced, 292–293; mispunctuated, 649–650; nonrestrictive, 483, 627–629; noun, 483; order, 292–293; parenthetic, 630–631; participial, 484, 600, 618; prepositional, 484, 603; prepositional-gerundial, 484; restrictive, 483, 627–630; useless repetition, 433–435; verb, 483–484, 608; verbal, 484 *See also* Comma; Dash; Semicolon

Places, punctuation, 633–634

Plagiarism, 169

Planning, faulty, 19

Plays, titles of, 681

Plenty, 452

Plural, 602

Plurals, apostrophe and, 672; figures, letters, words, 672; nouns, 464–465; pronouns, 468, 497; verbs, 599

Plus, 452

P.M., p.m., 442

Poe, Edgar Allan, quoted, 97–98

Poetic words, 385

Poetry, capitalization, 684; titles, 681

Point of view, consistency, 94–97; description, 118; mental, 96–97; narrative, 115; personal, 95; physical, 96; subjective or objective, 95–96; theme, 94–98

Polysyllabication, 427–428

Position, sentence, 325–330

Positive degree, 574, 602

Possessive case, 602; apostrophe, 669–671; gerund, 502–503; inanimate objects, 503; indication of time or measure, 503; joint possession, 671; nouns, 465–466, 669–671; pronouns, 497, 672–673

Post hoc error, 85

Practicable, practical, 452

Précis-writing, 114, 126–129; example, 129; suggestions, 127–129

Predicate, 489, 602; adjective, 530, 602; agreement, 508–513; and object, 634; complement, 498, 531, 602; complete, 602; compound, 490, 602; noun or pronoun, 512, 530, 602; simple, 602; verb, 472

Predication reduced, 309–311

Prepositional phrase, 484, 603

Prepositional-gerundial phrase, 484

Prepositions, 479–481, 602–603; and object separated, 302; at end of sentence, 326–327; compound, 480; idiomatic use, 480–481; list of, 479–480; object of, 498–499

Present participle, 540, 556, 603

Present perfect tense, 552, 555, 603

Present tense, 549, 553–554, 557, 603

Pretty, 452

Price, Stephen S., quoted, 69

Primary tenses, 607

Principal, principle, 452

Index

Principal clause, 485–486

Principal parts, verbs, 539–545, 603; change in form, 541–544; endings, 540–541; irregular verbs, 541–544; misused, 544–545; regular verbs, 541–544

Profile, 117–118

Progressive verb form, 549, 556, 561, 603

Prolixity, 311

Pronouns, 467–471, 603; agreement with antecedent, 518–520; agreement with predicate, 509–512; antecedent, 518–525; case, 589; consistency in use, 322; correct case forms, 497; declension, 592; defined 467–468; demonstrative, 469, 592; double reference, 524–525; implied reference, 521–523; indefinite, 470, 595, 672–673; intensive, 470, 520–521, 597; interrogative, 469–470, 497, 597; *it,* 523–524; kinds of, 468; number, 497; objects of verbs or prepositions, 498–499; personal, 468, 497, 521, 601, 672; plural, 599, 602; possessive case, 672–673; predicate, 530, 602; reciprocal, 471, 604; reference of, 604; reflexive, 470, 520–521, 604; relative, 468–469, 497, 511–512, 520, 604, 672; shift, 322; singular, plural, 509–512; subjects, 497–502; *they,* 524; *you,* 523

Pronunciation, aid in spelling, 361–363; dictionary use, 347–348

Proofreading, 30; printed materials, 108–109; proofreader's symbols, 106–107; theme, 104–105

Proper nouns, 463, 603; capitalization, 684–687

Proportion, paragraph, 228–230; theme, 59–60, 62–63

Proposition, 452

Proven, 452

Provided, provided that, providing, 452–453

Provincialisms, 386

Punctuation, 609–679, 701–706; abbreviations, 692; bibliographies, 176; business letters, 717–720; defined, 609–610; footnotes, 170–174; glossary of applied punctuation, 701–706; importance, 609–610; marks, 610; outlines, 56, 613; purposes, 610–612; to en-

close, 611; to end or terminate, 610–611; to introduce, 611; to separate, 611
    See also individual marks of punctuation

Pure conjunction, 580, 604; punctuation, 620–621, 635, 648–649

Purpose, central, 42–44; in themes, 77–78; of punctuation, 610–612

Question, direct, 492; indirect, 596, 615–616; punctuation, 612, 615–616

Question-begging error, 86–87

Question mark, 614–616; direct question, 615; doubt or uncertainty, 616; ellipsis periods, 613; misuse, 615–616; quotation marks, 678; series of questions, 616

Quite a, 453

Quotation marks, 674–679; and italics, 677, 681; chapter headings and titles, 677, 681; dialogue, 675–676; direct quotation, 675–677; indirect, 678–679; in pairs, 677–678; interrupted quotation, 675; level of usage, 676; misuse, 678–679; paragraphing, 676; position with other marks, 678; quotation within quotation, 677; several paragraphs, 676; single, 674, 677; technical terms, 676; titles, 677, 679, 681

Quotations, 604; capitalization, 684; colon, 655; comma, 619–620; direct, 592, 604, 675–677, 684; indirect, 596, 604, 678–679; within quotations, 677; words, 636

Radio and television, as source of ideas, 48; listening, 12–13

Raise, rise, 453, 474

Rambling sentences, 266–267

Readers, consideration for and study of, 29, 32–33, 41

Reader's Digest, 126

Readers' Guide to Periodical Literature, use illustrated, 148–149

Reading, as communication, 7–10; as source for ideas, 48; note taking, 160–163

Real, 453

Reason is *because,* 288–289, 453

Reason, paragraph development, 210–211

Reciprocal pronouns, 471, 604

Index

Recommendations, paragraphing for, 240–243
Reduced predication, 309–311
Refer back, 454
Reference books, 140–148
Reference of pronouns, 518–525, 604
References, parentheses and, 662
Reflexive pronouns, 470, 520, 604
Regionalisms, 386
Regular verbs, 541–545, 604
Relative clause, *see* Adjective clause
Relative pronouns, 468–469, 497, 520, 604–605, 672; and verbs, 511–512
Repetition, as transition, 235–236, 305–306; effective, 101–102; emphasis, 329; faulty, 311, 430, 433–435; ineffective, 214–215, 433–434, 438–439; passive voice, 329–330; useless, 311, 430–431, 433–435
Research paper, 163–192; bibliography, 175–177, 184–187, 191–192; choosing and analyzing subject, 164–166; documentation, 169–177; footnotes, 169–175; illustrations of, 178–192; investigation, 166–168; library research, 139–157, 167; note taking, 160–163, 167; outline, 168; revising, 169; writing, 168–169
Respectfully, respectively, 453
Restrictive modifiers, clauses and phrases, 483, 487, 605, 627–630; double restriction, 629–630
Reviewing, *see* Book reviewing
Revision, for clear thinking, 88–89; paragraphs, 243–246; research paper, 169; themes, 30, 103–109
Rhoads, C. P., quoted, 73
Rhyme, 437
Right along, right away, right then, 454
Rise, raise, 453, 474
Roberts, Paul, quoted, 421–422
Robinson, Francis P., quoted, 241–242
Roman numerals, form, 697–698; in outline, 56
Rules for spelling, 366–371
    See also Spelling
Running-on sentences, 281
Russell, Bertrand, quoted, 75

Salutation, and punctuation, 620, 655–656, 712–714
    See also Business letters

Salvadori, Mario G., quoted, 72
Schreiner, Olive, quoted, 675–676
Second person, 95, 468, 497
Seen, saw, 454
See-saw sentences, 281–282
Semicolon, 646–650, 678; conjunctive adverb, 647–648; coordinate clauses, 646–649; misused, 21, 649–650; phrases and dependent clauses, 649–650; series, 649; vs. colon, 650; vs. dash, 650
Sentence, 247–335, 489–493, 605; analysis, 741–742; appropriateness, 334–335; balanced, 492–493, 589; beginning, 326–327, 332–333; beginning with a numeral, 694; blended, 263–264; capitalization, 684; choppy, 323–324; clearness, 265–308, 335; climax, 328; comma splice, 20–21, 257–260, 264, 636; complex, 334, 490–491, 590; compound, 334, 490, 590; compound-complex, 334, 491, 591; conciseness, 309–311; consistency, 320–322; correctness, 248–264; dangling modifiers, 294–298; declarative, 335, 491, 592; defined, 247–248, 335, 489, 605; diagraming, 741–748; effectiveness, 309–335, 490–493; elliptical, 250; emphasis, 326–330; ending, 326–327; essentials, 247–249; exclamatory, 335, 491–492, 593; faulty coordination, 280–284; faulty subordination, 286–287; forms, 333; fragment, 20, 249–254, 605; fused, 20, 263–264; grammatical classification, 334–335, 490–491; imperative, 335, 491, 595; importance of, 247–249; incompleteness of meaning, 268–271, 273–275; incongruous ideas, 267; interrogative, 335, 492, 597; kinds, 490–493; length, 333, 335; logical dependent clauses, 288–290; loose, 492–493, 598; mixed and illogical constructions, 273–277; omissions, 268–271; outline, 52–53, 56; parallelism, 312–317; period, 612; periodic, 327–328, 492–493, 601; position and arrangement, 325–330; problems in writing, 248–249; punctuation, 612, 614–616; rambling, 266–267; running-on, 281; see-saw, 281–282; simple, 334, 490, 605; split constructions, 301–303; stringy, 281;

Index

telegraphic style, 271; thesis, 42, 53, 60; topic, 42; transition, 304–308; types of, 335, 490–493; unity, 265–267; varied length and structure, 331–333; variety, 331–333; word order, 291–293

Separation, unnecessary, 301–303

Sequence of tenses, 558–559, 605

Series, words, phrases, clauses, 624–625; misuse of punctuation, 635–636

Set, sit, 454, 474

Shakespeare, William, quoted 88

Shall, will, as auxiliary verbs, 454, 536, 554

Shift in mood, 570; number, 322; person, 322; point of view, 95; tense, 320, 557; voice, 321–322, 565

Ships, names of, 681

Shores, Louis, quoted, 73

Should, would, as auxiliary verbs, 454, 536–537, 559

Sign of the infinitive, 605

Signature, business letters, 716

Simile, 415, 418

Simple conjunction, 580

Simple object, 600

Simple predicate, 602

Simple sentence, 334, 490, 605

Simple tense form, 605–606

Simple to complex order, 119

Simple tone of verbs, 553–556, 605–606

Single quotation marks, 677

Singular, 606

Sit, set, 454, 474

Sketch, 118–119

Slang, forms of, 403–404; reasons for avoiding, 404–406

Slanting words, 86–87

So, overuse, 282–283, 454–455, 620

So . . . as, 455

Social letters, *see* Friendly letters

Somewheres, 443

Sort of, sort of a, 450

Space order, 225

Speaking as communication, 6–7

Specific diction, *see* Diction

Speech, figures of, 414–415, 418; parts of, 462–481, 600

Spelling, 22, 337, 360–379; aids, 347, 360–373; books on, 361 n; carefulness, 372; *ceed, cede,* 371; commonly misspelled words, 363–364, 372; diction-

ary use, 347, 365; doubling, 368–370; final *y,* 367; *ie-ei,* 366–367; inserted *k,* 371; memory devices, 365–366; pronunciation aids, 361–363; rules, 366–371; *s* and *es,* 371; silent *e,* 370–371; similar words confused, 363–364; spelling list, 363–364, 372–379

Splice, comma, 20–21, 257–260, 636

Split constructions, 301–303

Split infinitive, 303

Squinting modifier, 293

Stationery, business letters, 710; friendly letters, 734–735; themes, 27–28

Stevenson, Robert Louis, quoted, 205–206

Stoke, Harold W., quoted, 70, 74

Street numbers, 695

Strong verbs, 598

Structure, parallel, 312–317

Style, consistency, 98; kinds, 98; telegraphic, 271

Subheads, 51–59

Subject, agreement with verb, 508–513; at beginning, 332–333; case forms, 497–498; complement, 590, 602; complete, 606; compound, 490, 520, 606; consistency, 321–322; defined, 606; sentence or clause, 490; separation from predicate, 302; simple, 606

Subjective complement, 590, 602

Subjectivity, 95–96

Subjects, theme, analysis of, 40–46; development of, 44; improper choice and limiting, 19

Subjunctive mood, 472, 568–570, 606

Subordinate clause, *see* Dependent clause

Subordinating conjunctions, 580, 582–584, 606

Subordination, excessive, 287; faulty, 286–287; upside-down, 287

Substance, paragraph, 201–215; sources for, 202–203; theme, 47–49

Substantive, 606–607

Such as, punctuation, 633, 654–655

Suggestive values, words, 418–419

Summaries, writing of, 126–129; paragraphing of, 240–241, 242–243

Summarizing colon or dash, 655, 659

Superlative degree, 574–576, 607

Supposition, 569

Suppressed evidence, 85–86

Sure, 455

Index

Suspended expressions, 631–632
Suspicion, 455
Swenson, Eric, quoted, 67
Syllabication, 347
Sympathy, letter of, 736–737
Synonyms, 351–352; misuse, 410
Syntax, 607

Tautology, 311
Technical words, 413–414; quotation marks, 676
Telegraphic style, 271
Telephone numbers, 627, 695
Television listening, 12–13
Tense, 471, 549–559; compound, 607; consistency of use, 320–321, 556–559; defined, 607; formation of, 553–556; future, 552, 554, 594; future perfect, 552, 555, 593–594; in dependent and independent clauses, 558–559; infinitive, 555, 558; misuse of past and past participle, 545; participle, 556–558; past, 549, 554, 601; past perfect, 552, 555, 601; perfect, 607; present, 549, 553–554, 557, 603; present perfect, 552, 555, 603; primary, 549–552, 607; secondary, 552–553, 607; sequence of, 558–559, 605; shift in, 557; simple, 607; subjunctive, 559; tables illustrating, 532–533, 550–551, 562–563; timeless or universal truths, 557; verbals, 555–556
   See also Conjugation
Term report, *see* Research paper
Terrible, terrific, 444
"Thank-you" note, 735–736
That, 455, 468–469, 520
Theme, analysis of subject, 40–46; argument, 121–122; autobiographical, 116; basic forms, 114–122; beginning, 28, 63–71; central purpose, 42–44; clearness, 80–89; coherence, 78–80; consistency, 94–98; definition, 76; description, 118–119; development, 44; effectiveness, 99–103; ending, 71–75; exposition, 119–121; first themes, 14–22; length, 41; manuscript form, 27–30; mood, 97–98; narrative, 115–118; one-paragraph, 239–240; outlines, 50–60; paper, 27–28; paraphrase, 129–132; point of view, 94–97; précis, 126–129; proportion, 62–63; require-

ments, 25–27; revision, 30, 103–109; serious errors, 19–22; style, 98; subjects, 31–35; substance, 47–49; suggestions for writing, 15–17, 25–27; test questions, 26–27; title, 28, 37–39; tone, 44–46; topics, 31–35; unity, 76–78; work sheets, 25–26
   See also Research paper
Then, 442
There is, there are, etc., 512–513, 593
These kind, those kind, these sort, those sort, 455
Thesis sentence, 42, 53, 60
They, indefinite use, 524
Thinking, books on, 82 n; clear, 82–89; deductive, 83–84; errors in, 84–88; gaps in, 79, 236–237; inductive, 83–84
Third person, 95, 468, 497
This, that, 521–523
Thouless, Robert, quoted, 199–200
Thurber, James, quoted, 45–46, 69
Thusly, 455
Tigner, Hugh Stevenson, quoted, 211, 226
Time, use of numbers, 696
Time order, 119
Titles, 37–39, 677, 679; after names, 634; and subtitles, 656; capitalization, 39, 683–684; colon, 656; comma, 634; indirect reference to, 39, 64; italics and quotation marks, 677, 679, 681; phrasing, 38; position, 38–39; punctuation, 38–39; theme, 37–39; vague reference to, 39, 64; vs. subject, 37
Tone in themes, 44–46; unity of, 77–78
Tone in verbs, 471, 549, 553–556, 607–608; emphatic, 556, 593; formation of, 553–556; passive voice, 561–564; progressive, 556, 603; simple, 553–556, 605–606; tables of illustrations, 550–551, 562–563
Too, 456, 630; *to, too, two,* 455
Topic outline, 51–52, 56
Topic sentences, 42, 196–200; development of, 203–213; form, 196–198; ineffective development, 213–215; position, 198–200
Topics, assigned, 35; choice of, 31–35; kinds, 32–33; limiting, 34–35; research paper, 164–166; theme, 31–35
Trade names, capitalization, 685
Trains, names of, 681

Index

Transition, defined, 233–234, 304; devices, 79–80, 304–306; inexact and ineffective, 306–308; paragraph, 80, 233–237, 238–239; repetition, 235–236, 305–306; sentence, 79–80, 304–308; words and phrases, 79, 234–235, 304–305

Transitive verbs, 473–474, 608

Transposed expressions, 631–632

Trilling, Lionel, quoted, 207–208

Triteness, 424–426; list of trite expressions, 424–426

Try and, 456

Twain, Mark, quoted, 101–102

Type, 456

Type of a, 450

Typewriting, 29–30; business letters, 710; themes, 29–30

Uninterested, disinterested, 445

Unique, 456

United States Government Printing Office, *Style Manual,* quoted, 624, 693–694, 697–698

Unity, paragraph, 219–222; purpose, 77–78; sentence, 265–267; theme, 76–78; tone, 77–78; violation of, 77

Up, 456

Upside-down subordination, 287

Usage, 337–341; and quotation marks, 676; levels of, 339–340, 350–351, 421–423

Used, as auxiliary verb, 538

Vague words, 409–410

Van Putte, Roland, quoted, 244–246

Variety, effectiveness, 100; sentence, length and form, 331–333

Verb phrase, 483–484, 608; separated, 301–302

Verbals, 472–473, 608; dangling, 295–297; gerund, 594; infinitive, 596; participle, 600; phrases, 484; tense formation, 555–556

Verbs, active voice, 553, 561–565, 587, 608; agreement with subject, 21, 508–513; auxiliary, 471, 531–538, 588–589; conjugation, 591; copula, copulative, coupling, 598; correct form, 22; defined, 471, 608; emphatic tense forms, 556, 593; endings, 540–541, 599; finite, 593; gerund, 472–473, 594; infinitive, 473, 596; intransitive, 473–474, 597–598; irregular, 541–545, 598; joining, 598; linking, 530–531, 598; list of, 541–544; main, 534–535; misuse, 544–545; mood, 472, 567–570, 598; non-finite, 599; objects of, 498–499; participle, 472, 600; passive voice, 561–565, 601, 608; person, 601; phrases, 483–484, 608; plurals of, 599, 602; predicate, 472–473; principal parts, 539–545; progressive tense forms, 556, 603; regular, 540–545, 604; separated from object or complement, 302; simple verb forms, 553–556, 605–606; strong, 598; subject of, 497–498, 499–502; tense, 549–559, 607; tone, 549, 553–556, 607–608; transitive, 473–474, 608; uses, 471–472; verbals, 472–473, 608; voice, 561–565, 601, 608; weak, 604

Very, 456

Viewpoint, *see* Point of view

Vocabulary, building, dictionary aids, 346, 353–354; exercise in, 358–360

See also Words

Vocatives, 592, 633

Voice, 472, 561–565, 608; active, 553, 561–565, 587, 608; consistency, 321–322; formation of, 561–564; impersonal writing, 565; ineffective use of passive, 102–103; intransitive forms, 564–565; passive, 561–565, 601, 608; shift from active to passive, 565; table of forms, 562–563

Vulgarisms, 395, 422

Wallace, Ralph, quoted, **70**

Weak verbs, 604

Well, good, 448, 630

What, number of, 510

Where at, 456

Which, who, that, 468–469, 520–522

While, 456

White, E. B., quoted, 203–204, 240

Who, whom, whoever, whomever, **457,** 468–469, 500–502, 520

Whole lot, 451

Will, as auxiliary verb, 454, 536, 554

Wilson, Woodrow, quoted, 44–45

Word order, 291–293

Word Study, quoted, 327, 406

Wordiness, 429–431, 433–435

767

Index

Words, 337–457; Americanisms, 387; appropriateness, 338, 420–423; archaic, 385; as words, plural of, 672; as words, use of italics, 682; asserting, 471–474; barbarisms, 395; Briticisms, 387, 428; capitalization, 683–688; clearness, 409–415; colloquialisms, 387–389; compound, 664–667; conciseness, 429–431, 433–435; concrete, 417–418; connotative, 418–419; correctness, 340–407; defined, 337–341; derivation, 351; dialect, 386; dictionary use, *see* Dictionary; direct, 419; division, 667–668; effectiveness, 102, 417–439; emphatic diction, 417–419, 682; euphony, 436–439; faulty repetition, 430, 433–435; fine writing, 427–428; foreign words, 681–682; glossary of faulty diction, 440–457; homonyms and homographs, 363–364, 398–400; hyphenated, 664–668; idiomatic, 390–393; illiteracies, 395, 422; improprieties, 398–400; italics, 680–682; joining, 479–481; levels of usage, 339–340, 350–351, 421–423, 676; localisms, 386–387; misplaced, 291–293; mixed figures, 414–415; modifying, 476–479; naming, 463–471; nationalisms, 387; neologisms, 404, 406–407; obsolete and obsolescent, 384–385; or figures, 694–696; order, 291–293; parenthetic, 630–631; parts of speech, 462–463; plurals of, 672; poetic, 385; position, 326–329; precise, 409–411; provincialisms, 386; purposes, 463; quoted, 676; regionalisms, 386; simple, 419; slang, 403–407; specific, 409–410, 417–418; spelling, *see* Spelling; technical, 413–414; triteness, 424–426; useless repetition, 433–435; vocabulary, 353–354, 358–360; vulgarisms, 395, 422; wordiness, 429–431

    See also Diction; Grammar; Parts of Speech

Work sheets, 25–26

Worst kind, worst sort, worst way, 457

Would, as auxiliary verb, 454, 536–537, 559

Writing, autobiographical, 116; as communication, 5–6; basic forms of, 114–122; "fine," 427–428; purpose, 40–44; readers, study of, 29, 32–33, 41; serious errors in, 19–22

    See also Argument; Business letters; Description; Exposition; Friendly letters; Narration; Paraphrase; Précis; Research paper; Theme

Wyzanski, Charles E., Jr., quoted, 68

Yes, 630

"You" beginning, 68–69

You, indefinite use, 523

Theme Record (with Number of Serious Errors)

(Figures and letters in parentheses refer to Handbook sections)

Number of Theme	1	2	3	4	5	6	7	8	9	10	11	12	13	14	15	16
Grade on theme																
Adjective and adverb (83)																
Capitals, abbreviations, italics (96, 97, 98)																
Comma splice (32)																
Comma misuse (88)																
Coordination, subordination, parallelism (37, 38, 39, 45)																
Dangling modifiers (41)																
Diction (53-70)																
Fused sentences (33)																
Paragraphing (21-30)																
Possessive case (75j-l, 94a-e)																
Pronouns, nominative and objective case (75)																
Pronouns, antecedents—agreement, reference (77)																
Punctuation marks other than commas and semicolons (86, 87, 90-95)																
Semicolon misuse (89)																
Sentence fragment (31)																
Spelling (52)																
Subject, predicate—agreement in number (76)																
Variety in sentences (47, 48, 49)																
Verb forms—mood, tense, etc. (78-82)																

(Make a copy of this chart for additional theme records.)

Symbols Used in Indicating Errors in Writing

(Figures and letters in parentheses refer to *Handbook* sections)

ab use of abbreviations (98)

agr agreement of subject and predicate in number (76)

amb ambiguous word or meaning (60)

ant antecedent not clear (77)

awk awkward phrasing (63, 64, 69)

C to R not clear to reader

ca wrong case (75)

cap use a capital (97)

cl lacking in clearness (12, 60)

comb combine two or more simple sentences in a complex or compound-complex sentence (47)

comp faulty comparison (83e-h)

con consistency (13, 46)

coord faulty coordination (37)

cs comma splice (32)

cst awkward or faulty construction (35, 36, 39, 42)

d faulty diction (70)

da inappropriate diction (64)

dcol colloquialism (55)

dcon concise diction needed (67)

dem emphatic diction (63)

deu euphony (69)

dfw fine writing (66)

dict see your dictionary (51)

did idiom (56)

dil illiteracy (57)

dim impropriety (58)

dl localism (54)

dm dangling modifier (41)

dmf mixed figure (62)

dp precise diction (60)

dr useless repetition (68)

dsl slang (59)

dtc technical word (61)

dtr triteness (65)

dw word wrongly divided (93c)

e poor emphasis (63)

ef effectiveness of word or sentence construction (45, 48, 59, 63)

ff following rules or pages

fig use of numbers (99)

fs fused sentences (33)

fw use figures for words (99)

gl see Glossary (Diction, 70 Grammar, 85; Punctuation, 100)

gr grammatical error (75, 76, 77, 79, 83)

id wrong idiom, unidiomatic (56)

il illegible handwriting (1b)

imp important

ir irrelevant

it italics (96)

l illogical in thought (12c)

m wrong mood (82)